READINGS IN MANAGEMENT ACCOUNTING

Sixth Edition

S. Mark Young

Marshall School of Business
University of Southern California

Prentice Hall

Boston   Columbus   Indianapolis   New York   San Francisco   Upper Saddle River

Amsterdam   Cape Town   Dubai   London   Madrid   Milan   Munich   Paris   Montreal   Toronto

Delhi   Mexico City   Sao Paulo   Sydney   Hong Kong   Seoul   Singapore   Taipei   Tokyo

This book is dedicated to my mentors Professor Sydney S. Y. Young, Professor Jacob G. Birnberg and Professor John K. Shank

Editor-in-Chief: Donna Battista
Executive Editor: Stephanie Wall
Editorial Project Manager: Christina Rumbaugh
Senior Operations Specialist: Diane Peirano
Production Project Manager: Carol O'Rourke
Printer/Binder: Bindrite Graphics, Robbinsville

Prentice Hall
is an imprint of

www.pearsonhighered.com

10 9   8   7   6   5   4   3   2   1

ISBN-13: 978-0-13-702503-9
ISBN-10: 0-13-402503-3

Table of Contents

Preface

While this book can be used to supplement any management accounting or cost accounting text, the readings have been tailored to accompany Anthony Atkinson, Robert S. Kaplan, Ella Mae Matsumura, and S. Mark Young's textbook, *Management Accounting, 6th Edition* (Pearson Prentice Hall, 2011).

To Students

For each textbook chapter there is a corresponding set of readings that complements text material and introduces you to applications of the material in a wide variety of contexts. At the end of each reading, questions test your understanding of what you have read. The readings are taken from many sources including the *Wall Street Journal, Strategic Finance, Harvard Business Review*, and *Management Accounting Quarterly* among others. They represent both classic and contemporary readings on each of the topics covered in the text.

   The best way to use this book is to read each assigned article in one sitting. Then, read the article a second time taking notes and asking yourself how the article extends your understanding of the text material. In some cases, your instructor may assign specific questions that follow each of the readings. Taking the time to answer these questions thoughtfully will improve your understanding of the material. I hope you find the articles stimulating and thought-provoking.

To Instructors

Readings in Management Accounting, Sixth Edition contains 52 articles representing state-of-the-art thinking and examples on a wide variety of management accounting topics in many types of service and manufacturing contexts. Some of the articles are classics in the field, and others are very recent additions to the literature. Please note that several readings have been summarized rather than reprinted in their entirety. Those readings may be accessed by directly contacting the publisher of the article, by going to their Web site or obtaining hard or electronic copies from the library. While each of the readings has been listed for a specific chapter, in many cases, a particular article may be used as supplementary material for several chapters. If you have a favorite article that is not contained in this book, please send me the citation and I will gladly consider it for the next edition and acknowledge your contribution.

   The suggested solutions to the questions in this book can be found in the *Instructor's Manual* prepared for *Readings in Management Accounting*. The Instructor's Manual is posted at the following Web site: www.pearsonhighered.com. Instructors must have a login ID that can be obtained from Pearson. Please contact your local Pearson Prentice Hall representative for more detailed information. Thank you for adopting this text.

S. Mark Young
Marshall School of Business
University of Southern California
Los Angeles, CA 90089

Acknowledgments

I would like to thank Stephanie Wall, Christina Rumbaugh and Jane Avery for their editorial and administrative assistance. Also, I would like to thank Robert Kaplan, Harvard University, Ella Mae Matsumura, University of Wisconsin Madison, Anthony Atkinson, University of Waterloo, and Mike Shields, Michigan State University for their many contributions to this book.

S. Mark Young
University of Southern California

November 2010

About the Author

Dr. S. Mark Young holds the *George Bozanic and Holman G. Hurt Chair in Sports and Entertainment Business* and is also Professor of Accounting, Professor of Management and Organization at the Marshall School of Business, University of Southern California and Professor of Communication and Journalism at the Annenberg School for Communication at USC. Previously, Professor Young served as the Associate Dean for Academic Planning and Associate Dean and Academic Director of the Marshall MBA (Full-Time MBA) Program. Professor Young received an A.B. from Oberlin College (Economics), an M. Acc. from the Ohio State University, and a Ph.D. from the University of Pittsburgh.

Professor Young has published research in a variety of journals including *The Accounting Review, Accounting, Organizations and Society*, and the *Journal of Accounting Research*. Currently, he is on the editorial board of several major journals and was past Associate Editor for *The Accounting Review*. He will also serve as a member of the Advisory Board for the new journal, the *Journal of Management Accounting Studies.* In 2006, he was a co-winner of the Notable Contribution to the Accounting Literature (with Shannon Anderson) and has won the *Notable Contributions to the Management Accounting Literature* Award twice—with Frank Selto (1994) and Shannon Anderson (2003). He also received the *Jim Bulloch Award for Innovations in Management Accounting Education* in 2005.

Dr. Young has extensive executive teaching and consulting experience having taught in executive programs for Warner Brothers, Daimler-Chrysler, Texas Instruments, Shell Oil, AMGEN, and British Airways. Most recently, Young has had consulting or research relationships with the First Data Corporation, the Chrysler Corporation, Texas Instruments, and Southwest Airlines. He has won several outstanding teaching awards at the undergraduate and graduate levels, including the *Golden Apple Teaching Award* and is a Distinguished Fellow in the Center for Excellence in Teaching at USC. Currently he teaches courses in management accounting and entertainment management, and leads the entertainment management program within the Marshall School at USC.

Professor Young also maintains an interest in popular culture. His book, *The Mirror Effect: How Celebrity Narcissism is Seducing America (*with Drew Pinsky; Harper Collins, 2009) is a New York Times and Los Angeles Times Best Seller. Young also comments regularly in the business and entertainment presses and has appeared on the Situation Room (CNN), The View, Howard Stern's Satellite Radio show, National Public Radio, the BBC, Fox & Friends, and ABC News. He has been quoted in the New York Times, The London Times, Newsweek, Scientific American Mind, and many other publications.

Chapter 1

How Management Accounting Information Supports Decision Making

The readings in Chapter 1 all emphasize the changing role of management accounting information in today's business organizations. Even though Peter Drucker's well-known essay, *Be Data Literate—Know What to Know* (Reading 1.1), was written some time ago, it is still very relevant today. Drucker argues that there are three informational challenges facing executives. The first is to become information literate—to know what information they need, when, and in what form. The second challenge is how to obtain, test, and combine information and integrate it into the existing information system. The final challenge central to the study of management accounting is that data processing and accounting systems need to be brought together to decrease redundancy and increase compatibility. Drucker discusses the many new roles for accounting information and states, "Accounting has become the most intellectually challenging area in the field of management, and the most turbulent one."

The second article (Reading 1.2) by Bill Ferrara, *Cost/Management Accounting: The Twenty-First Century Paradigm*, traces the development of product costing and pricing through four management accounting eras or paradigms. In Paradigm A—from the early 1900s to the 1940s—standard costing was developed. Prices were determined by taking total cost per unit and adding a desired profit. In Paradigm B, the major advances made were the distinction between fixed and variable costs, the development of direct costing, and greater emphasis on volume and capacity considerations. In the late 1980s and through the early 1990s, Paradigm C arose with the development of activity based costing (ABC) and a new framework for creating greater accuracy in product costing by recognizing product complexity and product diversity as cost drivers. Paradigm D represents the current era and is characterized by the emphasis on target costing. Using this concept, the market determines selling prices, which in turn dictate allowable costs. The author predicts that a combination of Paradigms C and D will be the most useful for the 21st Century.

Alexander Mersereau argues in Reading 1.3, *Pushing the Art of Management Accounting* that, despite the many new advances in management accounting practices, the implementation effectiveness of these new practices has stalled in many organizations. Mersereau suggests that three things have to happen to increase effectiveness: (1) management accountants must know what information the organization needs, how it will be used, and how to communicate it to everyone, (2) managers must be trained to understand management accounting information, and (3) managers must be able to act on the information with which they are provided.

Reading 1.4, *Preserving Control* by Ramona Dzinkowski summarizes four issues that controllers of major U.S. companies say are major concerns to them. These are: (1) the effects of downsizing on the overall operational and control environment, (2) new reporting risks as a result of downsizing, (3) new metrics that arise as a result of restructuring, and (4) how new global accounting standards will have an impact on what they do.

Readings
Chapter 1

1.1 Be Data Literate—Know What to Know

by Peter F. Drucker

Executives have become computer literate. The younger ones, especially, know more about the way the computer works than they know about the mechanics of the automobile or the telephone. But not many executives are information-literature. They know how to get data. But most still have to learn how to use data.

Few executives yet know how to ask: What information do I need to do my job? When do I need it? In what form? And from whom should I be getting it? Fewer still ask: What new tasks can I tackle now that I get all these data? Which old tasks should I abandon? Which tasks should I do differently? Practically no one asks: What information do I owe? To whom? When? In what form?

A "database," no matter how copious, is not information. It is information's ore. For raw material to become information, it must be organized for a task, directed toward specific performance, applied to a decision. Raw material cannot do that itself. Nor can information specialists. They can cajole their customers, the data users. They can advise, demonstrate, and teach. But they can no more manage data for users than a personnel department can take over management of the people who work with an executive.

THE FIRST CHALLENGE

Information specialists are toolmakers. The data users, whether executive or professional, have to decide what information to use, what to use it for and how to use it. They have to make themselves information-literate. This is the first challenge facing information users now that executives have become computer literate.

But the organization also has to become information literature. It also needs to learn to ask: What information do we need in this company? When do we need it? In what form? And where do we get it? So far, such questions are being asked primarily by the military, and even there mainly for tactical, day-to-day decisions. In business such questions have been asked only by a few multinationals, foremost among them the Anglo-Dutch Unilever, a few oil companies such as Shell, and the large Japanese trading companies.

The moment these questions are asked, it becomes clear that the information a business most depends on are available, if at all, only in primitive and disorganized form. For what a business needs the most for its decisions—especially its strategic ones—are data about what goes on outside of it. It is only outside the business where there are results, opportunities and threats.

So far, the only data from the outside that have been integrated into most companies' information systems and into their decision-making process are day-to-day market data: what existing customers buy, where they buy, how they buy. Few businesses have tried to get information about their noncustomers, let alone have integrated such information into their databases. Yet no matter how powerful a company is in its industry or market, noncustomers almost always outnumber customers.

American department stores had a very large customer base, perhaps 30% of the middle-class market, and they had far more information about their own customers than any other industry. Yet their failure to pay attention to the 70% who were not customers largely explains why they are today in a severe crisis. Their noncustomers increasingly were the young affluent, double-earner families who were the growth market of the 1980s.

The commercial banks, for all their copious statistics about their customers, similarly did not realize until very late that more and more of their potential customers had become noncustomers. Many had turned to commercial paper to finance themselves instead of borrowing from the banks.

When it comes to nonmarket information—demographics; the behavior and plans of actual and potential competitors; technology; economics; the shifts signaling foreign-exchange fluctuations to come and capital movements—there are either no data at all or only the broadest of generalizations. Few attempts have been made to think through the bearing that such information has on the company's decisions. How to obtain these data; how to test them; how to put them together with the existing information system to make them effective in a company's decision process—this is the second major challenge facing information users today.

It needs to be tackled soon. Companies today rely for their decisions either on inside data such as costs or on untested assumptions about the outside. In either case they are trying to fly on one wing.

Finally, the most difficult of the new challenges: We will have to bring together the two information systems that businesses now run side by side—computer-based data processing and the accounting system. At least we will have to make the two compatible.

People usually consider accounting to be "financial." But that is valid only for the part, going back 700 years, that deals with assets, liabilities and cash flows; it is only a small part of modern accounting. Most of accounting deals with operations rather than with finance, and for operational accounting money is simply a notation and the language in which to express nonmonetary events. Indeed, accounting is being shaken to its very roots by reform movements—aimed at moving it away from being financial and toward becoming operational.

There is the new "transactional" accounting that attempts to relate operations to their expected results. There are attempts to change asset values from historical cost to estimates of expected future returns. Accounting has become the most intellectually challenging area in the field of management, and the most turbulent one. All these new accounting theories aim at turning accounting data into information for management decision making. In other words, they share the goals of computer-based data processing.

Today these two information systems operate in isolation from each other. They do not even compete, as a rule. In the business schools we keep the two apart with separate departments of accounting and of computer science, and separate degrees in each.

The practitioners have different backgrounds, different values, and different career ladders. They work in different departments and for different bosses. There is a "chief information officer" for computer-based data processing, usually with a background in computer technology. Accounting typically reports to a "chief financial officer," often with a background in financing the company and in managing its money. Neither boss, in other words, is information-focused as a rule.

The two systems increasingly overlap. They also increasingly come up with what look like conflicting—or at least incompatible—data about the same event; for the two look at the same event quite differently. Till now this has created little confusion. Companies tended to pay attention to what their accountants told them and to disregard the data of their information system, at least for top-management decisions. But this is changing as computer-literate executives are moving into decision-making positions.

UP FOR GRABS

One development can be considered highly probable: Managing money—what we now call the "treasury function"—will be divorced from accounting (that is, from its information component) and will be set up, staffed and run separately. How we will otherwise manage the two information systems is up for grabs. But that we will bring them together within the next 10 years, or at least sort out which system does what, can be predicted.

Computer people still are concerned with greater speed and bigger memories. But the challenges increasingly will be not technical, but to convert data into usable information that is actually being used.

Mr. Drucker is professor of social sciences and management at the Claremont Graduate School in California.

QUESTION

1.1 What does Drucker mean when he says: "Be data literate?"

1.2 Cost/Management Accounting: The Twenty-First Century Paradigm

by William L. Ferrara, CPA*

CERTIFICATE OF MERIT, 1994–95
What will the field of management accounting look like in the twenty-first century? To find out, let's consider four paradigms that cover its recent history. These paradigms provide us with an intriguing review of the current scene from a historical perspective (see Table 1)

and an opportunity to focus on unresolved issues. Ultimately, we can consider adjusting and even combining paradigms in anticipation of a new one for the twenty-first century.

For continuity and simplicity, we'll consider each paradigm in the context of both product costing and the

* From W. L. Ferrara, "Cost/Management Accounting: The Twenty-First Century Paradigm," *Management Accounting* (December 1995): 30–36. Reprinted with permission conveyed through Copyright Clearance Center, Inc.

3

determination of selling price. This context is useful especially because the current vogue of activity-based cost analysis emphasizes improved product costing in order to arrive at better pricing decisions.

PARADIGM A: TURN OF THE CENTURY UNTIL THE 1940S—THE ERA OF THE INDUSTRIAL REVOLUTION PLUS

Paradigm A conjures up the image of an early-day industrial engineering type such as Frederick Taylor who was interested in what costs should be, that is, standard costs. These engineering-driven standards were typically a function of product specifications, time and motion studies, and the like. The costs involved were direct materials, direct labor, manufacturing overhead, and even marketing and administrative costs, all of which were tied together in a total cost per unit of output.

Variable with product diversity (number of products)	XX
Variable marketing and administrative	XX
Total variance cost per unit	XX
Fixed costs	
Fixed manufacturing overhead	XX
Fixed marketing and administrative	XX
Total fixed cost per unit	XX
Grand total cost per unit	XX
Desired profit (markup)	XX
Target selling price per unit	XX

Costing/Pricing—Paradigm D
The 1990s and Beyond:
The Era of Market-Driven Standard (Allowable) Costs

Selling price (given competitive setting)	XX
Less desired profit	XX
Allowable or target cost per unit	XX

Added to the total cost per unit was a desired profit or markup, and the sum of total cost and desired profit yielded a target selling price per unit. In many instances, the total cost per unit excluded marketing and/or administrative costs, which were included as a factor in the desired profit. The ultimate result was still the target selling price per unit—the price that would yield desired profitability if projected costs per unit could be achieved.

Two issues of contention surface immediately with Paradigm A:

1. What volume of activity should be used to determine unit costs?
2. How should desired profit be determined?

The variety of answers typically offered is amazing even if both questions are put to an audience of practitioners representing various departments of the same company, as I have done over many years.

Table 2 shows possible answers for the "volume of activity" question, which must be addressed to determine total unit costs for Paradigms A, B, and C.

Answers usually lean in the direction of expected volume or something referred to as standard or normal volume. A rather difficult aspect of the expected volume answer is its implicit circular reasoning—expected volume assumes a selling price while it is being used to determine unit costs and ultimately a "target" selling price.

The answers for the "desired profit" question typically used to be very subjective or rule-of-thumb oriented. In recent years, however, up-to-date return on investment and cost of capital concepts have been considered in the most prevalent answers.

As we move on to subsequent paradigms, these two questions or issues of contention remain, and others emerge.

PARADIGM B: THE 1940S UNTIL THE 1980S— THE ERA OF COST-VOLUME-PROFIT ANALYSIS AND DIRECT COSTING

Paradigm B introduces the distinction between fixed and variable costs, which ultimately leads to cost-volume-profit analysis and direct costing. The fixed/variable cost dichotomy and its implications encompass the most dynamic developments in management accounting from the 1940s to the 1980s.

On the surface, not much seems to change between Paradigms A and B other than the distinction between fixed and variable costs as part of a total unit cost and a target selling price. However, even a cursory consideration of Tables 1 and 2 reveals a refinement of one of our issues of contention, that is:

1. Variable costs per unit are determined by engineering standards and analytic techniques, which means that the volume of activity issue relates essentially to fixed costs.

2. Furthermore, many variable costs have become more fixed over time. Union contracts and labor legislation have affected labor costs in just this fashion.

The issue of how to determine desired profit remains an issue of contention as we move to Paradigms C and D.

Variable costs per unit for direct materials and direct labor are determined easily by the engineering specifications for materials and labor requirements. Similarly, the per-unit amounts of other variable costs can be calculated. Techniques that typically are variations of regression analysis isolate the variable cost per unit as the "b" coefficient in flexible budget formulations.

Deriving variable costs per unit via engineering standards and analytic techniques leaves us with only the fixed costs to consider when determining the volume of activity to divide by in deriving per-unit

TABLE 2. THREE HISTORICAL PARADIGMS RELATIVE TO CALCULATING AND USING UNIT PRODUCT COSTS*

Paradigm A
Calculating and Using Unit Product Costs
Ignoring the Distinction Between Fixed and Variable Costs

Manufacturing costs	
Direct materials	$ 200,000
Direct labor	250,000
Manufacturing overhead	450,000
Marketing and administrative costs	500,000
Total	$1,400,000

Paradigm B
Calculating and Using Unit Product Costs
Using the Distinction Between Fixed and Variable Costs

Variable costs	
Direct materials	1.00 per unit
Direct labor	1.25 per unit
Manufacturing overhead	.50 per unit
Marketing and administrative	.25 per unit
Total	$ 3.00 per unit
Fixed costs	
Manufacturing overhead	350,000
Marketing and administrative	450,000
Total	$ 800,000

Paradigm C
Calculating and Using Unit Product Costs
The New Ideology of Activity-Based Costing

Variable costs	
Direct materials	$ 1.00 per unit
Direct labor	1.25 per unit
Variable manufacturing overhead	
Variable with number of units	.50 per unit
Variable with product complexity (number of batches)	.40 per unit
Variable with product diversity (number of products)	.35 per unit
Variable marketing and administrative	.25 per unit
Total	$ 3.75 per unit
Fixed costs	
Manufacturing overhead	$ 175,000
Marketing and administrative	450,000
Total	$ 625,000

Note: Volume levels to be considered for determining unit costs; actual volume—last period; average actual volume—e.g., past five years; expected volume—next period; average expected volume—e.g., next five years; capacity; other possibilities—standard or normal volume, given that these volume levels can be precisely defined.

* The numbers in the above illustrations are intended only to be illustrative in the broadest sense. They have no other intended purpose.

costs. None of the other issues related to the volume-of-activity question changes from our earlier discussion, except that many variable costs have become more fixed over time. In essence, the issue of volume of activity to divide by has become a larger issue as the relative amount of variable costs has diminished and the relative amount of fixed costs has increased.

PARADIGM C: THE LATE 1980S AND THE EARLY 1990S—THE ERA OF ACTIVITY-BASED COSTING

Much of the recent, exciting revival of interest in cost/management accounting relates to Paradigm C, which embodies activity-based costing (ABC). On the surface, Paradigm C considers only two additional variable costs in the development of a total cost per unit. Recognition of these additional variable costs is designed to improve the accuracy of a total unit cost, which then should improve the determination of selling prices and product mix decisions.

The new or additional variable costs of ABC relate to product complexity and product diversity. As shown in Tables 1 and 2, there are three elements of variable manufacturing cost under ABC:[1]

1. Costs that vary with units of product.
2. Costs that vary with product complexity, such as number of batches.
3. Costs that vary with product diversity, such as number of products.

The implications of the new categories of variable costs initially suggest a decreased number of fixed costs, but *further consideration of ABC leads me to suspect that the supposed additional variable costs are really fixed costs.*

This additional issue of contention could revive the controversy over "direct costing versus absorption costing," a paramount issue of the late 1950s and 1960s. Look at the ABC literature. It doesn't take much to see the possibility that ABC is nothing more than an updated, revised, and, most likely, more accurate version of absorption costing.

It's unfortunate that the advocates of ABC virtually have ignored the significance of Paradigm B's direct costing implications that were put forth so eloquently by J. S. Earley in 1955. According to Earley, the new management accounting "implied basing decisions on their estimated effects on marginal balances and contribution margins rather than upon 'full cost' calculations. It involves consistent references to variable costs and 'specific' fixed costs where these are relevant—and neglect of those costs unaffected by decisions."[2]

Another interesting facet of cost/management accounting virtually ignored by the advocates of ABC is the emergence of Paradigm D. This paradigm, which appears to have hail its origins in Japan (Hiromoto), has the potential to revolutionize cost/management accounting as it implicitly asks ABC enthusiasts, "What do costs have to do with the determination of selling prices? With the exception of cost-based pricing contracts, the market determines the price, and the role of cost is to help determine whether or not it is wise to enter the market or stay in the market."[3]

PARADIGM D: THE 1990S AND BEYOND—THE ERA OF MARKET-DRIVEN STANDARD (ALLOWABLE OR TARGET) COSTS AS OPPOSED TO ENGINEERING-DRIVEN STANDARD COSTS.

Under Paradigm D we no longer look to the development of a total unit cost in order to help determine a selling price. Instead we use the selling price we believe the market will allow to help us determine the cost that the market will allow. Peter Drucker has referred to this concept as price led costing as opposed to cost-led pricing.

The allowable or target cost per unit is a market-driven standard cost that has to be met if desired profits are to be achieved. Paradigm D questions the validity of any paradigm based on engineering-driven standard costs. Perhaps after some 90 years, the engineering-driven standard costs of Frederick Taylor and his contemporaries have been partially or wholly displaced by market-driven standard costs.

We still have the issue of how to determine desired profit with Paradigm D. However, Paradigm D creates a whole series of provocative new issues such as:

1. All that counts is that total cost per unit ultimately must not exceed the allowable or target cost if the desired profit is to be attained. This idea may mean that now the distinction between fixed and variable costs is either irrelevant or considerably less relevant.
2. If we truly believe in continuous improvement, then the allowable or target cost per unit must be reduced over time.
3. The way we work may have to change in order for us to reduce costs. Ultimately, this change can lead to the empowerment of our own work-force for, as we all know, often it is those closest to the action who can lead us on the path of continuous improvement.

This issue of continuous improvement via empowerment involves all people in the workforce—those in the factory, in procurement, in marketing and distribution, and in administrative offices.[4] Continuous improvement even creates the possibility of more positive relationships with suppliers and customers, again to reduce costs and increase quality and performance.[5] Tom Johnson, one of the early enthusiasts of ABC, stated the case for continuous improvement as follows: "Do activity costing if you must. But don't fool yourself into thinking that ABC will help you become a global competitor. For that, get busy with the improvement process!"[6]

REFINING AND FOCUSING ISSUES OF CONTENTION

Look at Paradigm D again. The two questions or issues of contention for Paradigm A concerning desired profit and level of volume remain, but they are easier to deal with in the era of Paradigm D. Given our current knowledge of cost of capital concepts, we can deal effectively with desired profit in terms of the level of profit needed to keep the suppliers of capital (debt and equity) satisfied given a particular profit planning horizon.

In terms of the volume of activity issue, Paradigm D can yield an answer that would have been considered only tentatively under earlier paradigms because of its implicit circular reasoning. For example, given the selling price being considered, one could argue for using the expected volume of activity at that selling price for the time period being considered—whether a month, or a quarter, or a year. The resultant expected cost per unit then could be compared to the allowable or target cost per unit of Paradigm D. An unfavorable comparison should produce a questioning attitude concerning what can be done about costs (fixed, variable, or other) or expected activity via alterations in pricing and promotion strategies that would improve the situation. The answers to such questions could provide the continuous improvements of which Johnson spoke.

When viewing volume of activity after the fact, one should shift to calculating actual costs per unit using the actual volume of activity. The result would be a comparison of allowable (target) costs, expected costs, and actual costs per unit. Especially useful would be the comparison of expected and actual costs per unit in terms of what caused the difference, if any, that is, inability to achieve anticipated continuous cost improvements and/or inability to achieve expected volume for the product promotion and pricing strategies chosen.

THE CURRENT SCENE

Table 3 is designed to point out some remaining issues of contention. The first, concerning the volume of activity to use under Paradigm D, was the one just discussed. The remainder follow.

Diminishing product life cycles. As life cycles for many new products decrease, the reasons for using Paradigm D increase.[7] Some products don't last long enough for engineering-driven standards to be established and utilized. Such products literally must achieve the allowable or target cost of Paradigm D in their design stage if a desired profit is to be realized.

Somewhat related to shorter product life cycles is the notion of idle capacity, which no longer may be as important a costing concept as it used to be. The suggested use of expected and actual volume of activity under Paradigm D surely enhances this thought.

Strategies concerning various product lines. If a company produces both commodity-type products and specialty-type products, it might be able to use both engineering- and market-driven standard costs. Market-driven standards probably would apply more to specialty products with their shorter life cycles. Engineering-driven standards could be more appropriate for the longer life cycles of commodity products. Nevertheless, market-driven standard costs must be determined for any intensely competitive product.

Standard cost variances/responsibility accounting. When we are looking toward a total cost per unit that must meet or better the allowable or target cost, cost variances by individual cost, activity, or department seem to be less relevant. Worker empowerment within a company requires a cooperative spirit rather than a focus on the individual department and cost center. Group or total success is the key today.

TABLE 3. OTHER ISSUES OF POSSIBLE CONTENTION

- Under Paradigm D, what volume of activity should be used when determining actual total cost per unit to compare with allowable or target cost per unit?
- Does the diminishing time frame for the product life cycle have an impact on the movement toward Paradigm D, especially the movement toward market-driven standard (allowable) costs as opposed to engineering-driven standard costs?
- Does a firm's strategic posture by product line allow for a possibility of different paradigms for different product lines?
- Is the old emphasis on cost variances by individual cost categories and departments less or no longer relevant in an era when the total cost from suppliers through to customers is emphasized?
- Where does the "theory of constraints" fit in? It looks like a refinement of the direct costing ideology.
- What method should be used for assigning costs to product lines and individual products within each product line?

The old individual cost and cost center focused control concepts inherent in standard costing and responsibility accounting may be counterproductive in today's world. The need for continuous improvement and forcing a continuous learning curve focused on total cost surely challenges one's training and earlier views.

The theory of constraints. Eli Goldratt, the Israeli physicist turned management consultant, has had an impact in recent years. His concentration on throughput, operating expense, and inventories has intrigued many management accountants. Interestingly, his theory of constraints (TOC) appears to be a refinement of direct costing coupled with linear programming.

TOC concentrates on only three variables: throughput, inventory, and operating expenses. Throughput relates to actual sales minus materials costs. Inventory consists only of purchased items at their purchased cost, and operating expenses are expenses other than materials. The objective is to focus on increasing throughput by eliminating constraints and decreasing both inventory and operating expenses.

In essence, the theory of constraints treats operating expenses as fixed and does not add any value to inventory whether it's in process or a finished state. All operating expenses plus the cost of inventory (materials) used to produce the actual throughput are considered in determining the true profitability of a period's throughput.

There is a direct costing flavor in the theory of constraints. The apparent success of TOC simultaneous with the development of ABC (a form of absorption costing) is worth examining. A detailed comparison of a number of users of both techniques certainly would be useful.

Assigning costs to product lines and within product lines. Ultimately, any cost accounting system has to deal with the twin issues of assigning costs between and within product lines. Activity-based costing may make a real contribution toward resolving both these issues.

ABC's concentration on three categories of variable costs may be especially useful. These three categories relate to the traditional notion of variability with units and the two new ideas of variability with product complexity (such as number of batches) and variability with product diversity (such as number of products). At this point in time, those of us concerned with these product-line issues must be open to alternative points of view.

LOOKING AHEAD—THE TWENTY-FIRST CENTURY PARADIGM

The best hope I see for a new Paradigm for the twenty-first century would be a combination of Paradigms C and D. An alternate variation could combine Paradigms C and D with elements from Paradigm B.

Regarding the first suggestion, in our intensely competitive world marketplace it is difficult to deny the efficacy of Paradigm D. The allowable or target standard cost permitted by our competitors in the marketplace cannot be ignored. Neither can we ignore the necessity for continuous improvement.

Paradigm D, however, is not sufficient. It must be combined with a before-the-fact determination of expected actual cost and an after-the-fact actual cost. The actual costs should be determined using the more precise ABC method, that is, Paradigm C.

The ongoing comparison of a cost per unit allowed by the marketplace (subject to continuous improvement) with the actual and expected actual cost per unit is vital. Such a system of comparison should seek answers to the following questions:

1. What adjustments to product promotion and pricing strategies most likely will yield expected and actual volumes capable of achieving allowable costs?
2. What adjustments to our current cost structure and work procedures will enhance our ability to achieve allowable costs?
3. What adjustments to our current cost structure and the way we cooperate with suppliers and customers will enhance our ability to achieve allowable costs?

What better use could be made of cost/management accounting data than to elicit answers to these questions? The combination of Paradigms C and D provides a meaningful environment in which to use ABC in the determination of product promotion and pricing strategies. Similarly, the combination gives real meaning to ABCs role in forcing consideration of alternative cost structures.

What happens when we add a touch of Paradigm B? Charles Horngren provides the idea for combining B with C and D to develop a new paradigm for the twenty-first century.[8] On numerous occasions he has cautioned us about using per-unit dollar amounts rather than total dollar amounts, especially in the context of fixed costs. By using per-unit amounts, we run the risk of treating fixed costs as variable costs and potentially concentrating too much on parts of the picture rather than the total picture.

Consider a product-line income statement, which has columns for individual products as well as a total column for the sum of individual products. The total column for the product line forces us to keep an eye on "total system" results while simultaneously looking at individual products or pieces of the system.

Shifting from the per-unit concentration of Paradigms C and D can be accomplished easily by multiplying the expected actual and actual volumes for each product by the per-unit amounts at each respective volume level for each product. Then the resulting total dollar amounts can be arranged in the format of a product line income statement as described above.

If we draw the distinction between fixed and variable costs, our product line income statement can include elements from Paradigm B with C and D. For example, if the only variable costs are materials, as assumed in the theory of constraints, we easily can develop contribution margins in the context of our product line income statements. The contribution margin as well as the net income by product and product line yields an opportunity to consider both short- and long-run aspects of profitability simultaneously as individual product and total system profitability are examined.

An intriguing result of combining Paradigm B with C and D is the ability to include, in our analysis of product line income statements, aspects of product life cycles and products that are expected to be cash users vs. cash generators during different stages of their life cycles. The product line income statement in this context looks at individual products and the sum total of a product line over a time frame that encompasses the life cycle of individual products or, at minimum, a three- to five-year period.

LOOKING BACKWARD TO SEE AHEAD

Often it is useful to reconsider where we have been during various stages of our development. Especially helpful would be case studies that could lead to the fine-tuning of a cost/management accounting paradigm for the twenty-first century. Of interest would be:

- A detailed comparison of a number of users of the theory of constraints and ABC.
- Historical analyses of early, prominent, and successful users of Paradigm B and their current status with regard to moving toward Paradigms C and D or combinations thereof.[9]
- Historical analyses of successful companies (defined in some reasonable manner) and their current status in regard to moving toward Paradigms C and D or combinations thereof, with or without elements from Paradigm B.

The suggestions in this article relative to a paradigm for the twenty-first century seem especially useful. There definitely seems to be a place in management accounting for the more refined and exacting calculations of ABC. But that place seems better suited in combination with Paradigm D and perhaps Paradigm B as well, especially as we proceed to the twenty-first century.

ENDNOTES
1. Depending on the product or service offered, one could have the same three elements of variable costs for marketing and administrative activities as well as manufacturing activities.

2. J. S. Earley, "Recent Developments in Cost Accounting and the 'Marginal Analysis'," *Journal of Political Economy*, June 1995, p. 237. The primary source for Earley's comments are the research studies of the Institute of Management Accountants, especially reports 16, 17 and 18 published during 1949 and 1950 on *The Analysis of Cost-Volume-Profit Relationships*.

3. For a discussion of how Paradigm B responds to this comment, see "Profit Planning and Pricing Strategies," Chapter 15 in *Managerial Cost Accounting; Planning and Control* by W. L. Ferrara, et al., Dame Publications, Inc., 1991.

4. See Thomas A. Stewart, "GE Keeps Those Ideas Coming," Fortune, August 12, 1991, for one company's approach to continuous improvement and empowerment.

5. See Dave Woodruff and Stephen Phillips, "Ford Has a Better Idea: Let Someone Else Have the Idea," Business Week, April 30, 1990.

6. H. T. Johnson, "Let's Set the Record Straight on ABC," Measurement Systems, Association for Manufacturing Excellence, March–April 1992.

7. See R. Cooper and P. B. B. Turney, Hewlett-Packard: Roseville Networks Division, Harvard Business School Case Study 189–117,1989, for an illustration of diminishing product life cycles and a resultant increase in new products as well as product modifications.

8. C. T. Horngren and G. L. Sundem, Introduction to Management Accounting, ninth edition, Prentice Hall, 1993, p. 201.

9. See Current Applications of Direct Costing, Institute of Management Accountants, Research Report 37, 1961, for a list of companies from which to choose.

William L. Ferrara, CPA, Ph.D., is the David M. Beights professor of accountancy at Stetson University, DeLand, Fla. He is a member of the Daytona Beach Area Chapter, through which this article was submitted, and can be reached at (904) 822-7421.

QUESTION

1.2 What does Ferrara see as the best combination of paradigms for the twenty-first century? Explain.

1.3 Pushing the Art of Management Accounting

Despite the many strides the profession has made over the years, some still believe that management accounting practices haven't taken as strong a hold in organizations as they should. FCMA Alexander Mersereau describes the challenges that are slowing the adoption of critical management accounting tools in broader business

by Alexander Mersereau, CMA, FCMA*

Management accounting practice has developed substantially over the past century, but recent studies suggest that the practice is no longer making the strides that it once did. Unless management accountants take a hard look at the effectiveness of current practice, this situation isn't likely to improve. In some companies, radical changes are needed to the structure of the finance function, the nature of the interactions management accountants have with other managers and the performance metrics used to guide the function itself.

THE GOOD NEWS

The early part of the 20th century was a period of rapid development for the field, when scientific management sought to identify what costs should be and economic organizations began to use budgets and relate returns to levels of investment. However little development occurred in the following years and, by the early 1980s, management accounting had reached a point of

* From: A. Mersereau, "Pushing the Art of Management Accounting," *CMA Management* (February 2006): 22–27. Reprinted with permission of Certified Management Accountants of Canada.

stagnation. H. Thomas Johnson and Robert S. Kaplan, writing in 1987, declared:

Today's management accounting information, driven by the procedures and the cycle of the organization's financial reporting system, is too late, too aggregated and too distorted to be relevant for managers' planning and control decisions.... Management accounting reports are of little help to operating managers as they attempt to reduce costs and improve productivity.[1]

This call for renewal was widely heeded. Their book *Relevance Lost: The Rise and Fall of Management Accounting* became a best seller for the editor of Harvard Business School Press and set off a wave of innovation and interest in the management accounting profession worldwide. Among the numerous technical innovations that came from this period were activity-based cost management, the Balanced Scorecard, benchmarking, life cycle costing, target costing, economic value added measures and strategic cost management. Management accounting was also able to build upon innovation in other fields such as Total Quality Management, Six Sigma, Kaizen and Business Process Reengineering. The development was rapid and interest spread well beyond the management accounting community. Peter Drucker, writing in the *Harvard Business Review* in 1990[2], declared that "the most exciting and innovative work in management today is found in accounting."

Fifteen years later, it's a good idea to ask ourselves what has happened to this reform. On one hand, the new tools that came from that period are evidently in use. Advanced management accounting practices such as ABC and non-financial performance measures are included in all major management textbooks. Studies of activity-based cost management (ABC) have reported generally positive user perceptions of benefits. Most of the larger companies appear to have experimented with Balanced Scorecard (BSC) techniques and studies have linked elements of scorecard use to higher profitability. Economic value added (EVA) research has reported positive results. On the other hand, despite these positive results it would appear that the adoption of advanced management accounting practices once again has slowed.

STIPPING STANDARDS

Studies estimate that the use of ABC has fallen and is now below 20%, and the percentage of those considering implementing ABC has also fallen. Of companies that have introduced activity-based techniques, only a minority claim that it is embedded in their organization. Strategic cost management techniques, such as attribute costing, seem little known outside academia. The majority of firms adopting EVA measures apparently don't use them significantly.

Balanced Scorecard researchers have concluded that most users make little attempt to link their non-financial performance to strategy and that only a small minority attempt to validate the cause and effect linkages included in their models. Moreover, Balanced Scorecard practice seems to have developed an independent momentum, excluding the finance function altogether in some organizations. There is even pressure for management accountants to do less. In his autobiography, Jack Welch complained: "The budget is the bane of corporate America (and) never should have existed" and research that would enable organizations to move beyond budgeting is underway.

Therefore, it isn't surprising that despite the wave of innovation in management accounting in the late 1980s and early 1990s, a recent study by IBM consulting reported that less than half of managers received role-specific information to support *ad hoc* decisions. Fewer still received frequent operational metrics related to processes under their control and very few could obtain information across functions, processes and geographies. A similar study by Accenture/Economist Intelligence Unit reported a significant gap between potential and actual practice.[3]

These indications of a slowing pace of management accounting change may be due to a range of factors. In some cases, new management accounting tools aren't adapted to organizational strategy or structure and can't be used. And in some cases, innovation has failed due to implementation-related factors. However, the main problems aren't technical or structural; they lie in the need for a better management of the management accounting process itself.

GETTING INVOLVED

At the heart of the management accounting process is a communications system, or a set of communications systems, that provide information to managers. The ability of management accountants to improve the scope, timeliness or quality of the information they provide depends on how well they understand and manage these systems. There are three main areas in management accounting systems in which communication problems can occur, which are illustrated here using the tale of *The Three Monkeys*.

The three monkeys that most people know are *Speak No Evil, Hear No Evil* and *See No Evil*. In this medieval Japanese illustration, a trio of monkeys is depicted with one having his hands over his mouth, another covering his ears and a third his eyes. The original use of this image seems to have been to illustrate wisdom. The three wise monkeys, as they were referred to, counselled the disciplined avoidance of evil. Conversely in modern times the image of the three monkeys has been used to emphasize stupidity and negligence, or the unwillingness of people to get involved. Here they are used in the latter sense to illustrate the need for management accountants to become more involved in this communications process.

The management accounting communications process begins with a set of inputs to the accounting information system. This data is then encoded into information using a language (accounting) and transmitted to a recipient. Here is our first monkey, the speaking one. The management accountant can't possibly observe, measure and report on everything. She must select from a wide field what to report, how to report it and when. To do this well, she must anticipate how this information ought to be used, have a language at her disposal that succinctly codifies the key data observed, and have a communication medium that reaches the intended audience efficiently and effectively.

The next leg of the communications process is the receipt of the information. Here we confront the second monkey, the hearing one. Managers must be able to correctly decode the reports they receive. They must therefore be familiar with the concepts used in the accounting models that are used to prepare the reports and understand what the variances in the numbers signify.

Finally, managers act on the information received. How they will act depends on how they interpret the message. This is a separate challenge and introduces the third monkey, the seeing one. Individuals interpret and act on information using personal decision rules that they have learned over time. A large part of any manager's decision strategy will be guided by how he views his organization and his role in it, and personal and corporate objectives are never completely aligned.

The actions that a manager takes as a result of receiving information (including actions taken in anticipation) and the consequences of these actions should be of great interest to the management accountant. These consequences become part of the world she must observe. This is the first monkey all over again, and so the cycle continues.

At the heart of the management accounting process is a communications system, or a set of communications systems, that provide information to managers. The ability of management accountants to improve the scope, timeliness or quality of the information they provide depends on how well they understand and manage these systems.

BIG PICTURE PROVIDERS
How do some organizations meet the challenges illustrated by the three monkeys? Let's look again at the first monkey, the speaking one. To be able to communicate to managers, accountants must have a clear picture of the strategic importance of the phenomena they observe, and they must have a clear idea of how operating decisions are made. Some of this can be learned in university but most of it comes from day-to-day experiences within operations. This requires frequent contact between management accountants and other managers.

However, the cycles of monthly, quarterly and annual planning and reporting are punishing and accountants regularly work overtime during these periods. To overcome these barriers, some organizations encourage contact by physically locating accountants with other managers. Some deliberately place accountants on interfunctional working groups and many ensure that management accountants have either dotted or solid line accountability to operating managers. Some organizations have adopted a structure in which some management accountants don't have routine reporting responsibilities.

A complicating factor is how management accountants are themselves received when dealing with operations personnel. Over the years in some quarters accountants have earned a reputation for bringing an unbalanced and overly financial point of view to problem solving, which has diminished their position in the hierarchy. Some managers have characterized financial managers as among those with the least mental flexibility, the most closed minds and the least willingness to take risks.

While some of the blame for this impression can be attributed to poor public relations, the selection and training of accountants remains a significant issue. Management accounting requires practitioners with a "big picture" point of view who are able to challenge operating managers as peers. Formal education may actually have a negative effect on recruitment. Several studies have suggested that accountants may follow a training regime that is too highly oriented to the financial aspects of their work and not sufficiently directed to the behavioural side. Others have observed that the financial bias to the educational component has the regrettable consequence of attracting candidates to the profession who are more comfortable with a formulabased approach to decision making and less at ease with the ambiguities that characterise managerial work.

EDUCATING OTHERS
Let's turn now to the hearing monkey, which refers to the ability of managers to understand the accounting reports they receive. When financial accounts are prepared and distributed externally, accountants are permitted to assume that the reader is trained in accounting. This isn't the case inside the organization, where a vast majority of managers haven't completed any significant formal accounting training, and those who have will have forgotten much of what they learned.

Some organizations are attempting to overcome this problem by supplementing or replacing financial reports with symbols or colours (green for OK, yellow to signal issues and red to announce a real problem). While such systems have the advantage of simplicity, questions need to be asked about the overall content of such communications. What does yellow or green really mean? What about the grey areas in between? And in the political context of organizations, how might these ambiguities be exploited for personal benefit?

Rather than reducing the content of accounting messages to one of three possible states, accountants need to help end users become more proficient in reading accounting reports. Some organizations have built accounting training modules for their managers that help them understand the specific reports they receive. Management accountants have an important role to play in preparing and delivering training materials. In today's complex managerial environment technical functions, especially accounting, need to become more than suppliers of information. They must become a kind of a school where managers can receive training. Yet in many organizations, accountants are too busy to become trainers and internal reward systems likely discourage such activities. Here the training activity itself needs to be repositioned to make it attractive to accountants.

As the scope of management accounting messages widens to include non-financial performance indicators, management accountants acquire an additional challenge. Many managers have difficulties visualizing the cause and effect relationships that link value drivers to financial returns. Yet this is the key knowledge needed to manage value, and training is often required to help managers understand better the cause and effect relationships that underlie shareholder value.

The third monkey, the seeing one, refers also to the manager, this time to the conflict that exists between shareholder values and the interests of individual managers. Increasing functional specialization means that managers are increasingly disconnected from shareholder values. Many managers are strongly committed to the organization without being committed to the financial goals that drive it. Management accountants have a role to play in instilling financial discipline and conveying financial values to non-financial managers. One method is to require operating managers (rather than accountants) to systematically prepare and present the financial analysis of their business unit. Shareholder value training is also important.

At the same time that the management accounting function must pay greater attention to the effectiveness of its internal communications processes, other demands are arising. There is increasing pressure to reduce the overall cost of the finance function as a percentage of revenues. There are increasingly time consuming demands for more detailed external reporting. While these latter goals are important and must be achieved, putting the priority there only increases the risk that internal accounting communications will fail to achieve their objectives and that management accounting system change will be further delayed.

THE WAY FORWARD

Improving management accounting begins with a commitment to change. For many organizations, this is a huge step. Accountants have been found to be the first to resist accounting change, and the failure of various ABC and scorecard projects has been linked to the unwillingness of accountants themselves to see the project through. Many accountants are afraid that radical change might endanger existing systems and processes. To ensure that change is permanent, commitment to change must come from the top and must be sustained.

As the previous examples illustrate, improving the management accounting function often requires structural reorganization. If everyone is consumed by the routine reporting cycles, there will be no one left to assume emerging roles in areas such as management training. In some organizations bringing in new people will be necessary. Management accounting is more than just accounting, it requires people who understand the behavioural consequences of numbers and who can link controls to strategy.

Last, but not least, the management accounting process requires new metrics. Most accounting functions measure timeliness, in terms of the delay between the end of the reporting cycle and the issuing of the report, and many measure the cost of the finance function relative to revenues. Few organizations measure the use or the usefulness of the management accounting information provided. The absence of such measures guarantees that things will remain the same.

DIAGNOSTIC

Management accountants should conduct frequent analyses of their communications processes. Such a diagnosis would include the following questions:

- What changes to management accounting practice have you initiated in the last two years?
- How many people are committed to real change?
- Do accounting personnel regard themselves as members of the operating team?
- How much time do management accountants spend with non-financial personnel?
- Are management accounting personnel physically located in such a way as to bring them in regular contact with nonfinancial managers?

- Do management accountants have a reporting responsibility to operational managers?
- Do reports to individual managers/units contain a maximum amount of information about that specific unit?
- Are accountants given responsibilities that can only be discharged by working with operational people?
- Do the accountants who have these responsibilities have sufficient status to maintain working relationships on the basis of mutual respect?
- How many accounting personnel do not have significant routine reporting responsibilities?
- How much financial training is provided for operating management?
- Does this training explain the links between financial and operational events?
- Does this training explain why financial goals are important?
- Are operating managers required to systematically prepare and present the financial analysis of their unit?
- Do performance measures other than cost and timeliness exist for the management accounting function?
- What priority is given to these metrics and how are they used?

The more management accountants can respond positively to these questions, the better organizations will become at managing the communications processes that underlie management accounting. This will create a better understanding of the role that management accountants can play in achieving success and it is in this context that significant management accounting change will occur.

Alexander Mersereau, CMA, FCMA, D.Sc., is a professor at HEC Montreal.

ENDNOTES

1. Johnson, H. & Kaplan, R. (1987), *Relevance Lost: The Rise and Fall of Management Accounting*, Boston, Harvard Business School Press, p 269.
2. Drucker, Peter (1990) The Emerging Theory of Manufacturing *Harvard Business Review* May/June pp. 94–102.
3. Accenture Finance Solutions (2004) *Best in Class How Finance Business Process Outsourcing Can Help Create a High Performance Finance Function.*

QUESTION

1.3. According to Mersereau who is often the first to resist accounting change? Why is this the case?

1.4 Preserving Control

*In today's still turbulent economy,
U.S. controllers are trying to do their best
to maintain the upper hand while being surrounded
by financial and operational distractions.*

by RamonaDzinkowski*

As part of the continuous restructuring activities of U.S. companies, corporate controllers have undertaken critical initiatives to ensure that financial and operational controls remain intact. Impacts of downsizing, new methods and metrics related to risk management, and a general rethink of supply chain strategies and procedures are just some of the issues controllers are dealing with. At the same time, they're keeping a close eye on what the next big operational challenge might be for the finance functions of their companies. Most agree that, after the dust of the U.S. recession clears, it could well be the adoption of International Financial Reporting Standards (IFRS).

---

* From: R. Dzinkowski, "Preserving Control," *Strategic Finance* (March 2010): 43-46. Reprinted with permission.

At a recent Controllers Roundtable discussion during the Financial Executives International (FEI) Current Financial Reporting Issues Conference, an expert panel of corporate controllers from U.S. companies provided their insights on these and other issues that will be keeping them awake at night in 2010.

DOWNSIZING

U.S. controllers are concerned with the impacts of downsizing, not only on the productive capabilities of the firm but also on the overall operational and control environment. According to Marsha Hunt, vice president and corporate controller of Cummins Inc., a global company that designs, manufactures, sells, and services diesel engines in 190 countries and territories, one of the critical issues surrounding the control environment during a period of downsizing or restructuring is to make sure that finance is aware of the decisions made for the company as a whole and to make sure a stop-gap strategy exists in advance.

Says Hunt, "One of the considerations as the corporate controller when we were going through [downsizing] decisions was to make sure that there was good awareness of exactly who was being impacted…and I don't mean just within the financial function, but also in other key functions, such as procurement or marketing, the people that make pricing decisions, the people with whom the finance organization may already have very good relationships. There's a lot of work involved to try and make sure that the controller is informed of those decisions and has the opportunity to put in place some alternative procedures in advance of people leaving the company."

At the same time, monetary controls remain a constant focus of the controller's office during periods of significant downsizing, particularly in companies with complex international operations. For example, with the ongoing restructuring at a decentralized company like Tyco, and the accompanying downsizing of the workforce, the emphasis was on a very structured approach to managing financial controls.

John Davidson, Tyco's senior vice president, controller, and chief accounting officer, explains: "We're a decentralized company, so we have lots of different points where accounting transactions or financial transactions are processed. We have ongoing monitoring to make sure that fundamental blocking and tackling is being done, such as your basic account reconciliations. There is a fair ly structured process that we have for reporting the status of those, and we make sure there is no significant slippage. As well, we have a structured balance sheet review process that we go through and make sure that our businesses are on top of their various accounts and that we're not slipping in any significant way." With respect to the impacts of loss of people, Davidson says, "We pay very close attention to the positions that have been vacated, and for any key position we make sure that we understand how those roles are being covered."

THE ROLE OF SOX REPORTING

New reporting risks may also occur as a result of downsizing that make internal controls over financial reporting even more critical. As Nicholas S. Cyprus, vice president, controller, and chief accounting officer at General Motors Corporation, explains, certain risks emerge when companies lay off a substantial number of the management team. He notes, "When you go through a downsizing, just simple things like certain blocking-and-tackling controls, reconciliations, get put to the side because people don't have enough time to do them, and, of course, depending on how significant the accounting is, it doesn't get reconciled. That sets you up for potentially an end-of-period adjustment and, if it's really bad, a restatement."

> "When you have a major restructuring, what do you do to make sure you haven't broken your control infrastructure?"
>
> —*Nicholas Cyprus, vice president, controller, and chief accounting officer, General Motors Corporation*

To address these risks, General Motors turned to its highly structured internal control evaluation and reporting architectures. "At GM," says Cyprus, "we took out about a third of our executive headcount and quite a [number] of our salaried employees. We tied that into our SOX [Sarbanes-Oxley Act] team structure. So one of the things I asked the other controllers to do was map out all the jobs that were going away. They didn't necessarily need to be finance jobs because a lot of operations jobs have accounting implications. We actually tied it back to our SOX process and then used that process to see how we were covering those jobs to make sure we didn't have any gaps."

KEY METRICS

Associated with restructuring efforts in a bad economy are the key metrics that are being used to monitor financial risks more closely. At Tyco and many other companies affected by the reduction in global consumer demand, managing working capital has taken on new meaning. As John Davidson explains, "Our focus is on working capital from an operating standpoint, also in terms of just understanding the financial performance of our businesses. This year and over the past year, we actually formed what we called a working capital management team." Each month the CFOs from Tyco's various businesses meet to talk about process performance around things such as accounts receivable. At the same time, Tyco increased its focus on inventories. Because of the downturn, Davidson says, "balance sheets have been tricky, so making sure that the inventories that we do have remain filled is a key thing."

In addition to managing internal financial and operational risks, companies increasingly are monitoring the financial positions of companies they rely on across their entire production and distribution processes. At Cummins, their focus has turned to scrutinizing the strength of the balance sheet of their suppliers as well as their supply policies. In several cases, Cummins was relying on a single source of supply, which, under distressed circumstances, would leave them exposed to risks of disruptions in production. This caused them to look for alternative sources in overseas markets, which then shifted their focus toward measuring inventory turnover related to longer shipping lead times.

As Marsha Hunt says, "We've had a number of areas where we had one source of supply, and in this economy we were concerned. We realize that our suppliers are struggling, so we're looking at alternative sources. In some cases those could be international suppliers." But according to Hunt, the change in the supply chain required a change in Cummins's way of thinking about inventories and how they were measured so that the metrics didn't undermine or mask what was considered a good business decision. "What you can have happening," she explains, "is that you are shifting some of your sourcing to an overseas environment, and you may have a lot of material that's sitting on a boat for 60 days before it gets to you. So now we look at certain measures, such as inventory turnover, for example. You can have a very smart business decision to actually source your material somewhere else, but if you don't take a look at how you measure your inventory turnover you could be actually driving a negative trend or masking the trends you want to measure."

IFRS OR U.S. GAAP? DIVERGENT VIEWS
The Securities & Exchange Commission (SEC) has yet to set a date for the U.S. adoption of IFRS. But with more than 150 countries around the world adopting them and the ongoing momentum by the International Accounting Standards Board (IASB) and Financial Accounting Standards Board (FASB) to produce one set of high-quality global standards, U.S. controllers are wondering whether they should turn up the heat on IFRS conversion in their companies in 2010. With the general understanding that converting to IFRS doesn't happen overnight, some international companies are paying closer attention to how the standards are being rolled out in publicly listed subsidiaries around the world, and others are choosing to wait until the SEC is satisfied that IFRS should be the standard for reporting in American firms.

Cummins Inc. owns 51% of a subsidiary in India that's a reporting registrant in that country. Traditionally, the company has been structured so that the corporate control function hasn't been engaged in local statutory reporting; rather, their subsidiaries report to them on a U.S. Generally Accepted Accounting Principles (GAAP) basis. But now that India is adopting IFRS, Cummins's control team will be monitoring what happens there very closely, which will help them make decisions around how to proceed elsewhere. Marsha Hunt says, "Largely it will be accelerating the positions we need to make around certain policies. We don't want to set up our Indian subsidiary in a situation where the parent company comes in, assuming the U.S. were to adopt [IFRS] at some point in the future, and then forces a restatement of the financial statements there. So we're trying to think through those judgment issues now."

To prepare for IFRS conversion now, Cummins has been encouraging training and has identified core team members they want to expose to IFRS, focusing first on the critical conversion areas that are expected to have the largest impact on the company. As Hunt explains, "We've actually taken two of the areas that we think will affect us to the greatest degree, as far as capturing information differently, and [those are] research and development expenses and fixed assets. We've already put together some project teams to try and think through and understand what the differences are between U.S. GAAP and those areas [under IFRS] because we want to be in a position to advise our subsidiaries in India." Cummins has also engaged Ernst & Young to advise the Indian subsidiary to help them move from local GAAP to IFRS and will be learning through the conversion process as it rolls out. "The core team in my group," she adds, "is going to be spending a lot of time on video conferences very early in the morning as we want to participate in those meetings with Ernst & Young and our Indian subsidiary to really understand what's going on."

Similarly, companies like Tyco—with an extensive global network—see the benefit of a unified standard and an early understanding of how IFRS is being adopted in their companies around the world. As John Davidson explains, "We have about 1,200 legal entities across the globe, of which roughly 900 are outside the U.S. For us, one standard, one reporting scheme would be really beneficial. Think about the benefits that would improve the company—to be able to move people from one countryor one business to the next and think they'll be talking about the same set of standards. I think it would be a great benefit. We're not there yet, and it's certainly going to be a lot of work, but we are working with the [business] units that are getting ready to adopt."

But as the economic downturn in the U.S. has limited discretionary spending across the board, it has also potentially impeded the progress toward understanding the likely impacts of IFRS in many companies. From a practical perspective, controllers are concerned that the budgetary aspects of adoption aren't being adequately considered at this time, and, without a hard adoption date, the argument for IFRS conversion resources remains weak.

As Marsha Hunt explains, "…we have people at Cummins who are engaged in other groups in other parts of the organization that don't understand necessarily that IFRS could advantage us. So one of the things that [has] happened is that…°the spending has been turned off on anything but the compliance function at this time. I'm sure we're not alone with other controllers that are a little concerned, or at least I'm concerned, about the budgetary aspects of this not being properly considered by some of those senior folks in the company. It's difficult, frankly, without any rules to put in front of someone to try and argue why we should be spending those resources and even doing the work to figure out what that cost is going to be. So, I think we've lost a little bit of time in being ready compared to where we might have been a couple years ago."

Others are taking a wait-and-see approach, looking to the FASB and the IASB to move further along the path to convergence of IFRS and U.S. GAAP. Says Nicholas Cyprus of GM, "I'm not moving GM forward in IFRS other than just a monitoring process of understanding what the rules are….I think we've got to get a heck of a lot closer to having one converged set of GAAP before we all go crazy trying to reconcile between the two." At the same time, given the business and legal environment in the U.S., he questions whether or not a less rules-based system makes sense. "I am still very skeptical in the way we do business in the United States," he says, "and the kind of litigation rules that we have, whether a principle-based philosophy's going to

work….You know, you get into a judgment-based thing and debates are going to reign…and we have enough even with the rules-based environment today, and all the complexities of the rules….So I think if the regulators want the preparer community to step up and get this done, they need to look at themselves and get convergence on the way, really on the way, before you're going to see General Motors step up and spend money. I don't want to spend it multiple times, and I'm worried about that."

SHIFTING FOCUS

From the three experts providing their views on what's keeping them up at night, we clearly see that controllers now have to do things differently in order to ensure that their control environments remain intact. A shift in effort toward monitoring the impacts of layoffs on control procedures, increasing the focus on accounts receivable, and scrutinizing the financial health of suppliers with greater rigor isn't likely to be unique to American controllers but is expected to characterize their jobs for many months to come. At the same time, some U.S. controllers are turning their attention toward adopting global accounting standards in 2010 in anticipation of eventual acceptance from the SEC. Others, like General Motors, continue to wait with caution for a level of comfort that the FASB and IASB are getting closer to finalizing their conversion projects.

Ramona Dzinkowski is a Canadian economist and business journalist living in Toronto. She is also executive director of the Canadian Financial Executives Research Foundation, the research institute of Financial Executives International (FEI) Canada. You can reach her at rndresearch@ interhop.net. ©2010 by Ramona Dzinkowski. For copies and reprints, contact the author.

QUESTION

1.4 Why are controllers concerned about the effects of downsizing on their organizations?

Chapter 2

The Balanced Scorecard
Strategy Map

John Shank and Vijay Govindarajan's article, *Strategic Cost Management and the Value Chain* (Reading 2.1), begins the series of articles for this chapter. The article discusses the value chain concept as the central building block of strategic cost management. Management accounting methods such as activity based costing and other tools can be incorporated into the value chain concept. The authors illustrate their method of developing a value chain within an organization and then use a case study of the paper industry to illustrate their argument. This article could also be used with material in Chapter 9 on managing costs across the value chain.

Readings 2.2 and 2.3, Kaplan and Norton's *Transforming the Balanced Scorecard from Performance Measurement to Strategic Management*, Parts I and II, respectively, extend the authors' work on the balanced scorecard into the area of organizational strategy. Together they introduce the idea of strategy maps and balanced scorecards to develop performance objectives and measures linked to strategy. The key relationships are shown in Figure 2 of the first installment, which is a comprehensive illustration of how factors in the learning and growth perspective affect processes within the internal perspective. In turn, these processes influence key variables in the customer perspective. Factors from both the internal and customer perspectives affect revenue growth and productivity strategies in the financial perspective, which ultimately improves shareholder value.

In Reading 2.4, *Measuring the Strategic Readiness of Intangible Assets*, Robert Kaplan and David Norton, focus on one of the most vexing aspects of successfully implementing the balanced scorecard—aligning intangible assets in the learning and growth perspective. More specifically, the article discusses the three key categories of intangible assets and their readiness to be deployed. The three categories are: (1) human capital, (2) information capital, and (3) organization capital. Because intangible assets are considered "softer" or more subjective than financial measures, managers often ignore them or don't know how to manage them. This article provides a compelling argument as to the importance of managing intangible assets to successfully implementing the balanced scorecard for the benefit of the organization as a whole.

Reading 2.5, *Strategy or Stakeholders: Which Comes First?* by Robert Kaplan argues that the traditional approach of putting stakeholders first, above corporate strategy, is misguided. Rather, organizations should first develop their corporate strategy, and then incorporate the interests of stakeholders. He argues that companies can account for any stakeholder considerations they view as important through their Balanced Scorecard and Strategy Map and mold performance to them without compromising strategy or their ability to adjust it to changing conditions.

Readings
Chapter 2

2.1 Strategic Cost Management and the Value Chain

by John K. Shank and Vijay Govindarajan*

Strategic Cost Management (SCM) is organized around the value chain concept. The value chain is the linked set of value-creating activities. In contrast, traditional management accounting uses the value-added perspective.

The value chain framework is a method for breaking down the chain – from suppliers of basic raw materials to end-use customers – into strategically relevant activities in order to understand the behavior of costs and the sources of differentiation. Gaining and sustaining competitive advantage requires the firm to understand the entire value delivery system.

The value-added concept has two big disadvantages – it starts too late and stops too soon. For instance the value added concept begins with payments to suppliers (purchases) and stops with charges to customers (sales). The key is to maximize the difference (the value added) between purchases and sales. Starting cost analysis with purchases misses all of the opportunities for exploiting linkages with the firm's suppliers.

Traditional management accounting relies on a single cost driver – output volume. Cost concepts relate to output volume – fixed versus variable cost, average cost versus marginal cost and others.

In contrast, in the value chain framework, output volume is seen to capture little of the richness of cost behavior. Instead, multiple cost drivers are used based on the various types of activities throughout the value chain. These cost drivers are broken into two types: structural and executional cost drivers.

STRUCTURAL COST DRIVERS INCLUDE:

- Scale – What is the size of investments in manufacturing, R&D and marketing?
- Scope – What is the degree of vertical integration?

- Experience – how many times in the past has the firm done what it is doing again?
- Technology – what process technologies are used in each step of the firm's value chain
- Complexity – how wide a line of products or services is being offered to customers?

EXECUTIONAL COST DRIVERS INCLUDE:

- Workforce involvement – Is the work force committed to continuous improvement?
- Total quality management (TQM) – Is the work force committed to total product quality?
- Capacity utilization – What are the scale choices on maximum plant construction?
- Plant Layout – How efficient, against current norms, is the plant's layout?
- Product Configuration - Is the design or formulation of the produce effective?
- Linkages with suppliers or customers – Is the linage with suppliers or customers exploited, according to the firm's value chain?

Shank and Govindarajan provide several examples to illustrate how to use both structural and executional drivers to derive the most benefit from using a value chain approach.

QUESTIONS

2.1a What is the difference between the value-added and value-chain concepts? Explain.

2.1b What are structural and executional cost drivers and how are they distinguished in Shank and Govindarajan's article?

---

* This article has been summarized from the original article by John K. Shank and Vijay Govindarajan, "Strategic Cost Management and the Value Chain," *Journal of Cost Management* (Winter 1992): 5–21.Reprinted with permission, Copyright © 1992, Thomson-Reuters.

2.2 Transforming the Balanced Scorecard from Performance Measurement to Strategic Management: Part I

by Robert S. Kaplan and David P. Norton*

Several years ago we introduced the Balanced Scorecard (Kaplan and Norton 1992). We began with the premise that an exclusive reliance on financial measures in a management system is insufficient. Financial measures are lag indicators that report on the outcomes from past actions. Exclusive reliance on financial indicators could promote behavior that sacrifices long-term value creation for short-term performance (Porter 1992; AICPA 1994). The Balanced Scorecard approach retains measures of financial performance—the lagging outcome indicators—but supplements these with measures on the drivers, the lead indicators, of future financial performance.

THE BALANCED SCORECARD EMERGES

The limitations of managing solely with financial measures, however, have been known for decades.[1] What is different now? Why has the Balanced Scorecard concept been so widely adopted by manufacturing and service companies, nonprofit organizations, and government entities around the world since its introduction in 1992?

First, previous systems that incorporated nonfinancial measurements used *ad hoc* collections of such measures, more like checklists of measures for managers to keep track of and improve than a comprehensive system of linked measurements. The Balanced Scorecard emphasizes the linkage of measurement to strategy (Kaplan and Norton 1993) and the cause-and-effect linkages that describe the hypotheses of the strategy (Kaplan and Norton 1996b). The tighter connection between the measurement system and strategy elevates the role for nonfinancial measures from an operational checklist to a comprehensive system for strategy implementation (Kaplan and Norton 1996a).

Second, the Balanced Scorecard reflects the changing nature of technology and competitive advantage in the latter decades of the 20th century. In the industrial-age competition of the 19th and much of the 20th centuries, companies achieved competitive advantage from their investment in and management of tangible assets such as inventory, property, plant, and equipment (Chandler 1990). In an economy dominated by tangible assets, financial measurements were adequate to record investments on companies' balance sheets. Income statements could also capture the expenses associated with the use of these tangible assets to produce revenues and profits. But by the end of the 20th century, intangible assets became the major source for competitive advantage. In 1982, tangible book values represented 62% of industrial organizations' market values; ten years later, the ratio had plummeted to 38% (Blair 1995). By the end of the 20th century, the book value of tangible assets accounted for less than 20% of companies' market values (Webber 2000, quoting research by Baruch Lev).

Clearly, strategies for creating value shifted from managing tangible assets to knowledge-based strategies that create and deploy an organization's intangible assets. These include customer relationships, innovative products and services, high-quality and responsive operating processes, skills and knowledge of the workforce, the information technology that supports the work force and links the firm to its customers and suppliers, and the organizational climate that encourages innovation, problem-solving, and improvement. But companies were unable to adequately measure their intangible assets (Johnson and Kaplan 1987, 201–202). Anecdotal data from management publications indicated that many companies could not implement their new strategies in this environment (Kiechel 1982; Charan and Colvin 1999). They could not manage what they could not describe or measure.

INTANGIBLE ASSETS: VALUATION VS. VALUE CREATION

Some call for accountants to make an organization's intangible assets more visible to managers and investors by placing them on a company's balance sheet. But several factors prevent valid valuation of intangible assets on balance sheets.

First, the value from intangible assets is indirect. Assets such as knowledge and technology seldom have a direct impact on revenue and profit. Improvements in intangible assets affect financial outcomes through chains of cause-and-effect relationships involving two or three intermediate stages (Huselid 1995; Becker and

* From: R. S. Kaplan and D. P. Norton, "Transforming the Balanced Scorecard from Performance Measurement to Strategic Management: Part I," *Accounting Horizons* (March 2001), 15(1): 87–104. ©American Accounting Association. Articles available online at http://aaahq.org/pubs/electpubs.htm.

Huselid 1998). For example, consider the linkages in the service management profit chain (Heskett et al. 1994):

- investments in employee training lead to improvements in service quality
- better service quality leads to higher customer satisfaction
- higher customer satisfaction leads to increased customer loyalty
- increased customer loyalty generates increased revenues and margins

Financial outcomes are separated casually and temporally from improving employees' capabilities. The complex linkages make it difficult, if not impossible, to place a financial value on an asset such as work force capabilities or employee morale, much less to measure period-to-period changes in that financial value.

Second, the value from intangible assets depends on organizational context and strategy. This value cannot be separated from the organizational processes that transform intangibles into customer and financial outcomes. The balance sheet is a linear, additive model. It records each class of asset separately and calculates the total by adding up each asset's recorded value. The value created from investing in individual intangible assets, however, is neither linear nor additive.

Senior investment bankers in a firm such as Goldman Sachs are immensely valuable because of their knowledge about complex financial products and their capabilities for managing relationships and developing trust with sophisticated customers. People with the same knowledge, experience, and capabilities, however, are nearly worthless to a financial services company such as etrade.com that emphasizes operational efficiency, low cost, and technology-based trading. The value of an intangible asset depends critically on the context—the organization, the strategy, and other complementary assets—in which the intangible asset is deployed.

Intangible assets seldom have value by themselves.[2] Generally, they must be bundled with other intangible and tangible assets to create value. For example, a new growth-oriented sales strategy could require new knowledge about customers, new training for sales employees, new data-bases, new information systems, a new organization structure, and a new incentive compensation program. Investing in just one of these capabilities, or in all of them but one, could cause the new sales strategy to fail. The value does not reside in any individual intangible asset. It arises from creating the entire set of assets along with a strategy that links them together. The value-creation process is multiplicative, not additive.

THE BALANCED SCORECARD SUPPLEMENTS CONVENTIONAL FINANCIAL REPORTING

Companies' balance sheets report separately on tangible assets, such as raw material, land, and equipment, based on their historic cost—the traditional financial accounting method. This was adequate for industrial-age companies, which succeeded by combining and transforming their tangible resources into products whose value exceeded their acquisition and production costs. Financial accounting conventions relating to depreciation and cost of goods sold enabled an income statement to measure how much value was created beyond the costs incurred to acquire and transform tangible assets into finished products and services.

Some argue that companies should follow the same cost-based convention for their intangible assets—capitalize and subsequently amortize the expenditures on training employees, conducting research and development, purchasing and developing databases, and advertising that creates brand awareness. But such costs are poor approximations of the realizable value created by investing in these intangible assets. Intangible assets can create value for organizations, but that does not imply that they have separable market values. Many internal and linked organizational processes, such as design, delivery, and service, are required to transform the potential value of intangible assets into products and services that have tangible value.

We introduced the Balanced Scorecard to provide a new framework for describing value-creating strategies that link intangible and tangible assets. The scorecard does not attempt to "value" an organization's intangible assets, but it does measure these assets in units other than currency. The Balanced Scorecard describes how intangible assets get mobilized and combined with intangible and tangible assets to create differentiating customer-value propositions and superior financial outcomes.

STRATEGY MAPS

Since introducing the Balanced Scorecard in 1992, we have helped over 200 executive teams design their scorecard programs. Initially we started with a clean sheet of paper, asking, "what is the strategy," and allowed the strategy and the Balanced Scorecard to emerge from interviews and discussions with the senior executives. The scorecard provided a framework for organizing strategic objectives into the four perspectives displayed in Figure 1):

1. *Financial*—the strategy for growth, profitability, and risk viewed from the perspective of the shareholder.

2. *Customer*—the strategy for creating value and differentiation from the perspective of the customer.
3. *Internal Business Processes*—the strategic priorities for various business processes that create customer and shareholder satisfaction.
4. *Learning and Growth*—the priorities to create a climate that supports organizational change, innovation, and growth.

From this initial base of experience, we subsequently developed a general framework for describing and implementing strategy that we believe can be as useful as the traditional framework of income statement, balance sheet, and statement of cash flows for financial planning and reporting. The new framework, which we call a "Strategy Map," is a logical and comprehensive architecture for describing strategy, as illustrated in Figure 2. A strategy map specifies the critical elements and their linkages for an organization's strategy.

■ Objectives for growth and productivity to enhance shareholder value.
■ Market and account share, acquisition, and retention of targeted customers where profitable growth will occur.

■ Value propositions that would lead customers to do more higher-margin business with the company.
■ Innovation and excellence in products, services, and processes that deliver the value proposition to targeted customer segments, promote operational improvements, and meet community expectations and regulatory requirements.
■ Investments required in people and systems to generate and sustain growth.

By translating their strategy into the logical architecture of a strategy map and Balanced Scorecard, organizations create a common and understandable point of reference for all organizational units and employees.

Organizations build strategy maps from the top down, starting with the destination and then charting the routes that lead there. Corporate executives first review their mission statement, why their company exists, and core values, what their company believes in. From that information, they develop their strategic vision, what their company wants to become. This vision creates a clear picture of the company's overall goal, which could be to become a top-quartile performer. The strategy identifies the path intended to reach that destination.

FIGURE 1. THE BALANCED SCORECARD DEFINES A STRATEGY'S CAUSE-AND-EFFECT RELATIONSHIPS

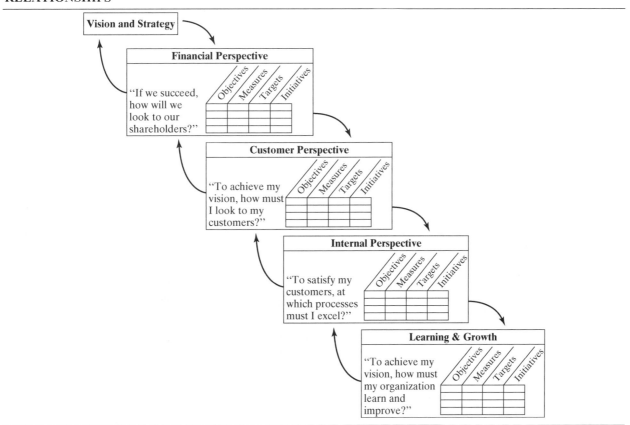

21

Financial Perspective. The typical destination for profit-seeking enterprises is a significant increase in shareholder value (we will discuss the modifications for nonprofit and government organizations later in the paper). Companies increase economic value through two basic approaches—*revenue growth* and *productivity*.[3] A revenue growth strategy generally has two components: build the franchise with revenue from new markets, new products, and new customers; and increase sales to existing customers by deepening relationships with them, including cross-selling multiple products and services, and offering complete solutions. A productivity strategy also generally has two components: improve the cost structure by lowering direct and indirect expenses; and utilize assets more efficiently by reducing the working and fixed capital needed to support a given level of business.

Customer Perspective. The core of any business strategy is the *customer-value proposition*, which describes the unique mix of product, price, service, relationship, and image that a company offers. It defines how the organization differentiates itself from competitors to attract, retain, and deepen relationships with targeted customers. The value proposition is crucial

because it helps an organization connect its internal processes to improved outcomes with its customers.

Companies differentiate their value proposition by selecting among *operational excellence* (for example, McDonalds and Dell Computer), *customer intimacy* (Home Depot and IBM in the 1960s and 1970s), and *product leadership* (Intel and Sony) (Treacy and Wiersema 1997, 31–45). Sustainable strategies are based on excelling at one of the three while maintaining threshold standards with the other two. After identifying its value proposition, a company knows which classes and types of customers to target.

Specifically, companies that pursue a strategy of operational excellence need to excel at competitive pricing, product quality, product selection, lead time, and on-time delivery. For customer intimacy, an organization must stress the quality of its relationships with customers, including exceptional service, and the completeness and suitability of the solutions it offers individual customers. Companies that pursue a product-leadership strategy must concentrate on the functionality, features, and performance of their products and services.

The customer perspective also identifies the intended outcomes from delivering a differentiated value proposition. These would include market share in targeted customer segments, account share with targeted

FIGURE 2. THE BALANCED SCORECARD STRATEGY MAP

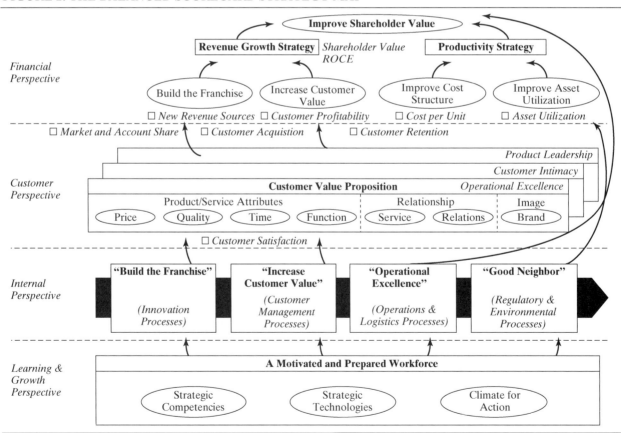

proposition. These would include market share in targeted customer segments, account share with targeted customers, acquisition and retention of customers in the targeted segments, and customer profitability.[4]

Internal Process Perspective. Once an organization has a clear picture of its customer and financial perspectives, it can determine the means by which it will achieve the differentiated value proposition for customers and the productivity improvements for the financial objectives. The internal business perspective captures these critical organizational activities, which fall into four high-level processes:

1. *Build the franchise* by spurring innovation to develop new products and services and to penetrate new markets and customer segments.
2. *Increase customer value* by expanding and deepening relationships with existing customers.
3. *Achieve operational excellence* by improving supply-chain management, internal processes, asset utilization, resource-capacity management, and other processes.
4. *Become a good corporate citizen* by establishing effective relationships with external stakeholders.

Many companies that espouse a strategy calling for innovation or for developing value-adding customer relationships mistakenly choose to measure their internal business process by focusing only on the cost and quality of their operations. These companies have a complete disconnect between their strategy and how they measure it. Not surprisingly, organizations encounter great difficulty implementing growth strategies when their primary internal measurements emphasize process improvements, not innovation or enhanced customer relationships.

The financial benefits from improvements to the different business processes typically occur in stages. Cost savings from increases in *operational efficiencies* and process improvements deliver short-term benefits. Revenue growth from enhancing *customer relationships* accrues in the intermediate term. Increased *innovation* generally produces long-term revenues and margin improvements. Thus, a complete strategy should generate returns from all three high-level internal processes.

Learning and Growth Perspective. The final region of a strategy map is the learning and growth perspective, which is the foundation of any strategy. In the learning and growth perspective, managers define the employee capabilities and skills, technology, and corporate climate needed to support a strategy. These objectives enable a company to align its human resources and information technology with the strategic requirements from its critical internal business processes, differentiated value proposition, and customer relationships. After addressing the learning and growth perspective, companies have a complete strategy map with linkages across the four major perspectives.

Strategy maps, beyond providing a common framework for describing and building strategies, also are powerful diagnostic tools, capable of detecting flaws in organizations' Balanced Scorecards. For example, Figure 3 shows the strategy map for the Revenue Growth theme of Mobil North America Marketing & Refining. When senior management compared the scorecards being used by its business units to this template, it found one unit with no objective or measure for dealers, an omission immediately obvious from looking at its strategy map. Had this unit discovered how to bypass dealers and sell gasoline directly to end-use consumers? Were dealer relationships no longer strategic for this unit? The business unit shown in the lower right corner of Figure 3 did not mention quality on its scorecard. Again, had this unit already achieved six sigma quality levels so quality was no longer a strategic priority? Mobil's executive team used its divisional strategy map to identify and remedy gaps in the strategies being implemented at lower levels of the organization.

STAKEHOLDER AND KEY PERFORMANCE INDICATOR SCORECARDS

Many organizations claim to have a Balanced Scorecard because they use a mixture of financial and nonfinancial measures. Such measurement systems are certainly more "balanced" than ones that use financial measures alone. Yet, the assumptions and philosophies underlying these scorecards are quite different from those underlying the strategy scorecards and maps are described above. We observe two other scorecard types frequently used in practice: the *stakeholder scorecard* and the *key performance indicator scorecard.*

FIGURE 3. MOBIL USES REVERSE ENGINEERING OF A STRATEGY MAP AS A STRATEGY DIAGNOSTIC

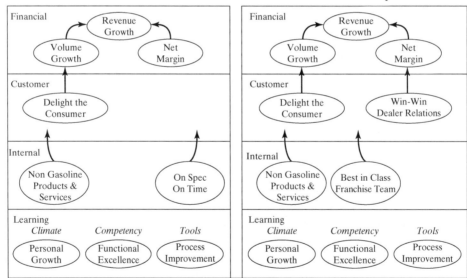

Stakeholder Scorecards. The *stakeholder scorecard* identifies the major constituents of the organization—shareholders, customers, and employees—and frequently other constituents such as suppliers and the community. The scorecard defines the organization's goals for these different constituents, or stakeholders, and develops an appropriate scorecard of measures and targets for them (Atkinson and Waterhouse 1997). For example, Sears built its initial scorecard around three themes:

■ "a compelling place to shop"
■ "a compelling place to work"
■ "a compelling place to invest"

Citicorp used a similar structure for its initial scorecard—"a good place to work, to bank, and to invest." AT&T developed an elaborate internal measurement system based on financial value-added, customer value-added, and people value-added.

All these companies built their measurements around their three dominant constituents—customers, shareholders, and employees—emphasizing satisfaction measures for customers and employees to ensure that these constituents felt well served by the company. In this sense, they were apparently *balanced*. Comparing these scorecards to the strategy map template in Figure 2 we can easily detect what is missing from such scorecards: no objectives or measures for *how* these balanced goals are to be achieved. A vision describes a desired outcome; a strategy, however, must describe *how* the outcome will be achieved, how employees, customers, and shareholders will be satisfied. Thus, a stakeholder scorecard is not adequate to describe the strategy of an organization and, therefore, is not an adequate foundation on which to build a management system.

Missing from the stakeholder card are the drivers to achieve the goals. Such drivers include an explicit value proposition such as innovation that generates new products and services or enhanced customer management processes, the deployment of technology, and the specific skills and competencies of employees required to implement the strategy. In a well-constructed *strategy scorecard*, the value proposition in the customer perspective, all the processes in the internal perspective, and the learning and growth perspective components of the scorecard define the "how" that is as fundamental to strategy as the outcomes that the strategy is expected to achieve.

Stakeholder scorecards are often a first step on the road to a strategy scorecard. But as organizations begin to work with stakeholder cards, they inevitably confront the question of "how." This leads to the next level of strategic thinking and scorecard design. Both Sears and Citicorp quickly moved beyond their stakeholder scorecards, developing an insightful set of internal process objectives to complete the description of their strategy and, ultimately, achieving a strategy Balanced Scorecard. The stakeholder scorecard can also be useful in organizations that do not have internal synergies across business units. Since each business has a different set of internal drivers, this "corporate" scorecard need only focus on the desired outcomes for the corporation's constituencies, including the communities and suppliers. Each business unit then defines how it will achieve those goals with its business unit strategy scorecard and strategy map.

Key Performance Indicator Scorecards. Key Performance Indicator (KPI) scorecards are also common. The total quality management approach and variants such as the Malcolm Baldrige and European Foundation for Quality Management (EFQM) awards generate many measures to monitor internal processes. When migrating to a "Balanced Scorecard," organizations often build on the base already established by classifying their existing measurements into the four BSC categories. KPI scorecards also emerge when the organization's information technology group, which likes to put the company database at the heart of any change program, triggers the scorecard design. Consulting organizations that sell and install large systems, especially so-called executive information systems, also offer KPI scorecards.

As a simple example of a KPI scorecard, a financial service organization articulated the 4Ps for its "balanced scorecard:"

1. Profits
2. Portfolio (size of loan volume)
3. Process (percent processes ISO certified)
4. People (meeting diversity goals in hiring)

Although this scorecard is more balanced than one using financial measures alone, comparing the 4P measures to a strategy map like that in Figure 2 reveals the major gaps in the measurement set. The company has no customer measures and only a single internal-process measure, which focuses on an initiative not an outcome. This KPI scorecard has no role for information technology (strange for a financial service organization), no linkages from the internal measure (ISO process certification) to a customer-value proposition or to a customer outcome, and no linkage from the learning and growth measure (diverse work force) to improving an internal process, a customer outcome, or a financial outcome.

KPI scorecards are most helpful for departments and teams when a strategic program already exists at a higher level. In this way, the diverse indicators enable individuals and teams to define what they must do well to contribute to higher-level goals. Unless, however, the link to strategy is clearly established, the KPI scorecard will lead to local but not global or strategic improvements.

Balanced Scorecards should not just be collections of financial and nonfinancial measures, organized into three to five perspectives. The best Balanced Scorecards reflect the strategy of the organization. A good test is whether you can understand the strategy by looking only at the scorecard and its strategy map. Many organizations fail this test, especially those that create stakeholder scorecards or key performance indicator scorecards.

Strategy scorecards along with their graphical representations on strategy maps provide a logical and comprehensive way to describe strategy. They communicate clearly the organization's desired outcomes and its hypotheses about how these outcomes can be achieved. For example, *if* we improve on-time delivery, *then* customer satisfaction will improve; *if* customer satisfaction improves, *then* customers will purchase more. The scorecards enable all organizational units and employees to understand the strategy and identify how they can contribute by becoming aligned to the strategy.

APPLYING THE BSC TO NONPROFITS AND GOVERNMENT ORGANIZATIONS

During the past five years, the Balanced Scorecard has also been applied by nonprofit and government organizations (NPGOs). One of the barriers to applying the scorecard to these sectors is the considerable difficulty NPGOs have in clearly defining their strategy. We reviewed "strategy" documents of more than 50 pages. Most of the documents, once the mission and vision are articulated, consist of lists of programs and initiatives, not the outcomes the organization is trying to achieve. These organizations must understand Porter's (1996, p. 77) admonition that strategy is not only what the organization intends to do, but also what it decides *not* to do, a message that is particularly relevant for the NPGOs.

Most of the initial scorecards of NPGOs feature an operational excellence strategy. The organizations take their current mission as a given and try to do their work more efficiently—at lower cost, with fewer defects, and faster. Often the project builds off of a recently introduced quality initiative that emphasizes process improvements. It is unusual to find nonprofit organizations focusing on a strategy that can be thought of as product leadership or customer intimacy. As a consequence, their scorecards tend to be closer to the KPI scorecards than true strategy scorecards.

The City of Charlotte, North Carolina, however, followed a customer-based strategy by selecting an interrelated set of strategic themes to create distinct value for its citizens (Kaplan 1998). United Way of Southeastern New England also articulated a customer (donor) intimacy strategy (Kaplan and Kaplan 1996). Other nonprofits—the May Institute and New Profit Inc.—selected a clear product-leadership position (Kaplan and Elias 1999). The May Institute uses partnerships with universities and researchers to deliver the best behavioral and rehabilitation care delivery. New Profit Inc. introduces a new selection, monitoring, and governing process unique among nonprofit organizations. Montefiore Hospital uses a combination of product leadership in its centers of excellence, and excellent customer relationships—through its new patient-oriented care centers—to build market share in its local area (Kaplan 2001). These examples demonstrate that NPGOs can be strategic and build competitive advantage in ways other than pure operational excellence. But it takes vision and leadership to move from continuous improvement processes to thinking strategically about which processes and activities are most important for fulfilling the organization's mission.

Modifying the Architecture of the Balanced Scorecard. Most NPGOs had difficulty with the original architecture of the Balanced Scorecard that placed the financial perspective at the top of the hierarchy. Given that achieving financial success is not the primary objective for most of these organizations, many rearrange the scorecard to place customers or constituents at the top of the hierarchy.

In a private-sector transaction, the customer plays two distinct roles—paying for the service and receiving the service—that are so complementary that most people don't even think about them separately. But in a nonprofit organization, donors provide the financial resources—they pay for the service—while another group, the constituents, receives the service. Who is the customer—the one paying or the one receiving? Rather than have to make such a Solomonic decision, organizations place both the donor perspective and the recipient perspective, in parallel, at the top of their Balanced Scorecards. They develop objectives for both donors and recipients, and then identify the internal processes that deliver desired value propositions for both groups of "customers."

In fact, nonprofit and government agencies should consider placing an over-arching objective at the top of their scorecard that represents their long-term objective such as a reduction in poverty or illiteracy, or improvements in the environment. Then the objectives within the scorecard can be oriented toward improving such a high-level objective. High-level financial measures provide private sector companies with an accountability measure to their owners, the shareholders. For a nonprofit or government agency, however, the financial measures are not the relevant indicators of whether the agency is delivering on its mission. The agency's mission should be featured and measured at the highest level of its scorecard. Placing an over-arching objective on the BSC for a nonprofit or government agency communicates clearly the long-term mission of the organization as portrayed in Figure 4.

Even the financial and customer objectives, however, may need to be re-examined for governmental organizations. Take the case of regulatory and enforcement agencies that monitor and punish violations of environmental, safety, and health regulations. These agencies, which detect transgressions, and fine or arrest those who violate the laws and regulations, cannot look to their "immediate customers" for satisfaction and loyalty measures. Clearly not; the true "customers" for such organizations are the citizens at large who benefit from effective but not harsh or idiosyncratic enforcement of laws and regulations. Figure 5 shows a modified framework in which a government agency has three high-level perspectives:

1. *Cost Incurred*: This perspective emphasizes the importance of operational efficiency. The measured cost should include both the expenses of the agency and the social cost it imposes on citizens and other organizations through its operations. For example, an environmental agency imposes remediation costs on private-sector organizations. These are part of the costs of having the agency carry out its mission. The agency should minimize the direct and social costs required to achieve the benefits called for by its mission.
2. *Value Created*: This perspective identifies the benefits being created by the agency to citizens and is the most problematic and difficult to measure. It is usually difficult to financially quantify the benefits from improved education, reduced pollution, better health, less congestion, and safer neighborhoods. But the balanced scorecard still enables organizations to identify the outputs, if not the outcomes, from its activities, and to measure these outputs. Surrogates for value created could include percentage of students acquiring specific skills and knowledge; density of pollutants in water, air, or land; improved morbidity and mortality in targeted populations; crime rates and perception of public safety; and transportation times. In general, public-sector organizations may find they use more output than outcome measures. The citizens and their representatives—elected officials and legislators—will eventually make the judgments about the benefits from these outputs vs. their costs.
3. *Legitimizing Support*: An important "customer" for any government agency will be its "donor," the organization—typically the legislature—that provides the funding for the agency. In order to assure continued funding for its activities, the agency must strive to meet the objectives of its funding source—the legislature and, ultimately, citizens and taxpayers.

After defining these three high-level perspectives, a public-sector agency can identify its objectives for internal processes, learning, and growth that enable objectives in the three high-level perspectives to be achieved.

FIGURE 4. ADAPTING THE BALANCED SCORECARD FRAMEWORK TO NONPROFIT ORGANIZATIONS

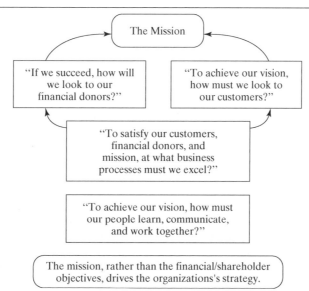

The Mission

"If we succeed, how will we look to our financial donors?"

"To achieve our vision, how must we look to our customers?"

"To satisfy our customers, financial donors, and mission, at what business processes must we excel?"

"To achieve our vision, how must our people learn, communicate, and work together?"

The mission, rather than the financial/shareholder objectives, drives the organizations's strategy.

FIGURE 5. THE FINANCIAL/CUSTOMER OBJECTIVES FOR PUBLIC SECTOR AGENCIES MAY REQUIRE THREE DIFFERENT PERSPECTIVES*

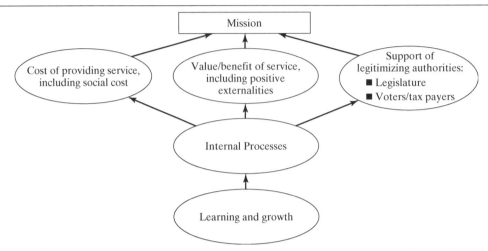

* Professor Dutch Leonard, Kennedy School of Government, Harvard University, collaborated to develop this diagram.

BEYOND MEASUREMENT TO MANAGEMENT

Originally, we thought the Balanced Scorecard was about performance measurement (Kaplan and Norton 1992). Once organizations developed their basic system for measuring strategy, however, we quickly learned that *measurement* has consequences far beyond reporting on the past. Measurement creates focus for the future. The measures chosen by managers communicate important messages to all organizational units and employees. To take full advantage of this power, companies soon integrated their new measures into a *management system*. Thus the Balanced Scorecard concept evolved from a performance measurement system to become the organizing framework, the operating system, for a new strategic management system (Kaplan and Norton 1996c, Part II). The academic literature, rooted in the original performance measurement aspects of the scorecard, focuses on the BSC as a measurement system (Ittner et al. 1997; Ittner and Larcker 1998; Banker et al. 2000; Lipe and Salterio 2000) but has yet to examine its role as a management system.

Using this new strategic management system, we observed several organizations achieving performance breakthroughs within two to three years of implementation (Kaplan and Norton 2001a, 4–6, 17–22). The magnitude of the results achieved by the early adopters reveals the power of the Balanced Scorecard management system to focus the entire organization on strategy. The speed with which the new strategies deliver results indicates that the companies' successes are not due to a major new product or service launch, major new capital investments, or even the development of new intangible or "intellectual" assets. The companies, of course, develop new products and services, and invest in both hard, tangible assets, as well as softer, intangible

assets. But they cannot benefit much in two years from such investments. To achieve their break-through performance, the companies capitalize on capabilities and assets—both tangible and intangible—that already exist within their organizations.[5] The companies' new strategies and the Balanced Scorecard unleash the capabilities and assets previously hidden (or frozen) within the old organization. In effect, the Balanced Scorecard provides the "recipe" that enables ingredients already existing in the organization to be combined for long-term value creation.

Part II of our commentary on the Balanced Scorecard (Kaplan and Norton 2001b) will describe how organizations use Balanced Scorecards and strategy maps to accomplish comprehensive and integrated transformations. These organizations redefine their relationships with customers, reengineer fundamental business processes, reskill the work force, and deploy new technology infrastructures. A new culture emerges, centered not on traditional functional silos, but on the team effort required to implement the strategy. By clearly defining the strategy, communicating it consistently, and linking it to the drivers of change, a performance-based culture emerges to link everyone and every unit to the unique features of the strategy. The simple act of describing strategy via strategy maps and scorecards makes a major contribution to the success of the transformation program.

ENDNOTES

American Institute of Certified Public Accountants (AICPA), Special Committee on Financial Reporting, 1994. *Improving Business Reporting—A Customer Focus: Meeting the Information Needs of Investors and Creditors*. New York, NY: AICPA.

Atkinson, A. A., and J. H. Waterhouse. 1997. A stakeholder approach to strategic performance measurement. *Sloan Management Review* (Spring).

Banker, R., G. Potter, and D. Srinivasan. 2000. An empirical investigation of an incentive plan that includes nonfinancial performance measures. *The Accounting Review* (January): 65–92.

Becker, B., and M. Huselid. 1998. High performance work systems and firm performance: A synthesis of research and managerial implications. In *Research in Personnel and Human Resources Management*, 53–101. Greenwich, CT: JAI Press.

Blair, B. B. 1995. *Ownership and Control: Rethinking Corporate Governance for the Twenty-First Century*. Washington, D.C.: Brookings Institution.

Chandler, A. D. 1990. *Scale and Scope: The Dynamics of Industrial Capitalism*. Cambridge, MA: Harvard University Press.

Charan, R., and G. Colvin. 1999. Why CEOs fail. *Fortune* (June 21).

Epstein, M., and J. F. Manzoni. 1998. Implementing corporate strategy: From Tableaux de Bord to Balanced Scorecards. *European Management Journal* (April).

Greenwood, R. G. 1974. *Managerial Decentralization: A Study of the General Electric Philosophy*. Lexington, MA: D. C. Heath.

Heskett, J., T. Jones, G. Loveman, E. Sasser, and L. Schlesinger. 1994. Putting the service profit chain to work. *Harvard Business Review* (March–April): 164–174.

Huselid, M. A. 1995. The impact of human resource management practices on turnover, productivity, and corporate financial performance. *Academy of Management Journal*: 635–672.

Ittner, C., D. Larcker, and M. Meyer. 1997. Performance, compensation, and the Balanced Scorecard. Working paper, University of Pennsylvania.

———, D. Larcker, and M. Rajan. 1997. The choice of performance measures in annual bonus contracts. *The Accounting Review* (April): 231–255.

———, and D. Larcker. 1998. Innovations in performance measurement: Trends and research implications. *Journal of Management Accounting Research*: 205–238.

Johnson, H. T., and R. S. Kaplan. 1987. *Relevance Lost: The Rise and Fall of Management Accounting*, Boston, MA: Harvard Business School Press.

Kaplan, R. S., and D. P. Norton. 1992. The Balanced Scorecard: Measures that drive performance. *Harvard Business Review* (January–February): 71–79.

———, and ———, 1993. Putting the Balanced Scorecard to work. *Harvard Business Review* (September–October): 134–147.

———, and E. L. Kaplan. 1996. United Way of Southeastern New England. Harvard Business School Case 197–036. Boston, MA.

———, and D. P. Norton. 1996a. Using the Balanced Scorecard as a strategic management system. *Harvard Business Review* (January–February): 75–85.

———, and ———. 1996b. Linking the Balanced Scorecard to strategy. *California Management Review* (Fall): 53–79.

———, and ———. 1996c. *The Balanced Scorecard: Translating Strategy Into Action*. Boston, MA: Harvard Business School Publishing.

———. 1998. City of Charlotte (A). Harvard Business School Case 199–036. Boston, MA.

———, and R. Cooper. 1998. *Cost and Effect: Using Integrated Cost Systems to Drive Profitability and Performance*. Boston, MA: Harvard Business School Press.

———, and J. Elias. 1999. New Profit, Inc.: Governing the nonprofit enterprise. Harvard Business School Case 100–052. Boston, MA.

———. 2001. Montefiore Medical Center. Harvard Business School Case 101–067. Boston, MA.

———, and D. P. Norton. 2000. Having trouble with your strategy? Then map it. *Harvard Business Review* (September–October): 167–176.

———, and ———. 2001a. *The Strategy-Focused Organization: How Balanced Scorecard Companies Thrive in the New Business Environment*. Boston, MA: Harvard Business School Press.

———, and ———. 2001b. Transforming the Balanced Scorecard from performance measurement to strategic management, Part II. *Accounting Horizons*. (forthcoming).

Kiechel, W. 1982. Corporate strategists under fire. *Fortune* (December 27): 38.

Lebas, M. 1994. Managerial accounting in France: Overview of past tradition and current practice. *European Accounting Review* 3 (3): 471–487.

Lipe, M., and S. Salterio. 2000. The Balanced Scorecard: Judgmental effects of common and unique performance measures. *The Accounting Review* (July): 283–298.

Porter, M. E. 1992. Capital disadvantage: America's failing capital investment system. *Harvard Business Review* (September–October).

———. 1996. What is strategy? *Harvard Business Review* (November–December).

Treacy, F., and M. Wierserma. 1997. *The Wisdom of Market Leaders*. New York, NY: Perseus Books.

Webber, A. M. 2000. New math for a new economy. *Fast Company* (January–February).

ENDNOTES

1. For example, General Electric attempted a system of nonfinancial measurements in the 1950s (Greenwood 1974), and the French developed the Tableaux de Bord decades ago (Lebas 1994; Epstein and Manzoni 1998).
2. Brand names, which can be sold, are an exception.
3. Shareholder value can also be increased through managing the right-hand side of the balance sheet, such as by repurchasing shares and choosing the low-cost mix among debt and equity instruments to lower the cost of capital. In this paper, we focus only on improved management of the organization's assets (tangible and intangible).
4. Measurement of customer profitability (Kaplan and Cooper 1998, 181–201) provides one of the connections between the Balanced Scorecard and activity-based costing.
5. These observations indicate why attempts to "value" individual intangible assets almost surely is a quixotic search. The companies achieved breakthrough performance with essentially the same people, services, and technology that previously delivered dismal performance. The value creation came not from any individual asset—tangible or intangible. It came from the coherent combination and alignment of existing organizational resources.

Robert S. Kaplan is a professor at Harvard University and David P. Norton is founder and president of the Balanced Scorecard Collaborative in Lincoln, MA.

QUESTIONS

2.2a   What is a strategy map?

2.2b   According to Kaplan and Norton, what are the two basic approaches to increasing economic value?

2.3 Transforming the Balanced Scorecard from Performance Measurement to Strategic Management: Part II

by Robert S. Kaplan and David P. Norton*

In a previous paper (Kaplan and Norton 2001b), we described the role for strategy maps and Balanced Scorecards to develop performance objectives and measures linked to strategy. With this paper, we show how organizations use their scorecards to align key management processes and systems to the strategy. We also discuss the relationship of the Balanced Scorecard (BSC) to other financial and cost measurement initiatives, such as shareholder value metrics and activity-based costing, and quality programs. We conclude with suggestions about opportunities for additional research on measurement and management systems.

THE FIVE PRINCIPLES OF A STRATEGY-FOCUSED ORGANIZATION

When asked to describe how the Balanced Scorecard helped them achieve breakthrough performance, executives of adopting organizations continually referred to two words: *alignment* and *focus* (Kaplan and Norton 2001 a, Chapter 1). Although each organization achieved strategic alignment and focus in different ways, at different paces and in different sequences, each eventually used a common set of five principles, which we refer to as the Principles of a Strategy-Focused Organization, portrayed in Figure 1.

Principle #1: Translate The Strategy to Operational Terms. Organizations translate their strategy into the logical architecture of a strategy map and Balanced Scorecard to specify in detail the critical elements for their growth strategies (Kaplan and Norton 2001 b). These create a common and understandable point of reference for all organizational units and employees.

Principle #2: Align the Organization to the Strategy. Organizations consist of numerous sectors, business units, and specialized departments, each with its own operations and often its own strategy. Functional departments, such as finance, manufacturing, marketing, sales, engineering, and purchasing, have their own bodies of knowledge, language, and culture. Functional silos arise and become a major barrier to strategy implementation since most

---

* From: R. S. Kaplan and D. P. Norton. "Transforming the Balanced Scorecard from Performance Measurement to Strategic Management: Part II," *Accounting Horizons* (June 2001): 147–160. ©American Accounting Association. Articles available online at http://aaahq.org/pubs/electpubs.htm.

FIGURE 1. THE PRINCIPLES OF A STRATEGY-FOCUSED ORGANIZATION

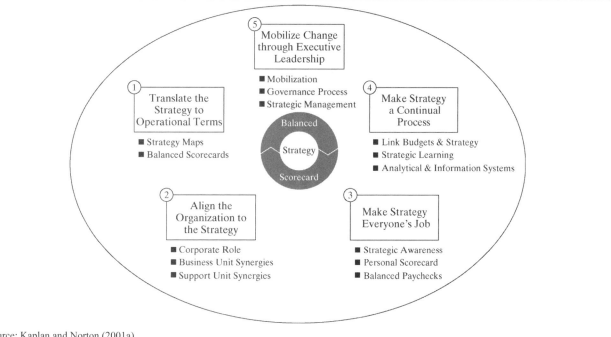

source: Kaplan and Norton (2001a)

organizations have great difficulty communicating and coordinating across these specialty functions. For organizational performance to be more than the sum of its parts, individual strategies must be linked and integrated. The corporate role defines the linkages expected to create synergy and ensures that the linkages actually occur.

Figure 2 shows the linkages at the Mobil North American Marketing and Refining division (NAM&R). The high-level strategic themes in #1 guide the development of the Balanced Scorecards in the business units in #2, which are either geographic regions or product lines, such as lubricants. Each unit formulates a strategy appropriate for its target market in light of the specific circumstances it faces—competitors, market opportunities, and critical processes—but that is consistent with the themes and priorities of NAM&R. The measures at the individual business-unit levels do not have to add to a divisional measure, unlike financial measures that aggregate easily from sub-units to departments to higher organizational levels. The business-unit managers choose local measures that *influence* but are not necessarily identical to the divisional scorecard measures.

Beyond aligning the business units, strategy-focused organizations must align their staff functions and shared service units, such as human resources, information technology, purchasing, environmental, and finance as in #3 of Figure 2. Often this alignment is accomplished with

service agreements between each functional department and the business units. Management and cost accounting textbooks describe how to assign the costs of support departments to production departments and selling units. The scorecard approach is much more comprehensive. In addition to contracting on price or cost, the staff functions and the line business units agree to the menu of services to be provided, including their functionality, quality level, response time, and cost. This service agreement becomes the basis of the Balanced Scorecard constructed by the functional department. The department's customers are the internal business units, the value proposition is defined by the negotiated service agreement, and the financial objectives are derived from the negotiated budget for the department. Next, the department identifies the internal process and learning and growth objectives that drive its customer and financial objectives.

When this process is complete, all the organizational units—line business units and staff functions—have well-defined strategies that are articulated and measured by Balanced Scorecards and strategy maps. Because the local strategies are integrated, they reinforce each other. This alignment allows corporate-level synergies to emerge in which the whole exceeds the sum of the individual parts.

Linkages can also be established across corporate boundaries, as in #4 of Exhibit 2. Several companies constructed Balanced Scorecards to define their relationships with key suppliers, customers, outsourcing vendors, and joint ventures. Companies use such

FIGURE 2. ALIGNING THE ORGANIZATION TO ITS STRATEGY

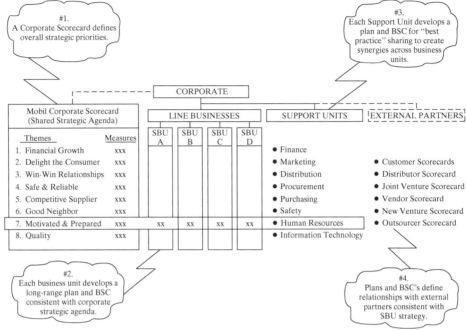

Source: Kaplan and Norton (2001a)

scorecards with external parties to be explicit about (1) the objectives of the relationship, and (2) how to measure the contribution and performance of each party to the relationship in ways other than just price or cost. Sometimes, particularly in governmental settings, scorecards are defined for high-level themes, such as salmon recovery in Washington State and economic development in the City of Charlotte, that encompass multiple departments and government agencies. No one department or agency has complete jurisdiction or ability to influence the desired outcomes. The scorecard for the high-level theme provides the mechanism that engages managers from multiple departments and agencies to discuss how they can contribute to achieving high-level strategic objectives.

Principle #3: Make Strategy Everyone's Everyday Job. The CEOs and senior leadership teams of adopting organizations understood that they could not implement the new strategy by themselves. They wanted contributions—actions and ideas—from everyone in the organization. The third principle of strategy-focused organizations requires that all employees understand the strategy and conduct their day-to-day business in ways that contribute to the success of that strategy. This is not top-down *direction*. This is top-down *communication*. Senior managers understand that individuals far from corporate and regional headquarters can create considerable value by finding new and improved ways of doing business.

Executives start this process by using the Balanced Scorecard to *communicate* and *educate* the organization

about the new strategy. Some observers are skeptical about communicating strategy to the entire organization, feeling that valuable information would be leaked to competitors. Mobil's Brian Baker's response was:

> Knowing our strategy will do them little good unless they can execute it. On the other hand, we have no chance of executing our strategy unless our people know it. It's a chance we'll have to take.

Companies can educate the employees about surprisingly sophisticated business concepts. To understand the scorecard, employees learn about customer segmentation, variable contribution margin, and database marketing. Instead of assuming that the workforce is incapable of understanding these ideas, managers make concerted efforts to educate employees at all levels of the organization about key strategic components.

Peter Drucker (1954) introduced management-by-objectives (MBO) nearly 50 years ago. But Drucker's excellent concept was implemented poorly in practice, leading to MBO in most organizations focusing on a myriad of local measures and initiatives not linked to high-level organizational objectives or coordinated with each other. The Balanced Scorecard enables personal objective setting to be integrated across the organization and linked to high-level strategic objectives.

Companies communicate their strategy and scorecard *holistically*. Instead of cascading objectives through the chain of command, as is normally done, they communicate the complete strategy down to individual employees. Individuals and departments at lower levels are challenged to develop their own objectives in light of the broader priorities; in some cases, personal scorecards are used to set *personal objectives*. Many pleasant surprises result from this process as individuals find new ways to do their jobs and identify areas outside their normal responsibilities to which they can contribute.

Finally, most organizations link *incentive compensation* to the Balanced Scorecard, typically after managing with the scorecard for a year. The executives must be confident that they are using sensible measures, have valid and reliable data collection processes to support the measures, and have measures not easily manipulated. Once they become confident about their measures and data, they turn the powerful compensation lever on. Brian Baker at Mobil declared:

> People got that scorecard out and did the calculations to see how much money they were going to get. We could not have gotten the same focus on the scorecard if we didn't have the link to pay.

Gerry Isom, CEO of Cigna Property and Casualty agreed:

> It would be hard to get people to accept a totally different way of measurement if you don't reinforce that change through incentive compensation.

A study of 214 companies reports that 88% of responding companies considered the use of Balanced Scorecard measures linked to reward systems to be effective (Mercer & Co. 1999).

Incentive systems based on the Balanced Scorecard vary widely. Some companies, such as Mobil, deploy a team-based incentive system, using business-unit and division scorecards as the basis for rewards. Others use a combination of business-unit, company, and individual performance rewards. Compensation can be based on up to 25 strategic measures. Instead of promoting confusion, as many fear, the scorecard compensation systems heighten the employees' interest in all components of the strategy and further their demand for knowledge and information about scorecard measures. Strategy becomes everyone's everyday job because employees now understand the strategy and are motivated to make it succeed.

Principle #4: Make Strategy A Continual Process.
Most organizations build their management processes around the budget and operating plan. The monthly

management meeting reviews performance vs. plan, discusses variances from past performance, and requests action plans for dealing with short-term variances. There is nothing wrong with this, *per se*. Tactical management is necessary. But in most organizations that's all there is. Besides the annual strategic-planning meeting, no meeting occurs where managers discuss strategy. We surveyed participants at conferences and learned that 85% of their management teams spend less than one hour per month discussing strategy.

The adopting BSC companies introduce a new "double-loop process" to manage strategy. The process integrates the management of tactics with the management of strategy, using three important processes, as depicted in Figure 3.

First, organizations *link strategy to the budgeting process*. They use the Balanced Scorecard as a screen to evaluate potential investments and initiatives. At Chemical Bank, where more than 70 different requests for funding were submitted, executives found that over 50% of the proposed initiatives had no impact on any scorecard measure. These were discarded as "nonstrategic." They also found that despite having more than three times as many proposed initiatives as scorecard measures, about 20% of the measures on the scorecard had no initiatives associated with improving them. A new process for managing strategic initiatives emerged that included authorizing funds for strategic initiatives within the annual budget process.

Companies usually have an *operational budget* that authorizes spending for producing and delivering existing products and services, and marketing and selling them to existing customers. They now introduce a *strategy budget* that enables them to develop entirely new capabilities, reach new customers and markets, and make radical improvements in existing processes and capabilities. This distinction is essential. Just as the Balanced Scorecard attempts to protect long-term objectives from short-term suboptimization, the budgeting process must protect the long-term initiatives from the pressures to deliver short-term financial performance.

The second step to make strategy a continual process introduces a *simple management meeting* to review strategy. As obvious as this step sounds, such meetings did not exist in the past. Now, management meetings are scheduled on a monthly or quarterly basis to discuss the Balanced Scorecard so that a broad spectrum of managers comes together to discuss the strategy. A new kind of energy is created. People use terms like "fun" and "exciting" to describe the meetings. One senior executive reported that the meetings became so popular, there was standing room only and he could have sold tickets to them.

Information feedback systems change to support the new management meetings. Initially, these systems are designed for the needs of the executive team. But organizations can go further by creating *open reporting* in which performance results are made available to everyone in the organization. Building upon the principle that "strategy is everyone's job," they empower "everyone" by giving them the knowledge needed to do their jobs. At Cigna Property & Casualty, a first-line underwriter sees performance reports before a direct-line executive if she happens to be monitoring the feedback system. This creates a set of cultural issues that revolutionize traditional, hierarchical approaches to information and power.

Finally, a *process for learning and adapting the strategy* evolves. The initial Balanced Scorecard represents hypotheses about the strategy; at time of formulation it is the best estimate of the actions expected to create long-term financial success. The scorecard design process makes the cause-and-effect linkages in the strategic hypotheses explicit. As the scorecard is put into action and feedback systems begin their reporting on actual results, an organization can test the hypotheses of its strategy. Some, like Brown & Root and Sears, did the testing formally, using statistical correlations between measures on the scorecard to determine whether, for example, employee empowerment programs were increasing customer satisfaction and improved processes. Others, like Chemical Bank, tested the hypotheses more qualitatively at meetings where managers validated and refined the programs being used to drive service quality and customer retention.

Still others use the meetings to search for new strategic opportunities that were not currently on their scorecard (see Mintzberg [1987] and Hamel [2000] for discussions of emergent strategy). Ideas and learning emerge continually from within the organization. Rather than waiting for next year's budget cycle, the priorities and the scorecards are updated immediately. Much like a navigator guiding a vessel on a long-term journey, constantly sensing the shifting winds and currents and constantly adapting the course, the executives of the successful companies use the ideas and learning generated by their organization to fine-tune their strategies. Instead of being an annual event, strategy formulation, testing, and revision became a continual process.

Using the Balanced Scorecard in this manner matches what Bob Simons (1995, Chapter 5; 2000, Chapter 10) describes as an interactive control system, characterized by four defining characteristics:

- Information in the control system provides an important and recurring agenda for senior management.
- The system demands frequent and regular attention from operating managers at all levels of the organization.
- Date generated by the system are interpreted and discussed in face-to-face meetings of superiors, subordinates, and peers.
- The system is a catalyst for the continual challenge and debate of underlying data, assumptions, and action plans.

Simons' research reveals how managers choose one system, such as the budget system, the revenue reporting system, or the project management system, and make it their interactive system. After that research was conducted, the Balanced Scorecard emerged to provide a general template for an organization's interactive system.

FIGURE 3. MAKING STRATEGY A CONTINUAL PROCESS

Source: Kaplan and Norton (2001a)

34

Rather than having to choose one from the many existing systems, executives can design their own interactive system to focus intensely on strategy and its implementation. And the process of constructing their customized interactive system provides the additional benefit of team building and gaining coherence and commitment within the senior management team for the strategy. This leads naturally to the discussion of the fifth principle to create a strategy-focused organization.

Principle #5: Mobilize Leadership for Change. The first four principles focus on the Balanced Scorecard tool, framework, and the processes to support it. To become truly strategy-focused, however, requires more than processes and tools. Ownership and active involvement of the executive team is the single most important condition for success. Strategy requires change from virtually every part of the organization. Strategy requires teamwork to coordinate these changes. Strategy implementation also requires continual focus on the change initiatives and on the performance against targeted outcomes. If those at the top are not energetic leaders of the process, change does not occur, strategy is not implemented, and the opportunity for breakthrough performance is lost.

A Balanced Scorecard program starts with the recognition that it is not a "metrics" project; it's a change project. Initially the focus is on *mobilization* and creating momentum, to get the process launched. Once mobilized, the focus shifts to *governance* to install the new performance model. Finally, and gradually over time, a new management system evolves, a *strategic management system* that institutionalizes the new cultural values and processes into a new system for managing. Convergence to the new management system can take two to three years.

In the mobilization phase, the leaders must make the organization understand why change is needed; the organization must be unfrozen. Kotter (1996) describes how transformational change begins at the top and with three discrete actions by the leaders: (1) establish a sense of urgency; (2) create the guiding coalition; and (3) develop a vision and a strategy. The leaders of successful Balanced Scorecard organizations clearly followed this mode. Several of the adopting companies were experiencing difficult times. The obvious threat of failure and loss of jobs was a motivator that created receptivity for change. But the role for the Balanced Scorecard to drive change and breakthrough performance is not limited to distressed or failing companies. Often, executives at companies currently doing well create stretch targets to ensure that the organization does not become complacent. They use the Balanced Scorecard to communicate a vision for dramatically better performance than the present. Executive leadership makes the need for change obvious to all.

Once the change process is launched, executives establish a *governance* process to guide the transition. This process defines, demonstrates, and reinforces the new cultural values to the organization. Breaking with traditional power-based structures is important. The creation of strategy teams, town hall meetings, and open communications are all components of the new management approach.

Embedding the new strategy and culture into a new management system, however, creates a risk that the organization fails to adapt to future shifts in opportunities and threats. Good executives recognize that strategies must continually evolve to reflect changes in the competitive landscape. The art of the leader is to delicately balance the tension between stability and change.

This concludes the summary of the five principles to become strategy-focused. We now turn to the relationship of the BSC to other improvement initiatives and to promising areas of future research.

RELATIONSHIP OF BSC TO OTHER ORGANIZATIONAL IMPROVEMENT INITIATIVES

The BSC emerged in the 1990s just as two other approaches—activity-based costing and shareholder value management—were being advocated as measurement systems to help managers improve organizational performance. The three approaches do not compete with each other; in fact they are highly compatible and while each can be implemented independently of the others, organizations will get the greatest benefit from integrating all three.

Shareholder Value Management. Shareholder value metrics, such as residual income, economic value-added, and shareholder value-added (Myers 1996, 1997), address two defects in traditional financial performance measurement: the overinvestment problem when only net income or earnings is used as the aggregate performance measure, and the underinvestment problem when a ratio—such as return-on-investment or return-on-equity—is used. We encourage managers who operate under a shareholder value discipline to use that metric as their overarching measure in the financial perspective. Within the financial perspective of the BSC, the shareholder value metric is decomposed into the subobjectives of cost reduction, improved asset productivity, and revenue growth (see strategy map template, Kaplan and Norton 2001b, Figure 2). Customer objectives define the strategy for revenue growth.

Managers operating only with shareholder value metrics, and without the more comprehensive BSC measurement framework, often take a low-risk and short-term path—reduce costs and dispose of underutilized assets—to achieve their financial improvements.

Growing revenues typically takes longer, involves more risk, and requires more near-term spending to develop new products, services, and markets, enhance customer relationships, improve service, and increase employee capabilities. Nothing in shareholder value management is incompatible with revenue growth. But the financial metrics in a shareholder value approach cannot serve as a vehicle for articulating a revenue growth strategy and the complementary processes for achieving it. The BSC complements shareholder value management by defining the drivers of revenue growth—explicit objectives and measures for targeted customers, the differentiating customer value proposition, the internal business processes for innovation and enhanced customer relationships, and the needed infrastructure investments in people, systems, and organizational alignment. It also helps executives manage the trade-offs between short-term productivity improvements and long-term sustainable revenue growth.

Activity-Based Costing. Activity-based costing (ABC) was developed to correct another defect in financial systems—the inability of traditional costing systems to identify the drivers of indirect and support costs (Kaplan and Cooper 1998). ABC operates by relating organizational spending to activities and processes that support the design, production, marketing and delivery of products and services to customers.

Operational Linkage. The first linkage between ABC and the BSC occurs in the operational measures of the BSC's internal process perspective. Three parameters—cost, quality, and time—usually define the operating performance of any process. Quality and time are relatively easy to measure since they are based on physical measurements. Cost, however, is an analytic concept that cannot be measured by a stopwatch or a laser-gauging instrument. Only with an ABC model can organizational expenses be accurately traced to processes of product development, marketing and sales, manufacturing, distribution, and service delivery.

Customer Profitability Linkage. A second linkage occurs when an ABC model is used to measure the profitability of individual customers (Kaplan and Cooper 1998, Chapter 10). The BSC customer perspective typically includes customer outcome measures such as acquisition, satisfaction, retention, account share, and market share. But com panies also need to measure whether their loyal, satisfied customers are profitable. Balancing measures such as customer profitability or percentage of unprofitable customers help managers ensure they are not improving their customer measures at the expense of high-level financial profitability measures.

Budgeting Linkage. A third linkage arises when the ABC model is used for activity-based budgeting: combining information on the forecasted volume and mix of products and services with anticipated activity and process efficiencies to construct a bottom-up budget for forthcoming periods (Kaplan and Cooper 1998, Chapter 15). With the BSC providing the management process for defining the strategic budget, and activity-based budgeting used to develop the operational budget (see discussion of these two budgets in Principle #4 above, "Making Strategy a Continual Process"), managers have powerful analytic tools for their budgeting processes.

ABC can also be combined with shareholder value management by applying ABC principles to assign assets to activities and then to cost objects. This enables capital costs and residual income to be calculated at the individual product and customer level.

Getting Started. Thus, shareholder value metrics, ABC, and the BSC play complementary roles. People often ask, "My organization has limited capacity for these major change initiatives. I can't do all three at the same time. Which should I do first?"

1. If the biggest problems facing an organization are large, growing indirect and support expenses, and inefficient processes, then implement ABC first. It gives managers a deep understanding of their cost structure, helps them to identify the most costly and nonvalue-added processes, and reveals how much of the growth in support resources can be reversed by taking appropriate actions with inefficient processes, complex products, or demanding customers.
2. If the organization has a low return on investment, a weak financial structure, a low sales-to-asset ratio, and high levels of working capital, then start with shareholder value management. The shareholder value approach highlights the inefficient use of capital and provides explicit incentives for managers to divest underperforming assets and increase the utilization of the remaining assets.
3. If the organization wishes to implement a major change in its strategy, or has just been restructured from a centralized, functional organization to a decentralized, customer-focused one, then start with the BSC. No other tool facilitates major changes in strategy better or faster.

Organizations ultimately benefit from all three measurement approaches: the financial and investment discipline that comes from adopting a shareholder value approach; the deep understanding of cost structure and cost drivers that activity-based costing provides; and the integrated framework for managing strategy, including value and revenue drivers, that the Balanced Scorecard delivers.

Total Quality Management. Many companies also engage in quality initiatives. The causal linkages in a BSC strategy map enhance quality programs by articulating the two ways that process improvements can link to strategic outcomes. First, quality improvements in the internal perspective should improve one or more outcome measures in the customer perspective; second, quality improvements can lead to cost reduction, an outcome in the financial perspective. The BSC enables managers to describe how they expect to translate quality improvements into higher revenues, fewer assets, less people, and lower spending.

The BSC process also guides organizations to redeploy their scarce resources of people and funds away from nonstrategic process improvements and toward those processes and initiatives most critical for implementing the strategy to achieve breakthrough customer and financial performance. In addition, building a Balanced Scorecard often reveals entirely new processes at which the organization must excel. Rather than just improving existing processes, the scorecard process focuses quality initiatives on improving the performance of these newly identified processes.

RESEARCH AGENDA ON ORGANIZATIONAL PERFORMANCE MANAGEMENT

During the past ten years, the Balanced Scorecard evolved from a performance measurement system to an organizing framework for successful strategy implementation. Changing what is measured profoundly affects the behavior of managers and employees, and helps organizations deliver dramatically improved performance. This is good news for accounting researchers. Accountants are in the measurement business and the experience of adopting companies reaffirms that *measurement matters*. Moreover, the experience affirms that *management control systems matter*. It's not just *what* is measured but *how* the measurements are used that determines organizational success. The impact of the scorecard is reinforced when it is used in a multiplicity of management processes: compensation (the most studied process by accounting researchers); alignment of diverse organizational units to a common strategy; communication and education; setting individual objectives; linking strategy, planning, resource allocation, and budgeting; setting targets; exploiting information technology for new reporting presentations; conducting management meetings interactively to promote testing, learning, and adaptation; and senior leadership's use of measurement to drive organizational change All these processes can be studied to assess their individual and collective effectiveness.

Some good empirical work tests the causal linkages that underlie the construction of strategy maps (Ittner and Larcker 1998; Banker et al. 2000). Interesting experimental work assesses how individuals respond to

reports containing financial and nonfinancial data (Lipe and Salterio 2000; Swain et al. 1999). But these are only the beginning of promising research initiatives on performance measurement and management.

Analytic research can expand beyond contracting issues to address how synergies—nonlinear returns—are created when diverse individuals do their tasks in ways that are in phase with and reinforce each other. The successful BSC implementers did not hire new, more skilled employees. They did not work their employees harder or longer. They achieved the benefits by having their existing employees focus and align their efforts around a common strategy. Understanding how measurement yields nonlinear performance returns by coordinating and focusing employees' effort could be fertile ground for analytic modeling.

Empirical and experimental research can explore several important issues. How can targets with comparable degrees of difficulty be established across diverse business and shared service units? Mobil adopted a process they called "leveling" to put all units on a level playing field for rewards. It called for active involvement of senior staff specialists and managerial peers to review, challenge, and eventually ratify the targets proposed by decentralized units. The form of the reward is also of interest. Mobil's previous policy rewarded managers who achieved their targets, but gave zero rewards when performance fell short of targets. The new policy was a continuous reward function that increased with the degree of difficulty of the targets. As the CEO stated, "I prefer to give a better rating for a manager who stretches for a target and falls a little short, than to someone who beats an easy target." Just how to implement such a process in practice, of course, is a nontrivial task for which additional research could certainly be beneficial. Analytic schemes already exist for rewarding the achievement of stretch targets (Kaplan and Atkinson 1998, p. 773–780), but our experience with implementing these schemes in practice is quite limited.

The visibility of a manager's ability and effort is heightened when the BSC is used as an interactive control system. A Mobil senior executive claimed, "The process enables me to see how managers think, plan, and execute. I can see the gaps." Such increased observability of managers' performance allows companies to use subjective rewards based on ability and effort, not the second-best approach of rewarding only on results. Again, empirical and experimental research can investigate the effectiveness of subjective rewards based on such increased observability. How well are people making subjective evaluations and judgments? What kind of subjective judgments can we confidently allow individuals to make and in what circumstances?

Many organizations obtain substantial commitment and contributions from their employees without introducing incentive compensation based on BSC measures. Individuals want to be part of and contribute to a successful organization. Without the guidance of a BSC, however, employees are often just given a job to do, not an opportunity to find new and better ways to help the organization achieve its strategic objectives. Thus, research on the mix between intrinsic and extrinsic motivation can be effectively conducted with the communication and personal goal-setting processes of the BSC management system.

The multiplicity of management processes required to create strategic focus in an organization can be studied. Are all critical? Is success a multiplicative model in which the performance breakthroughs come from all processes being implemented effectively? Or can some processes be effective and deliver significant results without being reinforced by others? This research will likely require intense field research, probably by studying an implementation in a multi-unit organization, where different units adopted different aspects of the BSC management system. For example, some units might have implemented all five principles of a strategy-focused organization, while others did only one or two. How did this affect the resulting performance of all these units?

During the past ten years, many organizations of all types and in all geographic areas adopted performance management systems that use a mixture of financial and nonfinancial metrics. In these two papers, we present a framework that describes the measurement and management systems of successful organizations we observe in practice. With the widespread availability of organizational implementations and a framework to describe how the implementations were performed, accounting researchers can now begin a systematic research program, using multiple research methods, to explore the key factors in implementing more effective measurement and management systems. Such a systematic exploration provides a valuable complement to the individual case studies to be produced in the years ahead.

ENDNOTES

Banker, R., G. Potter, and D. Srinivasan. 2000. An empirical investigation of an incentive plan that includes nonfinancial performance measures. *The Accounting Review* (January): 65–92.

Drucker, P. 1954. *The Practice of Management*. New York, NY: HarperBusiness.

Hamel, G. 2000. *Leading the Revolution*. Boston, MA: HBS Press.

Ittner, C., and D. Larcker. 1998. Are nonfinancial measures leading indicators of financial performance? An analysis of customer satisfaction. *Journal of Accounting Research*: 1–35.

Kaplan, R. S., and A. A. Atkinson. 1998. *Advanced Management Accounting*. Third edition. Upper Saddle River, NJ: Prentice Hall.

———, and R. Cooper. 1998. *Cost & Effect: Using Integrated Cost Systems to Drive Profitability and Performance*. Boston, MA: HBS Press.

———, and D. P. Norton. 2001a. *The Strategy-Focused Organization*. Boston, MA: Harvard Business School Press.

———, and ———. 2001b. Transforming the balanced scorecard from performance measurement to strategic management: Part I. *Accounting Horizons* (March): 87–104.

Kotter, J. 1996. *Leading Change*. Boston, MA: HBS Press.

Lipe, M., and S. Salterio. 2000. The balanced scorecard: Judgmental effects of common and unique performance measures. *The Accounting Review* (July): 283–298.

Mercer, William M. & Co. 1999. Rewarding employees: Balanced scorecard fax-back survey results. May 20. London, U.K.

Mintzberg, H. 1987. Crafting strategy. *Harvard Business Review* (July–August).

Myers. R. 1996. Metric wars. *CFO Magazine* (October).

———. 1997. Measure for measure. *CFO Magazine* (November).

Simons, R. 1995. *Levers of Control*. Boston, MA: HBS Press.

———. 2000. *Performance Measurement & Control Systems for Implementing Strategy*. Upper Saddle River, NJ: Prentice Hall.

Swain M., K. Krumwiede, and T. Eaton. 1999. Effects of balanced scorecard performance measures on decision process and design quality. Working paper, Brigham Young University.

Robert S. Kaplan is a Professor at Harvard University and David P. Norton is founder and president of the Balanced Scorecard Collaborative in Lincoln, MA.

QUESTION

2.3 Describe the five principles of a Strategy-Focused Organization.

2.4 Measuring the Strategic Readiness of Intangible Assets

by Robert S. Kaplan and David P. Norton*

How VALUABLE IS A COMPANY culture that enables employees to understand and believe in their organization's mission, vision, and core values? What's the payoff from investing in a knowledge management system or in a new customer database? Is it more important to improve the skills of all employees or focus on those in just a few key positions?

Measuring the value of such intangible assets is the holy grail of accounting. Employees's skills. IT systems, and organizational cultures are worth far more to many companies than their tangibles assets. Unlike financial and physical ones, intangible assets are hard for competitors to imitate, which makes them a powerful source of sustainable competitive advantage. If manages could find a way to estimate the value of their intangible assets, they could measure and manage their company's competitive position much more easily and accurately.

But that's simpler said than done. Unlike financial and physical assets, intangible assets are worth different things to different people. An oil well, for example, is almost as valuable to retail firm as it is to an oil exploration corporation because either company could sell it swiftly if necessary. But a workforce with a strong sense of customer service and satisfaction is worth far more to the retailer than it would be to the oil company. Also, unlike tangible assets, intangible assets almost never create value by themselves. They need to be combined with other assets. Investments in IT, for example, have little value unless complemented with HR training and incentive programs. And, conversely, many HR training programs have little value unless complemented with modern technology tools. HR and IT investments must be integrated and aligned with corporate strategy if the organization is to realize their full potential. Indeed, when companies separate functions like HR and IT organizationally, they usually end up with competing silos of technical specialization. The HR department argues for increases in employee training, while the IT department lobbies for buying new hardware and software packages.

What's more, intangible assets seldom affect financial performance directly. Instead, they work indirectly through complex chains of cause and effect. Training employees in Total Quality Management and Six Sigma, for instance, should improve process quality. That improvement should then increase customer satisfaction and loyalty— and also create some excess resource capacity. But only if the company can transform that loyalty into improved sales and margins and eliminate or redeploy the excess resources will the investment in training pay off. By contrast, the impact of a new tangible asset is immediate: When a retailer develops a new site, it sees financial benefits from the sales in the newly opened outlet right away.

Although these characteristics make it impossible to value intangible assets on a freestanding basis, they also point the way to a new approach for quantifying how intangible assets add value to the company. By understanding the problems associated with valuing intangible assets, we learn that the measurement of the value they create is embedded in the context of the strategy the company is pursuing. Companies such as Dell, Wal-Mart, or McDonald's that are following a low-cost strategy derive value from Six Sigma and TQM training because their strategies are predicated on continuous process improvement. The strategy of offering customers integrated solutions (rather than discrete products) pursued by Goldman Sachs, IBM Consulting, and the like requires employees good at establishing and maintaining longterm customer relationships. An organization cannot possibly assign a meaningful financial value to an intangible asset like "a motivated and prepared workforce" in a vacuum because value can be derived only in the context of the strategy. What the company *can* measure, however, is whether its workforce is properly trained and motivated to pursue a particular goal.

Viewed in this light, it becomes clear that measuring the value of intangible assets is really about estimating how closely aligned those assets are to the company's strategy. If the company has a sound strategy and if the intangible assets are aligned with that strategy, then the assets will create value for the organization. If the assets are not aligned with the strategy or if the strategy is flawed, then intangible assets will create little value, even if large amounts have been spent on them.

In the following pages, we will draw on the concepts and tools of the Balanced Scorecard to present a way to systematically measure the alignment of the company's human, information, and organization capital—what we

---

call its *strategic readiness*—without which even the best strategy cannot succeed.

THE STRATEGY MAP

The strategy map provides a framework for linking intangible assets to shareholder value creation through four interrelated perspectives. The *financial perspective* describes the tangible outcomes of the strategy in traditional financial terms, such as ROI, shareholder value, profitability, revenue growth, and lower unit costs. The *customer perspective* defines the value proposition the organization intends to use to generate sales and loyalty from targeted customers. This value proposition forms the context in which the intangible assets create value. The *internal process perspective* identifies the critical few processes that create and deliver the differentiating customer value proposition. At the foundation of the map, we have the *learning and growth perspective*, which identifies the intangible assets that are most important to the

strategy. The objectives in this perspective identify which jobs (the human capital), which systems (the information capital), and what kind of climate (the organization capital) are required to support the value-creating internal processes. These intangible assets must be integrated and aligned with the critical internal processes.

DEFINING STRATEGIC READINESS

In developing the Balanced Scorecard more than a decade ago, we identified, in its Learning and Growth Perspective, three categories of intangible assets essential for implementing any strategy:

- **Human Capital:** the skills, talent, and knowledge that a company's employees possess.
- **Information Capital:** the company's databases, information systems, networks, and technology infrastructure.

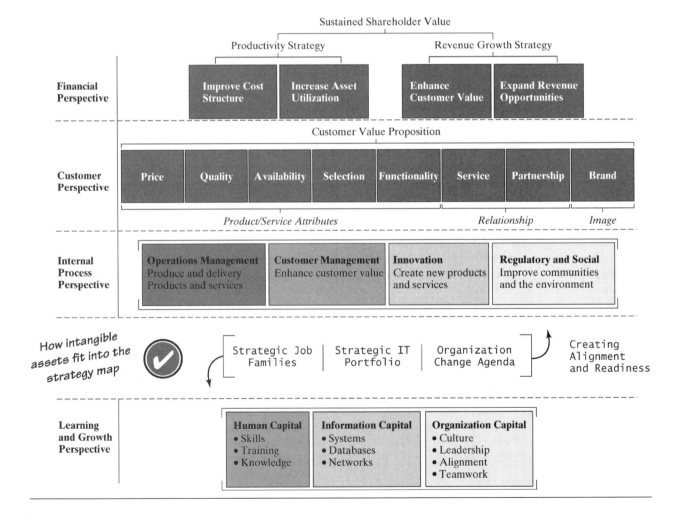

- **Organization Capital:** the company's culture, its leadership, how aligned its people are with its strategic goals, and employees' ability to share knowledge.

To link these intangible assets to a company's strategy and performance, we developed a tool called the "strategy map," which we first introduced in our previous article for *Harvard Business Review*, "Having Trouble with Your Strategy? Then Map It" (September–October 2000). As the exhibit "The Strategy Map" shows, intangible assets influence a company's performance by enhancing the internal processes most critical to creating value for customers and shareholders. Companies build their strategy maps from the top down, starting with their long-term financial goals and then determining the value proposition that will deliver the revenue growth specified in those goals, identifying the processes most critical to creating and delivering that value proposition, and, finally, determining the human, information, and organization capital the processes require.

This article focuses on the bottom—the foundation—of the map and will show how intangible assets actually determine the performance of the critical internal processes. Once that link has been established, it becomes easy to trace the steps back up the map to see exactly how intangible assets relate to the company's strategy and performance. That, in turn, makes it possible to align those assets with the strategy and measure their contribution to it. The degree to which the current set of assets does—or does not–contribute to the performance of the critical internal processes determines the strategic readiness of those assets and thus their value to the organization. The strategic readiness of each type of intangible asset can be thought of as follows:

Human Capital (HC): In the case of human capital, strategic readiness is measured by whether employees have the right kind and level of skills to perform the critical internal processes on the strategy map. The first step in estimating HC readiness is to identify the *strategic job families*–the positions in which employees with the right skills, talent, and knowledge have the biggest impact on enhancing the organization's critical internal processes. The next step is to pinpoint the set of specific competencies needed to perform each of those strategic jobs. The difference between the requirements needed to carry out these jobs effectively and the company's current capabilities represents a "competency gap" that measures the organization's HC readiness.

Information Capital (IC): The strategic readiness of information capital is a measure of how well the company's strategic IT portfolio of infrastructure and applications supports the critical internal processes. Infra-structure comprises hardware–such as central servers and communication networks—and the managerial expertise—such as standards, disaster planning, and security—required to effectively deliver and use applications. Two categories of applications, in turn, are built on this infra-structure: *Transaction-processing applications*, such as an ERP system, automate the basic repetitive transactions of the enterprise. *Analytic applications* promote analysis, interpretation, and sharing of information and knowledge. Either type may or may not be a *transformational application*—one that changes the prevailing business model of the enterprise. Levi's uses a transformational application to tailor jeans to individual customers. Home Shopping Network uses a transformational application to measure the "profits per second" being generated by currently offered merchandise. Transformational applications have the most potential impact on strategic objectives and require the greatest degree of organization change to deliver their benefits.

Organization Capital (OC): Organization capital is perhaps the least understood of the intangible assets, and the task of measuring it is correspondingly difficult. But in looking at the strategic priorities that companies in our database of Balanced Scorecard implementations used for their organization capital objectives, we found a consistent picture. Successful companies had a *culture* in which people were deeply aware of and internalized the mission, vision, and core values needed to execute the company's strategy. These companies strove for excellent *leadership* at all levels, leadership that could mobilize the organization toward its strategy. They strove for a clear *alignment* between the organization's strategic objectives and individual, team, and departmental goals and incentives. Finally, these companies promoted *teamwork*, especially the sharing of strategic knowledge throughout the organization. Determining OC readiness, we concluded, would involve first identifying the changes in organization capital required by the new strategy—what we call the "organization change agenda"—and then separately identifying and measuring the state of readiness of the company's cultural, leadership, alignment, and teamwork objectives.

Strategic readiness is related to the concept of liquidity, which accountants use to classify financial and physical assets on a company's balance sheet. Accountants divide a firm's assets into various categories, such as cash, accounts receivable, inventory, property, plant and equipment, and long-term investments. These are ordered hierarchically according to the ease and speed with which they can be converted to cash—in other words, according to the degree of their liquidity. Accounts receivable is more liquid than inventory, and both accounts receivable and inventory are classified as short-term assets since they typically convert to cash within 12 months, faster than the cash recovery cycle from such illiquid assets as plant and equipment. Strategic readiness does much the same for intangible assets—the higher their state of readiness, the faster they contribute to generating cash.

HUMAN CAPITAL READINESS AT CONSUMER BANK

Here we can see how human capital at our composite company, Consumer Bank, is linked to its critical strategic processes and how well the company scores in terms of the skills and capabilities it needs. The top row lists the internal processes the bank identified as critical to delivering its value proposition. The second row shows the jobs that have the greatest influence on those processes—the *strategic job families*. The third row lists the competencies needed for each job, and the fourth row specifies the number of people with those skills the company requires.

The bottom row shows how ready Consumer Bank's human capital is for its new strategy. Taken together, these internal assessments indicate the extent to which the bank actually has the capacity it needs. The bank is in excellent shape for its two operations management processes (100% and 90% readiness) but deficient for the two customer management processes (only 40% and 50% readiness) and for one of the innovation processes

(20% readiness). The aggregate measure of 65% human capital readiness (in the red zone) is a weighted average of readiness scores for all seven strategic job families. In terms of human capital, this report tells executives how quickly they can implement their new strategy.

HUMAN CAPITAL READINESS

All jobs are important to the organization; otherwise, people wouldn't be hired and paid to perform them. Organizations may require truck drivers, computer operators, production supervisors, materials handlers, and call center operators and should make it clear that contributions from all these employees can improve organizational performance. But we have found that some jobs have a much greater impact on strategy than others. Managers must identify and focus on the critical few that have the greatest impact on successful strategy implementation.

John Bronson, vice president of human resources at Williams-Sonoma, estimates that people in only five job families determine 80% of his company's strategic priorities. The executive team of a chemical company has identified eight job families critical to its strategy of offering customized innovative solutions. These job families employ, in aggregate, 100 individuals—less than 7% of the total workforce. Kimberlee Williams, vice president of human resources at Unicco, a large integrated facilities-services management company, says

	Operations Management		Customer Management		Innovation		Regulatory and Social	
Strategic Processes	Minimize problems	Provide rapid response	Cross-sell the product line	Shift to appropriate channel	Understand customer segments	Develop new products	Diversify workforce	
Strategic Job Families	Quality manager	Call center representative	certified financial planner	Telemarketer	Consumer marketer	Joint venture manager	Community recruiter	
Competency Profile	Six Sigma program

Problem management system | Customer interaction center

Problem management system

Team building | Solutions selling

Relationship management

Product-line knowledge

Professional certification | Phone selling

Product line knowledge

Older management system | Market research

Market communi-cation

Cross business process | Relationship management

Negotiation

E-commerce know-how | Community roots

Public relations

Legal frameworks | **Overall Assessment of Human Capital Readiness** |
| **Number Required** | 30 | 20 | 100 | 20 | 10 | 30 | 10 | |
| **Strategic Job Readiness** | 100% | 90% | 40% | 50% | 20% | 70% | 80% | **65%** |

42

that three job families are key to its strategy: project managers, who oversee the operations in specific accounts; operations directors, who broaden the relationships within existing accounts; and business development executives, who help acquire new accounts. These three job families employ only 215 people, less than 4% of the workforce. By focusing human capital development activities on these critical few individuals, the chemical company, Unicco, and Williams-Sonoma can greatly leverage their human capital investments. It is sobering to think that strategic success in these three companies is determined by how well they develop competencies in less than 10% of their workforces.

Once a company identifies its strategic job families, it must define the requirements for these jobs in considerable detail, a task often referred to as "job profiling" or "competency profiling." A competency profile describes the knowledge, skills, and values required by successful occupants in the job family. Often, HR managers will interview individuals who best understand the job requirements to develop a competency profile they can use to recruit, hire, train, and develop people for that position. To see how this might be done, consider Consumer Bank, a composite example distilled from our experiences in working with about a dozen retail banks.

Consumer Bank was migrating from its historic strategy of promoting individual products to one offering complete financial solutions and one-stop shopping to targeted customers. The map for this new strategy identified seven critical internal processes, one of which was "crosssell the product line." Human resources and line executives then identified the financial planner as the job most important to the effective performance of this process. A planning workshop further identified four skills fundamental to the financial planner's job: solutions selling, relationship management, product-line knowledge, and professional certification. For each internal process on its strategy map, Consumer Bank replicated this approach, identifying the strategic job families and critical competencies each required. The results are summarized in the exhibit "Human Capital Readiness at Consumer Bank."

To take the next step–assessing the current capabilities and competencies of each of the employees in each strategic job family–companies can draw from a broad range of approaches. For example, employees can themselves assess how well their current capabilities fit the job requirements and then discuss those assessments with a mentor or career manager. Alternatively, an assessor can solicit 360-degree feedback on employees' performance from their supervisors, peers, and subordinates. From these assessments, employees get a clear understanding of their objectives, meaningful feedback on their current levels of skill and performance, and specific recommendations for future personal development.

Consumer Bank estimated that it needed 100 trained and skilled financial planners to execute the cross-selling process. But in assessing its recent targeted hiring, training, and development programs, the bank's HR group determined that only 40 of its financial planners had reached a high enough level of proficiency. The bank's human capital readiness for this piece of the strategy was, therefore, only 40%, as the exhibit shows. By replicating this analysis for all its strategic job families, the bank learned the state of its human capital readiness and thus whether the organization could move forward quickly with its new strategy.

INFORMATION CAPITAL READINESS

Executives must understand how to plan, set priorities for, and manage an information capital portfolio that supports their organization's strategy. As with human capital, the strategy map serves as a starting point for delineating a company's IC objectives. In the case of Consumer Bank, the chief information officer led an initiative to identify the specific information capital needs of each of the seven internal processes previously identified as critical to the bank's new value proposition.

For the customer management process "cross-sell the product line," the workshop team identified an application for customers to analyze and manage their portfolios by themselves (a customer portfolio self-management system) as a transformational application. The workshop team identified an analytical application for the same process (a customer profitability system) and a transaction-processing application (an integrated customer file). The internal process "understand customer segments" also needed a customer profitability system, as well as a separate customer feedback system to support market research. The process "shift to appropriate channel" required a strong foundation of transactional systems, including a packaged CRM software suite that included modules for lead management, order management, and sales force automation. For the operations process "provide rapid response," participants identified a transformational application (customer self-help) as well as an analytic application (a best-practice community knowledge management system) for sharing successful sales techniques among telemarketers. Finally, the "minimize problems" process required an analytical application (service quality analysis) to identify problems and two related transaction-level systems (one for incident tracking and another for problem management).

After defining its portfolio of IC applications, the project team identified several required components of IT infrastructure. Some applications needed a CRM transactions database. Others required that a Web-enabled infrastructure be integrated into the bank's overall Web site architecture. The team also learned about the need for an internal R&D project to develop a

Information Capital Readiness at Consumer Bank

The first two rows of the information capital readiness report, like the human capital report, list the company's critical internal processes and its strategic job families. The remaining five rows specify the various items in the IC portfolio, assigning scores indicating how well developed each items is. In this example, Consumer Bank has the IC portfolio it needs to support innovation but is less able to support the job most critical to its customer management and operational excellence goals.

	Operations Management		Customer Management		Innovation	
Strategic Processes	Minimize Problems	Provide rapid response	Cross-sell the product line	Shift to appropriate channel	Understand customer segments	Develop new products
Strategic Job Families	Quality manager	Call center representative	Certified financial planner	Telemarketer	Consumer marketer	Joint Venture manager
	Strategic Information Capital Portfolio					
Transformational Applications		Customer self-help 4	Customer portfolio self management 4			
Analytical Applications	Service quality analysis 2	Best practice community knowledge management system 3	Customer profitability 3	Best practice community knowledge management system 2	Customer profitability 3	Best practice community knowledge management system 2
Transaction-Processing Applications	Incident tracking 6; Problem management 2	Workforce scheduling 3; Problem management 2	Integrated customer file 3	CRM/lead management 6; CRM/order management 6; CRM/sales force automation 4	Customer feedback 2	Project management 2
Technology Infrastructure	Web enabled 3; Computer telephony integration 4	Computer telephony integration 4; Interative voice response 3	CRM packaged software 2; Web enabled 3	Web enabled 3; Computer telephony integration 4	CRM packaged software 2	
Combined Readiness Level	✗	✗	?	✗	✓	✓

Ratings

1 — OK

2 — Minor enhancements needed

3 — New development under way

4 — New development behind schedule

5 — Major enhancements required

6 — New application required

new interactive voice-response technology. All together, the bank's planning process defined an information capital portfolio made up of 14 unique applications (some of which supported more than one internal process) and four IT infrastructure projects. (See the exhibit "Information Capital Readiness at Consumer Bank.")

The team then turned to assessing the readiness of the bank's existing portfolio of IC infrastructure and applications, assigning a numerical indicator from 1 to 6 to each system. A score of 1 or 2 indicates that the system is already available and operating normally, perhaps needing only minor enhancements. A score of 3 or 4 indicates that the system has been identified and funded but is not yet installed or operational. In other words, current capability does not yet exist but development programs are under way to close the gap. A score of 5 or 6 signals that a new infrastructure or application is needed to support the strategy, but nothing has yet been done to create, fund, and deliver the capability. Managers responsible for the IC development programs provided the subjective judgments for this simple measurement system, and the CIO was responsible for assessing the integrity of the reported numbers. In the IC exhibit, we can also see that Consumer Bank aggregated the readiness measures of individual applications and infrastructure programs—designating them green, yellow, or red, based on the worst-case application in the category—to create a portfolio status report. With such a report, managers can see the strategic readiness of the organization's information capital at a glance, easily pinpointing the areas in which more resources are needed. It is an excellent tool for monitoring a portfolio of information capital development programs.

Many sophisticated IT organizations already use more quantitative, objective assessments of their information capital portfolios than the subjective process we've just described for Consumer Bank. These organizations survey users to assess their satisfaction with each system. They perform financial analyses to determine the operating and maintenance costs of each application. Some conduct technical audits to assess the underlying quality of the code, ease of use, quality of documentation, and frequency of failure for each application. From this profile, an organization can build strategies for managing its portfolio of existing IC assets just as one would manage a collection of physical assets like machinery or a fleet of trucks. Applications with high levels of maintenance can be streamlined, for example, applications with high operating costs can be optimized, and applications with high levels of user dissatisfaction can be replaced. This more comprehensive approach can be effective for managing a portfolio of applications that are already operational.

ORGANIZATION CAPITAL READINESS

Success in performing the critical internal processes identified in an organization's strategy map invariably requires an organization to change in fundamental ways. Assessing OC readiness is essentially about assessing how well the company can mobilize and sustain the organization change agenda associated with its strategy. For instance, if the strategy involves focusing on the customer, the company needs to determine whether its existing culture is customer-centric, whether its leaders have the requisite skills to foster such a culture, whether employees are aware of the goal and are motivated to deliver exceptional customer service, and, finally, how well employees share with others their knowledge about the company's customers. Let's explore how companies can make these kinds of assessments for each of the four OC dimensions.

Culture. Of the four, culture is perhaps the most complex and difficult dimension to understand and describe because it encompasses a wider range of behavioral territory than the others. That's probably why "shaping the culture" is the most often-cited objective in the Learning and Growth section of our Balanced Scorecard database. Executives generally believe that changes in strategy require basic changes in the way business is conducted at all levels of the organization, which means, of course, that people will need to develop new attitudes and behaviors—in other words, change their culture.

Assessment of cultural readiness relies heavily on employee surveys. But in preparing surveys, companies need to distinguish clearly between the values that all employees share—the company's base culture—and the perceptions that employees have of their existing system—the climate. The concept of base culture has its roots in anthropology, which defines an organization's culture as the symbols, myths, and rituals embedded in the group consciousness (or subconscious). To describe a company's base culture, therefore, you have to uncover the organization's systems of shared meanings, assumptions, and values.

The concept of climate has its roots in social psychology and is determined by the way organizational influences—such as the incentive structure or the perceived warmth and support of superiors and peers—affect employees' motivation and behavior. The anthropological component reflects employees' shared attitudes and beliefs independent of the actual organizational infrastructure, while climate reflects their shared perception of existing organizational policies, practices, and procedures, both formal and informal.

Surveying perceptions of existing organizational policies and practices is a fairly straightforward task, but getting at the base culture requires a little more digging. Anthropologists usually rely on storytelling to identify shared beliefs and images, but that approach is inadequate for quantifying the alignment of culture to strategy. Organizational behavior scholars have developed measurement instruments, such as Charles O'Reilly and colleagues' Organizational Culture Profile, in which employees rank 54 value statements according to their perceived importance and relevance in the organization. Once ranked, an organization's culture can be described with a reasonable degree of reliability and validity. Then the organization can assess to what extent the existing culture is consistent with its strategy and what kinds of changes may be needed.

One caveat: Managers do need to be aware that some variations in culture are necessary and desirable in different operating units or functions. The culture of an R&D group, for example, should be different from the culture of a manufacturing unit; the culture of an emergent business unit should be different from the culture of a mature one. Executives should strive for agreement throughout the organization about corporatewide values such as integrity, respect, treatment of colleagues, and commitment to customer satisfaction. But some value statements in the survey instrument should refer to the culture of specific operating units. So, for example, surveys of the employees in operations and service-delivery units would include statements about quality and continuous improvement, whereas the R&D department survey might include statements about creativity and innovation. For employees involved in customer acquisition, statements might relate to retention and growth or to a deep understanding of individual customers' preferences and needs.

Leadership. If companies change their strategies, people will have to do some things differently as well. It is the responsibility of leaders at all levels of the organization—from the CEO of a retail chain down to the local store managers—to help employees identify and understand the changes needed and to motivate and guide them toward the new ways of working.

In researching the best practices in our Balanced Scorecard database, we were able to identify seven generic types of behavioral changes that build organization capital, and each fell into one of two categories: changes that support the creation of value—such as increasing people's focus on the customer—and those required to carry out the company's strategy—such as increasing accountability. The sidebar "Seven Behaviors for Transformation" describes these behavioral changes in more detail.

To ensure that it gets the kind of leaders it needs, a company should draw up a *leadership competency model* for each of its leadership positions. This is a kind of job profile that defines the competencies a leader is expected to have to be effective in carrying out the company's strategy. For example, one manufacturing company, attempting to create teams to solve customers' problems, identified and defined three competencies essential for people in team leadership positions:

- **Customer Focus**—Outstanding leaders understand their customers. They place themselves in the customers' minds and spend time with them to understand their current and future needs.
- **Fostering Teamwork**—Outstanding leaders work collaboratively with their own teams and across organizational and geographic boundaries. They empower their teams to achieve excellence.
- **Open Communications**—Outstanding leaders tell the truth. They openly share information with peers, managers, and subordinates. They tell the whole story, not just how it looks from their position.

Often, organizations will measure leadership traits, such as those listed above, through employee surveys. A staff or external unit solicits information from subordinates, peers, and superiors about a leader's mastery of the critical skills. This personal feedback is used mainly for coaching and developing the leader, but the unit can also aggregate the detailed (and confidential) data from the individual reviews to create a status report on the readiness of key leadership competencies needed throughout the organization.

Alignment. An organization is aligned when all employees have a commonality of purpose, a shared vision, and an understanding of how their personal roles support the overall strategy. An aligned organization encourages behaviors such as innovation and risk taking because individuals' actions are directed toward achieving high-level objectives. Encouraging and empowering individual initiative in an unaligned organization leads to chaos, as the innovative risk takers pull the organization in contradictory directions.

Achieving alignment is a two-step process. First, managers communicate the high-level strategic objectives in ways that all employees can understand. This involves using a wide range of communication mechanisms: brochures, newsletters, town meetings, orientation and training programs, executive talks, company intranets, and bulletin boards. The goal of this step is to create intrinsic motivation, to inspire employees to internalize the organization's values and objectives so that they want to help the organization succeed. The next step uses extrinsic motivation. The organization has employees set explicit personal and team objectives aligned to the strategy and establishes incentives that reward employees when they meet personal, departmental, business unit, and corporate targets.

Measuring alignment readiness is relatively straightforward. Many survey instruments are already available for assessing how much employees know about and how well they understand high-level strategic objectives. It is also fairly easy to see whether or not individuals' personal objectives and the company's existing incentive schemes are consistent with the high-level strategy.

For example, a large property and casualty insurance company adopted a new strategy intended to reduce its underwriting losses by creating a tighter link between the underwriters, who decide whether to accept a new piece of business, and the claims agents, who deal with the consequences from poor underwriting decisions. Historically, these specialists lived in different parts of the organization, and their incentives were totally unrelated to each other, which clearly did little to foster cooperation between them or with the line business units they supported. To reflect the new strategy, the company changed to a team-based compensation system in which everyone's incentive pay was based on a common set of measures (their Balanced Scorecard). Underwriters and claims agents, who worked in service departments shared by the various business units, were now rewarded using the Balanced Scorecard measures related to the business units they supported. The company used a survey instrument to capture the employees' perceptions of the improved teamwork created by aligning the incentive systems.

ORGANIZATION CAPITAL READINESS REPORT

The various measures for organization capital readiness should be put together in a readiness report, which shows, for all the components of organization capital, where the company needs to introduce changes to its behaviors and policies. The report shown here is a simplified version of one prepared by a company in our Balanced Scorecard database.

Attribute	Strategic Objective	Strategic Measure	Target	Actual	
Culture	Foster awareness and internalization of the mission, vision, and core values needed to execute the strategy	Customer-focused (customer survey; percentage who understand the organization's mission)	80%	68%	✗
		Other core values (employee change readiness survey)	80%	52%	✗
Leadership	Develop leaders at all levels who can mobilize the organization toward its strategy	Leadership gap (percentage of key attributes in competency model rated above threshold)	90%	92%	✓
Alignment	Align goals and incentives with the strategy at all levels of the organization	Strategic awareness (percentage of staff who can identify organization's strategic priorities)	80%	75%	✗
		Strategic alignment (percentage of staff whose objectives and incentives link to Balanced Scorecard)	100%	60%	✗
Teamwork	Ensure that knowledge and staff assets that have strategic potential are shared	Sharing best practices (number of knowledge management system hits per employee)	5.0	6.1	✓

Teamwork and Knowledge Sharing. There is no greater waste than a good idea used only once. Most organizations have to go through a cultural change to shift individuals from hoarding to sharing their local knowledge. No asset has greater potential for an organization than the collective knowledge possessed by all its employees. That's why many companies, hoping to generate, organize, develop, and distribute knowledge throughout the organization, have spent millions of dollars to purchase or create formal knowledge management systems.

The challenge in implementing such systems is motivating people to actually document their ideas and knowledge to make them available to others. Most organizations in our Balanced Scorecard database attempted to develop such motivation by selecting "teamwork" and "knowledge sharing" as strategic priorities in their Learning and Growth Perspective. Typical measures for these priorities included the number of best practice ideas the employees identified and used, the percentage of employees who transferred knowledge in a workout process, the number of people who actually used the knowledge management system, how often the system is used, the percentage of information in the knowledge management system that was updated, and how much was obsolete.

For knowledge sharing to matter, it must be aligned with the priorities of the strategy map. For example, one organization—a chemical company—created several best practice communities to complement the internal process objectives on its strategy map. The Improve Workplace Safety community consisted of the safety directors from every facility. They studied the best practices at the high-performing plants and created a best practice–sharing program. The company's output measure, "days away from work," dropped by 70%. In another example, a children's hospital was attempting to reduce costs without reducing the quality of patient care. Intensive discussions resulted in a top-ten list of best practices already being used somewhere in the hospital. The hospital then formed cross-functional medical practice teams of physicians, nurses, and administrators to implement as many of these procedures as they practically could. It measured success, the output of this knowledge-sharing process, by the "number of best practices utilized." The effective implementation of best practices over the next three years led to dramatic improvements in organizational outcomes: Readmission rates dropped by 50%, cost per case and length of stay each declined by 25%, and both customer satisfaction and quality of care increased. In these and many other examples in our case files, organizations enhanced their performance by aligning the teamwork and knowledge-sharing component of their organization capital with their strategy.

To get an overview of organizational readiness, companies can put the information they obtain from their various surveys and assessments together in a report like the one shown in "Organization Capital Readiness Report." In this exhibit, the leadership measure, drawn from the leadership competency model, displays the company's estimate, based on employee surveys, of the degree to which the company possesses the key attributes for leadership. At 92%, the company is above target on its leadership objective and can be considered strategically ready in terms of this dimension. The company's OC with respect to teamwork and knowledge sharing is also in good shape. But the firm is performing inadequately in alignment and in developing the right culture, and these problems are lowering its overall level of organization capital readiness.

The intangible assets described in the Balanced Scorecard's Learning and Growth Perspective are the foundation of every organization's strategy, and the measures in this perspective are the ultimate lead indicators. Human capital becomes most valuable when it is concentrated in the relatively few strategic job families implementing the internal processes critical to the organization's strategy. Information capital creates the greatest value when it provides the requisite infrastructure and strategic applications that complement the human capital. Organizations introducing a new strategy must create a culture of corresponding values, a cadre of exceptional leaders who can lead the change agenda, and an informed workforce aligned to the strategy, working together, and sharing knowledge to help the strategy succeed.

Some managers shy away from measuring their intangible assets because these measures are usually "softer," or more subjective, than the financial measures they conventionally use to motivate and assess performance. The Balanced Scorecard movement has encouraged organizations to face the measurement challenge. Using the systematic approaches set out in this article, companies can now measure what they want, rather than wanting only what they can currently measure. Even if the measures are imprecise, the simple act of attempting to gauge the capabilities of employees, information systems, and organization capital communicates the importance of these drivers for value creation. In the course of our work, we have seen many companies find new ways to measure—and consequently new ways to enhance the value of–their intangible assets. The measurement and management of these assets played a prominent role in their transformation into successful, strategy-focused organizations.

*Robert S. Kaplan (rkaplan@hbs.edu) is the Marvin Bower Professor of Leadership Development at Harvard Business School in Boston. **David P. Norton** (dnorton@bscol.com) is the founder and president of the Balanced Scorecard Collaborative (www.bscol.com) in Lincoln, Massachusetts. This article is based on their book* Strategy Maps: Converting Intangible Assets into Tangible Outcomes *(Harvard Business School Press, 2004).*

QUESTION

2.4   Where and how do intangibles fit into the strategy map? Explain.

2.5 Strategy or Stakeholders: Which Comes First?

by Robert S. Kaplan*

How far should organizations go in abiding by stakeholders' interests? According to stakeholder theory, strategy should take into account, if not be built around, stakeholder interests. Nonsense, argues Robert Kaplan. Such an approach is not only wrong-headed, it's impracticable. Besides, companies can account for any stakeholder considerations they view as important through their Balanced Scorecard and strategy map—and hold performance to them, without compromising strategy or their ability to adjust it to changing conditions.

---

*   From: R. Kaplan, Strategy or Stakeholders: Which Comes First? Balanced Scorecard Report (March-April, 2008); Volume 10, Number 2: 14-16. Reprinted with permission. Copyright © 2008 by the Harvard Business School Publishing Corporation; all rights reserved.

Many critics of "American" capitalism, whether from Europe, Japan, or emerging markets, believe that U.S. corporations focus too narrowly on shareholder interests at the expense of other stakeholders. The critics usually identify these other corporate stakeholders—those who have a stake in the performance and behavior of companies—as employees, customers, suppliers, and especially, communities and society in general, though some also include governmental agencies and political groups. The critics view U.S. corporations as operating under the philosophy expressed by notable (and Nobel Prize-winning) free market economist Milton Friedman, who stated: "The business of business is business," and "The social responsibility of business is to increase its profits."

These critics want to hold business accountable to performance beyond what it delivers to shareholders. Some have argued that companies need to start with determining the preferences of all their stakeholders andthen craft a strategy that meets the stakeholders' expectations. In the 1980s, Professor Edgar Freeman formatilzed the arguments for a stakeholder theory of the firm.[1] He and subsequent followers of this school of thought argued that companies need to consider and satisfy the interests of their various stakeholders as they conduct their business.

This "stakeholder view" has been reinforced in recent years by the corporate social responsibility (CSR) movement, which advocates that organizations take responsibility for the impact of their activities on customers, employees, shareholders, communities, and the environment in all aspects of their operations. CSR proponents urge companies to expand their traditional financial reporting framework to take into account their environmental and social performance as well, an approach now referred to as "triple-bottom-line" reporting.[2] Some have viewed the Balanced Scorecard as a mechanism for implementing the stakeholder, rather than the shareholder, perspective and as a framework that can be adapted for triple-bottom-line reporting.

Buiding on the stakeholder framework, some prominent management control scholars have criticized the Balanced Scorecard framework for putting financial performance for sharefholders at the top of a (private sector) strategy map, where it serves as the ultimate measure of the strategy's success. These writers advocate that "performance measurement design starts with stakeholders."[3] Their stakeholder approach to performance measurement starts by defining objectivs for what each stakeholder group expects from the corporation and how each group contributes to the corporation's success. Once stakeholder expectations or, even further, implicit and explicit contracts between the stakeholders and the corporation, are defined, the corporation then defines a strategy to meet these expectations and fulfill those contracts. Thus, while the Balanced Scorecard approach starts with a strategy for shareholder value creation, and then identifies the interrelationships and objectives for various stakeholders, the stakeholder approach starts with stakeholders and. In a second step, defines a strategy to meet shareholder expectations. The stakeholder scorecard would measure how well the company has performed for eacho f its various stakeholder groups, without ascribing any hierarchy to them.

STRATEGY PRECEDES STAKEHOLDERS

The great business historian Alfred Chandler taught us that strategy precedes structure. I strongly believe that strategy also precedes stakeholders. The stakeholder approach can essentially be viewed as a reaction to and rejection of the narrow shareholder-value-maximization view articulated in Friedman's glib statements. In this spirit, the stakeholder approach has served to highlight the multiple relationships that companies need to nurture and preserve in order to drive long-term, sustainable value creation. But stakeholder theory confuses means and ends. It therefore ends up as a less powerful, less actionable, and ultimately less satisfying approach than the strategy map/Balanced Scorecard approach. David Norton and I, following the thinking of Chandler and strategy scholar Michael Porter, have advocated selecting a strategy first, and only subsequently working out the relationship with other stakeholders, as needed by the strategy. I will illustrate the contrast between our point of view and that of stakeholder advocates with several examples.

YOU CAN'T BE ALL THINGS TO ALL CUSTOMERS

First, consider the case of Mobil's U.S. Marketing and Refining (USM&R), a well-documented Balanced Scorecard implementation.[4] Mobile learned, through market research, that its customer base was heterogeneous. Some valued only low price and wanted Mobil to offer the cheapest prices, matching or beating the prices of discount stations and other major gasoline companies. Other customers, however, were less price-sensitive and were willing to pay a premium, say up to $0.10–0.12 per gallon more, if they could have a superior buying experience—one including, for example, quick service, the ability to pay by credit card at the pump, clean restrooms, friendly and helpful employees, and a great convenience store. Stakeholder theory fails in this case. Which customers' expectations should Mobil satisfy? It could not satisfy both customer groups. Having larger gasoline stations equipped with more pumps and self-pay mechanisms;

having better-paid, better-trained, and more experienced employees; and having a full-service convenience store costs money. These costs would need to be covered by higher prices, thereby disappointing the price-sensitive customers. Conversely, if Mobil offered the lowest prices, it would not have been able to afford to invest in the larger stations with more self-service and self-pay pumps, the better-qualified employees, and the convenience store, thereby disappointing the customers desiring a great buying experience.

Strategy is about choice. Companies cannot meet the expectations of every possible customer. Wal-Mart meets the apparel needs of one customer segment, price-sensitive clothing purchasers. Nordstrom meets the needs of another segment, those seeking complete wardrobe solutions, with sales staff that know their style preferences, sizes, and clothing budget. High-end designer stores, such as Armani and Ferragamo, meet the expectations of a third segment, purchasers seeking product-leading fashion, fabric, and fit, who are willing to pay a great deal more to satisfy their clothing preferences. Similarly, customers of Southwest Airlines have different expectations of performance than the business- and first-class customers who fly British Airways. Strategy determines which customer segments a company has decided to serve and satisfy, and the value proposition that it will offer to win the loyalty of those customers. Determining strategy must precede defining measures of customer satisfaction and loyalty. Otherwise, the company would attempt to meet the expectations of all the existing and potential customers it could serve—an expensive, nondifferentiated approach. Yet this is precisely what stakeholder theory demands.

A similar situation occurs with employees. In creating the Balanced Scorecard, Dave Norton and I deliberately chose not to label the fourth perspective the "employee" or "people" perspective; instead we chose a more generic name, "learning and growth," to signal that we were not taking a pure stakeholder approach. Within the BSC framework, employee objectives always appear (in the learning and growth perspective), but they are there because employees are necessary for achieving the strategy, not because someone has identified them as a stakeholder class. Consider the example of a pharmaceutical company in the early 1990s. Among its most important employees (what we would not call a "strategic job family") are the chemists who perform research to identify new compounds for treating specific diseases. The stakeholder approach would call for interviewing these key employees to learn their career expectations, and then developing a strategy that would satisfy and meet the expectations of these employees.

Later in the 1990s, however, and continuing into this century, pharmaceutical companies shifted their strategies because of the new capabilities that became available from the scientific fields of molecular biology and genetics. With this new shift, molecular biologists and geneticists becauem the new key employees; the fate of pharmaceuticals' formerly key employee stakeholder, PhD chemists, became more tenuous, especially if they did not acquire dramatically new capabilities and competencies to enable them to contribute to new approaches for drug development. Again, the stakeholder view would lock a company into maintaining relationships with this soon-to-be obsolete employee group, preventing the company from moving swiftly enough to acquire entirely new employees to help implement the new strategy.

I might add that on a recent visit to Japan, for the 2007 Asia Pacific Balancred Scorecard Summit, several Japanese executives shared their version of the stakeholder theory. They told me that in their companies, employees cam first, not shareholders. I thought to myself (but did not respond) that this way of thinking has likely contributed to Japan's struggle for the past two decades to adapt to the reality of lower-cost production from China and Southeast Asia.

With respect to suppliers, stakeholder theorists also criticize the Balanced Scorecard for not having a separate perspective for this group—one of their firve essential stakeholder groups in their world-view. But as with employees, suppliers show up on the scorecard (typically in the internal process perspective) when they are essential to the strategy. So companies like Wal-Mart, Nike, and Toyota, for whom suppliers play a critical role in creating sustainable competitive advantage, would certainly feature supplier performance in their strategy maps. But consider a company like Mobil USM&R, whose main suppliers are petroleum exploration and production companies (which provide a commodity such as crude oil), and constructions companies (which build refineries and pipelines). These suppliers provide essential products and services, but don't provide any differentiation for or support of Mobil's strategy. Similarly, a community bank with a customer intimacy strategy gets its raw material, money, from the U.S. Federal Reserve system. Suppliers are not a critical component of its strategy. Thus, Mobil USM&R and the community bank may choose not to feature suppliers on their scorecares because suppliers don't contribute to their competitive differentiation and the sustainability of their strategies. Again, strategy precedes stakeholders—and, in these cases, may reveal that a stakeholder is not decisive for the strategy.

WHEN STAKEHOLDERS ARE KEY TO STRATEGY

When stakeholders are vitally important fot the success of a company's strategy, they should be included in the company's strategy map and scorecard. The organization's performance relative to society and communities does not appear as internal process objectives when such performance contributes to the differentiation of the organization's strategy.[5] This practive matches that articulated by Michael Porter when he advocated that environmental and social performance be aligned to support the company strategy.[6]

Occasionally, we find companies in which the shareholders themselves choose an explicit stakeholder value approach rather than having shareholder value be the unifying paradigm for their strategy. That's OK; that's their choice. And, it doesn't mean that they have to abandon the Balanced Scorecard methodology and switch to the stakeholder view. They can use a strategy map and Balanced Scorecardd to articulate their preference for simjultaneously creating economic, environmental, and social value. This will help them balanceand manage the tensions among those values. Ths is exactly the path taken by Amanco, a Latin Amnerican producer of water treatment solutions, whose founding shareholder believed deeply in triple-bottom-line permformance.[7]

In summary, stakeholder theory may have been useful for articulating a broader company mission beyond the narrow, short-term shareholder-value-maximizing model. To its credit, it has increased companies' sensitivity about how the failure to incorporate stakeholder preferences and expectations in their strategy can lead to an excessive focus on short-term financial results and even undermine long-term performance. The Balanced Scorecard, however, incorporates stakeholder interests endogenously, within a coherent strategy and value-creation framework, when outstanding performance in relation to those stakeholders is critical to the success of the strategy. The converse is not true for stakeholder theory. Stakeholder theory provides little guidance for companies when they wish to modify their strategy in a way that adversely impacts and existing stakeholder.

Because of the dynamics of competition, technology, regulation, and consumer preferences, companies at times need to shift their focus and priorities among multiple stakeholders. A strategy that is based on creating long-term shareholder value enables companies to be flexible in adapting to changing conditions, while still recognizing how the interests of all their stakeholders must be reflected in sustaining their value-creating strategies.

ENDNOTES

1. R. E. Freemah, Stratigic Management: A Stakeholder Approach (Pitman, 1984).
2. J. Elkington, "Towards the Sustainable Corporation: Win-Win-Win Business Strategies for Sustainable Development," California Management Review (1994).
3. A. Neely, C. Adams, and M. Kennerly, the Performance Prism: The Scorecard for Measuring and Managing Stakeholder Relationships (Pearson Education, 2002); A. Atkinson, J. Waterhouse, and R. Wells, "A Stakeholder Approach to Strategic Perforance Measurement," Sloan management Review (Spring, 1997).
4. Mobil U.S. Marking and Refining (A): Harvard Business School Case, by R. S. Kaplan (June 26, 1997: 197120); also R. S. Kaplan and D. P. Norton, "Creating the Strategy-Focused Organization: The Mobil NAM&R Experience," chapter 2 in The Strategy-Focused Organization (HBS Press, 2001).
5. R. S. Kaplan and D. P. Norton, "Regulatory and Social Processes," chapter 6 in Strategy Maps (HBS Press, 2003).
6. M. E. Porter and Mark R. Kramer, "Strategy and Society: The Link between Competitive Advantage and Corporate Social Responsibility," Harvard Business Review (December 2006).
7. Amanco: Developing the Sustainability Scorecard: Harvard Business School Case, by R. S. Kaplan and R. Reisen (January 25, 2007: 107038).

QUESTION

2.5 According to Robert Kaplan which should come first, stakeholders' interests or corporate strategy? Explain.

Chapter 3

Using Costs in Decision Making

The first article for this section is Reading 3.1, Robin Cooper and Robert Kaplan's *How Cost Accounting Distorts Product Costs*. In this now classic article, Cooper and Kaplan strongly question the relevance of the traditional cost accounting model and its applicability for product costing. The authors discuss problems with traditional cost accounting, including the inadequacy of both variable and full costing methods for accurate product costing and the failure of both marginal and fixed-cost allocations. Other topics, such as understanding the cost of complexity and transaction costing (an early name for activity-based costing), are introduced. This article helped set the stage for a great deal of research on the failings of traditional cost accounting methods.

Reading 3.2, Robin Cooper's *Does Your Company Need a New Cost System*, poses a critical question for managers: "Do I really know what my products cost?" Answering this question will allow managers to determine whether their costing system is reporting accurate product costs. In order to address this question, Cooper suggests that managers look for symptoms that often point to poor system design. For example, one symptom of a poor system occurs when a firm's customers completely ignore price increases, even though the firm's manufacturing costs haven't changed. In this instance, the cost system may be underestimating product costs, and thus, the associated markup is still below market. Cooper outlines a number of other design flaws that managers should understand as they attempt to develop more accurate systems.

Some critics of cost management practices today have suggested that the distinction between direct and indirect costs is no longer relevant for decision making. In Reading 3.3, *Distinguishing between Direct and Indirect Costs Is Crucial for Internet Companies*, L. Gordon and M. Loeb argue that the distinction between direct and indirect costs is still highly salient for e-commerce firms. In addition to using products, services, and departments as cost objects, the authors state that Internet companies must also treat customers as key cost objects—a notion highly consistent with the current view on the importance of assessing customer profitability.

In *Caution: Fraud Overhead* (Reading 3.4), John MacArthur, Bobby Waldrup, and Gary Fane describe a situation in which the "Wapello Manufacturing Inc." consultants were called in to investigate a potential fraud. Apart from uncovering a number of internal control problems, the analysis of the company's records revealed large overhead accounts. Because overhead contains a wide variety of costs and accounts such as indirect salaries, supplies, taxes, insurance, and depreciation, fraudulent expenses can often be hidden in journal entries and in overhead variance calculations. Due to complexity, the management of such large accounts is often left to the controller—someone who clearly understands what is contained in them. In this case, the controller was arrested for embezzlement.

Reading 3.5, *The Business of Making Movies* by S. Mark Young, James Gong, and Wim Van der Stede discuss the motion picture industry and provide an overview of the process and costs of making a feature film.

Readings
Chapter 3

3.1 How Cost Accounting Distorts Product Costs

The traditional cost system that defines variable costs as varying in the short-term with production will misclassify these costs as fixed.

by Robin Cooper and Robert S. Kaplan*

In order to make sensible decisions concerning the products they market, managers need to know what their products cost. Product design, new product introduction decisions, and the amount of effort expended on trying to market a given product or product line will be influenced by the anticipated cost and profitability of the product. Conversely, if product profitability appears to drop, the question of discontinuance will be raised. Product costs also can play an important role in setting prices, particularly for customized products with low sales volumes and without readily available market prices.

The cumulative effect of decisions on product design, introduction, support, discontinuance, and pricing helps define a firm's strategy. If the product cost information is distorted, the firm can follow an inappropriate and unprofitable strategy. For example, the low-cost producer often achieves competitive advantage by servicing a broad range of customers. This strategy will be successful if the economies of scale exceed the additional costs, the diseconomies of scope, caused by producing and servicing a more diverse product line. If the cost system does not correctly attribute the additional costs to the products that cause them, then the firm might end up competing in segments where the scope-related costs exceed the benefits from larger scale production.

Similarly, a differentiated producer achieves competitive advantage by meeting specialized customers' needs with products whose costs of differentiation are lower than the price premiums charged for special features and services. If the cost system fails to measure differentiation costs properly, then the firm might choose to compete in segments that are actually unprofitable.

FULL VS. VARIABLE COST
Despite the importance of cost information, disagreement still exists about whether product costs should be measured by full or by variable cost. In a full-cost system, fixed production costs are allocated to products so that reported product costs measure total manufacturing costs. In a variable cost system, the fixed costs are not allocated and product costs reflect only the marginal cost of manufacturing.

Academic accountants, supported by economists, have argued strongly that variable costs are the relevant ones for product decisions. They have demonstrated, using increasingly complex models, that setting marginal revenues equal to marginal costs will produce the highest profit. In contrast, accountants in practice continue to report full costs in their cost accounting systems.

The definition of variable cost used by academic accountants assumes that product decisions have a short-time horizon, typically a month or a quarter. Costs are variable only if they vary directly with monthly or quarterly changes in production volume. Such a definition is appropriate if the volume of production of all products can be changed at will and there is no way to change simultaneously the level of fixed costs.

In practice, managers reject this short-term perspective because the decision to offer a product creates a long-term commitment to manufacture, market, and support that product. Given this perspective, short-term variable cost is an inadequate measure of product cost.

While full cost is meant to be a surrogate for long-run manufacturing costs, in nearly all of the companies we visited, management was not convinced that their full-cost systems were adequate for its product-related decisions. In particular, management did not believe their systems accurately reflected the costs of resources consumed to manufacture products. But they were also unwilling to adopt a variable-cost approach.

Of the more than 20 firms we visited and documented, Mayers Tap, Rockford, and Schrader Bellows provided particularly useful insights on how product costs were systematically distorted.[1] These companies had several significant common characteristics.

* From: R. Cooper and R. S. Kaplan, "How Cost Accounting Distorts Product Costs," *Management Accounting* (April 1988): 20–27. Reprinted with permission conveyed through Copyright Clearance Center, Inc.

They all produced a large number of distinct products in a single facility. The products formed several distinct product lines and were sold through diverse marketing channels. The range in demand volume for products within a product line was high, with sales of high-volume products between 100 and 1,000 times greater than sales of low-volume products. As a consequence, products were manufactured and shipped in highly varied lot sizes. While our findings are based upon these three companies, the same effects were observed at several other sites.

In all three companies, product costs played an important role in the decisions that surrounded the introduction, pricing, and discontinuance of products. Reported product costs also appeared to play a significant role in determining how much effort should be assigned to marketing and selling products.

Typically, the individual responsible for introducing new products also was responsible for setting prices. Cost-plus pricing to achieve a desired level of gross margin predominantly was used for the special products, though substantial modifications to the resulting estimated prices occurred when direct competition existed. Such competition was common for high-volume products but rarely occurred for the low-volume items. Frequently, no obvious market prices existed for low-volume products because they had been designed to meet a particular customer's needs.

ACCURACY OF PRODUCT COSTS
Managers in all three firms expressed serious concerns about the accuracy of their product-costing systems.

For example, Rockford attempted to obtain much higher margins for its low-volume products to compensate, on an ad hoc basis, for the gross underestimates of costs that it believed the cost system produced for these products. But management was not able to justify its decisions on cutoff points to identify low-volume products or the magnitude of the ad hoc margin increases. Further, Rockford's management believed that its faulty cost system explained the ability of small firms to compete effectively against it for high-volume business. These small firms, with no apparent economic or technological advantage, were winning high-volume business with prices that were at or below Rockford's reported costs. And the small firms seemed to be prospering at these prices.

At Schrader Bellows, production managers believed that certain products were not earning their keep because they were so difficult to produce. But the cost system reported that these products were among the most profitable in the line. The managers also were convinced that they could make certain products as efficiently as anybody else. Yet competitors were consistently pricing comparable products considerably lower. Management

suspected that the cost system contributed to this problem.

At Mayers Tap, the financial accounting profits were always much lower than those predicted by the cost system, but no one could explain the discrepancy. Also, the senior managers were concerned by their failure to predict which bids they would win or lose. Mayers Tap often won bids that had been overpriced because it did not really want the business, and lost bids it had deliberately underpriced in order to get the business.

TWO-STAGE COST ALLOCATION SYSTEM
The cost systems of all companies we visited had many common characteristics. Most important was the use of a two-stage cost allocation system: in the first stage, costs were assigned to cost pools (often called cost centers), and in the second stage, costs were allocated from the cost pools to the products.

The companies used many different allocation bases in the first stage to allocate costs from plant overhead accounts to cost centers. Despite the variation in allocation bases in the first stage, however, all companies used direct labor hours in the second stage to allocate overhead from the cost pools to the products. Direct labor hours were used in the second allocation stage even when the production process was highly automated so that burden rates exceeded 1,000%. Figure 1 illustrates a typical two-stage allocation process.

Of the three companies we examined in detail, only one had a cost accounting system capable of reporting variable product costs. Variable cost was identified at the budgeting stage in one other site, but this information was not subsequently used for product costing. The inability of the cost system to report variable cost was a common feature of many of the systems we observed. Reporting variable product costs was the exception, not the rule.

Firms used only one cost system even though costs were collected and allocated for several purposes, including product costing, operational control, and inventory valuation. The cost systems seemed to be designed primarily to perform the inventory valuation function for financial reporting because they had serious deficiencies for operational control (too delayed and too aggregate) and for product costing (too aggregate).

THE FAILURE OF MARGINAL COSTING
The extensive use of fixed-cost allocations in all the companies we investigated contrasts sharply with a 65-year history of academics advocating marginal costing for product decisions. If the marginal-cost concept had been adopted by companies' management, then we would have expected to see product-costing systems that explicitly reported variable-cost information. Instead, we observed cost systems that

reported variable as well as full costs in only a small minority of companies.

The traditional academic recommendation for marginal costing may have made sense when variable costs (labor, material, and some overhead) were a relatively high proportion of total manufactured cost and when product diversity was sufficiently small that there was not wide variation in the demands made by different products on the firm's production and marketing resources. But these conditions are no longer typical of many of today's organizations. Increasingly, overhead (most of it considered "fixed") is becoming a larger share of total manufacturing costs. In addition, the plants we examined are being asked to produce an increasing variety of products that make quite different demands on equipment and support departments. Thus, even if direct or marginal costing were once a useful recommendation to management, direct costing, even if correctly implemented, is not likely a solution—and may perhaps be a major problem—for product costing in the contemporary manufacturing environment.

THE FAILURE OF FIXED-COST ALLOCATIONS

While we consistently observed managers avoiding the use of variable or marginal costs for their product-related decisions, we observed also their discomfort with the full-cost allocations produced by their existing cost systems. We believe that we have identified the two major sources for the discomfort.

The first problem arises from the use of direct labor hours in the second allocation stage to assign costs from cost centers to products. This procedure may have been adequate many decades ago when direct labor was the principal value-adding activity in the material conversion process. But as firms introduce more automated machinery, direct labor is increasingly engaged in setup and supervisory functions (rather than actually performing the work on the product) and no longer represents a reasonable surrogate for resource demands by product.

In many of the plants we visited, labor's main tasks are to load the machines and to act as troubleshooters. Labor frequently works on several different products at the same time so that it becomes impossible to assign labor hours intelligently to products. Some of the companies we visited had responded to this situation by beginning experiments using machine hours instead of labor hours to allocate costs from cost pools to products (for the second stage of the allocation process). Other companies, particularly those adopting just-in-time or continuous-flow production processes, were moving to material dollars as the basis for distributing costs from pools to products. Material dollars provide a less expensive method for cost allocation than machine hours because, as with labor hours, material dollars are collected by the existing cost system. A move to a machine-hour basis would require the collection of new data for many of these companies.

Shifting from labor hours to machine hours or material dollars provides some relief from the problem of using unrealistic bases for attributing costs to products. In fact, some companies have been experimenting with using all three allocations bases simultaneously: labor hours for those costs that vary with the number of labor hours worked (e.g., supervision—if the amount of labor in a product is high, the amount of supervision related to that product also is likely to be high), machine hours for those costs that vary with the number of hours the machine is running (e.g., power—the longer the machine is running the more power that is consumed by that product), and material dollars for those costs that vary with the value of material in the product (e.g., material handling—the higher the value of the material in the product, the greater the material-handling costs associated with those products are likely to be).

Using multiple allocation bases allows a finer attribution of costs to the products responsible for the incurrence of those costs. In particular, it allows for product diversity where the direct labor, machine hours, and material dollars consumed in the manufacture of different products are not directly proportional to each other.

For reported product costs to be correct, however, the allocation bases used must be capable of accounting for all aspects of product diversity. Such an accounting is not always possible even using all three volume-related allocation bases we described. As the number of product items manufactured increases, so does the number of direct labor hours, machine hours, and material dollars consumed. The designer of the cost system, in adopting these bases, assumes that all allocated costs have the same behavior; namely that they increase in direct relationship to the volume of product items manufactured. But there are many costs that vary with the diversity and complexity of products, not by the number of units produced.

THE COST OF COMPLEXITY

The complexity costs of a full-line producer can be illustrated as follows. Consider two identical plants. One plant produces 1,000,000 units of product A. The second plant produces 100,000 units of product A and 900,000 units of 199 similar products. (The similar products have sales volumes that vary from 100 to 100,000 units.)

The first plant has a simple production environment and requires limited manufacturing-support facilities. Few setups, expediting, and scheduling activities are required.

The other plant presents a much more complex production-management environment. Its 200 products have to be scheduled through the plant, requiring frequent setups, inventory movements, purchases, receipts, and inspections. To handle this complexity, the support departments must be larger and more sophisticated.

The traditional cost accounting system plays an important role in obfuscating the underlying relationship between the range of products produced and the size of support departments. First, the costs of most support departments are classified as fixed, making it difficult to realize that these costs are systematically varying. Second, the use of volume-related allocation bases makes it difficult to recognize how these support-department costs vary.

FIGURE 1. THE TWO-STAGE PROGRESS

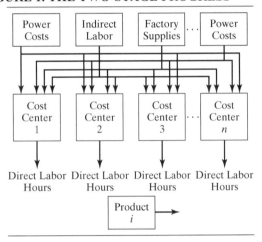

Support-department costs must vary with something because they have been among the fastest growing in the overall cost structure of manufactured products. As the example demonstrates, support-department costs vary not with the volume of product items manufactured, rather they vary with the range of items produced (i.e., the complexity of the production process). The traditional definition of variable cost, with its monthly or quarterly perspective, views such costs as fixed because complexity-related costs do not vary significantly in such a short time frame. Across an extended period of time, however, the increasing complexity of the production process places additional demands on support departments, and their costs eventually and inevitably rise.

The output of a support department consists of the activities its personnel perform. These include such activities as setups, inspections, material handling, and scheduling. The output of the departments can be represented by the number of distinct activities that are performed or the number of transactions handled. Because most of the output of these departments consists of human activities, however, output can increase quite significantly before an immediate deterioration in the quality of service is detected. Eventually, the maximum output of the department is reached and additional

personnel are requested. The request typically comes some time after the initial increase in diversity and output. Thus, support departments, while varying with the diversity of the demanded output, grow intermittently. The practice of annually budgeting the size of the departments further hides the underlying relationship between the mix and volume of demand and the size of the department. The support departments often are constrained to grow only when budgeted to do so.

Support-department costs are perhaps best described as "discretionary" because they are budgeted and authorized each year. The questions we must address are: What determines the level of these discretionary fixed costs? Why, if these costs are not affected by the quantity of production, are there eight people in a support department and not one? What generates the work, if not physical quantities of inputs or outputs, that requires large support-department staffs? We believe the answers to these questions on the origins of discretionary overhead costs (i.e., what drives these costs) can be found by analyzing the activities or transactions demanded when producing a full and diverse line of products.

TRANSACTION COSTING

Low-volume products create more transactions per unit manufactured than their high-volume counterparts. The per unit share of these costs should, therefore, be higher for the low-volume products. But when volume-related bases are used exclusively to allocate support-department costs, high-volume and low-volume products receive similar transaction-related costs. When only volume-related bases are used for second-stage allocations, high-volume products receive an excessively high fraction of support-department costs and, therefore, subsidize the low-volume products.

As the range between low-volume and high-volume products increases, the degree of cross-subsidization rises. Support departments expand to cope with the additional complexity of more products, leading to increased overhead charges. The reported product cost of all products consequently increases. The high-volume products appear more expensive to produce than previously, even though they are not responsible for the additional costs. The costs triggered by the introduction of new, low-volume products are systematically shifted to high-volume products that may be placing relatively few demands on the plant's support departments.

Many of the transactions that generate work for production-support departments can be proxied by the number of setups. For example, the movement of material in the plant often occurs at the commencement or completion of a production run. Similarly, the majority of the time spent on parts inspection occurs just after a setup or changeover. Thus, while the support departments are engaged in a broad array of activities, a considerable portion of their costs may be attributed to the number of setups.

Not all of the support-department costs are related (or relatable) to the number of setups. The cost of setup personnel relates more to the quantity of setup hours than to the actual number of setups. The number of inspections of incoming material can be directly related to the number of material receipts, as would be the time spent moving the received material into inventory, The number of outgoing shipments can be used to predict the activity level of the finished-goods and shipping departments. The assignment of all these support costs with a transactions-based approach reinforces the effect of the setup-related costs because the low-sales-volume items tend to trigger more small incoming and outgoing shipments.

Schrader Bellows had recently performed a "strategic cost analysis" that significantly increased the number of bases used to allocate costs to the products; many second-stage allocations used transactions costs to assign support-department costs to products. In particular, the number of setups allocated a sizable percentage of support-department costs to products.

The effect of changing these second-stage allocations from a direct labor to a transaction basis was dramatic. While the support-department costs accounted for about 50% of overhead (or about 25% of total costs), the change in the reported product costs ranged from about minus 10% to plus 1,000%. The significant change in the reported product costs for the low-volume items was due to the substantial cost of the support departments and the low batch size over which the transaction cost was spread.

Table 1 shows the magnitude of the shift in reported product costs for seven representative products. The existing cost system reported gross margins that varied from 26% to 47%, while the strategic analysis showed gross margin that ranged from –258% to +46%. The trends in the two sets of reported product profitabilities were clear: the existing direct-labor-based system had identified the low-volume products as the most profitable, while the strategic cost analysis indicated exactly the reverse.

There are three important messages in the table and in the company's findings in general.

- Traditional systems that assign costs to products using a single volume-related base seriously distort product costs.
- The distortion is systematic. Low-volume products are undercosted, and high-volume products are overcosted.
- Accurate product costs cannot, in general, be achieved by cost systems that rely only on volume-

related bases (even multiple bases such as machine hours and material quantities) for second-stage allocations. A different type of allocation base must be used for overhead costs that vary with the number of transactions performed, as opposed to the volume of product produced.

The shift to transaction-related allocation bases is a more fundamental change to the philosophy of cost-systems design than is at first realized. In a traditional cost system that uses volume-related bases, the costing element is always the product. It is the product that consumes direct labor hours, machine hours, or material dollars. Therefore, it is the product that gets costed.

In a transaction-related system, costs are assigned to the units that caused the transaction to be originated. For example, if the transaction is a setup, then the costing will be the production lot because each production lot requires a single setup. The same is true for purchasing activities, inspections, scheduling, and material movements. The costing element is no longer the product but those elements the transaction affects.

In the transaction-related costing system, the unit cost of a product is determined by dividing the cost of a transaction by the number of units in the costing element. For example, when the costing element is a production lot, the unit cost of a product is determined by dividing the production lot cost by the number of units in the production lot.

This change in the costing element is not trivial. In the Schrader Bellows strategic cost analysis (see Table 1), product seven appears to violate the strong inverse relationship between profits and production-lot size for the other six products. A more detailed analysis of the seven products, however, showed that product seven was assembled with components also used to produce two high-volume products (numbers one and six) and that it was the production-lot size of the components that was the dominant cost driver, not the assembly-lot size, or the shipping-lot size.

In a traditional cost system, the value of commonality of parts is hidden. Low-volume components appear to cost only slightly more than their high-volume counterparts. There is no incentive to design products with common parts. The shift to transaction-related costing identifies the much lower costs that derive from designing products with common (or fewer) parts and the much higher costs generated when large numbers of unique parts are specified for low-volume products. In recognition of this phenomenon, more companies are experimenting with assigning material-related overhead on the basis of the total number of different parts used, and not on the physical or dollar volume of materials used.

TABLE 1. COMPARISON OF REPORTED PRODUCT COSTS AT SCHRADER BELLOWS

Product	Sales Volume	Existing Cost System		Transaction-Based System		Percent of Change	
		Unit Cost[a]	Unit Gross Margin	Unit Cost[a]	Unit Gross Margin	Unit Cost	Unit Gross Margin
1	43,562	7.85	5.52	7.17	6.19	(8.7)	12.3
2	500	8.74	3.76	15.45	(2.95)	76.8	(178.5)
3	53	12.15	10.89	82.49	(59.45)	578.9	(645.9)
4	2,079	13.63	4.91	24.51	(5.97)	79.8	(221.6)
5	5,670	12.40	7.95	19.99	0.36	61.3	(93.4)
6	11,169	8.04	5.49	7.96	5.57	(1.0)	1.5
7	423	8.47	3.74	6.93	5.28	(18.2)	41.2

[a] The sum of total cost (sales volume × unit cost) for all seven products is different under the two systems because the seven products only represent a small fraction of total production.

LONG-TERM VARIABLE COST

The volume-unrelated support-department costs, unlike traditional variable costs, do not vary with short-term changes in activity levels. Traditional variable costs vary in the short run with production fluctuations because they represent cost elements that require no managerial actions to change the level of expenditure.

In contrast, any amount of decrease in overhead costs associated with reducing diversity and complexity in the factory will take many months to realize and will require specific managerial actions. The number of personnel in support departments will have to be reduced, machines may have to be sold off, and some supervisors will become redundant. Actions to accomplish these overhead cost reductions will lag, by months, the complexity-reducing actions in the product line and in the process technology. But this long-term cost response mirrors the way overhead costs were first built up in the factory—as more products with specialized designs were added to the product line, the organization simply muddled through with existing personnel. It was only over time that overworked support departments requested and received additional personnel to handle the increased number of transactions that had been thrust upon them.

The personnel in the support departments are often highly skilled and possess a high degree of firm-specific knowledge. Management is loathe to lay them off when changes in market conditions temporarily reduce the level of production complexity. Consequently, when the work load of these departments drops, surplus capacity exists.

The long-term perspective management had adopted toward its products often made it difficult to use the surplus capacity. When it was used, it was not to make products never to be produced again, but rather to produce inventory of products that were known to disrupt production (typically the very low-volume items) or to produce, under short-term contract, products for other companies. We did not observe or hear about a situation in which this capacity was used to introduce a product that had only a short life expectancy. Some companies justified the acceptance of special orders or incremental business because they "knew" that the income from this business more than covered their variable or incremental costs. They failed to realize that the long-term consequence from accepting such incremental business was a steady rise in the costs of their support departments.

WHEN PRODUCT COSTS ARE NOT KNOWN

The magnitude of the errors in reported product costs and the nature of their bias make it difficult for full-line producers to enact sensible strategies. The existing cost systems clearly identify the low-volume products as the most profitable and the high-volume ones as the least profitable. Focused competitors, on the other hand, will not suffer from the same handicap. Their cost systems, while equally poorly designed, will report more accurate product costs because they are not distorted as much by lot-size diversity.

With access to more accurate product cost data, a focused competitor can sell the high-volume products at a lower price. The full-line producer is then apparently faced with very low margins on these products and is naturally tempted to de-emphasize this business and concentrate on apparently higher-profit, low-volume specialty business. This shift from high-volume to low-volume products, however, does not produce the anticipated higher profitability. The firm, believing in its cost system, chases illusory profits.

The firm has been victimized by diseconomies of scope. In trying to obtain the benefits of economy of scale by expanding its product offerings to better utilize its fixed or capacity resources, the firm does not see the high diseconomies it has introduced by creating a far more complex production environment. The cost accounting system fails to reveal this diseconomy of scope.

A COMPREHENSIVE COST SYSTEM

One message comes through overwhelmingly in our experiences with the three firms, and with the many others we talked and worked with. Almost all product-related decisions—introduction, pricing, and discontinuance—are long-term. Management accounting thinking (and teaching) during the past half-century has concentrated on information for making short-run incremental decisions based on variable, incremental, or relevant costs. It has missed the most important aspect of product decisions. Invariably, the time period for measuring "variable," "incremental," or "relevant" costs has been about a month (the time period corresponding to the cycle of the firm's internal financial reporting system). While academics admonish that notions of fixed and variable are meaningful only with respect to a particular time period, they immediately discard this warning and teach from the perspective of one-month decision horizons.

This short-term focus for product costing has led all the companies we visited to view a large and growing proportion of their total manufacturing costs as "fixed." In fact, however, what they call "fixed" costs have been the most variable and rapidly increasing costs. This paradox has seemingly eluded most accounting practitioners and scholars. Two fundamental changes in our thinking about cost behavior must be introduced.

First, the allocation of costs from the cost pools to the products should be achieved using bases that reflect cost drivers. Because many overhead costs are driven by the complexity of production, not the volume of production, nonvolume-related bases are required. Second, many of these overhead costs are somewhat discretionary. While they vary with changes in the complexity of the production process, these changes are intermittent. A traditional cost system that defines variable costs as varying in the short term with production volume will misclassify these costs as fixed.

The misclassification also arises from an inadequate understanding of the actual cost drivers for most overhead costs. Many overhead costs vary with transactions: transactions to order, schedule, receive, inspect, and pay for shipments; to move, track, and count inventory; to schedule production work; to set up machines; to perform quality assurance; to implement engineering change orders; and to expedite and ship orders. The cost of these transactions is largely independent of the size of the order being handled; the cost does not vary with the amount of inputs or outputs. It does vary, however, with the need for the transaction itself. If the firm introduces more products, if it needs to expedite more orders, or if it needs to inspect more components, then it will need larger overhead departments to perform these additional transactions.

SUMMARY

Product costs are almost all variable costs. Some of the sources of variability relate to physical volume of items produced. These costs will vary with units produced, or in a varied, multiproduct environment, with surrogate measures such as labor hours, machine hours, material dollars and quantities, or elapsed time of production. Other costs, however, particularly those arising from overhead support and marketing departments, vary with the diversity and complexity in the product line. The variability of these costs is best explained by the incidence of transactions to initiate the next stage in the production, logistics, or distribution process.

A comprehensive product cost system, incorporating the long-term variable costs of manufacturing and marketing each product or product line, should provide a much better basis for managerial decisions on pricing, introducing, discontinuing, and reengineering product lines. The cost system may even become strategically important for running the business and creating sustainable competitive advantages for the firm.

THE IMPORTANCE OF FIELD RESEARCH

The accompanying article, coauthored with Robin Cooper, is excerpted from *Accounting & Management: Field Study Perspectives* (Boston, Mass., Harvard Business School Press, 1987) William J. Bruns, Jr. and Robert S. Kaplan (eds.). The book contains 13 field studies on management accounting innovations presented at a colloquium at the Harvard Business School in June 1986 by leading academic researchers from the U.S. and Western Europe. The colloquium represents the largest single collection of field research studies on management accounting practices in organizations.

The HBS colloquium had two principal objectives. First, the authors were to understand and document the management accounting practices of actual organizations. Some of the organizations would be captured in a process of transition: attempting, and occasionally succeeding to modify their systems to measure, motivate and evaluate operating performance. Other organizations were studied just to understand the system of measurement and control that had evolved in their particular environment.

A second, and even more important, objective of the colloquium was to begin the process by which field research methods in management accounting could be established as a legitimate method of inquiry. Academic researchers in accounting have extensive experience with deductive, model-building, analytic research with the design and analysis of controlled experiments, usually in a laboratory setting; and with the empirical analysis of large data bases. This experience has yielded research guidance and criteria that, while not always explicit, nevertheless are widely shared and permit research to be conducted and evaluated.

At a time when so many organizations are reexamining the adequacy of their management accounting systems it is especially important that university-based researchers spend more time working directly with innovating organizations. We are pleased that MANAGEMENT ACCOUNTING, through publication of this article, is helping to publicize the existence of the field studies performed to date.

The experiences described in the accompanying article, as well as in the other papers in the colloquium volume, indicate a very different role for management accounting systems in organizations than is currently taught in most of our business schools and accounting departments. We believe that present and future field research and casewriting will lead to major changes in management accounting courses. To facilitate the needed changes in curriculum and research, however, requires extensive cooperation between university faculty and practicing management accountants. As noted by observers at the Harvard colloquium:

> *There is a tremendous store of knowledge about management accounting practices and ideas out there in real companies. Academicians as a whole are far too ignorant of that knowledge. When academics begin to see the relevance of this data base, perhaps generations of students will become more aware of its richness. Such awareness must precede any real progress on prescribing good management accounting for any given situation.*
>
> *To observe is also to discover. The authors have observed interesting phenomena. We do not know how prevalent these phenomena are or under what conditions they exist or do not exist. But the studies suggest possible relationships, causes, effects, and even dynamic process in the sense that Yogi Berra must have had in mind when he said, "Sometimes you can observe a lot just by watching."*

With the research support and cooperation of the members of the National Association of Accountants, many university professors are looking forward to watching and also describing the changes now under way so that academics can begin to develop theories, teach, and finally prescribe about the new opportunities for management accounting.

Robert S. Kaplan

ENDNOTES

1. Mayers Tap (disguised name) is described in Harvard Business School, case series 9-185-111. Schrader-Bellows is described in HBS Case Series 9-186-272.

Robin Cooper is an associate professor of business administration at the Harvard Business School and a fellow of the Institute of Chartered Accountants in England and Wales. He writes a column, "Cost Management Principles and Concepts," in the Journal of Cost Management *and has produced research on activity-based costing for the CAM-1 Cost Management System Project.*

Robert S. Kaplan is the Arthur Lowes Dickinson Professor of Accounting at the Harvard Business School and a professor of industrial administration at Carnegie-Mellon University. Currently, Professor Kaplan serves on the Executive Committee of the CAM-1 Cost Management System Project, the Manufacturing Studies Board of the National Research Council, and the Financial Accounting Standards Advisory Committee.

QUESTION

3.1 What does the term "cost of complexity" mean in Cooper and Kaplan's article? Is this concept used in traditional cost-accounting systems?

3.2 Does Your Company Need a New Cost System?

*by Robin Cooper**

Today's cost management systems have to be scrutinized frequently in order to determine if they reporting accurate product costs. If they are not, they need to be overhauled, according to this article by Robin Cooper.

Cooper argues that managers need to ask themselves the following question, "Do I really know

what my products cost?" Answering this question requires an often elaborate and detailed study which can be very expensive. Cooper suggests that before undertaking such a study that management look for the following symptoms of a poorly designed or obsolete cost system as well as its design flaws.

---

* This article has been summarized from the original article by R. Cooper, "Does Your Company Need a New Cost System?" *Journal of Cost Management* (Spring 1987): 45–49. Reprinted with permission. Copyright © 1987, Thomson Reuters.

SYMPTOMS THAT YOU MAY NEED A NEW COST SYSTEM:

1. *Products that are very difficult to produce are reported to be very profitable even though they are not premium priced.*
   Intuitively products that are hard to produce should cost more to make and should either be selling at a premium or have low margins. If this is not the case there may be a problem with the cost system.
2. *Profits margins cannot be easily explained.*
   Managers should be able to state why some products are more profitable than others. Factors such as market share, quality differences and economies of scale influence profitability. If the cost system is reporting accurately then management should be able to explain the overall pattern of profitability.
3. *The results of bids are difficult to explain.*
   If management cannot predict which bids they think they can win, the cost system may be reporting inaccurate product costs. For instance if management thinks it is bidding too low and wins and bids too high and loses bids then problems probably exist.
4. *The competition's high-volume products are priced at apparently unrealistically low levels.*
   High volume products typically are less expensive to produce than low volume products and many cost systems fail to accurately account for these differences. If a company with no clear competitive advantage is pricing high volume products at very low levels and making a good profit then problems may exist.
5. *Vendor bids for parts are considerably lower than expected.*
   Companies often put parts out to bid as they may be too expensive to produce in-house. If outside vendor bids are much lower than expected the cost system may be at fault.
6. *Customers ignore price increases, even when there is no corresponding increase in cost.*
   When prices go up customers usually react negatively and demand goes down. If there is little to no reaction to a price increase then the cost system may be underestimating product costs.

FLAWS IN SYSTEM DESIGN:
Costing systems may be flawed in several ways. These flaws can result in severe distortion of product costs.

1. *Only direct labor hours (or dollars) are used to allocate overhead from cost pools (cost centers) to the products.*
   When direct labor was a significant part of the total cost of a product (say 30% to 40%) the use of direct labor as an allocation basis may have been appropriate. In today's environment direct labor is often less than 10% of total product cost and using it as an allocation basis can distort product costs.
2. *Only volume-related allocation bases (e.g. labor hours, machine hours, and material dollars) are used to allocate overhead from cost pools to products.*
   Using volume-related allocation bases assumes that the cost of producing a production lot varies in direct proportion to the number of items in the lot. This assumption may hold for volume related activities such as direct labor, supplies, etc. but does not hold for non-volume related activities such as inspection and setups. Such costs vary with the number of inspections and setups.
3. *Cost pools are too large and contain machines that have very different overhead structures.*
   Due to enormous increases in automation many cost centers now contain a mix of conventional and automated machinery. As these centers get larger and larger overhead get higher and higher as do overhead rates. Such high rates can lead to a distortion in product costs.
4. *The cost of marketing and delivering the product varies dramatically by distribution channel, and the cost accounting system effectively ignores marketing costs.*
   While we have been discussing production costs primarily in this article, other period costs need to considered when a manager is trying to determine overall product line profitability. Thus, factors such as different distribution channels and differential marketing costs must be considered for each product line. This line of analysis is called customer profitability analysis.

QUESTION

3.2   What are three of the symptoms that Cooper says accompany a poorly designed or obsolete costing system? Do each of these definitely mean that the existing system needs to be abandoned?

3.3 Distinguishing Between Direct and Indirect Costs Is Crucial for Internet Companies

by Lawrence A. Gordon, Ph.D., and Martin P. Loeb, Ph.D. *

EXECUTIVE SUMMARY

People who argue that distinguishing between direct and indirect costs is of no relevance in today's Information Economy are dead wrong! Indeed, the importance of the direct vs. indirect costs dichotomy (as well as with many other management accounting techniques) may be even more crucial to an Internet-based firm's survival than to other companies. The key paradigm shift here is that, when separating direct from indirect costs, we need to think of customers as a primary cost objective in such an environment.

Cost management is an important aspect of running a corporation successfully. A crucial part of costs management is the proper allocation of costs to various products and services. Indeed, the way costs are allocated plays a key role in determining the reported profitability of individual products and/or services. In addition, product-line decisions and pricing decisions (of both an internal and external nature) often are affected by cost allocation decisions.

At the heart of cost allocation decisions is the dichotomy between direct and indirect costs. Because a given cost can be direct with respect to one cost objective and indirect with respect to another cost objective, determining the appropriate cost objective is fundamental. This fact not-withstanding, there seems to be a growing concern, if not confusion, on the importance of the distinction between direct and indirect costs for Internet-based businesses. We argue that the distinction between direct and indirect costs is as important for Internet-based companies as it is for other companies. The e-commerce revolution, however, requires many companies to make a fundamental change in the way they consider the notion of a cost objective and, in turn, cost management. In particular, Internet-based companies need to view the *customer* as a primary cost objective for purposes of allocating costs.

DIRECT VS. INDIRECT COSTS: A TRADITIONAL VIEW

Direct costs can easily be traced to the cost objective and can be assigned to the cost objective in a straightforward manner. In contrast, *indirect costs* cannot be easily traced to the cost objective.[1] They need some sort of allocation scheme. Thus, the choice of cost objective is critical to the determination of whether a cost is considered direct or indirect.

A cost objective is the purpose for which a cost is being measured. Further, it is quite common for a given cost to be measured for multiple purposes. Thus, a given cost may be direct with respect to another cost objective and indirect with respect to another cost objective.[2] Traditionally, products, services, and departments have served as key cost objectives in managing the operations of a firm. In manufacturing firms, the primary cost objective is traditionally assumed to be the physical products being produced. A computer manufacturer, for example, would usually consider the need to determine the cost of producing a computer as the primary purpose for which costs (at least manufacturing costs) are being measured. As such, the costs of materials and labor that can easily be traced to the production of individual computers would be considered direct costs. Costs of materials and labor that cannot be directly related to the production of individual computers would be considered indirect costs. In a similar vein, the costs associated with depreciating machinery, utilities, and accident insurance would be additional indirect costs in most manufacturing firms.

Knowing the costs of manufacturing a product is important in determining the product's profitability, even where prices are market driven,[3] because in these markets the costs will determine the desirability of being in the market. In markets where prices are driven more by costs, knowing the cost of producing a product is all that more important. Further, many new cost management techniques, such as target costing, are focused on controlling product costs. Assessing the contribution of one subunit versus another subunit within a given company also requires a financial manager to determine product costs for transfer pricing purposes. Accordingly, choosing products as the primary cost objective seems quite logical for most manufacturing firms.

Whereas tangible products are logical choices for primary cost objectives in most manufacturing firms, services are logical choices for primary cost objectives in other firms. For example, in the banking industry, the

---

distinction between a direct and an indirect cost is usually considered in terms of whether the cost can or cannot be directly related to a particular service (e.g., processing a loan). Choosing departments as the primary cost objective seems to make sense in other firms. For example, in a retail department store, the distinction between direct and indirect costs is often thought of in terms of whether the cost can or cannot he related to a specific department (e.g., men's clothing). As with measuring the cost of products, measuring the cost of services and departments will facilitate profitability analysis as well as pricing decisions.[4]

Yet a fundamental change in the way many companies do business has taken place over the past five years. This change falls under the rubric of e-commerce (i.e., electronic commerce) and is largely the result of the Internet E-commerce has changed the way companies interact with their suppliers and, even more important, the way they interact with their customers. In fact, Internet commerce has changed the very essence of the way many companies do business. Now, many companies generate a large portion of their revenues via the Internet, and a growing number generate the *majority* of their revenues that way. We refer to these companies as Internet-based because they epitomize the essence of the new Information Economy.[5]

To date, most companies still consider costs as being direct or indirect in terms of products, services, or departments. This is true even for many Internet-based firms. Though the basic nature of doing business has changed for a large segment of our economy, the essence of cost management has not changed. In particular, many Internet-based firms have not abandoned the old way of thinking about cost objectives. Yet the important distinction between direct and indirect costs is becoming fuzzy. Some people even argue that distinguishing between direct and indirect costs is no longer a valid way to look at costs for a company operating in an e-commerce environment where intangible assets (e.g., intellectual capital) are so prevalent. For example, in the popular book *The Blur*, Davis and Myer argue that "direct costs are dead, and diminishing marginal returns died with them, a victim of intangibles." We disagree!

In our opinion, the need to differentiate between direct and indirect costs is as valid today in an e-commerce environment as it is in a traditional (brick-and-mortar) environment. Profitability analysis, product-line decisions, and pricing decisions are still significantly affected by the way costs are classified in terms of direct and indirect. The thing that is often no longer valid, however, is the focus on the old notion of cost objectives for firms that operate in an e-commerce environment. We believe companies actively involved in e-commerce need to view customers, as well as products, services, and departments, as key cost objectives. Nowhere is this need more important than in Internet-based firms.

Direct vs. Indirect Costs in Internet-Based Firms

The number of firms that derive the majority of their sales over the Internet has grown at a rapid rate. The U.S. Bureau of Census conservatively estimated that $5.3 billion (0.64%) of retail sales in the fourth quarter of 1999 was conducted using the Internet.[6] Furthermore, this estimate excludes the huge number of Internet sales from business to business. Clearly, the growth of the Internet is changing all facets of commerce. Understanding the impact of these changes on corporate cost management systems is vital.

The distinguishing feature of an e-commerce environment is that business transactions are handled electronically. The hallmark of such an environment has become the way firms interact with customers via the Internet. A logical way to decide whether to classify a firm as being dominated by an e-commerce environment is to use the percentage of the firm's sales generated from the Internet. For a firm to be eligible for the Dow Jones Internet Composite Index (which is further subdivided into the Dow Jones Internet Commerce Index and the Dow Jones Internet Service Index), the company must generate at least half of its sales via the Internet.[7]

Internet customers, be they households, businesses, or government agencies, can and do conduct quick and inexpensive shopping comparisons. These comparisons take place in a nanosecond, with the click of a mouse, Hence companies are required to continually adjust prices to respond to price changes initiated by competitors. At the same time, their competitors are making similar price adjustments. As a result, companies are required to expend continuous real-time efforts at attracting and tracking customers.

In the e-commerce environment, where information search costs approach zero and competitors match price cuts almost instantaneously, competing only in price is not likely to be the means to attracting and maintaining a loyal customer base. Pricing over the Internet has pushed firms to operate in highly competitive, if not purely competitive, economic markets. Businesses are quickly learning that a comparative advantage in the cyber marketplace (or, as some have called it, the marketspace) can be secured only by competing effectively in quality customer service to the point of becoming customer-centric. Understanding and managing such services requires the allocation of these costs among customers. The proper allocation, in this regard, requires that customers become a key, if not the primary, cost objective for the purposes of distinguishing between direct and indirect costs.

Most Internet-based firms use business models that are classified as business-to-business (B2B) or business-to-consumer (B2C). As the names of these models indicate, B2B means that the firm is using the Internet to generate sales of goods and services to other businesses, while B2C means that the firm uses the Internet to generate sales directly to consumers (i.e., retail sales). In addition, the business models used by some Internet-based firms would be classified as business-to-government (B2G) or consumer-to-consumer (C2C). B2G means that the firm sells its products and services primarily to government agencies. C2C means that the firm (for example, eBay) facilitates direct trades among consumers by providing a central marketplace in cyberspace. A firm using a C2C business model typically generates revenues from fees and commissions paid by consumers for participating in the electronic marketplace. Of course, many major corporations use more than one of the above business models.

Security analysts and the general investing public commonly use the B2B designation to refer to companies (e.g., Ariba and i2 Technologies) that produce products and services (e.g., software and consulting) to facilitate B2B transactions among businesses via the Internet. The products and services produced by such B2B firms use the Internet to help match sellers of inputs of production with the buyers of these inputs in an efficient manner so firms secure the right inputs at the right time at minimum cost. Such supply chain management benefits sellers by expanding their geographical market to the entire globe and benefits buyers by facilitating the search for low-cost suppliers, reducing the processing costs associated with materials acquisition, and reducing their inventory holding costs.

While the companies designated in the media as B2B firms have often been associated with generating high growth in revenues and profits, the larger effects of the B2B revolution are seen outside the firms given the B2B designation. The larger impact on the economy comes from the rapidly expanding number of firms that have embraced B2B for their supply chain management and for sales of their products to other businesses. Irrespective of whether a firm uses the Internet to sell its products and/or services to other businesses, to consumers, or to government agencies, the environment of electronic commerce requires successful firms to focus data collection on customers or customer classes. Because selling via the Internet empowers customers by reducing their information search costs and their costs of switching from one vendor to another, firms selling via the Internet have strong motivation to treat customers as key cost objectives than do firms that sell through non-Internet sources.

Whether using e-commerce for retail sales or business-to-business sales, companies must devote substantial resources to providing their customers with a user friendly, secure, and hassle-free shopping experience. The development, maintenance, and enhancement of software that keeps track of customer preferences is essential for ensuring such an experience. In essence, Internet-based firms rely much less on traditional infrastructure assets, such as buildings, and more on computers, specialized software, and intellectual capital that cater to customers in cyberspace.

When comparing one seller with another, customers cannot compare the service level that would be provided as easily as they can compare quoted prices. Nevertheless, with the wealth of information on the Web, including the seller's website, websites of consumer groups, bulletin boards, and message boards, customers can gather information about the quality of service at a fraction of the cost of a decade earlier. These comparisons result in diminishing customer loyalty. Moreover, with venture capitalists funding start-up companies on a regular basis and with more brick-and-mortar companies adding e-commerce divisions, new competition is constantly coming to the marketplace. Thus, companies face a dynamic, increasingly competitive environment.

In this new environment, companies that are going to be competitive need to devote substantial resources to attracting customers through advertising on the Internet as well as in traditional media (e.g., newspapers, magazines, and television) that direct customers to the firm's Internet sales site. During the actual sales, it is easier for competitive Internet-based firms than traditional firms to customize the physical product (e.g., specifications of a machine being purchased by one firm from another) or service (e.g., loan agreement) being sold. Internet-based sales provide an easy mechanism for direct and instantaneous contact with customers so companies can quickly modify products to new specifications (e.g., the addition it deletion of a clause in a loan agreement). It is also incumbent upon e-commerce firms to provide a high level of post-sale services to customers because such services are often carried out in an easy, quick, and inexpensive manner. Tracking delivery from the time of sale is a good example of the type of postsale service easily provided in an e-commerce environment.

For all the reasons we have noted, tracing costs to individual customers and/or customer classes is an essential competitive strategy for Internet-based companies. In other words, the customer must be a primary cost objective for them. Furthermore, tracing costs to customers cannot be considered a one-time or even periodic investment. Instead, tracing costs to customers must be done on a continuous basis and requires a real-time cost system. For many Internet-based companies, this requires a major change from the way they accumulate costs.[8] In fact, Internet-based firms that fail to treat customers as a primary cost objective face the danger of being outsmarted by the competition and left with the least profitable customers in the marketplace.[9]

For an Internet-based retailer, the costs of products a customer buys would be classified as direct costs for the customer. For an Internet-based manufacturing firm, the manufacturing cost of products would represent an intermediate cost objective, and the total cost (including costs which are indirect with respect to products) would be traced directly to the customers. Because software can identify the specific Internet advertising that routes a particular customer to the firm's e-store, the cost of this advertising can also be allocated to customers in logical manner. It may even be possible to trace specific software-related costs to particular customers in an e-commerce environment, thereby treating these costs as direct costs in terms of customers.[10] In essence, many of the costs of pre- and post-sale services, as well as the costs for services incurred during the actual sale, could be traced to individual customers and/or customer classes and treated as direct costs for e-commerce firms.[11] Costs that cannot be traced directly to individual customers and/or customer classes, such as the costs associated with computer hardware, would be treated as indirect costs.

By treating the customer as a primary cost objective, effective resource allocation decisions will be enhanced. In addition, effective customer profitability analysis, pricing decisions, and marketing decisions will be greatly facilitated. Finally, and of no small consequence, the use of customers as a primary cost objective will facilitate the very essence of being an Internet-based firm (i.e., an Internet-based cost management system will facilitate e-commerce business).

It is well known, and accepted, that focusing on the needs and desires of customers is fundamental to running a successful business. This is true whether the business is Internet-based or brick-and-mortar. Yet a fundamental cost objective for Internet-based firms needs to be the customer. In other words, in accumulating and allocating costs, Internet-based firms need to adopt a customer focus. Once they recognize this fact, it becomes clear that the distinction between direct and indirect costs is as important for them as it is for other firms.

Of course, the fact that Internet-based firms need to adopt a customer focus in allocating costs in no way mitigates the potential importance of knowing the costs of individual products (or services) as well as departments. Thus, Internet-based firms may well consider other cost objectives in differentiating between direct and indirect costs. To the extent that this is the case, the argument that distinguishes between direct and indirect costs is a relevant and important activity for Internet-based firms is only strengthened.

USE MANAGEMENT ACCOUNTING TECHNIQUES PROPERLY

Cost allocations are fundamental to effective cost management, and, as we have emphasized, a key aspect of cost allocations is the distinction between direct and indirect costs. Nevertheless, the clams that this distinction is not relevant to Internet-based companies have been promulgated lately. We disagree with this

claim, for the reasons given above. A fundamental aspect of our argument is the need for Internet-based firms to trace costs to customers. Hence, Internet-based firms need to treat the customer as a primary cost objective in differentiating between direct and indirect costs.

The new Information Economy has important implications for the field of management accounting. Direct vs. indirect costs is only one such implication. Other implications include the way companies need to consider performance measures, profit planning, and the use of cost information for pricing decisions. While the sum of these implications represents a fundamental shift in the management accounting paradigm, it does not represent the demise of management accounting. Indeed, the proper use of management accounting techniques is more relevant to the survival of firms in today's dynamic information economy than ever before in the history of commerce.

Lawrence A. Gordon, Ph.D., is the Ernst & Young Alumni Professor of Managerial Accounting at the Robert H. Smith School of Business, University of Maryland, College Park, Md. He can be reached at (301) 405-2255 or lgordon@rhsmith.umd.edu.

Martin P. Loeb, Ph.D., is professor of accounting and Deloitte & Touche Faculty Fellow at the Robert H. Smith School of Business, University of Maryland, College Park, Md. He can be reached at (301) 405-2209 or mloeb@rhsmith.umd.edu.

1. Indirect costs are often referred to as overhead costs. Because the term overhead is misleading, we will use indirect to refer to such costs.
2. For examples illustrating this point, see Chapter 3 of Gordon. *Managerial Accounting: Concepts and Empirical Evidence*, in Further Reading section.
3. In the extreme case of prices being set by the market-place, we have what economists refer to as a purely competitive market. In a purely competitive market, firms essentially take the market price as given and need to focus on cost management techniques to earn a desirable level of profit.
4. Of course, firms are interested in many cost objectives. Hence, the designation of one cost objective as primary does not preclude the use of other cost objectives.
5. Our definition of what constitutes an Internet-based firm is consistent with the way Dow Jones derives its list of such firms (i.e., for more information, see http://indexes.dowjones.com./djii/djiiabout.html).
6. The U.S. Department of Commerce reports (*Digital Economy 2000*, June 2000, p. 9) "private estimates for consumer e-commerce in the fourth quarter of 1999 ranged from approximately \$4 billion to \$14 billion."

7. Clearly, the trend is for all firms to increase their Internet-based sales. Accordingly, the distinction between Internet-based firms and non-Internet-based firms is one of degree rather that absoluteness. Over time, it seems logical to expect more and more firms to become Internet-based.

8. Although not the focus of this article, it is equally important for Internet-based firms to identify the revenues of individual customers and/or customer classes.

9. The growing emphasis on linking customers to the production process in the emerging literature on supply chain management is consistent with this argument. For an interesting discussion on the use of "customer-product maps," in the context of supply chain management, see Cloud in the Further Reading section.

10. In a non-e-commerce environment, computer-related costs are traditionally considered to be indirect with respect to a firm's products and services. Given that these assets are an important aspect of an e-commerce firm's assets, this reclassification has nontrivial implications.

11. Recent work in database design has centered on customer focused data models. This work has particular relevance to the arguments presented in this section.

FURTHER READING

R. J. Cloud, "Supply Chain Management: New Role for Finance Professionals," *Strategic Finance*, August 2000. pp. 28–32.

S. Davis and C. Myer, *Blur: The Speed of Change in the Connected Economy*, Addison Wesley, 1998.

Dow Jones Internet Indexes, Dow Jones Company, 2000, http://indexes.dowjones.com./djii/djiiabout.html.

L. A. Gordon, *Managerial Accounting: Concepts and Empirical Evidence*, 5th Edition, McGraw-Hill, 2000.

United States Commerce Dept., *Digital Economy 2000*, June 2000, http://www.esa.doc.gov/de2000.pdf.

QUESTIONS

3.3a Describe the differences between B2B, B2C, B2G, and C2C business models within the context of Internet firms.

3.3b Why is there a need among Internet firms to provide such a high level of service to customers? Furthermore, why do the authors state that customers must be considered a primary cost object for these types of firms?

3.4 Caution: Fraud Overhead

Overhead accounts are a breeding ground for fraud. What to do?

by John B. MacArthur, FCCA, Bobby E. Waldrup, CPA, and Gary R. Fane, CMA, CPA*

$1 MILLION FOUND

The forensic accountant/consultant investigated Wapello's accounting records, including the executive payroll, and discovered that the controller had been fraudulently issuing additional paychecks to himself. In addition to the payroll discrepancies, the consultant discovered that the controller had destroyed many of the accounting records from prior years. There were missing purchase invoices, which made it necessary for the consultant and Wapello people to reconstruct the payables accounts, especially the company's freight bills.

The consultant also found that the controller was embezzling money through the loans payable account. All the fraudulent transactions were charged to the manufacturing overhead account, mainly as fictitious tool purchases. How could this fraud have occurred?

"BLACK BOX" OVERHEAD ACCOUNTS

First, any company is likely to be more vulnerable to fraud if it has grown from microsize to midsize. A small company with a single or small group of owners tends to centralize all decision making at the executive management level, with little or no control policies in place. As the company's operations grow, there's a need to implement formal internal control procedures, but the legacy of "small firm" management style may linger through the growth period. And that usually means that putting adequate internal controls in place often gets

* From: J. B. MacArthur, B. E. Waldrup and G. R. Fane, "Caution: Fraud Overhead," *Strategic Finance* (October 2004): 28–32. Reprinted with permission conveyed through Copyright Clearance Center, Inc.

TABLE 1: SELECTED FRAUD SYMPTOMS

Analytical Symptoms

Ending inventory balances appear too high or are increasing too fast.

Reported cost of goods manufactured/sold (COGS) balances appear too high.

Overhead variances increase in frequency and/or size.

Increasing ratio of ending inventory account balances to ending inventory physical counts.

Accounting/Documentary Symptoms

Inventory and/or COGS transactions aren't recorded in a complete or timely manner.

End-of-period inventory and/or COGS adjustments are high or increasing in frequency.

Control Symptoms

Management overrides internal controls related to inventory or COGS.

Overhead application rates are raised or lowered by management throughout the year.

Behavioral/Verbal Symptoms

Management or employees give inconsistent or vague responses to inventory and/or COGS inquires.

Unusual delays occur in providing requested inventory and/or COGS information.

The behavior or responses of management are suspicious when management is asked about inventory and/or COGS transactions, vendors, or accounts.

Lifestyle Symptoms

Loan covenants benefiting officers have a collateral relationship to reported/physical inventory levels.

Managers or employees have significant personal financial pressures.

Tips/Complaints

Complaints from vendors/customers that relate to inventory.

Complaints from employees and other stakeholders about noninventory cash transactions. Often, a fraud in the overhead accounts can be traced to inappropriate overhead charges deliberately misdirected from operating expense and other accounts.

Source: Adapted from W. Steven Albrecht and Chad Albrecht, *Fraud Examination and Prevention*, Thomson South-Western, Mason, Ohio, 2003, pp. 272–273.

overlooked or deferred because available resources are used to support more "front-line" activities.

Moreover, the potential of fraud is exacerbated at midsize companies when the following types of conditions exist:

- Few—if any—controls over upper management, such as requiring duplicate signatures on payroll checks.
- Accounting record keeping is concentrated in a few hands, with little separation of duties.
- There's a culture of implicit employee trust, especially in long-standing employees and professional accountants.
- There's no external audit.
- Owners have little or no accounting knowledge.
- The company has relatively large overhead accounts where fraudulent expenses can be hidden.

Furthermore, overhead costing in midsize manufacturing companies is particularly susceptible to fraud because the costing is complex, the accounts have relatively large dollar values, and nonaccounting managers don't understand how they work.

To nonaccountants, overhead accounts are a confusing "black box" because accumulating and applying overhead is one of the least understood activities of the costing process. The manufacturing overhead account and associated subsidiary records such as the tooling account are some of the most exploitable accounting records. The manufacturing overhead account is a particularly large "sink" for all the various overhead items, such as plant depreciation, indirect salaries, plant supplies, and plant insurance. Fraudulent expenses can be hidden among the many journal entries that are made to this account that likely won't rise to the audit materiality threshold individually. Also, predetermined overhead rates are typically applied to production, and overhead variances for underapplied and overapplied overhead are to be expected. These overhead variances could include fraudulent expenses that can be explained as part of the estimating errors.

Because of this, nonaccountant owners/managers may find the whole costing process in general opaque and highly technical, with cost variances in particular difficult to understand. Consequently, they'll often leave the details to a controller or other trusted employee. But sometimes that employee can't be trusted.

A SETTING FOR FRAUD

At Wapello Manufacturing, the outside consulting accountant identified a number of accounting system issues and inadequacies after completing his three-month investigation. Among them were the following:

The use of a predetermined plant-wide overhead allocation method. The company had growing overhead variances because this allocation method tends to result in less accurate overhead cost assignments to products as the number and variety of products expand.

The accounting system lacked adequate separation of duties. The controller had sole control of both the product costing system and payroll preparation. The controller was authorized to prepare journal entries, sign payroll checks, and reconcile bank statements. Because no formal CFO had ever been hired, the controller effectively performed the duties of both positions.

The social characteristics of top management. The executive management displayed social attributes that concerned the consultant. First, the owner/CEO tried to keep executive payroll secret by delegating preparation of it to the controller, facilitating the fraudulent executive-payroll transactions. Next, the controller was uncooperative and resistant, refusing to speak with the consultant unless the president of the firm was present. Finally, both the CEO and president mistakenly trusted the skill level and honesty of the controller unconditionally.

INTERNAL CONTROLS

Robust internal controls of overhead accounts can help prevent fraud.

Wapello's consultant recommended strengthening the company's internal controls over its manufacturing overhead transactions by taking the following measures:

- All adjusting entries to manufacturing overhead and inventory accounts should be reviewed by an independent member of management.
- Significant manufacturing overhead variances should be analyzed both within and across time periods to identify anomalies.
- Nonaccounting management should be told about complaints concerning high product costs.
- The roles of product costing and payroll preparation should be separated.
- An improved overhead allocation system, such as departmental or activity-based costing, should be implemented if it is cost beneficial.

Other recommendations from the consultant included establishing an internal audit function and developing a formal system whereby the outside auditor would report control weaknesses separately to both accounting and nonaccounting management.

To that list, we recommend adding close monitoring of fluctuating cost of goods manufactured, cost of goods sold, inventory balances, and looking out for other symptoms of potential fraud, as shown in Table 1.

MORE MEASURES

Paradoxically, more money is fraudulently stolen from smaller companies, which have less elaborate accounting control systems, than is stolen from large ones, as shown in Table 2.

As companies grow in size and complexity, it's important to review and revise their internal controls to make sure they are adequate to deter fraudulent activity. In particular, as companies grow from micro/small to midsize businesses, owner/managers can no longer monitor all activities by physical observation alone, nor can they trust all new, nonfamily-member employees to be honest.

Among the lessons Wapello's CEO learned from this ordeal is to separate accounting duties; closely monitor accounts that are obvious places to hide fraudulent transactions, such as manufacturing overhead; and make sure proper internal controls are in place.

TABLE 2: OCCUPATIONAL FRAUD BY COMPANY SIZE

Firm Type	Median Loss Per Fraud Scheme	Firm Characteristics
Micro/Small	$127,500	1–99 employees. Executive management is owner concentrated. Has few or no formal accounting controls.
Midsize	$135,000	100–999 employees. Specialized nonowner executive management. Has minimal separation of accounting duties.
Large	$53,000	1,000–9,999 employees. Nonowner executive management. Has formal Internal controls and external audit.
Global	$97,000	10,000 or more employees. Executive management reports to formal board of directors. Has an Internal audit department and structured controls.

Adapted from: The Association of Certified Fraud Examiners, *2002 Report to the Nation: Occupational Fraud and Abuse*, pp. 17–18.

The authors thank University of North Florida graduate students Jamie D. Collis, Harry I. Eloranta, Melissa J. Gruebel, Aaron Kendrick III, Betty J. Saunders, and Christopher M. Shetzline for their work on the "Wapello" case.

John B. MacArthur, Ph.D., FCCA, is the Kathryn and Richard Kip Professor of Accounting and Cost Management at the Coggin College of Business at the University of North Florida in Jacksonville, Fla. You can reach John at (904) 620-1689 or macarth@unf.edu.

Bobby E. Waldrup, Ph.D., CPA, is an assistant professor of accounting at the Coggin College of Business at the University of North Florida in Jacksonville, Fla. You can reach Bobby at (904) 620-1669 or bwaldrup@unf.edu.

Gary R. Fane, Ph.D., CMA, CPA, is a professor of accounting and interim dean at the Coggin College of Business at the University of North Florida. You can reach Gary at (904) 620-1546 or gfane@unf.edu.

QUESTION

3.4   At Wapello Manufacturing what were some of the major accounting system issues and inadequacies that led to an environment in which fraud could occur?

3.5 The Business of Making Movies

The U. S. motion picture industry generates close to $100 billion in revenues, is one of the country's largest exporters, and exerts enormous cultural influence worldwide. But today it also faces pressures.

by S. Mark Young, James J. Gong, and Wim A. Van der Stede*

Going to the movies has always been one of society's most pleasurable pastimes. Over the past few years, though, enormous changes have occurred in the movie-making business: escalating production and marketing costs, the significant impact of increased piracy, the uncertainty in film financing, the proliferation of digital technology, and the increase in available entertainment options for consumers. These and other factors have implications for the motion picture business, the types of movies it will produce, and how and where people will view them.

Based on research sponsored by the Foundation for Applied Research (FAR) of the Institute of Management Accountants (IMA®), this is the first in a

* From: S. M. Young, J. Gong and W. Van der Stede, "The Business of Making Movies," Strategic Finance (February 2008): 26-32. Reprinted with permission conveyed through Copyright Clearance Center, Inc.

series of articles on the U.S. motion picture industry—one of the so-called creative industries. The goal of the series is to provide readers with current information about costs, revenues, and risks in this highly dynamic and influential industry. In this article we'll discuss how the industry operates, the challenges it faces, and what goes into making a movie.

In a subsequent article we'll discuss the business of selling movies—distribution, the importance of advertising, opening box-office revenues, and the increase in new revenue streams from various forms of mobile technology.

THE INDUSTRY IN PERSPECTIVE

Motion pictures aren't only a significant source of revenue for many countries—they're also instrumental in shaping worldwide impressions of a country's intellectual, historical, and cultural environment. For instance, most moviegoers would have little difficulty associating Akira Kurosawa's *Seven Samurai* with Japan, Federico Fellini's *La Dolce Vita* with Italy, or Peter Faiman's *Crocodile Dundee* with Australia.

Globally, more than 3,000 feature films reached movie theaters in 2006, bringing in $23.8 billion in box-office revenues. And total global annual revenues across all distribution channels such as video and DVD, cable, television, and mobile sources were forecasted to be $450 billion by the end of 2007, according to the Motion Picture Association of America (MPAA). The largest distributors of feature films in 2006 were India with 800, the U.S. with 599, and China with 255.

Let's now look at the organization of the U.S. motion picture business. Six major studios make up the core of the motion picture industry: 20th Century Fox, Walt Disney Pictures, Warner Brothers Pictures, Paramount Pictures, Columbia Pictures, and Universal Pictures. The MPAA represents these studios internationally and plays a number of roles: It advocates for the U.S. film industry, protects producers from copyright theft, and fights piracy. In 2006, the MPAA studios released 203 files (34%), and other independent distributors released 396 (66%).

Even though major studios have made their name in Hollywood, large, vertically integrated conglomerates own them today. These conglomerates also incorporate a number of other forms of entertainment and media, such as radio stations, cable and network television stations, newspapers, magazines, theme parks, and book publishing (see Table 1). As examples, News Corporation owns 20th Century Fox, Fox Broadcasting Company, Direct TV, *National Geographic*, and the *Sunday Times* (U.K.), while Disney owns Walt Disney Pictures, ESPN, ABC, Buena Vista Home Entertainment, and Disneyland. Vertical integration of this magnitude creates enormous barriers to entry for any entity trying to get into the business, in part because they have to gain access to major distribution channels.

Each major studio has subsidiary studios that produce medium- and small-budget films (see Table 1), and since Paramount purchased DreamWorks and Disney bought Pixar, there are only a few truly

TABLE 1: THE MPAA MOTION PICTURE STUDIOS, MAJOR SUBSIDIARY STUDIOS, DISTRIBUTORS, AND PARENT CORPORATIONS

MAJOR STUDIOS	MAJOR SUBSIDIARY STUDIOS	DISTRIBUTORS	PARENT CORPORATIONS
20th Century Fox Film Corporation	Fox Searchlight	20th Century Fox International Corporation	News Corporation
Walt Disney Pictures	Miramax Films Pixar Animation Touchstone Pictures	Buena Vista International, Inc.	The Walt Disney Company
Warner Bros. Pictures	New Line Cinema	Warner Bros. Pictures International Theatrical Distribution	Time Warner
Paramount Pictures	DreamWorks Pictures Paramount Vantage	Paramount Pictures Corporation	Viacom, Inc.
Columbia Pictures	Screen Gems Sony Pictures Classics	Columbia TriStar Motion Picture Group	Sony Corporation (Sony Pictures Entertainment)
Universal Pictures	Focus Features	Universal International Films, inc.	General Electric Company

independent studios. Currently the most notable independent film company, Lionsgate Entertainment, produces critically acclaimed films such as *Monster's Ball* and *Crash*. But even with the existence of these subsidiaries and a few independent film companies, critics have raised concerns that, because distribution is in the hands of a few large companies, the general public has the opportunity to see only a limited number and kinds of films. While this debate goes beyond the scope of our article, there's concern that independent filmmakers need more opportunities to showcase their work to the general public. For example, film festivals offer such opportunities. There are tens of thousands of films submitted to 3,000 film festivals, but less than one half of 1% ever make it as part of the 3,000 total feature films.

PRODUCING A FEATURE FILM

Making a movie follows six phases: (1) development, (2) pre-production, (3) production, (4) post-production, (5) marketing and distribution, and (6) exhibition. Here we'll focus on the first four phases—the business of making movies—and our subsequent article will address marketing and distribution as well as exhibition.

Central to creating any movie is the producer. People often confuse the roles of the producer and another key person—the director. The best way to describe the difference between a producer and a director is that the producer is considered the chief of staff, and the director is the senior line manager. The major creative force behind the project, the director is the person who actually makes the film, and top directors can earn from $3 million to $10 million per film.

The producer, however, has ultimate control of the film and shepherds it from idea inception through distribution. Producers of major films often garner seven-figure salaries plus potential bonuses and participation in the net profit. (The term net profit is one of the most controversial financial constructs in the entertainment industry because the calculation of net profits isn't straightforward. For instance, the revenues that are included in gross receipts and costs deducted as expenses are subject to protracted negotiations among the parties involved.)

There are many types of producers, such as executive producers, producers, co-producers, and associate producers, but we'll use the term "producer" to denote the key person responsible for the film. Who can actually call themselves a producer is a point of contention in the movie business. The Producers Guild of America (PGA) has developed a number of explicit criteria for someone to earn specific producer credits in terms of title. According to the PGA, a producer must play significant roles in many of the six phases of film production. While the PGA has guidelines, the studios argue they need flexibility in their negotiations to grant titles to individuals and their associates to entice them to participate in projects.

Development

In the development phase, the producer acquires intellectual property. A producer may purchase the rights to make a movie based on a novel, short story, play, or video game or as a sequel or remake of a film. Purchasing story rights can be very expensive. For instance, the cost of the story rights for M. Night Shyamalan's *Unbreakable* was reputed to be $5 million. The producer also hires a screenwriter, who must transform the basic story idea into a usable script. A major screenwriter in Hollywood can earn up to $1 million to write the first several drafts of a script. The producer often must obtain the initial financing, which is easier if he/she hires a well-regarded screenwriter and some key members of the cast, the director, and the crew.

This sequence of events is by no means linear. For instance, a producer may already be tied to a major studio or may operate independently. Because of a track record, being tied to a studio makes it more likely to find properties. An independent producer will have to put together a package with the script, some members of the cast, and then do a pitch to a studio.

With the major elements in place, studio decision makers then must determine whether the movie will be successful. A popular method in Hollywood uses the comparables approach where major parties to the film go through brainstorming sessions to identify a movie or movies that most closely resemble the project under consideration. Decision makers match characteristics of the proposed film with comparable films based on the movie's budget, theme, genre, actors, and director, among other factors. Scenario analysis of potential box-office revenue uses profitability data from large databases. The comparables approach combines rigorous analysis with gut feelings to determine whether the movie should move forward. Once executives are satisfied with the predicted profitability and they secure financing, the studio head green-lights the movie.

Major studio movies have become extremely expensive to produce. In 2006, the average cost of making an MPAA film was $100.3 million, broken down into $65.8 million in negative cost (that is, production costs) and $34.5 million in marketing costs. Some studios finance a film completely on their own using bank loans or other financing sources, while others enter into limited partnerships with other studios to reduce risk. In this case, the studios will negotiate a split of the revenues.

Since budgets of most major movies are extremely high, reducing risk is of paramount importance. Moreover, predicting which movies will be successful is very difficult, but we'll address this topic in the March issue of *Strategic Finance*. Consider *Napoleon Dynamite* from Fox Searchlight and *Stealth* from Columbia Pictures. Purchase from the Sundance Film Festival, *Napoleon Dynamite* cost $400,000 to produce and used a largely unknown cast, but the worldwide box office was $46 million, a return of 5,600%. *Stealth*, on the other hand, had a budget of $138 million and signed Jamie Foxx just after he won the Academy Award and Jessica Biel, a rising star in Hollywood. Worldwide box-office receipts for the film were $64 million—or a loss of 75% of its budget.

A method known as slate financing has recently become popular in Hollywood. In slate financing, a hedge fund manager, for example, will purchase the next 25 or 30 movies from a studio and split the profit with the studio. Over the past three years, hedge fund managers have invested more than $4 billion in Hollywood films, with most of the money going to the major studios. Today, all major studios have financing deals with a hedge fund. Universal, for instance, has a deal with Relativity Media, which states that it will put up $1.6 billion to fund movies from Sony and Universal. The studios are very much in favor of using hedge funds because they take all the work out of financing. But hedge fund managers seem to have mixed feelings about the results, and some are beginning to directly sponsor specific producers and directors rather than giving money to the studios. (For more information, see "Shaking the Money Tree," which appeared in the May 21–27, 2007, issue of *Variety*.

Pre-Production

In pre-production, the producer will hire the director, cinematographer, unit production manager, production designer, and principal cast. The producer also will scout locations and approve the final shooting script, production schedule, and budget.

A critical job of a producer and casting agents is to hire the right talent to work at the right price. A key element that sets the motion picture industry apart from others is that the people who produce, direct, and star in movies have recognizable names and faces on which they trade. This contrasts sharply to, say, the airline industry, in which skilled individuals go about their work every day, but each is essentially unknown (except perhaps the CEO) outside of their immediate customers. A-list talent in Hollywood can make up to $20 million per film, although studios are attempting to reduce these up-front payments in lieu of a larger percentage of net profits.

In addition, a small army of technical people, such as those who are set designers, camera operators, lighting specialists, transportation personnel, etc., work on the motion picture. The highest-paid member of the crew is the director of photography.

When negotiating the contracts to hire talent for the film, the producer and casting agents also need to consider conditions established by different types of unions. The term "union" in the creative industries describes labor organizations that represent technical personnel, and the term "guild" describes labor organizations that represent creative people, such as actors, producers, and directors. For major motion pictures, more than 40 unions can be represented on a production set. Apart from well-known guilds such as the Screen Actors Guild (SAG), which represents talent such as actors and actresses, another guild, the Writers Guild of America (WGA), has become very recognizable by the public as, at the time of this writing, its members are on strike for a greater share of DVD and Internet residuals from the major studios.

The budget for a film is split into above-the-line and below-the-line segments. Above-the-line costs include everyone who can share in the profits, including the producer, director, and actors. The below-the-line part of the budget consists of the cost of the technical people such as the crew, materials, locations, etc.

Actors are also represented by business managers, agents, publicists, and attorneys (some agents and business managers are attorneys) to help them manage their careers. The existence of these intermediaries provides a layer of complexity in the creative industries that doesn't exist in most other industries. The main job of intermediaries is to find jobs that suit their clients.

Production

Producers are also responsible for preparing production budgets, and the director implements the actual production (shooting) and post-production budgets. A film's negative cost—the cost of manufacturing the mast print—has several components. These costs include any up-front payments to the talent, such as actors and actresses, and other employees; costs of sets; and other costs incurred during the production process. If it's a studio film, then the studio also charges a fee for using its facilities as well as interest on the negative cost and overhead.

During production, the producer will hire a line producer to monitor the physical aspects of making the film and oversee the principal shoot. The line producer also helps monitor the budget closely to make sure there aren't any budget overruns. Physical production can involve many elements, and specific requests often must be negotiated carefully. For instance, to make the film *The Italian Job* in 2003, Paramount closed two blocks of Hollywood Boulevard for more than a week at the cost of several thousand dollars.

Of course, cost disasters can occur. Often cited as a way *not* to make a movie, Michael Cimino's 1980 *Heaven's Gate* had such enormous production delays and excessive filming costs that the final cost was approximately $40 million, compared to its original budget of $11.6 million. This film is reputed to have bankrupted the studio, United Artists.

Post-Production

In post-production, the producer will work with post-production personnel, including the editor, composer, and visual-effects staff. He/she consults with all creative and financial personnel on the answer print or edited master and works with the financial and distribution entities concerning the marketing and distribution plans for the motion picture in both domestic and foreign markets. Major companies such as Industrial Light & Magic can employ hundreds of people if the computer-generated imagery is extensive. Post-production work on *Hulk*, for instance, is estimated to have cost $10 million.

Another significant cost for a film is original music—whether it's original compositions or existing pieces. Major composers can garner seven-figure salaries for an original score. The cost of using an existing piece of music is exemplified in the film *Lords of Dogtown* where producers paid $3 million to use Led Zeppelin's *Whole Lotta Love.*

In Table 2 we provide a comprehensive example of each significant cost for a major motion picture using *Spiderman 2* as an example. One of the most expensive movies of all time, *Spiderman 2* in 2004 cost a staggering $200 million to produce, but it also grossed $784 million worldwide over its theatrical run. One of the biggest challenges facing the major motion picture studios is the pressure to outdo themselves, especially when it comes to sequels. Every sequel in the major Hollywood franchises has cost a lot more money to produce than the previous film in the series. A few examples include *The Lord of the Rings*, *Shrek*, *Pirates of the Caribbean*, and *Spiderman*. For example, *Spiderman 3*, which debuted in May 2007, is reputed to have cost $258 million but went on to gross $890.8 million in theatrical release worldwide.

THE RIGHT BLEND

Making a major motion picture is a complex task with many moving parts. It involves the blending of the right talent, money, management, technology, creativity, and a bit of luck. Even with all of these ingredients, though, a film's success is hardly guaranteed. In our next article, we'll explore the possibilities for success—the business of selling movies.

TABLE 2: COST BREAKDOWN FOR SPIDERMAN 2 (COLUMBIA PICTURES, 2004)

Story rights: $20 million

Screenplay: $10 million

Producers: (Stan Lee, Grant Curtis, Laura Ziskin, Avi Arad, Joseph M. Caracciolo, and Kevin Feige): $15 million

Director: Sam Raimi, $10 million

Cast: $30 million, broken down as follows: Tobey Maguire, $17 million; Kirsten Dunst, $7 million; Alfred Molina, $3 million; rest of cast, $3 million

Production shooting costs: $45 million

Visual effects: $65 million

Music: $5 million

Composer: Danny Elfman, $2 million

Total Production (Negative) Cost: $200 million

(Source: Discussions with industry executives and www.boxofficemojo.com)

We thank the Foundation for Applied Research (FAR) of the Institute of Management Accountants for their financial support; Tara Barker, FAR administrator; Sandy Richtermeyer, former IMA professor-in-residence; and the motion picture industry executives who shared their knowledge with us.

S. Mark Young, Ph.D., holds the George Bozanic and Holman G. Hurt Chair in Sports and Entertainment Business and is also a professor of accounting at the Marshall School of Business at the University of Southern California. You can reach Mark at (213) 740-4848 or mark.young@marshall.usc.edu.

James J. Gong, Ph.D., is a professor of accounting in the department of accountancy in the College of Business at the university of Illinois at Urbana-Champaign. You can reach James at gong@uiuc.edu.

Wim A. Van der Stede, Ph. D., is a professor of accounting in the department of accounting and finance at the London School of Economics. You can reach Wim at W.Van-Der-Stede@lse.ac.uk.

QUESTION

3.5 Discuss the six phases of making a feature film.

Chapter 4

Accumulating and Assigning Costs to Products

The linkages among variations in product and cost standards, cost behavior, and quality costs are highlighted in Harold Roth and Tom Albright's article, *What Are the Costs of Variability*, Reading 4.1. To illustrate the cost of variability, the authors cite a number of examples, including a study that sought to understand the sources of variation in the quality of paperboard output. In that study, data was collected on variables such as the shifts, crews, grades of product, grade changes, etc. The company under study was operating in a capacity-constrained environment, and the cost accountants developed a product cost analysis that showed the cost of products that were lost due to variations in the manufacturing process. Their model included the variable cost of materials and overhead, a fixed cost allocation, and the lost contribution margin. Using this model, the company was able to determine that the cost of certain grades of paperboard exceeded their selling price. The strategic implications of manufacturing products with high variation in product quality became much more evident as a result of the study.

An critical process for many firms is reducing costs without adversely affecting the mission and objectives of the organization. In *Effective Long-Term Cost Reduction: A Strategic Perspective* (Reading 4.2), authors Michael D. Shields and S. Mark Young caution against the most expedient, short-term, traditional method for reducing costs—firing employees. This traditional approach has a number of significant ramifications, such as reducing employee morale and motivation and losing valuable work-related knowledge as each employee is fired. Both morale and motivation can decline as remaining employees experience greater stress, given their greater workload and constant worry that they will be next. In turn, coordination problems—such as production delays, missed schedules, and decreases in quality and delivery time—can occur. Shields and Young argue for a much more strategic approach to cost reduction and develop a set of guidelines that firms can use to avoid the "slash and burn" traditional approach. These guidelines focus on reducing costs by improving organizational activities and processes and viewing employees as resources rather than as costs.

In Reading 4.3, S. M. Young, James Gong, Wim Van der Stede, Tatiana Sandino, and Fei Du build on Reading 3.5 and discuss how the major Hollywood studios market and distribute major feature films. The authors also present the results of a research study they conducted describing the most critical factors that lead to a financially successful film.

T. L. Estrin, J. Kantor, and D. Albers' *Is ABC Suitable for Your Company?* (Reading 4.4), presents a method for determining whether ABC is appropriate for a particular company. The authors develop what they call a contingency grid based on two dimensions: the potential for ABC to provide costing information that is significantly different from what a traditional system would generate and the propensity for the organization's managers to use the newly generated information. By answering a series of questions, an organization can score and locate itself on the grid. The authors state that while there is subjectivity in how an organization scores itself and the factors used are not exhaustive, the contingency grid provides some structure that will allow managers to determine whether ABC should even be attempted in their organizations. While the early applications of ABC were developed in manufacturing settings, more recent applications have surfaced in service organizations.

Readings
Chapter 4

4.1 What Are the Costs of Variability?

Knowing the answer is key to a company's quest for quality.

by Harold P. Roth, CMA, and Thomas L. Albright, CPA*

CERTIFICATE OF MERIT, 1992–93

Zero defects and robust quality are two quality philosophies used to help U.S. companies compete in the global marketplace. An important measure in any quality philosophy is the cost of product variability.

Although variation among products may affect the consumers' perceptions of quality, the importance of consistency to a producer depends on the quality philosophy it follows. For example, with a zero defects philosophy the only cost attributed to variation occurs when products fall outside the specification limits. Thus, the cost of variation depends on whether the product can be reworked, if there are constraints on production, and the distance between product specification limits.

On the other hand, a robust quality program claims that any variation is undesirable and causes costs to be incurred by the manufacturer, consumer, or society. An estimate of these costs is provided by the quality loss function.

TWO PHILOSOPHIES

The term "quality" has many different meanings depending on the context used. When quality is used to describe products, it may mean "conforming to specifications" or "fitness for use." Although these two definitions may mean the same thing to many people, they have different implications for how quality is evaluated and the importance of product variability.

The philosophy underlying the "conformance to specifications" definition generally leads to a zero defects approach to quality while the "fitness for use" philosophy leads to a robust quality approach.[1]

The role of product variability in evaluating quality depends on whether the company has adopted a zero defects or a robust quality philosophy. With a zero defects philosophy, the allowable variation is defined by specification limits, and any variation within those limits is accept able. According to the robust quality philosophy, any variation from a target value represents a condition that is less than ideal, with potential economic consequences. Thus, robustness is the result of meeting exact targets consistently—not from always staying within tolerances.

In turn, the cost of variation also depends on the philosophy. Generally, companies that adopt a zero defects philosophy will not attribute any cost to variability if the product is within specification limits. But the robust quality proponent will assign a cost to variability whenever a product varies from a target. Companies following a robust quality philosophy believe any variation from target results in a loss. Furthermore, greater losses will occur as the variation from target becomes larger.

VARIABILITY FROM TARGET

A case study at the Sony Corporation supports the idea that a relationship exists between variability and the zero defects and robust quality philosophies.[2] The study involved the color density of television sets produced in two manufacturing facilities—one in San Diego and the other in Tokyo.

The color density distribution associated with the output of each manufacturing site is illustrated in Figure 1. Three reference points: the lower specification limit, target value, and upper specification limit appear on the horizontal axis of the graph.

Generally, Sony considers any television set with color density measurement less than the lower specification limit or greater than the upper specification limit to be defective. However, the approach to quality differs between the two plants.

---

* From: H. P. Roth and T. L. Albright, "What Are the Costs of Variability?" *Management Accounting* (June 1994): 51–55. Reprinted with permission conveyed through Copyright Clearance Center, Inc.

FIGURE 1. DISTRIBUTION OF COLOR DENSITY

Sony of Tokyo Versus Sony of San Diego

Sony of Tokyo strives to produce at the target value and does not inspect each unit. Thus, some out-of-spec units are shipped to customers, as evidenced by the tails of the distribution that fall outside the specification limits. In contrast, Sony of San Diego uses 100% inspection to ensure that the televisions fall within the specification limits and to prevent the shipment of defective units to distributors.

After studying the output of the plants, Sony discovered that although the number of defective units was similar in both manufacturing plants, the variation around the target specification was not. As shown in Figure 1, there is less variation in the televisions produced in the Tokyo plant because more sets are near the target value. The distribution of color densities from the San Diego plant (which is shown by the rectangular distribution) indicates greater variability than that of the Tokyo plant because more sets fall farther away from the target value.

Customers who purchased television sets manufactured by Sony of Tokyo reported greater satisfaction and filed fewer warranty claims than those who purchased products manufactured by Sony of San Diego. The lesson to Sony was clear—variation from the target specification of a critical component has implications for customer satisfaction and, therefore, costs.

COST OF VARIABILITY

There are many costs associated with variability in product attributes. For example, raw material costs will be higher if products use more materials than specified by engineering standards (for example, the target value). Likewise, variability in material thickness or weight may result in added wear on down-stream machines that cause more maintenance and repair costs.

Also, products that exceed material usage targets may have higher delivery costs because they weigh more than the target weight. However, these costs are not attributed to variability with the zero defects philosophy.

Instead, costs of variability are recognized only when a product falls outside the specification limits. When products meet specifications, they are assumed to meet the customers' requirements.

The costs incurred when products fall outside the specification limits depend on three factors: whether the product can be reworked or repaired, production constraints, and where specification limits are set.

When products fall outside the specification limits, it may be less costly to rework or repair them than to discard them. When products are reworked and then sold, there is no loss of the materials and parts that comprise the final product. In addition, disposal costs are reduced or avoided by the producer, so costs are generally lower if rework is possible.

The constraints that exist in the production process also affect the cost. If excess capacity exists and additional units can be produced to replace nonconforming products, the costs incurred because a product fails to meet specifications depend on whether the nonconforming unit is sold or discarded. But if additional units cannot be produced, then the cost of variability includes an opportunity cost for the lost sales. Thus, the economic costs of lost production are higher when there are constraints than if no constraints exist.

A paper manufacturer provides an example of the costs of variability in a capacity-constrained environment.[3] A study was conducted to understand the sources of variation in the quality of paperboard output. The variables studied included crews, shifts, grades of product, rest interval between shifts, and whether a product was produced immediately following a grade change. The variability and cost data that resulted from the study had strategic implications for the company.

Because the company was operating in a capacity-constrained environment, the cost accountants developed a product cost analysis that captured the economic cost of a unit of product that was lost as a result of variability in the manufacturing process. The cost included the variable cost of materials and overhead (less any pulp or chemicals that could be recovered through reworking the product), a fixed cost allocation, and the lost contribution margin (a surrogate for the opportunity cost from producing a defective product in a capacity-constrained environment).

The revised cost numbers had strategic implications for the product mix manufactured by the plant. By analyzing the cost of each grade of product, the company discovered that the cost of certain grades far exceeded the selling price.

For example, the company learned that the production of uncoated paperboard resulted in a much larger proportion of defective units than that of coated paper-board. This knowledge helped the company analyze the strategic implications of manufacturing a product that exhibits extreme variation in the quality of production by attaching a cost to products exhibiting high rates of variability.

CALCULATING THE COSTS

Various costs are incurred when products fall outside the specification limits. These include out-of-pocket costs such as costs of inspection and rework.

If the product can be sold as a first-quality unit after the rework, these out-of-pocket costs are the total costs of variability. If the reworked unit cannot be sold as a first-quality unit, then the cost of variability also may include an opportunity cost. The opportunity cost will be relevant if the second-quality item replaces a sale for a first-quality item. In this case, the opportunity cost of variability is the difference between the contribution margin of the first-quality product and the actual contribution margin.

If a product falls outside the specification limits, cannot be reworked, and must be scrapped, then the cost of variability includes the materials, labor, and other costs incurred in producing the product. In addition, any cost incurred in disposing of the product also is a cost of variability.

To illustrate the computation of costs that are caused by variability, assume a company is producing a product that sells for $50 per unit. The variable production cost is $20, and the unit contribution margin is $30. During the last month, the company manufactured 100,000 units that used all the available machine hours. All units produced are sold.

The weight is a critical dimension for this product. The target value for the weight is 20 kg, and the specification limits are set at plus or minus 2 kg. For the units produced last month, the weights followed a normal distribution with an average of 20 kg and a standard deviation of 0.8 kg. Figure 2 illustrates the distribution of the weights from this production process.

As shown in Figure 2, most of the weights fall between 18 and 22 kg and, therefore, conform to the specifications. However, some of the weights are above the upper specification limit of 22 kg, and some are below the lower specification limits of 18 kg. These units that fall in the tails of the distribution are nonconforming. To determine the number of nonconforming units, a z-value is calculated, and a table for areas under the normal curve is consulted to determine the portion in the tails of the distribution.[4]

For this example, the calculated z-value shows that the specification limit is 2.5 standard normal deviates from the mean (see Figure 2). With z equal to 2.5, a table for the area under the normal curve shows that 0.0062% of the observations exceed 22 kg. Because the distribution is symmetrical, an equal portion falls below the lower specification limit of 18 kg. Thus, the number of nonconforming products manufactured last month was 1,240 [100,000 (2 × 0.0062)].

FIGURE 2. DISTRIBUTION OF PRODUCTS

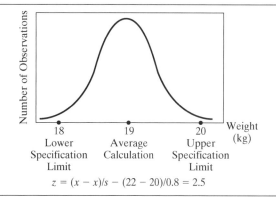

$$z = (x - \bar{x})/s - (22 - 20)/0.8 = 2.5$$

The cost attributed to the variability of these 1,240 units depends on their disposal. If the units can be reworked[5] for $12 a unit and then sold for the normal sales price of $50, the cost of variability is equal to the rework cost. But if the products only can be sold for $45 a unit, there is also an opportunity cost of $5 per unit, for a total cost of $17. If the product cannot be reworked, then the relevant cost of variability is the variable production cost, the opportunity cost, and any disposal cost.

Table 1 summarizes the cost of variability for various conditions. The total cost of variability for this product can be calculated by multiplying the unit cost by the number of nonconforming units. With 1,240 nonconforming units during the month, the cost of variability could range from a low of $14,880 ($12 × 1,240) if the units are reworked and sold as first-quality units to a high of $68,200 ($55 × 1,240) if the units cannot be reworked and must be disposed of at a cost of $5 per unit.

This example shows how organizations might estimate their costs of variability when they manufacture products that do not conform to specifications. But it ignores any costs incurred because products vary within the specification limits and any costs incurred by consumers because of variability in the products.

Thus, the philosophy of zero defects may understate the total cost of product variability. The quality loss function provides an alternative way to measure the cost of variability that is consistent with the robust quality philosophy.

QUALITY LOSS FUNCTION

The quality loss function (QLF) is a part of the Taguchi quality philosophy.[6] The QLF is based on the idea that any variability from a target value causes a loss to society. Thus, his proponents believe that any variability is costly even if the products still fall within the specification limits.

TABLE 1. COST OF VARIABILITY

Sales price per first-quality unit	$50
Sales price per second-quality unit	45
Variable production cost per unit	20
Normal contribution margin per unit	30
Rework cost per unit	12
Disposal cost per unit	5

Condition	Variable Production Cost	Rework Cost	Disposal Cost	Lost Contribution Margin	Total Unit Cost
Unit is reworked and sold for $50		$12			$12
Unit is reworked and sold for $45		12		$5	17
Unit cannot be reworked and has no disposal cost	$20			30	50
Unit cannot be reworked and has a $5 disposal cost	20		$5	30	55

characteristic (weight) represents a nominal-is-better function. In other words, the target value of 20 kg is the nominal value, and production should strive to manufacture products weighing 20 kg. Any variation from this value results in a loss under the quality loss function.

The quality loss function is a quadratic function where costs increase as the actual product characteristic deviates from the target value. Figure 3 shows the quality loss function for the nominal-is-better case, and Table 2 presents the formula for measuring the quality loss for an individual unit.

To determine the total loss for a period using the quality loss function, an average loss per unit can be calculated and multiplied by the total number of units. When the average and standard deviation are known, the average loss can be estimated using the formula also shown in Table 2.

With 100,000 units, the quality loss is $192,000 [$1.92 × 100,0001] which is much larger than the cost of variability estimated using the conformance to specification model. The reason for the greater cost is that the quality loss function includes a cost for any unit that varies from the target value regardless of whether it falls inside or outside the specification limits.

WHY VARIABILITY IS IMPORTANT

According to research, a lack of product consistency is a major factor in customers' perceptions of poor quality. The relationship between variability and quality is recognized in many quality control techniques such as statistical process control. It is also recognized by companies such as Oregon Cutting Systems where the operational definition of quality is to "reduce variability around the target."[7]

TABLE 2. MEASURING QUALITY LOSS

Quality Loss for an Individual Unit:
$$L = k(Y - T)^2$$
where L = unit loss,
Y = actual value of characteristic,
T = target value of characteristic, and
k = proportionality constant.

The value of k is usually computed by dividing the loss for a product, which falls at the specification limit by the squared distance form the target value to the specification limit, i.e.:

$$k = \frac{c}{d^2}$$

where c = loss associated with a unit produced at the spec. limit, and
d = distance from target value to spec limit.

In this example, if the loss for a unit at the specification limit is $12, then the proportionality constant is $3:

$$k = \frac{\$12}{(22 - 20)^2} = \frac{\$12}{2^2} = \$3$$

Average Loss per Unit:
$$\text{Average loss} = k[s^2 + (Y - T)^2]$$
where s = standard deviation
Y = average (mean)
T = target value, and
k = proportionality constant.

From the data given above, the average loss is $1.92:
$$\text{Average loss} = \$3[0.8^2 + (20 - 20)^2] = \$3 \times 0.64 = \$1.92$$

Measuring variability should provide managers with information that can help them improve operations by identifying opportunities for improving product quality. If specific parts of a product can be identified as the source of variability, then managers know where they should focus their quality improvement efforts.

FIGURE 3. QUALITY LOSS FUNCTION

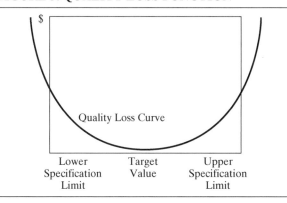

These efforts may involve educating and retraining employees, redesigning production processes, investing in equipment, and even redesigning products. If a product can be manufactured using a smaller number of components and parts, there is less likelihood that the sum of the individual variations will result in significant quality problems.

Measuring the cost of variability also should help managers in their quest for quality. If managers do not define quality in terms of variability, they may not be aware of the types of costs associated with variability and of the magnitude of the costs. With an estimate of the cost, managers may be more likely to understand the financial implication of variability and the savings that result from their efforts to reduce it. Unless cost savings are measured, the financial impact of the efforts will not be known.

Although all processes and products will show some variation because it is a law of nature, companies need to measure it and strive to reduce it if they want to be competitive. If they do not reduce variation, it is likely their competitors will, and the consistently performing product may be perceived as higher quality by customers.

ENDNOTES

1. For a discussion of robust quality see Genichi Taguchi and Don Clausing, "Robust Quality," *Harvard Business Review* January–February 1990, pp. 65–75.
2. This case study is discussed by Taguchi and Clausing, pp. 68–69; and by Ranjit Roy, *A Primer on the Taguchi Method*, Van Nostrand Reinhold, New York, 1990, pp. 12–13.
3. For further details on the study see T. L. Albright and J. M. Reeve, "A Case Study on the Impact of Material Yield-Related Cost Drivers on Economic Improvement," *Journal of Management Accounting Research*, Fall 1992, pp. 20–43.
4. Most statistics books provide tables showing Areas under the Normal Curve. For an example, see Eugene L. Grant and Richard S. Leavenworth *Statistics Quality Control*, 5th ed., McGraw-Hill Book Company, New York, 1980, pp. 628–629.
5. Because the example states that production uses all available machinery, this example assumes that the reworking is done by laborers using different machines than used for the initial production.
6. Genichi Taguchi is a Japanese engineer who has developed statistical approaches to improving product and process quality. His approaches are discussed in many books dealing with quality engineering and design. Examples include Ranjit Roy, *A Primer on the Taguchi Method*, Van Nostrand Reinhold, New York, 1990; Philip J. Ross, *Taguchi Techniques for Quality Engineering*, McGraw-Hill Book Company, New York, 1988; and Thomas B. Barker, *Engineering Quality by Design*, Marcel Dekker, Inc., New York, and ASQC Quality Press, Milwaukee, 1990.
7. Jack Bailes, Ilene Kleinsorge, and Larry White, "How Support Services Can Use Process Control," MANAGEMENT ACCOUNTING® October 1992, p. 45.

Harold P. Roth, CMA, CPA, Ph.D., is a professor of accounting at the University of Tennessee, Knoxville. He is past president of IMA's Knoxville Chapter, through which this article was submitted. Dr. Roth can be reached by calling (615) 974–1756.

Thomas L. Albright, CPA, is an assistant professor of accounting in the Culverhouse School of Accountancy at the University of Alabama. He holds a Ph.D. degree from the University of Tennessee. Dr. Albright is a member of IMA's West Alabama Chapter and can be reached at (205) 348–6131.

QUESTIONS

4.1a Is the "cost of variability" concept applied consistently under the zero defects and robust quality philosophies? Explain.

4.1b Describe the "quality loss function" in Roth and Albright's article.

4.2 Effective Long-Term Cost Reduction: A Strategic Perspective

by Michael D. Shields and S. Mark Young*

In the 1970's cost reduction programs relied on the traditional method of simply cutting costs by eliminating jobs and thus reducing payroll. A traditional cost reduction program is usually triggered by an immediate threat to the organization such as poor performance, loss of contracts, or price reductions. Traditional programs tend to be short term in nature and often are ineffective in developing long term sustained change.

While these programs do reduce costs in the short run the associated reduction in the value of human assets sets the stage for potential long-term failure. The five traditional cost reduction programs typically used are:

THE TECHNOLOGY APPROACH

This approach focuses on replacing direct labor with technology to increase operating efficiency and to reduce the influence of unions. This approach is usually adopted or intensified after performance measures indicate poor performance. This approach has not worked in many companies especially those in which labor cost is a small percentage of total product cost.

LEAN AND MEAN

The Lean and Mean approach uses a tough policy to reduce the number of employees. A common approach is to employ across-the-board cuts through layoffs and reductions in pay and benefits. Lean and mean is not effective in the long term, because it attempts to reduce costs by reducing workers, but it does not reduce the work that needs to be done to make and sell products.

OFFSHORE RETREAT

This approach relies on reducing costs by moving to locations such as Asia that offer the promise of lower labor costs. The success of this type of approach is often contingent upon how employees at home are treated and on the vagaries of exchange rates and currency fluctuations. Employee morale at home can be hurt if domestic or local employees are laid off when the firm moves jobs offshore.

MERGERS

Mergers purport to create economies of scale for the merging firms. The idea is to eliminate overlapping employees, products, plants and overhead. Problems arise, however, when the merging firms differ significantly on corporate culture, types of products and technologies. Those who remain in their jobs can suffer motivation and morale loss.

DIVERSIFICATION

Diversification into new industries is an approach that firms often used when they are searching for less expensive operating environments. If a firm expands beyond its core competency, however, it is likely to experience difficulties in developing and implementing new products, technologies, or distribution systems, with the result that costs are higher, rather than lower, than expected.

STRATEGIC COST REDUCTION

Strategic cost reduction as an alternative approach that focuses on a long term approach integrating competitive strategy, technological strategies, human resource strategies and organizational design considerations to provide a focused and coordinated basis for sustaining competitive advantage.

At the core of strategic cost reduction is the idea top management will be clearly involved in developing a sound and humane approach to cost cutting, that employees must be educated in being very cost conscious in the firm, and that employees are the ultimate source of competitive advantage. To this end, the organization must attempt to offer long-term employment to employees in order to gain their trust and support and to increase their motivation.

Organizations must attempt to develop these types of norms before engaging in cost reduction. Since the five approaches mentioned above have not been particularly successful to date, firms need to seriously consider the strategic cost reduction approach.

QUESTION

4.2   What are five of the most frequently used traditional cost reduction programs, and how effective is each one?

---

* This article has been summarized from the original article by Michael D. Shields and S. Mark Young, "Effective Long-Term Cost Reduction: A Strategic Perspective," *Journal of Cost Management* (Spring 1992): 16–30. Reprinted with permission. Copyright © 1992, Thomson Reuters.

4.3 The Business of Selling Movies

by S. Mark Young, James J. Gong, Wim A. Van der Stede, Tatiana Sandino, and Fei Du*

Once a movie is produced, it's all about getting as many eye- balls as possible to see it, as they say in the industry. But the competition is steep given the available entertainment options for consumers: Video games. Television. Home video. Music. Sports. In this sequel to "The Business of Making Movies" in the February issue of *Strategic Finance*, we'll present our research (which included data on more than 2,000 movies) on the key success factors that lead to box-office success. Now on with the show.

MARKETING AND DISTRIBUTION

The term "distribution" often covers both the marketing and placement of movies in theaters and, ultimately, other markets, such as DVD, video-on-demand (VOD), and television. For major studio movies, both the production and marketing budgets are committed simultaneously. While a studio makes the movie, its marketing division is developing a comprehensive marketing and distribution plan for the film.

Marketing

Many people now consider marketing to be the key factor that leads to box-office success. Over time, marketing costs have been escalating. An average amount for a Motion Picture Association of America (MPAA) film in 2006 was $34.5 million compared to $25 million in 1999, an increase of almost 40% in seven years.

A movie's marketing budget often reaches as high as 50% of its total negative cost (production cost) for blockbuster films (the ones that studios are betting will be their financial salvation for any bad decisions they made over the course of a year). Research from Harvard Business School shows a studio spends 90% of a film's marketing budget before the movie reaches theaters. While the marketing budget for each film is thought to be fixed, there's some discretion to increase it if the movie is faring well. According to an interview with William Murray, former executive vice president of the MPAA, television, print, radio, and outdoor billboards account for approximately 75% of the total marketing budget, with the lion's share (typically 40% or more) going to marketing on television. The remaining budget pays for trailers, posters, pre-release behind-the-scenes documentaries about the film, appearances, and, in general, attempts to develop a buzz about the film before the studio releases it.

Studios also use viral marketing techniques to promote their products, typically employing e-mail and other electronic media campaigns to encourage people to pass along messages about a new movie.

One of the best-known examples of viral marketing involved the 1999 release of The Blair Witch Project, an independent film that cost $60,000 to produce and that aired at the Sundance Film Festival. Artisan Entertainment purchased the rights to the film for $1 million, spent $20 million on a marketing campaign, and distributed the film. Launched on the Internet, the campaign suggested that the film was a real documentary about three students who disappeared in the secluded woods of Maryland. The movie went on to gross $249 million worldwide at the box office.

Licensing is another critical part of marketing. One of the best examples is the 10-year relationship between McDonald's and the Walt Disney Company. Said to be a $1 billion deal, McDonald's paid Disney $100 million a year and did 11 promotions of Disney films that included *Finding Nemo*, *The Incredibles*, *Cars*, and *Pirates of the Caribbean: Dead Man's Chest*. The deal ended when Disney decided to distance itself from the fast-food franchise.

Distribution

Regardless of its quality, a film will never see the light of day without a distributor. An independent company or a subsidiary of a major studio distributes the film by acting as a negotiator between the film-production company and theater owners, who are known as film exhibitors. A studio's distribution division distributes most major films, while a smaller proportion of films is distributed by independent distributors, such as Artisan's The Blair Witch Project. Distributors design and implement the marketing campaigns for the channels and territories in which they have distribution rights.

A distributor has a number of responsibilities. First, it must secure interest in its films by hosting industry screenings for exhibitors. Second, it contracts with exhibitors on the profit split for each party, which is based on a percentage of gross revenues after deducting the theater's overhead, known as the house nut. Third, it must determine the production company's share of the revenues and, if necessary, conduct an audit of the exhibitor's ticket receipts. The proceeds are then transferred to the production company. Finally, the distributor ensures that the studio provides the requisite

* From: S. M. Young, J. Gong, W. Van der Stede, T. Sandino, and F. Du, "The Business of Selling Movies," *Strategic Finance* (March 2008): 35–41. Reprinted with permission conveyed through Copyright Clearance Center, Inc.

number of film prints to the exhibitors for opening day. Then it monitors that contracted theaters are showing the films since they have guaranteed a certain number of seats, show times, etc. It's easy to see why all the major studios have distribution arms and how difficult it is to distribute a film without a distribution company.

Part of the distribution process also involves the MPAA movie rating. Industry analysts believe that different ratings have different revenue potential, a claim that has been examined in prior research. For instance, producers try to obtain the lowest rating they can since an R rating or above will limit the audience. On average, a movie rated R is estimated to make about 12% less revenue than it would if it had a lower rating.

Exhibition

Typically, a standard contract between the distributor and exhibitor specifies the general conditions that apply to all individual contracts. These terms include the profit-sharing rules and length of time the movie will be in the theater. Currently, movies run from four to eight weeks, but that can change based on how well a movie is performing. In these situations, holdover clauses allow the movie to run longer than the standard time.

A number of deals can be made between a distributor and an exhibitor. The type depends on each movie's perceived revenue potential and the relative bargaining power of the parties (e.g., a major studio vs. a small independent producer). The deal will also depend on the number of days the movie runs, when it opens, and many other factors.

There are two general types of deals. In the first, both distributor and exhibitor take a fixed percentage through- out the film's theatrical run. But most contracts involve a sliding-scale percentage of gross box-office receipts and have many variations, with the distributor getting the larger of two possible payments that change as the weeks go on. For example, consider the 90/10 deal. In the first week of a movie's run, the distributor will take the larger of two possible payments: 90% of ticket revenue after the exhibitor has deducted its overhead (the house nut) or a floor payment, which is a percentage of the box office (say 70%) before the exhibitor has taken out the house nut. As the weeks go on, the floor-payment percentage decreases, but the

overhead doesn't. At first glance, it might seem that the distributor has the better deal, but the exhibitor usually inflates overhead, and, most important, the distributor doesn't share at all in concession revenue.

So how profitable are concessions for the exhibitor? Analysts say there's an 85% gross margin on concessions in theaters. While concessions are approximately 20% of revenues, they account for about 46% of profits. Theaters depend enormously on their concessions, and some have quipped that a theater is actually a restaurant that happens to show movies. Now you know why a bag of popcorn costs $4.50 and a soft drink $5.

The five largest exhibitors are major theater chains, all of whom own many theaters and screens. They include Regal Entertainment Group; AMC, which recently bought Loews Cineplex Entertainment; Cinemark Theatres; Carmike Cinemas; and National Amusements (see Table 1). Across the top-five chains, the average number of screens per theater is just under 12. The advantage of these large chains is they can show many copies of the same movie simultaneously. Spiderman 3 holds the record for the widest opening of a film, filling 4,253 screens across the nation.

Today, the two most pressing issues for exhibitors are the pressure to install digital technology in their theaters and the pressure to provide a better movie-viewing experience for customers.

Digital cinema has a number of advantages for distributors since movies can be shown in theaters via DVD-like format, satellite, or hard drives. And distributors can save a lot of money on film since a single print can cost upward of $1,000. Thus, if a movie opens wide at 3,500 theaters, the cost savings would be $3.5 million. Multiplying this by the number of movies a studio releases a year amounts to substantial savings over other formats.

Satellite transmission is probably the most efficient, but it's prohibitively expensive. Although exhibitors see the benefits, they have balked at the overall conversion of their theaters. Currently, the cost to convert a theater to accommodate digital technology is approximately $250,000. Another critical factor is the cost of owning digital technology equipment because of the high risk of obsolescence and projected maintenance costs. With

TABLE 1: THE LARGEST THEATER CHAINS

THEATER	HEADQUARTERS	SCREENS	THEATERS
Regal Entertainment Group	Knoxville, Tenn.	6,403	539
AMC	Kansas City, Mo.	5,340	382
Cinemark Theatres	Plano, Texas	4,516	398
Carmike Cinemas	Columbus, Ga.	2,447	289
National Amusements	Dedham, Mass.	1,500	124

existing technology there's little risk to exhibitors since current projection equipment has an expected life of about 20 years. At this point, a key issue is who will pay for the theaters to change their technology. While there was initial agreement that the studios and exhibitors would split the cost, that agreement is no longer in place because negotiations failed.

The second issue for exhibitors relates to concerns that the movie-going experience has been degrading over time, which in part led to a box-office slump over the past few years. Many customers said discourteous patrons, ringing cell phones, and dirty theaters kept them away, so exhibitors recently launched campaigns to control rude behavior and cleaned up their theaters. Apparently their efforts are paying off as a three-year ticket slump ended with theaters selling 1.45 billion tickets in 2006.

Theatrical Release and the Box Office

In Hollywood, there's an obsession with a film's theatrical release and its opening weekend box-office performance. This box-office period is critical because the numbers from that three-day period establish most subsequent deals for DVD, international distribution, cable and satellite television, and free television. During opening week- end, executives nervously wait for the box-office numbers. On Saturday morning they obtain the numbers for opening day, and by late Sunday night they see the entire weekend's take. Yet while executives focus on opening weekend, even the global box office of the entire theatrical run accounts for only about 20% of the total revenues for a film released in today's environment. The other 80% of the revenues come from other forms of distribution, including DVDs, television, etc.

Success Factors

Because of all the concern about box-office revenues, as part of our research we conducted an empirical study to determine which factors seemed to be the best predictors of opening and cumulative box-office revenues (the entire box-office receipts over the entire domestic theatrical run) in the U.S.

We gathered production, marketing, and revenue data from 2,023 movies released between 1990 and 2006 that were listed by Boxofficeguru.com and the Motion Picture Investor. As an example of some data we were working with, and as a point of interest, Table 2 shows the Top-20 all-time highest-grossing box-office films worldwide and their associated production and marketing costs.

We also incorporated several control variables in our study that might affect movie revenues. These include measures of actor and director star power we obtained from such sources as Hollywood.com and The-Numbers.com, which gauge actor and director star power. Star power is measured by taking the average of the cumulative box-office receipts of the movies in which the star acted or directed. We also controlled for movie genre (it affects movie revenue) by obtaining data on genre from the Hollywood.com and IMDb.com databases.

There were other control variables, too. Prior research has documented that sequels also may affect movie revenues. Hollywood.com includes in its description whether a movie is a sequel. Further, we divided movies into those distributed by a major studio vs. those distributed by an independent distributor, and we controlled for the various types of ratings from G to R. Another factor, the season in which a studio releases a film, typically includes the following time periods: normal (January through April and September through October), summer (May through August), and holiday (November through December). Finally, the number of theaters showing a movie is expected to affect box-office receipts. Since we focused on cumulative box-office receipts, we used the largest number of theaters showing a movie during the movie's entire running period as a control variable.

After controlling for all these factors, we ran regressions and obtained the following results. We expected that star-studded and hi-tech (action with special effects) movies would have higher production costs than other types of motion pictures. Moreover, common wisdom in the industry suggested that sequels are costly to produce because expectations among moviegoers are higher. Finally, motion pictures can be distributed by three entities: major studios, independent producers (Indies), or distributors. Major studios often only finance those motion pictures that have large commercial potential, and, with this expectation, they're willing to heavily invest in those movies.

Our results support these expectations. We found that both acting and directing star power have significant positive effects on production costs. We also found hi-tech motion pictures and sequels have higher production costs than those that aren't hi-tech or sequels, and those that independent studios finance have lower production costs than those that major studios finance.

As for the determinants of marketing costs, we expected that production costs would, in turn, have a significant positive effect on marketing costs. Our results indeed indicate that the sheer size of production costs positively affects marketing costs where production costs account for 47% of the variation in marketing costs on average. We also expected that, similar to production costs, a movie's quality would drive marketing costs. Through marketing, for example, the studio can capitalize on the star as an input. And we found that movie features had similar effects on marketing costs; that is, sequels, motion pictures with big star power, those in the hi-tech genre, and those distributed by major studios have higher marketing costs. In addition, studios

TABLE 2: HIGHEST-GROSSING BOX-OFFICE MOVIES OF ALL TIME (in millions, rounded)*

RANK	MOVIE	STUDIO	PRODUCTION COST	MARKETING COST	DOMESTIC BOX OFFICE	WORLDWIDE BOX OFFICE
1	Titanic (1997	Paramount	$200	$31	$601	$1,845
2	The Lord of the Rings: The Return of the King (2003)	New Line	$94	$51	$377	$1,119
3	Pirates of the Caribbean: Dead man's Chest (2006)	Buena Vista	$225	$52	$423	$1,066
4	Harry Potter and the Sorcerer's Stone (2001)	Warner Brothers	$125	$44	$318	$977
5	Pirates of the Caribbean: At World's End (2007)	Buena Vista	$300	**	$309	$961
6	Harry Potter and the Order of the Phoenix (2007)	Warner Brothers	$150	**	$292	$939
7	The Lord of the Rings: The Two Towers (2002)	New Line	$94	$43	$342	$926
8	Star Wars: Episode 1—The Phantom Menace (1999)	Fox	$115	**	$431	$924
9	Shrek 2 (2004)	DreamWorks SKG	$70	$52	$441	$921
10	Jurassic Park (1993)	Universal	$63	$33	$357	$915
11	Harry Potter and the Goblet of Fire (2005)	Warner Brothers	$150	$59	$290	$892
12	Spiderman 3 (2007)	Sony	$258	$120	$337	$891
13	Harry Potter and the Chamber of Secrets (2002)	Warner Brothers	$100	$46	$262	$877
14	The Lord of the Rings: The Fellowship of the Ring (2001)	New Line	$93	**	$315	$871
15	Finding Nemo (2003)	Buena Vista	$94	$46	$340	$865
16	Star Wars: Episode 3 – Revenge of the Sith (2005)	Fox	$113	$43	$380	$850
17	Spiderman (2002)	Sony	$139	$51.1	$404	$822
18	Independence Day (2002)	Fox	$75	$46	$306	$817

TABLE 2 (Continued)

RANK	MOVIE	STUDIO	PRODUCTION COST	MARKETING COST	DOMESTIC BOX OFFICE	WORLDWIDE BOX OFFICE
19	Shrek the Third (2007)	DreamWorks SKG	$160	**	$323	$798
20	Harry Potter and the Prisoner of Azkaban (2004)	Warner Brothers	$130	$49	$250	$790

*All data come from Boxofficemojo.com.
**Unavailable—Some movie marketing costs are guarded very carefully and not reported publicly.

spend more money on marketing non-R-rated motion pictures than R-rated motion pictures and more money on movies released in the summer than on those released in other seasons.

We also found that both production and marketing costs have a positive effect on cumulative box-office receipts, but marketing costs appear to have stronger positive effects on box-office revenues. Overall, the results of our cost-revenue association tests indicate that marketing costs are much more strongly associated with revenue streams throughout a motion picture's product life cycle. In our regressions, a 10% change in production cost is associated with roughly only a 2% change in cumulative box-office revenue, whereas the same percentage change in marketing cost is associated with roughly a 10% change in cumulative office revenue. Thus, our findings show that star-laden motion pictures, sequels, and hi-tech motion pictures have high production costs. On the other hand, motion pictures financed by independent studios are less costly than major studio motion pictures, yet our results indicate that motion pictures released by major studios don't earn higher cumulative box-office receipts than those released by independent distributors.

Therefore, the success of a motion picture depends on many factors. First, the movie has to be well made and appeal to a wide audience. Second, there must be a clear marketing plan and a distribution deal with exhibitors. Third, our research shows that the more money spent on marketing the better, as this will lead to greater returns at the box office.

ACCOUNTING IMPLICATIONS

Finally, we believe our study also has implications for accounting practices and regulations in the motion picture industry. The American Institute of Certified Public Accountants' (AICPA) Statement of Position (SOP) No. 00-2, "Accounting by Producers or Distributors of Films," requires capitalization of production costs of released movies and subsequent amortization for up to 10 years. On the other hand, SOP No. 00-2 requires immediate expensing of marketing costs even before studios release movies. Yet our results show that not only do production and marketing costs have positive effects on movie revenues, but the effect of marketing costs is larger than that of production costs for both opening box office and, particularly, cumulative box-office revenues. As such, from a matching-principle perspective, our findings call into question the rationale for the differential treatment of marketing costs—that is, expensing rather than capitalizing. To this end, we hope our results provide evidence that will further the debate in the movie industry much like that regarding the accounting treatment of research and development investments.

We thank the Foundation for Applied Research (FAR) of the Institute of Management Accountants for financial support; Tara Barker, FAR Administrator; Sandy Richtermeyer, former IMA professor-in-residence; and the motion picture industry executives who shared their knowledge with us.

S. Mark Young, Ph.D., holds the George Bozanic and Holman G. Hurt Chair in Sports and Entertainment Business and is also a professor of accounting at the Marshall School of Business at the University of Southern California. You can reach Mark at (213) 740-4848 or mark.young@marshall.usc.edu.

James J. Gong, Ph.D., is a professor of accounting in the department of accountancy in the College of Business at the University of Illinois in Urbana-Champaign. You can reach James at gong@uiuc.edu.

Wim A. Van der Stede, Ph.D. is a professor of accounting in the department of accounting and finance at the London School of Economics. You can reach Wim at W.Van-Der-Stede@lse.ac.uk.

Tatiana Sandino is an assistant professor in the Marshall School of Business at the University of Southern California. You can reach Tatiana at Tatiana.sandino@marshall.usc.edu.

Fei Du is a doctoral student in the Marshall School of Business at the University of Southern California. You can reach Fei at Fei.du@marshall.usc.edu.

QUESTION

4.3a   Why is the opening box office weekend so important for a feature film?
4.3b   Based on the list of the Highest-Grossing Box Office Movies of All Time (Table 2) which of these films wasn't worth the production and marketing costs that the studio spent?

4.4 Is ABC Suitable for Your Company?
An impartial analysis of overall operations can tell you yes or no.

by T. L. Estrin, CMA, Jeffrey Kantor, and David Albers*

How do you know if activity-based costing (ABC) would be right for your company? There's an objective way to decide before your company takes the plunge. For ABC to be effective, a majority of all costs incurred by a significant unit of a business must be analyzed systematically. These costs include not only most fixed and variable factory burden costs, but also some fixed and variable marketing and administrative costs. Implementation of ABC requires a complex, comprehensive process that is costly and time-consuming, so naturally managers would want to be assured of the advantages before embarking on the implementation of ABC.

The potential benefits of ABC can be analyzed in advance along two separate dimensions. The first is based on the probability that, in a given application, ABC will produce costs or other results that are significantly different from ones that could be generated with more conventional or less costly methods. The ABC-generated costs may or may not be "better" or more accurate, but they are different in amount. The second dimension of the model seeks to establish that, given that cost information generated by ABC is indeed different, management will use it for significant decisions. Managers must regard ABC information as superior, and the nature of the organization and its competitive, legal, and social environments must allow managers to use the information freely.

The factors involved in the first dimension include the number and diversity of products or services produced, the diversity and differential degree of support services used for different products, the extent to which common or joint processes are used, the effectiveness of current cost allocation methods, and the rate of growth of period costs. The factors involved in the second dimension are management's freedom to set prices, the ratio of period costs to total costs, strategic considerations, the climate and culture of cost reduction in the company, and the frequency of analysis that is desirable or necessary.

A CONTINGENCY APPROACH TO IMPLEMENTING ABC

This methodology is based on a company's analysis of itself. It consists of weighting and combining the weights of the above factors and dimensions in order to evaluate the likelihood of success of implementing ABC. The combined weighted scores are plotted as a point on one of the four quadrants of a graph. Meanings are attached to the quadrant and the location of the final score in that quadrant. The methodology is not designed to produce a ratio-scale number indicating the relative benefits of ABC but to structure a systematic analysis by which the managers of a company can discuss the common factors that support or reject implementation.

To start, management must analyze the nature of the company in light of responses to two key questions:

1. For a given organization, is it likely that ABC will produce costs that are significantly different from those that are generated with conventional accounting, and does it seem likely that those costs will be "better"?

---

*   From: T. L. Estrin, J. Kantor, and D. Albers, "Is ABC Suitable for Your Company?" *Management Accounting* (April 1994): 40–45. Reprinted with permission conveyed through Copyright Clearance Center, Inc.

2. If information that is considered "better" is generated by the new system, will the new information change the dependent decisions made by the management?

FINDING THE ANSWERS

Ten mediating factors can guide management in determining the answers. The first five address the potential advantages of ABC versus traditional costing methods, and the second five deal with management's need and ability to react to product costing distortions.

Product diversity (PD). Product diversity refers to the quantity or range of distinct products or the variety of product families offered. Minor product variations should not be confused with product diversity. For example, it is unlikely that .20 cm. diameter ball bearings are a different product offering from .21 cm. diameter ball bearings. Differences in the complexity of various products also should be reflected in this analysis. Products that appear relatively homogeneous but that vary greatly in complexity are indicative of high diversity (such as 64K memory chips versus 1024K memory chips). Color variations, if applicable, need to be examined carefully. Does changing the color materially change the product? Is the function color dependent? (For example, contrast red ink versus blue ink pens and red versus blue cars.)

There are numerous considerations in evaluating the extent and degree of product diversity:

- Accounting product classifications. Does the general ledger incorporate different product classifications? Are there internal reports that attempt to split sales, margins, or earnings by product lines?
- Markets served. Are they broken into geographical or industrial groups that purchase different types of products? Is the manufacturing department organized sequentially or in parallel? Sequential organization suggests limited product differentiation; parallel organization can indicate product diversity.
- Stockrooms. Are different stockrooms handling the same inventory classification (for example, raw material, finished goods) for different products?
- Sales. Does the company sell both OEM and manufactured items?
- Advertising. Does the company advertise only its name and/or one product, or does its advertising reflect different products?

Support diversity (SD). Support diversity refers to the range or variation of support overhead given to products. Assumptions can't be based on size. Even if the organization is only a cost center or a production facility, if it has more than one basic product or family of products, diversity in product support requirements probably exists. In this connection, reference to the manufacturing activities required is particularly useful. A superficial look at the organization may indicate little diversity, but a closer examination may reveal that actual activities vary greatly by product.

To determine and evaluate the degree of support diversity, companies should answer the following questions:

- Do departmental titles contain product names, and/or are departmental activities driven by specific products? Are there engineering support departments, and, if so, are their efforts skewed toward specific products?
- Are different manufacturing locations included in the one costing system?
- Are the manufacturing products relatively complex? (As a rule of thumb, complex products require more support, so the likelihood of diversity in support requirements increases.)
- Do different products use different distribution channels, have separate advertising requirements, or go to different markets?
- Is research and development homogeneous or product oriented?
- Is the company organized in (product-focused) modules, or do product task forces exist?
- Do different products require different material handling processes? Do different stockrooms exist?
- Is the organization operating in or moving toward a JIT environment?
- Are there major differences in product volumes or lot sizes?
- Is there a "new product introduction" organization?
- Does the company sell both OEM and manufactured items?

Common process (CP). Common process refers to the degree of commonality of processes among the different product offerings. "Processes" encompass all identifiable activities including manufacturing, engineering, marketing, distribution, accounting, material handling, quality control, research and development, and administration. If there is a high degree of commonality of processes or activities among products, period costs required by each product cannot be separated using conventional management accounting. ABC, by its nature, may be more effective.

Before assigning a common process value, companies should answer the following questions:

- If the organization examines profitability by product, are many expenses captured directly, or are they based on allocation or other arbitrary factors? Direct capture of most expenses may indicate a high degree of process segregation.

- Do different products require different production processes? Do production departments have more than one product to which to charge time?
- Are there distinct material handling processes? Do various products use different stockrooms? Is purchasing organized by product type or by type of material purchased? What degree of commonality exists between suppliers?
- Are engineering or shop support departments organized by product? Do engineers or technicians frequently support different products? Can they charge their time to different products?
- Is more than one distribution channel used?
- Is quality control organized by products?
- Do research and development personnel concentrate on specific products, or is the R&D more general in nature? Are R&D costs captured by product?
- Is administration organized by product?

Period cost allocation (CA). Period cost allocation refers to the existing costing system's conceptual ability to allocate period costs properly. In essence, period cost allocation is an analysis of the allocation methodology to determine if it is capable of mimicking the results of ABC. It is a premise of ABC that, over time, so-called period costs (indirect, variable, and fixed costs) are attributable to the activities required in making various products. Thus, a major focus of ABC analysis is on associating period costs with products. ABC also suggests that many nonmanufacturing costs, such as marketing costs, also are a function of product activity and should be loaded onto the products responsible for their incurrence.

- Is the general ledger set up to capture support expenses by product through the use of product-specific departments, engineering time sheets, indirect labor classifications, and the like?
- To what extent are indirect expenses not identified by product?
- How many concurrent bases of allocation are used?
- Are they consistent with the major cost drivers?
- How many levels are in the allocation hierarchy? If multi-level, are the allocations on a product-specific basis?
- Is the allocation hierarchy riddled with estimates or arbitrary factors?
- How many cost centers exist, and how product-specific are the cost centers?
- If only one allocation basis is used, can it distribute the costs by product accurately despite the probable lack of correlation between output and the consumption of resources? Would the distribution of costs still be accurate if there were significant changes in the nature of the period costs? (Assume that the more allocation bases are used, the more readily changes can be reflected in product costs.)

- Can the allocation bases reflect the impact of product volume fluctuations accurately? (For instance, burden rates are established based upon anticipated product volumes. Will the allocation bases recognize the probable change in support requirements if the product mix changes significantly?)

Rate of growth of period costs (PG). Rate of growth of period costs refers to the growth in period costs as an indicator of the dynamism required by the costing system. One of ABC's strengths is its ability to capture changes in the support requirements of products quickly through its direct measurement of activity levels. If period costs, as a percentage, remain relatively stable over years, management can to some extent adjust implicitly for the distortions produced by a conventional cost system. Also, given period cost stability for several years, a traditional costing system can be structured to provide product costs similar or identical to those calculated by ABC (excluding below-the-line, cost of goods manufactured costs).

HOW DOES MANAGEMENT USE COST INFORMATION IN DECISIONS?

If management agrees that the nature of the products, the productive processes, and the marketing of the products are such that the costs generated by ABC will be significantly different from traditional management accounting costs and that ABC costs reflect true product costs more accurately, it still may not be able to, or may not want to, use this better information. A number of factors will influence management's desire for or ability to use cost information in its deliberations. Among these factors are pricing freedom, period expense ratio, strategic considerations, cost reduction efforts, and analysis frequency.

Pricing freedom (PF). Pricing freedom refers to the company's degree of power and freedom to set prices and therefore establish product profitability. The more freedom a company has, the less important product costs become. Pricing will be set to maximize profits and will depend on market elasticity. Where monopoly conditions apply and demand is inelastic, high prices will be set. Where there are pure competition, many competitors, and good substitute products available, however, prices will be determined entirely by market forces.

Because the vast majority of organizations face situations somewhere between the two extremes, companies should answer the following questions as they evaluate this factor:

- Are all product prices regulated? If so, are the prices based on costs and subject to appeal and revision?
- How competitive is the market? Are price surveys common or available? Does the profitability of the

industry appear unusually high or low? Are the competitive aspects based on some factor other than price?

- Are there high barriers to entry?
- Do the company's products occupy a unique position within the market? Can premium prices be justified due to service?
- Where are the products within their life cycle?
- Is the company a price leader or a price follower?
- How dynamic are the products' prices? What are the causes of the changes or lack thereof?

Period expense ratio (FE). Period expense ratio addresses the possible materiality of product cost distortions directly. If possible distortions are so minimal that no management actions would result from their correction, then the distortions become irrelevant. Although the materiality of this factor also should be evaluated from the perspective of percentage change in reported costs, the primary focus should be on the impact upon product profitability. (For example, a reported cost change of 5% may be immaterial to a jeweler operating on 300% markup, but it is extremely significant to a volume-based grocery working with 2%–4% margins.)

Although there is no specific formula for quantifying possible product cost distortions and determining the materiality of those distortions, the following questions may help the appraisal process. When answering these questions, companies should consider only period costs that must be allocated; variable costs that can be loaded directly onto products should be ignored.

- What is/would be the plant average or blanket burden rate? Is it a large multiple of labor? How does it compare to various product or cost center rates?
- Are period costs a "significant" proportion of the total cost structure (including direct costs)? What would be the impact upon total profitability if the percentage of period costs increased 10%? 50%? 100%?
- Are cost reduction activities focused upon product costs (such as reduction of supplier prices) or upon period costs? Is it management's belief that focusing upon direct costs offers greater potential benefits? Is this belief appropriate?

Strategic considerations (SC). Strategic considerations refer to the constraints imposed upon management's decisions by its explicit or implicit strategies—in other words, the degree to which strategies override costs in the decision-making process. These strategies are not limited to marketing strategies; they also include secondary strategies and objectives related to technology, manufacturing, quality, and the like.

- Is a "market niche" strategy being employed? Is the strategy dependent upon product profitability/costs?
- Are capital expenditures for new products, manufacturing changes, or capacity expansions frequently justified explicitly on the basis of "strategic reasons" instead of economic returns?
- Are capital expenditures frequently initiated implicitly and driven by strategic considerations, with the financial benefits of the project being used merely to obtain project approval?
- What type of analysis and justification is necessary for approval of R&D expenditures? Is the true rationale more strategic in nature?
- Does the organization establish customer prices based upon costs or market? If the company sells to related entities using prices based upon costs, would changes in the transfer pricing result in changes in volume or in the receiving location's decisions?
- Are make-versus-buy comparisons performed frequently? Does the organization have this option, or do technological or policy restrictions constrain it?
- Are changes in product design or manufacturing processes driven mainly by costs, or are other sources such as market or product requirements critical?
- Are product discontinuation analyses performed regularly in an attempt to (indirectly) reduce costs or for reasons such as fostering specific market perceptions?

Cost reduction (CR). Cost reduction involves the corporate culture as it affects the relationship between internal cost-related decisions and the indirect component of the total cost of products. It involves the nature of internal cost-related decisions and the degree to which the decisions depend upon accurate allocations of period costs. A number of potential internal decisions depend on accurate costs—manufacturing process changes, product design modifications, make-versus-buy comparisons, product scrubbing, capacity expansion evaluation, and so on. Analysis of these activities will indicate the likelihood of management action resulting from changes in reported product costs due to the elimination of distortions in the period cost allocation.

- How extensive are cost reduction activities within the organization? Do any engineering groups focus exclusively upon cost reduction? Is there an employee suggestion plan?
- Are there numerous or frequent cost-oriented task forces? Are cost reduction metrics tracked internally? Are there frequent changes in head count unrelated to load?

- Are the above cost reduction activities general in nature and not related to specific products? Are cost reduction targets established in total only, or by function/activity, or by product?
- Do the cost reduction activities focus upon nonperiod targets? Are there material or labor variance targets?
- Are make-versus-buy comparisons applicable? If so, how frequent are the analyses? How close are the decisions?
- Are product scrubbing decisions both frequent and dependent upon costs? Are period costs a major factor in the decision?
- Are process modifications focused upon the manufacturing organization? Are period costs relevant?
- Are capacity changes dependent upon costs? Are allocated period costs incorporated into—or even relevant to—the decisions?

Analysis frequency (AF). Analysis frequency refers to the frequency, either routine or special, of product cost analyses and incorporates both the current and the desired frequencies. A measure of dynamism, it also embodies the other management action factors. A discrepancy between the existing and desired frequencies of analysis indicates dissatisfaction with the existing costing system.

- Are product profitability reports issued routinely from the existing costing system? Are they believed, or are "adjustments" made? If believed, are they used fruitfully?
- How frequently are special studies or ad hoc analyses of product costs performed or requested? Is there a lack of credibility in the existing data, or are the existing data insufficient? If studies/analyses are infrequent, why? Is it due to a low requirement or to the difficulty of obtaining "accurate" data?
- What prompts special cost study requests, volume fluctuations, pricing requests, and the like? Do these changes occur often?
- Would management like more frequent or more detailed product cost analyses? For what purpose?

PLOTTING THE ANSWERS

Now let's assign values to the factors listed above and plot them on a chart to provide a focus for a discussion among managers and give them a mechanism for highlighting their differences in order to reach a consensus in a more effective manner.

Figure 1 shows a grid that may be used to plot the situational factors in an evaluation of the potential of ABC for a particular situation. Each of the 10 factors is scored on a –5 to +5 scale, and the scores of each of the two sets of five factors are weighted and combined into the two scores, which are plotted on the grid. A weighted aggregate score of the five factors affecting "product cost distortion," which indicates the potential benefits of ABC for the company, is plotted on the "Y" axis of the grid. A weighted composite score of all the factors affecting management's need and ability to act on better cost information in making decisions is plotted on the "X" axis.

FIGURE 1. THE CONTINGENCY GRID

Potential for ABC Due to Product Cost Distortions

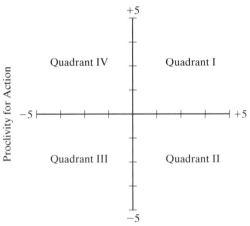

"X" Axis, Proclivity to Use Cost Information in Business Decisions	"Y" Axis, Basic Potential for ABC Based on Cost Distortions
PF—Pricing Freedom	PD—Pricing Diversity
FE—Fixed Expense Ratio	SD—Support Diversity
SC—Strategic Considerations	CP—Common Processes
CR—Cost Reduction Effort	CA—Cost Allocation
AF—Analysis Frequency	FG—Growth of Indirect Costs

In order to show the scores from the two sets of factors on the two-dimensional contingency grid, we must combine the scores of each set into a single score on that characteristic. It is necessary to weigh each of the five factors in both classifications to recognize that differences exist in the relative importance of each factor in a given company.

Each of the five factors on each dimension of the grid can be assigned a score depending on management's analysis of its situation. The weighting process begins with the presumption of equal ranking (i.e., weighting of 20%). Then managers examine each factor to determine if the weighting should be changed. This end can be achieved in a "Delphi" process where managers from all pertinent areas submit scores and their reasoning for all factors by mail. Then they receive the high, low, and average scores with rationales and revise their estimates. The first rounds of this process can be on an area-by-area basis (such as accounting or production), and the last rounds of this process can be done with broadly representative members of management meeting to determine the scores.

The examination is based on three main criteria:

1. If this factor had the extreme value of + or –5, to what extent is the main characteristic impacted? For example, without product diversity, will product cost distortions occur? Without material pricing freedom, will management actions occur?
2. If this factor has the extreme value of + or –5, what is the impact upon the other factors?
3. Is this factor extremely subjective or difficult to measure, and should weighting be structured to ameliorate its impact?

INTERPRETING THE RESULTS

Quadrant I. Results that are plotted in Quadrant I (both "X" and "Y" are positive) initially suggest because product cost distortions are likely and management is free to act upon corrected product costs, an ABC system should be implemented. It is possible, and even likely, however, that the source of the cost distortions is included in the category of "below-the-line" (selling and administrative) expenses and that the current traditional allocation technique is providing adequate overhead cost information. Because recommendations differ depending on the source of the distortions (traditional "overhead" or the "below-the-line" category), managers must perform the "potential for ABC due to product cost distortions" section of the analysis again, omitting any consideration of nonoverhead, organizations, activities, or similar expenses.

If the revised composite score remains Quadrant I, it is an indication that the source of the distortions is within the category defined as traditional overhead. In this case, companies should consider implementing a full ABC system or a costing system that incorporates ABC concepts. Product cost distortions probably are occurring, and because those costs are being used extensively within the organization, it is likely that less than optimal decisions are being made.

If the revised composite score shifts to Quadrant II, the source of the distortions is within the category known as "below-the-line" (selling and marketing, administration, and research and development). In this case, implementation of a full ABC system is not warranted—the existing traditional allocation technique is providing adequate cost information for the overhead component of the product costs, and there is no reason to incur the implementation and maintenance costs of a full-blown ABC system. If "below-the-line" expenses for total product cost purposes are the main culprits in reporting incorrect products costs, however, managers should scrutinize the allocation methodology of those analyses for possible errors. A stand-alone system using ABC concepts and addressing only "below-the-line" costs may be appropriate.

Quadrant II. If the results of the analysis are plotted in this quadrant, it indicates that although management is free to utilize product cost information, it is unlikely that those costs contain material distortions. Because there are no direct benefits, implementing ABC at this time is not recommended. The situation should be monitored for changes over time, however, particularly if the "Y" value is relatively small.

Quadrant III. Results plotted in this quadrant clearly indicate that ABC is not recommended. It is unlikely that material product cost distortions are present, and management has limited ability to utilize or react to modified costs.

Quadrant IV. Results occurring in this quadrant suggest that although product cost distortions are likely, management has little ability to modify its decisions that are cost dependent. Management should re-examine its use of product cost information and its freedom to react to changes, including performing the "management action" section of the model analysis again. Although management may be constrained from acting on cost information in the short run, many valuable long-term uses for this information may appear. Only when management is satisfied that it would *not* use corrected product cost information should it reject possible implementation of an ABC system.

THE FINAL DECISION

After reading about ABC, attending ABC seminars, or being approached by ABC consultants, many managers still may be in a quandary as to whether the implementation of this technique will improve the competitiveness of their particular companies. These executives need some method of evaluating whether the potential claimed benefits of ABC would outweigh the certain and substantial costs of its implementation. Our contingency analysis model should help them by matching the characteristics of their company, its products, and the costing system used with the factors that make ABC most effective.

The factors we presented are neither mutually exclusive nor collectively exhaustive. While the scoring system is subjective, it is grounded on factors cited in the ABC literature as being causal in determining the superiority of ABC over traditional costing. Most important, it presents a structure for managers to use in their deliberations and encourages them to arrive at some consensus with regard to the degree to which the factors are present in their company and ultimately to convince themselves as to either the uselessness, the desirability, or the critical necessity for the implementation of ABC.

T. L. Estrin, CMA, Ph.D., is an associate professor of business administration at the University of Windsor,

Windsor, Canada, and a director of the Cost Management Group there. He is a member of the Society of Management Accountants of Canada and the Inst. of Mgmt. Accountants. He may be reached at (519) 253-4232, ext. 3457.

Jeffrey Kantor, Ph.D., CA, is a professor of business administration at the University of Windsor and a director of the Cost Management Group.

David C. Albers is the regional support international manager for Multimedia Communication Systems and has done process analysis with Northern Telecom Inc. for several years.

QUESTION

4.4 Using Estrin, Kantor, and Albers' contingency grid, if an organization's score puts it in Quadrant III, is ABC implementation recommended? Explain. Is their method "foolproof?"

Chapter 5

Activity-Based Cost Systems

Four articles on activity-based costing are included in this section. Taken together, the articles discuss various applications of ABC and some new directions in thinking on the topic.

Reading 5.1, *Unbundling the Cost of Hospitalization*, by Larry Carr, illustrates the implementation of an ABC system at Braintree Hospital in Boston. This application was designed to tease apart (or unbundle) the fixed cost allocation of nursing services. In the past, nursing costs were simply allocated into the cost per day of a hospital room. However, since nurses have different professional qualifications and skills, and patients require different care and have differential lengths of stay; devising a more accurate costing system would be beneficial to patients and the hospital. Certainly a patient would no longer be charged the average cost of nursing, especially if he or she required little nursing care, and the hospital would have a much more diagnostic system for activity and cost control.

Mitchell Max discusses the resurgence of interest in applying activity-based costing in the banking industry in Reading 5.2, *ABC Trends in the Banking Sector: A Practitioner's Perspective*. The resurgence has occurred as banks are finding new ways to leverage cost and profitability information. Some of these include, activity-based pricing for Business-to-Business services, linking ABC with performance management scorecards, and providing information to support cost improvements and for use in customer profitability analysis.

Ronald Lewis' article, *Activity-Based Costing for Marketing* (Reading 5.3), focuses on the problem of how to account for marketing costs, and in particular, distribution costs. Since marketing costs constitute more than 50 percent of the total costs in many product lines, not considering them appropriately can result in inaccurate product costing and pricing. Using data from the Atlanta Company, Lewis develops an activity-based costing approach to handling marketing costs. Cost drivers for activities such as selling, advertising, warehousing, packing, shipping, and general office are developed, and costs are assigned accordingly. Analyses can then be undertaken by product, sales territory, and product line.

In Reading 5.4, *Rethinking Activity Based Costing*, Robert Kaplan and Steven Anderson state that for many large-scale operations, ABC can be difficult to implement and maintain. In this article they develop a simplified activity based costing approach that they call Time-Driven Activity Based Costing and demonstrate how it works.

Readings
Chapter 5

5.1 Unbundling the Cost of Hospitalization
ABC can keep health care providers off the critical list.

*by Lawrence P. Carr**

In the health care industry, the insurance companies leverage their considerable power by scrutinizing the billing practices of the health care providers. A serious concern of insurers is the cost of hospital nursing care and related services.

Traditionally, the cost of nursing is factored into the daily room charge for a hospital stay. For example, a rate of $500 to $800 per day covers the 24-hour nursing availability for the patient. Nursing expenses, primarily labor costs, are part of the overhead rate comprising the daily $500 to $800 billing to the patient. Charges are aggregate in nature with the same average fixed fee applied to all patients.

The problem with this typical convention is that not all patients use nursing services in equal amounts. Patient utilization of nursing services is individualistic. Fixed charges are not always related to the services rendered. Further, nursing services are available "on call" to handle possible patient emergencies where the value may not be readily quantifiable.

Braintree Hospital is a private rehabilitation hospital providing in-patient and outpatient treatment. It is one of the largest rehabilitation network care providers in the country with 168 beds on site and management contracts covering 200 more beds. Generally patients are referred to Braintree by other hospitals or private physicians.

The patient's average stay is approximately 21 days, during which time the individual progresses through a comprehensive program aimed at restoring and maintaining functional abilities (basic living skills). Patients enter with physical disabilities due to neurological and orthopedic diseases or injury and normally are diagnosed as one of the following: stroke, spinal cord injury, congenital deformity, amputation, major multiple trauma, fracture of femur, brain injury, polyarthritis & joint replacement, neurological disorders, burns and neoplasms.

An activity-based costing system enabled Boston's Braintree Hospital to satisfy, in the near term, the insurance industry's changing approach to reimbursement. In the medium term, it positioned the hospital to enter the 1990s with the shifting payment paradigm of managed care. Knowing the cost of nursing care provided to each individual patient by diagnosis gave management reliable data to negotiate per diem rates.

NURSING SERVICES PROVIDED

Typically, nursing services in the hospital consist of a varied skill mix: professional registered nurses (RNs), licensed practical nurses (LPNs), and ancillary nursing assistants (NAs). These professionals have different levels of education, training, and hospital experience.

For example, the north wing of the second floor of Braintree Hospital has 43 beds. The nursing staff consists of a nurse manager, RNs, LPNs, and NAs who work varying shifts to cover the unit 24 hours, seven days a week. The staff is reduced for the 11 p.m. to 7:30 a.m. shift due to workload distribution.

Teams of nurses perform many different functions. They administer medication, maintain daily patient records, assist the physicians with medical care, monitor medical devices, conduct routine tests, and so on. They are responsible for the routine jobs of feeding the patients, administering to their bodily needs, bathing, ensuring patient safety, and evaluating the care provided. Perhaps most important, they provide personal comfort and care for the patient.

The professional RN is licensed and can perform all of the many nursing functions in the hospital. But he or she concentrates primarily on the more intense and demanding patients and functions. At the same time, RNs are responsible for the delivery of care to a specific group of patients on a floor or ward.

The other nursing team members normally work with the RNs to deliver care to their group of patients. Thus, the array of services is delivered by a team with varying skill levels. There is a hierarchy of nursing from the RN to the NA with the top level capable of doing all of the functions of the levels below. Pay scales vary from

$26 per hour to $8 per hour, depending on the personal skill/educational level and specific position.

As you might imagine, there is a wide variation in the amount of nursing services consumed by patients, just as there is a wide variety of patient ailments that require differing degrees of nursing attention. The health care industry has recognized this phenomenon, and third-party payers are pushing very hard to pay only for services used by the patient and at the lowest price.

Patients are becoming more aware of and interested in the distribution of care and the inherent costs, probably due to the economy and media attention focused on health care costs. Such comments as, "Mrs. Smith is getting all of the nursing attention. She needs it and, thankfully, I don't, but I have to pay for it. This doesn't seem fair," are quite common.

NO HARD DATA

Mary-Jean Crockett, the progressive-thinking vice president of nursing, recognized that nursing services delivery needed to be understood better. She felt the growing pressure from the insurance companies that pay for most of Braintree's patient care and heard the "buzz" at national professional conferences. She was determined to find an easy, reliable, and fair method to ascertain the amount, mix, and resulting cost of nursing services consumed by individual patients. She also wanted a more accurate approach to forecasting the skill mix associated with care of the different diagnostic groups. She remained cognizant that she also needed to monitor the high level of quality, comfort, and safety that leads to positive patient outcomes.

Two years ago, Mary-Jean initiated the nursing services analysis project by chairing a project team of nurses and administrators. Team members included the staff development instructor, nursing MIS project manager, and the nursing supervisor/coordinator of quality assurance. All the team members worked as staff members on the nursing care units and were familiar with the actual work flow at Braintree.

After the first organizational meeting and the sharing of the concerns for the nursing service issues, the team realized it had no hard data upon which to make its assessment. Everyone had anecdotal stories with the constant theme of the imbalance between the actual delivered nursing and the fixed single billing rate. Additionally, Mary-Jean was very interested in the efficiency as well as the effectiveness of the current nursing staffing levels and delivery of care system.

THE PILOT STUDY

A literature review and discussion with "experts" in the field did not provide insight into assessing the workflow in the Braintree environment. Then a process analysis was conducted that produced time, motion, and frequency studies of the routine and special medical events on all of the nursing units.

The routine events such as vital sign test, medication, and bed changing were easy to predict and consistent across all units. The percentage of baseline routine nursing time could vary from 5% to 70%, depending on the medical problem and length of hospital stay. For example, a new brain injury patient requires constant care, and routine nursing, may comprise just 5% of the total daily nursing services consumed. On the other hand, a burn patient about to be discharged may be quite self-sufficient, and the routine care would consist of 70% of the total daily nursing care. The team concluded that it needed more data to predict the nonroutine, variable, or special events that consumed considerable nursing, time. It believed the non-routine events were the driving forces behind the varying levels of services needed and provided.

The team, after many additional meetings, developed a simple but quite reliable data gathering instrument to capture variable and unpredictable events and build a database. Figure 1 shows the nursing service classification data form. The established procedure provided that the nurses from each shift simply checked the appropriate boxes for the service rendered for each individual patient. The sheets were collected daily for the previous 24 hours and entered into the database system created for the study. The nursing staff openly accepted the study and, with very few exceptions, completed the form accurately and in a timely manner.

This cooperation reflects the strength of employee empowerment because the nursing staff assisted with the system implementation. The project manager reviewed the input daily and followed up quickly to correct any data collection problems. Currently this system is automated with touch-screen data entry at the locations and automatic download to the database.

The staff became very proficient at completing the form, and the project team members monitored the process. They were very pleased with the data integrity. Table 1 shows a daily summary of the data. Panel A shows the distribution of nursing care by types of activities. The unit in this case is the floor and wing of the hospital (2N-2nd floor North Wing). Panel B shows the distribution of nursing by diagnosis (illness for which the patient was admitted to the hospital). Panels C and D organize the data around the hospital unit.

Table 2 shows an individual patient classification summary of the data over a 44-day period. Using a database system, the team was able to organize the fields of data in an appropriate configuration. Mary-Jean immediately saw how she could use this information for nurse staffing and operational planning. Team members were pleased with the process insight provided by the amassed data, but they were not clear how to use the information in the managed care environment. The missing element was the assignment of the percentage of nursing time used for each skill level.

FIGURE 1. SERVICE CLASSIFICATION FORM

PRIMARY DIAGNOSIS _____ CLASSIFIER'S NAME _____ DATE _____	 ADDRESSOGRAPH

PILOT CLASSIFICATION TOOL   DRAFT 3

In each of the following sections, place a check mark in the most appropriate box corresponding to the most complex level of case documented in the past 24 hours.

FEEDING
A1 ☐ Setup
A2 ☐ Enteral Feed
A3 ☐ Distant Supervision
A4 ☐ 1:1 Supervision
A5 ☐ Dependent P.O. Feed

MOBILITY
B1 ☐ Contact Guard, Walker
    Independent, Stand Pivot Min-Mod
    of 1, Sliding Board Independent or
    Assist Min-Mod of 1
B2 ☐ Hoyer Lift/Transiad
B3 ☐ Max of 1, Mod-Max of 2, Stand
    Pivot, Squat, Sliding Board Max 1

ADL
C1 ☐ Setup or Min Assist
C2 ☐ Min-Mod Assist
C3 ☐ Mod Assist
C4 ☐ Mod-Max Assist
C5 ☐ Total Dependence
C6 ☐ Dependent Shave
C7 ☐ Dependent Bed Shampoo

MEDICAL
D1 ☐ Routine Medical Supervision
D2 ☐ VS Q VShift
D3 ☐ Assist with M.D. Procedure
D4 ☐ # of Procedures Performed in 24 Hours
D5 ☐ Frequent Vital Signs
    (Q 1-2 hrs over 24 hrs)
D6 ☐ Precautions, Respiratory
D7 ☐ Precautions, Wound/Skin, Enteric

MEDICATIONS
E1 ☐ Routine Meds, P.O.
E2 ☐ Meds IM, SC
E3 ☐ Meds PR, Enteral, or Topical
E4 ☐ Meds PRN (any route)
E5 ☐ Receiving Meds and/or Hydration IV

ELIMINATION
F1 ☐ Continent Bowel/Bladder
    or Continent of Bowel with
    Foley Catheter
F2 ☐ Incontinent Bowel and/or Bladder
F3 ☐ Assist-Dependent Ostomy Care
F4 ☐ Texas Cath
F5 ☐ Straight Cath

ELIMINATION
G1 ☐ Teaching, Psych/Soc Support, Safety Interventions
    (Non-Aggitated Patient)
G2 ☐ Q 15 Minute Safety Checks
    by M.D. Order
G3 ☐ 1:1 Observation
G4 ☐ # Shifts
G5 ☐ Skill (RN, LPN, RT, NA)
G6 ☐ Frequent Aggressive or
    Aggitated Behavior Requiring
    Intervantion of Only 1 Staff Member
G7 ☐ Frequent Aggressive or Aggitated
    Behavior Requiring Intervention
    More Than 1 Staff Member

SKIN CARE
H1 ☐ Routine Skin Care, Includes
    Topical Treatments
H2 ☐ Wound Care
H3 ☐ # Treatments in 24 Hrs.
H4 ☐ Central Line

RESPIRATORY
I1 ☐ Routine TCDB, O2 Equipment
I2 ☐ Routine Tracheostomy Care
    (include up to one additional
    suctioning per shift)
I3 ☐ Requires Suctioning Two or
    More Times Per Shift
I4 ☐ Manage Meds by Nebulizer
    Incentive Spirometry,
    Humidification

TABLE 1. PATIENT CLASSIFICATION SUMMARY (PANELS A AND B)

PANEL A UNIT	CENSUS	NUTR	MOBIL	ADL	MEDICAL	MEDS	ELIM	SAFETY	SKIN	RESP	INDIR	OTHER	HOURS	AVERAGE
					DISTRIBUTION OF CARE ACTIVITIES			CLASSIFICATION DATE				11/05/92		
2N	41	7.0%	8.0%	10.0%	1.0%	5.0%	10.0%	5.0%	3.0%	0.0%	45.0%	5.21%	208.4	5.1
2S	30	11.0%	10.0%	13.0%	1.0%	5.0%	9.0%	4.0%	1.0%	1.0%	40.0%	5.21%	170.4	5.7
3N	40	6.0%	7.0%	10.0%	1.0%	5.0%	8.0%	6.0%	1.0%	0.0%	49.0%	5.21%	187.9	4.7
3S	41	5.0%	5.0%	12.0%	3.0%	5.0%	6.0%	5.0%	2.0%	1.0%	49.0%	5.21%	191.0	4.7
	152	7.2%	7.5%	11.2%	1.7%	5.1%	8.2%	5.3%	2.0%	0.4%	46.1%	5.2%	757.7	5.0

PANEL B CASE MIX	DX	CENSUS	NUTR	MOBIL	ADL	MEDICAL	MEDS	ELIM	SAFETY	SKIN	RESP	INDIR	OTHER	HOURS	AVERAGE
			BY DIAGNOSIS												
32%	1	49	25.1	23.8	30.8	2.6	12.3	23.4	12.3	3.4	0.0	112.7	13.5	259.9	5.3
16%	6	24	3.1	8.3	11.0	1.2	6.0	10.4	6.0	2.9	0.0	55.2	5.7	109.9	4.6
15%	12	23	6.7	6.8	12.6	4.6	5.8	7.8	7.8	3.3	1.5	52.9	6.0	115.7	5.0
11%	8	17	0.9	3.7	7.4	0.9	4.3	3.4	4.3	1.8	0.0	39.1	3.6	69.1	4.1
9%	7	13	9.8	6.3	9.0	0.8	4.0	6.6	3.3	0.9	1.5	29.9	4.0	75.9	5.8
7%	9	11	3.9	3.2	5.3	0.6	2.8	3.8	2.8	0.7	0.0	25.3	2.6	50.8	4.6
4%	4	6	0.3	1.8	2.7	0.3	1.5	2.0	1.5	1.4	0.0	13.8	1.4	26.7	4.4
3%	11	5	3.0	2.5	3.4	1.7	1.3	3.4	1.3	0.8	0.0	11.5	1.6	30.3	6.1
1%	5	2	0.1	0.3	0.8	0.1	0.5	0.4	0.5	0.0	0.0	4.6	0.4	7.8	3.9
1%	2	2	1.8	0.3	1.8	0.1	0.5	1.2	0.5	0.3	0.0	4.6	0.6	11.7	5.8
0%														0.0	0.0
		152													

TABLE 1. PATIENT CLASSIFICATION SUMMARY (PANEL C)

UNIT	CLASSIFIED HOURS		HOURS WORKED	PRODUCTIVITY CLASSIFIED HAVE	APPROPRIATE STAFFING HAVE CLASSIFIED
2N	208.398		186	112%	89%
	93.779	DAY	85.225	110%	91%
	73.9812	EVE	62	119%	84%
	40.6375	NOC	38.75	105%	95%
2S	170.418		186	92%	109%
	76.688	DAY	77.5	99%	101%
	60.4983	EVE	62	96%	102%
	33.2314	NOC	46.5	71%	140%
3N	187.931		201.5	93%	107%
	84.5688	DAY	85.25	99%	101%
	66.7154	EVE	69.75	98%	105%
	36.6465	NOC	46.5	79%	127%
3S	190.955		178.25	107%	93%
	85.9298	DAY	77.5	111%	90%
	67.789	EVE	69.75	97%	103%
	37.2362	NOC	31	120%	83%
TOTAL	757.701		751.75	101%	99%
	340.965	DAY	325.5	105%	95%
	268.984	EVE	263.5	102%	98%
	147.752	NOC	162.75	91%	110%

WORKLOAD DISTRIBUTION

DAY	45.0%	EVE	35.5%	NOC	19.5%

TABLE 1. PATIENT CLASSIFICATION SUMMARY (PANEL D)

Panel D UNIT	Dx 1	Dx 2	Dx 3	Dx 4	Dx 5	Dx 6	Dx 7	Dx 8	Dx 9	Dx 10	Dx 11	Dx 12
					DIAGNOSTIC DISTRIBUTION BY UNIT							
CENSUS	49	2	0	6	2	24	13	17	11	0	5	23
2N	31%	0%	0%	100%	50%	25%	0%	24%	9%	0%	0%	35%
2S	31%	0%	0%	0%	0%	0%	100%	0%	9%	0%	20%	0%
3N	18%	0%	0%	0%	0%	38%	0%	41%	36%	0%	20%	43%
3S	20%	100%	0%	0%	50%s	38%	0%	35%	45%	0%	60%	22%

TABLE 2. PATIENT CLASSIFICATION SUMMARY

Sample patient listing of a single patient throughout hospitalization

CLASSIFIER	DENUM, M	LAURENCE, J	DENUM, M	BRODERICK, K	GILMORE, J
PATIENT			MYPATHY		
REC#			092131		
UNIT			2S		
ROOM#			217A		
SEX			M		
DATE	12/29/92	01/13/93	01/29/93	02/10/93	02/22/93
ADM	12/24/92	12/24/92	12/24/92	12/24/92	12/24/92
NUTR	1.70	0.33	0.05	0.33	0.05
MOBIL	1.00	0.17	0.17	0.17	0.17
ADL	0.72	0.58	0.72	0.58	0.42
MEDICAL	0.05	0.05	0.05	0.05	0.05
MEDS	0.25	0.25	0.25	0.25	0.25
ELIM	1.00	1.00	1.00	1.00	0.20
SAFETY	0.25	0.25	0.25	0.25	0.25
SKIN	0.02	0.02	0.22	0.02	0.02
RESP	0.00	0.00	0.00	0.00	0.00
INDIR	2.30	2.30	2.30	2.30	2.30
OTHER	0.40	0.27	0.28	0.27	0.20
UNIT	2S	2S	2S	2S	2S
DX	1	1	1	1	1
HOURS	7.68	5.22	5.28	5.22	3.90
DAY	5	21	36	48	60
RN	2.54	2.18	2.32	2.18	1.79
LPN	1.68	1.13	1.19	1.13	0.82
NA RT	3.47	1.91	1.77	1.91	1.30

MODEL OF ACTIVITIES

The pilot team met with a consultant, who explained how to assign the skill mix information by activity. The consultant, using activity-based costing principles, revealed to team members how they had captured the nursing resources consumed by the various patients' diagnosis.

A further analysis of these data also demonstrated that the nursing resource consumption changed with the length of stay of the patient. Most patients have a large consumption of nursing services during the initial period of their stay, and, over time, the consumption declines. Thus, the consumption of nursing services is a function of both the mix of patient diagnosis and the length of hospital stay.

The team reviewed each activity and assigned a percentage of time spent for each skill level of nursing (RN, LPN, and NA). In this manner, a matrix was built where all the activities performed by the various skill levels were determined for each category of patient illness. This relationship was tracked over the length of hospital stay by patient category.

The data were reconfigured to provide the nursing skill level needed to deliver care (based on their activities) for each type of patient. In addition, the total amount of the time each skill level spent in each activity was readily available. The team now had a model of the activities consumed by each patient by classification based on the patient's use of all skill levels as well as the amount of nursing services. The team had developed the nursing resource consumption model for the hospital.

For example, a patient entered the hospital on 12/24 with a traumatic head injury and was released on 2/22 for a total stay of 60 days. As shown in Table 3, the total nonroutine nursing services used on 12/29 were 7.68 hours with RN 2.54 (33%), LPN 1.68 (22%), and NA 3.47 (45%) hours. On 2/22, 57 days later, the total nonroutine nursing is 3.90 hours, 50% less than the initial consumption. The distribution also has changed with RN 1.79 (45%), LPN .82 (21%), and NA 1.30 (34%). This trend over time and composition mix change has economic and staffing implications for the hospital.

As demonstrated, nursing costs by skill level were applied to the data, producing a predictable and reliable cost of nursing service by diagnosis over the length of the patient stay model. This information is invaluable when the hospital contracts with the insurance companies for a fixed daily hospital fee for specific rehabilitation diagnosis.

TABLE 3. PATIENT CARE SUMMARY

MYPATHY	12/29	5	7.68	33%	22%	45%
	1/14	21	5.22	42%	22%	36%
	1/29	36	5.28	44%	22%	34%
	2/10	48	5.22	42%	22%	36%
	2/22	60	3.9	45%	21%	34%

IT WORKS

The system unbundled a previously fixed cost allocation for nursing. The consumption of nursing services based on patient diagnosis and length of stay, coupled with the other cost elements of a hospital stay, enabled the hospital to contract knowledgeably with the third-party payers. Prior to this information, the hospital cost management called for full bed occupancy and hoped for the right mix of patients to allow the hospital to cover its costs. Or, it operated with a more costly, inefficient mix. The new system produced the costs for those nursing services actually used by the patient. This information changes the management economic focus from filling all beds to looking at the nursing skill level and seeking those patients who have a consumption level compatible with the available nursing services. Or, adjust the nursing mix for the forecasted consumption level.

The team was elated with the model and its potential use. To confirm the model's accuracy, extensive validity and reliability tests were performed. These tests showed a 99% accuracy as correlated to actual staffing patterns and standards of practice as established by the nursing department. The model works!

At present the hospital uses these data to structure its contract negotiations with insurance carriers and for management decisions concerning nursing work flow trends and stalling. Mary-Jean Crockett uses the database to aid in the management of the delivery and quality of nursing services. She points out that "the purpose of our patient classification system is to provide quality nursing care by providing a sufficient number and skill mix of staff necessary to do so, based upon actual patient care requirements." She can match the necessary total staff by skill mix with the actual staff by skill mix and make the necessary adjustments to ensure both quality of care and cost effectiveness.

The new data permit the hospital to unbundle the previously fixed single nursing services charge. The effect on patient mix and length of stay by diagnosis on the economic structure of the hospital becomes apparent. In an environment of reduced third-party payments and increased competition, the hospital can use this new information. Jeffrey Goode, vice president-finance, said, "Rates are negotiable depending on circumstance. The third-party payers are very sophisticated today. I use the new information to help negotiate per diem rates with the insurance companies. Rate negotiation is one of the keys to our success. Having this information is critical in today's health care environment."

Financially, the hospital matches the daily revenues with the daily expenses to arrive at a hospital profit. Normally the daily patient stay is 40% of the revenue, with inpatient ancillary services representing 60% of the daily revenue. Wherever possible, ancillary services such as physical therapy, medication, and so on are billed directly. The costs of the ancillary services are captured directly, while the costs of a patient's daily stay are rolled into the fixed daily charge. Nursing services costs are approximately 50% of the total fixed daily charge. With the new activity-based system, 50% of the fixed patient overhead—nursing services—can be allocated based on the direct consumption by the patient.

Armed with this new information, financial forecasting is more reliable. The patient load and mix projections can be translated into a cost behavior model based on resource consumption. More important, the hospital armed with new cost data can negotiate rates and fees more intelligently with the third-party payers.

KEY SUCCESS FACTORS

The ability to understand the nursing services delivery process and to unbundle the nursing tasks was critical to the success of the project. The project team members were nurses with many years of practice. Even the designer and manager of the database was an RN. The project leader, Mary-Jean, understood the balance of delivering quality nursing care in the changing economic structure of our health care delivery system. She was determined to maintain and value appropriately the quality and caring of nursing services.

The hospital senior management fully supported the project. Team members worked well together and they communicated their progress and findings regularly. The output was nonthreatening. The nursing staff viewed this information as an enabler, which permitted better staffing.

The enthusiasm and seriousness of the team sent a clear and positive message to the hospital staff. The data collection was made simple and easy, first the paper form and later the electronic form. It was part of the nursing delivery process. The Braintree nurses shared Mary-Jean's concerns and knew that the data somehow would benefit them and make their job better understood. The high validity of the pilot test was very convincing.

The accounting and finance departments became involved after the consultant showed the team how to add cost data to the operational data. They saw which operational factors drove the costs and arrived at an activity-based costing and management system. This linkage is invaluable for doing business and managing in the new managed care economic health care environment.

HEALTH RESULTS

The success at Braintree Hospital was communicated to the 32 other rehabilitation facilities throughout the parent company. The model has been replicated successfully at many of the network facilities. In fact, the parent company's Big 6 auditing and consulting firm has incorporated the model into the financial program of all of company facilities. Now the activity-based cost model is a key part of the entire company's cost accounting system.

Using basic process analysis and sensible data collection, they developed an activity-based cost management system (ABC-MS). It provided valuable operational information for managing nursing services delivery and the cost consumption data to meet the changing health care reimbursement practices. This information changed the way Braintree Hospital conducts business. By understanding the delivery process, the hospital is compensated for the actual services delivered, and the third-party payers have a feeling of equity. The ideal health care system is where we pay for what we use and we use only what we need. The activity-based cost management system moves us toward this goal.

Lawrence P. Carr, Ph.D., is the Trivisonno term chair and assistant professor, Babson College. He can be reached at (617) 239–5138.

Note:

This work was made possible by the openness and cooperation of the Braintree Hospital staff. A special thanks is extended to the members of the CMS project team (M. DiBlasi, P. Flaherty and K. Sampson) and Mary-Jean Crockett, vice president of nursing.

QUESTION

5.1 In Lawrence Carr's article on the cost of healthcare, the consumption of nursing services is a function of what factors? Did the system work?

5.2 ABC Trends in the Banking Sector–A Practitioner's Perspective

*by Mitchell Max, Managing Partner, The Performax Group**

Ten years ago, in *The Information Executives Truly Need*, Peter Drucker observed that service industries - including banks - "have practically no cost information at all[1]". Today, not only has Activity-Based Costing (ABC) become common in the financial services arena, but it is in the midst of an unprecedented resurgence as organizations move quickly to replace, revise or extend their ABC systems and processes. Organizations that have avoided ABC due to perceptions of it being too complex or not producing enough value relative to initial and ongoing effort are now embracing ABC as a new weapon in their arsenals. Individuals with skills in this area are in high demand. Technology developments and investments are stronger than ever, as the tools have caught up with the aspirations of leaders in the field, enabling them to operate in new ways. What is driving this change? Is this truly an evolution or merely a fad which will pass?

From a practioner's perspective, this change is being driven by a number of critical business needs which are outlined in this paper. Today's implementers are leveraging advanced technologies and approaches in new ways to deliver sustained value for their organizations through Activity-Based Costing information. This paper seeks to present the reader with a compelling justification for advancing their ABC initiatives, and an understanding of how the new technologies and approaches can be effectively leveraged. It draws on direct experience and interaction with organizations that are raising the bar for value from their ABC investments and looks to measure the progress we have made over the past decade, along with some thoughts for the future.

THE NEED FOR ABC INFORMATION

Drucker noted that "Enterprises are paid to create wealth, not control costs.... They have to be managed for … wealth creation. To do that requires information that enables executives to make informed judgments.[2]" Today's CFO's are responding to an unprecedented need for improved, sustained bank performance to meet growing stakeholder expectations. Sophisticated banks - and their stakeholders - realize that improved performance cannot come from cost-cutting alone. Comprehensive performance management approaches, systematic management of central costs, razor-sharp pricing and customer profitability information are emerging by enlightened banks as the keys to their profitable future.

The demand for actionable, accurate and transparent cost and profitability information is growing. Bank mergers have promised significant savings, but obvious resource duplication is only one source of cost reduction, and scale efficiencies have not materialized to the extent promised. Technology

* From: M. Max, "ABC Trends in the Banking Sector – A Practitioner's Perspective," *Journal of Performance Management* (2004): 23–40. Reprinted with permission of the Association for Management Information in Financial Services (AMIfs), www.amifs.org.

innovation has also been slow to dramatically drive down operating costs. As a result, banks are looking for more comprehensive and deep understanding of cost information as they strive to meet stakeholder expectations.

Banks have traditionally used average costs as part of their profitability analysis. For those banks that do use ABC, it often takes the form of standard unit costs, with some transactional differentiation - for example, using different costs for assisted vs. self-service transactions - applied to channel-specific transaction volumes. While providing directionally correct information at a high level, accurate costing often remains elusive to these banks, particularly when viewed at the detailed level.

As differentiation of service increases in financial institutions, it drives multiple levels of complexity. In turn, complexity drives highly different levels of cost consumption, for example:

- Product customization, which often requires special back-office processing
- Special compliance functions/procedures
- Manual reporting/government filings
- Significant effort to explain product features to clients
- High error rates triggering significant levels of manual adjustments
- Degree of online self-service capability
- Product complexity driving level of sales/advisory effort
- Electronic versus manual transactions
- Straight-through vs. manual processing

Studies have shown unit cost factors, due to differing demand intensity impacting consumption, to be in some cases 5 or 10 times higher or lower than the "average". As a result, *average costs have never been more inappropriate!* In fact, the level of cost differentiation has become so significant that even business unit executives are rejecting the use of average costs as a basis for decision-making. Only when costs are based on actual consumption, and demonstrated in a transparent fashion, will they be truly accepted by all parts of the business. In fact, when presented in a transparent way, cost information forms a powerful tool in dialog with customers.

NEW APPLICATIONS FOR ABC
Today's banks are identifying new and unique ways to leverage cost and profitability information, including:
- Activity-Based Pricing, particularly for Business-to-Business services;
- Linking ABC information into Performance Management scorecards and processes;

- Providing information on a process view of costs, both to support cost improvement needs and to enable ongoing accountability for management by business process; and
- Information on the profitability of discrete customer relationships.

ACTIVITY-BASED PRICING
Financial services organizations are recognizing that significant value can be derived from pricing which leverages ABC information. In situations where pricing is determined solely by reference to the market, organizations can do little but select and nurture customer relationships with high yields and lower cost to serve. There are many situations however, where pricing can and must be based on an understanding of the cost to serve for each product and customer. In particular, business-to-business services have significant potential for profit optimization when the cost to serve can be transparently calculated, and in many cases discussed with clients during price negotiation. As a result, there is great demand for accurate, transparent and reliable cost information by the customer-facing sides of the business.

In one case, a transaction processing outsourcer has been highly successful in using this information to target specific clients and, through training of its sales force has begun to improve the profitability of client relationships. Previously, discussions could only refer refer subjectively to the level of complexity of their interactions. With new information, specific measures of transaction intensity can be described with clients, and additional opportunities to capture pricing for special "value-added" services become more evident.

INTEGRATING ABC AND PERFORMANCE MANAGEMENT
In their initial work with ABC, most banks focused their implementations narrowly, developing isolated unit costs, product cost data and departmental cost studies, with a focus on understanding specific unit costs - generally focused on product and organizational profitability. Many of these studies were static, and quickly became outdated.

Increasingly, we are witnessing a need to develop more comprehensive cost and profitability information, looking for example at the cost of an entire business process which now encompasses multiple channels and organizational units. Further, organizations recognize the significant value that can be derived from weaving cost and profitability information into more comprehensive and integrated performance management applications across the organization. Cost data now forms an integral part of Balanced Scorecard applications, and internal performance benchmarks are used to identify opportunities for performance improvement. The need for external bench-marking is growing rapidly. Cost and profitability are now critical elements in assessing and managing the *ongoing* performance of branches, channels and customers.

As a result, banks are experiencing the need to develop linkages between ABC tools, data warehouses and Corporate Performance Management (CPM) platforms. IT groups are becoming more directly involved in ABC applications, as they begin to treat cost information as a corporate asset, and identify the way it is foundational to other information - such as CRM data or CPM applications. This technical data integration is expected to continue at an increasing pace as CPM rises in prominence due to a heightened focus by many of the technology analysts. New approaches to Performance Management, such as Beyond Budgeting[3], are reinforcing the need for the integration of these components by demonstrating the need for open and transparent information as the basis for relative performance management and interactive control processes.

THE NEW GOALPOST: TRUE CUSTOMER PROFITABILITY

Studies continue to show that banks that manage the profitability of customer relationships outperform banks managing without this data. Experience has demonstrated that non-profitability-based segmentation (e.g., based on revenue, balances or number of products) can produce behaviors that reward retention of high touch - and generally less profitable - customers. (One retail broker found that over 20% of their "high target" customers were in the lowest two profitability deciles.)

The sheer fact that *customers have multiple channel and process options* for sales and service interaction with banks, means that only by understanding and managing customer demand can cost and profitability be understood and managed. Best practice organizations explicitly measure and manage the true profitability of each customer relationship.

All banks recognize the criticality of customer profitability information. The information is increasingly used in developing and executing customer acquisition and retention strategies, with leading organizations incorporating this information into their customer relationship management (CRM) systems. As the more sophisticated banks divest themselves of low-profitability customers, other banks must be wary of accepting their "hand-me-down" accounts. Banks that market "free checking" models run the risk of being selected by the very low-profitability customers that have "terminated" relationships with other banks. Consequently, profitability analysis at the customer level is no longer optional.

Accurate analysis across multiple dimensions requires cost assignment down to the lowest cost object level-the account. The best way to understand costs across dimensions-including customer, product and channel dimensions-is to actually cost them out at the account level. Understanding that lowest level and then developing rollups of the information across all cost object dimensions results in truly accurate information that can be used across the organization. Traditional applications which cascade costs from one profitability dimension to another (organizational, product, channel, and customer) do not meet the test of accuracy.

Based on these observations, it is anticipated that:

- *Large banks will continue to refine and extend their customer profitability platforms.* Many of the largest banks calculate standard unit costs for each channel-specific transaction type, and multiply those costs by transaction volumes to determine and store customer profitability information in massive data warehouses. While these solutions continue to meet many of the profitability analysis needs within those large banks, such as supporting CRM solutions, they do not address operational cost management needs, or the cross functional process costing analysis requirements for these complex organizations. With new, more scalable costing technology offerings becoming available, larger organizations, with tens or hundreds of millions of customers, are looking towards newer solutions in meeting their costing needs. One major brokerage company, for example, recently converted their in-house ABC application to a commercial software product, enabling them to efficiently and effectively prepare and analyze the profitability of each of its 8 million customers on a monthly basis. By integrating their previously separate unit cost and profitability models, they are able to better use more discrete (and hence, more accurate) cost information and "Black Belts", who drive their teams towards more discrete and detailed measures of process performance. This forces a greater level of interest in true qualitative cost drivers (e.g., the level of training) and on process performance measures (e.g., error rates) which in some cases can force additional detail into ABC models. While this is not news to our manufacturing colleagues, this is a clear shift in emphasis as banks realize the degree to which some parts of their organizations resemble factory operations.

This trend creates a number of demands on costing systems and professionals:

- *Greater need for process costing information and management.* Organizations need more detailed process costing information for management reporting. ABC models need to be able to report on costs both by department and process. As banks begin to appoint process owners, information on the cost of business processes is being increasingly demanded - in addition to traditional departmental cost data.

- *Need for better, ongoing measures of performance.* When it comes to measuring performance, financial institutions need more granular, rigorous, accurate and timely information. A shift is on to better understand the factors of cost causation, including qualitative cost drivers and the management of demand intensity.

- *Linkages from ABC foundations to other initiatives.* Scorecards, performance measurements, and other components of the CPM tool sets are linked to ABC and changes in costing- and are thus becoming more critical. Software vendors are becoming increasingly aware of the need to demonstrate integration amongst the various performance management tools.

MANAGING THE BANK AS AN ECONOMIC UNIT

Financial services organizations are clearly becoming more sophisticated about how they manage costs. As banks expand and enhance their costing capabilities, we are witnessing a return to the use of *Activity-Based Management* as a key weapon in the war on costs. Over their history, banks have inadvertently made ABM more difficult to implement, by breaking up their operations into discrete organizational units in the drive for consolidation and efficiency. This has made it difficult to manage activities as an entire process. For example, customer transactions are handled in one area, branch back-offices are often consolidated in a geographic area, major processing is handled in a central unit or outsourced. Understanding and managing total economic costs through process "swim lanes" has become a major undertaking.

Banks are beginning to apply process management techniques. More recently, as they seek innovative ways to reduce costs, banks have begun to organize around processes and look at costs from a customer perspective, including recognition that costs will cross multiple sales and delivery channels. Early analysis here often focuses on the total cost of a process (i.e. mortgage origination cost). Since most banks continue to organize and operate in functional silos, ABM information is increasingly in demand, and ABC software is being utilized increasingly to tag activities by business process regardless of where it resides for organizational convenience.

At the same time, process improvement techniques are becoming more sophisticated, with an increasing

prevalence of Six Sigma and other detailed process techniques. The Six Sigma approaches popularized by such companies as Motorola and GE are now being embraced by the financial services sector; back-office processing facilities are starting to introduce Lean Manufacturing techniques. At one large transaction processor, multi-disciplinary ABC project teams include "Black Belts", who drive their teams towards more discrete and concrete action and provide more transparent profitability measures to their business segments.

- *Mid-size banks and non-retail lines of business in large banks also require scalable customer profitability platforms.* Mid-size banks and non-retail lines of business need access to comparable customer profitability tools scaled to support customer levels in the ten-million range. Newer ABC tools are making this possible.

- *Need for effective integration of transactional information across the organization.* Pulling data into large data warehouses and understanding how to use and leverage it effectively will ultimately determine the success of the financial institution's customer profitability initiative. As organizations begin to collect and manage a variety of information at the customer level, there is an increasing need to optimize not only the physical storage of this but also the leveraging of this related data amongst all information consumers within the bank.

- *An end to the separation of cost and profitability information at the customer level.* Increasingly, banks now look to solutions which combine unit cost and customer profitability, along with other profitability measures, in a single product or model. While this was previously not possible, advances in technology have begun to open this solution up to all but the largest banks. One regional bank has retained the use of its A/LM package for Funds Transfer Pricing at a customer level, and is linking it to customer-level cost data from a new ABC system.

- *Strain between detail required for ABC and causal factors needed for reengineering and Six Sigma programs.* As financial institutions take more strategic approaches to building costing systems, they need to develop ABC information at a level of detail that will support the causal factor requirements of reengineering and Six Sigma programs. This granularity is much lower than that required for strategic (product, channel) cost analysis. Greater care and the use of professional judgment are needed in the development of cost models to meet these often-conflicting scenarios.

NEW CHALLENGES FOR ABC IMPLEMENTATIONS

The new needs presented above are matched with a new set of challenges facing ABC implementers.

While the need for this information is rising, the appetite for spending on ABC systems and supporting infrastructure is clearly waning as finance continually looks to optimize the value it provides to the bank. ABC groups are being constantly challenged to "do more with less":

- *Need for regular updates and ongoing reporting is driving the need for lower total cost of ownership (TCO).* Early adopters of ABC were plagued by the size of the staff groups that were needed to maintain their systems; without large staff complements, ABC models quickly became outdated. It is not uncommon to find ABC teams with over 20 people, plus a dedicated systems group supporting them. As a result, frustration with the significant maintenance costs associated with ABC has become rampant. As ABC becomes more critical to success and corporations are increasingly in flux, organizations are focusing on how they can develop and maintain accurate costing systems while keeping down costs-particularly ongoing labor costs. Time-baseding down costs-particularly ongoing labor costs. Time-based cost models and strong data automation, discussed later in this paper, are supporting a renewed ABC approach with a lower ongoing cost of ownership.

- *Survey tools falling out of favor.* Surveys have traditionally been used to capture the assignment of resources to activities in ABC models. With variable staffing models on the rise, and the frequency of organizational change, survey information has become increasingly inaccurate and requires significant maintenance resources. Different approaches are needed.

- *Focus on data integrity for external and regular management reporting.* As line-of-business profitability and costing information increasingly finds its way into externally published reports, organizations will need to ensure that the information meets generally accepted accounting principles (GAAP) and regulatory requirements and complies with Sarbanes-Oxley legislation. Tying ABC information to authoritative and certified back-office systems is becoming a new theme in advanced applications. CFO's must demonstrate that the information presented in segmented reporting has the same integrity as that presented under the GAAP statements. The same standards apply to the use of ABC information in supporting decisions made by management or the board. ABC practitioners are now coming to realize that cost systems must be as complete and accurate as the information produced for external and other internal reporting, and that compliance will be fully required. Approximates or estimates are coming under greater scrutiny when used as the basis for cost allocation.

At the same time, changes in the structure of bank operations are presenting new challenges to ABC implements, both for initial design and also for ongoing application maintenance:

- *Use of non-banking concepts in cost modeling.* Banks combine both product "manufacturing" (marketing, operations) and "distribution" (sales and service channels). As they reorganize, banks have increasingly been working to separate these functions, and separate cost information is required to support the accountabilities that management is introducing. The traditional non-banking approach of separating product manufacturing from service fulfillment/delivery allows greater flexibility in costing than the single - model approach which has been historically employed. With separate accountabilities, the organization can discretely flow costs between different parts of the organization. For example, mortgage applications and mortgage processing on the product side would be kept separate from loan distribution. Standard costs at the transfer point can be used to measure the efficiency of each group separately. This is a new approach to cost modeling which is being addressed. Traceback of costs through these separate models is a requirement of many new systems.

- *Shared Services are here to stay.* Banks are unique in the high levels of common cost base and infrastructure which is used to support its products and customers. When costs are fully allocated to branches, many banks find that the level of indirect costs is over 50% of total non-interest costs. To better measure and manage this high level of common costs, Shared Service approaches are becoming commonplace in banks. IT, HR, financial and customer service applications are being centralized and shared. Accountabilities are created for cost and profitability information at discrete levels in the organization. Best practice execution of shared services methodologies require cost allocation models tuned to the organization's culture - taking it out of the technical implementation approach and relying to a much greater extent on the use of Change Management specialists.

- *The need to reflect a systemic view of costs. A financial institution cannot manage technology without considering operations, and vice versa.* When examining the cost of processing a mortgage application, for example, a bank needs to consider both the technology and labor costs of the activity or process. If a bank wants to know how much it will cost to process an ATM deposit, it needs to look at the technology costs of running the machines, the costs of servicing the machines, and the costs of the courier systems and item processing areas that handle deposit slips. Interestingly, many banks have begun a move to combine organizational responsibility for technology and back-office operations. These new Chief Technology and Operations Officers need new information on the total cost of transaction or service handling if they are to make effective decisions. Costs must therefore flow together to support this ongoing analysis - for example, by helping to analyze the business case for a technology investment in terms of its ability to reduce manual effort - and to track the achievement of benefits post-implementation. This requires a more integrated approach to modeling than is done when the items are treated in distinct models silos.

■ *Banks change fast-traditional costing systems can't keep up!* To a greater degree than ever before, change is the only constant.

As a result, banks are seeking ABC platforms that can meet a wide variety of needs - concurrently and over time. No one ABC approach or model design will fit all parts of an organization. The organization must find tools flexible enough to meet a variety of needs and evolve as those needs change. Limitations in software design are tolerated less than ever before, simply because the future is so unknown.

CHANGE MANAGEMENT IMPACTS
In addition to the systems changes that these needs and challenges drive, a number of organizational and "people" impacts are becoming prevalent:

■ More widespread use and greater access to ABC models and information. ABC no longer lives predominantly in the realm of finance. Learning that usage and sponsorship are critical to driving value from ABC, Operations, Marketing, HR and IT departments-as well as various lines of business-are increasingly driving the application of ABC - with Finance in a supporting role.

■ Need for broad change management and links to regular decision-making. Bringing ABC information more broadly into the organization shifts the focus from costing as an accounting science to costing as a management and behavioral science. ABC

departments are beginning to re-tool, building competencies in training and change management to augment the purely technical modeling and analysis skills.

■ Centers of excellence approach to ABC support. Centralized costing groups actively encourage the use of ABC information across the organization, changing the way that information is used and deployed. This reinforces the need for improved training, and also for leveraging technologies which support distributed cost modeling and analysis.

CLOSING THE GAP: NEW APPROACHES AND TECHNOLOGIES
ABC approaches and technologies are responding to the challenges presented above. While history doesn't always exactly repeat itself, some concepts do re-emerge when the time is right. Advances in ABC technologies have facilitated a return to original principles in costing in financial services.

Resurfacing of time-based approach. Over the past 10 years, ABC implementation approaches have shifted from the use of time-based standards to the use of periodic (or often continuous) survey tools. The high level of effort associated with maintaining survey information on resource consumption - which frequently changes - is often cited as a reason for abandonment of ABC initiatives. The tide has now turned: in recent implementations, we have begun to see engineering-style estimates for time standards-once the basis for leading banking applications - returning into vogue as part of the ABC lexicon. This approach is consistent with a more rigorous and scientific approach to the use of metrics in operations. In fact, a natural linkage exists between time-based analysis and productivity standards in back-office operations (e.g., daily applications processed per FTE), which have become stronger as a result of centralization. This approach is only now feasible with the technological innovations that allow for time to be dynamically assigned based on transactional activity in operational areas.

Awareness and management of key capacity drivers. The use of time-based costing is also facilitating a renewed interest in the cost of capacity. More sophisticated than a simple fixed/variable cost analysis, our clients are increasingly looking to better measure and manage capacity, both in order to support more refined pricing, and to find ways to focus the organization on developing more flexible platforms. One major organization, for example, has begun to look at alternatives to internal technology capacity as a result of this newly focused attention, with the potential savings of millions of dollars annually. Similarly, significant capacity exists in fixed staffing models; organizations that are able to create flexible work environments can better respond to dynamically changing business volumes and price more aggressively in the market.

Flexible, less specialized business models require adaptive ABC approaches. In the recent past, organizations focused on fixed, specialized business models. As organizations look to better leverage their investment in human capital in a rapidly changing environment, there is a movement back towards flexibility - particularly with staffing models that must incorporate such trends as job sharing, flexible hours, cross training and seasonality. As staffing needs change daily or even hourly, fixed percentages are increasingly irrelevant in allocating resource costs.

Weights and estimates are arbitrary. ABC practitioners have long used weights and estimates as proxies for average complexity. However, each customer drives distinct consumption levels based on product/channel/service mix. Only systems and approaches based on actual behavior and costs derived from real transactions - using the actual sales or delivery usage by the customer - will give the most accurate, reliable and supportable cost and profitability information.

CONCLUSIONS

Clearly, ABC is becoming the sophisticated foundation for enterprise performance management in the financial services sector. The movement of ABC into the mainstream, the renewal of earlier costing ideas, the emergence of process management and new business models, the intensification of differentiation, and attainable customer profitability - all highlight a renewed need for accurate costing implementations.

We have come a long way from Drucker's original challenge. While it is difficult to predict the future, ABC software vendors and consultants report an increasing level of interest from banks in dramatically advancing their cost and performance management capabilities. As bank mergers continue, and stakeholders' performance expectations continue to rise, the demand for - and investment in - costing resources, processes and technologies will also be sustained.

Improved technologies and new financial leadership are critical in supporting this new evolution. Technology is delivering on the promise of ABC that practitioners have looked forward to for many years. However, technology alone can't completely fulfill ABC's potential. ABC thought leaders and practitioners must continue to use ABC-generated information to capture value that supports more investments in the technology.

The true value of ABC is limited only by the creativity of practitioners and the support of corporate leadership. Thankfully, more CFO's, COO's and CIO's now understand the value of this information. With their support, financial institutions can continue to invest in the technology and human resources that will lead to even more successful ABC initiatives, and ultimately, sustained performance improvement of their organizations.

ENDNOTES

1. Drucker, Peter F., *The Information Executives Truly Need*, Harvard Business Review, January-February 1995
2. Ibid
3. For more information, see Max Mitchell, "Budgeting Revisited: Cracks in the Foundation of Bank Performance Management", Journal of Bank Cost and Management Accounting, Vol. 15 No. 3; and also www.bbrt.org.

QUESTION

5.2 Discuss the challenges faced by banks as they implement activity based costing.

5.3 Activity-Based Costing for Marketing

by Ronald J. Lewis*

CERTIFICATE OF MERIT, 1990–91

Manufacturing costs and traditional cost accounting systems are not the only cause of America's problems in the world-class Competitiveness arena. Marketing functions, particularly physical distribution, are a significant cost factor, yet marketing costs are being ignored in the mainstream discussions today. Also, activity-based costing (ABC) techniques and total cost management (TCM) concepts have been recommended and used by some companies for marketing activities since the late 1960s. How can they be merged with the concepts being promoted today?

THE PROBLEM'S HIDDEN CAUSE

Critics of traditional cost control systems who concentrate on production costs alone are overlooking a significant portion of the total costs of many manufactured products.

A major cause of the higher cost of these products is the cost of physical distribution activities and other marketing functions. Marketing costs make up more than 50% of the total costs in many product lines and approximately 20% of the U.S. Gross National Product.

Physical distribution is a major cost factor in the United States. It may not be a major cost factor in geographically small countries, such as Japan or Great Britain, within their own domestic markets. Nevertheless, when foreign companies establish factories in the United States, they face the same logistics problems that U.S. companies encounter.

The theoretical advantages of just-in-time (JIT) methods may not work in all real-life situations, even in Japanese transplants. In addition, the familiarity that U.S. companies have had with physical distribution problems may be an advantage for them over their foreign competitors. For example, a Japanese-American joint venture established a plant in Michigan to provide parts to a Japanese assembly plant in Ohio. In the Michigan plant, observers found that boxes of parts were stacked to the ceiling in all available floor space of the factory. When asked about JIT and other inventory reduction methods, the plant manager explained that parts were shipped from Japan by freighter to the West Coast, then by rail to Chicago, and finally by truck to Michigan. Therefore, it was more economical to ship in large quantities and store the extra supplies on the factory floor.

The joint-venture supplier in this example is majority owned by the Japanese company, which supplies another Japanese company, an automobile manufacturer, with these particular parts. Competition is not a factor because the two Japanese companies have prearranged agreements, so these physical distribution costs are considered unavoidable under the circumstances.

Although this example illustrates the fallacy of assuming that the Japanese have some magic formula for manufacturing efficiency, it also indicates that marketing costs, particularly the costs of physical distribution, are a major factor in worldwide competition and should not be ignored in discussions of performance measurements and integrated cost systems.

ABC TECHNIQUES FOR MARKETING

The objective of marketing cost analysis is to provide relevant quantitative data that will assist marketing managers in making informed decisions regarding such important areas as profitability, pricing, and adding or dropping the product lines or territories. In achieving this objective it is necessary to be able to trace costs directly to product lines or to territories where possible and to establish a rational system of allocating nontraceable costs to the cost objective. The accounting profession has not pursued this challenge!

ABC principles can be applied in attempting to trace marketing costs to product lines and territories in order to measure profitability. I'll show you how. All you have to do is follow the procedure outlined next.

1. Establish activities performed as advertising, selling, order filling, shipping, and warehousing.
2. Accumulate direct costs for each activity, and separate into variable and fixed categories.
3. Determine cost drivers for each activity. For *selling*, the cost driver is gross sales, or orders received, or number of sales calls. For the activity of *order filling, shipping*, and *warehousing*, the cost driver would be number, weight, or size of units shipped. For the activities of *credit* and *collection* and *general office*, the cost driver is number of customer orders or number of invoice lines.
4. Calculate unit costs for each activity. The unit cost of each activity is determined by dividing the total activity cost by the cost driver selected. Where

---

* From R. J. Lewis, "Activity-Based Costing for Marketing," *Management Accounting* (November 1991): 33–36. Reprinted with permission conveyed through Copyright Clearance Center, Inc.

conditions justify the practice, the unit cost can be used as the basis for budgeting and for the establishment of standards in a standard cost system.

5. Apply contribution cost analysis. The accumulation of direct costs and the allocation of indirect costs to marketing activities enables management to assign total cost responsibility to each marketing activity although the identification of total costs does not always provide relevant information for specific decisions. Only by applying contribution analysis will the company be able to determine profit contribution by product line or by territory.

Tables 1-5 were prepared by the controller of Atlanta Company to provide information about marketing profitability. Table 1 shows selling prices, unit manufacturing costs, units sold, and other bases of variability. Table 2 shows total variable and fixed costs for each activity and develops unit rates for variable and fixed costs of each major marketing activity: selling, warehousing, packing and shipping, and general office.

Selling. The selling function is represented by the dollar value of sales. There may be justification for basing variability of selling cost on other factors, such as the number of sales calls or orders obtained, and the controller must select the basis that has the main causal effect on cost variability. Atlanta Company uses the basis of dollar value of sales.

Advertising. Advertising is a promotional activity, similar to selling, which possibly could be attributed to the cost factors. Atlanta selected units of product sold. Note that advertising may or may not have variable cost characteristics. Some companies increase their advertising when sales are down, so the cost may bear an inverse relationship with sales. Atlanta found that a portion of advertising varies with sales and that a larger portion is fixed.

Warehousing. Warehousing is the general distribution function of storage terminating. The factor of variability selected by Atlanta is weight of product sold.

Packing and Shipping. Another physical distribution function, packaging and shipping, usually has a greater proportion of variable expenses and is related to the quantity of units of product shipped. Atlanta assumes units shipped are equal to units sold.

General Office. Atlanta needs clerical accounting, credit and collection, and other activities to service the overall marketing function. Each service has its own variability, but Atlanta assumes that number of orders affects all.

Table 3 provides additional product and territory transactions data. For example, the quantity of product C sold in the West territory during the period was 14,000 units. Customers' orders for product A in the South total 50. These data form the basis for the determination of the cost calculations in subsequent tables.

The profitability analysis by territory (shown in Table 4) reveals that both territories show a profit from operations. Table 5 shows the total company profitability by product line. The profitability statement by product line provides additional information for marketing managers. Product lines A and B are profitable, whereas product line C shows an operating loss of $16,000. This statement has revealed that although the overall company shows a profit and that both territories are profitable, one product line requires further analysis. Additional tables could be presented with data by product line for each territory separately to further isolate the operating loss of product C.

As you can see, "Charging costs direct eliminates the need to allocate or assign costs. Costs that cannot be charged directly should be assigned to the product through activitybased costing."[1]

This modern advice dovetails with my illustration, which demonstrates that the techniques recommended for marketing cost analysis at least 20 years ago are conceptually equal to those now being recommended for production costs by Robert Kaplan, William Ferrara, Michael Ostrenga, and others contributing to the deluge of activity-based costing literature.[2] The only differences are that only marketing costs were involved, the state of technology was less developed, and the accounting profession did not recognize the importance of marketing costs and the methods being recommended.

WE MUST EMPHASIZE MARKETING COSTS

The main theme of management accounting journal articles in recent years has been world-class competition emphasizing the gradual slipping of U.S. manufacturers, particularly in comparison with Japanese manufacturers. Production costs have been the center of attention, while marketing costs have been ignored. We must focus on marketing costs as an important component of the total cost of a product.

The use of activity-based costing techniques for marketing functions arose during the years 1968 through 1973 when marketing executives urged members of the accounting profession to develop a better system of identifying, classifying, and allocating physical

TABLE 1. ATLANTA COMPANY PRODUCT LINE DATA YEAR 19X1

Product Line	Product Line		
Information	**A**	**B**	**C**
Selling price	$10.00	$8.00	$12.00
Unit manufacturing cost	$ 8.00	$5.00	$11.00
Quantity of units sold and shipped	50,000	30,000	20,000
Average weight of units sold	2.0 lbs.	3.0 lbs.	4.0 lbs.
Number of customers' orders	100	200	200
Variable portion of manufacturing cost	60%	60%	60%

TABLE 2. ATLANTA COMPANY CALCULATION FOR PER UNIT COST RATES

TOTAL COSTS

Marketing Activity	Cost Driver	Total Volume	Cost of Marketing Activity Total	Unit Rate
Selling	Dollar value of sales	$980,000	$49,000	5.0%
Advertising	Quantity of units sold	100,000	$40,000	$.40
Warehousing	Weight of shipped	270,000 lb.	$27,000	$.10
Packing and shipping	Quantity of shipped	100,000	$20,000	$.20
General office	Number of customers' orders	500	$10,000	$20.00

VARIABLE AND FIXED COST RATES

Marketing Activity	Variable Cost	Unit Rate	Fixed Cost	Unit Rate
Selling	$29,400	3.0%	$19,600	$2.0%
Advertising	$10,000	$ .10	$30,000	$.30
Warehousing	$13,500	$ 05	$13,500	$.05
Packing and shipping	$12,000	$ .12	$ 8,000	$.08
General Office	$ 2,000	$4.00	$ 8,000	$16.00

TABLE 3. ATLANTA COMPANY SALES AND ORDERS BY TERRITORY (IN UNITS) YEAR 19XI

Transaction by Territory	Total	A	B	C
Products sold:				
West	60,000	26,000	20,000	14,000
South	40,000	24,000	10,000	6,000
Total	100,000	50,000	30,000	20,000
Customers' Orders:				
West	280	50	80	150
South	220	50	120	50
Total	500	100	200	200

TABLE 4. ATLANTA COMPANY PROFITABILITY STATEMENT BY TERRITORY (ALL PRODUCTS) YEAR 19X1

	Total Company	Territory West	Territory South	Allocation Basis
Sales revenue	$980,000	$588,000	$392,000	
Less cost of soles	770,000	462,000	$308,000	
Gross margin	$210,000	$126,000	$ 84,000	
Less Expenses				
Selling	$ 49,000	$ 29,400	$ 19,600	5% of sales
Advertising	40,000	24,000	16,600	$.40/unit sold
Warehousing	27,000	16,800	10,200	10/lb. shipped
Packing and shipping	20,000	12,000	8,000	$.20/unit sold
General office	10,000	5,600	4,400	$20/order
Total expense	$146,000	$ 87,800	$ 58,200	
Operating Income (Loss)	$ 64,000	$ 38,200	$ 25,800	

distribution costs. At that time, several articles (including one of mine[3]) isolated the activities in the major marketing functions. Cost drivers, a modern euphemism for activity bases, were identified for each activity within the marketing functions.

Techniques that resemble the recently discovered activity-based costing system and the total cost concept which is the forerunner of total cost management were discussed thoroughly and recommended for physical distribution costs at the request of the marketing managers of several hundred U.S. corporations. The accounting profession largely ignored the recommendations of the practitioners and overlooked the fact that physical distribution activities have cost characteristics similar to those of production activities. Now, 20 years later, accountants are attaching new names to these same techniques. Activity-based costing techniques have been and should continue to be applied to marketing costs to assist companies in management decision making.

TABLE 5. ATLANTA COMPANY: PROFITABILITY STATEMENT BY PRODUCT LINE (ALL TERRITORIES) YEAR 19X1

	Total Company	A	Product Line B	C	Allocation Basis
Sales revenue	$980,000	$500,000	$240,000	$240,000	
Cost of sales	770,000	400,000	150,000	220,000	
Gross margin	$210,000	$100,000	$90,000	$20,000	
Less: Expenses					
Selling	$ 49,000	$25,000	$12,000	$12,000	5% of sales
Advertising	40,000	20,000	12,000	8,000	$.40/unit sold
Warehousing	27,000	10,000	9,000	8,000	$.10/lb. shipped
Packing and shipping	20,000	10,000	6,000	4,000	$.20/unit sold
General office	10,000	2,000	4,000	4,000	$20/order
Total expense	$146,000	$67,000	$43,000	$36,000	
Operating income (Loss)	$ 64,000	$33,000	$47,000	$(16,000)	

ENDNOTES

1. Michael R. Ostrenga, "Activities: The Focal Point of Total Cost Management." MANAGEMENT ACCOUNTING®, February 1990, pp. 42–49.
2. Robert S. Kaplan, "The Four-Step Model of Coat Systems Design." MANAGEMENT ACCOUNTING® February 1990, pp. 22–26. Also, William L. Ferrara, "The New Cost/Management Accounting: More Questions than Answers," MANAGEMENT ACCOUNTING®, October 1990, pp. 48–52.
3. Ronald J. Lewis, "Strengthening Control of Physical Distribution Costs," *Management Services* (AICPA), January–February 1968. Also, J. L. Heskett, R. M. Ivie, and N. A. Glaskowsky, Jr., *Business Logistics Management of Physical Supply and Distribution,* The Ronald Press Company, New York, N. Y., 1964.

Ronald J. Lewis is Professor of accounting at Central Michigan University in Mt. Pleasant, Mich., and a member of the Saginaw Valley Chapter of the IMA, through which this article was submitted. He holds A.B. and A.M. degrees from Wayne State University and a Ph.D. degree from Michigan State University. Formerly he was the vice-president of academic affairs at Tri-State University, Angola, IN. He may be reached at (517) 774–3796.

QUESTION

5.3 In Lewis' article, what are the appropriate cost drivers for selling, advertising, warehousing, packing and shipping, and general office activities? Is there any flexibility in the choice of cost drivers for these categories? Explain.

5.4 Rethinking Activity-Based Costing

*by Robert S. Kaplan and Steven R. Anderson**

EXECUTIVE SUMMARY:

Editor's Note: Activity-based costing, ABC, would seem to be an accurate way for managers to assign costs to the customers and products that use a department's services. But real-world use has shown ABC loses power in large-scale operations, and can be difficult to implement and maintain. In their *Harvard Business Review* article, excerpted here, authors Kaplan and Anderson suggest the process be simplified through an approach they call "time-driven ABC." Here's an overview.

The solution to the problems with ABC is not to abandon the concept. ABC after all has helped many companies identify important cost- and profit-enhancement opportunities through the repricing of unprofitable customer relationships, process improvements on the shop floor, lower-cost product designs, and rationalized product variety. Its potential

---

on a larger scale represents a huge opportunity for companies. Fortunately, simplification is now possible through an approach that we call time-driven ABC, which we have successfully helped more than 100 client companies implement, including those described

estimates of only two parameters are required: the cost per time unit of supplying resource capacity and the unit times of consumption of resource capacity by products, services, and customers. At the same time, the new approach provides more accurate cost-driver rates by allowing unit times to be estimated even for complex, specialized transactions.

Estimating the cost per time unit of capacity. Instead of surveying employees on how they spend their time, managers first directly estimate the practical capacity of the resources supplied as a percentage of the theoretical capacity. There are various ways to do this. As a rule of thumb, you could simply assume that practical full capacity is 80 percent to 85 percent of theoretical full capacity. So if an employee or machine is available to work 40 hours per week, its practical full capacity is 32 to 35 hours per week. Typically, managers would allot a lower rate—say 80 percent—to people, allowing 20 percent of their time for breaks, arrival and departure, communication, and training. For machines, managers might allot a 15 percent differential between theoretical and practical capacity to allow for downtime due to maintenance, repair, and scheduling fluctuations. A more systematic approach, perhaps, is to review past activity levels and identify the month with the largest number of orders handled without excessive delays, poor quality, overtime, or stressed employees. Whichever approach you prefer, it's important not to be overly sensitive to small errors. The objective is to be approximately right, say within 5 percent to 10 percent of the actual number, rather than precise. If the estimate of practical capacity is grossly in error, the process of running the time-driven ABC system will reveal the error over time.

The capacity of most resources is measured in **terms of time availability.**

Returning to our example, let's assume that the customer service department employs 28 reps to do the frontline work and that each puts in eight hours per day. In theory, therefore, each worker supplies about 10,560 minutes per month or 31,680 minutes per quarter. The practical capacity at about 80 percent of theoretical is therefore about 25,000 minutes per quarter per employee, or 700,000 minutes in total. Since we already know the cost of supplying capacity—the $560,000 in overhead costs—we can now calculate the cost per minute of supplying capacity ($0.80).

The capacity of most resources is measured in terms of time availability, but the new ABC approach can also recognize resources whose capacity is

in this article. In the revised approach, managers directly estimate the resource demands imposed by each transaction, product, or customer rather than assign resource costs first to activities and then to products or customers. For each group of resources, measured in other units. For example, the capacity of a warehouse or vehicle would be measured by space provided, while memory storage would be measured by megabytes supplied. In these situations, the manager would calculate the resource cost per unit based on the appropriate capacity measure, such as cost per cubic meter or cost per megabyte.

Estimating the unit times of activities. Having calculated the cost per time unit of supplying resources to the business's activities, managers next determine the time it takes to carry out one unit of each kind of activity. These numbers can be obtained through interviews with employees or by direct observation. There is no need to conduct surveys, although in large organizations, surveying employees may help. It is important to stress, though, that the question is not about the percentage of time an employee spends doing an activity (say, processing orders) but how long it takes to complete one unit of that activity (the time required to process one order). Once again, precision is not critical; rough accuracy is sufficient. In the case of our example, let's suppose that managers determine that it takes 8 minutes to process an order, 44 minutes to handle an inquiry, and 50 minutes to perform a credit check.

Deriving cost-driver rates. The cost-driver rates can now be calculated by multiplying the two input variables we have just estimated. For our customer service department, we obtain cost-driver rates of $6.40 (8 multiplied by $0.80) for processing customer orders, $35.20 (44 by $0.80) for handling inquiries, and $40 (50 by $0.80) for performing credit checks. Once you have calculated these standard rates, you can apply them in real time to assign costs to individual customers as transactions occur. The standard cost rates can also be used in discussions with customers about the pricing of new business.

Note that these rates are lower than those estimated using traditional ABC methods (see the exhibit "Doing ABC the Traditional Way").

DOING ABC THE TRADITIONAL WAY

This table provides a traditional ABC analysis for a customer service department for its first fiscal quarter. The percentage of time spent on activities is determined from employee surveys. Once activity quantities are known or forecast, cost-driver rates are used to allocate the department's costs on customers' utilization of the department's activities.

ACTIVITY	% OF TIME SPENT	ASSIGNED COST	ACTIVITY QUANTITY	COST-DRIVER RATE
Process customers orders	70%	$392,000	49,000	$8 per order
Handle customer inquiries	10%	$56,000	1,400	$40 per quantity
Perform credit checks	20%	$112,000	2,500	$44.80 per credit check
Total	**100%**	**$560,000**		

The reason for this difference becomes obvious when we recalculate the quarterly cost of performing the customer service activities. In the exhibit "The Impact of Practical Capacity," time-driven ABC analysis reveals that only 83 percent of the practical capacity (578,600 of the 700,000 minutes) of the resources supplied during the quarter has been used for productive work, and hence, only about 83 percent of the total expenses of $560,000 were assigned to customers or products during this period. This takes care of the technical drawback of traditional ABC systems we mentioned earlier—the fact that surveyed employees respond as if their practical capacity were always fully utilized.

THE IMPACT OF PRACTICAL CAPACITY

This table shows the effect on cost assignment when we use rates based on practical capacity (700,000) minutes, assumed here at 80 percent of theoretical full capacity. We can see that only about 83 percent of the customer service department's practical capacity was actually put to productive use during the first fiscal quarter.

ACTIVITY	UNIT TIME (minutes)	QUAN-TITY	TOTAL MINUTES	TOTAL COST
Process customers orders	8	49,000	392,000	$313,600
Handle customer inquiries	44	1,400	61,600	$49,280
Perform credit checks	50	2,500	125,000	$100,000
Total			**578,600**	**$462,880**

In the case of our customer service department, the traditional ABC survey produced a work distribution of 70 percent, 10 percent, and 20 percent of the employees' time performing the department's three activities. But while that distribution did reflect how workers spent their productive time, the fact that their total productive time was significantly less than their practical capacity of 32 hours per worker per week was completely ignored. The calculation of resource costs per time unit forces the company to incorporate estimates of the practical capacities of its resources, allowing the ABC cost drivers to provide more accurate signals about the cost and the underlying efficiency of its processes.

Analyzing and reporting costs. Time-driven ABC enables managers to report their costs on an ongoing basis in a way that reveals both the costs of a business's activities as well as the time spent on them. In our customer service department example, a time-driven ABC report would look like the exhibit "ABC, the Time-Driven Way."

ABC, THE TIME-DRIVEN WAY

This reporting template for time-driven ABC shows the customer service department's costs in the second quarter of operations. Here we assume that the department processes 51,000 customer orders, handles 1,150 inquiries, and performs 2,700 credit checks. The data reveal that the company supplied $85,120 worth of unused resource capacity during this period, representing opportunities for savings or growth depending on the company's circumstances.

Note that the report highlights the difference between capacity supplied (both quantity and cost) and the capacity used. Managers can review the cost of the unused capacity and contemplate actions to determine whether and how to reduce the costs of supplying unused resources in subsequent periods; they can then monitor those actions over time. In some cases, the information can save companies that are considering expansion from making unnecessary new investments in capacity. For example, the vice president of operations at Lewis-Goetz, a hose and belt fabricator based in Pittsburgh, saw from his time-driven ABC model that one of his plants was operating at only 27 percent of capacity. Rather than attempt to downsize the plant, he decided to maintain the capacity for a large contract he expected to win later that year, for which he otherwise would have created new capacity.

ACTIVITY	QUANTITY	UNIT TIME	TOTAL TIME USED (in minutes)	COST-DRIVER RATE	COST ASSIGNED
Process customers orders	51,000	8	408,000	$6.40	$326,400
Handle customer inquiries	1,150	44	50,600	$35.20	$40,480
Perform credit checks	2,700	50	135,000	$40.00	$108,000
Total Used			**593,600**		$474,880
Total Supplied			**700,000**		$560,000
Unused Capacity			**106,400**		$85,120

Updating the model. Managers can easily update their time-driven ABC models to reflect changes in operating conditions. To add more activities for a department, they don't have to reinterview personnel; they can simply estimate the unit time required for each new activity.

Managers can also easily update the cost-driver rates. Two factors can cause these rates to change. First, changes in the prices of resources supplied affect the cost per time unit of supplying capacity. For example, if employees receive an 8 percent compensation increase, the resource cost rate in our example increases from $0.80 per supplied minute to $0.864 per minute. If new machines are substituted or added to a process, the resource cost rate is modified to reflect the change in operating expense associated with introducing the new equipment.

The second factor that can cause a change in the activity cost-driver rate is a shift in the efficiency of the activity. Quality programs, continuous improvement efforts, reengineering, or the introduction of new technology can enable the same activity to be done in less time or with fewer resources. When permanent, sustainable improvements in a process have been made, the ABC analyst recalculates the unit time estimates (and therefore the demands on resources) to reflect the process improvements. For example, if the customer service department gets a new database system, the reps may be able to perform a standard credit check in 20 minutes rather than 50 minutes. To accommodate the improvement, just change the unit time estimate to 20 minutes, and the new cost-driver rate automatically becomes $16 per credit check (down from $40). Of course, you then have to add back in the cost impact of purchasing the new database system by updating the cost per time unit estimate, so the final figure may be somewhat higher than $16.

By updating the ABC model on the basis of events rather than on the calendar (once a quarter or annually), you get a much more accurate reflection of current conditions. Any time analysts learn about a significant shift in the costs of resources supplied or the practical capacity of those resources, or about a change in the resources required to perform the activity, they update the resource cost per time unit, or resource cost rate, estimates. And any time they learn of a significant and permanent shift in the efficiency with which an activity is performed, they update the unit time estimate.

QUESTION

5.4 How does time-driven activity based costing differ from traditional activity-based costing?

Chapter 6

Measuring and Managing Customer Relationships

Reading 6.1 is Kenneth Manning's article, *Distribution Channel Profitability*. Many companies still do not scrutinize their sales, general, and administrative costs (SG&A) to the same extent that they do their manufacturing costs. Without such detailed scrutiny, revenue and cost trade-offs related to the various distribution channels through which companies deliver products cannot be made. This article discusses three approaches to distribution channel profitability—a standard approach, an ABC approach, and a strategic cost management approach. Manning develops a four-step process to developing accurate channel and customer costs, which is applied to two companies facing different competitive issues.

In Reading 6.2, *A Strategic Approach to Building Online Customer Loyalty: Integrating Customer Profitability Tiers*, Dennis Pitta, Frank Franzak, and Danielle Fowler, develop a framework for managing online customer loyalty. They exploit the concept of customer value tiers and show how managers can use their scarce service resources by serving profitable customers.

V. Kuman and Bharath Rajan discuss how to better manage customer relationships. In Reading 6.3, *Nurturing the Right Customers*, the authors state that loyal customers aren't necessarily profitable and that the relationship between loyalty and profitability is a complex one. They develop a metric that they call Customer Lifetime Value (CLV) that allows companies to make consistent decisions about which customers to retain.

Reading 6.4 is R. Kaplan and V. Narayanan's article, *Measuring and Managing Customer Profitability*. The authors provide a very insightful table (Exhibit 2) that can be used to identify high versus low cost-to-serve customers. Another key contribution of the article is the portrayal of the whale curve of cumulative profitability. This diagram describes the overall contribution of the most profitable and least profitable customers to cumulative profitability. Using the whale curve, managers can begin the process of turning unprofitable customers into profitable ones by focusing on three areas: process improvements, pricing decisions, and relationship management. The authors close the article with a discussion of barriers to implementation success.

Readings
Chapter 6

6.1 Distribution Channel Profitability
ABC concepts can help companies make strategic decisions

by Kenneth H. Manning*

Which of your distribution channels is most profitable? If you analyze them using an approach built on activitybased costing (ABC) concepts, you may find an unexpected answer.

Distribution costs are a fact of life for almost every manufacturer, distributor, and supplier. As major retailers, wholesalers, distributors, and manufacturers reconfigure their supply chains, all participants in the supply chain need to understand the revenue and cost tradeoffs associated with the various channels through which they deliver products and services.

To evaluate strategic issues within the distribution system, formulate potential responses to those issues, and estimate the impact of improvements on the overall business, you need reliable and accurate information. One approach to gaining the necessary data is constructed around activity-based costing (ABC) concepts that many companies have adopted over the last several years.[1] ABC provides a more accurate view of a company's cost structure than a standard cost approach, particularly for companies that produce a broad range of products and volumes. The benefits of ABC have been discussed in great detail in other publications and will not be presented here.[2] Building on these ABC concepts, the methodology presented here allows practitioners to determine the relative profitability of their distribution channels and customer groups. The methodology assumes that the practitioners have at least a conceptual view of an ABC approach, although a working knowledge of ABC techniques is highly recommended.

COMPARISON OF THREE APPROACHES
The typical approach to developing knowledge of channel profitability, using standard product costing, is shown in Figure 1. This approach creates two cost pools:

product costs and sales, general, and administrative (SG&A) costs. The product costs are transferred to the channels based on standard unit costs and the product mix sold through that channel. The SG&A expenses typically are allocated to the channels based on net revenue or sales volume by channel.

If the organization is aligned by channel or customer group, this approach may yield accurate profitability figures. But most often, companies are aligned by region, product line, or facility location, which makes the translation to channel or customer difficult using conventional approaches.

This approach may help answer some questions related to distribution costs, but there are numerous issues that it cannot address. In addition, it has all the drawbacks associated with traditional standard product costing, which have been shown to distort costs in many situations. Because this approach makes no attempt to adjust product costs, the analysis related to product costs can be misleading.

A more refined approach to channel profitability is to use an ABC methodology. Figure 2 illustrates the more accurate ABC approach to this problem. The ABC approach has one large advantage over the conventional approach: It costs products more accurately. Overhead costs are allocated to product lines in a more logically related fashion than under the conventional approach. The result is improved accuracy over the typical standard costing approach.

The drawback to this approach is that while we are allocating cost in a much more logical and rigorous manner, the analysis is based on one major assumption that is probably not true: that all costs are product-driven costs and therefore must be traced or allocated to products. For most companies, organizational costs are driven by more than just the products they produce.

---

* From K.H. Manning, "Distribution Channel Profitability," *Management Accounting* (January 1995): 44–48.
Reprinted with permission conveyed through Copyright Clearance Center, Inc.

FIGURE 1. STANDARD APPROACH TO CHANNEL PROFITABILITY

FIGURE 2. ABC APPROACH TO CHANNEL PROFITABILITY

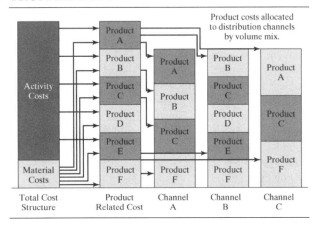

The strategic cost management approach outlined below recognizes that cost is not driven solely by the products produced but also by the customers served and the channels through which the product is offered. Removing the restriction that all costs must be related to products allows the development of a more accurate view of cost consumption. Under the traditional ABC methodology, it was not possible to detect if product costs were high due to certain customer groups or to certain channels. However, this approach gives us additional insight into the reasons for the product line cost position by creating three different types of costs: product-related costs, channel-related costs, and customer-related costs. Examining the cost structure from this perspective allows management to understand cost differences related to any one of these categories or related to interactions between these categories. (See Figure 3.)

FIGURE 3. SCM APPROACH TO CHANNEL PROFITABILITY

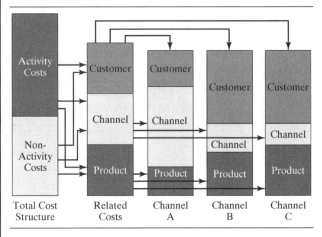

DEVELOPING ACCURATE CHANNEL AND CUSTOMER COSTS

The approach used to develop this view of costs relies on several guidelines:

■ Include all costs (direct, indirect, overhead, implicit).
■ Focus on relevance over precision.
■ Use issues to drive analysis.

The methodology follows a four-step process, which is outlined below.

1. *Separate the organization's cost structure into activity costs and nonactivity costs.* The cost structure of the organization should be translated into activity and nonactivity components that reflect the operations of the enterprise. The number and detail of these components should be determined by the issues the study is addressing. Table 1 lists several activity and nonactivity components one would expect to see in a manufacturing company. Through the use of traditional ABC concepts, the cost associated with each of these components should be estimated. The sum of these component costs should equal the organization's total cost structure.

2. *Identify the cost behavior of all activity and nonactivity costs.* The activity and nonactivity components are organized into three categories of cost behavior: product-related, customer-related, and channel-related (see Table 1). Each cost component should be related to only one category. If a cost component cannot be related to just one category, either further decompose the activity or nonactivity definition, or, if it is judged immaterial, assign the component to the primary behavior category.

3. *Trace these costs to the individual products, channels, and customers.* Once the different cost components are classified as product-related, channel-related, or customer-related, it is necessary to identify the tracing factor that relates those costs back to the appropriate products, channels, or customers. *Tracing factors are quantifiable, repeatable measures that closely approximate the level of effort associated with an activity.* They are used to trace the activity cost to the individual component groups, e.g., product line A, product line B, channel A, and so on.

For example, the activity cost of "non-EDI order processing" was determined to be $432,500 for the one-year period. The number of order lines filled was identified as the tracing factor, as shown in Table 2.

This same procedure is performed for all cost components to develop a total cost view for the three types of cost categories. Nonactivity costs are treated in a similar manner, except direct cost linkages are easier to find for these items. In most cases it will be possible to allocate those costs directly to the product, customer, or channel that created them.

TABLE 1. COST BEHAVIOR OF ACTIVITY COSTS AND NONACTIVITY COSTS

	Product Related	Channel Related	Customer Related
Activity Costs	■ Schedule Production	■ Attend Trade Shows	■ EDI and Computer Interfaces to Customer
	■ Setup and Changeover for Machine A	■ Order/invoice Processing	■ Special Shipping and Handling Requests
	■ Test Quality Parameters	■ Sales Force	■ Collect Bad Debt
	■ Maintain Equipment	■ Telemarketing	■ Technical Support for Customer A
		■ Advertising Brand A	■ Prepare/Deliver Annual Sales Bid
		■ Arrange for Shipping	
Nonactivity Costs	■ Material Costs	■ Trade Discounts	■ Bad Debt Expense
	■ Royalties	■ Freight	■ Customer Rebates

TABLE 2. ACTIVITY COST OF NON-EDI ORDER PROCESSING

	Activity: Non-EDI Order Processing	Tracing Factor: Number of Order Lines
Channel A	$78,140	$123,045
Channel B	208,358	328,095
Channel C	146,002	229,903
Total	$432,500	$681,043

4. *Translate the product, channel, and customer cost elements into a total cost view for the business.* The final step requires that two matrices be constructed for the purpose of linking these three views. The first matrix links the product and customer view by capturing the customer purchases by product. The second matrix links the customer and channel view by capturing the customer purchases by distribution channel. These two matrices then are used to translate the costs driven by each channel into a total cost view for product, customer, or channel.

Following this methodology will provide any necessary cost view of the organization. Obviously, it is also necessary to capture revenue information for the same products, channels, and customers for which costs were calculated.

PRODUCT VIEW VS. CHANNEL/CUSTOMER VIEW

The traditional ABC approach is probably most consistent with the way corporate planners think about business strategy and planning: by product area. The majority of businesses are formed around product lines and product groups, a fact that obviously influences the way we think about them. But alternative views certainly are becoming more important as products are served through increasingly varied channels—distributors, catalogs, mega-stores, direct mail, and so on. As companies develop future business plans, understanding the cost and profitability of serving different channel and customer groups will become critical to making good business decisions.

In essence, we have recast the entire company's costs and created a database of costing information around several new views: activity, nonactivity, product, channel, and customer. Attempting to perform these manipulations without the assistance of a powerful PC would be impossible, but with the introduction of the PC and numerous software applications, it is now relatively easy. The data are organized in a way that encourages analysis of number of different issues.

The best results have been obtained when this methodology was used in an issues-driven approach—the type and nature of the decision being made should drive the level of detail and direction of the analysis. The effort to arrive at good, accurate channel and customer costs is worth making only if you need to address business issues. The key issues should be identified, documented, and articulated in advance of any analysis. For instance, the sections below describe how two companies facing different competitive issues could use the approach to develop their strategic responses.

FOCUSED COMPETITOR ENTERING MARKET

A specialty chemical manufacturer supplied products to a broad range of customers in the food, consumer products, and manufacturing industries. The products were made primarily in-house although some were purchased and repackaged and then sold through a network of representatives, a direct sales force, and a telemarketing customer service center. Customers could opt for several delivery and pricing options including customer pick-up, bulk delivery, or less-than-truckload (LTL) delivery.

It recently had become known that a new competitor was planning to enter a key segment of the company's market. The management team knew that the impact would be negative but did not know to what extent. The vice president of sales & marketing particularly was concerned. He believed that the targeting segment provided a significant portion of the division's profit although the financial report indicated that it was not very profitable due to above average discounts. The head of sales and marketing decided to sponsor a study to understand the "true" profitability of the various delivery options and customer groups (or market segments).

The study team uncovered several significant findings:

- The large customers did provide a disproportionate percentage of the division's profits, despite their much lower gross margin, due primarily to less customer service, lower bad credit expenses, and reduced handling charges on large orders.
- Cost differentials within the large customer grouping depended on the use of the product. Customers in the food industry consumed more technical marketing, demanded more research support, and required a finer grade product, which slowed process run rates.
- The "true" cost difference among the different delivery options was surprising. The conventional cost approach assumed that the only difference between these options was the freight costs. The study revealed that the customer pick-up option after adjustment for freight charges actually cost less than the other delivery options due to much lower

damage claim losses and reduced freight scheduling costs.

- The gross sales generated by small customers did not cover even the cost of selling and servicing these accounts. It turned out that smaller customers often had limited resources with which to solve technical problems and relied on the company's assistance in this area. Because there was no rationing mechanism or internal R&D tracking system, these costs went undetected for the most part.
- Several of the large-volume outsourced products did not provide sufficient margin to cover their full distribution costs. While they appeared profitable under the standard cost and profit reporting system, the study indicated they were unprofitable once the inbound logistics cost and purchasing cost were taken into account.

Given this information, the head of sales & marketing worked with the vice presidents of operations, R&D, and finance to develop the following set of responses:

1. Technical resources were shifted away from smaller customers and assigned to work exclusively on the large consumer product and manufacturing accounts. The sales force then attempted to discover customer problems that could be solved by making these valuable resources available to the customers. The R&D department also created a simple time reporting system to track these "soft" costs better.
2. The customer pick-up delivery price was lowered to attract more volume through this channel. This move was intended to attract the largest-volume users of the product—consumer product and manufacturing. It also had the advantage of encouraging the competitor to take away our lowest-margin business, food processors, because these companies did not use sufficient volume to take advantage of the new price discounts.
3. The company began to look actively for other suppliers for the products they outsourced so as to improve the profitability of this operation. In addition, they decided to redesign the vendor relations group and reengineer the purchasing process with the goal of reducing the overall handling cost by 50% for purchased goods.

Using the cost and revenue information in the model management was able to estimate the impact of these changes on the overall results under several different scenarios. While the impact of the new competitor definitely would be negative, the overall effect would be mitigated substantially by these responses.

SALES FORCE RESTRUCTURING

An industrial equipment supplier had one of the oldest and most capable sales forces of all the suppliers in its field. As a result, several competitors recently had started to shift their focus to other distribution channels. While competitors moved away from dedicated sales forces, the management team chose not to pursue these alternative methods because they still considered the in-house sales force a source of real advantage in the marketplace. Due to several periods of unsatisfactory results and the continued growth of alternative distribution and sales channels, however, the company's management decided to undertake a distribution profitability study focused on understanding the strategic value of the sales force.

The primary issues management wanted to address was sales force effectiveness, so the analysis was structured to focus on this aspect of the cost structure. The detailed log of sales-force activity was tracked to customers or channels, depending on the activity. By creating a very detailed cost picture of the various channels, the company could see the relative profitability of the various channel configurations and the source of cost differentials. By building this detail, management was able to see the sales force costs consumed by different customer and product groups.

With this cost baseline, management estimated the impact of several changes to the structure. In addition, the cost differential between the company and its competitors was estimated from knowledge of how its competitors' activities and sales volumes differed across their sales forces. Combining these cost and profitability views with an understanding of the customer buying factors provided insight into several issues.

A FRAMEWORK FOR DISTRIBUTION ISSUES

After performing the analysis, management became aware of several points that had not been clear before:

- Some high-margin product lines that were thought to be profitable were, in fact, unprofitable due to the channel-related costs.
- Sales volume did not correlate with restated customer profitability.
- The cost of selling product differed dramatically depending on the customer application.
- One product line that was low margin and thought to be a loss leader was, in fact, relatively profitable.

Based on these findings, management formulated several changes in response to this new information:

- The loss leader was priced lower to attract additional volume from existing customers.
- Another product line was dropped because the primary customer base for it was extremely unlikely to buy any of the other products, and the revenue from these single-product customers would never justify the cost to serve them through a sales force.
- In addition, several representatives were taken on to serve those customers who were small- to medium-volume purchasers and did not require technical expertise from the sales force. These reps were offered a margin that encouraged them to deal exclusively with this company. The cost savings from shifting the sales force more than compensated for the margin passed on to the distributors.

The sales force then was refocused on those customers who valued their technical expertise and would be likely to buy additional product lines from this supplier in the future.

By assessing the cost and profit differentials among customers and channels, this company was able to shift its sales resources to those opportunities that provided better long-term growth and profitability.

The analysis described above forms the basis for multiple types of decisions including: pricing levels, warehouse investments, cost reduction targets, make/buy decisions, new channel options, channel rationalization, and selection of target markets and key customers.

This approach is not presented as the complete solution to the distribution issues of the 1990s, but it is a very important analytical framework that should accompany most distribution strategy developments. It forms the basis for developing a solid quantitative understanding of the current distribution and customer situation. The findings and models developed in this phase can be used to evaluate current performance, estimate future impacts, and track improvements from new distribution strategies.

ENDNOTES

1. Robin Cooper and Robert S. Kaplan, "Measure Cost Right Make the Right Decision," *Harvard Business Review*, September/October 1988, pp. 96–103.
2. Philip Rhodes, "Activity-Based Costing: What Will It Do for You," *APICS*, August 1992, pp. 29–31.

Kenneth H. Manning is with Deloitte & Touche in Atlanta, Ga. He can be reached at (404) 220–1147.

QUESTIONS

6.1a Discuss the four-step process that Manning uses for developing accurate channel and customer costs.

6.1b In developing the four-step process, Manning discusses both activity and nonactivity costs. What are two examples of two nonactivity customer-related costs? Why are these labeled as "nonactivity costs?"

6.2 A Strategic Approach to Building Online Customer Loyalty: Integrating Customer Profitability Tiers

by Dennis Pitta, Frank Franzak, and Danielle Fowler*

ABSTRACT

Purpose—The purpose of this paper is to present a strategic framework to managing online loyalty.
Design/methodology/approach—The paper integrates concepts including a range of recently published (1993–2006) theoretical works in consumer loyalty and ongoing case developments in internet practice.
Findings—Provides information and action approaches to consumer marketers that may increase the success providing want satisfying market offerings. Outlines the costs and benefits of some online customer loyalty building practices. By integrating the literature supporting lifetime customer value with the literature concerned with generating online customer relationships, it provides a pathway to profitable relationships. It also exposes the unintended problems that some online customer loyalty initiatives may create.
Research limitations/implications—The theoretical concepts that form the foundation of the paper appear to have a significant application to consumer marketing but have not been tested empirically.
Practical implications—Uncovers a previously unreported strategy for generating profitable online customer loyalty.
Originality/value—This paper describes the nature and application of customer value tiers to an important marketing process. It offers the potential of increasing marketing success by allowing firms to maximize the value of their scarce service resources by serving profitable customers.
Keywords—Customer loyalty, Customer relations, Internet shopping, Profit maximization, Electronic commerce
Paper type—Conceptual paper

INTRODUCTION

During the 1980s customer loyalty was on most marketers' minds. Numerous companies spent millions on customer relationship management programs with the goal of building customer loyalty. It is ironic that the concept of customer loyalty is not something that consumers recognize. For most companies the customer or brand loyalty issue is, in behavioral terms, nothing more than repeat purchasing. In fact, many company efforts aim solely at increasing the percentage of repeat purchases among current customers. Supporting this effort, marketing strategists have developed predictive models that show the important profitability effects of increasing the repeat purchase rate among existing customers.

The problem may lay in the current nature of customer relationship management initiatives. The 1-to-1 Marketing concept (Pepper and Rogers, 1993) generated a groundswell of interest in getting closer to the customer. The concept is grounded on information technology as a way to capture relevant consumer preferences so that repeat customers might enjoy easier future transactions (Pitta, 1998). The authors note that in a typical service encounter, such as checking into a hotel, numerous questions need to be answered. Thus, guests are conducted through the series of choices that supposedly reveal their true preferences. The genius of the concept is that capturing each of these decisions using appropriate hardware and software identifies the customer and a specific set of preferences. It is assumed that the preferences are somewhat persistent and once they are revealed they tend to remain largely unchanged. In principle, the customer is relieved of the burden of repeating the list of answers each time he or she stays at a hotel in the same chain. Since larger firms with numerous locations realized that each of their units could access the information in their central customer databases, the firms invested heavily in the technology. Thus, technology was a complement, and sometimes a substitute for a personal interaction. The situation is analogous to police forces removing "cops on the beat," police officers who walk through their assigned area and get to know the neighborhood, the law abiding people, and threats to their safety. When police departments put officers in automobiles, they lost the intimacy with their neighborhoods and the people they swore to protect and became less effective at recognizing symptoms of crime before crimes occurred. For marketers, losing touch with their customers signals the loss of proactive marketing.

Despite the good intentions of trying to regain lost familiarity, there are a few defects in the system. First, the technology did not always perform flawlessly. Some systems failed to reach the "once and for all" standard. The result required customers to

---

answer that initial list of questions, each time they arrived at a destination, even if they stayed at the chain or the specific hotel before. Even the most unaware consumer would be bored and probably irritated by the repetition. Some have complained about the number of a company's customer service personnel who have asked the same questions over and over.

With many companies embarking on programs to get to know their customers, a second flaw emerged. While companies continued to collect customer data, there was an expectation that the exercise was more of a discrete act than a process. Just because someone ordered a smoking room and a Coke did not guarantee that those selections would not change over time. Humans develop during their lifetimes and change their behavior based on numerous factors. To be really effective, such programs require continuous refreshing of customer preferences. They also should be based on a clear understanding of the elements that comprise customer loyalty.

Perhaps the most important focus should be the "right" customer. Organizations must not only boost repeat purchases and customer satisfaction, they need to discriminate among their customer base. There is a recent awareness that customers are not only different in terms of their needs but deliver different amounts of profitability over their lifetimes. When firms fail to focus on customers who will increase profit and reduce costs, they run the risk of working hard with little to show for the effort. Any attempts at building customer loyalty must be based on a foundation of customer profitability.

THE CORE OF CUSTOMER LOYALTY

Consumer loyalty seems to be based on a collection of factors. The first is trust. Consumers must trust the vendor or product they encounter. Second, the transaction or relationship must have a positive perceived value greater than that supplied by competitors. Third, if marketers build on the first two factors, they may be able to create a level of positive customer emotional attachment. That emotional response may be commitment to their brands that is resistant to change. Each of the factors requires some discussion.

Trust

Much of the customer loyalty literature has attempted to define what the concept entailed. Numerous researchers have focused on the elements that support and grow loyalty. As a result there is a list of concepts that have been studied in isolation and in combination with others. Trust, has been emphasized as a determinant of customer loyalty (Schlosser et al., 2006; Smith, 2002; Reichheld et al.,

2000a) throughout the literature. Trust is vital in situations in which informational cues are incomplete. In a world of perfect knowledge, trust is unnecessary. In the real world, it helps reduce perceived risk by lessening the likelihood that a customer will suffer a loss. Essentially, trust bolsters the customer's belief in the likelihood of a positive outcome. The effect may be expressed in terms of a feeling that the vendor will "make things right." In some relationships the initial transaction is based on no previous history and, absent positive word of mouth, is essentially based on faith. After one successful interaction, a consumer will have evidence that the vendor delivers as promised, or not. That evidence supplants faith as a basis for interaction. Early in a relationship, elements such as company or brand name assume increasing importance. They serve as surrogate indicators of probable performance. Thus, international brands such as Toyota have brand equity that bolsters consumers' perception of trust (Ward and Lee, 2000). In fact, in a new relationship, brand or company names and perceptions take on the burden of trust creation. In the online world, trust is still a major concern among online consumers. The prospect of divulging credit card information to an online "stranger" is an e-commerce obstacle to some consumers who in reality could shop securely (Dunn, 2004).

It is known that trust is a living element in a relationship and can grow in strength by successful interactions or be diminished to the point of extinction by a failure to deliver. In extreme cases, when trust is damaged, so is the transactional relationship.

Schlosser et al. (2006) explored three underlying components of trust: the vendor's ability to deliver, benevolence and integrity. Ability, benevolence, and integrity beliefs are acknowledged as conceptually distinct measures of trusting beliefs. Schlosser and her coauthors investigated the effect of web site design investments on consumers' trusting beliefs and online purchase intentions. They found that such investments signal the component of trusting beliefs most strongly related to online purchase intentions: ability. They also found that the effects were strongest when consumers sought to search for products rather than to browse and when purchases involved risk.

There are specific activities that combine to bolster trust. They include overtly ethical activities that can be recognized by customers. Integrity and performance are other key elements. Overall, energetic attempts to provide customers with appropriate levels of information about products and services, privacy, prices, security as well as the company's policies, practices and procedures will increase consumer trust levels (Smith, 2002; Reichheld et al., 2000a). There are ways of operating a business that can be called traditional customer retention practices. They are the bedrock of customer loyalty and include transaction security, trustworthiness, on-time delivery, reasonable prices, product and service performance, as well as follow-up service and support. These elements comprise a set of "trust generating activities." Without these in place and operating, trust building is not possible.

The literature notes that trust is perhaps the one element that must be established early and nurtured throughout the lifetime of the customer relationship. The literature also notes that the economics of an individual transaction are insufficient to insure firm profitability. Customers must buy multiple times for a relationship to be profitable. The lifetime approach takes this economic view into account. The focus on lifetime relationship should not be minimized. Many businesses spend inordinate amounts of time and money trying to attract new customers in contrast to retaining existing customers. For all companies that make serious efforts to attract first time customers, only 40 percent devote equal effort in designing customer retention and repeat purchase strategies. In addition, some companies try to maximize individual marketing transactions, ignoring the value of establishing and exploiting relationships with customers. The emphasis seems to be misdirected. Marketers know the economic benefits of customer retention and efforts to boost repeat purchase. There are numerous reports of the positive benefits of increasing customer retention rates on profits. For example, Reichheld et al. (2000a) found that a 5 percent increase in customer retention rates could produce a 25 to 95 percent increase in profits for many companies. That multiplier effect merits attention and action.

Consequently, Zeithaml et al. (2001) emphasize the lifetime customer value (LCV) concept as a means of increasing profitability and success. They suggest that companies should evaluate each customer on his or her LCV and court those with high scores and ignore those with low scores. There are techniques that can be used to accomplish these goals.

Net perceived value

The relevant research offers a selection of other factors that affect loyalty. Next after trust in developing loyalty is the consumer's perceived sense of value resulting from a transaction or relationship. Perceived value has been defined as a customer's overall evaluation of the benefits versus the costs involved in a marketing context. Specifically, perceived value can be viewed as a broad construct focusing on prices, costs incurred and benefits delivered by a marketer versus competitors. The literature notes that customer satisfaction may be based on a foundation of perceived value but the constructs are different. Different consumers view value in different ways. However, most consider costs and benefits. Looking at benefits and costs helps consider the variety of elements involved in a marketing transaction.

Value

For some customers, just finding a product is valuable. For example, in the specialty gift market, finding that one gift that perfectly matches a recipient may be a triumph. For others, finance terms or ability to use credit cards is an expected level of service and valued. Other marketing activities such as home delivery of new products and disposal of old ones can determine whether a purchase takes place. Similarly, setup and service may be critical in product categories with a high technological component such as computer or high definition television.

Some but not all customers recognize value in the convenience of their transactions. For some customers, time is a critical element. Thus, mechanisms that reduce the time to search for information about products and vendors, to evaluate that information and make a purchase decision, to speed payment and delivery, and reduce the effort in customer service and satisfaction might be valued. This customer segment may be more sophisticated in its understanding of marketing and its set of preferences and can be targeted for further carefully crafted offers. Specifically, bundling a product of acceptable quality with a set of services aimed at increasing convenience and reducing consumer worry or effort may yield profitable results.

Costs

The basic value computation would seem to look at benefits versus costs.

They include monetary costs, the well known price of products and services. Costs also include the amount of time, effort, worry, and uncertainty that are involved with a transaction. The idea of "cutting out the middleman" describes a consumer assuming some of the duties of a channel member to get a lower price. For example, pre-paying for an automobile before it is delivered assumes the financial role of a middleman. Similarly, buying in quantity is a middleman practice that should result in lower prices. The practice does not really lower costs, but shifts them to a different set of non-monetary costs. The shifted costs may be considerable and unattractive to particular buyers but is a choice.

The basic conceptualizations not only have elements that pertain to the value a consumer realizes from an interaction but have elements of personal emotional factors as well. Perceived value and emotional factors interact with each other. For example, a consumer who interacts with a retailer can evaluate the outcome using logic. If the interaction is "valuable" in economic or needs satisfaction terms, the consumer may develop a positive emotional response toward the retailer.

The emotional elements

If a marketer has established trust with particular customers by conducting business focusing on trust generating activities, the stage is set for a deeper relationship. The role of commitment has received special attention (Amine, 1998; Reichheld et al., 2000b). While brand loyalty can be assessed by observing consistent purchases of a brand over a period of time, it is really more than a set of repetitive discrete transactions between consumers and brands. It is not only repeat purchase behavior but also a set of motives that underlie that behavior. Those motives can help to distinguish between spurious loyalty which can be described as inertia and true loyalty which signifies a commitment to the brand or company. This differentiation helps to understand whether a given consumer's repeat purchased will continue (true loyalty) or may stop when a change in the store assortment or the selling conditions occurs (inertia).

Inertia may be rather durable since it is formed based on habits or routines that enable consumers to cope effectively with time pressures and search efforts. Inertia repeat purchasing of a brand appears has been described as habitual behavior to reduce two types of work. The first is mental and involves comparing product or company attributes. The second is physical and focuses on information search activities like visiting stores or searching the internet. Without the bond of commitment, marketers run the risk that apparent consumer loyalty may evaporate when there is a change in the habitual supply conditions, encouraging brand switching. How may true customer loyalty develop? One mechanism involves customers making repeat purchases from a vendor with or without any commitment. Over time, if the vendor takes measures to boost trust, perceived value, and emotional connections, then commitment may follow. Other emotional bonds may assume equal importance.

Recent work on the emotional bonds between customers and brands highlighted a construct that describes the levels of customer engagement. The idea emerged from research done by the Gallup organization. Gallup developed a set of rating scales that measure four critically important emotional states. Gallup's research was done professionally and yields efficient and reliable measures. While its strength will vary, emotion is inherent in most consumer decisions. Together, these states represent the strength of the emotional connection existing between a customer and a brand or a company. The measures are labeled: confidence, integrity, pride, and passion. Specifically, confidence is confidence in the brand's promise of benefits. Every product makes claims about the benefits it will convey but consumers have become jaded by too many claims from too many new and improved products. If consumers feel confident about a product or company's benefits, that product or company has achieved a difficult to get accolade.

Consumers must also believe in the brand or company's integrity. A recent list of the ten worst automobiles included the 1977 Honda Accord. Today the Accord is the standard of a valuable and reliable car. In 1977 it was a new product and suffered engine and body problems that were severe. They threatened to sink the model and the company in the American market. Honda took ownership of the issues and fixed each one, mostly at its own expense. That significant investment in its product's reputation paid dividends almost immediately. Honda is a perfect example of a company that stands behind its products and it has a loyal following of customers who believe in the company's integrity.

The higher level emotions are pride in being a customer, and passion for the brand. Pride reflects the degree to which consumers feel appreciated by the company and proud of their personal association with the brand. When consumers seek to wear company logo clothing, or select a company credit card, they manifest that pride in being the company's customer. The Breitling watch company targets some of its owners for exclusive logo merchandise sales. Like the externally branded clothing of the 1990s, Breitling merchandise billboards the corporate name. Exclusive clothing sales to Breitling owners reinforces their pride in being customers.

Passion reflects the belief that the brand is essentially irreplaceable and represents a seemingly perfect fit with the customer's personal needs. It's hard to surpass the consumer passion shown by Harley-Davidson motorcycle owners whose behavior may border on obsession.

The literature has investigated the underlying dimensions of loyalty and loyalty intentions. Some have attempted to map the dynamic mechanism that forms consumer loyalty over time (Johnson et al., 2006). Analysis of responses to the individual items in this set of measures has revealed that customers develop emotional attachment to a brand in a cumulative way, with confidence as the foundation of a brand relationship and passion as the pinnacle.

THE ROLE OF THE TRANSACTION

Another relevant factor in customer loyalty is the interactivity inherent in the buyer-seller relationship (Schlosser, 2000). However, the most valuable views have been multidimensional.

Marketers have long recognized the importance of transactional elements in marketing relationships. Notions of convenience and transactional success have been studied over time. Examples such as the marketing use of transaction cost accounting were attempts to increase customer satisfaction and ultimately loyalty while maximizing profitability. There are numerous variations in terms of transactions. Some, like a visit to a doctor's office may be highly involving and require deep thought and response from patients. Others, such as using a vending machine, are relatively low involvement interactions. The main classification of interest here is the face-to-face versus online transaction.

Face to face transactions in a retail setting

The face to face (F2F) transaction environment is an information rich, multimedia communication arena. Potentially, each of the senses can play a part. The typical retail environment may involve informational sources such as point of purchase advertising or video based infomercials, apparent product features, price and warranty information, and human salespeople.

Building customer loyalty in a face to face interaction Face to face transactions involve what is arguably the most powerful communicator in marketing, the product or service. Well-engineered products broadcast their benefits. For example, bicycle stores have a varied inventory that might include examples with titanium and steel frames. Customers who examine and compare the different units will understand the differences in weight readily. Salespeople, knowledgeable about their products and those of their competitors can point out differences, highlight benefits and costs and in doing so offer great aid. In computer terms, a customer can pose "random access" questions to a salesperson and get tailored answers without the need to search through literature or a list of frequently asked questions. Moreover, the professional salesperson can use his or her selling skills to diagnose customer wants and needs and even offer information which the customer did not anticipate asking. During the interaction, customers may form a positive bond with the salesperson, an emotional response. Thus, salespeople who demonstrate honesty, integrity, care and concern can foster a feeling of trust. They can also engender a perception of value by their helpful behavior.

Face-to-face retail interactions may vary greatly. By definition they include the most basic form, customer interactions with a vending machine without other human contact. Even this kind of transaction has some basic elements of the human touch since new vending machines now display questions and express thanks for the business.

However, face-to-face transactions between humans are more complicated. Perhaps the checkout line in a retail store is the least likely human-to-human contact to aid in building a customer relationship. And yet, numerous retailers train their check out personnel to make eye contact with customers, greet them and ask if there is anything further aid they might offer. In repetitive purchase situations like grocery shopping, some customers and check out clerks can develop an acquaintance that is like friendship.

High involvement products require increasing levels of salesperson interaction – "consultative interaction." Helzberg Diamonds, a US jewelry retailer, is known for its high quality gemstones at reasonable prices. Diamonds are high involvement products characterized by high cost, and relatively clear criteria that can aid selection. Helzberg's sales process is highly personalized and may require a trial and error approach that moves a customer to a final choice. Handling that process may be a salesperson's ultimate selling challenge. It requires guiding a series of decisions and really understanding the customer's wants. Salespersons' personalities play an important role in building a relationship with customers and Helzberg selects its personnel carefully. During that consultative interaction, the customer has the opportunity to evaluate the salesperson's comments. In general they may be scaled on a number of continua. One relevant scale ranges from "high pressure" to "intelligent advice." If a salesperson can make a sale while conveying the impression of care, concern and offering intelligent, unbiased advice, a positive relationship may result. That relationship may be the basis for strong customer loyalty and repeat purchases. Some Helzberg salespeople have a stable group of customers who return periodically for repeat purchases.

Differences between the face-to-face and online environments

Early in the evolution of e-commerce, in the early 1990s, the literature discussed terms such as "bricks and mortar" versus "virtual retailers." It became clear that the bricks and mortar competitors had an advantage over the pure internet retailers. Consumers felt more confidence in dealing with a "real" company rather than a comparatively intangible virtual organization. Consumer fears that some internet stores were in actuality ghost storefronts with no inventory and little reputation to defend sometimes were realized. Some consumers lost money when undercapitalized retailers went bankrupt. At the time, bricks and mortar retailers who started internet stores had an instant advantage. Their "clicks and mortar" retail operations had the confidence enhancing real store backing up the benefits of their internet operations. The situation demonstrated that trust is easier to generate for an existing store brand name. A similar situation exists for products.

Danaher et al. (2003) compared the brand loyalty of grocery products for closely matched samples of brands purchased either online or offline. The results were straightforward. They found that for purchases made offline, brand market share is not related to the differences in brand loyalty. However, for online purchases a comparison of actual with model-estimated brand loyalty shows that "excess brand loyalty" exists. In particular, greater brand loyalty is observed for brands with high market share, and vice versa for low share brands.

There is strong evidence of higher brand loyalty for online purchases compared with offline. The findings are consistent with those of Degeratu et al. (2000) who found that brand name was important in the sense that a "strong" brand, characterized by a large market share, did better in an online environment compared with a "weak" brand, characterized by a low market share. Danaher et al. (2003), offer possible explanations for this phenomenon. They include:

- online shoppers may infer product quality from the brand name and the greater relative salience of the brand name online compared with offline means that consumers are likely to place more emphasis on the importance of brand name when shopping online (Moore and Andradi, 1996); and
- buying a well-known rather than a lesser-known brand online has less perceived risk (Ernst & Young, 1999).

One or both of these reasons are plausible explanations for the finding that online brand loyalty for high market share brands exceeds that of a traditional shopping environment, with the reverse effect for low share brands.

The nature of online transactions
Commerce on the internet, or e-commerce, has experienced rapid and continued growth over time.

Online shoppers are attracted by the ease with which they can find products on the internet, the detailed product information available, and the variety of choices offered. The economics of e-commerce make it easy for vendors to do business online and too many smaller retailers have started internet operations. The result is retailer information clutter. Consumers have demonstrated a tendency to bypass these problems by relying on branded products or themselves (Pitta and Fowler, 2005). The phenomenon, if widespread, could limit the success of new product introductions via the web. Ernst & Young reported that 69 percent of those surveyed stated that brand names play a significant role in their online buying decisions. Thus, marketing through established brands may be required on the internet, even though consumers' cost of information gathering seems quite low.

There is speculation about the source of the differences between online and offline purchases. Compared to communications with the mass media, internet communications feature enhanced interactivity which empowers customers. They can decide how to approach the information. They can decide what to look at and what to ignore and how to evaluate it. In this context, interactivity is an invitation to choose among different message and product alternatives. While the control is in the hands of the consumer (Schlosser, 2000), one of the glaring contrasts between the online and face-to-face retail environments is the relative lack of interactivity online.

In an online transaction there are no face-to-face props to aid in consumer decision making. As a result, consumers tend to rely on substitutes and analogs to help them make choices. Over time, they tend to increase their experience with online companies as well as their search proficiency and need to rely less on brand names (Ward and Lee, 2000).

BUILDING CUSTOMER LOYALTY ONLINE
Marketing managers must establish consumers' trust in a variety of contexts. The specific case of computer-mediated environments such as the internet is particularly difficult (Naquin and Paulson, 2003). One approach involves explicit statements about the security of customers' personal data. However, evidence on the effectiveness of such statements is mixed. Some research has shown that such statements help instill consumer confidence in e-commerce sites (Palmer et al., 2000). In contrast, others suggest that they are not necessarily the most important predictor of online trust (Montoya-Weiss et al., 2003). Findings from a recent large-scale study

suggest that consumers use "surface" elements, such as web site design (Fogg et al., 2002) in judging security and trust. Schlosser et al. (2006) found that investments in web site design can boost trusting beliefs and online purchase intentions. Other web site design elements can aid in relationship building.

One innovative relationship-building example comes from the UK. Online travel services have exploited the internet's strengths such as ease of search and matched them to the specifics of travel. Travel services require information rich communications ranging from schedules to destination details and terms of service. The information load can be overwhelming to a novice traveler. Online, several major travel services vie for dominance in the marketplace using standard website design features to lure customers. In contrast, a group of UK travel agents has designed its website to deliver immediate primary contact with a real person. The UK travel agents provide a toll free number at the beginning of an online transaction to convey the visitor directly to a helpful human. This helps agencies with a limited internet presence and establishes a human bond immediately. Another example from the travel industry comes from the USA. In the US airline industry, retirees can be the human being at the other end of the line. Technology allows individuals to work from home and be available for extended hours. Southwest Airlines has a number of customer service agents who work from homes all over the USA. They are scattered across the four continental time zones and Hawaii and comprise a six-hour time zone window. The agents can offer extensive around the clock coverage. The retiree agents are well trained and selected for personality and helpfulness. For many travelers, a friendly grandparent on the other end of the line is comforting and relationship building.

The travel industry offers yet another example that online marketers should consider. Since trust is necessary for any relationship, third party comments can be valuable. Companies like Orbitz solicit customer evaluations and travel recommendations to boost their credibility. These efforts may involve sponsored online forums that invite seasoned travelers to share their personal experiences for the benefit of others. Such online community forums have been shown to alert consumers to opportunities and help them avoid problems. One recent example focused on Easter Island, part of Chile. Travelers warned others to avoid the largest hotel on the island and instead seek one or two smaller venues. The alternatives did not advertise but were excellent. The main hotel advertised heavily but was deemed a place to avoid. The community forum, reachable from the sponsor's web site, adds credibility and value to the sponsor and thus helps build a consumer relationship.

One other technique is to allow customers to join a vendor-sponsored "club." Online customer "members" can reap the benefits of "club members only" deals. They can get early warning of impending offers and often get preferential pricing. Since they are readily available to retailers through an online database, these customers provide lower transaction costs. Since they are experienced customers, in the sense that they have purchased from the retailers before, they have a higher probability of purchasing again. Therefore, they are more valuable than customers with no purchase history.

In summary, online marketers face a different challenge than their face to face competitors. They need to generate trust immediately, offer clearly perceived value and establish a long term relationship with selected customers (Smith, 2002). If online marketers are successful in generating brand loyalty, they should treat it as a valuable commodity not to be wasted.

THE CUSTOMER VALUE PYRAMID

Marketing textbooks have recognized differences among consumers in their value to firms. Some of the literature deals with heavy versus light users of products and services and notes that heavy users are valuable not only for their contribution to volume and revenue but also for their positive effects on profit. Most firms are aware at some level that their customers differ in profitability, and recognize the "80/20 rule" – 20 percent of customers produce 80 percent of sales or profit for the company. Empirical studies have supported that rule of thumb. In particular, long-term studies of bank patrons' account behavior and perceptions of service quality, the 80/20 rule was shown clearly (Zeithaml et al., 2001). Specifically, the authors noted that the top 20 percent produced 82 percent of the bank's retail profits, an almost perfect confirmation of the 80/20 rule in this profit setting.

Moreover, the more profitable 20 percent held more sophisticated views of service quality. The highest tier described service quality in terms of three factors: attitude, reliability, and speed. The lowest tier viewed only attitude and speed. In addition, when analyzing the drivers of repeat purchases, the highest tier focused on speed; the lowest on attitude. That evidence offers an opportunity to focus on the more profitable customers with customer loyalty building strategies to which they will respond.

The customer pyramid framework

As an example Zeithaml et al. (2001) postulated a framework for categorizing customers using a four tier system based on different expected levels of profit. They called the classification system the customer pyramid. Using the customer pyramid is helpful whenever the company has customers that differ in profitability but is delivering the same levels of service to all customers. In these situations, the firm is using limited resources to stretch across a wide group of customers, possibly under-serving its best customers.

Their framework used the names of four metals to indicate value and included the following four tiers, Platinum, Gold, Iron and Lead. Platinum and Gold customers are valued while the Iron and Lead tiers are less attractive.

The Platinum tier describes the company's most profitable customers. They are often heavy users of a product or service and not overly price sensitive. They show a commitment to the firm and seem willing to invest in and try new offerings. The other valuable tier, the gold tier is still attractive. It differs from the platinum tier with lower but still good profitability levels. Gold customers may seek price discounts that limit margins. Also their commitment to the firm is lower than that of the platinum tier. Typically, they may be heavy users of the product category but may value minimizing risk by multi-sourcing rather than working with one company.

The two less attractive tiers, Iron and Lead represent much lower profit potential than others. Iron tier customers are valuable in that they provide the volume needed to utilize the firm's capacity. They should be retained as customers. However, their spending levels, loyalty, and profitability are not substantial enough for special treatment.

In contrast, Lead tier customers represent losses to the company. They tend to cost more than they generate. They may demand more service than they are merit given their spending and profitability. Moreover they may pose a potential threat to the company. Since Lead tier customers expect more than they deserve, they may be dissatisfied with the service they do get and complain to others about the company.

The usefulness of the customer pyramid classification lies in its focus. While many firms conduct usage segmentation, this approach focuses on a group of variables other than sales that are responsible for profitability of the tiers. It is a robust concept that applies to both online and face-to-face selling situations.

In distinguishing a customers' value, keywords can be important. Labels such as "premier customer," "preferred customer," and "valued customer," can communicate an individual's appropriate service levels quickly. For example, using its own version of the customer pyramid method,

Bank of America classifies its customers into three levels roughly equivalent to excellent, good, and average based on their contributions to bank profitability. Each level has access to a range of bank services, with the most profitable customers having the greatest selection and paying the lowest rates. Thus premier customers may have several no fee checking accounts, a free safety deposit box, no charges for currency conversions or money orders, and even preferred rates on loans. In addition, premier customers also are assigned a private banker, available via telephone, who can offer personalized service, increasing the strength of the customer-bank relationship and the potential for profits. Personal contact with a private banker is an expensive service that represents a scarce resource best restricted to the most profitable clients.

The less important preferred customers have to pay for some or all of the services and get higher, less favorable loan rates. They typically do not have access to a private banker. The least important, "valued" customers pay for most services and when applying for loans, get the least favorable, ordinary loan rates. Thus the bank offers a higher level of service to the more profitable customers their own platinum and gold clients. They treat their Iron customers professionally with respect. The Lead clients are missing from the bank's customer service strategy.

Customer pyramid concepts can be applied equally well to online and face-to-face retail situations. The key seems to value both your customers and your products appropriately.

Using the customer pyramid to build online loyalty

We have seen that the first level of loyalty, trust, plus the second level, perceived value, can lay the groundwork for the third level, relationship building. Presumably, customers who have online purchase relationships with companies have already reached a level of trust. Their perceptions of value may differ depending on the tier that they are in. Zeithaml and her coauthors recognize four different articulations of value: value as low price; value as desired product or service benefits; value as the quotient of quality divided by price; and finally value as the sum of all the received benefits minus the costs.

The first articulation, low price, probably applies to Lead tier customers who want low price even if they have to accept less. Customers who concentrate on desired product benefits without consideration of cost are probably in the Platinum tier. These customers would be satisfied by firms that provide high value, high margin products and services. In between these two are the Gold and Iron customers who are both service and price sensitive. This view supports the reality that some customers are willing to pay for enhanced services and others are not. To support this view, Zeithaml and her coauthors site the numerous levels of express package delivery services offered by FedEx ranging from slow and cheaper to fast and expensive.

Once customers are identified and classified into profitability tiers, firms can attempt to build relationships to enhance customer loyalty while, more importantly, build profitability. For example, Gold tier customers are valuable but can be even more profitable if they morphed into Platinum customers. The requirement is to know the Gold customer very well to build new product offerings that serve the client better. Some strategies that have been used to enhance the relationship include becoming a full service provider. Home Depot is an example of a company that succeeded in turning its Gold customers into Platinum. It opened high end Expo Design Centers that carried exclusive, extensive, and expensive home renovation items targeted to specific Gold customers. It thereby offered a full service alternative to satisfy their needs and found that their purchase volume increased significantly.

Largeart.com, a Maryland-based online provider of large art pieces including murals and sculptures, found that commissioning an artist to create a painting large enough to hang in a bank foyer was the easy part. Getting the piece to an international buyer proved more difficult and became an obstacle to purchase. The solution was to become a full service provider. The company decided to roll the finished painting in a shipping tube, insure it and send it not to the customer, but to a certified framing contractor near the customer. The local framing provider was responsible for unrolling the art at its destination, reframing it, delivering it to the site and hanging the painting for the client. The company now has a network of local experts on contract to provide this technical service around the globe. By providing full service for an unwieldy piece of art, Largeart.com gained valuable customer loyalty and saw improvements in its customers' purchase volume.

Online providers are especially concerned about service problems. Such issues can lead to dissatisfaction and customer relationship extinction. It is imperative that companies learn when service problems occur and resolve them quickly and completely. The Dell computer company sells its systems online. It provides as much information as possible online and uses knowledgeable, well-trained consumer service personnel to guide customers through the design and ordering process. It also offers a service guarantee. Dell assures customers that they will be satisfied or else they receive some form of compensation commensurate with their problem. When a system arrives, Dell service representatives can help with setup via telephone. If there is a problem, such as a defective part, it can be expressed to the customer for installation by a local technician. There are several types of service guarantees. Marketers should choose the type of service guarantee geared to the pyramid tier. The very best customers should get a complete satisfaction guarantee. The worst, Lead tier customers, should get one with fewer features.

One of the best examples of building customer loyalty and moving customers from Gold to Platinum levels involves outsourcing. The practice involves providing an entire function that a customer firm formerly performed for itself. BJ's Wholesale Warehouse is one of the large warehouse discount retailers. It had responsibility for all data processing in each of its stores. While it was successful, an outside vendor consultant offered to integrate each store into a centrally processed system based near company headquarters in Massachusetts. The system was much more complex than any BJ's had run internally. The vendor then offered to run and maintain the more extensive system. In a short time, the vendor became the provider of all the company's transaction processing and moved BJ's from a Gold to a Platinum customer. Notably, there was a widespread system failure on Memorial Day, 2006. The vendor's service team solved the problem in less than an hour. While the time lapse seemed like an eternity, and cost the chain lost sales, it was much shorter than the in-house BJ's data processing operation could have delivered. BJ's top management was concerned but upon reflection realized that the glitch would have been a disaster without outside help. Even this problem increased the strength of the customer-vendor bond.

One reason for its value is that outsourcing reduces the nonmonetary costs of providing these services to the client firm, freeing it to concentrate on its core competencies. For example, the expertise and effort required to keep pace with new information technology, threats to security and fixing problems, and keeping qualified staff can become a distraction for a client firm. Once a vendor performs well for a customer, it can bind the customer to the organization and make the customer's business predictable, and increase its value to the company.

IMPLICATIONS FOR MARKETERS

While online marketers can make astute decisions that boost consumer trust, increase perceived value and build loyal customer relationships, it should be clear that companies must be selective. In an environment typified by turmoil and scarce resources, marketers must consider whom they wish to serve carefully. In fact, the typical strategies for building online volume may be counterproductive in building attractive customer relationships. In contrast, setting requirements to be a customer may raise a firm's perceived exclusivity, making existing customers proud.

For example, some of the specific techniques for building online loyalty involve electronic coupons and e-mail newsletters that contain special offers. The idea is that customers will respond to special offers that reduce price and thereby increase perceived value. Using a classification system like the customer pyramid offers guidance in the search for profitability. In fact, price reduction offers are a bad idea for lead tier customers. The discounts may be popular with lead customers but they may reduce profitability. There are examples of customers delaying routine purchases in anticipation of a price break, reducing profits further. Moreover, discount offers may be irrelevant to platinum or gold tier customers and should be avoided.

The economics of e-commerce make personal contact too expensive to extend to all online customers. Thus, marketers tend to reject the concept out of hand. However, contact with a human can be valuable and boost company profits. Marketers may wish to use personal contact relationship building strategies only with their most profitable customers. By restricting it to the Platinum or Gold customer tiers, human contact can become affordable and the firm can enjoy its profit enhancing benefits.

Finally, some of the techniques that foster online volume building should be applied very carefully to the customer pyramid. The examples used above like members only clubs pose a danger to profits if applied to lead tier customers. Price discounts may be wasted on them. In contrast, Platinum tier members can be alerted to new purchase opportunities before the general public. If price is not part of the offer, Platinum tier customers may appreciate the advanced notice, which will increase their bond with the marketer.

Another example, sponsored online community forums can offer value if restricted to satisfied customers. Presumably, the Platinum and Gold tier customers are satisfied and will appreciate third party recommendations. The danger, again, is focused on Lead tier customers. They will probably enjoy the lowest level of services and if they find a way to join such a forum, may complain about the sponsor and tarnish the experience for others. The final caveat is that discriminating against Lead tier customers makes economic sense. However, it must be done carefully to avoid angering them and causing further damage.

REFERENCES

Amine, A. (1998), "Consumers' true brand loyalty: the central role of commitment", *Journal of Strategic Marketing*, Vol. 6, pp. 305–19.

Danaher, P.J., Wilson, I.W. and Davis, R.A. (2003), "A comparison of online and offline consumer brand loyalty", *Marketing Science*, Vol. 22 No. 4, pp. 461–76.

Degeratu, A., Rangaswamy, A. and Wu, J. (2000), "Consumer choice behavior in online and traditional supermarkets: the effects of brand name, price, and other search attributes", *International Journal of Research in Marketing*, Vol. 17 No. 1, pp. 55–78.

Dunn, J. (2004), "Survey shows online security perception gap between experts, users", *Knight Ridder Tribune Business News*, Vol. 17, p. 1.

Ernst & Young (1999), The Second Annual Ernst & Young Internet Shopping Study: The Digital Channel Continues to Gather Steam, Ernst & Young, New York, NY, available at www.ey.com/publicate/consumer/pdf/internetshopping.pdf (accessed October 18).

Fogg, B.J., Soohoo, C., Danielson, D., Marable, L., Stanford, J. and Tauber, E. (2002), "How do users evaluate the credibility of web sites? A study with over 2,500 participants", available at: http://portal.acm.org/citation. cfm?doid ¼ 997078.997097 (accessed December 6, 2005).

Johnson, M.D., Herrmann, A. and Huber, F. (2006), "The evolution of loyalty intentions", *Journal of Marketing*, Vol. 7 No. 2, pp. 122–32.

Moore, K. and Andradi, B. (1996), "Who will be the winners on the internet?", *Journal of Brand Management*, Vol. 4 No. 1, pp. 57–64.

Montoya-Weiss, M.M., Voss, G.B. and Grewal, D. (2003), "Determinants of online channel use and overall satisfaction with a relational, multichannel service provider", *Journal of the Academy of Marketing Science*, Vol. 31, pp. 448–58.

Naquin, C.E. and Paulson, G.D. (2003), "Online bargaining and interpersonal trust", *Journal of Applied Psychology*, Vol. 88 No. 1, pp. 113–20.

Palmer, J.W., Bailey, J.P. and Faraj, S. (2000), "The role of intermediaries in the development of trust on the WWW: the use and prominence of trusted third parties and privacy statements", *Journal of Computer-Mediated Communication*, Vol. 5, March, pp. 1–25.

Pepper, D. and Rogers, M. (1993), *The One-to-One Future: Building Relationships One Customer at a Time, Century Doubleday*, New York, NY.

Pitta, D.A. (1998), "Marketing one-to-one and its dependence on knowledge discovery in databases", *Journal of Consumer Marketing*,

Vol. 15 No. 5, pp. 468–80.

Pitta, D. and Fowler, D. (2005), "Online consumer communities and their value to new product developers", *Journal of Product and Brand Management*, Vol. 14 No. 5, pp. 283–91.

Reichheld, F.F., Markey, R.G. Jr and Hopton, C. (2000a), "The loyalty effect—the relationship between loyalty and profits", *European Business Journal*, Vol. 12 No. 3, pp. 134–9.

Reichheld, F.F., Markey, R.G. Jr and Hopton, C. (2000b), "E-customer loyalty—applying the traditional rules of business for online success", *European Business Journal*, Vol. 12 No. 4, pp. 173–9.

Schlosser, A.E. (2000), "Harnessing the power of interactivity: implications for consumer behavior in online environments", in Hoch, S.J. and Meyer, R.J. (Eds), *Advances in Consumer Research*, Vol. 27, Association for Consumer Research, Provo, UT, p. 79.

Schlosser, A.E., White, T.B. and Lloyd, S.M. (2006), "Converting web site visitors into buyers: how web site investment increases consumer trusting beliefs and online purchase intentions", *Journal of Marketing*, Vol. 70 No. 2, pp. 133–48.

Smith, A.D. (2002), "Loyalty and e-marketing issues", *Quarterly Journal of Electronic Commerce*, Vol. 3 No. 2, pp. 149–61.

Ward, M.R. and Lee, M.J. (2000), "Internet shopping, consumer search and product branding", *Journal of Product & Brand Management*, Vol. 9 No. 1, pp. 6–20.

Zeithaml, V.A., Rust, R.T. and Lemon, K.N. (2001), "The customer pyramid: creating and serving profitable customers", *California Management Review*, Vol. 43 No. 4, p. 118.

FURTHER READING

Pastore, M. (2000), "Internet retailers look toward profitability", InternetNews.com, August 30.

ABOUT THE AUTHORS

Dennis Pitta is the J. William Middendorf Distinguished Professor at the Merrick School of Business, University of Baltimore. He has authored numerous articles in product management and healthcare marketing. His current research interests are new product development, and the effect of new technologies on marketing.

Frank Franzak is Associate Professor and Chair of the Marketing Department at the Virginia Commonwealth University. His research interests focus on creativity and new product development. In addition, he is engaged in research detailing the relationship between the creative culture in nations and their new product development success.

Danielle Fowler is an Assistant Professor at the Merrick School of Business, University of Baltimore. She is an expert in e-commerce and information technology and its application to business and marketing. Her current research investigates emerging marketing applications for smart cards and other technology.

QUESTION

6.2   What are the key factors that lead to customer loyalty?

6.3 Nurturing the Right Customers

By measuring and improving Customer Lifetime Value, you'll be able to grow your most profitable customers

by V. Kumar and Bharath Rajan*

Companies Companies often measure their success by the number of loyal customers they can count. Statements like "I've owned six Hondas" or "I always shop at Target" are music to a marketer's ears. But this devotion doesn't always translate to the bottom line. Our research has proven that loyal customers *aren't necessarily profitable* and that the relationship between loyalty and profitability is more complex than is often perceived. In addition, firms regularly use traditional loyalty metrics to measure the value of their customers, and these can lead managers to implement flawed marketing strategies that drain the firm's resources.

How can companies address this issue? Through something we call Customer Lifetime Value (CLV). When companies adopt a CLV-based approach, they can make consistent decisions over time about which customers and prospects to acquire and retain, which customers and prospects not to reach out to, and the level of resources to be spent on each of the various customer segments.

CLV: A FORWARD-LOOKING METRIC

Customer Lifetime Value can be defined as: *"The sum of accumulated cash flows—discounted using the weighted average cost of capital (WACC)—of a customer over his or her entire lifetime with the company."* Yet most companies have a much shorter horizon for computing CLV. This is because of changes in product life cycle, changes in customer life cycle, and the fact that, for a variety of reasons, 80% of profit can generally be accounted for in three years. Figure 1 shows how to measure CLV.

The CLV framework can be modeled using three main components: contribution margin, marketing cost, and probability of purchase in a given time period. Each of these components will have its own set of drivers/predictors, and each set is estimated simultaneously. The CLV calculation helps companies rank customers on the basis of their contribution to the firm's profits. This allows a company to treat each person differently based on his or her contribution rather than approaching everyone in a similar fashion.

An analysis of CLV can help companies across all industries answer three important questions they typically face. Let's take a closer look at each one.

1. WHICH CUSTOMERS AND FUTURE PROSPECTS SHOULD WE RETAIN, GROW, ACQUIRE, OR WIN BACK?

Before your business can answer this question with any certainty, you should first ascertain the following:

Whom Should We Acquire and Retain?

Every company seeks the answer to this fundamental question. The CLV metric suggests that acquiring and retaining profitable customers should be the guiding principle. When companies pursue this approach, however, they encounter three common pitfalls: They consider customer acquisition and retention rates as principal metrics of marketing performance; they focus too much on the current cost of customer acquisition and retention and not enough on the customer's long-term value; and they treat acquisition and retention as independent activities and attempt to maximize both rates.

In the first pitfall, the two metrics—rates of customer acquisition and retention—are easy to understand and track, and companies have naturally had a long-standing attraction toward garnering more market share. Though these two metrics may have relevance in a contractual setting, such as in subscriptions to magazines or cable services, in most cases, using acquisition and retention rates as measures of overall performance is misguided and may lead to the problem of diminishing returns. In other words, as acquisition and retention rates increase, the firm's profits don't always increase beyond a certain point. Therefore, companies should make decisions to acquire or retain the next customer *only* if the cost of doing so is less than the value the customer brings to the firm.

In the second pitfall, companies focus too much on short-term profits and not enough on establishing a long-term relationship with the customer. This problem occurs when managers group their customers into one

* From V. Kumar and B. Rajan, "Nurturing the Right Customers," Strategic Finance (September 2009): 27-33. Reprinted with permission conveyed through Copyright Clearance Center, Inc.

of the following four buckets: those who are both easy to acquire and retain, those who are hard to acquire but easy to retain, those who are easy to acquire but hard to retain, and those who are both hard to acquire and retain. Based on this classification system, guess who the managers will target first? Right: only the low-maintenance easy pickings. This wouldn't be a problem if each set of customers were equally profitable, but that's often not the case.

In the third pitfall, companies treat the acquisition and retention departments independently of one another. The result: The acquisition department tries to gather the most customers possible (often concentrating on loyal customers instead of profitable ones), and the retention department works on retaining *everyone* (often vainly throwing money at the profitable transient/"blow in" customers). In other words, the marketing dollars aren't spent on attracting potentially highly profitable customers who are hard to acquire.

How Can We Make Customers Profitably Loyal?
After selecting the "right" customers to acquire and retain, the next step is to segment them based on profitability and loyalty. Through our research, we've found that such segmentation yields four distinct types:

True Friends (high loyalty and high profitability) are the most valuable customers. They're satisfied with what the company has to offer, buy steadily and regularly over time, and offer the highest profit potential. In managing these true friends, firms should indulge in consistent yet intermittent communication so as not to seem overly aggressive.

Butterflies (low loyalty and high profitability) are profitable but transient. They enjoy flitting around to find the best deals, and they avoid building a stable relationship with any single provider. Companies make the classic mistake of continuing to invest in these customers and, in some cases, invest even after they stop purchasing. To manage this type of customer, firms should lock in their profits while the can and find the right moment to sever the relationship.

Barnacles (high loyalty and low profitability) are long-term customers, yet they don't generate a satisfactory return on investment because they don't spend enough often enough. But they can become profitable when managed properly. It comes down to this: Do they simply not have the money to spend, or are they buying the same or similar items from a competitor? If cash flow is their problem, then the company should cut back on the efforts it makes to reach these customers—and reduce its losses in the process. On the other hand, if the customer is spending elsewhere, specific up-selling and cross-selling can be done to boost profits. Since Barnacles don't offer high profits, the marketing resources directed to them should be diverted to Butterflies.

Strangers (low loyalty and low profitability) have very little fit with the company's products and services; these customers have no loyalty toward the firm and bring in no profits. The key strategy in

FIGURE 1. MEASURING CLV

managing these customers is to identify them early and refrain from making any major investment in them.

When they do come knocking, however, the company's aim should be to extract the maximum profit from every transaction since these customers may not come back again.

How Can We Realize Revenue Growth from Customers?

The answer to this question lies in multichannel shopping (via walk-in stores, telephone, the Internet, etc.). Since each channel caters to a different set of customers and provides varying levels of services, this approach reduces the overall service cost, thereby increasing profitability. What are these multichannel shoppers, and how can a firm identify them? We conducted a study in a business-to-business (B2B) format and cited the following drivers:

Customer characteristics: Includes the number of different product categories in which a customer has made a purchase, amount of product returns, frequency of Web-based contacts, the customer's tenure with the company, and frequency of purchases. The higher the incidence of these factors, the greater the likelihood of multichannel shopping.

Supplier-specific characteristics: Includes the number of different channels used to contact the customer, type of contact channel, and channel mix. Again, the higher the degree of supplier-specific factors, the greater the likelihood of multichannel shopping.

Customer demographics: Refers to the number of customer-service employees, the company's annual sales, and its industry category

Through research, we've found that as a customer shops across more channels (from one channel to three or more), he or she (1) spends more with the company, (2) spends a higher proportion on the focal firm (rather than with a competitor), (3) has a higher past profitability (which is correlated with future profitability), and (4) is more likely to buy from the company in the future. A successful company will evaluate which customers show the right signs of being potential multichannel shoppers based on the drivers and try to leverage those drivers to encourage multichannel shopping behavior.

But how can a company know which channel a customer is likely to adopt next and when this is likely to happen? Several behavioral and psychological aspects that determine the choice and timing of channel adoption are:

- The travel cost involved in purchasing and the immediate product availability.
- The total quantity of items a customer purchases in a single shopping trip, in

which product categories, and the level of price discounts.
- The customer's purchase frequency and the frequency of marketing communications.
- Customer heterogeneity, which increases the acceptance of new channels and shopping across different channels.

Using test and control groups, we've found in a business-to-business (B2C) scenario that adding one more channel resulted in an average net gain of about 80%. After accounting for marketing costs, the increase in revenue translated into a return on investment (ROI) of 800%. By knowing how a customer buys, and the number and type of channels he/she buys from, a company can make informed decisions about customer profitability. It can then contact the right customers at the right time to encourage adopting another channel, thereby increasing revenues.

How Can We Retain Customers and Prevent Churn?

Retaining customers is a crucial function for any organization. Customer attrition impacts a firm in several ways. The most obvious is the loss of revenue from the profitable customers who have defected. Second, the company doesn't get a chance to recoup its initial costs to acquire the customer. The firm also loses the opportunity to up-sell/cross-sell to people who have defected, a potential revenue loss. Finally, there are some lost "social" effects, such as influencing other customers through either positive or negative word of mouth.

Many companies have realized the importance of controlling the churn and have adopted or are in the process of adopting analytic tools to predict and prevent attrition. The key questions that need to be answered before developing this intervention strategy are: (1) How can firms identify the customers who are likely to defect? (2) When are they likely to defect? (3) Should the firm intervene and, if so, when? And (4) How much should firms spend to avoid the attrition of a particular customer?

Most churn models can answer these questions by building a "propensity to quite" model. These models indicate the probability of a customer quitting at a particular point in time. Based on when the customer is likely to leave, firms can provide appropriate intervention strategies that will aid retention. Figure 2 show the intervention strategies. The dotted lines indicate the propensities to quit of the customers had they *not* been targeted with intervention strategies.

The decision on the channel of intervention and the type of offer through which the intervention is to be made is based on individual customer characteristics.

FIGURE 2. PROACTIVE INTERVENTION STRATEGIES

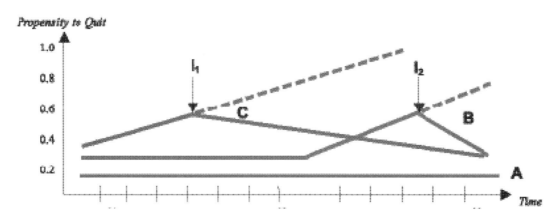

The amount of resources to be spent on each customer is directly linked to the Customer Lifetime Value. If it costs the company $100 per customer to intervene, it isn't product to promote to a customer whose CLV is only $50. The company should intervene with an offer that costs less than $50.

We studied the effect of the customer intervention strategy in a telecom firm on test and control groups. Using our strategy, the firm realized a net revenue gain of $345,000 after accounting for the cost of intervention, and the ROI was close to 806%. This demonstrates that the key to retaining customers is to identify those who are likely to quit and reach them with appropriate messages.

2. WHICH CUSTOMERS AND FURTHER PROSPECTS SHOULD WE NOT RETAIN, GROW, ACQUIRE, OR WIN BACK?

Any company that offers a variety of products serving multiple customer segments should want to know how it can measure and understand individual marketing actions that affect purchase behavior. This is achieved in part by identifying those types of customers who *aren't* to be retained, and CLV can help in accomplishing this task.

To analyze this facet of CLV, we considered more than 300,000 customers of an apparel retailer, calculated their individual CLV scores, and obtained a distribution. Based on the results, we segmented the customers into 10 deciles. The customers in the top two deciles constituted high CLV, the ones in segments three through five represented medium CLV, and those in the bottom five deciles represented low CLV. We observed that the top 20% of the customers accounted for 95% of the profits, and the retailer was actually losing money with 30% of them. This is because several customers in low CLV segments have negative CLV scores. Profile analyses on these high and low

customers helped us put a face on the CLV scores and thereby allowed the retailer to manage their customers effectively.

We then segmented the customers based on CLV and their current share of wallet (SOW) to develop a two-by-two matrix. (Share of wallet indicates the degree to which a customer meets his or her needs in the category with a particular brand or firm. For instance, if a customer spends $200 monthly on groceries, and $150 of her purchases is with Walmart, then Walmart's share of wallet for that customer is 75%.) We suggested that the retailer spend the minimum on customers with low CLV scores and high current SOW. In the case of customers with high CLV scores and high current SOW, we recommended maintaining the current level of spending. Low CLV and low current SOW customers were encouraged to cross-buy from different product categories and purchase more-expensive products. We found that a 15% increase in cross-purchase of customers in the top two deciles resulted in a 20% increase in their CLV. In other words, future customer profitability increases if the customer purchases in more product categories from the retailer.

In the case of customers with high CLV and low current SOW, all firms—not just this particular clothing retailer—should stimulate interest among customers by cross-selling across different product categories and by promoting higher-margin purchases.

3. HOW MUCH SHOULD WE SPEND TO RETAIN, GROW, ACQUIRE, AND WIN BACK CUSTOMERS?

CLV-based strategies, such as optimal resource allocation for a given buying level and sup-selling and cross-selling to retain customers, can help firms ascertain how much they should spend on customer segments in order to strengthen them.

Optimal Resource Allocation

Most managers are faced with budgetary constraints when making decisions regarding where, how, and on whom they're going to spend their marketing dollars. It wouldn't be prudent to contact *all* the customers. So what's the solution?

The answer lies in evaluating customers based on their profitability and *not* on how easy it is to acquire and retain them. The optimal allocation strategy evaluates customers based on their future profitability and recommends appropriate marketing initiatives. Once the decision about whom to contact has been made, the following questions arise:

1. How responsive are these customers to various channels of contact, and what is the optimal contact mix?
2. If a mix of communication strategies is used, how does the firm extract the most from every effort?

Generating the maximum "bang for the buck" depends significantly on factors such as the cost involved in communicating through a particular channel, the customer's response when contacted through a particular channel, the frequency of communication, the customer contact levels across different channels, and the expected profit level from each customer.

After considering these issues, companies can segment their customers based on their current SOW and CLV. Through this, we can see that low SOW/low CLV customers are of little value, and, to avoid losses, managers should refrain from investing in them. For high CLV/low SOW customers, companies should adopt a conversion strategy and invest in up-selling and cross-selling. Resources should be shifted away from high SOW/low CLV customers to high CLV/low SOW customers. Finally, high SOW/high CLV customers should be the main targets for loyalty programs, and firms should invest heavily in these people to maintain their loyalty and maximize profitability.

When a B2B firm implemented our optimal resource allocation strategy, they unlocked the true potential of their high-value customers and realized 100% more revenue and 70% more profit. Figure 3 provides a comparison between the B2B firm's original resource allocation strategy and our optimal strategy. As you can see, by carefully monitoring the customers' purchase frequency, the interpurchase time (the average number of days between two purchases), and the contribution of each type of customer toward profits, managers can tailor their marketing initiatives in order to maximize CLV.

Up-selling and Cross-selling

Companies need to exercise caution when cross-selling. We've found that not all profitable customers buy more products and not all customers who buy more products are profitable. The decision to cross-sell should also be evaluated in comparison with up-selling and not-selling decisions.

It is essential for a company that sells multiple products to know what product a particular customer is going to buy next. This information helps in developing the message and timing of the customized communication strategy. Firms can achieve this through a purchase sequence mode. Ours addresses the following questions:

1. What is the sequence in which a customer is likely to buy multiple products or across multiple product categories?
2. When is the customer expected to buy each product?
3. What is the expected revenue from that customer?

Traditionally, a company estimates the purchase sequence by accounting for product choice and purchase timing *independently*. Using Bayesian estimation, however, we've developed an advanced model that accounts for product choice and purchase timing *together*. We discovered this from our research involving 20,000 customers of a high-tech B2B company. Using this model, the B2B firm was able to improve its profits by an average of $1,600 per customer, representing an increase in ROI of 160%. We also found that the traditional model can accurately predict which products customers will buy, but it performs poorly in predicting the purchase timing.

By linking these CLV-based initiatives with continuous organizational improvement, companies can customize their marketing messages based on the customer's value to the firm. As such, marketing costs will decrease, and overall profitability will increase. In a nutshell, CLV-based strategies can enable firms to achieve a sustainable competitive advantage and be successful in the marketplace.

This article is the result of a study supported by IMA's Foundation for Applied Research (FAR). For more information, see the authors' article "Profitable Customer Management: Measuring and Maximizing Customer Lifetime Value" in the Spring 2009 issue of *Management Accounting Quarterly* and the C-Suite report, *For Acquiring, Retaining & Winning Back Profitable Customers, Using Customer Lifetime Value.* You can find all three in the Library at www.linupima.com.

FIGURE 3. OPTIMAL RESOURCE ALLOCATION STRATEGY FOR A B2B FIRM

HIGH CLV	**BUTTERFLIES** COST REDUCTION ($): CELL 1 Current Spending: $1,008 Optimal Spending Limit: $2,197 FACE-TO-FACE MEETINGS: Current Frequency: once every 7 months Optimal Frequency: once every 5 months DIRECT MAIL/TELESALES: Current Interval: 6 days Optimal Interval: 2 days PROFITS: Current Profit: $109,364 Optimal Profit: $178,092	**TRUE FRIENDS** COST REDUCTION ($): CELL 2 Currently Spending: $1,385 Optimal Spending Limit: $2,419 FACE-TO-FACE MEETINGS: Current Frequency: once every 3 months Optimal Frequency: once every month DIRECT MAIL/TELESALES: Current Interval: 6 days Optimal Interval: 5 days PROFITS: Current Profit: $534,888 Optimal Profit: $905,224
LOW CLV	**STRANGERS** COST REDUCTION ($): CELL 3 Currently Spending: $819 Optimal Spending Limit: $433 FACE-TO-FACE MEETINGS: Current Frequency: once every 5 months Optimal Frequency: once every 13 months DIRECT MAIL/TELESALES: Current Interval: 10 days Optimal Interval: 13 days PROFITS: Current Profit: $7,435 Optimal Profit: $12,030	**BARNACLES** COST REDUCTION ($): CELL 4 Currently Spending: $1,291 Optimal Spending Limit: $612 FACE-TO-FACE MEETINGS: Current Frequency: once every 2 months Optimal Frequency: once every 10 months DIRECT MAIL/TELESALES: Current Interval: 8 days Optimal Interval: 8 days PROFITS: Current Profit: $10,913 Optimal Profit: $28,354

V. Kumar, Ph.D. is the Richard and Susan Lenny Distinguished Chair Professor of Marketing and executive director of the Center for Excellence in Brand and Customer Management at the J. Mack Robinson College of Business, Georgia State University, Atlanta, Ga. You can reach him at (404) 413-7590 or vk@gsu.edu. For additional information, you can visit www.drvkumar.com.

Bharath Rajan is a research manager at the Center for Excellence in Brand and Customer Management at Georgia State University. You can reach Bharath at brajan2@gsu.edu.

QUESTION

6.3 What is Customer Lifetime Value (CLV)? Why is it important?

6.4 Measuring and Managing Customer Profitability

by Robert S. Kaplan and V. G. Narayanan*

In this article R. Kaplan and V. G. Narayanan discuss the issue of customer profitability analysis. They argue that today organizations have invested in enterprise resource planning (ERP) systems and data warehouses to track detailed data about individual customer transactions and relationships and in customer relationship management (CRM) to improve customer satisfaction. Despite these innovations, many companies don't know if they are actually making money from their customers. The difficulty is that in an age of heightened customer demands, companies are customizing products and services but not necessarily linking the costs of doing so on a customer-by-customer basis.

Activity-based costing (ABC) and associated software can be used as the conceptual framework for linking customer transactional data from ERP and CRM systems with financial information.

ABC can be used to calculate individual customer profitability. The output from the ABC analysis is called a whale curve (see Exhibit 1), which plots cumulative profitability against customers. While cumulative sales usually follow the typical 20/80 rule (e.g. 20% of the customers provide 80%) of the sales), the whale curve for cumulative profitability usually reveals that the most profitable 20% of customers generate between 150% and 300% percent of total profits. The middle 70% break even and the least profitable 10% of customers lose from 50% to 200% of total profits, leaving the company with its 100% of total profits.

Many large customers often turn out to be the most unprofitable. Companies cannot afford to lose large sums of money from small customers as they simply do not do enough business with them to incur large losses. Only a large customer can be a large-loss customer. Large customers tend to be either the most profitable or the least profitable in the entire customer base. It is unusual for a large customer to be in the middle of the total profitability ratings.

Exhibit 2 identifies dimensions that help companies identify diversity in their cost of serving individual customers. For service companies, customer profitability is more important than product profitability as the costs of providing service are usually determined by customer behavior.

Once a company studies its whale curve of customer profitability, several actions to transform unprofitable customers to profitable ones can take place. These include improving processes by lowering costs to serve, changing pricing strategies to include menu pricing, and improving customer relationship management and measurement.

EXHIBIT 1. THE WHALE CURVE OF CUMULATIVE PROFITABILITY

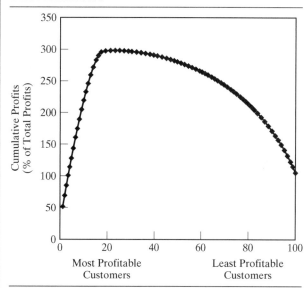

EXHIBIT 2. IDENTIFYING DIVERSITY IN VARYING COST-TO-SERVE CUSTOMERS

High Cost to Serve Customers	Low Cost to Serve Customers
Order custom products	Order standard products
Order small quantities	Order large quantities
Unpredictable order arrivals	Predictable order arrivals
Frequent changes in delivery requirements	Standard delivery
Manual processing	Electronic processing
Large amount of pre-sales support	Little to no pre-sales support
Large amounts of post-sales support	No post-sales support
Require company to hold inventory	Replenish as produced
Pay slowly (high accounts receivable)	Pay on time

QUESTIONS

6.4a   What does the whale curve of cumulative profitability illustrate?

6.4b   Describe the characteristics of high-cost-to-serve and low-cost-to-serve customers.

* This article has been summarized from the original article by Robert S. Kaplan and V. G. Narayanan, "Measuring and Managing Customer Profitability," *Journal of Cost Management* (September/October 2001): 5–15. Copyright © 2001. Thomson Reuters.

Chapter 7

Measuring and Managing Process Performance

In Reading 7.1, *The CFO's Best Friend*, Richard Gerardo and Andrew Spanyi, make the case that purchasing is a key value-adding market activity that can make a significant contribution to profitability. Many organizations have now developed a new position in their companies known as the CPO or the chief procurement officer whose job it is to manage the entire procurement process. Because profitability can really be improved through a carefully managed purchasing system, Gerardo and Spanyi label the CPO as the CFO's new best friend.

In Readings 7.2 and 7.3, John Gillett, Ross Fink, and Nick Bevington, discuss *How Caterpillar Uses 6 Sigma to Execute Strategy*, describing how Caterpillar was able to successfully implement this approach to total quality management. In a related article Keith Jones and Clement Chen, also discuss the effects of 6 Sigma in, *The Pervasive Success of 6 Sigma at Caterpillar,* as well as the new transparent financial reporting system that supports all of the changes that take place.

Reading 7.4 by Tom Albright and Stan Davis, *The Elements of Supply Chain Management*, provides a very good overview of what companies should consider before starting a supply chain management (SCM) program within the context of the Mercedes M-Class Sports Utility Program. The article covers numerous topics including: (a) developing and improving alliances with suppliers, (b) synchronizing flow of products, services, and information across the value chain, (c) supplier involvement with JIT and TQM, (d) target costing, and (e) outsourcing. This article can also be used as a supplement to Chapter 6 on activity and process decisions.

Readings
Chapter 7

7.1 The CFO's Best Friend

Purchasing isn't just a supply-chain activity—it's a value-adding market activity that can make a significant contribution to profitability.

by Richard A. Gerardo and Andrew Spanyi*

Many companies have long recognized the importance of cutting costs to become globally competitive. Consequently, organizations have put more emphasis on their supply chain activities, including purchasing. Everyone knows that if you spend a dollar less on purchasing, it goes right to the bottom line. The chief financial officer (CFO) and most other senior executives understand that if their company could cut the cost of all goods and services purchased by just 1% or 2%, it would have a substantial positive impact on profits. That's why many, if not most, companies have put a functional leader in place with the title of "Purchasing VP." To some extent, many companies have consolidated their supplier base by centralizing and aggregating the critical "buys" and assigning them to strategic purchasing teams. As a result, these companies feel they've addressed the opportunity adequately. So, the job is done—or is it?

Here's the simple question that few organizations can answer: When purchasing, do we have the most competitive price in the market? The corollary question is: When purchasing, did we "test" the market to determine if we had the most competitive price? The answers to these two questions determine the degree of impact that procurement has on overall competiveness. The scope of opportunity for improvement can be significant because many CFOs consider purchasing to be an underperforming unit. In fact, a recent report by the Aberdeen Group estimates that less than 20% of CFOs "view procurement's impact on overall competitiveness as very positive." A major improvement in this area and the consequent impact on profitability could make the chief procurement officer (CPO) the CFO's best friend.

In many organizations, the value of the total cost of purchased goods and services is often larger than the value of any individual business unit, but the subject of "effective and competitive" purchasing doesn't regularly make the agenda of the executive team. Yet with executive committee focus and aggressive buy-side market testing, purchasing can become a competitive advantage. The scope of opportunity for purchasing-driven profitability to make a significant incremental contribution to the bottom line is considerable for most companies.

Table 1 depicts the scope of impact on the bottom line for two representative companies on reducing the total cost of purchases, assuming that all other factors remain constant. In the situation at Company A, the total value of purchased goods and services is assumed to be 40% of revenues, earnings as a percent of sales is assumed to be 3%, and the positive impact on the bottom line based on reducing the total cost of purchases by just 5% is 66%. In the situation at Company B, the percent of revenues of purchased goods and services is assumed to be 60%, earnings as a percent of sales is assumed to be 5%, and the percent improvement to the bottom line based on reducing the total cost of purchases by just 5% would be 60%. Generally, a 5% reduction in the total cost of purchasing goods and services (all other factors remaining constant) may produce an improvement to the bottom line of anywhere from 28.5% to 100% for the typical company, depending on the specific circumstances. This potential, if realized, would bring a smile to the face of even the most cantankerous CFO.

The unfortunate truth, however, is that many senior executives think purchasing is a mechanical, necessary part of the supply chain rather than a value-adding "market activity" that can make a substantial contribution to the company's profitability. To find out how your company is doing, take the "purchasing challenge" test shown in Table 2. It only takes a few minutes.

THE PURCHASING CHALLENGE: A SELF-TEST
Table 2 outlines the major factors to consider and provides the means for a self-assessment.

---

* From: R. Gerardo and A. Spanyi, "The CFO's Best Friend," *Strategic Finance* (December 2008): 24–30. Reprinted with permission conveyed through Copyright Clearance Center, Inc.

TABLE 1. EARNINGS IMPACT: THE SCOPE OF OPPORTUNITY

	COMPANY A	COMPANY B
The value of all purchased goods and services as a % of Sales	40%	60%
Earnings (EBIT) as a % of Sales	3%	5%
% improvement in Earning (EBIT) by reducing the overall cost of purchased goods and services by 5%	66%	60%

TABLE 2. ASSESSING THE SCOPE OF OPPORTUNITY

FACTOR	TRUE	FALSE
The purchasing organization sets criteria such as reliability of supply, quality, and on-time delivery as prerequisites for being accepted as a supplier.		
We have centralized the purchasing of all key products and services such that the same or similar products or service is not purchased by different decision makers across the company.		
The senior purchasing people are clearly of the same caliber as their peers in sales, marketing, R&D, finance, and information systems.		
The purchasing people use a team-based approach with key resources from the appropriate business unit, manufacturing, and technical services to supplement their purchasing team on all critical buys.		
We understand our suppliers' cost structures as well as they do.		
We have the right data to identify the opportunity for purchasing-driven profitability.		
The purchases of goods and services are "tested" for the best price on the buy side in the same way as our sales organization continuously tests the market on the sell side.		
The purchasing team establishes enduring relationships with key people in the suppliers' organizations on the buy side just as well as is done on the sell side.		
The training program for purchasing managers is at least on par with what we systematically do for sales managers.		
Purchasing is seamlessly connected to an end-to-end supply chain process such that procurement of product, delivery, use, replenishment, and inventory control are in a single, integrated process.		
The chief purchasing officer is on par with his/her peers on the executive committee.		
The chief purchasing officer is part of our most senior management body—often called the "executive committee"—or at a minimum has a regular agenda item on executive committee meetings.		
Business units value the contribution made by purchasing and regularly invite the appropriate purchasing manager to participate in business meetings.		
The senior purchasing executive has been clearly tasked by the CEO and CFO with making a specific, measureable contribution to profitability.		

If you answered "FALSE" to three or more of the statements in Table 2, then your company could have a major opportunity to improve its purchasing practices. The extent of your success will depend on how much executive attention the CFO and CPO bring to theseopportunities and the amount of organizational energy they invest.

While the most important "missed opportunities" in purchasing today are "market testing" and "executive focus," much more is involved, including, but not limited to, the mental model and behaviors of your purchasing team, the extent you understand your suppliers' cost structures, the caliber and development of the people on the buy side, and assuring that purchasing is seamlessly connected to an end-to-end supply chain process so that procurement of product, delivery, use, replenishment, and inventory control are in a single, integrated process.

EXECUTIVE FOCUS IS CRUCIAL

It all begins with executive focus and attention. The CFO can play an essential role in laying the right framework for the CPO in this respect. We know that the key activity areas for manufacturing companies are to design, buy, produce, sell, and distribute goods. If you accept the proposition that the value of the total cost of purchased goods and services is larger than any individual business unit, then ask yourself these two questions: *How many hours a month does the executive team spend talking about individual business unit sales and marketing issues, reviewing sales data, market share, key accounts, etc.? How much time is spent reviewing the reciprocal data on the purchasing side?*

Now look at the agendas for the past year or two to determine how many hours were devoted to strategic purchasing, competitive acquisition of goods and services, purchasing profitability contribution, and other related practices. For many companies, the ratio is 5 to 1, or 25 to 1, or maybe the attention devoted to purchasing by the executive committee is so small that it isn't even meaningful. What is it for your organization? The best way to elevate the buy-side issues to the executive committee level is to have the senior purchasing officer (the CPO) sit on the highest decision-making body in the company or at least have a regular time slot on the executive committee meeting agenda to put the relevant buy-side business issues on the table. This is where the CFO can partner with the CPO in framing these issues in clear financial terms.

A STRONG CPO

Given adequate executive focus, the caliber of the purchasing team, their mental model, and their business practices will determine the degree of success an organization can realize in assuring that purchasing makes a significant contribution to overall profitability. First, the CEO and CFO need to reach agreement on the value of having a powerful chief purchasing officer. Typically, to put the right executive in place as the CPO involves taking a high-profile person, with a sales/marketing or a Strategic Business Unit (SBU) leadership background, and putting this person (with weight and influence) in charge of procurement. This individual should have a strong, historical track record of success in line management, a passion for getting results, a deep understanding of your business or industry, senior sales experience, and the ability to go toe-to-toe with other members of the executive committee. The CEO, CFO, and this new CPO will then jointly agree on a goal with respect to the incremental

improvement in the bottom line that will be driven by purchasing. The CEO and the new CPO will jointly create an environment such that when this person enters a room, everyone knows that they have to pay attention to him or her—like it or not. There are very few companies in the United States who have such a person as their current chief purchasing executive. Does your organization?

The CPO then needs to have a capable, performance-oriented purchasing team. This is a team of people who believe that:

- Key suppliers must demonstrate "a priori" their commitment to quality, on-time delivery, reliability, long-term commitment, ethical behavior, etc.
- All key buys such as raw materials, inbound and out-bound logistics, and energy, including items such as capital purchases, laptops, and key services such as contract labor, should be centralized, consolidated, and managed strategically.
- A team approach on the buy side, involving key people from the relevant departments and business units, is just as important as it is on the sell side.

But mind-set or attitude alone isn't enough. The CPO and the purchasing team need to have the right knowledge and set of skills that will earn the respect of people throughout the organization and enable an effective team approach to gather better data on suppliers' costs than you have ever had before through tight collaboration with IT resources. They also need the measurement and management skills to connect the supply chain processes of the supplier to those of the purchaser—and focus on the elimination of waste and cost in the entire supply chain, eliminating errors and driving inventory control. These skills don't come easily. Ask yourself this question: *Has your organization invested in the development of your procurement team members to the same extent that you have in the development of your sales team?*

Now let's consider the key principle of "market testing" on the buy side. When it comes to purchasing, this is a relatively simple, but frequently unapplied, principle of marketing dynamics. Think of it as the mirror image of "testing the market" on the sell side. In general, to determine if your selling organization has extracted the maximum value proposition from the marketplace, the selling organization increases price until this has an adverse effect on sales volume to such an extent that it decreases total revenue or market share. Using this method, the sales organization can defend its position that it has extracted the maximum value proposition available during any given set of market conditions. Likewise, the same mentality can and should be brought to the table when purchasing.

It's interesting to consider that when purchasing or selling, the parties involved are at the same table, but often with two very different mandates. The seller is most likely trying to get the maximum price without losing volume. The purchaser at the table is often willing to accept a "fair price" as long as an extensive laundry list of supply chain criteria is met, such as quality, on-time delivery, reliability, long-term commitment, ethical behavior, and more. These supply chain criteria are important, but they shouldn't be an excuse to pay a premium. The buy-side organization should assess, determine, and qualify those suppliers who can meet the supply chain criteria and then "test" these sellers' willingness to supply in the same way that many sales and marketing organizations test the market—i.e., by the impact on volume. Testing the selling market to determine the volume available should be done aggressively to the point that suppliers refuse to sell. Only when the buyer has "tested" the market and determined the seller's "no sell price" can the buyer know that they've found the bottom of the market. Only by knowing the market bottom and backing off it slightly can the CPO demonstrate to his or her organization that the most competitive buying price in the market has been obtained. This is precisely what CFOs need to encourage.

It goes without saying that there are many buy/sell relationships—some with true partnership components that share profits or those that involve special agreements such as takeout agreements—that don't lend themselves to this approach. But much of what's purchased today could be obtained at a more cost-competitive price if a "buy price/available volume" test were used. And this doesn't just apply to the most important raw materials purchases. It applies equally to all key purchases of both products and services, such as IT equipment, software, contract labor, etc. Only by applying market testing on the buy side with the discipline outlined above can a company optimize the potential contribution of purchasing to overall company profitability.

WHERE TO START

How does this journey begin? Consider the following story of one purchasing executive.

When we started on this program, we had to capture the imagination of senior management that there was an opportunity for purchasing to make a major contribution to profitability. What we said was that if we're purchasing $5 billion of stuff and we cut the cost of purchasing by 5%, then we would make a contribution of around $250 million. But we also said that we're not going to be so foolish as to stand up here

and promise you such a large sum of money at the beginning, so our first target was $50 million.

We are going to go and kill elephants first. We did a typical Pareto. Out of the $5 billion, the biggest

---

5 TIPS FOR GETTING STARTED

1. The CEO and CFO agree on the value of having a powerful CPO and take action to put the right person in this role.
2. The CEO, CFO, and CPO jointly agree on the incremental contribution to profitability to be made by purchasing.
3. The CPO assembles an action-oriented purchasing team and identifies the top priority areas of focus.
4. The CPO and the purchasing team take the set of actions needed for success and, in particular, implement "market testing."
5. The CFO and CPO work together to maintain executive attention on the company's progress on achieving the target incremental contribution to profitability.

---

category was raw materials at around $3 billion. Then we took all the buys of $100 million or more and said we could work out the math later. So we built the list, and the top 10 or 20 products represented around 80% of the total. Then we had something that was very bite size, and we could get our minds around it. Of these top 20 or so, the top two or three were the ones we were going to go after first because we had very large purchases in a bunch of different locations, and they were being handled by different people. So we went to each of those locations and told the people: "Guess what—you don't do this anymore. This now will be handled centrally, and here's why. We will have one standardized, aggregated, and leveraged buy, and one person will be in charge." For example, we took all raw material feedstock purchases and put the purchasing responsibility under one individual who reported to the CPO, and we also took all major IT purchases, including hardware and contract labor, and put the purchasing responsibility for these items under one individual who reported to the CPO.

But we got a lot of pushback. Some of the people who previously had the responsibility for purchasing locally were very unhappy. I explained that we still needed them desperately because each of them had all the critical information, so they weren't out of a job. Their new job would be to support the global negotiation, and they would be on the global negotiating team. But in the future there would be only ONE outside spokesperson who could look suppliers in the eye and say, "If you want to take your business from X to 5X—you have the opportunity—all you have to do is cut the price by Y." We figured out what the suppliers' actual costs were—in a very detailed engineering analysis (raw materials, capital costs, conversion costs)—and what their profitability was—so that we knew when we asked them for a price, we knew how much we were leaving them and that it would be sustainable for them, but it would be a significant reduction to what we were paying them at the time—at least that was our suspicion.

Of course we found in a few cases that there simply wasn't a lot of margin available. But in most cases we were paying somewhat of a premium. The research was actually fairly easy. We had some pretty sophisticated engineers who could drive by a plant and get capacity statistics, etc. The whole idea was that we were going to know more about our suppliers than the suppliers knew about themselves. That was a big mind-shift, and it allowed us to aggressively "test" the market on the buy side. We saw that information is power, and we needed the right mind-set and the right carrot so that when the supplier's sales guy left, he understood that if he gives you the right price he can double his volume with you and maybe even justify expansion of his own business. In the end, every company wants to grow. What you are leveraging is the profit motive on their part. And even if the supplier can't take all the business at that point in time, they can see that in future years it would be an opportunity to grow their business as a key supplier. That's why our suppliers were also interested in engaging with us in tough but fair negotiations.

While we began with modest goals, by the end of our first year we exceeded the $50 million target, and by the end of three years we exceeded the contribution to profit target of $250 million.

WHAT ABOUT YOUR COMPANY?

You determine the size of the prize. Is purchasing worth focusing on? If so, the effective change management implied and performance measurement practices in Table 2 are necessary, and these must be executed with tenacious determination. The CPO needs to ensure that purchasing takes advantage of a team-based approach, engaging some of the best resources from business units, manufacturing, quality, technical services, and other departments. The culture of the purchasing team needs to be shaped such that there's a continuing focus on testing the marketplace for the best price, and this means assuming a certain degree of risk. The entire end-to-end supply chain process needs to be measured and managed in order to deliver the targeted contribution through purchasing-driven profitability. Given a degree of success, the CPO may indeed become the CFO's best friend.

Richard A. Gerardo is the former vice president of Global Supply Chain for The Dow Chemical Company.

Andrew Spanyi is the author of More for Less: The Power of Process Management *(Meghan-Kiffer Press, 2006) and* Business Process Management is a Team Sport: Play It to Win! *(Meghan-Kiffer Press, 2003). You can reach the authors at andrew@spanyi.com.*

QUESTION

7.1 What is the purpose of the Purchasing Challenge: Self-Test?

7.2 How Caterpillar Uses 6 SIGMA to Execute Strategy

*by John Gillette, Ross Fink, and Nick Bevington**

In 2001, Caterpillar launched its 6 Sigma program to drive change to achieve the company's long-term strategic goals (Caterpillar uses 6 Sigma to identify its Six Sigma initiatives). This 6 Sigma process was, and continues to be, extremely successful. Some of the results include first-year benefits that exceeded implementation cost and achievement of the revenue goal two years earlier than planned. We'll briefly

discuss Six Sigma in general, describe Caterpillar, and show the entrenchment of 6 Sigma within the company's strategic planning process.

WHAT IS SIX SIGMA?

Six Sigma is a total quality management (TQM) technique pioneered by and applied to Motorola processes in the 1980s by Bill Smith, a Motorola

* From: J. Gillett, R. Fink and N. Bevington, "How Caterpillar Uses 6 SIGMA to Executive Strategy." *Strategic Finance* (April 2010): 22–28. Reprinted with permission conveyed through Copyright Clearance Center, Inc.

engineer who became known as the "father of Six America, Honeywell International, Raytheon, and General Electric, have taken these learned processes and expanded them. Even though many people have reservations about the potential savings from Six Sigma, a story by Charles Waxer ("Six Sigma Costs and Savings: The financial benefits of implementing Six Sigma at your company can be Significant," www.isixsigma.com/index.php?option=com_k2&view = item&id=1228&ltemid=187) reports that GE saved more than $12 billion over five years, Honeywell saved $800 million, and Motorola saved $15 billion over 11 years. Each company takes the Six Sigma process and best practices and makes the technique its own.

The methodology, which was created in the 1920s, comes from mathematician Walter Shewhart's introduction of how processes could be corrected. It uses the Greek symbol "sigma" to represent a standard deviation away from the mean. The sixth sigma is a representation of six standard deviations away from the mean of the population. In the most common use of Six Sigma, the goal is to create only 3.4 defects per million parts manufactured. Contrary to the name of the process, 3.4 defective parts per million is only 4.5 standard deviations away from the mean.

To combat the defects referenced in the Six Sigma goal, companies have adopted methodologies to make a linear map of the process. Two common methodologies are DMAIC (Define, Measure, Analyze, Improve, Control) and DMEDI (Define, Measure, Explore, Develop, Implement). The website www.iSixSigma.com defines DMAIC as "a data-driven quality strategy for improving processes, and is an integral part of the company's 6 Sigma Quality Initiative." DMEDI is defined as "a creative approach to designing new robust processes, products and services." Thus the difference between DMAIC and DMEDI is that DMAIC examines processes already in place, and DMEDI helps put a new process in place.

A Six Sigma project is designed to improve a process. Each step of the process that needs improving is mapped to analyze where problems exist. The problems are analyzed with many different tools, such as Pareto diagrams, tree diagrams, root cause analysis, and process mapping. Then a Six Sigma team takes on the improvement project. Many companies have defined the mastery of Six Sigma with the terminology of the belt system of martial arts and use Green Belts, Black Belts, and Master Black Belts to undertake and lead projects. Black Belts generally drive and run projects with the help of Green Belts. Green Belts assist the Black Belts with projects but aren't working full-time on a project, whereas Black Belts are fully dedicated to process improvements and are responsible for leading the team of Green Belts in completing the Sigma.: Since then, other companies, such as Bank of projects. Master Black Belts are teachers of the process and lend a hand to Black Belts as coaches.

Caterpillar embraced this methodology in 2001 when then CEO Glen Barton challenged the company to change. To introduce his ideas, he had three karate Black Belts put on a dramatic show of power by breaking pieces of wood that represented quality, cutting costs, and a goal of attaining $30 billion in revenue. Barton realized that he needed a tool that would allow the company to analyze where changes were needed, to help make the changes, and to help the company grow, so he chose 6 Sigma. Caterpillar had a long road in front of it, but the initial rollout of 6 Sigma used more than 300,000 hours of training in its first year. Dan Campion, Caterpillar Master Black Belt, points out that when Allied Signal sent its people through Black Belt training, the average number of years of company experience was five to seven. At Caterpillar, the average number of years of company experience was more than 20.

WHO IS CATERPILLAR TODAY?

Caterpillar, or Cat, is the world's largest manufacturer of construction and mining equipment (most consumers would recognize the huge yellow equipment), diesel and natural gas engines, and industrial gas turbines. It also delivers many related services, including financial, logistics, and remanufacturing.

Caterpillar reaches every continent with its products and services and, as of 2008, employs approximately 113,000 people. Caterpillar typically doesn't sell to the end customer but uses a global dealer distribution network. As of 2008, 180 dealerships span North America, Europe, Africa, the Middle East, Asia, and Latin America. These dealerships, which have more than 131,000 employees, act as the contact from the end customers to Cat.

The company has had great financial success as well. In 2006, Caterpillar recognized $41.5 billion in total sales and revenues, easily exceeding its 2001 goal, and this led to $3.5 billion in profit from a highly capital-driven industry. The company spent $1.6 billion in plant, property, and equipment as capital expenditures in 2006. Cat has an aggressive growth strategy that requires high levels of funding. For example, Caterpillar spent $1.4 billion in research and development in 2006. Caterpillar is also on the list of Fortune 100 companies. According to the 2009 Fortune 100 list, Caterpillar is first in its class, is No. 44 overall, has $51.3 billion in revenue, and has almost $3.6 billion in profit.

6 SIGMA AT CATERPILLAR

Caterpillar CEO Glen Barton started the 6 Sigma culture change in 2001 when he challenged every officer for his or her personal commitment to the program. And he got it. But many in the company became worried when Barton announced his retirement in 2004 and that the helm would be passed on to Jim Owens. In Owens's first speech, however, it became obvious that he believed in the program that Barton had started. His speech was short, but his commitment was apparent. The Black Belts, Master Black Belts, and anyone else associated with 6 Sigma projects were relieved as they realized that the methodology and their roles in the company would continue.

Many individuals throughout Caterpillar participate in 6 Sigma projects each year, from the factory workers to the group presidents who support the strategies. According to the company, there are approximately 2,000 active Black Belts at Cat. Each employee knows and understands that major initiatives and changes will take place using the 6 Sigma strategy. If a problem exists, 6 Sigma is the tool that will help solve it. On a side note, employees even take the lessons they learn from work to other organizations in which they volunteer their time.

The 6 Sigma culture has permeated Caterpillar in all aspects of the business. Craig Brabec, the current Global Finance and Strategic Support 6 Sigma Division Champion, came from a consulting business that helped companies go through change. He noticed something different about 6 Sigma at Cat: 6 Sigma didn't exist only in the manufacturing or the engineering side of the business—it also entered the financial world and the human resources side. When the company faced the challenge of the general population of its workforce retiring, it turned to 6 Sigma, using a 6 Sigma team to identify whether its benefits package was competitive with ones at other top companies. For example, Cat matches up to 6% of an employee's base salary in a 401(k) program from the day the employee begins, and its compensation plan is rated in the top 10% of plans in the S&P 500. Caterpillar recognized that its greatest asset was its people and that it would have to competitively replace the knowledge base that was going to be leaving the company.

In 1990, Caterpillar reorganized to a business unit structure, which sometimes makes the transfer of knowledge between business units more difficult. But 6 Sigma provided an effective change mechanism and a means of integrating the knowledge learned through 6 Sigma projects across the various business units.

In addition to its own use of 6 Sigma, the company has taught its suppliers and dealers about the benefits of using the technique to refine the entire sales model. Caterpillar has introduced 850 suppliers worldwide to 6 Sigma, which has created more than 1,000 supplier Black Belts to help run the projects. One supplier that said it was interested in the Caterpillar 6 Sigma methodology allowed Cat to consult and transform the business. When implementing 6 Sigma, Caterpillar used facts and data to show the results the supplier could expect, so it didn't take long for the supplier to totally buy in to the methodology.

Dealers have also taken on the 6 Sigma commitment. More than 165 dealerships have produced more than 1,000 Black Belts to help with projects. Dealers find it amazing that they can share their projects with one another on a Caterpillar website that depicts best practices among the dealers. Even though each dealership is run as a separate business, 6 Sigma has helped give all of them a common feel across the world. Not only are dealerships learning about projects that need to be done in their business, but they're following the steps of the process and learning which projects to do first. Just as Caterpillar embraced the methodology, dealers have also accepted the idea of making 6 Sigma a top-down methodology that pushes the training and concept down to the workers at the lowest level.

ATTAINING STRATEGIC GOALS

When Glen Barton introduced 6 Sigma to Caterpillar, he envisioned using it to help the company achieve the $30 billion mark in revenue by 2006. Instead, it achieved this goal in 2004—two years ahead of plan. Current Chairman and CEO Jim Owens continues to execute strategy using the 6 Sigma methodology. New strategic goals include People; Performance Product & Process; and Profitable Growth. Metrics have been developed for each of the strategic goals for the years 2010, 2015, and 2020. For simplicity, the following metrics will be used in Caterpillar's 2010 strategic goals: People's metrics include a highly engaged workforce and achieving world-class safety. Performance Product & Process's metrics include being No. 1 in quality, market leadership, and market-leading availability. Finally, Profitable Growth's metrics include $50 billion in revenue and earnings per share growth in the top half of the S&P 500 companies.

Over the last eight years, Caterpillar has demonstrated the usefulness of 6 Sigma in achieving its strategic goals. This was accomplished by fully integrating the methodology and its principles into all aspects of the business, including suppliers and dealers. It also allowed the integration of knowledge from Black Belt projects across business units. Further, Caterpillar believes that, by using 6 Sigma to drive change, its new goals are obtainable.

One example that exemplifies Caterpillar's continuing integration of 6 Sigma into all aspects of the business is a project that will improve threaded joint design in the assembly process. This project focuses on continuous improvement in Caterpillar's quality culture and provides an opportunity to leverage best practices and replicate solutions across the enterprise.

The company is also working on a 6 Sigma project that focuses on ergonomic improvement. This project is helping Caterpillar put processes in place that allow a proactive and, ultimately, preventive approach to ergonomic injuries—providing a better work environment for employees.

As you can see, Caterpillar is continuing to embrace the 6 Sigma methodology, not only in manufacturing and engineering, but across the organization. This way of working and thinking continues to be successful in driving the company's strategy for change.

John W. Gillett, CPA, Ph.D., is professor of accounting and chair of the Department of Accounting at Bradley University in Peoria, Ill. He also is a member of IMA's Central Illinois Chapter. You can reach John at (309) 677-2290 or jwg@bradley.edu.

Ross L. Fink, Ph.D., is professor of operations management in the Department of Business Management and Administration at Bradley University. You can reach him at (309) 677-2271 or rf@bradley.edu.

Nick Bevington is a staff accountant at Caterpillar Inc. in Griffin, Ga.

QUESTION

7.2 What is 6 Sigma and why was Caterpillar's adoption of it so successful?

7.3 The Pervasive Success of 6 SIGMA at Caterpillar
Accounting and finance efforts are a good example.

*by Keith T. Jones and Clement C. Chen**

The increasingly competitive marketplace has for some time now made it necessary for organizations of all types and sizes to reexamine their business processes—from engineering and production to marketing and financial functions—in order to determine how they can improve them. As if it weren't enough to tackle everything once, continuous improvement has become the standard in today's global, constantly changing environment.

Organizations from banks to manufacturers have used Six Sigma to improve their operations. Conceived as a tool to improve product quality to certain standards, it has been used by many companies to transform their operations in other areas, too, such as accounting and finance. For example, companies have used Six Sigma to reduce cycle time and improve reporting processes (see "Near Zero-Defect Accounting with Six Sigma" by Peter Brewer and Nancy Bagranoff in *The Journal of Corporate Accounting and Finance*, January-February 2004, and "Using Six Sigma to Improve the Finance Function" by Peter Brewer and Jan Eighme in the May 2005 issue of *Strategic Finance*). Yet this management tool has met with varying levels of success as companies have tried to apply it to areas outside production. A recent series of articles in *Business Week* warned that some companies that had achieved initial success with Six Sigma encountered road-blocks because of a tradeoff between efficiency and creativity. Some people even suggest that Six Sigma has run its course.

Caterpillar's experience with 6 Sigma (Caterpillar refers to Six Sigma as 6 Sigma) has been highly positive, despite traditional challenges inherent in any large top-down management initiative. We met with company representatives to learn how they achieved and have sustained a high level of success. While an article in *Six Sigma* magazine discussed Caterpillar's overall success, the focus here is on how they applied it successfully in the finance and accounting functions. A specific example will illustrate briefly how this company-wide process has been applied successfully in the accounting and finance arena.

A CULTURAL TRANSFORMATION
Caterpillar implemented 6 Sigma on a global level from day one, beginning in January 2001. The company never intended to try it in production, see how it worked, and then try it somewhere else. From their perspective, anywhere there was an outcome, there was a process. If there was a process, there was variation in

---

* From: K. Jones and C. Chen, "The Pervasive Success of 6 SIGMA at Caterpillar," *Strategic Finance* (April 2010): 29–33. Reprinted with permission conveyed through Copyright Clearance Center, Inc.

146

performance. If there was variation in performance, the process was subject to 6 Sigma. No area of the company was excluded, from production to revenue recognition to client services.

The company rolled out the program in "waves," and, by the end of 2001, had 700 Black Belts. Today there are roughly 2,000. Black Belts at Caterpillar are trained by Master Black Belts and receive a minimum of 160 hours of training while also working on their first project. The company develops its future leaders through the Black Belt program, administering a tight screening process to select employees for the Black Belt role. For example, they are looking for employees who are recognized to have strong project management skills. Within Global Finance, approximately one in three leaders has held a full-time 6 Sigma position.

Caterpillar used a "transformational" deployment strategy in implementing 6 Sigma as opposed to a functional or targeted strategy. The latter two focus on specific processes or individuals and, although they require less initial investment, make it difficult to integrate 6 Sigma into other parts of the company, largely because there's no common language and company-wide commitment. In Caterpillar's case, company leadership was committed up front and made it clear that 6 Sigma was here to stay. Everyone—every single employee—was trained in the basic concepts of 6 Sigma and equipped with common terminology. In fact, trainees were asked to formulate an "elevator speech" in which they would be able to describe in two minutes what 6 Sigma was about at Caterpillar. The training was the same for accounting Black Belts as for the production people in Beijing. The intent—and the ultimate result—was that 6 Sigma would permeate every corner of the company from day one. Every area—from research and development to production, marketing, finance, and accounting—has provided major inputs into implementation and used 6 Sigma to review and change internal processes. In fact, Caterpillar also rolled it out across their supply chain, bringing nearly all dealers and many suppliers on board.

RIGOR AND REALITY

From the beginning, Caterpillar appointed a "metrics manager" who was responsible for establishing criteria to ensure that the benefits of every project were "real." Calculating real, credible benefits is critical to a project's success, and tracking the benefits requires great rigor and attention to detail, according to the company's representatives who have managed 6 Sigma metrics. Rigorous standards are set for measurement of projected and actual benefits that are applied across the board, regardless of the process under review. This precision helps remove emotion and cynicism by providing real data. Policies are very specific about

what counts and what doesn't, but the company is still careful to ensure that this need for exactitude doesn't stifle creativity and impede progress. The full intent behind the metrics is to drive desired behaviors and lead employees into making fact-based decisions.

The company stresses a budgetary, zero-based approach, focusing on relevant, incremental benefits. It first establishes a benchmark of what the outcome would be if 6 Sigma weren't implemented. Then, once the project is complete, the company compares the cost benefits because of 6 Sigma methodology. There are three levels of benefits that must be quantifiable and subject to an independent review, and each level is designed to drive particular types of results. Level 1 benefits must indicate a clear, causal relationship between the project outcomes and the bottom line. Level 2 benefits involve redeploying resources made available from process improvements to other value-added positions, avoiding the need for additional headcount. Level 3 benefits are more varied and generally involve cost avoidance or longer-term value creation that requires upfront investment. For instance, there may be an engineering change that produces a quality improvement and results in increased future sales. All levels of benefits are critical. While Level 3 includes a focus on long-term benefits, Level 1 and 2 benefits are intended to drive behaviors toward short-term benefits.

During earlier stages of implementation, rewards were tied to Level 1 and 2 benefits achieved during the first year of a project, with Level 3 benefits incorporated in the second year. Employees initially viewed the Black Belt role as a risky career move, but then they saw that top management supported them and recognized their success with noticeable financial rewards. Yet if the Black Belts and 6 Sigma teams didn't deliver the results, management didn't deliver the rewards, so accountability for the results was clearly established. Such linking of specific rewards to 6 Sigma success was important in driving the global cultural change.

AN EXAMPLE: TRANSPARENCY IN FINANCIAL REPORTING

Following a reorganization in the early 1990s, there were three separate, distinct financial views of the entire organization: SEC/legal entity, business units accountable (internal management reporting ledgers), and enterprise product profitability. In the early 2000s, burdensome accounting headaches, coupled with changes in the regulatory landscape, motivated a move toward greater transparency in reporting. The company had accountants involved in the three different views of the organization, with approximately 75% working on legal entity reporting or business accountable reporting (legal reporting to the Securities & Exchange

TABLE 1. CATERPILLAR'S "RECIPE" FOR 6 SIGMA SUCCESS

CLARITY

✔ Everyone understands the terminology, expectations, and their reasons.

✔ There is a clear link from process improvement initiatives to company strategy and quantifiable benefits.

CONSISTENCY

✔ Every project is subject to the same rigor.

✔ The same principles are applied globally.

COMMITMENT

✔ Leadership is committed to 6 Sigma principles at all levels.

✔ Management is committed to 6 Sigma leaders and to their success.

Commission (SEC) and only 25% on insightful analysis. There were multiple business accountable ledgers and software packages, contributing thousands of reconciling journal entries made on a monthly basis just for internal management purposes. Extra hours worked during closing cycles sometimes approached 60%. In short, far too much time was being spent on generating reports and not enough time on generating insights from the numbers, not to mention the effect on the morale of the finance and accounting staff. Importantly, business decisions could be less than optimal as a result.

The goal was to implement an integrated, transparent financial reporting system to allow a clearer path to value creation. An analysis of stakeholders' views determined that it was still important to keep the separate views of the company—reporting and analyzing results by principal lines of business and by geographical region—but the numbers must be easily reconcilable to the external view. The intent was to simultaneously create a substantial shift from "adding up" to "adding value." A dedicated team was responsible for following the established methodology based on the 6 Sigma recipe of the "Three C's," that is, clarity, consistency, and commitment (see Table 1). Every business unit had a Black Belt assigned to it to apply the rigor of 6 Sigma and to improve leverage and communications across Caterpillar. A small core team in the company's Peoria, Ill., headquarters were "subject matter experts" on such things as cost of sales. This team worked with the business unit Black Belts to create and implement changes in methodology and communicate the necessary changes and training plans.

What were the results? The company began the massive project in early 2003 and started to understand the impacts by August of that year and aligned and tested the financial reporting systems. Caterpillar went from thousands of reconciling differences to none almost immediately. Their cascaded financial reporting system now links SEC reporting directly with results for product lines, eliminating the need for reconciling journal entries.

The benefits were twofold. First, complexity and risk in the numbers were removed, and managers were able to use one set of numbers, with multiple views, to manage the company. Second, significant effort was redeployed from reconciling to analysis. This redeployment saved the company from having to hire additional support people during a period of tremendous growth. Table 2 shows a partial list of the benefits to Caterpillar.

THE FOLLOW-THROUGH

There are challenges not only in the implementation of any major management initiative but in sustaining the emphasis once it has been established. One danger with any major process change such as 6 Sigma is that it will lose steam with a change in management. Caterpillar is significantly into its second chairman since implementing 6 Sigma and has experienced no such loss in momentum. When current CEO Jim Owens took over, he continued the emphasis on using 6 Sigma methodologies to capitalize on the talents of the people, firmly expressing a belief that the rigors of this methodology will continue to combine very powerfully with the talents of the people to tackle all business problems. A significant issue lies in how to avoid an initiative becoming a project of some time horizon, such as five years, regardless of the initial high level of success and apart from concerns about CEO changes. As one company representative aptly characterized the challenge, "How do we change from building the house to living in it?" Caterpillar continues to carry out projects in the same way as before—and with the same rigor—following up and holding the process owner responsible for the results. The company intentionally puts its best people on the most important projects.

TABLE 2. THE BENEFITS

✔ Caterpillar's strategy is carried out with more focus and clarity.

✔ Cynicism is minimized as a result of consistent methodology and rigor.

✔ There is one way of doing business, thereby increasing familiarity and commitment.

✔ Everyone can see the results . . . reconciled to the "bottom line."

✔ Significant resources are saved or redeployed to more value-added purposes.

✔ 6 Sigma is a "win/win" proposition because employees are rewarded for their success.

Black Belt experience is an important factor in determining promotability, and Master Black Belt graduations are characterized by large ceremonies that afford the honorees the opportunity to interact with the CEO and other high-ranking company individuals.

In the early stages of implementation, tying rewards to 6 Sigma results was important. Those who participated early received rewards tied to benefits. Such links to financial incentives are important in driving behavior, and the incentives should be more than "tokens." Significant incentives will signal that management believes in 6 Sigma and that others should get on board or be left behind. After 6 Sigma was well established, the direct rewards tied to specific results gave way to salary increases that naturally result when individuals are promoted to increasing levels of responsibility, again largely because of their participation and success within the 6 Sigma culture.

At the core, Caterpillar employees at all levels view 6 Sigma as the way they work to solve problems and make decisions that involve rigor and discipline, with a goal of process excellence. From a management perspective, it's a way of implementing strategy more effectively and efficiently. It is data driven and structured, which minimizes the effects of cynicism that could have derailed early efforts to implement the initiatives. The company doesn't have multiple management philosophies and tools; all projects are 6 Sigma projects. Employees understand the terminology and why they are doing it. Rather than turning into a "flavor of the month," as top-down initiatives often do, 6 Sigma is ingrained into the company's culture to the point that many can't imagine Caterpillar without it.

Keith T. Jones, CPA, Ph.D., is associate professor of accounting at Illinois State University and is a member of IMA's Central Illinois Chapter. You can reach him at (309) 438-2473 or kjones@ilstu.edu.

Clement C. Chen, CPA, Ph.D., is associate professor of accounting at the University of Michigan-Flint and is a member of IMA's Detroit Chapter. You can reach him at (810) 762-3267 or clementc@umflint.edu.

QUESTION

7.3 What's is Caterpillar's recipe for 6 Sigma success?

7.4 The Elements of Supply Chain Management

*by Tom Albright and Stan Davis**

EXECUTIVE SUMMARY

- *Supply chain management* (SCM) has received increasing attention as companies seek to gain and maintain a competitive advantage in the market.

- This article discusses points that companies beginning a SCM program should consider. Although it provides many illustrations, the article concentrates on the supply-chain practices followed by Mercedes U.S. International in developing the new M-class sports utility vehicle.

- SCM encompasses not only planning and controlling the flow of materials from suppliers to end users *(logistics-based SCM)* but also the philosophy adopted by a company toward supplier relationships *(strategic SCM).*

- SCM seeks to unify skills and resources of business functions found both within an enterprise and outside. The thrust is to develop relationships and to synchronize the flow of products, services, and information.

- Supply-chain considerations arc an integral part of an organization's value chain and essential to many business initiatives, including just-in-time (JIT) manufacturing, total quality management (TQM), electronic data interchange (EDI), outsourcing, and target costing.

Supply chain logistics is a primary activity in an organization's value chain. To engage in strategic cost management, managers must identify and assess primary and secondary activities and the processes necessary for the organization to compete. These activities and processes are referred to as an organization's *value chain.*

A company's value chain includes primary activities that create value for customers both *inside and outside* the firm (Thompson and Strickland 1996). Understanding the costs associated with each activity of the value chain provides an understanding of the organization's cost structure, which allows a firm to set cost or niche strategies. Typically, a value chain includes six primary activities (Thompson and Strickland, 1996):

1. Purchased supplies and inbound logistics;
2. Operations;
3. Outbound logistics;
4. Sales and marketing;
5. Service; and
6. Profit margin.

Supply chain management is integrally involved in the first three links in the chain and is becoming integrated into a firm's strategy. In developing a strategic plan, a company should carefully analyze potential relationships with suppliers. Because successful SCM is a key element in other management techniques, such as JIT, TQM, EDI, target costing, and outsourcing, assessing the power relationship is important. Given the demands that these programs place on suppliers, proper relationships with key suppliers are essential.

ALLIANCES WITH SUPPLIERS

Successful SCM practices begin with the selection of key suppliers, then developing trusting, mutually beneficial relationships that last over long periods. Alliances with suppliers are usually necessary only for vendors that supply integral, strategically important components to the manufacturing process.

The objective of aligning closely with suppliers is not to acquire the lowest possible price but, rather, to secure acceptable prices in return for superior service and reliability. Another benefit of developing strong alliances with suppliers of key components is the assistance suppliers can offer in designing new components and production processes.

But developing strong alliances is often difficult because of mistrust on both sides of the purchase arrangement. The supplier-purchaser relationship has long been an arm's-length transaction, with both sides seeking as much short-term gain as possible. Thus, developing long-lasting ties and sharing sensitive information is often difficult. Seeking to develop alliances built on trust and mutually beneficial outcomes requires a change in mind-set at many companies.

* From: T. Albright and S. Davis, "The Elements of Supply Chain Management," *International Journal of Strategic Cost Management* (Autumn 1999): 49–65. Reprinted with permission.

IMPROVING RELATIONSHIPS WITH SUPPLIERS OF STRATEGIC PARTS

The following four practices help foster improved relations with suppliers of strategic parts (Landry 1998):

1. *Power balancing.* In buyer-supplier relationships in which a buyer represents a large proportion of a supplier's business, the buyer may be in a position to demand price (or other) concessions. Such an uneven power distribution is not conducive to building a healthy strategic alliance. Equal dependence between partners occurs when the proportion of a supplier's total output that is sold to a customer roughly equals the proportion of total purchases acquired by a customer from that supplier. For example, if a supplier sells about 25% of its total output to a strategic partner, then a power balance is achieved if the buyer's proportion of total purchases is 25% for that supplier. Maintaining relative dependence between suppliers and buyers increases the likelihood that both parties will have a vested interest in the success of the other partner as the degree of relative dependence increases.

2. *Codependency.* Apart from balancing power in a supplier-buyer relationship, developing a code-pendency in the relationship can benefit the alliance. When a supplier commits substantial specialized resources to meeting the demands of a purchaser and the purchaser chooses to single-source with that supplier, both parties have a vested interest in the success of the purchaser. This relationship reduces maneuvering for short-term gains by suppliers and strengthens the desire for mutually beneficial outcomes for both parties.

3. *Target costing.* Instead of seeking the lowest bid, establishing target costs for components, then rewarding suppliers when those targets are reached encourages joint problem solving.

4. *Personal ties.* Developing trust between suppliers and purchasers usually begins at the individual level. Establishing joint teams consisting of employees from both the purchaser and the supplier helps foster good working relationships. Trust increases as each side begins to feel more comfortable with members from the other organization.

Many organizations often single-source numerous strategic components yet fail to establish the trust and partnership ties that can provide additional benefits for both parties. As the following example illustrates, treating suppliers as partners in strategic alliances provides long-term benefits other than obtaining low costs on supplied components.

THE MERCEDES M-CLASS SPORTS UTILITY VEHICLE

During the recession that began in the early 1990s, Mercedes-Benz struggled with product development, cost efficiency, material purchasing, and problems in adapting to changing markets. In 1993, these problems caused the worst sales slump in decades, and Mercedes lost money for the first time in its history.

In a search for additional market share, new segments, and new niches, Mercedes started developing a range of new products. Perhaps the largest and most radical of these new projects was the M-class, a sports utility vehicle that moved from concept to production in a relatively short time.

To design vehicle and production systems, Mercedes-Benz US. International used *function groups* that included representatives from every area of the company (marketing, development, engineering, purchasing, production, and controlling). The role of these function groups was to develop specifications and cost projections. Note also that a modular construction process was used to produce the M-class. First-tier suppliers provided modular systems (rather than individual parts or components) for production of about 65,000 vehicles annually.

Mercedes included suppliers early in the design stage of the vehicle. By including suppliers as members of the function groups, Mercedes was able to take advantage of their expertise and advice on matters such as supplier capability, cost, and quality. The synergy generated by these cross-function groups also allowed the groups to solve larger design issues, such as how to more efficiently and economically switch from manufacturing left-side-drive vehicles to right-side-drive vehicles. Significant time savings were recognized because of the design improvements implemented by the function groups. Because supplier personnel were at the Mercedes plant on a full-time basis during the launch, other issues (such as quality problems or slight modifications to the product) could be addressed in a more timely fashion.

SUPPLIER INVOLVEMENT IN JIT AND TQM

Initiating cost savings and quality programs requires a commitment not only from an organization itself, but also from parties outside the organization, such as transporters and suppliers of goods. Management initiatives such as JIT, TQM, target costing, and outsourcing require significant cooperation between suppliers and purchasers.

The JIT philosophy advocates *waste elimination*, including wasted materials resulting from a manufacturing process and wasted time in delivery and movement of goods. Additional sources of waste include machine setups, rework, warehouse space required by large inventories, and capital required to carry large inventory levels (which can mask production problems).

The success of JIT and TQM depends on developing innovative *performance measures* for suppliers. These measures include quality, response time, and number of delivery points. The ability to sustain a long-term relationship enables purchasers to work with suppliers over time to achieve acceptable performance on such measures. Buyers that frequently change suppliers end up buying from companies that are at the beginning of the learning curve. Thus, many benefits of a long-term relationship are foregone.

In addition to quality issues, lower inventory levels require suppliers to provide more shipments in smaller quantities. Suppliers must be able to respond quickly to orders and ship in lot sizes desired by the purchaser. In some cases, manufacturers may also require delivery of goods *to the point of production*, thus reducing the need for inventory and also reducing the expense and time of moving materials from a receiving dock to a holding area, then to the point of production.

These demands have caused a different type of relationship to develop between purchasers and suppliers. Many purchasers and suppliers are forging relationships based on long-term commitments, thus saving negotiation, inspection, and other costs associated with contracting with many suppliers. Properly orchestrated, a close relationship between suppliers and purchasers can be a win-win situation when organizations initiate programs such as JIT and TQM. Buyers receive high-quality goods delivered on schedule, and suppliers gain long-term commitments that enable them to plan for future orders with the understanding that buyers will continue to assist them in improving quality and service. These quality and service improvements can then be transferred to other customers the supplier may service.

MERCEDES AND IN-SEQUENCE DELIVERY

Mercedes designed its manufacturing facility consistent with the JIT philosophy, so there is little warehouse space at the factory where the M-class is made. Instead, Mercedes relies on *in-sequence delivery*, a system whereby preconstructed modules arrive in a prescribed sequence and are placed on the manufacturing line.

For example, from the moment a new vehicle order is initiated, manufacturers of the cockpit module have 169 minutes to manufacture (to specifications) and deliver the module to the proper place in the manufacturing line at the Mercedes plant. Mercedes and its suppliers stay in constant contact through EDI facilities that transmit order specifications and other information between the plant and first-tier suppliers.

Exhibit 1 illustrates Mercedes' in-sequence delivery system. When an order is initiated, suppliers are notified through an EDI transmission of the specifications for the new vehicle. Suppliers are then expected to deliver their products in a predetermined order as each module is needed in the manufacturing process. This system moves one step beyond the simple JIT philosophy by requiring various suppliers to synchronize their efforts so that production can occur uninterrupted.

TARGET COSTING

Because most costs are designed into a product, target costing must begin at the design stage of product development. It is at this stage that supplier selection becomes most critical. The indexes developed by Mercedes allowed the company and its suppliers to work closely to align the cost of a function group with its perceived value, as defined by customers. (All numbers provided here have been altered for proprietary reasons; however, the tables illustrate the actual process used in the development of the M-class.)

MERCEDES AND TARGET COSTING

During the concept development phase for the M-class, Mercedes team members used various indexes to help determine critical performance, design, and cost relationships. To construct the indexes, various forms of information were gathered from customers, suppliers, and members of the design team.

Although the actual number of categories used by Mercedes was much higher, Exhibit 2 illustrates the calculations used to quantify customer responses to the M-class concept. For example, values shown in the *importance column* resulted from asking a sample of potential customers whether they consider each category extremely important when considering the purchase of a new Mercedes product. Customers could respond affirmatively to all categories that applied.

EXHIBIT 1. IN-SEQUENCE DELIVERY

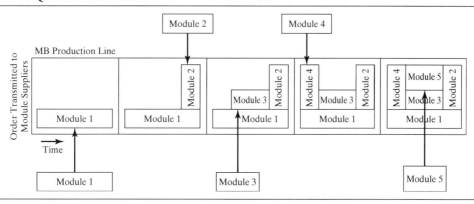

EXHIBIT 2. RELATIVE IMPORTANCE RANKING BY CATEGORY

Category	Importance	Relative Percentage
Safety	32	41%
Comfort	25	32
Economy	15	18
Styling	7	9
Total	79	100%

WORK OF THE FUNCTION GROUPS

To gain a better understanding of various sources of costs, function groups were identified together with target cost estimates. As shown in Exhibit 3, the relative target cost percentage of each function group was computed.

Exhibit 4 summarizes how each function group contributed to the consumer requirements identified in Exhibit 2. For example, potential customers identified safety as an important characteristic of the M-class; some function groups contributed more to the safety category than did others. Mercedes engineers determined that chassis quality was an important element of safety (50% of the total function group contribution).

Exhibit 5 combines the category weighting percentages from Exhibit 2 with the function group contribution from Exhibit 4. The result is an importance index that measures the relative importance of each function group across all categories. For example, potential customers weighted the categories of safety, comfort, economy, and styling as .41, 32, .18, and .09, respectively. The rows in Exhibit 5 represent the contribution of each function group to the various categories. The importance index for the function group is calculated by multiplying each row value by its corresponding category value, then summing the results. For example, the chassis importance index of .33 is computed as follows: $(.50 \times .41) + (.30 \times .32) + (.10 \times .18) + (.10 \times .09) = .33$.

As shown in Exhibit 6, the target cost index is calculated by dividing the importance index by the target cost percentage by function group. Managers at

Mercedes used indexes such as these during the concept design phase to understand the relationship of the *importance* of a function group to the *target cost* of a function group. Indexes less than one may indicate a cost in excess of the perceived value of the function group. Thus, opportunities for cost reduction—consistent with customer demands— may be identified and managed during the early stages of product development.

OUTSOURCING

A popular trend among manufacturing organizations is to minimize on-site value-added activities by outsourcing significant portions of the assembly processes. Original equipment manufacturers (OEMs) have increasingly begun to outsource their production processes to contract manufacturers in an effort to reduce costs.

OEMs now outsource some of the manufacturing processes that they formerly considered core competencies. OEMs are focusing their efforts on design and innovation issues. It has been estimated that contract manufacturers will achieve a cumulative annual growth rate of 25% between 1996 and 2001. EDI and partnering with suppliers are essential for OEMs that seek to reduce costs by using contract manufacturers (Roberts 1998).

Outsourcing Manufacturing Assembly Processes at Mercedes. Many manufacturers contract with suppliers for parts, then manage assembly in-house, but Mercedes took a different strategy by outsourcing assemblies of the M-class to suppliers. Engineers divided the M-class into systems that were combined to form a completed vehicle. As many as 18 modules to be delivered in sequence have been outsourced to suppliers, which purchase the sub-components and assemble the module for Mercedes.

By assembling the modules off-site, Mercedes has reduced plant and warehouse space requirements. In addition, the number of suppliers used has been drastically reduced by this outsourcing of systems. For example, the cockpit requires more than 150 parts from about 35 vendors. By outsourcing the cockpit to one vendor, Mercedes has reduced its involvement from potentially 35 vendors to only one.

EXHIBIT 3. TARGET COST AND PERCENTAGE BY FUNCTIONAL GROUP

Function Group	Target Cost	Percentage of Total
Chassis	$x,xxx	20%
Transmission	$x,xxx	25
Air conditioner	$x,xxx	5
Electrical system	$x,xxx	7
Other function groups	$x,xxx	43
Total	$xx,xxx	100%

EXHIBIT 4. FUNCTION GROUP CONTRIBUTION TO CUSTOMER REQUIREMENTS

	Category			
Function group	Safety	Comfort	Economy	Styling
Chassis	50%	30%	10%	10%
Transmission	20	20	30	
Air conditioner		20		5
Electrical system	5		20	
Other systems	25	30	40	85
Total	100%	100%	100%	100%

EXHIBIT 5. IMPORTANCE INDEX OF VARIOUS FUNCTIONAL GROUPS

	Category				
Function group	Safety .41	Comfort .32	Economy .18	Styling .09	Importance Index
Chassis	.50	.30	.10	.10	.33
Transmission	.20	.20	.30		.20
Air conditioner		.20		.05	.07
Electrical system	.05		.20		.06
Other systems	.25	.30	.40	.85	.35
Total	1.00	1.00	1.00	1.00	

EXHIBIT 6. IMPORTANCE INDEX OF VARIOUS FUNCTIONAL GROUPS

	(A) Importance	Index (B) % of Target Cost	(c) A/B Target
Function group	Index	Index	Cost
Chassis	.33	.20	1.65
Transmission	.20	.25	.80
Air conditioner	.07	.05	1.40
Electrical system	.06	.07	.86
Other systems	.35	.43	.81
Total		1.00	

First- and Second-Tier Suppliers. Note that Mercedes has developed a two-tier supplier network. First-tier suppliers provide finished modules to Mercedes. Second-tier suppliers are the vendors from which first-tier suppliers purchase parts. At the beginning of the production process, Mercedes maintained strict control over both first-tier and second-tier suppliers with respect to cost and quality issues. As the level of comfort and trust grew between Mercedes and first-tier suppliers, Mercedes gave first-tier suppliers more freedom to make their own arrangements with second-tier suppliers. Exhibit 7 illustrates Mercedes' two-tier relationship with suppliers.

The benefits to Mercedes are numerous. By outsourcing more than 80% of vehicle components to a limited number of first-tier suppliers, Mercedes reduces the overhead associated with purchasing activities and also saves on labor and employee-related costs. Further, by having established strong alliances with first-tier suppliers, Mercedes enjoys a higher level of service from suppliers and benefits from the expertise developed by suppliers as they seek ways to improve current operations. Finally, because much of the product is manufactured off-site, suppliers of major modules are encouraged to work together to continuously improve not only their own module but the integrated product as well.

DEVELOPING SUPPLIER RELATIONSHIPS

Developing strategic alliances with suppliers can be very rewarding. Although each organization's experience with building supplier relationships is unique, three suggestions can make a venture more likely to succeed.

Commit to Partnering Before Seeking Partners. Because developing strategic alliances with suppliers will change many practices, top management must be committed to establishing these relationships and accepting the changes that they will bring. Some of these changes include:

- Accepting a smaller vendor base from which to purchase supplies;
- Including suppliers in the early stages of design and development of new products; and
- Developing the ability to share information with vendors that will make their jobs easier.

An organization's commitment also may include agreeing to train a supplier's employees in various areas of importance (e.g., the organization's production practices), developing joint objectives with suppliers (e.g., joint profit levels), and striving to be a better customer.

Before seeking strategic partners, however, organizations need to accept the fact that the best supplier may not necessarily be the cheapest provider of goods and services. Higher-quality products and smaller, more frequent deliveries (as required by TQM and JIT) are more costly, and suppliers should not be expected to bear the entire burden of increased costs. Such an arrangement would not foster the trust between suppliers and buyers that is necessary in a long-term, mutually beneficial partnership (Duncan and Breen, 1988; Adair- | Heeley, 1988; Hay, 1990b; Kepp, 1994; Tait, 1998).

EXHIBIT 7. MERCEDES TWO-TIER SUPPLIER NETWORK

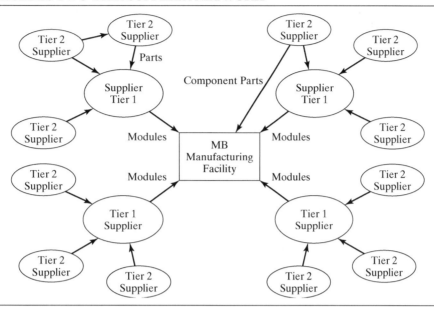

Select Appropriate Suppliers for Alliances. The first thing to remember when selecting suppliers is that the best supplier may not be among the current set of companies that provides goods to your organization. It may be necessary to sever business relations with some current vendors (even if they have been suppliers for a long time) if they are unwilling or unable to commit to a partnering relationship.

Make sure that a supplier can provide the level of service and quality your business will require. Some vendors, eager to earn business, may "promise the world" but lack the capacity, manpower, or infrastructure required to deliver on their end of the bargain.

Another important point to consider is the supplier's commitment to entering into a partnership arrangement. Because a strategic alliance requires two-way commitment, suppliers should be willing to accept their responsibilities in the partnership, such as the requirements imposed on suppliers under such initiatives as TQM or JIT, or a commitment to continuous improvement. Finally, inquire about the performance of suppliers with a few of their other customers to ensure that their dependability, quality, and service are acceptable (Hay, 1990a; Anonymous, 1994).

Be Prepared to Sell the Relationship. Ask the question, "Why would a supplier want to align itself with this organization?" A cursory glance at the requirements imposed by TQM or JIT programs may leave a vendor asking, "What's in it for me?"—a valid question. A supplier's willingness to enter into such a relationship

depends in part on its ability to meet the increased requirements.

Key selling points include the fact that, because fewer vendors will be supplying like goods, the result should be an increased volume for supplier partners. Other rewards for suppliers include the assurance of business, technical, production, and training assistance; financial help (if necessary) to acquire facilities needed to meet the customer's needs; and the ability to take advantage of any production or technological gains that result from doing business with other customers. Unless the arrangement is mutually beneficial, the prospects that suppliers will enter into helpful strategic alliances are greatly reduced (Duncan and Breen, 1988; Morgan, 1993a, 1993b).

LOGISTICS-BASED SUPPLY CHAIN MANAGEMENT

Logistics-based supply chain management (LSCM) has long held a prominent place within operations management as an area for cost savings. Traditionally, LSCM has involved management of material flow from supplier to manufacturer (inbound logistics) or from manufacturer to customer (outbound logistics). This approach, however, was restricted because it ignored material flow *within* an organization. Recent approaches have encompassed total materials flow: from the supplier of materials, through the manufacturing organization, to purchasers of finished goods.

Specifically, LSCM activities include (Copacino, 1997):

- Sourcing and purchasing;
- Conversion (manufacturing), including capacity planning and operations management;
- Production scheduling and materials planning;
- Distribution planning and warehouse operations:
- Inventory management (including inbound and outbound transportation); and
- The linkage with customer service, sales, promotion, and marketing activities.

LSCM can provide value-added activities in many areas including transportation, inventory, and information (Ross, 1998). Each is discussed in more detail here.

Transportation. The primary goal of transportation is to have goods delivered on time, undamaged, and cost-effectively. Deregulation of the transportation industry has made contracting for the delivery of inbound and outbound freight more beneficial. Although a common practice is to contract with the lowest bidder for transportation services, many shippers are beginning to demand not only low prices but also a higher level of service. Given the increased importance of JIT deliveries and maintaining low inventories, managers often incorporate the cost of missed delivery schedules into the cost of transportation.

Two philosophies exist toward selecting carriers:

- Repeatedly soliciting bids for individual transportation engagements; and
- Developing a relationship with certain carriers to encourage higher quality performance.

By sharing shipment responsibilities, sellers and buyers can include carriers in negotiations and reach agreements on such issues as:

- Traffic volume;
- Frequency and quality of service;
- Rates; and
- The carrier's liability for loss, delay, or damage.

Agreements that include all three parties—buyer, supplier, and transporter—will likely be more beneficial to all parties. The buyer gets to specify its issues of importance (e.g., on-time delivery vs. cost; damaged goods vs. on-time delivery), whereas the seller gets to specify its own issues of importance. The transporter gains a better understanding of what the buyer expects, what the seller expects, and what services are most important to customers-including what services the customers are willing to pay for (Carter and Ferrin, 1995).

Inventory. LSCM can also aid in controlling inventory levels and ensuring that goods are delivered in good order to other manufacturing units or to buyers outside the organization. Marketing, manufacturing, and purchasing personnel should all participate in forecasting material needs to achieve an effective purchasing and delivery plan.

Traditional solutions for inventory management include mathematical formulas such as the *economic order quantity* (EOQ) formula and *materials requirement planning* (MRP) techniques, which are used to optimize production schedules. Many computerized programs exist to aid manufacturers and wholesalers in maintaining an effective inventory management system (software packages used for SCM are discussed later in this article).

In managing inventory levels, it is essential for businesses to know with as much certainty as possible the lead time for delivery of supplies and for the production of goods. Without understanding the time required between recognizing the need for a good and its production, maintaining an optimal inventory balance is difficult. Unknown lead times increase the chance of over- or understocked inventory, both of which are costly to a business (Ross, 1998; Copacino, 1997).

LSCM at Hewlett-Packard. AtHewlett-Packard(HP), benchmarking is used to aid LSCM planning. Inventory is an insurance against uncertainty HP attacks this uncertainty at three sources: suppliers, manufacturing, and customers. Although not all sources of uncertainty can be eliminated, tracking certain measures enables manufacturing organizations to reduce their exposure to uncertainty. At HP, benchmark indicators include the following:

1. *Suppliers*. HP tracks on-time performance, average days or hours late, and the degree of inconsistency (the standard deviation of late measures). Tracking these measures helps HP know how much extra stock to keep on hand per supplier while minimizing the probability of stockouts.
2. *Manufacturing*. Downtime (for the process, not just a machine), repair time, and variation in repair time are key performance indicators. HP uses a probability distribution of performance and focuses on the reliability of the process.
3. *Customers*. Greater levels of order variation require greater levels of safety stock. HP tracks average demand and the variability of demand by customer (Davis, 1993).

Vendor-Managed Inventory. To control costs and improve the supply chain, leading companies use vendor managed inventory (VMI). By yielding (or at least sharing) the responsibility of managing inventories with suppliers, buyers reduce inventory carrying costs and receive improved service from suppliers (Tyndall et al., 1998). Suppliers benefit by gaining better insight into buyers' requirements and processes, and also from the increased information flow concerning future demands. By entering into a VMI agreement with a supplier, one wholesaler reduced delivery and administrative charges and also average inventory (from 10 days to 6 days) while keeping service levels constant. The company also reduced the time from order to delivery from 48 hours to 10 hours. Finally, the company gained a competitive advantage by sharing some of the associated cost savings with customers (Holstrom, 1998).

Organizing suppliers into a consortium can enable manufacturers to control inventory costs. Coordinating the activities of first and second tier suppliers can yield lower transaction costs by sharing operating insights and best practices. The increased cooperation among consortium members facilitates the sharing of information learned about third-tier suppliers and thus helps identify substandard suppliers. FedEx, among other organizations, has begun offering management services explicitly to help other companies set up consortium buying arrangements. Toyota has also developed supplier associations that foster communication and cooperation across major suppliers. The associations do the following (Stuart et al., 1998; Tyndall et al., 1998):

■ Standardize quality control;
■ Facilitate supplier interaction; and
■ Provide forums that build trust.

Information Technology. With shorter turnaround times and smaller orders becoming the norm, the ability to withdraw information from a logistics management system is crucial. Many buyers and suppliers set up EDI facilities that provide an unfettered information flow to ensure that orders and inventory levels are constantly monitored and maintained.

Characteristics of an LSCM system include:

■ Rapid and accurate transaction processing;
■ Real-time technologies integrated with other functions in the organization; and
■ Advanced decision-support capabilities.

These systems also should include modeling, transportation, routing, and scheduling capabilities that are linked to suppliers and purchasers (Copacino, 1997).

By choosing to link with suppliers through some form of EDI, companies can share long-term and short-term forecast demands to aid upstream suppliers in their scheduling requirements. One Volvo plant uses EDI hookups with a supplier to share forecasts of goods three to four days in the future. The EDI system then creates sales orders and initiates purchase orders so that the forecast can be met. Further, EDI links are planned for suppliers of Volvo's suppliers (second-tier suppliers) to further expedite the transfer of information and maintain proper materials flow among suppliers and Volvo (Anonymous, 1998a).

Other organizations use the Internet to share information with key suppliers. Using secure websites, manufacturers such as Boeing, Dell, and Thompson Consumer Electronics have designed ways to improve communications with suppliers and customers. Boeing allows customers to browse its catalog and order spare parts from an Internet site, which processes about 4,000 transactions per day. This has reduced order-processing costs by 25% and also shortened delivery time.

Thompson Consumer Electronics receives customer demand forecasts on its secured Internet site. This information is entered into Thompson's SCM software for scheduling and production requirements (Thompson uses SCM software manufactured by i2 Technologies). Further, Thompson posts its demand forecasts on line, thereby allowing suppliers to know when components are needed. As a result, Thompson has shortened lead times from three or four weeks to as little as one week in many cases.

Dell has taken information-sharing one step further. By customizing about 30 web pages for top suppliers, Dell allows the suppliers to view its customers' demands so that the suppliers can better plan for future demands. Dell also has linked websites to bulletin boards where suppliers can post messages and share information. Manufacturers on the leading edge of SCM continually seek ways to increase information flow between suppliers and its customers (Stein and Sweat, 1998).

SCM SOFTWARE
SCM software integrates external communications (i.e., communications with suppliers and purchasers through either the Internet or EDI) and internal communications. SCM software includes (but is not limited to) products from:

■ Manugistics, Inc.
■ American Software, Inc.
■ i2 Technologies, Inc.
■ Numertrix Ltd.
■ Red Pepper Software Co.

Using the PC-based Manugistics Routing and Scheduling Version 10 (MRS 10), Domino's Pizza updates and optimizes its routing schedules for delivery to production sites on a daily basis. Domino's previous system allowed updates only on a semiannual basis. Given dramatic changes in demand, Domino's hopes to save $1 million during its first year by optimizing its trucking routes on a daily basis.

By linking with suppliers and purchasing an integrated SCM software package, Molson Breweries not only notifies suppliers in various manufacturing locations of upcoming demand but also gains valuable information about margins for particular production sites. Production scheduling and transportation now is handled more efficiently based on profit margins of products, demand in given areas, and supplier capabilities at a given time.

3-Com Corp., a network equipment supplier, relied on linked Excel spreadsheets to keep production lines near target utilizations. As volume grew, planning and scheduling became more difficult. Therefore, 3-Com started using Red Pepper's Response Agent to aid in its SCM efforts. Now schedules that balance material and capacity constraints are generated and what-if scenarios can be run in a matter of hours; previously, what-if scenarios took days to run (Mayer, 1996).

By using Internet technology, EDI, and SCM software, suppliers know what a customer needs before the customer asks (or, possibly, before the customer even realizes that it needs anything). Thus, technology has made the concept of a "seamless" supply chain a reality. Developing creative links with suppliers and customers appears to be a rich opportunity for innovative manufacturers to enjoy a competitive advantage over competitors that are unwilling or unable to invest the time and resources into improving their supply chains.

FUTURE TRENDS IN LSCM
Trends in LSCM include the following:

- A greater emphasis on establishing a balance between cost and service in the logistics function;
- Increasing third-party services for LSCM activities;
- Increasing emphasis on channel integration, and
- Expanding roles for EDI relationships between suppliers and purchasers.

The transportation and warehousing industry is slowly transforming itself into a full-service logistics manager for manufacturing organizations that outsource logistics functions. Successful third-party providers of logistics services will tailor their services to specific industries and manufacturers to develop an expertise and relationship not offered by ordinary transportation providers. Included in these services are EDI hookups linking suppliers and purchasers to further facilitate transactions among organizations (Copacino, 1997). Competition among third-party transportation providers (transporters of goods other than the supplier or the purchaser of the goods) is increasing. Thus, customers can not only demand lower prices but also expect more

extensive services, furthering the benefits to businesses deciding to outsource logistics functions (Mireles, 1998).

Channel integration is the management of inventory, warehousing, and transportation across corporate boundaries (Copacino, 1997). Strategic supply chain management and logistical supply chain management techniques discussed in this article enable managers to reduce interorganizational barriers. Segmenting product offerings into channels allows manufacturers to better determine profitable and unprofitable product lines, differentiate between the levels of service required by these channels, and possibly eliminate unneeded layers within some channels.

Another major trend in LSCM is an increased dependence on EDI. Organizations are just beginning to realize the vast array of benefits available from EDI and advanced information systems capabilities. Unfortunately, a recent survey conducted by KPMG as part of a Global Supply Chain Benchmark Study reports that many organizations are not taking advantages of recent information technology advances. The report indicates that organizations are making more use of SCM software for internal purposes, but that the exchange of information between organizations is still far behind where it could be with the capabilities of today's information technology (Anonymous, 1998b).

ENDNOTES
C. B. Adair-Heeley, "JIT Purchasing: Seven Steps for Successful Implementation," *Production and Inventory Management Review and APICS* 8 (1988): 22–23.

Anonymous, "Service Is the Difference When Choosing a Copier Supplier," *Managing Office Technology* 39 (1994): 79–80.

Anonymous, "Make Supply Chain Technology Work for You," *Works Management* (July 1998a): 37–41.

Anonymous, "Key Trends and Analysis," *Stores* (April 1988b): S9–S20.

J. R. Carter and B. G. Ferrin, "The Impact of Transportation Costs on Supply Chain Management," *Journal of Business Logistics* 16 (1996): 207.

W. C. Copacino, *Supply Chain Management: The Basics and Beyond.* (Boca Raton, FL: St. Lucie Press, 1997).

T. Davis, "Effective Supply Chain Management," *Sloan Management Review* (Summer 1993): 35–46.

W. L. Duncan and S. Breen, "Making JIT Attractive to Suppliers," *Manufacturing Systems* 6 (1988): 54–55.

E. J. Hay, "Implementing JIT Purchasing: Phase III-Selection," *Production and Inventory Management Review and APICS News* 10 (1990a): 28–29.

E. J. Hay, "Implementing JIT Purchasing: Phase IV-Relationship Building," *Production and Inventory Management Review and APICS News* 10 (1990b): 38–40.

J. Holmstrom, "Implementing Vendor-Managed Inventory the Efficient Way: A Case Study of Partnership in the Supply Chain," *Production and Inventory Management Journal* (3rd Quarter 1998): 1–5.

M. Kepp. "Relationship-Building," *Business Latin America* 29 (1994): 6–7.

J. T. Landry, "Supply Chain Management," *Harvard Business Review* (November 1998): 24–25.

J. H. Mayer, "Supply-Chain Tools Cut Inventory Fat," *Applications Software Magazine* (May 1996): 77–80.

R. C. Mireles, "Supply Chain Management Trends," *Transportation and Distribution* (July 1998): 75.

J. Morgan, "Building a World Class Supply Base from Scratch," *Purchasing* (August 19, 1993a): 56–61.

J. Morgan, "Supplier Programs Take Time to Become World Class," *Purchasing* (August 19, 1993b): 61–63.

B. Roberts, "Ties that Bind," *Electronic Business* (August 1998): 62–68.

D. F. Ross, *Competing Through Supply Chain Management: Creating Market Winning Strategies Through Supply Chain Partnerships*. (New York: Chapman & Hall, 1998.)

T. Stein and J. Sweat, "Killer Supply Chain," *Information Week* 708 (1998): 36–41.

I. Stuart, R. Deckert, D. McCutcheon, and R. Kunst, "Case Study: A Leveraged Learning Network," *Sloan Management Review* 39 (1998): 81–93.

D. Tait, "Make Strong Relationships a Priority," *Canadian Manager* 23 (1998): 21–28.

A. A. Thompson and A. J. Strickland, III. *Strategic Management Concepts and Cases* (9th ed.). (Chicago: Irwin, 1996.)

G. Tyndall, C. Gopal, W. Partsch, and J. Kamauff, "Ten Strategies to Enhance Supplier Management," *National Productivity Review* (Summer 1998): 31–44.

Tom Albright is the J. Reese Phifer Faculty Fellow and Stan Davis is a doctoral student, both at the Culverhouse School of Accountancy at the University of Alabama in Tuscaloosa. Alabama. The authors thank Ola Kallenius and Bob Birch of Mercedes for their generous contributions.

QUESTIONS

7.4a   What are the four practices that help organizations foster improved relations with suppliers of strategic parts? Explain.

7.4b   What is the latest improvement in logistics-based supply chain management (LSCM)? What are its key elements?

Chapter 8

Measuring and Managing Life-Cycle Costs

R. Cooper and W. B. Chew's article, *Control Tomorrow's Costs Through Today's Designs* (Reading 8.1), discusses the importance of target costing for many of today's manufacturing organizations. In short, target costing is a management process in which companies work backwards to arrive at product costs, after making a detailed assessment of what customers' requirements are for a given product. Once the level of quality and functionality are set and a target price and volume are determined, companies focus on developing manufacturing processes and materials sourcing at a target cost to achieve a target profit. This process is distinct from many traditional Western approaches in which the manufacturing cost plus a desired profit determines selling price. Using examples from Japanese firms such as Olympus Optical Company, one of the world's leaders in single-lens reflex cameras, and Komatsu, manufacturer of earth-moving products, Cooper and Chew detail the process of developing target costs at each firm. The authors also discuss how target costing can be applied in process and service industries.

Reading 8.2, *The Use of Target Costing in Developing the Mercedes-Benz M-Class*, by Tom Albright describes how Mercedes-Benz used target costing in the design and production of the M-class, a sports utility vehicle (SUV). Mercedes used cross-functional teams and included project and process engineers, marketing people, engineers, and customers to help define key features that potential customers would value in an SUV. Professor Albright traces the development of the SUV through the concept, product realization and production phases. The article provides great insight into the target costing process.

Susan Borkowsi, Mary Jeanne Welsch and Kristin Wentzel discuss Johnson & Johnson's sustainability reporting system in Reading 8.3, *Johnson & Johnson: A Model for Sustainability Reporting*. The authors detail how Johnson & Johnson accounts for the nonfinancial factors related to environmental, social, and governance issues that affect the company's future performance.

In the third article in their series on the motion picture industry, Reading 8.4, *The Business of Making Money with Movies*, (see Readings 3.5 and 4.3), S. Mark Young, James Gong, and Wim Van der Stede discuss how the life-cycle revenues are captured by the numerous revenue streams that are generated after a feature film leaves theatrical release. These revenue streams include home video sales, pay-per-view opportunities, premium pay channels, network and cable television, international distribution, and Internet and mobile distribution.

Readings
Chapter 8

8.1 Control Tomorrow's Costs Through Today's Designs

by Robin Cooper and W. Bruce Chew*

Over the past 15 years, company after company has learned that quality must be designed into products before they are manufactured—that it is expensive, if not misguided, to attempt to inspect in quality after the product has left the production line. Today the most competitive companies are applying the same logic to determining the price of new products. Before a company launches a product (or family of products), senior managers determine its ideal selling price, establish the feasibility of meeting that price, and then control costs to ensure that the price is met. They are using a management process known as *target costing*.

Target costing drives a product development strategy that focuses the design team on the ultimate customer and on the real opportunity in the market. Leading Japanese electronics and vehicle manufacturers have used target costing to their advantage, and companies are now introducing it in the United States, Germany, and elsewhere. Its rigorous cost-management technique helps prevent senior managers from launching low-margin products that do not generate appropriate returns to the company, but its greater value lies in its ability to bring the challenge of the marketplace back through the chain of production to product designers. Target costing ensures that development teams will bring profitable products to market not only with the right level of quality and functionality but also with appropriate prices for the targeted customer segments. It is a discipline that harmonizes the labor of disparate participants in the development effort, from designers and manufacturing engineers to market researchers and suppliers.

The logic of target costing is simple. Looking at tomorrow's marketplace, the organization maps customer segments and targets the most attractive ones. It determines what level of quality and functionality will succeed within each segment, given a predetermined target price (and volume and launch date). The organization then designs the sourcing, production, and delivery processes that will enable it to achieve its desired profits at this target. In effect, the company reasons backward from customers' needs and willingness to pay instead of following the flawed but common practice of cost-plus pricing. Target costing ensures that success with the customers will yield economic success for the company.

COST DISCIPLINE: WHY NOW?

The logic of target costing is so simple and compelling that one may wonder why it has only recently begun to receive attention. After all, at any time in the past, senior managers could have gained much from becoming involved in the process of pricing and costing a product before it was designed. Their lack of involvement gave engineers and enthusiasts, who were unlikely to see the whole picture, undue influence over the company's competitive position. When senior managers tried to drive costs out of their operations ex post facto by cutting staff, eliminating frills, outsourcing, or reengineering downstream processes, they often discovered that as much as 70% to 80% of a product's costs were effectively immutable after it left the designers' hands. As product and process technologies have become more integrated, a product's cost has become even more strongly tied to its design.

Nevertheless, although a preemptive and disciplined approach to costs has always been reasonable, it has not always been urgent, and companies do not usually undertake difficult tasks if the tasks are avoidable. These days, however, price and cost targeting are no longer avoidable, largely because of the erosion of important first-mover advantages in the new global economy. In the past, many leading companies, especially those led by technical differentiation, found that they could take a cost-plus approach to releasing new products because they anticipated profiting from serial generations of products. They believed that being first to market was most important; that in preparing to be first, design teams needed to focus only on selecting and executing well the appropriate bundle of product attributes; and that ultimately, over several iterations of the product, the marketplace would allow the company to earn a reasonable return on total capital employed.

By that logic, when the product was first released, it might carry a comparatively high price considered affordable by only a small number of lead users, such as businesses hoping to turn a new technology to their advantage or comparatively wealthy, adventurous technologies. Lead users would pay a premium for the first-generation product and help create excitement for its new features; they would even help establish the brand. The revenues from lead users would rarely cover the cost of developing the product. Hewlett-Packard Company, for example, did not expect the first releases of its laser printers to recover R&D costs. But first-mover companies have assumed that they would have time to scale up to mass production and introduce serially cheaper versions of products for increasingly broader segments of customers. The mass market would be the source of most profits—as indeed it was for consumer products such as the 35-millimeter camera and the fax, and for components such as ABS brakes and digital TV controls.

Today that strategic assumption would be disastrous for all but the most advanced products, those with highly proprietary technologies. Global markets no longer allow a company time to introduce a product and then scale up. Now imitators—usually lean enterprises—can bring "me too" products to market so rapidly that first-mover companies have no time to inculcate brand loyalty, let alone recover their development costs. Lean competitors, with faster reflexes than old mass-production companies, work on shorter product-development and life cycles, and they manufacture almost anywhere—Korea, Mexico, Israel.

The growing number and increasing ubiquity of lean competitors means that copycat versions of most new products will be available within months, not years. So if market leaders can't recover costs as they used to, they have no choice but to manage costs from the design phase forward and to launch products at prices that will attract broad segments of customers and forestall imitation. How long they can hold on to their market, then, will often depend on how quickly they can offer greater functionality without raising price.

For companies to gain and hold market leadership today, they have to design the cost out of their products when they set initial levels of quality and functionality and they have to calibrate product performance to an identified price niche. In other words, senior managers need to approach new product development controlling for tomorrow's costs, not just today's. And tomorrow comes more quickly than it used to.

OLYMPUS: FROM COST TARGETS TO TARGET COSTING

In Japan, competition among lean companies has become so intense that aggressive cost management is critical to survival in sonic sectors. It is thus no accident that leading organizations such as Olympus Optical Company and Komatsu developed and adapted target costing early on.

Olympus was a leader in single-lens reflex (SLR) cameras, which had no technological competitor for a generation. But by 1987, "compact" cameras built around a miniaturized electronic shutter had absorbed so many advanced electronic controls—features such as automatic exposure and zoom—that consumers began to view them as a serious alternative to the SLR. Olympus had introduced a compact of its own as early as 1978, but not as a main focus of its product portfolio. In the mid-1980s, Olympus began losing money, and by 1987 its losses were substantial.

Senior managers saw severe problems. Cameras incorporating the new electronic technologies suffered from poor quality and there were no individual product "hits." The managers concluded that the planning and development of product families needed improvement. Externally, Olympus suffered from the sudden shift from SLR cameras to competitors' compact cameras and from a steady appreciation of the yen.

The company reacted first with an effort to regain lost share by introducing a number of new products—for example, SLRs with advanced electronics and compacts with an advanced zoom. A second initiative was aimed at improving quality, which historically had been high at Olympus and which continued to be crucial to its ability to lower the total costs associated with its products.

But most important to Olympus was the third initiative: reconciling production costs to a volatile market. Managers believed that the company's ability to manufacture cameras at a cost that would meet the increasingly stringent expectations of its customers would be central to the success of any new product. Moreover, the company's product development process would have to meet challenging price and profit targets within 18 months of their being set—before the competitive environment could shift again.

This was not the first time that Olympus managers had set cost targets for new products, but earlier targets had been more or less hypothetical. Senior managers had created no imperative to meet them, and missed targets did not prevent products from being launched. Essentially, designers did their best on functionality, manufacturing engineers pursued efficiency, and marketing sold what was produced. All that changed in 1987.

First, Olympus tried to establish a clearer picture of what features future customers would value in new product families. It produced a corporate plan that identified the future mix of businesses by major product line, the desired levels of profitability, and the contribution of each product to the cultivation of the brand, and it performed a technology review to learn how current and future technologies would affect the camera business. The technology review included an audit of Olympus's proprietary technologies that could be turned to the company's advantage. Its market mapping included an analysis of the general business environment to determine how macro-economic factors, such as changing exchange rates and the further segmentation of income groups, were likely to affect consumer demand. Finally, the marketing research included a survey of information collected from such sources as Olympus questionnaires, group interviews, interviews at fashion centers, and interviews with photographers as well as a competitive analysis that examined areas such as competitors' capabilities, likely price points, and filed patents.

With a clearer sense of what the camera market would bear and what Olympus's profitability goals required, the company identified the price points at which new compact cameras would sell. The U.S. market price for basic compact-camera models in 1991 was about $100. With that price as a baseline, Olympus analyzed consumer trends, competitors' performance, and forward-looking technology to establish what relationship it could anticipate between distinctive camera features, such as magnification capability or smaller size, and higher price points. From each price point, Olympus subtracted the appropriate margins for dealers and its U.S. subsidiary and also subtracted import costs, such as freight and duties, to arrive at the price that would be paid to the factory for any new model. Then, by subtracting its own margin requirement, Olympus finally arrived at a preliminary target cost for each new product.

Now what it needed was a disciplined process for developing products that could be made at those costs. The responsibility for ensuring that the company could produce cameras with the features customers wanted and at costs within the targeted limits fell to a product-development management team at Tatsuno, the site of Olympus's primary manufacturing operations. Only when designers and manufacturing engineers could demonstrate that estimated production costs did not exceed target costs would a camera be submitted for release to production.

OLYMPUS MOVES TO CLOSE THE GAPS

This process may sound straightforward, but it was not: Only about 20% of proposed new models cleared Olympus's hurdle on the first pass. However, the 80% that missed were not abandoned. As at many companies, it was not uncommon at Olympus for product managers to design "nice-to-have," but not "need-to-have" features into their products. The product-development management team's job was to ask whether the value those features added really outweighed their costs. Correspondingly, they would ask whether an enhanced

product could justifiably be moved to the next higher price point so that its estimated costs would generate acceptable returns.

Soon enough, those reviews ended. If target costs could not be met or price points could not be changed, the team returned the product to research and development for redesign.

In the context of this review, Olympus managers used a life-cycle analysis to reckon the costs of important new technologies incorporated in new product designs. That is, they assessed the value of a technology's contribution to features that could be expected to serve a variety of models over the life cycle of a whole product family; they did not attribute the technology's costs only to the first models introduced. Further, they separated the whole cost of a new technology into its two components: the costs of research and development and the costs of production.

The Olympus product-development team determined that in allocating research and development costs, product designers should consider how long a camera family is likely to be on the market (on the order of three years) or how long a specific feature is likely to find application in other camera families. As for production costs, Olympus managers learned that even after a product family comes to market, the costs associated with new technology often decline quickly and dramatically with the adoption of manufacturing programs that actually increase product quality—for instance, by reducing the number of parts in a subassembly, eliminating labor-intensive mechanical adjustments, or moving from metal or glass to plastic. The number of parts in the shutter unit of one entire class of compact cameras, for example, fell from 105 to 56, a reduction that led to a 58% decrease in production costs for this widely used component. By 1990, Olympus managers had discovered that the company could generally reduce its production costs by approximately 35% across the production lifetime of its new products. The product-development management team incorporated this figure into its target costing of future products.

On the whole, life-cycle analysis helped many potentially profitable products clear the hurdle. The practice may sound vaguely like the old strategy of distributing costs over successive generations of buyers, from lead users to mass markets, but it is different. There is no thought here of introducing the product family at high prices that then fall as volume increases. Cost, not price, is expected to fall.

Cost reductions of this magnitude don't happen without strenuous effort. For existing products and processes, Olympus monitored and managed fixed costs, purchased-parts costs, routine production costs, the costs of defective production, capacity utilization targets, and overhead expenses. And Olympus used its falling production costs in a number of ways. At times, it raised margins; at other times, it selectively dropped price points. On the whole, however, the company used cost savings to improve its products over time. The one thing it did not do was take a short-term profit, which, in the unforgiving environment of lean competition, would have been the most dangerous option. A company that just cashes in its market advantage invites imitation and invests nothing in sustaining its technical differentiation.

KOMATSU'S SUPPLIERS BRING COSTS DOWN

As the Olympus experience illustrates, target costing issues a clear-cut but daunting challenge to product designers. They cannot call a design a success unless they meet the functionality needs of the customer, the price demands of the distribution channel, the manufacturability requirements of the plant, and the financial projections of the corporation.

Komatsu's experience illustrates another way to use target costing—in this case to pressure suppliers to drive their costs down. Komatsu's earth-moving products contain many more components than do Olympus's cameras, and the company relies more heavily on outside suppliers for complete subsystems: hydraulic devices, electrical subassemblies, and the like. In 1993, for example, Komatsu manufactured roughly 30% of the content in its heavy equipment products, designed and subcontracted 50%, and purchased the remaining 20% from outside suppliers.

Moreover, the number of choices Komatsu must make regarding components makes it difficult to control development costs. Which features will the F company offer on which models? Which teams need additional support? Where should the company be refining designs and where should it be rethinking entire design approaches? Komatsu must involve suppliers in product design early in order to make informed decisions in those and other important matters.

Throughout the entire product-development process, Komatsu poses a challenge to its suppliers: to maintain the performance specifications of components and deliver at prices consistent with Komatsu's overall target costs. Komatsu's target costing program provides the parameters that guide its negotiations with suppliers and subassembly makers to ensure a profitable product launch. By linking performance needs and the company's margin requirements back to each major subassembly, Komatsu's design team can track the performance of whole vehicle and keep an eye on the integrated goal: a product launched at a price the end user will find attractive, not simply a subassembly that satisfies product designers.

To develop system and component targets for its suppliers, Komatsu relies on data on historical performance and cost that it has recorded in function and cost tables. Function tables, containing information about the physical characteristics of each component, help designers determine the company's best-performing components, Cost tables, containing information about the costs of components, help designers identify the low-cost components. By, in effect, overlaying one table on the other, Komatsu engineers identify the target cost of the best component for a given project. This target cost becomes the suppliers' target price.

In developing the target cost of an excavator's cooling system, for instance, Komatsu's engineers determined that the most important performance factor was the surface area of the system's radiator, They consulted function tables to calculate he minimum radiator surface area required. They consulted cost tables to calculate the most cost-effective design. Then they calculated the target cost of their radiator to reflect both minimums: least surface area and minimum cost per unit of area. In demanding that the radiator in the excavator's cooling system be both the most efficient at cooling and the most cost-effective, Komatsu forced its suppliers to push the frontiers of their own technology to achieve more efficient designs.

It is important to remember that subsystem target costs must fit within an overall target cost, which has been derived from a projected market price. But if a subsystem's cost exceeds its projected share of the product's target cost, Komatsu does not automatically reject the design or reduce the cost targets for other components. Like Olympus, Komatsu focuses not on some mechanistic algorithm but on the complex relationship between cost and price and the effects of both on value. Komatsu asks whether particular functions need to be continued. It provides engineering support to suppliers that cannot meet targets. It seeks unexploited opportunities to reduce costs even further among components that have already met their targets. Komatsu managers do not measure success one department at a time. They know that the marketplace does not reward an outstanding component, only an outstanding integrated design.

SMOOTHING OUT THE TARGET-COSTING PROCESS

Clearly, target costing involves more than listing dollar targets and projected margins. It is a highly structured product-development discipline, adapted to such specific elements of a company's strategic positioning as industry pricing dynamics, product-complexity and life-cycle analyses, and supplier relations. It requires a company to make a series of decisions that include defining the product that customers want, ascertaining the economics required for profitability, allocating targets to components, and identifying the gap between target costs and initial projections of manufacturing costs. (See the diagram "The Target-Costing Process.")

On the other hand, as the experiences of Olympus and Komatsu suggest, target costing is not an exact.science. It depends on credible data and on people who have the courage to make difficult judgments. Target costing is an iterative process that cannot be decoupled from the ordinary push and pull of the design process. The targets evolve as teams seek to balance functionality, price, volumes, capital investment, and costs. Also, because target costing is integrative, responsibility for achieving targets must be shared across functions. Finally, if they are to use target costing, companies must treat their suppliers as partners both during the design process and when they are setting cost targets.

Our description may make target costing sound like a smooth ride, but troublesome roadblocks can show up at different stages.

Defining the Product, Targeting the Marketplace. The choices that drive the entire target-costing process are the customer's. What prices will customers accept? What functionality will they insist on? What will competitors offer them? Because the ultimate goal of target costing is to maximize a product's total profitability, not minimize its cost, companies must do their best to understand how their customers' preferences and their competitors' products will evolve over time. That requires a thorough understanding of the customers' behavior in each market segment.

When the Japanese targeted the luxury car market, for example, they already knew one critical feature of luxury cars: They had to be quiet. For years, manufacturers had tried to lower sound levels in luxury cars and found the task inherently difficult. Sound level not only traded off against acceleration—high-revving engines tended to be loud—but was also an integrative challenge, because sound came from many other design components, including the drive train, tires, and door seals. Japanese researchers discovered, however, that frequency was as important to customers as decibel level; that is, the nature of the sound was as important as its loudness. This discovery pointed to a different design challenge: Instead of minimizing, sound, designers could try to "tune" the car in a pleasing fashion—an approach with enormous ramifications for the way companies set their target costs.

The relationship between volume and frequency points to the challenge facing anyone engaged in product positioning. Any approach that asks customers, "Do you like this offering better than that one?" and stops there will not yield much insight. Marketers need an approach that will reveal deeper patterns of customer preference. Fortunately, researchers can use sophisticated surveying techniques such as conjoint analysis to reveal how potential customers cluster around multiple product features and functionalities. These preferences must then be expressed as innovative design options—what we might think of as quality and functionality targets. It is at this point that companies might use such interfunctional design techniques as the House of Quality, which maps the relationship between customers' desired features and specific engineering characteristics.

It is not enough to focus on the customer; competitors are a parallel concern. Most companies define competitors as "companies that make things similar to what we make," which is the producers' view of competition. In target costing, the Japanese companies we have studied tend to define competitors from the customers' perspective: "I am about to make a purchase, so what are my options?" Olympus, for example, benchmarked itself not only against camera manufacturers but also against the makers of CD players and Walkman-type products. The company understood that it was competing for discretionary dollars against makers of all kinds of consumer gadgets, not just against camera makers.

Computing Overall Target Costs. Companies derive overall targets in a number of different ways but the purpose is always the same: to think rigorously about the company's future profitability. In fact, some Japanese companies classify target costing as a profit-management tool rather than as a cost-control tool. In any case, the task is to compute the costs that must not be exceeded if acceptable margins from specific products at specific price points are to be guaranteed.

For most companies, this order of logic represents a radical shift in thinking. Traditionally, companies perform the financial analysis associated with product development only after much of the development work has been done, and then only to determine whether to continue investment. In contrast, a financial analysis done early in the design process can accomplish much more. In target costing, it can tell design teams and general managers a great deal about what is required to make the product a success. The nature of the analysis may be the same, but shifts in timing and focus make a huge difference.

One U.S. vehicle maker we have worked with performed a financial analysis to estimate a likely return on investment for a redesigned product launched under a single set of hypothetical conditions. The purpose of the analysis was to make senior managers more comfortable with their decision to go ahead. So although the analysis aided the approval process, it provided little guidance to the design team. It displayed no sensitivity to the fact that conditions such as launch date, cost, and volume are variable and that small changes matter. Our analysis of the company's data showed that to miss cost targets would have been catastrophic: A 5% error would have eliminated any return on the company's $200 million investment.

Allocating Target Costs, Identifying the Gap. Once a target cost has been calculated for a new product, the design team has to divide it up among the product's various functions. How much can the team spend on one function as against all the others? The team must first calculate the gap between the target cost and what it estimates it would cost to build the product with today's processes, suppliers, productivity levels, and materials. The difference is a good approximation of the excess cost that must be wrung out of the new product.

It usually makes no sense to apply cost-reduction requirements uniformly across all the components and subsystems of the contemplated product. Rather, the design team can consult customer-value surveys, historical trends, and other data to guide it in determining how much cost it can remove from each component or subassembly. The team will allocate more costs to critical features (allowing for increased engine cost in a car that is intended to have a peppier ride, for example). But every extra dollar it allocates to improving one product feature must come from another function's allocation, because the target cost remains fixed.

Isuzu Motors' target-costing system, like others, aims to keep prices constant while adding as much functionality as possible to each new generation of vehicles. The system therefore attaches great importance to determining what features and level of performance the customer will want most, and it uses those preferences as the basis for allocating costs to major functions and group components. Market researchers ask customers to estimate how much they would pay for a given function. Then they develop ratios of preference by asking customers to estimate the relative importance of each function on a 100-point scale.

Isuzu uses this information to spread a product's target cost among the major specified function improvements. If the target cost for a component is too low to allow a sufficiently attractive or safe version to be produced, the component's target cost is increased and the target cost of other components is decreased. Thus, Isuzu continually uses its best sense of customer value to drive its design team's cost allocation decisions.

Obeying the Cardinal Rule. All design-team members, whatever their function specialty, must regard the overall final cost target as an unalterable commitment; target commitments outrank design commitments. The idea is that aggressive targets focus the efforts of the design team on creative solutions and press value engineering to its limits.

In other words, to say that target costing is an iterative process is not to say that target costs, once set, are then subject to ongoing debate. They are not. Targets must fall under the protection of what we call the *cardinal rule:* If you cannot meet the targets, you cannot launch the product. That being the case, the process of product definition and target generation continues, but not in the factory.

Some companies have a layered set of targets. The first pass is the simplest, and failure here leads to a more sophisticated life-cycle analysis. But this approach must not become a game with ever lower hurdles, each test becoming less rigorous than the one before. As one manager puts it, "In the past, if a specific project failed the test for funding, we just kept changing the assumptions for the project or revising the test until the project passed. Target costing will not tolerate that."

The cardinal rule applies to the product as a whole. When targets are assigned to individual subassembly teams, some teams will beat their targets, some will meet them, and some will fall short. But success is not determined component by component; it is achieved—or not— by the final product. When components turn out to be more expensive than anticipated, that cost must be offset somewhere else in the design. This requirement demands a degree of cooperation and team spirit that will necessitate change for many organizations.

TARGET COSTING AND THE ORGANIZATION

Any system that cuts across organizational boundaries and communicates so many vital economic and market objectives is bound to have a profound impact on how the organization does business. One of the main benefits of target costing is that it forces companies to delineate their product-development goals very precisely and in a single vernacular.

In many companies, clarity of communication may be sacrificed to a general commitment to decentralization. At one large U.S. industrial company we have worked with, for example, nearly every functional department was using a unit of analysis that it had developed to answer a question of importance to itself only and that varied subtly from every other functional department's unit of analysis. Competitors' specifications were collected by product, existing costs were computed by part, customers' needs were defined in terms of product attribute, manufacturing constraints were determined by installation point, and the capabilities of the supplier were measured by module.

All those measures were related, but none addressed overall cost targets. There was no overall context within which to work. As a result, a product designer assigned to a particular subsystem could not get a clear answer to the question: "How much do customers value this subsystem?" or "What does this subsystem cost?"

Target costing requires that such problems be addressed directly. It forces companies to be specific about what customers want and what prices they are prepared to pay. Finally, target costing creates opportunities to demonstrate a commitment to customers. If targets cannot be met, the company cannot simply raise the price and launch the product. Such discipline may be painful to the people who work on a project, but it sends an important message to the organization as a whole: that customers come first and that if the company doesn't create value for them, a competitor will.

MAKING IT WORK

For target costing to succeed, targets must not only be valid, people must also see them as valid. They cannot be the outcome of a "political" process. The market analysis that yields the target prices, the financial analysis that generates the target costs, and the disaggregation procedures that allocate costs among components and subassemblies—all must be trusted. The target-costing process must, therefore, be highly transparent.

Moreover, cost-reduction objectives must be achievable most of the time. Setting the bar too high can be as damaging as having no bar at all; in fact, the Japanese set a series of what they call *tip-toe objectives*, that is, objectives that may be reached by "standing on tiptoes"—a stretch that strains the organization but does not defeat it. Also, the requirements for product functionality must be clearly and publicly articulated so that nobody tries to achieve the target cost by reducing product functionality below acceptable levels. It is no good to reduce costs by shortchanging customers. When target costing works well, quantifiable hurdles are established in a transparent process, and senior managers commit themselves to what the numbers show. Engineers receive goals that are clear and achievable, and everyone adheres to the cardinal rule. A company that meets those requirements is not guaranteed a victory in the markets it enters. It does earn the right to compete.

TARGETING COSTS IN PROCESS AND SERVICE INDUSTRIES

Target costing has made its mark in industries in which products require a good deal of production assembly—cars, cameras, and bulldozers, for example. However, the discipline target costing offers has uses outside the assembly environment.

In processing companies, where the characteristics of the process—time, temperature, and pressure—determine the performance of the product, the focus of target costing shifts from the product to the process. A steel company would tend to focus on the costs associated with routings and processing time; a paper mill, on those associated with speed and breakage. The key issues—understanding market needs, ensuring satisfactory financial performance at a given price, and not exceeding the target cost—remain.

Similarly, target costing can be applied to services, for which the focus is the service delivery system. As in process—intensive manufacturing, process is inextricable from product. Think of the issues that are important to the delivery of health care and fast-food functions. Where services and process-intensive manufacturing diverge is in their flexibility. It is enormously expensive to convert a paper machine so that it can produce a grade or weight that was not considered in its initial design. Service delivery systems, however, are a different matter. In people-intensive, customer-responsive service-delivery systems, it is not only possible to add new services, it can be hard not to. Menus are easy to extend. Room services can easily be added. Consulting firms or law firms can always enter a new area of practice. Where is the discipline that ensures that these extensions are profitable?

Because a single service-delivery system may be used to deliver a wide range of services, determining the profitability of individual services becomes an exercise in the arbitrary allocation of costs. In services, particularly those in which waiting time is critical, it is the systemic effects of individual new service—for instance, the extent to which they make the process more complex—that determine whether their revenues and value to customers offset their costs. Target costing can still facilitate a discussion of the appropriateness of a new service, but only if it focuses on the systemic impact of the service extension and questions whether this impact aligns with company strategy and profitability goals. In service industries as in other industries, target costing can help organizations resist the urge to create new market offerings simply because they have the ability.

The authors gratefully acknowledge the assistance of Bernard Avishai in developing and writing this article.

Robin Cooper is a professor at the Claremont Graduate School's Peter F. Drucker Graduate Management Center in Claremont, California, and author of When Lean Enterprises Collide: Competing Through Confrontation (Harvard Business School Press, 1995), which draws on Cooper's five-year study of the management systems of 20 Japanese companies. W. Bruce Chew is a senior consultant at Monitor Company, a global consulting firm in Cambridge, Massachusetts. He is a former associate professor of technology and operations management at the Harvard Business School in Boston, Massachusetts.

QUESTIONS

8.1a Describe the procedure (as characterized by Cooper and Chew) that Isuzu Motors goes through to allocate its target cost among major functional improvements to its vehicles.

8.1b What are "tip-toe" objectives as discussed in the Cooper and Chew article, and what is their role in target costing?

8.2 The Use of Target Costing in Developing the Mercedes-Benz M-Class

by Tom Albright*

EXECUTIVE SUMMARY

- Target costing techniques are important tools for controlling costs in the early stages of product development.
- This article describes how Mercedes-Benz used target costing in the design and production of the M-class, a new sports utility vehicle.
- Mercedes' marketing research showed that customers in this market segment hold established expectations about product characteristics and price levels.
- This marketing information was used to design a vehicle with the characteristics that customers wanted, at a selling price that customers would pay, and that would produce an acceptable level of profitability for investors.

Target costing systems have three major characteristics (Cooper, 1995):

- Targets for price, quality, and function are set in advance.
- Major costs are identified in the design phase.
- The approach is multifunctional.

To develop the M-class, Mercedes used multifunctional teams that included product and process engineers, marketing professionals, and suppliers. The company held focus groups to help define features that potential customers expected to see in a sports utility vehicle from Mercedes.

Target costing was a logical cost management technique for Mercedes to use because the company was designing a completely new vehicle and concurrently constructing a new production facility. As a result, Mercedes could define a significant portion of the production costs that would be incurred before the costs were actually committed.

SUCCESS AT TARGET COSTING

Successful implementation of target costing principles requires managing many interrelated components, including the following (Ansari and Bell, 1997):

- Price-led costing
- Customer orientation
- Focus on product and process design
- Cross-functional teams
- Life-cycle cost reduction
- Value chain involvement

Price-led costing. In many industries, pricing has traditionally been a function of cost. Markups, or profit margins, are simply added to the estimated cost of a product to set an initial market price. If customers reject a price determined in this manner, producers have little recourse other than to reduce their margin, though they can also attempt to trim production costs.

* From: T. Albright, "The Use of Target Costing in Developing the Mercedes Benz M-Class," *International Journal of Strategic Cost Management* (Autumn 1998): 13–23. Reprinted with permission.

Target costing practices treat selling prices and margins as uncontrollable variables, because the markets determine selling prices, and companies must earn adequate margins to remain in business over the long term. Thus, cost is the only variable that can be influenced by management.

Customer orientation. Delivering products customers want at a price they are willing to pay is a fundamental premise "of target" costing. Lean enterprises survive by gaining a series of short-term advantages over their competitors in one of three customer-oriented variables (the *survival triplet*) (Cooper, 1995):

- Price
- Quality
- Functionality

Ultimately consumers determine minimum acceptable standards for quality and functionality and they define a maximum acceptable market price.

Short-term competitive advantage can be gained by managing the elements of the survival triplet more effectively than does the competition. For example, competitive advantage can be gained if a company can deliver comparable quality and functionality at a price significantly below that of its competitors. Similarly, a company can also gain a competitive advantage by providing greater functionality, higher quality, or both at comparable prices.

Focus on product and process design. Many production costs derive from decisions made during the design phase. Consequently, cost-reduction efforts should focus on phases before production begins. Mercedes, for example, made decisions early in the product-development process to reduce the level of value-added (or conversion) activities and costs within its planned facility.

Traditionally, purchased components have made up from 55% to 60% of unit production costs at Mercedes, which means that value-added percentages have ranged from 40% to 45%. During the product- and process-design phase for the M-class, Mercedes made the strategic decision to rely heavily on systems suppliers. As a result, the value-added percentage in the new plant where the M-class is made is only 20% to 25% of manufacturing cost.

Cross-functional teams. Target costing begins with customer needs. It should end with a product that meets or exceeds customer expectations. For this to happen, however, a wide variety of professional expertise is required. At Mercedes the cross-functional design team included cost planners, design engineers, systems suppliers, and marketing professionals had to coordinate their work to enhance quality and control costs.

Life-cycle cost reduction. Target costing also encourages designers to consider costs that extend beyond the manufacturing stage. Because target costing principles are customer-oriented, design decisions should seek to minimize both manufacturing costs and the ownership costs that customers will incur.

For example, although the Mercedes E300 diesel has a relatively high sticker price, it is the choice of many European cab companies because its maintenance costs are low, and its life commonly exceeds 300,000 miles. Lower operating costs during the vehicle's useful life and higher resale values are examples of life cycle cost-reduction strategies affected by engineering design choices.

Value chain involvement. Target costing principles stress the importance of managing costs throughout the value chain. Involving "upstream" suppliers early in development is crucial. Involving suppliers early during the design phase helped Mercedes improve quality and reduce costs. "Downstream" input—the involvement, for example, of the marketing and customer service departments—is also necessary to achieve the strategic benefits of target costing.

BACKGROUND OF THE MERCEDES M-CLASS PROJECT

To explain how Mercedes used target costing techniques in developing the M class, the following sections discuss each of the major target costing characteristics mentioned previously. Also discussed are innovations Mercedes developed, which include various indexes that explicitly link engineering and financial concepts.

Background. In the early 1990s, Mercedes struggled with problems in product development, cost efficiency, material purchasing, and adapting to changing markets. By 1993 Mercedes had experienced its worst sales slump in decades, and it lost money for the first time in its history.

Since that time, Mercedes has streamlined its core business, reduced parts and system complexity, and established simultaneous engineering programs with suppliers.

New products. In a search for additional market share, new segments, and new niches, Mercedes started developing a range of new products. The new C-class debuted in 1993, the E-class in 1995, the new sportster SLK in 1996, and both the A-class and the M-class All Activity Vehicle in 1997. Perhaps the largest and most radical of all the new projects was the M-class.

In April 1993, Mercedes announced it would build its first passenger vehicle manufacturing facility in the United States. The decision emphasized the company's globalization strategy and desire to move closer to customers and markets. After an intensive, six-month effort to evaluate locations suitable for a new plant costing $300 million, Mercedes chose Tuscaloosa County, Alabama. Annual production at the plant is now about 65,000 vehicles, with North American and export volumes approximately equal.

The M-class project can justifiably be called a radical, high-stake experiment (Woodruff and Miller, 1995). Mercedes had to build a new factory in a new country and also develop a new product for a new market segment. While Japanese manufacturing plants built outside Japan typically copy Japanese factories and models (at least at first), Mercedes simultaneously had to debug a new product, a new manufacturing process, and a new work force. During the early stages of product and rocess development, the popular press described the Mercedes venture as a prescription for disaster because of the many variables and unknowns involved.

THE M-CLASS PROJECT PHASES

The M-class moved from concept to production relatively quickly. The *concept phase* began in 1992, which led to a feasibility study that the board of directors approved. The project *realization phase* began in 1993. Finally, *production* began in 1997. Key elements of these various phases are described next.

Concept phase (1992–1993). The cross-functional team at Mercedes compared the company's existing product line with various market segments in order to find opportunities to introduce new types of vehicles. The analysis revealed opportunities in the rapidly expanding market for sports utility vehicles, dominated by Jeep, Ford, and GM.

The team conducted market research to estimate potential sales opportunities worldwide for a high-end sports utility vehicle having the characteristics of a Mercedes-Benz. A rough cost estimate was developed that included materials, labor, overhead, and one-time development and project costs. Then cash flows were projected and analyzed over a 10-year period. Net present value (NPV) analysis was used to acquire approval of the project from the board of directors. Because of the capital-intensive nature of the automobile manufacturing industry, estimates of production volume are critical factors in the NPV calculation.

Risks and opportunities. The sensitivity of the NPV calculation was analyzed by simulating various "what-if" scenarios involving different risks and opportunities. The risk factors that were tested included fluctuations in monetary exchange rate, different sales levels due to consumer substitution of M-class vehicles for other Mercedes products, and product and manufacturing costs that differed from projections.

Based on the economic feasibility study of the concept phase, the board approved the project. The search for manufacturing locations included sites in Germany, other European countries, and the United States. Partly because of Mercedes globalization strategy,

the decisive factor in placing the plant in the United States was the desire to be close to the biggest market for sports utility vehicles.

Project realization phase (1993–1996). The target costing process requires broad, cross-functional activities to acquire market information necessary to develop a new vehicle. Mercedes used customer focus groups to obtain this information. The company held regular customer clinics to explain the new vehicle concept and to view the prototype. These clinics elicited important information about how the proposed vehicle would be received by potential customers and the press. Customers were asked to rank the importance of various characteristics including safety, comfort, economy, and styling. Engineers organized in function groups designed systems to deliver these essential characteristics.

Furthermore, Mercedes would not lower its internal standards for components, even if initial customer expectations were lower than the Mercedes standard. For example, many automotive experts believe the handling of Mercedes products results from manufacturing a world-class chassis. Thus, each new class within the Mercedes line must meet strict standards for handling, even though these standards may actually exceed customer expectations for some classes.

Mercedes did not use target costing to produce the lowest-priced vehicle in an automotive class. Rather, the company's strategic objective was to deliver products that were slightly more expensive than competitive models but with a greater perceived value on the part of the customer.

Goal-oriented approach. Another difference between Mercedes' and other companies' use of target costing lies in the goal-oriented approach to achieving target cost. Cooper cites examples of Japanese companies that strive in a single-minded effort to achieve a static target cost. In contrast, the M-class (and M-class target cost) remained alive throughout the product realization phase because of changing dynamics.

Mercedes found it beneficial to place the design and testing team members in close physical proximity to other functions within the project to promote fast communication and decision making. In this way the company was able to respond quickly to changing conditions. For example, while the vehicle was under development, the market moved toward the luxury end of the spectrum. Crash test results were also incorporated into the evolving M-class design. In addition, Mercedes developed new technical features such as side airbags. (The decision to include this new feature on all Mercedes lines was made at the corporate level because experience has shown that customers' reactions to a vehicle class can affect the entire brand.)

As demonstrated above, Mercedes recognized the importance of flexibility in setting and achieving target costs.

Production phase 1997–present. The M-class project was monitored by annual updates of the net present value (NPV) analysis. In addition, a three-year plan (including income statements) was prepared annually and reported to the headquarters in Germany. Monthly departmental meetings were held to discuss actual cost performance compared with standards developed during the cost estimation process. Thus, the accounting system served as a control mechanism to ensure actual production costs conformed to target (or standard) costs.

TARGET COSTING AND THE M-CLASS

The target costing process was led by cost planners who were engineers, not accountants. Because the cost planners were engineers with manufacturing and design experience, they could make reasonable estimates of costs that suppliers would incur in providing various systems. Also, Mercedes already owned much of the tooling, such as dies to form sheet metal, used by suppliers to produce components. Tooling costs are a substantial part of the one-time costs in the project phase.

Mercedes divided the vehicle into function groups that included doors, sidewall and roof, electrical system, bumpers, powertrain, seats, heating system, cockpit, and front end. As shown in Exhibit 1, the process of achieving target cost for the M-class began with an estimate of the existing cost for each function group. Next, components of each function group were identified with their associated costs. Team members set cost reduction targets by comparing the estimated existing cost with the target cost for each function group. Finally, cost reduction targets were established for each component. As part of the competitive benchmarking process, Mercedes purchased and disassembled competitors' vehicles to help understand costs and manufacturing processes within the competitor's manufacturing plant.

A modular construction process that relied on high-value-added systems suppliers was used to produce the M-class. Advantages of this process include higher quality, shorter development time, and greater cost efficiency. First-tier suppliers provide entire systems rather than individual parts or components. For example, the entire cockpit was purchased as a unit from an external vendor.

Systems suppliers were part of the development process from the beginning of the project. Approximately 70 suppliers worked with teams from finance and controlling, engineering, purchasing, marketing, sales, logistics, and quality control to ensure the delivery of systems that meet expectations. Mercedes expected suppliers to meet established cost targets. To enhance function group effectiveness, suppliers were brought into the discussion at an early stage in the process.

Index development to support target costing. During the concept development phase, Mercedes team members used various indexes to help determine critical performance, design, and cost relationships for the M-class. The purpose of the indexes is to ensure that resources are applied in the most effective manner. An importance index is created by to conceptually linking the contribution of each major function group to an attribute desired by a customer. In the final stage of analysis, the value of each function group is compared with its cost. Thus, engineers can assess cost/benefit relationships during the design phase.

Index development to support target costing. During the concept development phase, Mercedes team members used various indexes to help determine critical performance, design, and cost relationships for the M-class. The purpose of the indexes is to ensure that resources are applied in the most effective manner. An importance index is created by to conceptually linking the contribution of each major function group to an attribute desired by a customer. In the final stage of analysis, the value of each function group is compared with its cost. Thus, engineers can assess cost/benefit relationships during the design phase.

EXHIBIT 1. FUNCTION GROUPS OF THE MERCEDES-BENZ M-CLASS SPORT UTILITY VEHICLE

Function Group: Chassis
Component 1
Component 2
Component 3
Component 4
Component 5
Component 6

Influence Factors
Materials
Labor
Overhead

Tooling,
Development,
Marketing, and Sales costs;
Startup and
Project Costs

Function Group: Chassis
Component 1
Component 2
Component 3
Component 4
Component 5
Component 6

Exhibits 2–6 illustrate the calculations used to quantify various aspects of the target costing process. (All numbers have been altered for proprietary reasons; however, the tables illustrate the actual process used in the development of the M-class.) To construct the indexes, various forms of information were gathered from customers, suppliers, and the M-class design team. Though the actual number of categories used by Mercedes was much greater, Exhibit 2 illustrates the calculations used to quantify customer responses to the M-class concept. For example, values shown in the importance column of Exhibit 2 resulted from asking a sample of potential customers, whether they consider each category important when contemplating the purchase of a new Mercedes product. Individuals could respond affirmatively to all categories that applied.

Target costs for functions. To gain a better understanding of the various sources of costs, function groups were identified together with their target cost estimates. Exhibit 3 shows the function groups, the target cost for each, and what percentage of the total cost each represents. The target cost percentage is used in the calculation of a target cost index.

Exhibit 4 summarizes how each function group contributes to the consumer requirements identified in Exhibit 2. The rows explain the relative importance of each function group to satisfying each category defined by customers. An interesting aspect of this table is that it makes explicit the link between consumer preferences and engineering components. For example, a large proportion of potential customers identified safety as the most important characteristic of the M-class; some function groups contributed more to safety than others. Mercedes engineers determined that chassis quality was an important element of safety (60% of the total function group contribution in this example).

Exhibit 5 combines the category weighting percentages from Exhibit 2 with the function group contribution from Exhibit 4. The key point is to understand which function groups contribute the most (least) to important (less important) consumer categories. The result is an importance index that measures the relative importance of each function group across all categories. For example, potential customers weighted the categories of safety, comfort, economy, and styling as .47, .32, .05, and .16, respectively. The rows in Exhibit 5 represent the contribution of each function group to the various categories. The importance index for the chassis is calculated by multiplying each row value by its corresponding category value and summing the results: $(.47 \times .60) + (.32 \times .20) + (.05 \times .05) + (.16 \times .05) = .36$.

EXHIBIT 2. RELATIVE IMPORTANCE RANKING BY CATEGORY

Category	Importance	Relative Percentage
Safety	45	47
Comfort	30	32
Economy	5	5
Styling	15	16
Total	95	100

As shown in Exhibit 6, the target cost index is calculated by dividing the importance index by the target cost percentage by function group. Managers at Mercedes used indexes such as these during the concept design phase to understand the relationship of the *importance* of a function group to the *target cost* of a function group. Indexes less than one may indicate a cost in excess of the perceived value of the function group. Choices made during the project realization phase were largely irreversible during the production phase because approximately 80% of the production cost of the M-class represented materials and systems provided by external suppliers. Thus, opportunities for cost reduction, known as value engineering, are best identified and managed during the early stages of product development.

VALUE ENGINEERING

Having established a target cost index, value engineering techniques may be applied to align target cost and perceived value. As defined by Cooper (1995), value engineering is the systematic, interdisciplinary examination of factors affecting cost to devise a means of achieving cost, quality, and functionality at the target cost.

Many value-engineering techniques are available. For example, purchasing, disassembling, and analyzing competitors' products provide insights into manufacturing processes and costs. This technique often is used as part of a competitive benchmarking program. Redesigning production processes and key components involves the cross-functional analysis of each component within a function group. Cooper describes how camera manufacturers may substitute a plastic lens to reduce costs when designing a new product. Supplier involvement early in the design phase can create opportunities for cost reduction, such as recycling reusable materials or adjusting tolerances where feasible.

EXHIBIT 3. TARGET COST AND PERCENTAGE BY FUNCTION GROUP

Function Group	Target Cost	Percentage of Total
Chassis	$x,xxx	25
Transmission	$x,xxx	20
Air conditioner	$x,xxx	8
Electrical system	$x,xxx	15
Other function groups	$x,xxx	32
Total	$xx,xxx	100

EXHIBIT 4. FUNCTION GROUP CONTRIBUTION TO CUSTOMER REQUIREMENTS

Category–Function Group	Safety	Comfort	Economy	Styling
Chassis	60%	20%	5%	5%
Transmission	20	30	30	
Air conditioner		20		5
Electrical system	5	5	25	
Other systems	15	25	40	90
Total	100%	100%	100%	100%

EXHIBIT 5. IMPORTANCE OF VARIOUS FUNCTION GROUPS

Category–Function Group	Safety .47	Comfort .32	Economy .05	Styling .16	Importance Index
Chassis	.60	.20	.05	.05	.36
Transmission	.20	.30	.30		.21
Air conditioner		.20		.05	.07
Electrical systems	.05	.05	.25		.05
Other systems	.15	.25	.40	.90	.31
Total	1.00	1.00	1.00	1.00	

EXHIBIT 6. TARGET COST INDEX

Index–Function Group	(A) Importance Index	(B) % of Target Cost	(C)A/B Target Cost Index
Chassis	.36	.25	1.44
Transmission	.21	.20	1.05
Air conditioner	.07	.08	.87
Electrical system	.05	.15	.33
Other systems	.31	.32	.97
Total		1.00	

SUMMARY

The Mercedes organization produced an entirely new vehicle from concept to production in four years, on time, and within budget. Mercedes launched the M-class in September 1997 in the United States market; the export market launch occurred in March 1998. The production facility originally constructed to produce 65,000 M-class vehicles annually is currently being expanded to permit annual production of 80,000 vehicles.

The M-class project used a streamlined management structure in order to facilitate efficient and rapid development. Target costing proved to be a key management element in the success of this venture.

REFERENCES

Albright, T. L. *Cases in Strategic Cost Management: Mercedes-Benz AAV*. (1998). The Institute of Management Accountants–REAP Program.

Ansari, S. and Bell, J. *Target Costing, The Next Frontier in Strategic Cost Management*. Chicago: Irwin, 1995.

Cooper, R. *When Lean Enterprises Collide*. Boston: Harvard Business School Press, 1995. Woodruff & Miller. 1995.

Tom Albright is J. Reese Phifer Faculty Fellow at the Culverhouse School of Accountancy at The University of Alabama. The author thanks Ola Kallenius, Jonathan DeHart, Jason Hoff, Henrik Jönsson, Josef Pfau, and Günther Thuss of Mercedes-Benz for their generous contributions to this article.

QUESTIONS

8.2a What are the six critical components of a target costing system?

8.2b Was the M-class project a risky one for Mercedes Benz? Explain.

8.3 Johnson & Johnson: A Model for Sustainability Reporting

*This article is based on a study supported by the IMA®
Foundation for Applied Research (FAR).*

by Susan C. Borkowski, Mary Jeanne Welsh, and Kristin Wentzel*

As an accountant or financial professional, you've probably heard lots lately about sustainability reporting. The concept, which is relatively new and gaining wider acceptance, refers to how firms handle nonfinancial factors related to environmental, social, and governance issues that potentially impact the company's future performance, income, and value. Viewed as a companion to financial reporting, the increased use of sustainability reports (SRs, for short) symbolizes the ever-growing demand by stakeholders for more transparency and accountability.

A Statement on Management Accounting (SMA), *The Evolution of Accountability—Sustainability Reporting for Accountants*, issued by IMA® in 2008, details the evolution of sustainability reporting. Recognizing that this phenomenon is still in its "infancy," IMA observed that "while some organizations . . . are leading the way, many are either ignoring the issues, have not yet made a start, or are trying to figure out what to do, how to do it, and how to take action in a way that adds value."

Toward that end, to provide guidance for nonreporting or newly reporting firms, we conducted a case study of a publicly traded company at the forefront of sustainability reporting: Johnson & Johnson. Based in New Brunswick, N.J., and employing approximately 119,000 people worldwide, J&J began issuing formal sustainability reports in 1993 for which it has received widespread praise over the years. Using both content analysis and interviews with company executives, we reviewed Johnson & Johnson's trend toward broadening its sustainability reporting in ways that increase both value and transparency, with the purpose of providing a framework for other firms to model.

HOW SUSTAINABILITY REPORTING CAME ABOUT

Sustainability reporting includes terms such as corporate social responsibility (CSR), environmental reporting, and triple bottom line, although a 2008 website examination of the Global 100 Most Sustainable Companies revealed that "sustainability" was the term they used most frequently. Sustainability encompasses a wide range of corporate initiatives related to issues such as environmental impacts, employee programs for healthier living, community development programs, customer safety programs, and fair trade practices. Multiple stakeholders—including socially responsible investors, consumers who want "green" products, and community groups concerned about environmental impacts—show growing interest in these issues. As evidence of this trend, professionally managed assets invested with a social responsibility focus have grown dramatically, with IMA reporting that socially responsible investments in the United States increased from $639 billion in 1995 to $2.29 trillion in 2005.

Though SRs lack reporting standards analogous to Generally Accepted Accounting Principles (GAAP), efforts to establish standards for sustainability reporting are ongoing. In 1997, the Boston-based nonprofit CERES (Coalition for Environmentally Responsible Economies) started a Global Reporting Initiative (GRI). The United Nations Environment Programme (UNEP) joined as a partner in 1999, the same year that an exposure draft of *GRI Sustainability Reporting Guidelines* was released. In 2002, CERES set up the GRI as an independent body with a mission to "integrate and unify the many standards in the marketplace into a single, generally accepted sustainability reporting framework, encompassing environmental, social, and economic performance." The GRI released its first reporting framework and guidelines in 2000, its G2 revision in 2002, and its current iteration, G3, in 2006. (For more information, go to www.globalreporting.org.)

The G3 guidelines, which the GRI says more than 1,500 companies worldwide have voluntarily adopted, set out core content for sustainability reports. Part 1 covers reporting principles, including materiality, stakeholder inclusiveness, sustainability context, and completeness. Part 2 covers standard disclosures in three areas that should be included

* From: S. Borkowski, M. Welsch and K. Wentzel, "Johnson and Johnson: A Model for Sustainability Reporting," *Strategic Finance*. (September 2010): 29-38. Reprinted by permission conveyed through Copyright Clearance Center, Inc.

174

in a sustainability report: strategy and profile, management approach, and performance indicators.

There's no regulation requiring U.S. companies to provide stand-alone sustainability reports, but the trend to provide these disclosures is definitely growing. Though only 32% of the top 100 U.S. companies in terms of revenue that were surveyed in 2005 issued stand-alone sustainability reports, the reporting rate increased to 73% by 2008, according to KPMG. IMA recognizes Johnson & Johnson as a "leading organization" in this growing trend for social accountability.

For this article, we conducted interviews with two executives who hold key roles in the preparation of J&J's sustainability reports: Brian Boyd, worldwide vice-president for Environmental, Health and Safety, and Elizabeth (Tish) Lascelle, then senior director, Environmental, Health and Safety Strategy and Assurance. We also analyzed the company's SRs from inception using robust content-analysis techniques. Overall, our findings show how sustainability reporting has evolved at Johnson & Johnson to become fully integrated with its culture and mission.

SUSTAINABILITY REPORTING AT J&J

Johnson & Johnson has a relatively long history of sustainability reporting compared to most U.S. companies. It first began setting environmental goals in 1990. Public reports followed in 1993 and 1996, with annual SRs beginning in 1998. The early reports focused primarily on environmental issues and employed "Environmental, Health and Safety" in the title. By 2003, however, Johnson & Johnson's sustainability reporting efforts had clearly broadened and evolved into what was then renamed the "Sustainability Report." Our word count analysis shows a roughly fourfold increase in the length of these reports, suggesting that the content and topics covered expanded dramatically over the years. Table 1 presents a summary of J&J's 13 sustainability reports from 1993 through 2008.

According to Brian Boyd, who was responsible for the sustainability reporting process from 1999 until 2008, when it moved to Corporate Communications, the over-riding reason Johnson & Johnson publishes SRs is to engage with external shareholders. The purpose is twofold:

1. To detail what Johnson & Johnson is doing with regard to sustainability issues and what the firm's strategies are, and

2. To engage stakeholders in the process by sharing information.

Boyd speculates that one of the primary drivers of the early reporting initiatives included increased demand from external stakeholders for information about the company's environmental policies. This supports prior research suggesting that voluntary SRs reduce information asymmetry between firms and the public. Overall, Johnson & Johnson produces SRs for the full range of its stakeholders, from the neighbor living near a manufacturing plant to the global investment community.

WHY REPORT?

Sustainability reporting remains voluntary, but research suggests two distinct theories on why firms do it: ethical vs. economic. Ethical views purport that firms hold societal and moral obligations to engage in socially responsible activities and thus report on these activities because it's the "right thing to do." Economic theories, on the other hand, assert that sustainability reports create better corporate reputations that, in turn, create shareholder wealth via increased profits.

Our interviews at Johnson & Johnson lend credence to both views. For instance, the firm's corporate culture is strongly rooted in its credo, which challenges internal decision makers "to put the needs and well-being of the people we serve *first*" (http://www.jnj.com/connect/about-jnj/jnj-credo). Robert Wood Johnson, former chairman of the company and one of its founders, crafted the credo in 1943, prior to J&J going public and long before anyone used the term "corporate social responsibility." The company's website explains: "Our Credo is more than just a moral compass. We believe it's a recipe for business success. The fact that Johnson & Johnson is one of only a handful of companies that have flourished through more than a century of change is proof of that."

Our review of Johnson & Johnson's SRs reveals continuing specific references to the credo and the company's responsibilities to its four groups of stakeholders, in this order: customers (including doctors, nurses, patients, parents, consumers, suppliers, and distributors), employees, the community (both local and global), and, finally, shareholders. J&J management believes that if the needs of the first three groups of stakeholders are met, then a fair profit should accrue to investors, hence supporting the economic theory for producing SRs. Table 2 shows how the emphasis on each group of stakeholders has shifted over the years.

Brian Boyd acknowledged a number of benefits of the company's sustainability reporting, although he admits that they aren't necessarily financial. In other words, while there's no straight line connecting SR activities to cost savings, intangible benefits often follow. For instance, in the absence of information,

TABLE 1. JOHNSON & JOHNSON'S SUSTAINABILITY REPORTS, 1993–2008

	2008	2007	2006	2005
Title of Report	Sustainability Report	Sustainability Report	Sustainability Report	Sustainability Report
Catchphrase	Caring for the world … commitment	Profiles in possibilities	Passion, performance, preserving the planet	Engaging more people, one person at a time
Number of pages	38	45	36	52
Location of credo	Back cover	Back cover	p. ii	p.2

	2004	2003	2002	2001
Title of Report	Sustainability Report	Sustainability Report	Environmental, Health and Safety Sustainability Report	Environmental, Health and Safety Sustainability Report
Catchphrase	Living our credo	Healthy people, healthy planet	Healthy people, healthy planet	Healthy people, healthy planet
Number of pages	44	50	34	34
Location of credo	p.7	Back cover	Back cover	Back cover

	2000	1999	1998	1996
Title of Report	Environmental, Health and Safety Sustainability Report	Environmental, Health and Safety Sustainability Report	Environmental, Health and Safety Sustainability Report	Sustaining Our Worldwide Environmental Sustainability Commitment
Catchphrase	Healthy people, healthy planet	Healthy people, healthy planet	n/a	Sustaining our worldwide environmental commitment
Number of pages	30	18	39	24
Location of credo	Back cover	Back cover	p. 2	Not included

	1993
Title of Report	A Special Responsibility
Catchphrase	A Special Responsibility
Number of pages	31
Location of credo	Not included

many people will assume the worst about a company's environmental, health, and safety activities. By producing one comprehensive SR annually, Johnson & Johnson satisfies the information needs of many stakeholders, in addition to its credo stakeholders. The advocacy community, for instance, wants to know what large companies are doing, and SRs can encourage discussion. They also provide information to agencies that rate companies based on their sustainability activities. Those ratings, in turn, influence financial analysts' recommendations and investors' decisions. Examples of ratings and agencies include the Dow Jones Sustainability Index (DJSI), the FTSE4Good Index, and Innovest Strategic Value Advisors.

The reporting process also mitigates risk. A 1997 study by Tom Brown and Peter Dacin, "The Company and the Product: Corporate Associations and Consumer Product Responses," found that negative perceptions regarding corporate social responsibility produce negative effects on consumer behavior, and vice versa. Boyd points out that SRs reduce the possibility that a nongovernmental organization (NGO) will launch a negative ad campaign on an issue. A negative campaign could cascade into reduced sales and decreased profits, thereby lending support to economic reasons for reporting.

TABLE 2. CHANGES IN STAKEHOLDER COVERAGE, CONTENT, AND TONE

TOTAL PARAGRAPHS = 2,783	EARLY REPORTS (1993–1999)	MIDDLE REPORTS (2000–2003)	NEWEST REPORTS (2004–2008)	CHANGE FROM EARLIEST TO NEWEST REPORTS
STAKEHOLDER				
Customers	2.2%	2.0%	13.2%	+ 501.9%
Employees	30.6%	37.8%	21.0%	− 31.3%
Community	8.2%	21.2%	20.7%	− 26.6%
Investors	0.0%	0.3%	2.5%	n/a
Two or more groups	16.7%	19.4%	34.1%	+ 104.2%
No specific focus	22.3%	19.3%	7.9%	− 64.4%
PARAGRAPH CONTENT				
Community issues	8.4%	13.5%	15.7%	+ 87.0%
HR/Diversity issues	2.5%	5.4%	5.9%	+ 137.1%
Environmental issues	57.7%	31.3%	30.6%	− 47.0%
General content	8.0%	18.6%	20.3%	+ 153.1%
Health & safety issues	22.4%	29.0%	11.7%	− 47.8%
Supply chain issues	1.0%	2.2%	15.9%	+ 1,485.8%
PARAGRAPH TONE				
Positive	93.1%	84.1%	85.0%	− 8.7%
Negative	2.2%	4.2%	2.8%	+ 26.0%
Neutral	4.7%	11.7%	12.2%	+ 160.4%

* Chi-square significant at a = .0001.

WHO'S RESPONSIBLE FOR SUSTAINABILITY REPORTING?

Numerous functional groups participate in J&J's sustainability reporting process, including Worldwide Environmental, Health and Safety, Corporate Contributions, Corporate Communications, Investor Relations, Procurement, Worldwide Operations, Human Resources, and other relevant business unit leaders. For example, if the sustainability report contains a story on the company's HIV pharmaceutical advances, that business unit leader has participated in that part of the discussion and reporting process.

Management accountants and finance professionals also participate in Johnson & Johnson's reporting process since they're in a position to manage and measure key components of the report. Although much of the financial data in the SRs comes directly from the current year's annual report, accounting and finance staff also contribute information that isn't readily available from it. They address questions about how financial information should be reported to reflect Securities & Exchange Commission (SEC) regulations and other reporting guidelines and requirements.

Interestingly, there are no specific systems in place at Johnson & Johnson to provide data for the SR. Each function leader uses his or her own internal systems to collect and report relevant data to the project leader, with Human Resources being the exception. HR is included to validate the SR process but not necessarily to provide data for the report. J&J also lacks a formal policy regarding confidentiality, instead relying on the judgment of function heads to avoid the release of any data that's sensitive in a competitive, legal, or business context. While Boyd has argued for greater transparency in the SR process, some function leaders are uncomfortable with that view.

As mentioned earlier, J&J's Corporate Communications department now produces the sustainability reports along with the annual reports, collecting data from the respective function heads, who identify the relevant issues in their departments. The group of 10 or so function leaders, including Boyd, continues to meet during the process.

WHAT GOES INTO THE REPORT?

In general, Johnson & Johnson produces its reports in accordance with GRI guidelines, with the more recent SRs providing a key at the end of the report that references the GRI codes. Our content analysis suggests that the amount and type of information reported has changed significantly over the years, reflecting J&J's own internal struggle to determine what should be reported— and in what quantity and depth—to satisfy its responsibilities as defined by its credo and by external validating organizations and outside agencies. For example, we found that both employee health indicators (tobacco use, high cholesterol, inactivity, and such) and economic factors (sales revenue, net earnings, share price, and the like) appeared more frequently in recent reports, while the number of employee safety factors (fleet car accidents, lost workdays, and such) remained largely consistent throughout the time frame. Table 3 summarizes the evolution of the content of Johnson & Johnson's 13 SRs, including the economic, employee health, employee safety, and environmental indicators reported from 1993 through 2008. (Details about each set of indicators are available from any of the authors; see the end of the article for their contact information.)

External forces also influence content. Boyd explained that when competitors started reporting certain index line items, J&J chose to include the same metrics, even though they're of no use or benefit to the company. Yet the DJSI requires certain metrics when ranking companies that even now Johnson & Johnson feels aren't important to report. As a result, Boyd says, the company receives a lower ranking on the DJSI because it chooses to measure and manage what's vital to itself and to its stakeholders rather than what's important to rating agencies.

While the GRI indicator list doesn't drive the content of Johnson & Johnson's SRs, it helps the company coordinate what's reported and provides consistency from year to year. What J&J wants to manage comes from its strategy, credo, and stakeholders, suggesting that a clear mission statement aids corporate sustainability reporting. Boyd feels that Johnson & Johnson is ahead of the sustainability reporting curve because it stays true to its credo and because it closely monitors global trends in what data is reported worldwide, not just in the pharmaceutical industry or in the U.S. For example, the company began reporting on carbon emissions before there was much public push for the information.

USE OF EXTERNAL ASSURANCE

Because of fears of internal bias, some advocates for transparency argue for independent third-party assurance, citing research that finds sustainability reports tend to focus on positive outcomes and that descriptive information rarely accompanies benchmark data. Our content analysis supports this finding. We coded each paragraph of Johnson & Johnson's SRs as positive, negative, or neutral and found that positive information dramatically outweighed negative or neutral information (see Table 2). Over the past 15 years, however—perhaps in response to external pressures—changes in tone have been significant: Positive coverage has decreased about 9%, while negative and neutral coverage has increased 26% and 160%, respectively.

The Global Reporting Initiative recommends the use of external assurance, although it isn't required for companies declaring a reporting level (more about that later). There are several sources of external assurance, including professional assurance providers (such as public accounting firms), stakeholder panels, or other groups. KPMG reports that most Fortune Global 250 (G250) companies that use third-party assurance rely on a major accountancy organization, yet a majority of firms it surveyed for its 2008 report didn't use any form of external assurance. Moreover, assurance rates are lowest in the United States and Canada.

The number of G250/N100 companies that reported formal assurance in their reports has increased in recent years but was still just 40% in 2008. As of June 2009, 338 of the reports filed with the GRI had "+" with their application level, indicating third-party assurance. Although that's only a third of the 1,002 reports filed since January 1, 2008, it represents 48% of the 701 reports filed with an application level and 72% of the 285 reports at the A application level. (Application levels provide an indication of the extent to which sustainability reports employ GRI guidelines. Levels include A, B, or C, with the aforementioned "+" for external assurance. Higher application levels require additional disclosures and more performance indicators.)

Johnson & Johnson currently does *not* declare a reporting level. Instead, its most recent SR includes an index with reference to the G3 indicators cited within the report. According to J&J's Elizabeth Lascelle, the company plans to eventually self-declare an application level without third-party assurance. While external assurance potentially increases the credibility and validity of SRs, firms will only seek it when the net benefits exceed the net costs. Johnson & Johnson avoids external assurance because it finds the process very expensive and time-consuming with no value added, at least from Brian Boyd's perspective. J&J sought formal assurance for an earlier SR, but the process was so tedious that Boyd's office made the decision to stop the process three-fourths of the way through.

Another option includes pursuing some form of external assurance from stakeholder groups. Johnson & Johnson maintains frequent contact with many of these groups (including investors, academics, consultants, NGOs, and community organizations) in order to better understand what the company needs to do to remain

TABLE 3. CHARACTERISTICS OF JOHNSON & JOHNSON'S SUSTAINABILITY REPORTS, 1993–2008

	2008	2007	2006	2005	2004	2003	2002
Number of awards/recognitions	25	18	14	16	19	22	21
Number of organizational partners	18	n/a	6	13	20	20	20
Organizational chart included	No	No	No	No	Yes	Yes	Yes
Indicators presented in tables and/or graphs							
Economic	11	9	9	4	5	5	1
Employee health	4	4	4	4	4	4	4
Employee safety	2	4	5	5	5	5	5
Environmental	11	10	9	12	13	12	17
Total indicators	28	27	27	25	27	26	27

	2001	2000	1999	1998	1996	1993	
Number of awards/recognitions	18	14	7	27	4	0	
Number of organizational partners	18	17	0	14	10	13	
Organizational chart included	Yes	Yes	No	Yes	Yes	No	
Indicators presented in tables and or graphs							
Economic	1	3	4	4	4	2	
Employee health	4	0	3	0	0	0	
Employee safety	5	5	5	5	0	0	
Environmental	16	12	10	11	7	10	
Total indicators	26	20	22	20	11	12	

socially and environmentally responsible. Currently, however, the company doesn't ask these groups to provide any assurance of the final SRs or of the reporting process itself. This interaction simply helps J&J define its strategy and goals to meet the needs of its stakeholders.

ROLE OF STAKEHOLDERS AND DISTRIBUTION OF SRS

At Johnson & Johnson, stakeholders remain valued participants in defining strategies, such as Healthy Planet 2010, which outlines the company's major environmental goals and improvement projects. Meanwhile, each year J&J sends final, approved SRs electronically to all employees, with hard copies going to the board of directors, the executive committee, and top senior managers worldwide. All self-identified "socially responsible" investors, relevant governmental agencies, and competitors also receive copies, as do other interested parties on request. In addition, new and older reports are always available on the Johnson & Johnson website.

Stakeholder feedback continues to shape J&J's sustainability reports. The introduction to the 2007 SR notes the impact of feedback from employees and external parties, including NGOs, and from three external evaluations on the format of the report. Based on data gathered from these sources, Johnson & Johnson concluded that report users typically want in-depth discussion about issues important to them rather than having to read the reports cover to cover. In response, the company modified its 2007 SR to provide more comprehensive coverage of key issues.

It's clear from the Johnson & Johnson experience with sustainability reporting that there must be management buy-in for the process to be successful. As we mentioned earlier, sustainability reporting is entirely voluntary in the United States and imposes additional costs on a firm, yet the benefits may be intangible. Also, in the absence of information, stakeholders will assume the worst.

Johnson & Johnson has found that for sustainability reporting to be truly beneficial to the company, the data needs to be driven by what the company wants to measure and manage, as well as by what external stakeholders demand. A focused analysis of your stakeholders' needs should prove beneficial to enhancing your own firm's sustainability reporting. J&J's reporting process provides a shining example of the right way to proceed.

For Further Reading

Here are a few resources about sustainability. You can find many more on the Internet and on the IMA website at www.imanet.org.

Laurie Brannen, "The Sustainability Reporting Evolution," *Business Finance*, February 2007, p. 4.

Tom J. Brown and Peter A. Dacin, "The Company and the Product: Corporate Associations and Consumer Product Responses," *Journal of Marketing*, November 1, 1997, pp. 68–84.

Marc J. Epstein, *Making Sustainability Work: Best Practices in Managing and Measuring Corporate Social, Environmental and Economic Impacts*, Berrett-Koehler Publishers, San Francisco, Calif., 2008.

Lori Holder-Webb, Jeffrey R. Cohen, Leda Nath, and David Wood, "The Supply of Corporate Social Responsibility Disclosures Among U.S. Firms," *Journal of Business Ethics*, February 2009, pp. 497–527.

Graham Hubbard, "Measuring Organizational Performance: Beyond the Triple Bottom Line," *Business Strategy and the Environment*, December 2006, pp. 177–191.

KPMG International Survey of Corporate Responsibility Reporting 2008. Available at: http://www.kpmg.com/CN/en/IssuesAndInsights/ArticlesPublications/Pages/ Corporate-responsibility-survey-200810-o.aspx. Accessed August 6, 2010.

Karen Paul, "Corporate Sustainability, Citizenship and Social Responsibility Reporting: A Website Study of 100Model Companies," *The Journal of Corporate Citizenship*, December 2008, pp. 63–78.

Roger Simnett, Ann Vanstraelen, and Wai Fong Chua, "Assurance on Sustainability Reports: An International Comparison," *The Accounting Review*, May 2009, pp. 937–967.

Statement on Management Accounting, *The Evolution of Accountability—Sustainability Reporting for Accountants*, IMA®, Montvale, N.J., 2008.

The authors gratefully acknowledge IMA's Foundation for Applied Research (FAR) for its support of this research project.

Susan C. Borkowski, Ph.D., is a Lindback Professor of Accounting at La Salle University in Philadelphia and a member of IMA's Philadelphia Chapter. You can reach Susan at (215) 951-1491 or borkowsk@lasalle.edu.

Mary Jeanne Welsh, Ph.D., is a professor and chair of accounting at La Salle University and a member of IMA's Philadelphia Chapter. You can reach her at (215) 951-1883 or welsh@lasalle.edu.

Kristin Wentzel, Ph.D., is an associate professor of accounting at La Salle University and a member of IMA's Philadelphia Chapter. You can reach Kristin at (215) 951-5176 or wentzel@lasalle.edu

QUESTION

8.3 What is the purpose of sustainability reporting?

8.4 The Business of Making Money with Movies

This article is based on a study supported by the IMA®
Foundation for Applied Research (FAR).

by S. Mark Young, James Gong, and Wim Van der Stede*

Despite an ever-changing entertainment landscape, motion pictures are still the cornerstone of the U.S. entertainment industry with consumers spending nearly $50 billion in 2008 to watch U.S. movies in a variety of formats. In the February and March 2008 issues of *Strategic Finance*, we discussed the cost side of the motion picture industry, focusing on how films are produced and marketed. In 2008, the average feature film cost the major studios $72 million to produce and $37 million to promote.

In this article, we discuss how the major film studios are constantly changing their revenue-generating models to extend the economic life of a film by adapting to new competitive forces and technological changes. After all, studios need to think beyond the box office since more than four-fifths of a film's revenue typically comes from home video, pay TV, and other downstream sources. The Foundation for Applied Research (FAR) of the Institute of Management Accountants (IMA®) sponsored our research (see FAR Research Study, p. 39). Let's begin.

Until the early 1970s, consumers in the U.S. had only a few ways in which they could enjoy a movie: They could see it during its theatrical release, attend a film festival or revival, or view it long after theatrical release on one of the three major television networks (ABC, NBC, or CBS). During this era, the main sources of revenues for the studios came from theatrical release, international sales, and network television.

In 1972, the options for consumers increased when Home Box Office (HBO) became the first cable television network to offer a subscription service. HBO's offerings included recent and well-known films, sporting events, and original programming. A truly significant technological innovation occurred in 1975 when Sony Corporation introduced Betamax, the first home video system. The Victor Company of Japan (JVC) quickly entered the market, offering the VHS format (video home system) as an alternative. Ultimately, VHS became the industry standard. In 1977, the Video Club of America opened the first video

store from which movies could be purchased, and George Atkinson opened the first video rental store. Home video provided new opportunities for the studios to generate more revenues from their existing film libraries.

Today the viewing options for consumers and, hence, the revenue streams for the studios have increased significantly as content delivery systems continue to evolve. Since studios rely on a variety of revenue streams, new technologies allow the industry to remain viable in turbulent times. Nevertheless, the theatrical release of a movie is still the single most important indicator of success and offers a critical means by which to evaluate industry trends. Table 1 shows the various revenue streams, beginning with the domestic box office. Let's now look at factors affecting the box office.

THE DOMESTIC BOX OFFICE

Without a doubt, opening box office performance (and cumulative box office receipts to a lesser extent) is still the critical indicator of a film's success. As we pointed out in "The Business of Selling Movies" in the March 2008 issue of *Strategic Finance*, the level at which the film performs on opening weekend (Friday through Sunday) influences all downstream contracts regarding digital versatile disk (DVD), international, network, satellite, and cable television, as well as Internet and mobile sales. Depending on ticket sales, movies stay at the box office from three weeks, like the movie *Gigli*, to eight months, like *Lord of the Rings: The Two Towers*.

According to Boxofficemojo.com, in 2009, overall box office performance reached an all-time high of $10.6 billion, thanks in large part to five huge blockbusters: *Transformers: Revenge of the Fallen*, *Harry Potter and the Half-Blood Prince*, *Up*, *The Twilight Saga: New Moon*, and *Avatar*. This is the first time ever that the domestic box office exceeded $10 billion. While this number is portrayed as good news, the studios are still concerned. These box office

* From: S. M. Young, J. Gong, and W. Van der Stede, "The Business of Making Money with Movies," *Strategic Finance*, (February 2010): 35-40. Reprinted by permission conveyed through Copyright Clearance Center, Inc.

TABLE 1. WINDOWS OF EXHIBITION FOR MOVIES

SOURCES	WINDOW
Domestic Box Office (Theaters)	Initial theatrical release of three weeks to eight months
Home Video (VHS/DVD)	Exclusive window of only six weeks before pay-per-view
Pay-Per-View	Exclusive window of from two to six weeks before premium channels
Premium Pay Channels (Pay TV)	Exclusive window for up to 18 months before network and cable TV
Network (Free) and Cable TV	Up to 12 to 18 months before syndication
Syndication	60 months on either network television or cable network

Note: Omitted from the distribution channels and windows are foreign sales, hotels, airlines, college campuses, the video game sec- tor, consumer products merchandising, and theme parks. Foreign sales usually begin after the initial theatrical release in the U.S. Each territory has different windows for different channels. Video games based on blockbuster movies sometimes earn equivalent revenues as the theatrical releases.

numbers mask several critical factors related to the current theater-going audience.

First, the studios are under enormous pressure to create blockbusters to obtain these kinds of results. It's no accident that the top three movies listed above cost between $210 million and $250 million, not including about $100 million in marketing costs. If such movies had failed, the studios would be in dire straits. Also, over time, the percentage of people who actually go to a movie theater has declined from a high of 65% of the population in 1930 (before television) to about 10% over the last several decades and to 9.9% in 2009. In 2009, however, attendance was up by about 10% over the previous year, and some believe that the recession caused many to go to the movies as an escapist route. Box office attendance has been decreasing for several reasons—chief among them the smorgasbord of entertainment options, such as video games, music, movies, television, and user-generated content (as might be viewed on social network sites) in a variety of formats and through innovative methods of delivery that include online and mobile devices.

These easy-to-access options compete with the motion picture industry for consumer dollars—a scenario very different from that of the 1930s when consumers had no other option but to attend a theater if they wanted to see a movie. Today approximately three out of four people prefer to watch movies in locations other than a theater because their satisfaction with the movie theater experience has declined, citing high ticket prices, boring commercials, rude behavior among other patrons, and dirty theaters.

Second, box office revenues have reached this record level primarily because of the large increases in ticket prices. For instance, in 1930 the average ticket price was $0.24, in 1990 it was $4.25, and in 2008 it was $7.18. In major cities, the average movie ticket costs $11 on a weekday and $13 on weekends, so, at these prices, many consumers wait to see a film in DVD or on pay-per-view in the comfort of their own homes.

Third, movie piracy, especially illegal downloads from the Internet, affects revenue. The Motion Picture Association of America (MPAA) estimates that more than $6.1 billion of revenue was lost because of piracy. While most piracy occurs in China, Russia, and India, the U.S. has its fair share. Piracy takes many forms, the most common being the unlawful release of a stolen print that is then uploaded to a file-sharing site, such as Pirate Bay. The most recent high-profile case of piracy involved the film *X-Men Origins: Wolverine*. In early April 2009, an almost completed, illegal copy leaked onto the Internet, and approximately one million people illegally downloaded it. Fortunately for 20th Century Fox, the film had a very strong box office weekend opening of $85 million. Nevertheless, while hard to estimate, a great deal of revenue was still lost because of piracy.

ASSESSING DIFFERENT FORMATS AND REVENUE STREAMS

Faced with a decline in patrons at the box office, increased competition from other entertainment options, and piracy of its content, the major studios are constantly assessing new revenue streams. The main goal for any entertainment company in these times is to develop content that can be distributed through as many channels as possible. Currently, the major sources of revenue outside theater releases come from home video, network, satellite and cable television, international distribution, the Internet, and mobile devices. In the following sections, we'll discuss the development and growth or decline of each of these market segments.

Home Video

The development of home video in the mid-1970s as a highly profitable post-theatrical release option fundamentally altered the economic structure of the film industry and its market practices. Initially, the studios priced their video releases for sale to video rental outlets rather than to consumers. At $100 or more each, few individuals could afford to purchase them. By 1986, the major studios earned more revenue in the domestic home video market through sales and rentals than they did from theatrical release.

By 1990, movies were either rented or sold at much more reasonable prices directly to consumers (known as sell-through). Video rentals reached a plateau, but video sell-through sales continued to grow. By 1992, the value of video sell-through sales exceeded the domestic theatrical box office for the first time. Home video caused a significant downward shift in the box office; for instance, the domestic box office represented 80% of studio revenues in 1980, but by 1992 it decreased to no more than 25%.

In 1997, the first DVD players were sold in the U.S. DVDs quickly became the industry standard, and today VHS tapes are no longer produced for new films. In 2006, *A History of Violence* was the last VHS tape made of a major feature film. According to Standard & Poor's, DVD sales in 2008 accounted for $16.2 billion, and DVD rentals generated revenues of $7.5 billion. But DVD sales are on the decline. Based on a 9% drop in 2008, Adams Media Research projects that DVD sales will decline 8% in 2009. The decline is attributed to the high price of DVDs, the downturn in the economy, and the popularity of DVD rental sites.

Industry analysts suggest that Blu-ray discs will replace DVDs once the prices of Blu-ray players and Blu-ray discs drop significantly. Yet market penetration of Blu-ray has been much slower than anticipated. Some suggest that all discs will be phased out and consumers will then obtain their films by direct streaming from Internet sources like Netflix, iTunes, and movielink or via satellite, thereby avoiding any physical discs. No one knows if physical discs will actually be completely phased out, though. For years, LP records became obsolete as CDs became the standard, but LPs are making a comeback as many consumers believe the sound quality of records is more authentic and pleasing.

Television

When television was born in the 1940s, the Hollywood studios initially viewed it more as a threat than an opportunity, but eventually they discovered that it was quite profitable to license movies to television. The six major studios earned revenues of about $17.7 billion in 2005 by licensing their movies and TV series to television networks and stations.

To maximize their television license revenue, studios divide the licensing of their movies into discrete time periods, known as "windows of exhibition." Table 1 describes the six major windows, including four

television windows (pay-per-view, premium pay channels, network and cable TV, and syndicated TV).

Video/DVD

As Table 1 shows, after the initial theatrical run, which typically lasts from two weeks to six months, the next window is for home video, which lasts up to six weeks with guaranteed exclusivity. According to Larry Gerbrandt, senior analyst at Paul Kagan & Associates, a little-known secret in the home video rental market is that the video rental companies make their largest profits from late fees.

Pay-Per-View (PPV)

The next window is pay-per-view (PPV), which allows subscribers to cable and satellite television to order movies directly through a joint venture that licenses the films from all the major studios. Initially this window was timed to open about seven months after the theatrical release to avoid delaying or competing with the video release. But when studios began releasing the DVDs in the late 1990s and their popularity soared, the window had to be moved up when cable and satellite suppliers complained that they received their movies too late to compete with DVDs. Despite claims that PPV would provide another strong cash stream, the six studios' revenues from it have remained relatively modest.

Premium Pay Channels

The next window, which opens one year after the movie appears in theaters, is premium pay channels. The three major pay TV channels are HBO, Showtime, and Starz. This window remains open for up to 18 months. The licensing fee to show a major studio movie over a one-year period is based on domestic box office performance and can be as high as $20 million to $25 million for a blockbuster, although the average is more like $7 million per film.

Network or Cable TV

The fifth window, which lasts between 12 and 18 months, is network or free television. The networks and cable stations compete to determine who will obtain the rights to broadcast each film and typically pay from $3 million to $15 million for a movie, depending on the title's box office success and number of runs.

Syndicated TV

The final window is syndicated television stations, which means that local stations can bid for the right to show the movie and can air it for up to five years. In the largest TV markets, studios may charge up to $5 million for syndicated television rights to a strong film.

International Distribution

The international box office has accounted for slightly less than half of the major studios' total income from theatrical markets since the 1960s. The international market for U.S. films continues to grow. Standard & Poor's estimates that, in 2008, foreign consumers spent nearly $18 billion watching U.S. movies (the worldwide box office is $28 billion, including nearly $10 billion of domestic box office revenue). The largest foreign consumers of films are those in the U.K., Japan, Germany, France, Spain, and Australia/New Zealand. Of course, not all of the $18 billion in revenues went to U.S. studios because the exhibitors kept approximately 50% of box office receipts.

Television licensing is equally profitable overseas. Studios typically sell their movies in blocks of six to 10 films to foreign television networks. The license fee for the package is then allocated across the movies at the studio's discretion. In 2003, overseas TV licensing was valued at approximately $1.76 billion, half from conventional broadcast stations and networks and the other half from pay TV.

The overseas nontheatrical market grew in the late 1980s as a result of growth of cable and video, making the home video market a larger source of overseas revenue for Hollywood studios than the overseas theatrical market in the 1990s. Standard & Poor's predicts that the overseas revenue from U.S. movies will increase to $41.6 billion by 2011.

Internet and Mobile Technology

As has been the case historically, new technology will pave the way for perhaps the most significant revenue streams yet to come. The rate at which the new technology (such as smart phones) penetrates the market is the limiting factor for new product proliferation, such as downloadable movies. Hollywood has taken note of how file sharing almost destroyed the music industry, and it is now preparing to deal with a similar threat. Like their experience with television, VHS, and DVD, the film industry is trying to determine a new revenue-generating model to exploit the Internet as a new revenue source.

The greatest concern is protecting copyright. Studios fear that once they release a film online in digital format, they will lose all control over its subsequent use and distribution. In one effort to maintain control over online content, the studios are working with the computer industry to build copy-protection technology into hard drives. For instance, Microsoft's Windows Vista contains a DRM (digital rights management) system called the Protected Media Path, which contains the Protected Video Path (PVP). PVP tries to stop DRM-restricted content from playing while unsigned software is running in order to prevent the unsigned software from accessing the content.

DVD rental companies and studios have come up with a new business model, although it will take some time before digital downloading and video-on-demand

(VOD) become significant revenue streams. Netflix and Blockbuster, through an alliance with TiVo, the digital video recording service, are creating a digital entertainment service that reportedly will allow customers to order a movie online, which will then be loaded onto their TiVo sets, providing DVD-quality movies on demand. Walt Disney recently joined News Group and Universal Studios to finance and supply content to Hulu.com, which Hulu operates on a revenue-sharing basis with its content partners. Walt Disney will not only supply archived TV programs but also titles from Disney's movie library.

Consumers already can download films directly to their iPods, BlackBerries, and other mobile devices. It's estimated that the number of those so-called smart phones will reach 2.6 billion worldwide by 2011, so movie downloads potentially offer a significant revenue source for the studios, assuming they can put in place the right business models. Predictions are hard to make, but *Screen Digest* has estimated a potential $1.3 billion of revenues from Internet movie downloads in the U.S. and Western Europe in the next couple of years.

EXPLOITING INTELLECTUAL PROPERTY

Through analysis of the movie industry, we've illustrated the roles of costs and revenues in a setting distinct from traditional goods and service industries. Motion pictures are just one of the information industries in which value is created through knowledge and intellectual property. Firms generate revenues by developing, selling, and reselling the same content using different formats and in different markets. For professionals in accounting and finance, understanding and managing lifecycle costs and revenues in knowledge-based industries such as motion pictures can help them create value by exploiting intellectual property.

S. Mark Young, Ph.D., holds the George Bozanic and Holman G. Hurt Chair in Sports and Entertainment Business and is a professor of accounting at the Marshall School of Business at the University of Southern California. He also is a member of IMA's San Gabriel Valley Chapter. You can reach Mark at (213) 740 4848 or at mark.young@marshall.usc.edu.

James J. Gong, Ph.D., is an assistant professor in the department of accountancy in the College of Business Administration at the University of Illinois at Urbana-Champaign. You can reach James at gong@illinois.edu.

Wim A. Van der Stede, Ph.D., is the CIMA professor of accounting and financial management in the department of accounting at the London School of Economics. He is also an IMA member. You can reach Wim at W.Van-der-Stede@lse.ac.uk.

FAR RESEARCH STUDY

The research we conducted for FAR involved two stages. In the first stage, we gathered information about the various revenue streams from published sources as well as in-depth interviews with a number of professionals working in the motion picture industry. This research forms the foundation of the current article. In the second stage, we conducted an empirical study to determine which variables had the greatest effect on cumulative box office. We found that two variables, movie critics' reviews as an indicator of product quality and the amount of money spent on advertising the film, were the two most important factors affecting the total (cumulative) box office receipts over the theatrical run of the film. Our research also found that cumulative domestic box office revenues positively affect international box office revenues as well as home video sales and rentals. Of note, the effects of the domestic box office revenues on each downstream revenue stream decrease as the time interval between the theatrical release window and downstream windows increases. Consistent with findings in the box office revenue analysis, critics' reviews have very strong positive effects on all three downstream revenues.

We used a sample of 1,276 films from 1997 to 2003 and obtained film critic reviews from *Entertainment Weekly* (*EW*), which publishes its own film critic reviews, film opinion results from an online survey, and critic reviews from other sources. *EW* reports eight or nine critic reviews of the same film in one place over three or more weeks. We calculated an overall indicator of each week's critic reviews collected from EW. Merging the critic review data with the theatrical box office data reduced our sample size to 856 films, which we used to perform the domestic box office revenue analyses.

We also collected advertising and production costs on the films in our sample from the Motion Picture Investor—a motion picture industry publication by Paul Kagan & Associates that publishes these cost data shortly after a film is released and then updates them in the next year. We collected foreign box office revenues and DVD/VHS rental revenues from various Internet sources, including www.worldwideboxoffice.com. We were able to obtain a proprietary database on DVD/VHS sales under confidentiality conditions from one of the six major motion picture studios. We also used a large set of control variables, including film production cost, actor and director star power, genre, original or sequel, distributor, rating, and season and size of release. Many of these variables are publicly observable features of the film and thus may influence filmgoers' expectations, such as their perceptions of the film's quality.

Authors' Note: *We thank Brian Mulligan, managing director and vice chairman for Media & Telecommunications Investment Banking Group at Deutsche Bank Securities, Inc., and Jill Stern for their valuable input for this article. We also thank Tara Barker, FAR administrator at IMA, and Sandy Richtermeyer, IMA Chair-Elect, for their continued support.*

QUESTION

8.4 Without all of the available post theatrical release revenue streams, do you think that the motion picture industry would survive?

Chapter 9

Behavioral and Organizational Issues in Management Accounting

---

Kenneth Merchant's classic article, *The Control Function of Management*" (Reading 9.1), presents a framework for determining the appropriate use of management controls. Merchant discusses specific action controls, those designed to make sure that individuals take the most appropriate actions; controls over results, those related to meeting targets such as budgets; and personnel controls, those based on hiring people who will do what is best for the organization. Using this framework, Merchant discusses a number of topics, including how to choose among the various forms of control and the kinds of financial and behavioral costs that are incurred in using each form of control.

Tom Lin's article, *Effective OEC Management Control at China Haier Group*, Reading 9.2, describes a Chinese company that implemented a very clear cultural change based on modern day operations and control principles. The company began as a refrigerator company but expanded into other electronic household items in the 1990s. Today Haier is considered one of the top worldwide brands. The company's cultural change strategy involves developing OEC management. The *O* stands for *overall*, the *E* for *everyone, everything, and everyday*, and the *C* for *control and clear*. The article details how this management system was successfully implemented.

David Gebler's *Creating an Ethical Culture*, (Reading 9.3), was published shortly before Kenneth Lay and Jeffrey Skilling were convicted of fraud and conspiracy. (Lay subsequently died of a heart attack while awaiting sentencing in July 2006.) The article is very timely, as major fraud by very senior company officials has clearly been on the rise over the past decade. Gebler states that despite an increase in the number of ethics programs in companies, reduced levels of misconduct have not occurred. Companies need to build the right organizational culture first, rather than superimposing an ethics program a culture that cannot respond.

Reading 9.4 by Kasthuri Henry, *Leading with Your Soul*, describes a Comprehensive Leadership Model whose goal is to create an ethical workplace that will lead to sustainability for companies. Central to the model are six leadership traits including: (1) Purpose Driven, (2) Courage of Conviction, (3) a Whole Person Approach, (4) Empowerment, (5) Succession Planning, and (6) Emotional Intelligence.

Reading 9.5 by T. Grant and G. Grant, *Can Regulations Curb Excessive Executive Pay*, traces the history of attempts to regulate CEO compensation. The authors provide reasons why regulations have failed and describe what can be done in the future to control escalating compensation.

Alfie Kohn's *Why Incentive Plans Cannot Work* (Reading 9.6), argues strongly that incentive plans that link rewards to measured performance are fundamentally flawed. Citing research evidence, Kohn believes that employees who expect to receive a reward for their efforts do not perform as well as those who do not expect rewards. What is lacking with current pay-for-performance systems is that they do not foster a work environment in which employees can experience intrinsic rewards. Ultimately, the preoccupation with extrinsic rewards does not lead to organizational commitment, discourages risk taking, and reduces creativity and innovation. Ever controversial, Kohn closes with the following, "Managers who insist that the job won't get done right without rewards have failed to offer a convincing argument for behavioral manipulation. Promising a reward to someone who appears unmotivated is a bit like offering salt water to someone who is thirsty. Bribes in the workplace simply won't work."

I (S. Mark Young) wrote Reading 9.7, *Implementing Management Innovations Successfully: Principles for Lasting Change*, based on many years of listening to managers complain about why management innovations, such as TQM, ABC, reengineering, and so on, continue to fail in their companies. These complaints were also borne out by articles in the business press that cited very low success rates at innovation implementation. The article defines a successful innovation implementation as one in which, "Managers and employees permanently alter the way they perform their job responsibilities to conform to the principles dictated by a particular innovation." The distinction I was trying to make in this article was that organizations often don't do what is necessary to get managers and employees behind an innovation. I then suggest eight principles that organizations should consider as they are deciding whether to adopt an innovation.

Readings
Chapter 9

9.1 The Control Function of Management

by Kenneth A. Merchant, Harvard University*

After strategies are set and plans are made, management's primary task is to take steps to ensure that these plans are carried out, or, if conditions warrant, that the plans are modified. This is the critical control function of management. And since management involves directing the activities of others, a major part of the control function is making sure other people do what should be done.

The management literature is filled with advice on how to achieve better control. This advice usually includes a description of some type of measurement and feedback process:

> *The basic control process, wherever it is found and whatever it controls, involves three steps: (1) establishing standards, (2) measuring performance against these standards, and (3) correcting deviations from standards and plans.*[1]
>
> *A good management control system stimulates action by spotting the significant variations from the original plan and highlighting them for the people who can set things right.*[2]
>
> *Controls need to focus on results*[3]

This focus on measurement and feedback, however, can be seriously misleading. In many circumstances, a control system built around measurement and feedback is not feasible. And even when feasibility is not a limitation, use of a feedback-oriented control system is often an inferior solution. Yet, good controls can be established and maintained using other techniques.

What is needed is a broader perspective on control as a management function: this article addresses such a perspective. The first part summarizes the general control problem by discussing the underlying reasons for implementing controls and by describing what can realistically be achieved. In the second part, the various types of controls available are identified. The last part discusses why the appropriate choice of controls is and should be different in different settings.

WHY ARE CONTROLS NEEDED?

If all personnel always did what was best for the organization, control—and even management—would not be needed. But, obviously individuals are sometimes unable or unwilling to act in the organization's best interest, and a set of controls must be implemented to guard against undesirable behavior and to encourage desirable actions.

One important class of problems against which control systems guard may be called *personal limitations*. People do not always understand what is expected of them nor how they can best perform their jobs, as they may lack some requisite ability, training, or information. In addition, human beings have a number of innate perceptual and cognitive biases, such as an inability to process new information optimally or to make consistent decisions, and these biases can reduce organizational effectiveness.[4] Some of these personal limitations are correctable or avoidable, but for others, controls are required to guard against their deleterious effects.

Even if employees are properly equipped to perform a job well, some choose not to do so, because individual goals and organizational goals may not coincide perfectly. In other words, there is a *lack of goal congruence*. Steps must often be taken either to increase goal congruence or to prevent employees from acting in their own interest where goal incongruence exists.

If nothing is done to protect the organization against the possible occurrence of undesirable behavior or the omission of desirable behavior caused by these personal limitations and motivational problems, severe repercussions may result. At a minimum, inadequate control can result in lower performance or higher risk of poor performance. At the extreme, if performance is not controlled on one or more critical performance dimensions, the outcome could be organizational failure.

WHAT IS GOOD CONTROL?

Perfect control, meaning complete assurance that actual accomplishment will proceed according to plan, is never

---

possible because of the likely occurrence of unforeseen events. However, good control should mean that an informed person could be reasonably confident that no major unpleasant surprises will occur. A high probability of forthcoming poor performance, despite a reasonable operating plan, sometimes is given the label "out of control."

Some important characteristics of this desirable state of good control should be highlighted. First, control is future-oriented: the goal is to have no unpleasant surprises in the future. The past is not relevant except as a guide to the future. Second, control is multidimensional, and good control cannot be established over an activity with multiple objectives unless performance on all significant dimensions has been considered. Thus, for example, control of a production department cannot be considered good unless all the major performance dimensions, including quality, efficiency, and asset management, are well controlled. Third, the assessment of whether good performance assurance has been achieved is difficult and subjective. An informed expert might judge that the control system in place is adequate because no major bad surprises are likely, but this judgment is subject to error because adequacy must be measured against a future that can be very difficult to assess. Fourth, better control is not always economically desirable. Like any other economic good, the control tools are costly and should be implemented only if the expected benefits exceed the costs.

HOW CAN GOOD CONTROL BE ACHIEVED?

Good control can be achieved by avoiding some behavioral problems and/or by implementing one or more types of control to protect against the remaining problems. The following sections discuss the major control options.

Control-Problem Avoidance. In most situations, managers can avoid some control problems by allowing no opportunities for improper behavior. One possibility is automation. Computers and other means of automation reduce the organization's exposure to control problems because they can be set to perform appropriately (that is, as the organization desires), and they will perform more consistently than do human beings. Consequently, control is improved.

Another avoidance possibility *is centralization,* such as that which takes place with very critical decisions at most organization levels. If a manager makes all the decisions in certain areas, those areas cease to be control problems in a managerial sense because no other persons are involved.

A third avoidance possibility is *risk-sharing* with an outside body, such as an insurance company. Many companies bond employees in sensitive positions, and in so doing, they reduce the probability that the

employees' behavior will cause significant harm to the firm.

Finally, some control problems can and should be avoided by *elimination* of a business or an operation entirely. Managers without the means to control certain activities, perhaps because they do not understand the processes well, can eliminate the associated control problems by turning over their potential profits and the associated risk to a third party, for example, by subcontracting or divesting.

If management cannot, or chooses not to, avoid the control problems caused by relying on other individuals, they must address the problems by implementing one or more control tactics. The large number of tactics that are available to help achieve good control can be classified usefully into three main categories, according to the *object* of control; that is, whether control is exercised over *specific actions, results,* or *personnel.* Table 1 shows many common controls classified according to their control object; these controls are described in the following sections.

Control of Specific Actions. One type of control, specific-action control, attempts to ensure that individuals perform (or do not perform) certain actions that are known to be desirable (or undesirable). Management can limit the incidence of some types of obviously undesirable activity by using *behavioral constraints* that render the occurrence impossible, or at least unlikely. These constraints include physical devices, such as locks and key personnel identification systems, and administrative constraints, such as segregation of duties, which make it very difficult for one person to carry out an improper act.

A second type of specific-action control is *action accountability*—a type of feedback control system by which employees are held accountable for their actions. The implementation of action-accountability control systems requires: (1) defining the limits of acceptable behavior, as is done in procedures manuals; (2) tracking the behaviors that employees are actually engaged in; and (3) rewarding or punishing deviations from the defined limits. Although action-accountability systems involve the tracking and reporting of actual behaviors, their objective is to motivate employees to behave appropriately in the future. These systems are effective only if employees understand what is required of them, and they feel that their individual actions will be noticed and rewarded or punished in some significant way.

A third type of specific-action control is *preaction review.* This involves observing the work of others before the activity is complete, for example, through direct supervision, formal planning reviews, and approvals on proposals for expenditures. Reviews can provide effective control in several ways by: correcting potentially harmful behavior before the full damaging

TABLE 1. A CONTROL TOOL CLASSIFICATION FRAMEWORK

Object of Control Specific Actions	Results	Personnel
Behavioral Constraint: —Physical (e.g., locks, security guards) —Administrative (e.g., separation of duties)	Results Accountability: —Standards —Budgets —Management by Objective (MBO)	Upgrade Capabilities: —Selection —Training —Assignment Improve Communication: —Clarify Expectations —Provide Information for Coordination
Action Accountability: —Work Rules —Policies and Procedures —Codes of Conduct		Encourage Peer Control: —Work Groups —Shared Goals
Preaction Review: —Direct Supervision —Approval Limits —Budget Reviews		

effects are felt; or influencing behavior just by the threat of an impending review, such as causing extra care in the preparation of an expenditure proposal. One advantage of reviews is that they can be used even when it is not possible to define exactly what is expected prior to the review.

Control of Results. Control can also be accomplished by focusing on results: this type of control comes in only one basic form, results accountability, which involves holding employees responsible for certain results. Use of results-accountability control systems requires: (1) defining the dimensions along which results are desired, such as efficiency, quality, and service; (2) measuring performance on these dimensions; and (3) providing rewards (punishments) to encourage (discourage) behavior that will lead (not lead) to those results. As with action-accountability systems, results-accountability systems are future-oriented; they attempt to motivate people to behave appropriately. But they are effective only if employees feel that their individual efforts will be noticed and rewarded in some significant way.

Control of Personnel. A third type of control can be called *personnel control* because it emphasizes a reliance on the personnel involved to do what is best for the organization, and it provides assistance for them as necessary. Personnel controls can be very effective by themselves in some situations, such as in a small family business or in a professional partnership, because the underlying causes of the needs for controls (personal limitations and lack of goal congruence) are minimal. However, even when control problems are present, they can be reduced to some extent by: (1) upgrading the capabilities of personnel in key positions, such as tightening hiring policies, implementing training programs, or improving job assignments; (2) improving communications to help individuals know and understand their roles better and how they can best coordinate their efforts with those of other groups in the organization; and (3) encouraging peer (or subordinate) control by establishing cohesive work groups with shared goals.

FEASIBILITY CONSTRAINTS ON THE CHOICE OF CONTROLS

The design of a control system often depends partly on the feasibility of the various types of controls: not all of these tools can be used in every situation. Personnel controls are the most adaptable to a broad range of situations.

To some extent, all organizations rely on their employees to guide and motivate themselves, and this self-control can be increased with some care in hiring, screening, and training. Even in a prison, where administrators are faced with a sharp lack of goal congruence and where few control options are available other than physical constraints, inmates are screened so that dangerous ones are not assigned to high-risk positions, such as in a machine shop.

Most situations, however, require reinforcing personnel controls by placing controls over specific actions, results, or a combination of the two. This is where feasibility becomes a limiting factor.

For control over specific actions, management must have some knowledge of which actions are desirable. While it may be easy to define precisely the required behavior on a production line, the definition of preferred behavior for a research engineer cannot be as precise. Being able to keep track of specific actions is also necessary to enforce actions accountability; however, this is usually not a limiting factor, except in rare situations such as a remote outpost, because actions can be observed directly or assessed indirectly through action reports, such as hours worked, sales calls made, or procedural violations.

For control over results, the most serious constraint is the ability to measure the desired results effectively.

(Management usually knows what results are desirable.) Ideally, measurements should: (1) assess the *correct* performance areas—the ones for which results are truly desired; (2) be *precise*—not determined by only crude estimations; (3) be *timely* and (4) be *objective*—not subject to manipulation. While perfect measures are rarely available, reasonable surrogates can often be found or developed. For example, "complaints received" might be a good (negative) indicator of the performance of hotel staff personnel along the customer-service dimension. Significant difficulty in achieving any of these four measurement qualities, however, can lead to failure of a results-oriented control system.

Figure 1 shows how the two factors most limiting control feasibility knowledge of desirable actions and the ability to measure results on the important performance dimensions—can influence the choice of controls used.[5] The most difficult control situation, shown in box 4 of Figure 1, is one in which the desirable actions are not known and the important result areas cannot be measured well. Only personnel controls (or problem avoidance) are available options. In a research laboratory, for example, success might be difficult to assess for years, yet prescription of specific actions could be counterproductive. Fortunately, in this specific setting, control is not a serious problem because research scientists tend to be professional—well trained and responsible to the standards of their profession. They tend to control themselves, and consequently, control of research laboratories tend to be dominated by controls over personnel.

In box 3 of Figure 1, where knowledge of desirable specific actions is poor but good results measurements are available, control is best accomplished by controlling results. Movie production is a good example. It is probably impossible to dictate what a movie director should do or even to observe his or her behavior and predict whether the finished product will be good. It is, however, a relatively easy task to measure the economic performance of the movie and the artistic merit, if that is a concern. In this situation, the best control system would seem to be a results accountability system that defines to the director the results expected, holds him or her responsible for achieving them, and provides some reinforcement in the form of compensation and/or recognition.

For similar reasons, results controls tend to be dominant at most upper-management levels. It is usually not possible to prescribe and keep track of the specific actions each manager should be performing, but it is relatively easy to define the results desired, in terms similar to those desired by shareholders.

Specific-action controls should dominate where there is knowledge about which actions are desirable but where results measurement is impossible or difficult, as indicated in box 2 of Figure 1. Consider, for example,

control over a real-estate development business where large capital investment decisions are made frequently. Results of these decisions are difficult to measure in a timely, accurate fashion because of their long-term nature; they tend to be inseparable from the results of other actions and are confounded by changes in the environment. However, the techniques of investment analysis are well developed (e.g., net present value analysis with tests of the sensitivity of assumptions), and control may be accomplished by formally reviewing the techniques used and the assumptions made.

FIGURE 1. KEY CONTROL OBJECT FEASIBILITY DETERMINANTS

| | | Ability to Measure Results on Important Performance Dimensions | |
		High	Low
Knowledge of Which Specific Actions are Desirable	Excellent	1. Specific-Action and/or Results Control	2. Specific-Action Control (e.g., real-estate venture)
	Poor	3. Results Control (e.g., movie director)	4. Personal control (e.g., research laboratory)

HOW TO CHOOSE AMONG THE FEASIBLE OPTIONS

Often managers cannot rely completely on the people involved in a given area and cannot employ one or more of the avoidance strategies mentioned earlier. When this is the case, the best situation is one in which either specificaction or results controls, or both, can be chosen, as is shown in box 1 of Figure 1. In general, the choice of one or more tools should involve consideration of: (1) the total need for control; (2) the amount of control that can be designed into each of the control devices; and (3) the costs of each, both in terms of money spent and unintended behavioral effects, if any. These decision parameters will be described more fully.

Need for Controls. The need for controls over any particular behavior or operation within an organization depends very simply on the impact of that area on overall organizational performance. Thus, more control should be exercised over a strategically important behavior rather than over a minor one, regardless of how easy it is to control each. For example, controlling the new-product-development activity is far more important in many companies than making sure that the production of existing products is accomplished as efficiently as possible. Consequently, more resources should be devoted to controlling the new-product activity, even though it is a far more difficult area to control.

Amount of Control Provided by Feasible Options. The amount of control provided by each of the control tools depends both on their design and on how well they fit the situation in which they are used. Personnel controls should usually provide some degree of control. But although they may be totally effective in some situations, such as in a small business, they provide little or no warning of failure. They can break down very quickly if demands, opportunities, or needs change.

Specific-action and results controls can provide widely varying amounts of control. In general, reasonably certain (or tight) control requires: (1) detailed specification of what is expected of *each individual;* (2) prevention of undesired actions, or effective and frequent monitoring of actions or results; and (3) administration of penalties or rewards that are significant to the individuals involved.

For example, with specific-action-accountability systems, the amount of control can be affected by changing one or more of the elements of the system. First, tighter control can be effected by making the definitions of acceptability more specific. This might take the form of work rules (e.g., no smoking) or specific policies (e.g., a purchasing policy to secure three competing bids before releasing the purchase order), as opposed to general guidelines or vague codes of conduct (e.g., act professionally). Second, control can be made tighter by improving the effectiveness of the action-tracking system. Personnel who are certain that their actions will be noticed relatively quickly will be affected more strongly by an action-accountability system than will those who feel that the chance of their being observed is small. Thus, constant direct supervision should provide tighter control than would an audit sampling of a small number of action reports some time later. Third, control can be made tighter by making the rewards or punishments more significant to the individuals involved. In general, this impact should vary directly with the size of the reward (or the severity of the punishment), although different individuals may react differently to identical rewards or punishments.

Results-accountability systems can be varied along similar lines. Expected performance can be defined broadly, for instance, with a goal for annual net income. Alternatively, expected performance can be defined in more detailed form by prescribing goals for specific result areas (for example, sales growth, efficiency, quality) and by using line items with short time horizons (e.g., month or quarter). Control is tighter when the performance dimensions for which desired results are defined explicitly and, of course, correctly: this type of control is particularly effective if well-established results standards are available, perhaps in the form of output from an engineering study, industry survey, or historical analysis. Results-accountability control can also be tightened by improving the measurement of results. This can be accomplished by making the measures more precise, more timely, and/or less subject to manipulation.

In addition, reviews can be used to provide either tight or loose assurance. Tight assurance is more likely if the reviews are detailed, comprehensive, and frequent.

Of course, managers do not have to rely exclusively on a single type of control in a control system. Use of more than one type of control—in effect, overlapping controls—will often provide reinforcement. For example, most organizations rely on selecting good people, establishing some set procedures, implementing some accountability for results, and reviewing some key decisions before they are made.

Costs: Outlay and Behavioral. The cost of a control depends on two factors: the incremental dollar cost of the tool and the cost of any unintended behavioral effects. The actual dollar cost of a control might be considerably less than it first appears because some devices that provide control may already be in place for other reasons. For example, a budgeting process for a small firm does not have to justify its cost on the basis of control reasons alone. Creditors probably already require pro forma financial statements, so the incremental cost might involve only additional detail (e.g., down to the operations level) and involvement of a greater number of participants.

The costs of any unintended negative effects must also be considered, and these can be very significant. It is beyond the scope of this article to provide an exhaustive enumeration of the many negative side effects possible. Indeed, they come in many different forms, but it is nevertheless useful to mention a few examples.

A common problem with specific-action controls is that they cause operating delays. These can be relatively minor, such as delays caused by limiting access to a stockroom, but they can also be major. For example, after the executives of Harley-Davidson Motor Company bought the firm from AMF, Inc., they were able to implement a rebate program in ten days, rather than the six to eight weeks it would have taken with all the reviews required in the multilayered AMF organization.[6] Obviously, where timely action is important, delays caused by control processes can be very harmful.

Another problem with specific-action controls is that they can cause rigid, bureaucratic behavior. Individuals who become accustomed to following a set routine are not as apt to sense a changing environment, nor are they likely to search for better ways of doing the tasks at hand in a stable environment.

Results controls can create severe, unintended negative effects when all the measurement criteria are not met satisfactorily. Perhaps the most serious common problem is a failure to define the results areas correctly. This causes goal "displacement," a situation where individuals are encouraged to generate the wrong results—in response to the goals defined in the control system—rather than those results truly needed by the organization. For example, a department store introduced an incentive compensation plan to pay employees on the basis of sales volume. The immediate impact was indeed an increase in sales volume, but the increase was accomplished in ways that were inconsistent with long-term organizational goals. The employees competed among themselves for customers and neglected important but unmeasured and unrewarded activities such as stocking, and merchandising.[7] Another common example of goal displacement is caused by the practice of rewarding managers on the oft criticized return-on investment criterion.[8]

Data distortion is another dangerous potential side effect of results controls. If the measurement methods are not objective, then the employees whose performances are being measured might falsify the data or change the measurement methods, and, in so doing, undermine the whole organization's information system.

Many of the ramifications of these unintended effects of control systems are not well understood, and their costs are very difficult to quantify. However, consideration of these effects is an important control-system design factor: they cannot be ignored.

WHERE DOES FEEDBACK FIT IN?
Because feedback does not appear prominently in the preceding discussion, it is useful for clarification purposes to consider where feedback fits in. Control is necessarily future-oriented, as past performance cannot be changed, but analysis of results and feedback of variances can often provide a particularly strong addition to a control system. A prerequisite, of course, is the ability to measure results, so feedback can only be useful in the situations presented in boxes 1 and 3 of Figure 1.

There are three reasons why feedback of past results is an important part of many control systems. First, feedback is necessary as reinforcement for a results-accountability system. Even if the feedback is not used to make input adjustments, it signals that results are being monitored. This can heighten employee awareness of what is expected of them and should help stimulate better performance.

Second, in repetitive situations, measurement of results can provide indications of failure in time to make useful interventions. This is shown in the simple feedback control model presented in Figure 2. When the results achieved are not satisfactory, the inputs, which include the specific actions and types of persons involved, can be changed to provide different results. Obviously, these input adjustments are more likely to improve results when there is a good understanding of how inputs relate to results; otherwise, the interventions are essentially experiments.

Third, analysis of how the results vary with different combinations of inputs might improve understanding of how the inputs relate to results. This process is depicted in loop A of Figure 3, a slightly more complicated feedback control model. As this input results understanding improves, it provides the opportunity to shift the control system from a results-oriented to a specific-action-oriented focus. If managers discover that certain specific actions produce consistently superior results, then it might be beneficial to inform employees of the specific actions that are expected of them, for example, by publishing these desired actions in a procedures manual. The greater the knowledge about how actions bring about results, the greater the possibilities of using a tight, specific-action-oriented control system.

Note that these latter two reasons for analyzing feedback—for making interventions and for learning—are only useful in situations that at least partially repeat themselves. If a situation is truly a one-time occurrence, such as a major divestiture or a unique capital investment, management has little use for feedback information. In these cases, by the time the results are available, it is too late to intervene, and a greater understanding of how results are related to inputs is not immediately useful.

FIGURE 2. A SIMPLE FEEDBACK CONTROL MODEL

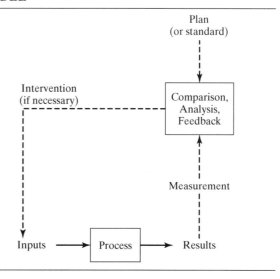

There are other circumstances where feedback need not, and perhaps should not, be a part of a good control system. In many cases, although feedback control systems are not really feasible, they are used anyway. This occurs because of the consistent tendency "to concentrate an matters that are concrete and quantifiable, rather than intangible concepts," which may be equally or more important.[9] Invariably, this will lead to dysfunctional effects, as will all other failures to satisfy the measurement criteria or to define results appropriately.

Cost considerations also commonly lead to decisions not to include feedback in a control system. The design, implementation, and maintenance of results-tracking information systems can often be very expensive. Thus, it is not feasible to have feedback as part of every control system, nor is it necessarily desirable even when feasibility constraints are not present.

FIGURE 3. A FEEDBACK CONTROL MODEL WITH LEARNING

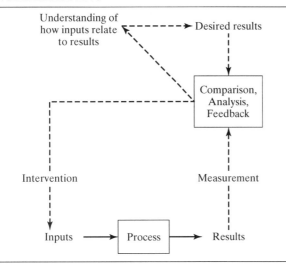

THE DESIGN PROCESS
As discussed at the beginning of this article, management control is a problem of human behavior. The challenge is to have each individual acting properly as often as possible. Thus, it seems logical to start the control-system design process by considering the personnel component of the organization by itself. In some situations, well-trained, highly motivated personnel can be expected, with a high degree of certainty, to perform their jobs satisfactorily without any additional control steps being taken. A confident reliance on personnel controls is a very desirable situation because additional controls cost money and may have undesirable side effects.

If, however, management determines that personnel controls should be supplemented, the first step should be to examine the feasibility of the various control options. To do this, management must assess two factors: how much is known about which specific actions are desirable, and how well measurement can be accomplished in the important performance areas. This feasibility test might immediately determine whether the controls that can be added should be oriented toward specific actions or results. Control can be made tighter by strengthening the controls in place, along the lines discussed earlier, or by implementing overlapping

controls, such as controls over results and specific actions.

In most cases, management has same, but less than complete, knowledge of which specific actions are desirable and some, but not perfect, ability to measure the important result areas. This situation usually calls for implementation of both specific-action and results controls, with feedback loops to improve understanding of the relevant processes.

AN EXAMPLE: CONTROL OF A SALES FORCE
The above observations about control can be illustrated by describing how control of a sales force might work. Generally, personnel controls are some part of every sales force control system. Consider, for example, this statement by a sales and marketing consultant:

> *I think I can tell a good salesman just by being around him. If the guy is experienced, confident, well prepared, speaks well, maintains control of situations, and seems to have his time planned, I assume I have a good salesman.*

If a sales manager feels confident about all of the salespeople employed, he or she might wish to allow personnel controls to dominate the control system. This is likely, for example, in a small business with a sales force comprised solely of relatives and close friends. But most sales managers are not willing to rely exclusively on hiring and training good people.

What controls should be added? The answer, of course, depends on the type of sales involved. In a single-product, high-volume operation, the volume of sales generated is probably a good simple factor on which to base a results-oriented control system. It provides a reasonable, although not perfect, surrogate for long-range profitability, and the measurements are very inexpensive because the data are already gathered as a necessary input to the financial reporting system. The results-accountability system can then be completed by providing reinforcement in the form of sales commissions. This simple solution will also work where multiple products with varying profitability are involved, if the commission schedules are varied so that rewards are assigned in proportion to the profitability of the sales generated.

Consider, however, a situation where salespeople sell large-scale construction equipment and where sales come in very large but infrequent chunks. A commission-type, results-accountability system is still feasible. Measurement of results is not difficult and can be accurate to the penny. The amount of control provided, however, is not high because the measurements fail on the timeliness dimension. Because sales are infrequent, zero sales are not an unusual situation in any given month. Therefore, a salesperson could be drawing advances on hypothetical future commissions for many months without performing any of the desired promotional activities.

Two solutions are possible. One is to augment the commission system with some specific-action controls, such as activity reports. Some activities are probably known to be desirable, such as the number of hours worked and the quantity of calls made. If the product mix and market environment are fairly stable, then requiring and monitoring activity reports is not as costly as it might seem, because it could provide an important side benefit—an activity-oriented data base. The patterns in this data base can be analyzed and compared with results over time to add to knowledge about which activities yield the best results.

An alternate solution is to improve the results-accountability system. It might be possible to define some factors that are strong predictors of sales success, such as customer satisfaction with the salesperson or customer familiarity with the company's products. Measurement of these intangibles, of course, would have to be done by surveying customers. Even though these measures do not directly assess the desired result area (long-range profitability), and measurement is imprecise, they could provide a better focus for a results-oriented control system than a sales-generated measure because of the improvement in timeliness. Over time, it is likely that the choice of measures and measurement methodologies could be improved. The advantage of this results-oriented solution over an action-oriented system is that it is more flexible and less constraining to the salespeople; they can continue to use styles best suited to their personalities.

CONCLUSIONS

This article has taken a new look at the most basic organizational control problem—how to get employees to live up to the plans that have been established. In the course of discussion, the following major points were made:

1. Management control is a behavioral problem. The various control tools are only effective to the extent that they influence behavior in desirable directions.
2. Good control can often be achieved in several different ways. In some circumstances, the control problems can be avoided, for example, by centralizing or automating certain decisions. If problems cannot be avoided, one or more types of controls are usually desirable or necessary. The options can be classified according to the object of control, labeled in this article as specific actions, results, and personnel.
3. Not all types of controls are feasible in all situations. Figure 4 presents the questions to ask when assessing the feasibility of control types. If none of the controls is feasible, the probability of undesirable results occurring is high.

4. Control can be strengthened either by employing a tighter version of a single type of control or by implementing more than one type of control. However, tighter control is not always desirable because of additional system costs and the potential of undesirable side effects, such as destruction of morale, reduction of initiative, or displacement of employee focus toward measurable result areas only. Some of the qualities, benefits, and costs of each of the major control types are listed in Table 2.
5. The basic management control problems and alternatives are the same in all functional areas and at all levels in the organization, from the lowest supervisory levels to the very top levels of management. The best solutions, however, vary between situations.

An understanding of control can be an important input into many management decisions. For example, control problems should be considered in making some types of investments. An investment in an operation in which control is very difficult—such as a highly specialized and technical area where control must depend heavily on personnel controls—is, by definition, risky. Thus, investments in such areas should promise high returns to compensate for this risk.

Similarly, control considerations should affect the design of the other parts of the management system. Consider, for example, the organizational structure. If independent areas of *responsibility* cannot be carved out as part of the organizational structure, results-accountability control systems will not work well because employees will not feel that their individual actions have a noticeable effect on results. (It should be noted that many of the prescriptions calling for "responsibility accounting" only provide the illusion of results independence because of the many allocations of the costs and/or benefits of shared resources.) If independent areas of *authority* are not established, specific-action-accountability control systems cannot work. This principle underlies the internal control principle of "separation of duties." In addition, if tighter reviews of specific actions are necessary for adequate performance assurance, it is likely that the supervisory spans of control will have to be reduced. Similar observations can be made about other management functions, but they are beyond the scope of this article.

This article has attempted to provide a new look at this basic, but often overlooked, management problem. The control area is decidedly complex, and there is much that is not known about how controls work and how employees respond to different types of controls. For example, it would be worthwhile to know more about how controls can be designed to maximize the amount of control provided while minimizing the cost in the form of employee feelings of lost autonomy. However, an

FIGURE 4. QUESTIONS TO DETERMINE FEASIBILITY OF CONTROL TYPES

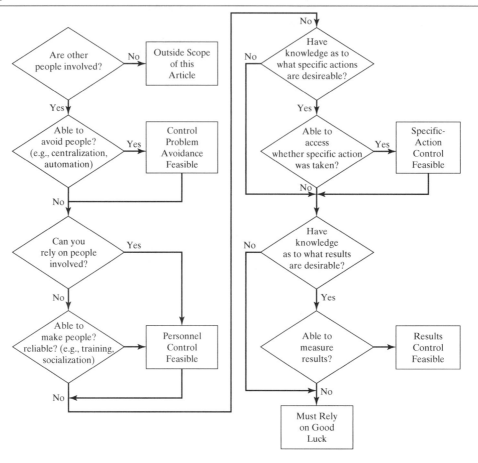

TABLE 2. QUALITIES OF CONTROL TOOLS

Object of Control:	Constraint	SPECIFIC ACTIONS Accountability	Review	RESULTS Accountability	PERSONNEL
Amount of Control Provided (tight or loose)	Tight	Tight if Specific; Loose if Vague	Tight if Detailed And Frequent	Tight if Expectations Are Specific And Detailed	Loose
Out-of Pocket-Cost (relative)	Low	Low	High	High	Varies
Possible Unintended Effects (examples)	Slight Operating Delays	Rigid Bureaucratic Behavior	Operating Delays	Goal Displacement Data Distortion	

increased awareness of the control problem, of what can be accomplished and of the options available should provide a new perspective that will suggest ways to improve control systems and overall organizational performance.

The author wishes to acknowledge Robert N. Anthony, Peter Brownell, and Martha S. Hayes for their helpful comments.

The control function of management can be a critical determinant of organizational success. Most authors discuss control only through feedback and adjustment processes. This article takes a broader perspective on control and discusses the following questions: What is good control? Why are controls needed? How can good control be achieved? If multiple control strategies are feasible, how should the choice among them be made? Ed.

ENDNOTES

1. See H. Koontz, C. O'Donnell, and H. Weihrich. *Management*, 7th ed. (New York: McGraw-Hill, 1980), p. 722.
2. See W. D. Brinckloe and M. T. Coughlin, *Managing Organizations* (Encino, CA: Glencoe Press, 1977), p. 298.
3. See P. F. Drucker, *Management: Tasks, Responsibilities, Practices* (New York: Harper & Row, 1974), p. 497.
4. A recent summary of many of the findings in this area (illustrating such cognitive limitations as conservative revision of prior subjective probabilities when new information is provided, and the use of simplifying decision-making heuristics when faced with complex problems) is provided by W. F. Wright, "Cognitive Information Processing Biases: Implications for Producers and Users of Financial Information," *Decision Sciences* (April 1980): 284–298.
5. A similar scheme is presented in W. G. Ouchi, "A Conceptual Framework for the Design of Organizational Control Mechanisms," *Management Science* (September 1979): 833–848.
6. See H. Klein, "At Harley-Davidson, Life without AMF Is Upbeat but Full of Financial Problems," *Wall Street Journal*, 13 April 1982, p. 37.
7. See N. Babchuk and W. J. Goode, "Work Incentives in a Self-Determined Group," *American Sociological Review* (1951): 679–687.
8. For a summary of criticisms of return-on-investment (ROI) measures of performance, see J. Dearden, "The Case against ROI Control," *Harvard Business Review*, May–June 1969, pp. 124–135.
9. See D. Mitchell, *Control without Bureaucracy* (London: McGraw-Hill Book Company Limited, 1979), p. 6.

Kenneth A. Merchant is Assistant Professor of Business Administration at Harvard University. Dr. Merchant holds the B.A. degree from Union College, the M.B.A. degree from Colombia University, and the Ph.D. degree from the University of California, Berkeley. His main interests lie in the areas of accounting, information systems, and planning and control. Dr. Merchant has published articles for such journals as The Accounting Review and Accounting, Organizations, and Society.

QUESTION

9.1 Merchant discusses specific action, results, and personnel controls. Provide three examples of each. Can organizations focus on just one major type of control method (e.g. action controls)?

9.2 Effective OEC Mamagement Control at China Haíer Group

The company has become successful through excellent customer service, product quality, operating efficiency, innovation, and speed to market.

by Thomas W. Lin, CMA*

In 1984, Zhang Ruimin took over a nearly bankrupt refrigerator factory in Qingdao, China. In 2003, the company's global sales hit $9.7 billion with a growth rate of 70% during the previous 19 years. Today, Haier Group is recognized as a worldwide brand. On January 31, 2004, the firm ranked 95th after such household names as Coca-Cola, McDonald's, and Nokia, which were the top three on the World Brand Laboratory's list of the 100 most recognizable brands. Haier was the only Chinese brand on the list.

So how did they achieve their success? As one of China's fastest-growing companies, Haier Group fits a 1999 Gallup survey profile for a successful company.

Customer service, product quality, operating efficiency, innovation, and speed to market are among the top seven factors for success. Haier excels in all these areas.

To achieve success the company developed its corporate culture, business strategy, and OEC management-control system, which enforces firm work rules and discipline. Haier's Human Resource Management Director Wang Yingmin explains the OEC acronym: "O stands for Overall; E stands for Everyone, Everything, and Everyday; C stands for Control and Clear. OEC means that every employee has to accomplish the target work every day. The OEC management-control system aims at overall control of

* From: T. W. Lin, Effective OEC Management Control at China Haier Group," *Strategic Finance* (May 2005): 39–45. Reprinted with permission conveyed through Copyright Clearance Center, Inc.

everything that every employee finishes on his or her job every day, with a 1% increase over what was done the previous day."

Why did Haier choose to implement the OEC system? According to CEO Zhang, "If you observe Chinese people's behaviors at the traffic lights, when the red light is on, people simply ignore it and cross the street anyway. At the workplace, Chinese people also tend to ignore rules and do not pay enough attention to details. We need a tough management system with fair rewards and penalty features to help our workers get things done properly."

OEC works. When I visited Haier's air conditioner manufacturing facility in the Haier High Tech Industrial Park at Yellow Island in July 2004, the factory floors were clean, and workers, wearing uniforms with photo ID badges, operated in an orderly manner at the assembly lines. Banners featuring quotes such as "A Product with Defects Is Useless" and "Innovation Is the Soul of Haier Culture" line the factory walls. One large bulletin board says, "Every day is a new day; all activities are completed in the same day by innovations." The OEC management-control system implementation has resulted in satisfied customers, efficient and effective processes, motivated and prepared employees, sustainable revenue, and profit growth.

Let's look at how OEC helped turn the company into one of the world's top brands.

BUSINESS STRATEGY

Haier CEO Zhang Ruimin and President Yang Mianmian say the firm developed three major strategies over three stages: brand building or recognition strategy, expansion or diversification strategy, and globalization strategy (see Figure 1). Called the famous-brand strategy, the first stage lasted from 1984 to 1991. During this period, the company created and built Haier-brand products and set up a quality-assurance system. In April 1985, Zhang gathered all employees and battered the first poor-quality refrigerator with a hammer, and then the employees responsible for these goods battered 76 defective refrigerators. The event woke up the quality awareness of all employees and established the concepts of "defective products are wasters" and "excellent products are produced by talented employees." The thinking shifted from volume as the priority to quality and brand recognition being the priorities.

From 1991 to 1998, the second stage featured an expansion or diversification strategy within China. Since the firm bases itself on quality instead of quantity, it decided that if someone bought a Haier Group refrigerator, then maybe they would want to buy something else from the firm. The business was developed primarily through mergers and acquisitions to cover all kinds of household electrical appliances and electronic consumer goods instead of just one product.

At this time it also focused on building great distribution channels all over China and improving product development speed and quality.

FIGURE 1: THREE STAGES OF STRATEGY DEVELOPMENT

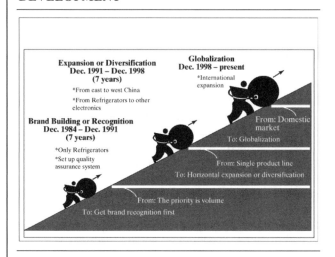

Since December 1998, the third stage has focused on the globalization strategy. Haier exported its products to Germany first, then to other European countries, the U.S., Southeast Asian countries, Middle Eastern countries, and India. In 2000, the firm opened a $35 million refrigerator factory in Camden, S.C., and started selling products through Wal-Mart and many other national and regional chains. In 2002, Haier opened its American headquarters in New York City.

The firm's international promotion framework encompasses global networks for design, production, distribution, and aftersales services. It established 18 design institutes, 10 industrial complexes, 22 overseas production factories, and 58,800 sales agents worldwide. Haier sells its products in 12 out of 15 European chain supermarkets and 10 of America's chain stores. And it has design, production, and sales facilities in the United States and some European countries with local employees primarily running them. None of the employees at its New York headquarters is Chinese.

Two other key business strategies at Haier relate to winning over consumers: speed and differentiation. Speed means to satisfy the consumer's needs as quickly as possible; differentiation means to introduce brand-new products or products with features to meet different needs. For example, the firm's U.S. president requested that the Haier headquarters design a new refrigerator that has pullout drawers in the freezer chest for the U.S. market, and in 17 hours a micro-freezer prototype was built. This really exemplifies the firm's speed strategy. Another example of the firm's differentiation in action: One employee discovered through visiting rural customers in the western part of China that they frequently used their washing machines not only to launder clothes but to also clean vegetables. Later, the firm marketed the machines as versatile enough to wash both clothing and vegetables for China's rural areas.

Haier differs from other appliance companies in that it will build products to order and it doesn't compete on price. Its philosophy is: "Customer is the king for every Haier salesperson." All employees learn that they have to give customers what they want. For example, if a customer buys a refrigerator, an employee goes to the customer's home to set it up for them.

HOW DOES OEC MANAGEMENT WORK AT HAIER?

For constant business growth, a company needs to continuously raise its goals and quality through innovation. That's where OEC comes in. Based on market competition, OEC management strives to continuously raise the firm's goals and improve management skills to achieve a sustainable competitive advantage. Every employee at Haier attends one month of corporate culture and OEC management training before being put to work.

Haier's OEC management-control system and enterprise culture have the following characteristics:

- Focus on and understand customer value, product quality, operating efficiency, innovation, and speed to market.
- Commit top management and leadership to creating a "new way of management" and a performance culture.
- Involve management and employees in creating the OEC management-control system. Allow them to become familiar with OEC so they feel included and share in ownership of the system.
- Educate management and employees. Use seminars and weekly company newsletters to explain the firm's strategy, customer value, OEC management, and the idea of every employee being a strategic business unit (SBU) to enable them to understand the concept and appreciate the benefits. (SBU means that each employee is a profit center with the responsibility to make a profit. Each employee generates his or her revenue by providing the best service to the employee in the next step downstream and incurs expense or cost by receiving service from the employee in the previous step upstream and resources from various supporting departments.)
- Create desired incentives, and reassure employees that they will be properly evaluated in accordance with their performance.

The OEC management-control system has three subsystems: target setting; control, checking, and clearance;

and incentive mechanism. Here's how these subsystems work.

TARGET SETTING

Every December, Haier headquarters sets the next year's guidelines and goals for each division by considering past performance, market demand forecast, group long-term goals, and each division's input on specific market-development needs (see Table 1).

Each division submits a divisional action program form with respect to its annual guidelines and goals. Also called the divisional management account, it includes specific annual goals, specific targets, and action programs, deadlines, responsible divisions, quality criteria, evaluation method, and frequency (see Table 2).

3E Card Evaluation Criteria
(Note: U.S. $1 = 8.27 Yuans)

The 3E cards feature seven criteria items with 30 checkpoints. Employees complete a 3E card every day, which a supervisor then reviews. Beyond the seven criteria there are additional sections on the card relating to penalties and rewards as well as inspections. Here are examples from each of the seven OEC items.

PRODUCTION PLAN

If less-than-plan production occurs because of external factors, production plan should be achieved by nonpaid overtime.

QUALITY

Daily defective product costs should be fined according to the defective product prices announced by the Quality inspection department.

TECHNOLOGY LEVEL AND PRODUCTION DISCIPLINE

Employees who fail to follow the technical requirements in production should be fined ¥20.

EQUIPMENT

Employees who violate equipment operation procedures should be fined ¥50.

MATERIAL

Employees who produce defective products should be fined an amount of up to 10% of the material price.

LABOR DISCIPLINE

Employees who are late for work should be fined ¥2; those who leave early from work should be fined the daily wage.

PRODUCTION SAFETY

Employees who operate without knowledge of safety operation rules and procedures should be fined ¥10.

TABLE 1: DIVISION _____ FISCAL YEAR GUIDELINES AND GOALS

GUIDELINES	X-1 YEAR:		X YEAR:				X+1 YEAR:	
GOALS	**CONTRAST ITEMS**		**CURRENT LEVEL HOME AND ABROAD**	**HIGHEST**	**FACTS OF _____ DIVISION**			
			LEVEL	COMPANY	X-1 YEAR	X YEAR	INCREASED BY %	PLAN OF X+1 YEAR	INCREASED BY %
Capacity	Output (00,000 units) Variety								
Financial Performance	Sales ($000,000,000) Profit ($000,000,000)								
Productivity	Productivity (Units per person, year)								
	Profit per person ($10,000 per person, year) Income per person								
Management	Quality Institutional Reform Infrastructure Management								
Market		New Products							
	Market Products	Star Products Cash Cow Products Dog Products							
	Target Market Market Position								
Development	Science and Technology New Projects Fields or Business Lines								

Prepared by: Verified by: Approved by:

OTHER AWARDS AND PENALTIES

This section will handle actions not mentioned above.

ENDORSEMENT

Additional explanations from the operators or inspectors will be recorded in this section.

INSPECTION AND REVIEW

Inspectors (team chiefs) are required to schedule inspections of the 3E card and give comments on evaluation and endorsement results. Reviewers are required to schedule reviews of the 3E card and release a review opinion. Employees' wages will be determined according to review results.

A department management account is the same as the divisional action program. Before the 26th day of each month, every department head submits an OEC monthly control general ledger to his or her superior for approval. It includes a list of items, target value, last month's value, expected evaluation result, last month's error-correction numbers, this month's error-correction numbers, responsible persons, work hours, and daily clearance control evaluation summary.

Every employee also completes a daily activity control clearing account called an employee management account. It consists of task items, evaluation criteria (benchmark, past-period performance, and this-period goal), values, name of the responsible employee, daily actual results, evaluation results, actual compensation, and reviewer. To track performance, each job is assigned to a specific employee along with a clear delineation of the job's supervising manager, the responsible employee, the employee's partner, and the quality-check person. For example, each piece of glass in a particular building is associated with an employee who must take care of it.

CONTROL, CHECKING, AND CLEARANCE: THE OEC DAILY CLEARING ROUTINE

The second subsystem—control, checking, and clearance—includes the OEC daily clearing routine, which involves a nine-step list of procedures:

1. Each team supervisor gives a daily briefing to workers before they start their work.
2. Production workers conduct their activities by following the seven OEC criteria to check and control: production quantity, quality, material consumption, technology level, equipment maintenance and condition, production safety and workplace condition, and labor discipline. For other workers, the criteria consist of activity items and specific targets.
3. Supervisors conduct on-site inspection tours every two hours, detect and solve problems, and complete

TABLE 2: DIVISIONAL MANAGEMENT ACCOUNT

_____ Division _____ Fiscal Year

GUIDELINES

(1) NUMBER	ADVANCED GOALS (2) GOALS	(3) TARGET VALUES	(4) EXISTING PROBLEMS	(5) ACTION PROGRAMS
(1)	(2)	(3)	(4)	(a) Through the daily clearance control procedure, we should integrate daily clearance into worker's daily life to ensure goal realization: task assignment, daily worksheet, error correction, result review, and salary compensation.
5	Management	■ Reforms of daily clearance management to achieve group's A level.	■ Lower error-correction rate of daily clearance.	
			■ Problems in on-spot management and low standards.	(b) Achieve goals of: daily plan control; scheduled work achievement inspection timetable; error correction controlled by daily clearance; 100% item controlled rate; 100% "A level" goal attainment; larger than 95% "B level" goal attainment.
		■ Raise team management skill level.		(c) Use the industrial engineering method to streamline on-site management model.
		■ Benchmark goals to achieve the competitive advantage.		(d) Cultivate, educate, and select future higher-level managers and executive elites.
				(e) Set up a bulletin board to announce monthly job rotation and promotion results.
				(f) Prepare a compensation reform plan to solve unfairness in compensation.
				(g) Strengthen factory safety system to ensure zero occurrence rates in major accidents and less than 0.3% minor accidents.
				(h) Train and establish six to eight honor teams.
				(i) Train and establish three self-management teams and 10 exam-waiver teams.

Note: This table skips 1 to 4 and shows only No. 5 as an example.

(6) PERIOD	(7) DEPARTMENTS RESPONSIBLE HR	FRANCE	PLANNING	MATERIAL	⊗ RESPONSIBLE QUALITY	EQUIPMENT	* ASSISTANT INSPECTION	AFTER SALE SERVICE	X SUPPORTING FACTORY I	FACTORY II	FACTORY III	(8) STANDARD	(9) VERIFICATION MATERIALS	(10) REVIEW METHODS
(a) Aug	✪	*	*	*	*	*	*	*	*	*	*	New Standard	Mode Material	Monthly Review
(b) All Year	*		✪			*						Q19509A	Exam Sheet Evaluation Result	Monthly Report and Review
(c) May						✪			*	*	*	:	:	Monthly Plan Review
(d) All Year	✪					*						New Standard	Operation Evaluation Result	Quarterly Plan Review
(e) March	✪											:	Announce Result	Monthly Review
(f) March	✪					*						:	Evaluation Result	:
(g) All Year	✪				*			*	*	*	*	954401-954405	Not Exceeding Standard; Announce	Daily Report, Monthly Review
(h) Sept.	✪	×	×	×	*	×	×	*	*	*	*	:	Evaluation Result	Monthly Plan Review
(i) Oct.	*	*			*	✪	*		*	*	*	929501-929504	Standard Attainment Result	Monthly Report and Review

Prepared by: _____ Approved by: _____

the production site OEC form with the seven OEC criteria items.

4. At the end of the day, all workers conduct a self-check of their own work with the OEC criteria, fill out their 3E (Everyone, Everything, and Everyday) cards with seven OEC criteria items, and submit them to their supervisors. The OEC evaluation criteria include 30 items (see "3E Card Evaluation Criteria" sidebar on p. 41 for examples as well as fines if employees don't uphold the criteria related to the seven OEC areas).

5. Each supervisor examines the 3E cards, corrects errors, gives a comprehensive evaluation, and submits the evaluation results to the work area manager. Evaluation results are graded as A, B, and C. If an employee achieves an A, ¥5 are added to that employee's daily compensation; if an employee receives a C, it's minus ¥5.

THE EMPLOYEES WHO ARE ACKNOWLEDGED AS THE BEST WORKERS FOR THREE CONSECUTIVE DAYS HAVE THE HONOR OF TELLING THEIR EXPERIENCES TO FELLOW WORKERS.

6. Each work area manager checks the sample 3E cards then fills out his or her own 3E card and submits it to the factory director.

7. Each factory director reviews the 3E cards and records the results in the factory OEC account. He or she then files a daily progress report to the Deputy Division General Manager regarding problems that have been solved, problems that haven't been solved, and suggested solutions to unsolved problems.

8. The Deputy Division General Manager reviews daily progress reports and suggested solutions and provides feedback before reporting to the Division General Manager.

9. If necessary, all production and supporting department heads get together to discuss and analyze problems found through the OEC process and work together to suggest corrections, improvement, and prevention that are needed.

INCENTIVE MECHANISM

Haier's third subsystem is the incentive mechanism, and its incentive policies are openness and fairness. The company adopts a point system for production workers using the 3E card, and if an employee earns more points, he or she makes a higher wage and bonus (this way, both management and employee know the daily wage and why).

The firm also uses quality-check coupons to provide an additional incentive mechanism. Each employee has a quality-check coupon booklet with red and yellow coupons for rewards and penalties. The booklet lists all quality problems the firm has detected and provides guidelines for checking each defect. If an employee failed to self-check a quality problem that was later found by his or her team member during a cross-check or by the superior during a managerial check, the employee will lose a red coupon and receive a yellow coupon that will be counted against that day's wage and bonus.

As further motivation, each employee receives a daily grade for actual performance and progress toward achieving his or her target. Daily evaluation results are shown to workers the next day on the bulletin boards in the factory. The employees who are acknowledged as the best workers for three consecutive days have the honor of telling their experiences to fellow workers. The employees who become the best workers most frequently in one month are considered the best workers of the month. They have more opportunities to attend job training and more social benefits, while employees who become the worst workers most frequently in one month are demoted to probation workers.

Finally, the firm has an open competitive bidding system for job placement. When there's a job opening within the group, employees who have reached the qualified skill level through internal training seminars or on-the-job training can bid for that job. Management then makes the final decision and selects the best candidate based on the submitted bids.

SUSTAINABILITY

From a nearly bankrupt company to a recognized worldwide brand, Haier has come a long way. Through making employees responsible for meeting OEC criteria, Haier will continue to excel and achieve its short-term goal of becoming one of the world's top three white-goods manufacturers. In this current competitive market economy, many companies have much to learn from Haier's culture and OEC management-control system.

Thomas W. Lin, CMA, Ph.D., is a professor of accounting and the Leventhal International Faculty Fellow in the Marshall School of Business at the University of Southern California in Los Angeles. You can reach him at (213) 740-4851 or wtlin@marshall.usc.edu.

The author acknowledges the financial support provided by the IMA Foundation for Applied Research and would like to thank Haier University President Zou Xiwen for providing the tables, which were originally in Chinese.

QUESTION

9.2 What are the five characteristics of Haier's OEC management control system and enterprise culture?

9.3 Creating an Ethical Culture

*Values-based ethics programs can help employees
judge right from wrong.*

by David Gebler*

While the fate of former Enron leaders Kenneth Lay and Jeffrey Skilling is being determined in what has been labeled the "Trial of the Century," former WorldCom managers are in jail for pulling off one of the largest frauds in history.

Yes, criminal activity definitely took place in these companies and in dozens more that have been in the news in recent years, but what's really important is to take stock of the nature of many of the perpetrators.

Some quotes from former WorldCom executives paint a different picture of corporate criminals than we came to know in other eras:

"I'm sorry for the hurt that has been caused by my cowardly behavior." —*Scott Sullivan, CFO*

"Faced with a decision that required strong moral courage, I took the easy way out.... There are no words to describe my shame."
—*Buford Yates, director of general accounting*

"At the time I consider the single most critical character-defining moment of my life, I failed. It's something I'll take with me the rest of my life."
—*David Myers, controller*

These are the statements of good people gone bad. But probably most disturbing was the conviction of Betty Vinson, the senior manager in the accounting department who booked billions of dollars in false expenses. At her sentencing, U.S. District Judge Barbara Jones noted that Vinson was among the lowest-ranking members of the conspiracy that led to the $11 billion fraud that sank the telecommunications company in 2002. Still, she said, "Had Ms. Vinson refused to do what she was asked, it's possible this conspiracy might have been nipped in the bud."

Judge Jones added that although Ms. Vinson "was among the least culpable members of the conspiracy" and acted under extreme pressure, "that does not excuse what she did."

Vinson said she improperly covered up expenses by drawing down reserve accounts—some completely unrelated to the expenses—and by moving expenses off income statements and listing them as assets on the balance sheet.

Also the company's former director of corporate reporting, Vinson testified at Bernie Ebbers's trial that, in choosing which accounts to alter, "I just really pulled some out of the air. I used some spreadsheets." She said she repeatedly brought her concerns to colleagues and supervisors, once describing the entries to a coworker as "just crazy." In spring 2002, she noted, she told one boss she would no longer make the entries. "I said that I thought the entries were just being made to make the income statement look like Scott wanted it to look."

Standing before the judge at her sentencing, Vinson said: "I never expected to be here, and I certainly won't do anything like this again." She was sentenced to five months in prison and five months of house arrest.

PRESSURE REIGNS

While the judge correctly said that her lack of culpability didn't excuse her actions, we must carefully note that Betty Vinson, as well as many of her codefendants, didn't start out as criminals seeking to defraud the organization. Under typical antifraud screening tools, she and others like her wouldn't have raised any red flags as being potential committers of corporate fraud.

Scott Sullivan was a powerful leader with a well-known reputation for integrity. If any of us were in Betty Vinson's shoes, could we say with 100% confidence that we would say "no" to the CFO if he asked us to do something and promised that he would take full responsibility for any fallout from the actions we were going to take?

Today's white-collar criminals are more likely to be those among us who are unable to withstand the blistering pressures placed on managers to meet higher and tougher goals. In this environment, companies looking to protect themselves from corporate fraud

---

* From: D. Gebler, "Creating an Ethical Culture," *Strategic Finance* (May 2006): 29–34. Reprinted with permission conveyed through Copyright Clearance Center, Inc must take a hard look at their own culture. Does it promote ethical behavior, or does it emphasize something else?

In most companies, "ethics" programs are really no more than compliance programs with a veneer of "do the right thing" messaging to create an apparent link to the company's values. To be effective, they have to go deeper than outlining steps to take to report misconduct. organizations must understand what causes misconduct in the first place.

We can't forget that Enron had a Code of Ethics. And it wasn't as if WorldCom lacked extensive internal controls. But both had cultures where engaging in unethical conduct was tacitly condoned, if not encouraged.

BUILDING THE RIGHT CULTURE

Now the focus has shifted toward looking at what is going on inside organizations that's either keeping people from doing the right thing or, just as importantly, keeping people from doing something about misconduct they observe. If an organization wants to reduce the risk of unethical conduct, it must focus more effort on building the right culture than on building a compliance infrastructure.

The Ethics Resource Center's 2005 National Business Ethics Survey (NBES) clearly confirms this trend toward recognizing the role of corporate culture. Based on interviews with more than 3,000 employees and managers in the U.S., the survey disclosed that, despite the increase in the number of ethics and compliance program elements being implemented, desired outcomes, such as reduced levels of observed misconduct, haven't changed since 1994. Even more striking is the revelation that, although formal ethics and compliance programs have some impact, organizational culture has the greatest influence in determining program outcomes.

The Securities & Exchange Commission (SEC) and the Department of Justice have also been watching these trends. Stephen Cutler, the recently retired SEC director of the Division of Enforcement, was matter of fact about the importance of looking at culture when it came to decisions of whether or not to bring an action. "We're trying to induce companies to address matters of tone and culture.... What we're asking of that CEO, CFO, or General Counsel goes beyond what a perp walk or an enforcement action against another company executive might impel her to do. We're hoping that if she sees that a failure of corporate culture can result in a fine that significantly exceeds the proverbial 'cost of doing business,' and reflects a failure on her watch— and a failure on terms that everyone can understand: the company's bottom line—she may have a little more incentive to pay attention to the environment in which her company's employees do their jobs."

MEASURING SUCCESS

Only lagging companies still measure the success of their ethics and compliance programs just by tallying the percentage of employees who have certified that they read the Code of Conduct and attended ethics and compliance training. The true indicator of success is whether the company has made significant progress in achieving key program outcomes. The National Business Ethics Survey listed four key outcomes that help determine the success of a program:

- Reduced misconduct observed by employees,
- Reduced pressure to engage in unethical conduct,
- Increased willingness of employees to report misconduct, and
- Greater satisfaction with organizational response to reports of misconduct.

What's going to move these outcomes in the right direction? Establishing the right culture.

Most compliance programs are generated from "corporate" and disseminated down through the organization. As such, measurement of the success of the program is often based on criteria important to the corporate office: how many employees certified the Code of Conduct, how many employees went through the training, or how many calls the hotline received.

Culture is different—and is measured differently. An organization's culture isn't something that's created by senior leadership and then rolled out. A culture is an objective picture of the organization, for better or worse. It's the sum total of all the collective values and behaviors of all employees, managers, and leaders. By definition, it can only be measured by criteria that reflect the individual values of all employees, so understanding cultural vulnerabilities that can lead to ethics issues requires knowledge of what motivates employees in the organization. Leadership must know how the myriad human behaviors and interactions fit together like puzzle pieces to create a whole picture. An organization moves toward an ethical culture only if it understands the full range of values and behaviors needed to meet its ethical goals. The "full-spectrum" organization is one that creates a positive sense of engagement and purpose that drives ethical behavior.

Why is understanding the culture so important in determining the success of a compliance program? Here's an example: Most organizations have a policy that prohibits retaliation against those who bring forward concerns or claims. But creating a culture where employees feel safe enough to admit mistakes and to raise uncomfortable issues requires more than a policy and "Code training." To truly develop an ethical culture, the organization must be aware of how its managers deal with these issues up and down the line and how the values they demonstrate impact desired

Figure 1: SEVEN LEVELS OF AN ETHICAL ORGANIZATION

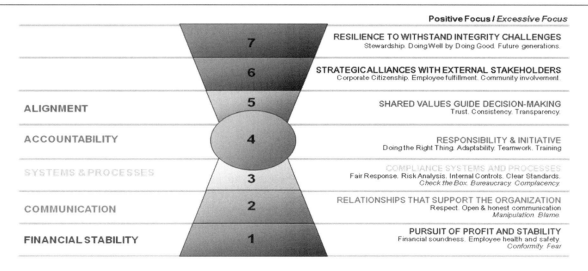

behaviors. The organization must understand the pressures its people are under and how they react to those pressures. And it must know how its managers communicate and whether employees have a sense of accountability and purpose.

CATEGORIZING VALUES

Determining whether an organization has the capabilities to put such a culture in place requires careful examination. Do employees and managers demonstrate values such as respect? Do employees feel accountable for their actions and feel that they have a stake in the success of the organization?

How does an organization make such a determination? One approach is to categorize different types of values in a way that lends itself to determining specific strengths and weaknesses that can be assessed and then corrected or enhanced.

The Culture Risk Assessment model presented in Figure 1 has been adapted from the Cultural Transformation Tools® developed by Richard Barrett & Associates. Such tools provide a comprehensive framework for measuring cultures by mapping values. More than 1,000 organizations in 24 countries have used this technique in the past six years. In fact, the international management consulting firm McKinsey & Co. has adopted it as its method of choice for mapping corporate cultures and measuring progress toward achieving culture change.

The model is based on the principle, substantiated through practice, that all values can be assigned to one of seven categories:

Levels 1, 2, and 3—The Organization's Basic Needs

Does the organization support values that enable it to run smoothly and effectively? From an ethics perspective, is the environment one in which employees feel physically and emotionally safe to report unethical behavior and to do the right thing?

Level 1—Financial Stability. Every organization needs to make financial stability a primary concern. Companies that are consumed with just surviving struggle to focus enough attention on how they conduct themselves. This may, in fact, create a negative cycle that makes survival much more difficult. Managers may exercise excessive control, so employees may be working in an environment of fear.

In these circumstances, unethical or even illegal conduct can be rationalized. When asked to conform to regulations, organizations do the minimum with an attitude of begruding compliance.

Organizations with challenges at this level need to be confident that managers know and stand within clear ethical boundaries.

Level 2—Communication. Without good relationships with employees, customers, and suppliers, integrity is compromised. The critical issue at this level is to create a sense of loyalty and belonging among employees and a sense of caring and connection between the organization and its customers.

The most critical link in the chain is between employees and their direct supervisors. If direct supervisors can't effectively reinforce messages coming from senior leadership, those messages might be diluted and confused by the time they reach line employees. When faced with conflicting messages, employees will usually choose to follow the lead of their direct supervisor over the words of the CEO that have been conveyed through an impersonal communication channel. Disconnects in how local managers "manage" these messages often mean that employees can face tremendous pressure in following the lead established by leadership.

Fears about belonging and lack of respect lead to fragmentation, dissension, and disloyalty. When leaders meet behind closed doors or fail to communicate openly, employees suspect the worst. Cliques form, and gossip becomes rife. When leaders are more focused on their own success, rather than the success of the organization, they begin to compete with each other.

Level 3—Systems and Processes. At this level, the organization is focused on becoming the best it can be through the adoption of best practices and a focus on quality, productivity, and efficiency.

Level 3 organizations have succeeded in implementing strong internal controls and have enacted clear standards of conduct. Those that succeed at this level are the ones that see internal controls as an opportunity to create better, more efficient processes. But even those that have successfully deployed business processes and practices need to be alert to potentially limiting aspects of being too focused on processes. All organizations need to be alert to resorting to a "check-the-box" attitude that assumes compliance comes naturally from just implementing standards and procedures. Being efficient all too often leads to bureaucracy and inconsistent application of the rules. When this goes badly, employees lose respect for the system and resort to self-help to get things done. This can lead to shortcuts and, in the worst case, engaging in unethical conduct under the guise of doing what it takes to succeed.

Level 4—Accountability

The focus of the fourth level is on creating an environment in which employees and managers begin to take responsibility for their own actions. They want to be held accountable, not micromanaged and supervised every moment of every day. For an ethics and compliance program to be successful, all employees must feel that they have a personal responsibility for the integrity of the organization. Everyone must feel that his or her voice is being heard. This requires managers and leaders to admit that they don't have all the answers and invite employee participation.

Levels 5, 6, and 7—Common Good

Does the organization support values that create a collective sense of belonging where employees feel that they have a stake in the success of the ethics program?

Level 5—Alignment. The critical issue at this level is developing a shared vision of the future and a shared set of values. The shared vision clarifies the intentions of the organization and gives employees a unifying purpose and direction. The shared values provide guidance for making decisions.

The organization develops the ability to align decision making around a set of shared values. The values and behaviors must be reflected in all of the organization's processes and systems, with appropriate consequences for those who aren't willing to walk the talk. A precondition for success at this level is building a climate of trust.

Level 6—Social Responsibility. At this level, the organization is able to use its relationships with stakeholders to sustain itself through crises and change. Employees and customers see that the organization is making a difference in the world through its products and services, its involvement in the local community, or its willingness to fight for causes that improve humanity. They must feel that the company cares about them and their future. Companies operating at this level go the extra mile to make sure they are being responsible citizens. They support and encourage employees' activities in the community by providing time off for volunteer work and/or making a financial contribution to the charities that employees are involved in.

Level 7—Sustainability. To be successful at Level 7, organizations must embrace the highest ethical standards in all their interactions with employees, suppliers, customers, shareholders, and the community. They must always consider the long-term impact of their decisions and actions.

Employee values are distributed across all seven levels. Through surveys, organizations learn which values employees bring to the workplace and which values are missing. Organizations don't operate from any one level of values: They tend to be clustered around three or four levels. Most are focused on the first three: profit and growth (Level 1), customer satisfaction (Level 2), and productivity, efficiency, and quality (Level 3). The most successful organizations operate across the full spectrum with particular focus in the upper levels of consciousness—the common good—accountability, leading to learning and innovation (Level 4), alignment (Level 5), sustainability (Level 6), and social responsibility (Level 7).

Some organizations have fully developed values around Levels 1, 2, and 3 but are lacking in Levels 5, 6, and 7. They may have a complete infrastructure of controls and procedures but may lack the accountability and commitment of employees and leaders to go further than what is required.

Similarly, some organizations have fully developed values around Levels 5, 6, and 7 but are deficient in Levels 1, 2, and 3. These organizations may have visionary leaders and externally focused social responsibility programs, but they may be lacking in core systems that will ensure that the higher-level commitments are embedded into day-to-day processes.

Once an organization understands its values' strengths and weaknesses, it can take specific steps to correct deficient behavior.

STARTING THE PROCESS

Could a deeper understanding of values have saved WorldCom? We will never know, but if the culture had encouraged open communication and fostered trust, people like Betty Vinson might have been more willing to confront orders that they knew were wrong. Moreover, if the culture had embodied values that encouraged transparency, mid-level managers wouldn't have been asked to engage in such activity in the first place.

The significance of culture issues such as these is also being reflected in major employee surveys that highlight what causes unethical behavior. According to the NBES, "Where top management displays certain ethics-related actions, employees are 50 percentage points less likely to observe misconduct." No other factor in any ethics survey can demonstrate such a drastic influence.

So how do compliance leaders move their organizations to these new directions?

1. **The criteria for success of an ethics program must be outcomes based.** Merely checking off program elements isn't enough to change behavior.

2. **Each organization must identify the key Indicators of its culture.** Only by assessing its own ethical culture can a company know what behaviors are the most influential in effecting change.

3. **The organization must gauge how all levels of employees perceive adherence to values by others within the company.** One of the surprising findings of the NBES was that managers, especially senior managers, were out of touch with how nonmanagement employees perceived their adherence to ethical behaviors. Nonmanagers are 27 percentage points less likely than senior managers to indicate that executives engage in all of the ethics-related actions outlined in the survey.

4. **Formal programs are guides to shape the culture, not vice versa.** People who are inclined to follow the rules appreciate the rules as a guide to behavior. Formal program elements need to reflect the culture in which they are deployed if they are going to be most effective in driving the company to the desired outcomes.

Culture may be new on the radar screen, but it isn't outside the scope or skills of forward-thinking finance managers and compliance professionals. Culture can be measured, and finance managers can play a leadership role in developing systematic approaches to move companies in the right direction.

David Gebler, J.D., is president of Working Values, Ltd., a business ethics training and consulting firm specializing in developing behavior-based change to support compliance objectives. You can reach him at dgebler@workingvalues.com.

QUESTIONS

9.3a What are the four key outcomes that determine the success of an ethics program?

9.3b What are the seven levels of an ethical organization? Does an organization need all seven levels?

9.4 Leading with Your Soul

The Comprehensive Ethical Leadership Model^{TM} shows you how to create an ethical workplace that will lead to sustainability for your company.

One of the fundamental challenges of our time is ethical leadership. It has been discouraging to see the parade of corporate executives epitomizing corruption and wrongdoing in the recent past. The breach of trust brought about by Enron, Tyco, Arthur Andersen, WorldCom, and others exposed the degree of corporate and social risk in our modern capitalist society. The Sarbanes-Oxley Act (SOX) was supposed to be the magic pill to guard against the culture of short-term profits at all costs that was turning its back on long-term value creation for sustainability. But what followed was the sub-prime mortgage crisis, fueled by questionable hedge fund strategies and the weakening of the financial system. Our recent history has illustrated that legislation can't fix moral lapses and impaired judgment. Instead, the fix needs to address the source of our dilemma—the lack of leadership values rooted in ethical choices.

The United States has evolved from an industrial economy into an information economy, causing a shift from laborers to knowledge workers. This shift calls for a caliber of leader different from those in the past. The age of globalization demands we recognize international interdependencies of resources and stakeholders. This interconnectedness requires mutual respect for societal impacts and mindfulness of the collective ramifications. Effectively balancing all these considerations with a social conscience to create value for corporate sustainability is at the heart of value-centric leadership.

Finance professionals are key strategic partners in creating value. Today, understanding the need for character development, ethics, and value-centric behavior is as important as technical skills. When technical skills and value-centric leadership are employed in concert, a sustainable professional capable of commanding a viable team emerges. The presence of such a finance team will be valuable to a corporation that relies on fair disclosure of business results to raise capital, do business, and sustain growth. The

Comprehensive Ethical Leadership Model^{TM} for sustainability depicts the blueprints for building an ethical foundation.

CHARACTER IN ETHICAL DECISION MAKING

It's a natural human tendency to seek happiness. Obviously, what constitutes happiness for one individual will differ from another. What an individual will do to obtain happiness, however, is reflective of the person's essence, which the Greek philosopher Aristotle and 19th Century utilitarian philosopher John Stuart Mill referred to as the "soul." From that soul emanates character that is an embodiment of who a person is—the foundation of the choices the person makes leading to the consequences that follow. It would serve us all well to keep in mind the words of the anonymous author who said, "Who we are speaks so loud that no one hears what we are saying."

Many believe business ethics somehow differs from everyday ethics. In *There's No Such Thing As "Business" Ethics: There's Only One Rule For Making Decisions*, John Maxwell addresses this notion by explaining that "There is no such thing as business ethics; one is ethical or not." There's also an opinion in business that compliance with the letter of the law is all that's necessary to be an ethical entity. We are a nation of laws where individuals and institutions are bound by legal agreements and contracts. Almost every aspect of human life—including birth, marriage, employment, organized leisure activity, healthcare, and even pet ownership—involves some form of agreement execution. But we must remain cognizant of the difference between legal and ethical grounds. The former is contract-based, open to interpretation, and has loopholes. The latter is covenant-based, driven by a moral compass representing integrity. Founded in self-governance, ethics is rooted in doing the right thing.

---

* From: K. Henry, "Leading with Your Soul," *Strategic Finance* (February 2009): 44-51. Reprinted with permission conveyed through Copyright Clearance Center, Inc.

Individuals struggle with ethics in the professional arena. Some of the reasons they cite are not having the emotional strength to stand up for what is right, not willing to confront issues, and not willing to sacrifice the impending personal material gain. The conscious choice to walk away from ethical decisions includes the following rationale:

1. It's easy to take the course of least resistance and do what's convenient.
2. You can fall into the trap of believing that winning is the goal and, hence, you must do what's needed to win.

Irrespective of the reasoning, what is right is always right, and what is wrong is always wrong. Aristotle was quite emphatic about "courage being a character virtue" integral for leading a moral life. Lack of courage will inevitably hinder an individual's ability to lead a life in keeping with their duty—to humanity and the workplace.

It isn't always easy to lead a moral life. It takes effort and a keen sense of self-awareness in the context of society. The Josephson Institute of Ethics illustrates this difficulty in its definition of ethics: "Ethics is about how we meet the challenge of doing the right thing when it will cost more than we want to pay." The choice to act ethically is imperative to sustain society, making moral behavior socially responsible and necessary. How an individual touches the lives of others is the true measure of the person, not the position held, income earned, or power exerted.

ROADBLOCKS TO ETHICAL DECISIONS

Like all things in life, ethics has its set of hindrances. For example, consider a finance department run by a CFO motivated by showing strong financial results to promote personal monetary gains and quick career ascent. This CFO will be inclined to overwork the team, reward results beneficial to that cause, and exert power to further the personal agenda. This will unequivocally breed a toxic work environment for finance professionals on the team and place an enormous risk on the corporation. If the company hasn't adjusted to the paradigm shift of managing the knowledge worker, embracing empowerment, and giving the voice of reason a venue to be heard, the situation won't bode well for long-term viability. Such a toxic environment will pressure reasonable financial professionals to do the expedient thing and earn the kudos in the interest of meeting the team goals and seeking professional recognition. An overworked team won't have the work-life balance or the time to contemplate what's right; they will automatically follow orders. Self-interest and career survival will take the front seat in such situations. Corporate sustainability, social interest, and the greater good become sacrificial lambs. Thus, the hindrances to ethical actions can be summarized as:

1. Professional and social pressures,
2. Pursuit of pleasure,
3. Desire for power,
4. Pride and the need to be a winner at any cost, and
5. Conflicting priorities.

The viable antidote to the pressures is for individuals to tap into their humanity to ask themselves, "How would I like to be treated in this situation?" This Golden Rule has a proven track record of being a win-win philosophy. It transcends culture and generations because it is universally acceptable, easily understood, and reliable as a directional compass. Corporations can certainly apply it to the workplace. It ensures the top-of-mind awareness that actions of one person impact others, for better or worse.

RELATIONSHIP BETWEEN ETHICAL LEADERSHIP AND SUSTAINABILITY

Business doesn't thrive in spite of ethical leadership but because of it. Organically embedding character virtues in businesses allows values to guide decision making. Any entity that doesn't conduct itself with honesty and a sense of fair play will be vulnerable to competition and lose its customer base. Such a firm will lose its ability to command loyalty from its stakeholders. Trade is predicated on fair play and honesty; market share is rooted in loyalty. At a time when the motto of "profit at all costs" has made the business world seem at crossroads with society, embracing trustworthiness and a sense of fair play gives organizations a strategic competitive advantage that leads to sustainability.

A prime example of this concept is apparent in the choices Johnson & Johnson made in 1982. When the company determined its Extra-Strength Tylenol was laced with cyanide, CEO James Burke took a stand that the company's commitment to its customers across all walks of life took precedence over corporate profits. In an extraordinary move, he backed up J&J's value proposition with a 31-million-bottle recall that cost the company more than $100 million. In the long run, this move sustained brand loyalty and boosted consumer confidence, proving corporations that stand the test of time are those that see themselves as part of the society while systemically exhibiting moral virtues.

ETHICAL LEADERSHIP TRAITS

The Comprehensive Ethical Leadership Model™ in Figure 1 is a blueprint to drive the strategic vision of

FIGURE 1. COMPREHENSIVE ETHICAL LEADERSHIP MODEL™

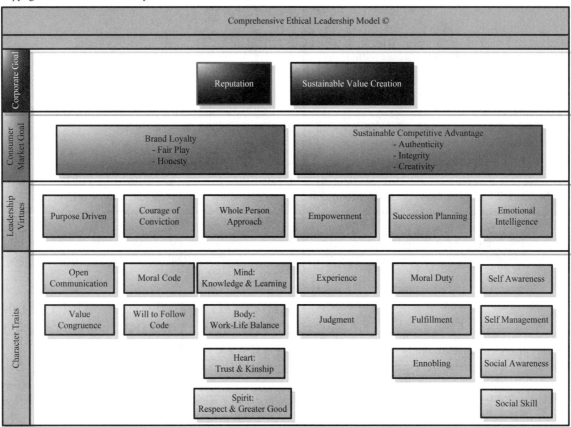

ethical leadership. Let's look at the six ethical leadership traits (Leadership Virtues) in the model.

1. Purpose Driven

Purpose lays the foundation for pursuing the defined greater good, the corporate vision. Far loftier than just going after corporate profits, purpose stifles an individual's tendency to move toward greed and worldly pleasures. The corporate vision provides an anchor and acts as a beacon when we're navigating the high seas of corporate decision making. Vision clearly taps into what is good in everyone and leads to prosperity through a moral course. Vision will also challenge individuals and entities to make the choice between living with purpose and pursuing profits for profit's sake.

In the Spring 2007 issue of *Leader to Leader*, Nikos Mourkogiannis, senior partner at Panthea, a global consulting firm, says, "For any organization, the starting point of greatness is not in meeting expectations, but in fulfilling a purpose that fits the identity of the organization." In such an organization, purpose-driven leaders will create an environment of open communication and value congruence to promote moral choices. Lack of purpose leads to socio-economic degradation, as we have seen. The credit crisis, stock market decline, corporate corruptions, and leadership lapses are all clear indicators of how important purpose-driven leadership is for sustainability.

2. Courage of Conviction

Ethics has two key components: having a standard to follow and the courage to follow that standard. Courage in a person's values and moral convictions is symbolized by guts, which enables some leaders to walk their talk while others merely talk. People gravitate toward courageous leaders. Based on their research on gutsy leaders, Kevin and Jackie Freiberg pointed out in the Summer 2004 issue of *Leader to Leader* that courageous leaders must do the following:

"You have to be gutsy enough to stand up to those who stand in your way. You have to be big enough to admit your mistakes. You have to be vulnerable enough to say 'I don't know.' You have to care enough to lead with love and trust, rather than power and fear. You have to be humble enough to surround yourself with people smarter and more capable than you, and then have the faith to get out of their way. You have to be open and flexible enough to adjust to ever-changing circumstances. You have to do what is right even when it's not politically correct."

Courage gives us the will to execute and stay the course. In the leader's willingness to be vulnerable lies the source of strength, power of charisma, and spirit worthy of emulation.

3. Whole Person Approach

In the Summer 2006 issue of *Leader to Leader*, Stephen Covey made the case for a paradigm shift in management philosophy corresponding to the shift of workforce from laborer to knowledge worker. He reasoned that "The fundamental reality is, human beings are not things needing to be motivated and controlled; they are four-dimensional—body, mind, heart, and spirit." Covey conveyed the message of respect for individuals as complete human beings, recognizing their need for survival (body), relationships (heart), continued learning (mind), and social contribution (spirit). This endeavor, if not followed through with utmost commitment, has the potential to cripple individuals and society because sustaining individuals is at the heart of sustaining the global society. Covey also said, "A new era is for greatness. It's for fulfillment, passionate execution, and significant contribution…. Leadership in the knowledge worker age will be characterized by those who find their own voice and who, regardless of formal position, inspire others to find theirs."

4. Empowerment

Different organizational situations demand different combinations of skills to take the reins. It's also true that supporting leadership roles emerge across all corporate initiatives. Stephen Guastello of Marquette University has conducted research to understand "how leaders really emerge." His findings, which were published in the September 2007 issue of *American Psychologist*, indicate that "more than leaders emerging from leaderless groups, a whole social structure emerges that consists of primary leaders, secondary leaders, and non-leaders."

In practice, the main individual leading a financial process-improvement effort will have in the team secondary leaders from treasury, financial systems, and financial reporting. The same finance leader could become a secondary leader in the subsequent financial system implementation initiative. This line of thinking presents an intriguing perspective of the need to arm all employees with the set of tools to be effective leaders via empowerment. Experiences gained by collaboration of empowered leaders will yield prudent business judgment, paving the way for long-term viability.

5. Succession Planning

Succession planning enables leaders and organizations to attract, nurture, retain, and develop talent. It also presents the opportunity to build a community of empowered individuals who are value centric. Such an environment of lifelong learning creates an atmosphere conducive for both technical and principles-based development. Without a succession plan, the organization's sustainability loses viability. Simon Hollington, director of Values Based Leadership Ltd, echoed this sentiment in the February 2007 issue of *Engineering Management*, saying, "Succession planning is vital to ensure that business success will continue when the current management structure is no longer there." Failure to take responsibility for succession planning, according to Hollington, results in two primary negative impacts: "the failure of the individual to realize his or her potential and the failure of the organization to look forward."

It's highly irresponsible to fail in this leadership responsibility and foolish to turn a blind eye to the opportunity to mentor, coach, and develop future leaders who will carry the torch by leveraging their developmental experience. This aspect of ensuring propagation of leaders, mentors, and coaches is an ethical responsibility of every leader in every organization. Like planting a tree, nurturing and developing individuals with talent and potential pays back over time. The succession-planning process is an ideal venue for honing moral leadership qualities and ethical decision-making abilities.

Another way to acquire ethical values and decision-making capabilities as part of succession planning is through a structured teaching methodology—a methodology that doesn't merely target the technical skill development in a specialized field or area of concentration, laying the foundation for professional goal attainment, but one that challenges the mind, empowers the mentees, and evokes them through "ennobling." Ennobling represents the process through which the mentor makes the mentee become noble. Many successful world-class companies, such as GE and Kimberly-Clark, have structured in-house holistic training programs to harness the benefits of the ennobling process as part of their succession planning. They also partner with universities and translate this practice of ennobling for succession planning into building a renewable pipeline of young talent. This collective effort of pursuing leadership duty to fulfill the promise of a future will strengthen the societal-corporate interconnectedness, fulfilling all those who are actively engaged.

6. Emotional Intelligence

Albert Bandura, Stanford University professor of psychology and author of *Self Efficacy: The Exercise of Control*, said that "modeling is the first step in developing competencies." Expanding on Bandura's reasoning, James M. Kouzes and Barry Z. Posner pointed out in the Spring 2003 issue of *Leader to Leader* that "To increase the quality and supply of exemplary leaders in the world, it's essential to give aspiring talent the chance to observe models of exemplary leadership. To develop ethical leaders, allow aspiring talent to observe leaders behaving ethically." They also highlighted that "Leadership is a relationship. If leaders are going to emerge, grow, and thrive in these disquieting times, they must become socially competent." This social competence is predicated on emotional intelligence comprising self-awareness, self-management, social awareness, and social skills. It's easy to understand how emotional intelligence embodying a sense of self and being in tune with those around us becomes an ingredient for ethical leadership. It makes possible empathy, care, consideration, and a whole host of character virtues that breed loyalty and sense of fair play much needed in commercial success.

APPLYING THE MODEL

The Comprehensive Ethical Leadership Model™ is a tangible way to institutionalize the six leadership virtues. When I had my own finance organization, every sub-group and its members within my team had career paths. Developed in partnership with the employees and their respective manager, career paths identified strengths and opportunities for professional growth. The manager nurtured their team members to progress along the path, recognizing that employees are "whole people," while delivering business results. This career path then became the basis of the performance management plan, which contains four sections that influence the ethical leadership model.

1. **Knowledge Development and Relationship Development:** This component recognized the whole person approach. Relationship building was vital—not just for driving results through collaborative partnership with other teams, but for developing the emotional intelligence of the members and helping them along in career path pursuits. This area of development also integrated the following virtues: communicating in an open and honest way, commanding respect through the work process, and having the courage to make decisions to keep deliverables on track.

2. **Process Development:** The plan empowered employees to continuously improve their processes by leveraging technology. The improved processes were quicker and less prone to errors, effectively reducing work hours and resulting in work-life balance. Managers also encouraged employees to partner with one another to join forces on improvements and ensure synergy without duplicating efforts across different parts of the finance value chain.

3. **Team Development and Succession Plan Realization:** This was a project approach to targeted employee development. A viable succession plan would come out of a systematic process of weekly team lunch-and-learn sessions, cross training, vacation planning with resource back-up, and job rotation. When opportunities within the firm opened up, the members were able to move up and along because executing the succession plan backfilled the position of the promoted employee. The plan wasn't an entitlement; employees had to earn positions with internal competition built into the process. But the process was collaborative and not divisive because everyone had a stake in the growth and success of the others.

4. **Process Delivery:** This included activities such as accounting, analysis, planning, management reporting, cash management, and disclosure reporting to develop technical skills. Routine accounting, close activity, SOX compliance, cash management, planning, and financial analysis for decision support were standard processes. The business unit had the goal of delivering revenue growth and profits; the compliance requirements necessitated adherence to policy guidelines regardless of growth implications; accounting regulations have to be followed for reporting and audit purposes. These competing goals existed in a matrix organization where duel reporting to a business executive and CFO was the norm. The only way to successfully execute our role was to do the right thing and ennoble each other in the process.

The finance organization that was built on this foundation continues to be supportive of its members, even though the members have grown into roles with more responsibility across various parts of the organization.

ETHICS LEADS TO SUCCESS AND SUSTAINABILTY

The Comprehensive Ethical Leadership Model™ presented here provides a road map for practitioners. Teams should spend quality time discussing these traits in relation to their own environment and develop a personalized game plan that's transferable into practice. This model will also add value to the process of performance management where value-centric leadership is embraced as an organizational success trait. Needless to say, ethical leadership will create an environment that cares about its employees in a holistic manner. In such an exemplary organization, employees will proudly and willingly take care of business and processes, realizing fulfillment. This approach of leading with your soul establishes a collective purpose through kinship, making the greater good front and center. This ultimately leads to marketplace loyalty, business growth, financial profits, and corporate sustainability. An organization of this caliber will be a market leader engaged in business alongside being an exemplary member of our civil society.

Kasthuri V. Henry, CTP, is the president of Kas Henry Inc, a consulting and training firm serving the corporate finance space. She is a visiting assistant professor at Southern Illinois University and an adjunct faculty member at North Park University (NPU) in Chicago. You can reach Kas at (224) 595-7418 or kas@kashenry.com.

QUESTION

9.4   What are the major roadblocks to making ethical decisions?

9.5 Why Incentive Plans Cannot Work
When reward systems fail, don't blame the program— look at the premise behind it.

*by Alfie Kohn**

It is difficult to overstate the extent to which most managers and the people who advise them believe in the redemptive power of rewards. Certainly, the vast majority of U.S. corporations use some sort of program intended to motivate employees by tying compensation to one index of performance or another. But more striking is the rarely examined belief that people will do a better job if they have been promised some sort of incentive. This assumption and the practices associated with it are pervasive, but a growing collection of evidence supports an opposing view. According to numerous studies in laboratories, workplaces, classrooms, and other settings, rewards typically undermine the very processes they are intended to enhance. The findings suggest that the failure of any given incentive program is due less to a glitch in that program than to the inadequacy of the psychological assumptions that ground all such plans.

TEMPORARY COMPLIANCE
Behaviorist theory, derived from work with laboratory animals, is indirectly responsible for such programs as piecework pay for factory workers, stock options for top executives, special privileges accorded to employees of the Month, and commissions for salespeople. Indeed, the livelihood of innumerable consultants has long been based on devising fresh formulas for computing bonuses to wave in front of employees. Money, vacations, banquets, plaques—the list of variations on a single, simple behaviorist model of motivation is limitless. And today even many people who are regarded as forward thinking—those promote underlie our behaviors. They do not create an enduring *commitment* to any value or action. Rather incentives

teamwork, participative management, continuous improvement, and the like—urge the use of rewards to institute and maintain these very reforms. What we use bribes to accomplish may have changed, but the reliance on bribes, on behaviorist doctrine, has not.

Moreover, the few articles that appear to criticize incentive plans are invariably limited to details of implementation. Only fine-tune the calculations and delivery of the incentive—or perhaps hire the author as a consultant—and the problem will be solved, we are told. As Herbert H. Meyer, professor emeritus in the psychology department the College of Social and Behavioral Sciences at the University of South Florida, has written, "Anyone reading literature on this subject published 20 years ago would find that the articles look almost identical to those published today." That assessment, which could have been written this morning, was actually offered in 1975. In nearly forty years, the thinking hasn't changed.

Do rewards work? The answer depends on what we mean by "work." Research suggests that, by and large, rewards succeed at securing one thing only: temporary compliance. When it comes to producing lasting change in attitudes and behavior, however, rewards, like punishment, are strikingly ineffective. Once the rewards run out, people revert to their old behaviors. Studies show that offering incentives for losing weight, quitting smoking, using seat belts, or (in the case of children) acting generously is not only less effective than other strategies but often proves worse than doing nothing at all. Incentives, a version of what psychologists call extrinsic motivators, do not alter the attitudes that merely—and temporarily—change what we do.

As for productivity, at least two dozen studies over

the last three decades have conclusively shown that people who expect to receive a reward for completing a task or for doing that task successfully simply do not perform as well as those who expect no reward at all. These studies examined rewards for children and adults, males and females, and included tasks ranging from memorizing facts to creative problem-solving to designing collages. In general, the more cognitive sophistication and open-ended thinking that was required, the worse people performed when working for a reward. Interestingly enough, the researchers themselves were often taken by surprise. They assumed that rewards would produce better work but discovered otherwise.

The question for managers is whether incentive plans can work when extrinsic motivators more generally do not. Unfortunately, as author C. Douglas Jenkins, Jr., has noted, most organizational studies to date—like the articles published—have tended "to focus on the effects of *variations* in incentive conditions, and not on whether performance-based pay per se raises performance levels."

A number of studies, however, have examined whether or not pay, especially at the executive level, is related to corporate profitability and other measures of organizational performance. Often they have found slight or even *negative* correlations between pay and performance. Typically, the absence of such a relationship is interpreted as evidence of links between compensation and something other than how well people do their jobs. But most of these data could support a different conclusion, one that reverses the causal arrow. Perhaps what these studies reveal is that higher pay does not, produce better performance. In other words, the very idea of trying to reward quality may be a fool's errand.

Consider the findings of Jude T. Rich and John A. Larson, formerly of McKinsey & Company. In 1982, using interviews and proxy statements, they examined compensation programs at 90 major U.S. companies to determine whether return to shareholders was better for corporations that had incentive plans for top executives than it was for those companies that had no such plans. They were unable to find any difference.

Four years later, Jenkins tracked down 28 previously published studies that measured the impact of financial incentives on performance. (Some were conducted in the laboratory and some in the field.) His analysis, "Financial Incentives," published in 1986, revealed that 16, or 57%, of the studies found a positive effect on performance. However, all of the performance measures were quantitative in nature: a good job consisted of producing more of something or doing it faster. Only five of the studies looked at the quality of performance. And none of those five showed any benefits from incentives.

Another analysis took advantage of an unusual situation that affected a group of welders at a Midwestern manufacturing company. At the request of the union, an incentive system that had been in effect for some years was abruptly eliminated. Now, if a financial incentive supplies motivation, its absence should drive down production. And that is exactly what happened, at first. Fortunately, Harold F. Rothe, former personnel manager and corporate staff assistant at the Beloit Corporation, tracked production over a period of months, providing the sort of long-term data rarely collected in this field. After the initial slump, Rothe found that in the absence of incentives the welders' production quickly began to rise and eventually reached a level as high or higher than it had been before.

One of the largest reviews of how intervention programs affect worker productivity, a meta-analysis of some 330 comparisons from 98 studies, was conducted in the mid-1980s by Richard A. Guzzo, associate professor of psychology at the University of Maryland, College Park, and his colleagues at New York University. The raw numbers seemed to suggest a positive relationship between financial incentives and productivity, but because of the huge variations from one study to another, statistical tests indicated that there was no significant effect overall. What's more, financial incentives were virtually unrelated to the number of workers who were absent or who quit their jobs over a period of time. By contrast, training and goal-setting programs had a far greater impact on productivity than did pay-for-performance plans.

WHY REWARDS FAIL

Why do most executives continue to rely on incentive programs? Perhaps it's because few people take the time to examine the connection between incentive programs and problems with workplace productivity and morale. Rewards buy temporary compliance, so it looks like the problems are solved. It's harder to spot the harm they cause over the long term. Moreover, it does not occur to most of us to suspect rewards, given that our own teachers, parents, and managers probably used them. "Do this and you'll get that" is part of the fabric of American life. Finally, by clinging to the belief that motivational problems are due to the particular incentive system in effect at the moment, rather than to the psychological theory behind all incentives, we can remain optimistic that a relatively minor adjustment will repair the damage.

Over the long haul, however, the potential cost to any organization of trying to fine-tune reward-driven compensation systems may be considerable. The fundamental flaws of behaviorism itself doom the prospects of affecting long-term behavior change or performance improvement through the use of rewards.

Consider the following six-point framework that examines the true costs of an incentive program.

1. **"Pay is not a motivator."** W. Edward Deming's declaration may seem surprising, even absurd. Of course, money buys the things people want and need. Moreover, the less people are paid, the more concerned they are likely to be about financial matters. Indeed, several studies over the last few decades have found that when people are asked to guess what matters to their coworkers—or, in the case of managers, to their subordinates—they assume money heads the list. But put the question directly—"what do you care about?"—and pay typically ranks only fifth or sixth.

   Even if people were principally concerned with their salaries, this does not prove that money is motivating. There is no firm basis for the assumption that paying people more will encourage them to do better work or even, in the long run, more work. As Frederick Herzberg, Distinguished Professor of Management at the University of Utah's Graduate School of Management, has argued, just because too little money can irritate and demotivate does not mean that more and more money will bring about increased satisfaction, much less increased motivation. It is plausible to assume that if someone's take-home pay was cut in half, his or her morale would suffer enough to undermine performance. But it doesn't necessarily follow that doubling that person's pay would result in better work.

2. **Rewards punish.** Many managers understand that coercion and fear destroy motivation and create defiance, defensiveness, and rage. They realize that punitive management is a contradiction in terms. As Herzberg wrote in HBR some 25 years ago ("One More Time: How Do You Motivate Employees?" January–February 1968), a "KITA"—which, he coyly explains, stands for "kick in the pants"—may produce movement but never motivation.

   What most executives fail to recognize is the Herzberg's observation is equally true of rewards. Punishment and rewards are two sides of the same coin. Rewards have a punitive effect because they, like out right punishment, are manipulative. "Do this and you'll get that" is not really very different from "Do this or here's what will happen to you." In the case of incentives, the reward itself may be highly desired; but by making that bonus contingent on certain behaviors, managers manipulate their subordinates, and that experience of being controlled is likely to assume a punitive quality over time.

   Further, not receiving a reward one had expected to receive is also indistinguishable from being punished. Whether the incentive is withheld or withdrawn deliberately, or simply not received by someone who had hoped to get it, the effect is identical. And the more desirable the reward, the more demoralizing it is to miss out.

   The new school, which exhorts us to catch people doing something right and reward them for it, is not very different from the old school, which advised us to catch people doing something wrong and threaten to punish them if they ever do it again. What is essentially taking place in both approaches is that a lot of people are getting caught. Managers are creating a workplace in which people feel controlled, not an environment conducive to exploration, learning, and progress.

3. **Rewards rupture relationships.** Relationships among employees are often casualties of the scramble for rewards. As leaders of the Total Quality Management movement have emphasized, incentive programs, and the performance appraisal systems that accompany them, reduce the possibilities for cooperation. Peter R. Scholtes, senior management consultant at Joiner Associates Inc., put it starkly, "Everyone is pressuring the system for individual gain. No one is improving the system for collective gain. The system will inevitably crash." Without teamwork, in other words, there can be no quality.

   The surest way to destroy cooperation and, therefore, organizational excellence, is to force people to compete for rewards or recognition or to rank them against each other. For each person who wins, there are many others who carry with them the feeling of having lost. And the more these awards are publicized through the use of memos, newsletters, and awards banquets, the more detrimental their impact can be. Furthermore, when employees compete for a limited number of incentives, they will most likely begin to see each other as obstacles to their own success. But the same result can occur with any use of rewards; introducing competition just makes a bad thing worse.

   Relationships between supervisors and subordinates can also collapse under the weight of incentives. Of course, the supervisor who punishes is about as welcome to employees as a glimpse of a police car in their rearview mirrors. But even the supervisor who rewards can produce some damaging reactions. For instance, employees *may be* tempted to conceal any problems they might be having and present themselves as infinitely competent to the manager in control of the money. Rather than ask for help—a *prerequisite* for optimal performance—they might opt instead for flattery, attempting to convince the manager that they have everything under control. Very few things threaten an organization as much as a hoard of incentive-driven individuals trying to curry favor with the incentive dispenser.

4. **Rewards ignore reasons.** In order to solve problems in the workplace, managers must understand what caused them. Are employees inadequately prepared for the demands of their jobs? Is long-term growth being sacrificed to maximize short-term return? Are workers unable to collaborate effectively? Is the rigidly hierarchical that employees are intimidated about making recommendations and feel powerless and burned out? Each of these situations calls for a different response. But relying on incentives to boost productivity does nothing to address possible underlying problems and bring about meaningful change.

Moreover, managers often use incentive systems as a substitute for giving workers what they need to do a good job. Treating workers well—providing useful feedback, social support, and the room for self-determination—is the essence of good management. On the other hand, dangling, a bonus in front of employees and waiting for the results requires much less effort. Indeed, some evidence suggests that productive managerial strategies are less likely to be used in organizations that lean on pay-for-performance plans. In his study of welders' performance, Rothe noted that supervisors tended to "demonstrate relatively less leadership" when incentives were in place. Likewise, author Carla O'Dell reports in *People, Performance, and Pay* that a survey of 1,600 organizations by the American Productivity Center discovered little in the way of active employee involvement in organizations that used small-group incentive plans. As Jone L. Pearce, associate professor at the Graduate School of Management, University of California at Irvine, wrote in "Why Merit Pay Doesn't Work: Implications from Organization Theory," pay for performance actually "impedes the ability of managers to manage."

5. **Rewards discourage risk-taking.** "People will do precisely what they are asked to do if the reward is significant," enthused Monroe J. Haegele, a proponent of pay-for-performance programs, in "The New Performance Measures." And here is the root of the problem. Whenever people are encouraged to think about what they will get for engaging in a task, they become less inclined to take risks or explore possibilities, to play hunches or to consider incidental stimuli. In a word, the number one casualty of rewards is creativity.

Excellence pulls in one direction; rewards pull in another. Tell people that their income will depend on their productivity or performance rating, and they will focus on the numbers. Sometimes they will manipulate the schedule for completing tasks or even engage in patently unethical and illegal behavior. As Thane S. Pittman, professor and chair of the psychology department at Gettysburg College, and his colleagues point out, when we are motivated by incentives, "features such as predictability and simplicity are desirable, since the primary focus associated with this orientation is to get through the task expediently in order to reach the desired goal." The late Cornell University professor, John Condry, was more succinct: rewards, he said, are the "enemies of exploration."

Consider the findings of organizational psychologist Edwin A. Locke. When Locke paid subjects on a piece-rate basis for their work, he noticed that they tended to choose easier tasks as the payment for success increased. A number of other studies have also found that people working for a reward generally try to minimize challenge. It isn't that human beings are naturally lazy or that it is unwise to give employees a voice in determining the standards to be used. Rather, people tend to lower their sights when they are encouraged to think about what they are going to get for their efforts. "Do this and you'll get that," in other words, focuses attention on the "that" instead of the "this." Emphasizing large bonuses is the last strategy we should use if we care about innovation. Do rewards motivate people? Absolutely. They motivate people to get rewards.

6. **Rewards undermine interest.** If our goal is excellence, no artificial incentive can ever match the power of intrinsic motivation. People who do exceptional work may be glad to be paid and even more glad to be well paid, but they do not work to collect a paycheck. They work because they love what they do.

Few will be shocked by the news that extrinsic motivators are a poor substitute for genuine interest in one's job. What is far more surprising is that rewards, like punishment, may actually undetermined the intrinsic motivation that results in optimal performance. The more a manager stresses what an employee can earn for good work, the less interested that employee will be in the work itself.

The first studies to establish the effect of rewards on intrinsic motivation were conducted in the early 1970s by Edward Deci, professor and chairman of the psychology department at the University of Rochester. By now, scores of experiments across the country have replicated the finding. As Deci and his colleague Richard Ryan, senior vice president of investment and training manager at Robert W. Baird and Co., Inc., wrote in their 1985 book, *Intrinsic Motivation and Self-Determination in Human Behavior*, "the research has consistently shown that any contingent payment system tends to undermine intrinsic motivation." The basic effect is the same for a variety of rewards and tasks, although extrinsic motivators are particularly destructive when tied to interesting or complicated tasks.

Deci and Ryan argue that receiving a reward for a particular behavior sends a certain message about what we have done and controls, or attempts to control, our future behavior. The more we experience being controlled, the more we will tend to lose interest in what we are doing. If we go to work thinking about the possibility of getting a bonus, we come to feel that our work is not self-directed. Rather, it is the reward that drives our behavior.

Other theorists favor a more simple explanation for the negative effect rewards have on intrinsic motivation: anything presented as a prerequisite for something else—that is, as a means toward another end—comes to be seen as less desirable. The recipient of the reward assumes, "If they have to bribe me to do it, it must be something I wouldn't want to do." In fact, a series of studies, published in 1992 by psychology professor Jonathan L. Freedman and his colleagues at the University of Toronto, confirmed that the larger the incentive we are offered, the more negatively we will view the activity for which the bonus was received. (The activities themselves don't seem to matter; in this study, they ranged from participating in a medical experiment to eating unfamiliar food.) Whatever the reason for the effect, however, any incentive or pay-for performance system tends to make people less enthusiastic about their work and therefore less likely to approach it with a commitment to excellence.

DANGEROUS ASSUMPTIONS
Outside of psychology departments, few people distinguish between intrinsic and extrinsic motivation. Those who do assume that the two concepts can simply be added together for best effect. Motivation comes in two flavors, the logic goes, and both together must be better than either alone. But studies show that the real world works differently.

Some managers insist that the only problem with incentive programs is that they don't reward the right

things. But these managers fail to understand the psychological factors involved and, consequently, the risks of sticking with the status quo.

Contrary to conventional wisdom, the use of rewards is not a response to the extrinsic orientation exhibited by many workers. Rather, incentives help create this focus on financial considerations. When an organization uses a Skinnerian management or compensation system, people are likely to become less interested in their work, requiring extrinsic incentives before expending effort. Then supervisors shake their heads and say, "You see? If you don't offer them a reward, they won't do anything." It is a classic self-fulfilling prophecy. Swarthmore College psychology professor Barry Schwartz has conceded that behavior theory may seem to provide us with a useful way of describing what goes on in U.S. workplaces. However, "It does this not because work is a natural exemplification of behavior theory principles but because behavior theory principles … had a significant hand in transforming work into an exemplification of behavior theory principles."

Managers who insist that the job won't get done right without rewards have failed to offer a convincing argument for behavioral manipulation. Promising a reward to someone who appears unmotivated is a bit like offering salt water to someone who is thirsty. Bribes in the workplace simply can't work.

Alfie Kohn is the author of four books, including No Contest: The Case Against Competition *and the newly published* Punished by Rewards: The Trouble with Gold Stars, Incentive Plans, A's, Praise, and Other Bribes, *from which this article is adapted. Kohn lectures widely at universities, conferences, and corporations on education and management.*

ON INCENTIVES
"The Pay-for-Performance Dilemma"
by Herbert H. Meyer, *Organizational Dynamics*, Winter 1975.

"Financial Incentives"
by G. Douglas Jenkins, Jr. in *Generalizing from Laboratory to Field Settings* edited by Edwin A. Locke Lexington, MA: Lexington Books, 1986,

"Why Some Long-Term Incentives Fail"
by Jude T. Rich and John A. Larson in *Incentives, Cooperation, and Risk Sharing* edited by Haig R. Nalbantian, Totowa, NJ: Rowman & Littlefield, 1987.

"Output Rates Among Welders: Productivity and Consistency Following Removal of a Financial Incentive System"
by Harold E. Rothe, *Journal of Applied Psychology*, December 1970.

"The Effects of Psychologically Based Intervention Programs on Worker Productivity: A Meta-Analysis"
by Richard A. Guzzo, Richard D. Jette, and Raymond A. Katzell, *Personnel Psychology*, Summer 1985.

"One More Time: How Do You Motivate Employees?"
by Frederick Herzberg, *Harvard Business Review*, January–February 1968.

"An Elaboration on Deming's Teachings on Performance Appraisal"
by Peter R. Scholtes in *Performance Appraisal: Perspectives on a Quality Management Approach* edited by Gary N. McLean, et al., Alexandria, VA: University of Minnesota Training and Development Research Center and American Society for Training and Development, 1990.

People, Performance, and Pay
by Carla O'Dell, Houston: American Productivity Center, 1987.

"Why Merit Pay Doesn't Work: Implications from Organization Theory"
by Jone L. Pearce in *New Perspectives on Compensation* edited by David B. Balkan and Luis R. Gomez-Mejia, Englewood Cliffs, NJ: Prentice-Hall, 1987.

"The New Performance Measures"
by Monroe J. Haegele in *The Compensation Handbook*, Third Edition edited by Milton L. Rock and Lance A. Berger, New York: McGraw-Hill, 1991.

"Intrinsic and Extrinsic Motivational Orientations: Reward Induced Changes in Preference for Complexity"
by Thane S. Pittman, Jolee Emery, and Ann K. Boggiano, *Journal of Personality and Social Psychology*, March 1982.

"Enemies of Exploration: Self-Initiated Versus Other-initiated Learning"
by John Condry, *Journal of Personality and Social Psychology*, July 1977.

"Toward a Theory of Task Motivation and Incentives"
by Edwin A. Locke, *Organizational Behavior and Human Performance*, Volume 3, 1968.

Intrinsic Motivation and Self-Determination in Human Behavior
by Edward L. Deci and Richard M. Ryan, New York: Plenum Press, 1985.

"Inferred Values and the Reverse-Incentive Effect in Induced Compliance"
by Jonathan L. Freedman, John A. Cunningham, and Kirsten Krismer, *Journal of Personality and Social Psychology*, March 1992.

The Battle for Human Nature: Science, Morality and Modern Life
by Barry Schwartz, New York: W. W. Norton and Company, 1986.

RECOMMENDED READING
"A Model of Creativity and Innovation in Organizations"
by Teresa M. Amabile in *Research in Organizational Behavior*, Volume 10 edited by Barry M. Staw and L. L. Cummings, Greenwich, CT: JAI Press, Inc., 1988.

Out of the Crisis
by W. Edwards Darning, Cambridge, MA: MIT Center for Advanced Engineering Study, 1986.

"Merit Pay, Performance Targeting, and Productivity"
by Alfie Halachmi and Marc Holzer, *Review of Public Personnel Administration*, Spring 1987.

No Contest: The Case Against Competition
Revised Edition by Alfie Kohn, Boston: Houghton Mifflin, 1992.

Punished by Rewards: The Trouble with Gold Stars, Incentive Plans, A's, Praise, and Other Bribes
by Alfie Kohn, Boston: Houghton Mifflin, 1993.

The Market Experience
by Robert B. Lane, Cambridge, England: Cambridge University Press, 1991.

The Hidden Costs of Reward: New Perspectives on the Psychology of Human Motivation
edited by Mark R. Lepper and David Greene, Hillsdale, NJ: L. Erlbaum Associates, 1978.

The Great Jackass Fallacy
by Harry Levinson, Cambridge, MA: Harvard University Press, 1973.

The Human Side of Enterprise
by Douglas McGregor, New York: McGraw-Hill, 1960.

Wealth Addiction
by Philip Slater, New York: Dutton, 1980.

Money and Motivation: An Analysis of Incentives in Industry

by William Foote Whyte and Melville Dalton, et al. New York: Harper, 1955.

QUESTION

9.5 What are the six reasons that incentive programs fail, according to Alfie Kohn? Explain.

9.6 Can Regulations Curb Excessive Executive Pay?

*by C. Terry Grant and Gerry H. Grant**

On the heels of the Securities & Exchange Commission's (SEC) executive compensation disclosure requirement that became effective in 2007, regulators are once again considering measures to curb escalating executive pay. Spawned by shareholder resolutions of companies such as Aflac and Boeing, a bill that would give shareholders a nonbinding vote on executive compensation was passed by the U.S. House of Representatives in April 2007. A similar bill is pending in the U.S. Senate. Executive compensation continues to be a primary concern of shareholders, analysts, and corporate governance advocates. No surprise, especially since CEO compensation is almost nine times as high as 1992 levels and consumes a growing percentage of income and cash flows despite continuous scrutiny from Congress, regulators, and the financial press.

In their defense, corporate compensation committees argue that executive compensation must be competitive to attract and maintain the best available management talent. Excesses such as the well-publicized case of Home Depot former CEO Robert Nardelli, however, continue to stoke concerns that executive compensation reforms still have a long way to go. While Home Depot suffered from sluggish stock price performance, the company's proxy statement revealed that Nardelli received more than $190 million in compensation during his approximately six years on the job. When he agreed to step down from his CEO post in January 2007, he received a severance package worth $210 million, according to a Home Depot press release.

We will discuss the move toward shareholders' "say on pay," highlight key compliance disclosures the

SEC has targeted in its initial review of the new 2007 compensation disclosures, and illustrate vague performance-based disclosures that prompted SEC comment letters to approximately 300 companies.

HISTORICAL PERSPECTIVE

Over the past 16 years, the SEC, Congress, and the Financial Accounting Standards Board (FASB) have taken action on executive compensation. In the early 1990s, regulators started addressing the issue of escalating executive compensation with a series of requirements intended to improve governance and provide shareholders more transparent compensation disclosures. Here's a snapshot look at the milestones.

In 1992, the SEC adopted a new executive compensation rule mandating specific executive compensation disclosures in corporate proxy statements. The rule required companies to use tables, rather than narrative form, to disclose the total compensation paid to the CEO and the company's next four highest-paid executives. The general shift in executive compensation from traditional salary and bonus awards toward more long-term compensation, such as stock options, contributed to the SEC's 1992 disclosure rule modifications. This change in compensation practices made it more difficult for shareholders to understand the total amount paid to executives—especially since most stock options weren't expensed at that time.

A year later, Congress passed the Revenue Reconciliation Act of 1993, which set an annual corporate tax deduction ceiling of $1 million for CEO compensation and the next four highest-compensated officers. On the surface, the 1993 Act caps the

---

* From: C. T. Grant and G. H. Grant, "Can Regulations Curb Excessive Executive Pay?" *Strategic Finance* (September 2008): 31-39. Reprinted with permission conveyed through Copyright Clearance Center, Inc.

deductibility of executive compensation at $1 million per year per employee. The annual deduction cap, however, applies only to remuneration "for services performed." Compensation committees quickly learned to structure executive compensation packages toward performance-based compensation to avoid the $1 million ceiling. This common tactic simply shifted the bulk of compensation to stock options.

After the passage of the 1993 Act, executive stock options thrived as the "Holy Grail" of executive compensation. Their popularity stemmed from their unique ability to elude the $1 million tax deductibility ceiling while still completely avoiding financial statement expense recognition under Accounting Principles Board (APB) Opinion No. 25, "Accounting for Stock Issued to Employees." Even though most companies didn't recognize any income statement expense under APB Opinion No. 25, when they exercised stock options they received a tax deduction amounting to the difference between the exercise price of the options and the market price of the stock on the exercise date.

Collectively, the SEC's 1992 disclosure rule and the Revenue Reconciliation Act of 1993 provide a baseline for disclosure and deductibility of executive compensation. In the eyes of many, both fell far short of achieving effective executive compensation governance.

In 1995, the FASB joined the attempts to achieve consistency and transparency in the accounting for all forms of executive compensation—particularly stock options. Because of political interference, the FASB failed in its attempt to require expensing of stock options and settled for improved footnote disclosures in Statement of Financial Accounting Standards (SFAS) No. 123, "Accounting for Stock-Based Compensation." But the FASB made a significant impact on the transparency of executive compensation when it issued SFAS No. 123(R), "Share-Based Payment," in 2004, which requires amortization of the fair value of stock options as an income statement expense over the vesting period of the options. Of course, SFAS No. 123(R) doesn't affect the tax deductibility of exercised options. Stock options retain their exclusion from the $1 million tax deductibility cap, so they remain an attractive form of compensation to many corporations.

The most recent move by the SEC to improve the clarity of executive compensation disclosures occurred in 2006 with the passage of a new regulation, "Executive Compensation and Related Person Disclosure." Unlike the 1992 SEC disclosure rule that applied to the CEO and the next four highest-paid executives, the 2006 rule applies to the CEO, CFO, and the remaining three highest-paid executives. The rule's intent is to provide a clear picture of executive compensation. The new rule requires corporate proxy statements to disclose all components of compensation in a single location, the *Summary Compensation Table*. A new total compensation column sums all components to ensure shareholders can easily determine an executive's total compensation.

The disclosure requirements include salary and bonus awards, as well as stock option grants, stock appreciation rights, long-term incentive plan awards, pension plans, and perquisites, such as the personal use of corporate aircraft and personal security services. These disclosures should improve governance as shareholders, and even compensation committees, get a single, high-definition picture of all components and total costs of executive compensation. Table 1 summarizes the four key regulations that affect executive compensation.

SEC TARGETS COMPLIANCE WITH 2006 RULE

With near completion of the second proxy season (2008) under the new SEC rule, the SEC staff has been actively reviewing companies' executive compensation compliance, including the adequacy of explanatory disclosures. John White, director of the SEC's Division of Corporation Finance, tipped his hand on the Commission's early review of executive compensation proxy disclosures in an August 2007 speech to the American Bar Association in San Francisco. To narrow the scope of this massive task, White explained that the SEC's initial examination would target larger companies. White described their general findings as well as their prime areas of interest:

"We are looking for analysis, particularly on the different components of compensation and on change of control and termination payments. We also are looking at performance targets. Is the description adequate? We're seeing a lot of really vague disclosure in this area about 'individual performance goals and targets' without further discussion."

According to the August 31, 2007, edition of *The Wall Street Journal*, approximately 300 companies, including Pfizer, Inc., received comment letters from the SEC requesting additional explanations about executive compensation disclosures in 2007. The following excerpt from Pfizer's 2007 proxy statement explains how the company will calculate the 2007 bonus for CEO Jeffrey B. Kindler. Given the lack of specificity regarding these performance targets, Pfizer's proxy statement illustrates the type of vague disclosures the SEC is trying to eliminate.

TABLE 1. KEY REGULATIONS AFFECTING CEO COMPENSATION

REGULATIONS AFFECTING EXECUTIVE COMPENSATION	BRIEF DESCRIPTION FO MAJOR IMPACT
SEC: **Executive Compensation Disclosure, 1992**	This requires companies to disclose tabular information relating to executive compensation components in their proxy statements for the CEO and the next four highest-paid executives. This disclosure change was motivated by a shift toward stock option compensation. There is no total compensation column summarizing all components of compensation.
Congress: **Revenue Reconciliation Act, 1993**	This law sets the threshold for the deductibility of executive compensation for publicly held corporations. The maximum allowable tax deduction for employee remuneration for services rendered is $1 million.
FASB: **SFAS no. 123(R), December 2004**	This accounting standard requires fair value measurement of stock options and expense recognition in the income statement over the vesting period. Corporate tax deductions are unchanged. The deductible amount is measured on the exercise date as the difference between the exercise price of the options and the market price of the stock.
SEC: **Executive Compensation and Related Person Disclosure, 2006**	This regulation requires detailed compensation disclosures for the CEO, CFO, and the three remaining highest-paid executives. These proxy disclosures summarize all types and amounts of executive compensation and provides a total compensation column. The proxy should also identify the *specific* targets that must be achieved before management earns performance-based compensation. This rule also expands director compensation disclosures. Related person disclosures reveal executive officers who are members of the compensation committee, as well as executives from different companies who serve on each other's compensation committee.

"In 2007, 60% of Mr. Kindler's bonus will be based on the Committee's assessment of the Company's financial performance in the following measures as well as total shareholder return, as disclosed by the Company:

- *Total Revenues*
- *Adjusted Diluted Earnings per Share*
- *Cash Flow From Operations*

The other 40% of his bonus will be based on the following strategic objectives:

- *Research products and pipeline development*
- *Establishing lower, more flexible cost base and instituting fundamental change within the organization*
- *Implementing business development strategy to drive additional sources of revenue*
- *Improving internal and external relationships and engaging collaboratively with patients, customers and business partners"*

In contrast to Pfizer, Lowe's Companies, Inc., which wasn't identified as having received an SEC comment letter, disclosed in its 2007 proxy statement *specific* performance-based targets the company must achieve before its CEO can earn cash incentive-based compensation. For fiscal year 2006, Lowe's compensation committee based the award of bonuses on achieving specific earnings targets:

"For the Fiscal Year ended February 2, 2007, the performance measure selected by the Compensation Committee was the percentage increase in the Company's earnings before interest and taxes ("EBIT") over the immediately preceding year. The Compensation Committee established a threshold rate of 8% EBIT growth that must be achieved before any non-equity incentive compensation amounts would be earned, a 14% EBIT growth rate for which target non-equity incentive compensation amounts would be earned

and a 20% EBIT growth rate for which the maximum non-equity incentive compensation amounts would be earned. The Company's EBIT growth rate for the 2006 Fiscal Year was 10.7%. Based on that EBIT growth rate, Mr. Niblock (CEO) earned non-equity incentive compensation equal to 109.25% of his base salary."

GROWTH IN CEO COMPENSATION

Table 2 tracks the changes in median CEO compensation, median net income, and median cash flows for S&P 500 companies from 1992 through 2006. We obtained financial statement and CEO compensation data from Standard & Poor's Compustat Database. (Since companies release 2007 executive compensation data in their 2008 proxy statements, 2007 data was unavailable on Compustat for most companies as of this writing.) Total CEO compensation includes the fair value of stock options measured on the grant date in accordance with SFAS No. 123(R). Despite repeated attempts to regulate executive compensation over this period, total median CEO compensation jumped from $1.1 million in 1992 to $9.1 million in

2006. Perhaps more alarming, the rate of growth in CEO compensation outpaced the rate of increase in both net income and operating cash flows.

Figure 1 shows a timeline of changes in median CEO compensation. Changes in median net income and median operating cash flows provide benchmarks to help assess the reasonableness of the increases. The data spans from 1992 through 2006 to incorporate the passage of the four major regulations we discuss. Each component (compensation, net income, and cash flows) is graphed relative to its respective 1992 base-year figure. Ironically, CEO compensation rapidly accelerated after the passage of the Corporate Pay Responsibility Act of 1991.

As Figure 1 shows, by 1997 CEO compensation at S&P 500 companies was almost five times higher than 1992 levels. This vastly outpaced the rise in net income, which grew only 2.5 times as high as 1992 levels, and operating cash flows, which increased slightly more than 1.5 times its 1992 level. CEO compensation dropped sharply in 1998 but continued to increase well beyond increases in net income and operating cash flows through 2006. Despite a sharp drop in net income

TABLE 2. S&P 500 MEDIAN CEO COMPENSATION, MEDIAN NET INCOME, AND MEDIAN OPERATING CASH FLOWS (Dollars in Millions)

YEAR	MEDIAN TOTAL COMPENSATION CEO	MEDIAN NET INCOME	MEDIAN OPERATING CASH FLOWS
1992	$1.1	$95.2	$247.5
1993	1.7	123.0	257.2
1994	2.1	173.9	297.9
1995	2.4	178.1	298.7
1996	4.1	195.8	337.1
1997	5.1	231.3	386.4
1998	3.2	242.3	413.8
1999	4.0	282.0	458.1
2000	5.0	308.3	517.8
2001	5.7	236.5	626.0
2002	5.6	239.5	650.8
2003	6.2	365.3	686.6
2004	6.8	467.4	798.8
2005	7.2	577.4	840.9
2006	9.1	629.5	948.3

FIGURE 1. GROWTH OF S&P 500 MEDIAN CEO COMPENSATION, MEDIAN NET INCOME AND MEDIAN OPERATING CASH FLOWS GRAPHED RELATIVE TO 1992 BASE-YEAR AMOUNTS

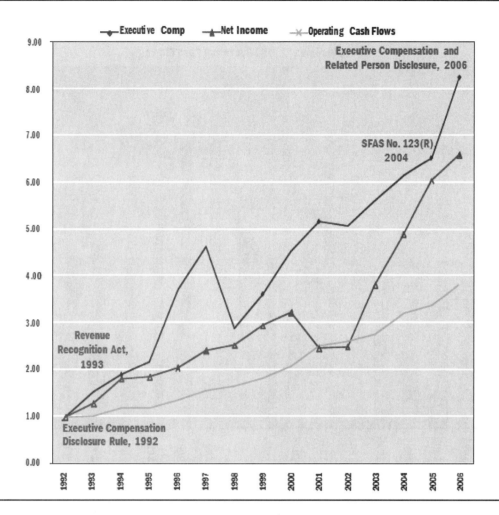

in 2001, CEO compensation continued to rise annually through 2006, except for a slight decrease in 2002. Unexpectedly, after the enactment of SFAS No. 123(R) and the SEC's 2006 "Executive Compensation and Related Person" rule, CEO compensation shot up from about 6.5 times 1992 levels in 2005 to well over 8.0 times 1992 levels in 2006.

Figure 2 expresses median CEO compensation at S&P 500 companies as a percent of median net income and median cash flows from 1992 through 2006. In 2006, CEO compensation accounted for approximately 1.5% of net income and 1% of operating cash flows. Perhaps of most interest to governance advocates: CEO compensation consumed about twice as much operating cash flows in 2006 vs. 1992 and accounted for more than 2% of median net income during four of the 15 years. The percentages can be considerably higher for specific companies. In our sample, CEO compensation

is as high as 8.1% of net income and 12.6% of operating cash flows.

WHY REGULATIONS HAVE FAILED

The SEC has been a strong advocate of full disclosure to enhance transparency and accountability, and its 1992 and 2006 executive compensation disclosure rules significantly improved clarity. Proxy statements now prominently display tabular summaries of all types of compensation awarded to top executives and are generally easy for shareholders to understand.

But it seems that an unintended effect has proven more powerful since full details of total compensation packages are now available to everyone, not just the shareholders of affected companies. Compensation disclosures have fueled bidding wars for top talent. Compensation committees may feel intense pressure to ensure their top management team is competitively compensated. When Aflac CEO Daniel P. Amos was

FIGURE 2. S&P 500 CEO COMPENSATION AS A PERCENT OF MEDIAN NET INCOME AND MEDIAN OPERATING CASH FLOWS

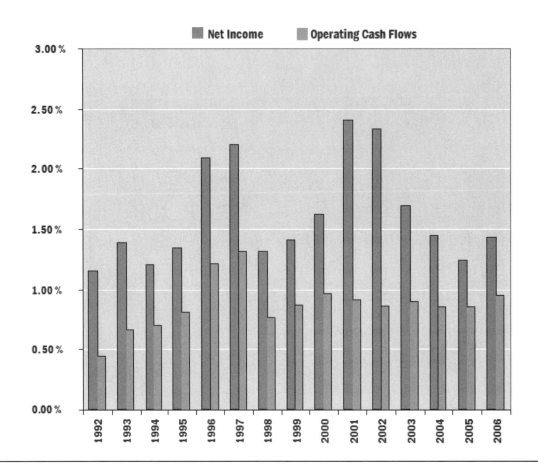

asked what his reaction would be if shareholders wanted him to stop receiving stock options, he provided an interesting insight about his perception of CEO compensation. As quoted in the March 7, 2008, edition of the *The Wall Street Journal*, Amos replied:

> *"I will have to make a decision at that time. Will I be as motivated if you cut my pay below everybody else's? The answer is no. I would be insulted that a rookie CEO that has never done anything his whole life could walk in and make more than I do. I have more money than I will ever spend. But there's got to be a scorecard to tell what you are worth. And compensation is the way the scorecard is kept."*

Not surprisingly, as 2008 proxy statements began to appear, top management compensation continued to rise, frequently without regard to company performance. Based on 2008 proxy statements filed through March 2008, the April 5 edition of *The New York Times* identified John Thain, CEO of Merrill

Lynch, as the highest-paid CEO in 2007. His total compensation of $83.8 million consisted of a $750,000 base salary, $15 million cash bonus, $33 million in stock awards, $35 million in stock options, and approximately $4,000 in perquisites. Although governance advocates would probably applaud the compensation committee's structuring of Thain's pay package to ensure maximum tax deductibility, perhaps the more important issue is whether his total annual compensation is fair and reasonable from the shareholders' perspective. Considering Merrill's stock price declined 42% in 2007, many shareholders may question the fairness of his compensation. Oracle's CEO Larry Ellison was next on the list with total 2007 compensation of $61.2 million, but Oracle's stock price did increase 29% in 2007.

GOVERNANCE ADVOCATES INFLUENCE SAY-ON-PAY INITIATIVES

The latest legislative initiative targets the advisory role of shareholders in executive pay decisions. In April

2007, the U.S. House of Representatives passed H.R. 1257, "The Shareholder Vote on Executive Compensation Act." Although only a simple majority was required to pass the bill, H.R. 1257 passed with a 67% favorable vote. A similar bill is pending in the U.S. Senate. Senator Barack Obama introduced S. 1181, "Shareholder Vote on Executive Compensation Act," which was referred to the Senate's Committee on Banking, Housing, and Urban Affairs. The bill, which the Senate hasn't yet approved, proposes an amendment to the Securities Exchange Act of 1934, giving shareholders an annual nonbinding advisory vote on executive compensation as well as a vote on new severance agreements. A spokesman for Obama's presidential campaign said the candidate would push for the bill's passage if he is elected this fall, according to the February 27, 2008, edition of *The Wall Street Journal*. Similarly, at the June 10 National Federation of Independent Business and eBay 2008 National Small Business Summit in Washington, D.C., presidential hopeful John McCain pledged to give shareholders approval rights for CEO pay and severance arrangements.

Critics of this latest legislative proposal claim the SEC's disclosure regulations on executive compensation are adequate. Others believe government regulators should let the private sector determine executive compensation decisions. While advisory shareholder approval isn't required in the U.S., a nonbinding vote on executive compensation is common in Australia and several European countries.

In May 2008, Aflac became the first U.S. public company to permit its shareholders a say-on-pay vote on the company's executive compensation policies and procedures. Although Aflac's shareholder vote is nonbinding, it opens the door for increased scrutiny of executive compensation. In its March 24, 2008, proxy statement, Aflac described the shareholder vote as follows:

> *"Resolved, that the shareholders approve the overall executive pay-for-performance compensation policies and procedures employed by the Company, as described in the Compensation Discussion and Analysis and the tabular disclosure regarding named executive officer compensation (together with the accompanying narrative disclosure) in this Proxy Statement."*

According to Aflac's May 6, 2008, press release, its shareholders overwhelmingly approved the measure, casting 93% of their votes in favor of Aflac's compensation policies and procedures as well as the CEO's 2007 compensation package. The 2008 proxy statement provided to shareholders before the vote reported Aflac CEO Daniel P. Amos's total compensation in 2007 was $14,834,713, only a slight increase from his 2006 compensation. His 2007 compensation package was composed of $1.3 million in salary, $2.8 million in stock awards, $5.6 million in stock options, $2.8 million in incentive compensation, $2 million in pension benefits, and approximately $300,000 in perquisites.

So far, at least seven other companies have approved say-on-pay votes for their shareholders. Beginning in 2009, shareholders of Verizon, Par Pharmaceuticals, Risk-Metrics, Blockbuster, H&R Block, Tech Data, and MBIA will cast their nonbinding votes on executive compensation. Shareholders of numerous other U.S. companies have passed say-on-pay resolutions but must await board approval before an actual say-on-pay vote takes place. According to the Lawyer Links database, Motorola and Ingersoll-Rand shareholders passed resolutions in 2007 and again in 2008, but the companies' boards of directors haven't yet approved the resolutions clearing the way for a say-on-pay vote. In addition, activist groups targeted about 100 companies in 2008 with similar say-on-pay resolutions, according to the March 7, 2008, edition of *The Wall Street Journal*.

Despite growing support for increased shareholder governance, approval of say-on-pay initiatives is far from a sure thing. For example, a dissident shareholder of Rackable Systems added a proposed say-on-pay amendment to the May 2008 annual shareholder meeting. Management opposed the measure and stacked the deck in its favor by establishing ground rules that counted shareholder abstentions as a negative vote, according to the company's proxy statement. Although shareholders cast more votes in favor of say-on-pay than against, the amendment failed because of counting abstentions as negative votes.

THE FUTURE

It's very difficult to regulate fairness in executive compensation. Ultimately, payment of equitable executive compensation is the board of directors' responsibility. Linking executive pay to performance is a good first step, but recent actions by the SEC and the U.S. Congress indicate compensation committees may need stronger criteria and specific performance targets to justify their executive compensation decisions. Compensation performance targets must be meaningful, challenging, and measurable. The SEC has already demonstrated companies can no longer justify executive compensation by simply stating that it is similar to that of executives of competitor companies.

Although regulations generally have been ineffective in controlling what many observers view as excessive compensation, regulations have mobilized shareholders to scrutinize executive compensation decisions. Armed with transparent executive compensation data, compensation committees should expect shareholders and others to continue demanding accountability for the stewardship of corporate assets. Careful compliance with the latest SEC disclosure rules and design of equitable executive compensation packages is imperative if companies hope to satisfy governance advocates. To counter criticism and avoid further regulations, boards may want to consider voluntarily giving their shareholders a nonbinding advisory vote on executive compensation. Otherwise, Congress may act further. This time it could include a mandatory shareholder vote on executive compensation.

C. Terry Grant, CPA, Ph.D., is a professor of accounting in the Stetson School of Business & Economics at Mercer University in Atlanta, Ga. You can reach Terry at (678) 547-6328 or grant_ct@mercer.edu.

Gerry H. Grant, CPA, Ph.D., is an associate professor of accounting in the Mihaylo College of Business and Economics at California State University in Fullerton. You can reach Gerry at (714) 278-2242 or ggrant@fullerton.edu.

The authors acknowledge the assistance of Ritu Rampuria on an early draft of this article.

QUESTION

9.6 Why have regulations designed to curb escalating CEO compensation failed?

9.7 Implementing Management Innovations Successfully: Principles for Lasting Change

*by S. Mark Young**

Over the past decade, the pace with which organizations worldwide have been experimenting with innovations to remain competitive has increased frenetically. Activity-based cost management (ABCM), Total Quality Management (TQM), and business process reengineering (BPR) have been attempted by many organizations separately, and in some cases, simultaneously. The financial and human resources that have been poured into these innovation attempts are truly staggering, but unfortunately, many innovations have failed.

The purpose of this article is to offer some principles for successful implementation that often are not explicitly incorporated, or are underemphasized in many approaches to implementation.

Successful implementation occurs when, "Managers and employees permanently alter the way they perform their job responsibilities to conform to the principles dictated by a particular innovation."

Principle 1: The Importance of organizational culture.
Some organizational cultures embrace change while others retreat from change. Knowing what kind of culture exists is an extremely important factor to understand.

Principle 2: Only adopt those innovations consistent with current corporate, divisional, and plant strategies.
The assumption underlying this principle is that employees will be more willing to adopt an innovation if it is consistent with the organization's strategy to which they have already committed.

Principle 3: Don't attempt an innovation if an organization is simultaneously engaging in downsizing.
Employees have great difficulty committing to change when they see that their organization is not committing to them. Have a strong feeling of job security allows employees to accept change more easily.

Principle 4; Spend as much time and resources on managing the human side of change as the technical side.
Managing the technical side of an innovation is often not the most significant problem for organizations.

---

* This article has been summarized from the original article by S. Mark Young, "Implementing Management Innovations Successfully: Principles for Lasting Change," in the *Journal of Cost Management* (September/October 1997): 16–20. Copyright © 1997, Thomson Reuters.

Successful change involves placing a great deal of effectively managing people so that they may embrace change.

Principle 5: Educate and train employees at all levels of the organization regarding the purpose and benefits of the innovation.

Educating employees only at the managerial level as to why change is occurring is an enormous mistake. Because most innovation success rests on improvements in variables related to quality, cost and time, employees at the point of production and service need to be included in any training and education programs. Only then can the entire organization embrace change.

Principle 6: Use medium- and long-term performance measures to gauge innovation success.

Many organizations simply rely on short term (often financial) performance measures such to gauge success. The key to assessing real change is to use measures that will answer questions such as, "Is the innovation leading to the intended consequences?" and "Are employees thinking differently about problems and are they making better decisions?" Answers to these questions may require more qualitative measures such as attitudinal surveys and direct observation of behavior. Such measures serve as medium term assessments of true behavioral change. The organization should also rely on long-term (3 to 5 year) measures as it takes several years for true change to occur.

Principle 7: Generate useful and understandable reports to illustrate the effects of change programs.

Managers are typically inundated with a lot of information and many reports that don't provide them with the answers they need. Reports related to change programs must be easily understandable and useful. They should detail measures that a manager can look at to determine if change is occurring.

Principle 8: Make explicit agreements regarding when and if existing information systems should be turned off once a new system is in place.

Determining when to switch off an old system and turn on the new one is of immense importance. Once a system like ABC has been implemented the old direct labor based system must be turned off quickly. If this does not happen then managers will be constantly looking at both the old and new systems. The numbers generated from both may cause confusion and reliance on the old system may not allow managers to make the transition to the new system.

QUESTION

9.7a Principle 4 says, "Spend as much time and resources on managing the human side of change as the technical side." Why is this so important?

9.7b Why does Young advocate in Principle 6 that organizations should use both medium- and long-term measures to gauge innovation success?

Chapter 10

Using Budgets for Planning and Coordination

Reading 10.1, *Continuous Budgeting at the HON Company*, by Drtina, Hoeger, and Schaub illustrates this large furniture maker's approach to staying competitive with the help of its budgeting process. Unlike many companies, HON uses a continuous, quarterly, budgeting system. For each quarter a budget is prepared, which includes plans not only for that particular quarter, but also for the next three quarters. As each new quarter arrives, the budgeting process is repeated. HON employees believe that the information generated is timely and comprehensive and provides them with information to respond quickly to their volatile environment. The article provides a detailed step-by-step approach to illustrate HON's method.

Reading 10.2, Christopher Bart's, *Budgeting Gamesmanship*, describes the games that managers play with their budgets. Bart defines budgeting gamesmanship as "the deliberate and premeditated manipulation of current year sales, cost, and profit forecasts by product managers to project an overly conservative image into their product budgets." Using interview and company data from eight large diversified companies, Bart documents how, and why, managers pad their budgets. Two key factors for why such padding occurs are the fear that senior management will arbitrarily slash their submitted budgets, and the managers' own concerns about uncertainty in the competitive environment in which they work.

In *Budgeting Made Easy*, Reading 10.3, Steve Hornyak discusses the enormous amounts of time and energy devoted to traditional budgeting. Among the many difficulties are incompatible software programs, time delays that mount up based on the difficulty of hooking up remote-user participants, and the inaccessibility of historical data that many managers need to help them gauge what resources they will need for the coming time period. Hornyak suggests that organizations begin to consider e-budgeting as a way to overcome many of these problems. E-budgeting can completely automate the budgeting process and include participants from remote locations world-wide. Web-based budgeting also allows access to important budget data from anywhere increasing the flexibility for all concerned. Other benefits include reductions in administrative resources, an increase in employee participation (shown by research to be a determinant of employee satisfaction), and more time to focus on strategic aspects of the budgeting process rather than the minutia of the process.

Michael Jensen's thesis in Reading 10.4, *Corporate Budgeting is Broken—Let's Fix It*, is that traditional corporate budgeting is a joke. The process takes an inordinate amount of time and causes usually honest people to be dishonest as they strive to low-ball targets and inflate results. Jensen suggests that the root cause of this dysfunctional behavior is that many companies link the achievement of certain goals to their compensation. To overcome this problem, Jensen suggests that managers be rewarded using a linear bonus scheme rather than one that provides them with a bonus once they achieve a certain level of performance.

The article, *Beyond Budgeting*, Reading 10.5 by Jeremy Hope and Robin Fraser, is another strong critique of traditional budgeting. The authors discuss two new approaches to budgeting—devolution and strategic performance management. *Devolution* involves flattening organizational hierarchies, reengineering processes, and using teamwork more effectively. One problem with this approach is that while delegation of control occurs, it is often within the strict regime of coordination and accountability with budgets as the key tool for policing control. *Strategic performance management* involves the use of a wide-ranging system for controlling the business, driving management behavior, and rewarding results. Although these systems have been effective, they often do not square nicely with a company's budgeting system. The *Beyond Budgeting* approach combines effective devolution and effective performance management systems.

In *Games Managers Play at Budget Time* (Reading 10.6), Richard Steele and Craig Albright describe five archetypes of bad behavior that are used by managers to subvert the budgeting system for their own ends. This article is a very good companion to Reading 10.2 and fleshes out specific types of dysfunctional managerial budgeting behavior. The authors argue that managerial game playing occurs sometimes because of lack of the appropriate skills to get the job done, very clear self-interested behavior, lack of clarity about performance expectations, or a response to an organization's culture. While game playing will never go away, the authors offer some prescriptions for curbing dysfunctional behavior with the budget.

Readings
Chapter 10

10.1 Continuous Budgeting at the HON Company

This furniture manufacturer builds a solid competitive strategy with progressive quarterly budgets.

by Ralph Drtina, CPA; Steve Hoeger, CMA; and John Schaub, CMA*

Survival in today's competitive environment means that businesses must be flexible and innovative, largely through development of new products and services, while simultaneously improving productivity and customer service. But building the effects of innovation into the annual budget can be difficult because actions and outcomes often are evolutionary and only become known as the year progresses. Under these conditions it is understandable that the annual budget is not an effective control tool because revenue and spending targets are based on operating conditions different from those actually encountered.

Standard cost accounting systems are not helpful either when budgeting for continuous change because of built-in contradictions. One shortcoming of standard costs for companies seeking continuous improvement, for example, is that they presuppose the goal is to optimize efficiency within a given state of operating conditions rather than to strive for ongoing improvement. Consequently, when production processes undergo continuous change, standards developed annually for static conditions no longer offer meaningful targets for gauging their success.

The HON Company, the largest maker of mid-priced office furniture in the United States and Canada, has overcome these obstacles through use of a continuous three-month budget cycle. The budget has become the integral planning and control device for achieving two strategic objectives: ongoing new product and service development and rapid continuous improvement. The budget also serves as an important vehicle for ensuring that the corporate culture is unified in its understanding of—and commitment to—strategic objectives.

VOLATILE FURNITURE INDUSTRY

The largest of nine operating companies that compose HON Industries, the HON Company operates exclusively as a manufacturer of office furniture and accessories. Organized along functional lines, it has 14 production plants located throughout the United States and operates as an independently run profit center with its operations tied to its parent through its strategic plan and budget.

Highly dependent on the overall economy's health, the office furniture industry is characterized by cyclical demand and uncertainties that make planning difficult, even in the short term. Furniture buyers often postpone purchases until their own business operations are profitable, and demand is normally seasonal with sales much higher in the second half of the calendar year.

Dominated by larger but fewer customers, the office furniture industry is faced with an increasing level of industry competition. As these customers continue to consolidate and grow, they put tremendous price pressure on their suppliers. Manufacturers that do win contracts often expand capacity to meet increased volume. As time passes, the large customers pressure suppliers to maintain or even lower prices, thereby disallowing cost increases incurred by suppliers to be passed on. Suppliers often find they are victims of their own success—their revenues increase, but profits are squeezed by rising costs. Yet they become captive suppliers to the large customers whose volume is needed to absorb the cost of expanded capacity. Given these highly uncertain industry conditions, considerable planning and coordination is needed to ensure that production capacity is used fully and unit costs are maintained or reduced.

---

* From: R. Drtina, S. Hoeger, and J. Schaub, "Continuous Budgeting at the HON Company," *Management Accounting* (January 1996): 20–24. Reprinted with permission conveyed through Copyright Clearance Center, Inc.

DOVETAILING STRATEGY AND BUDGET

Managers at the HON Company communicate and coordinate operating plans through a process called continuous quarterly budgeting. All departments work together to produce an updated four-quarter budget at the beginning of each quarter. Thus, as shown in Figure 1, a budget prepared for the third quarter 1996 includes plans for the third and fourth quarters of 1996 and the first and second quarters of 1997. Each quarterly budget requires the next four quarters to be completely re-budgeted. By having a detailed quarterly budget that is up-to-date and comprehensive, managers and employees in all areas are prepared to deal with rapid change.

In the HON Company's aggressive but realistic budget philosophy, senior management expects each quarter's performance to exceed the previous one. New products and services drive company growth, and research to define and meet emerging customer demand is ongoing. In 1996, for example, the company expects to launch dozens of new product series in addition to introducing hundreds of variations to the size, shape, and features of existing models. Recognizing that service is critical, too, HON offers two- and three-week delivery for orders of any product size and combination. Competitors typically require four- to five-week lead time for single product orders.

Budget targets must be supported by action plans that coordinate operational improvements throughout the organization. For example, when the strategic plan calls for a specified increase in productivity (8% in 1995), all departments are expected to work together to bring about needed change. In manufacturing, production processes repeatedly are challenged and bottlenecks removed. Sales and marketing are expected to generate increased sales volume to make full use of capacity gained through manufacturing improvements. Distribution then must develop plans to handle increased deliveries while reducing the cost of delivery per sales dollar.

PREPARING THE BUDGET

The typical quarterly budget process is done in five basic steps over a six-week period. (See Figure 2.)

Step 1—Develop sales budget. Preparation of the sales budget begins with the territory sales managers when they submit quarterly sales budgets to the sales department for consolidation. Then the sales budget is summarized by geographic territory and by distribution channel. At the same time the sales department is preparing territory budgets, the marketing department independently prepares a sales budget based on general product types and distribution channels. These two sales budget submissions typically differ, largely due to divergent perspectives and sources of information. While the sales department bases its estimates on historical patterns of existing products, marketing has more detailed information about new products and their introduction dates and about special promotion programs.

After the marketing and sales departments have made their separate sales forecasts, the two groups compare forecasts, analyze differences, and reach agreement on the final sales targets. If the two sales targets differ by a substantial amount, more detail about sales derivation and rationale is shared and discussed. Negotiations over acceptable targets continue until the two parties reach a consensus.

Once sales and marketing reach agreement, their sales targets are compared to the strategic plan at a top-level meeting attended by the president and senior staff. The purpose of the meeting is to identify major product group sales levels that appear too low or too high. As a result of discussions on the issues causing these discrepancies, changes are made to reconcile budgeted sales and market share with the strategic plan. Upon final approval, sales dollar targets are sent to production scheduling for conversion to production units and shipping volume.

FIGURE 1. OVERVIEW OF CONTINUOUS QUARTERLY BUDGET

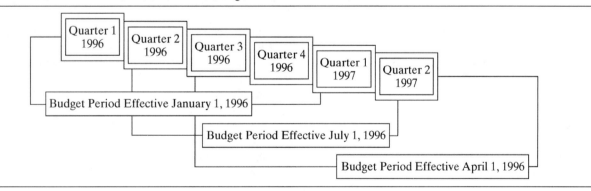

FIGURE 2. QUARTERLY BUDGET PROCESS

| Step 1.
Develop the sales budget by product line (2 weeks). | Step 2.
Convert the sales budget to a plant production and shipping schedule (1 week). | Step 3.
Prepare cost/expense budgets for production and distribution and for sales and general administration (1 week). | Step 4.
Consolidate department and plant budgets and compare budget results with the strategic plan (1 week). | Step 5.
Prepare a complete budget package for the parent company (1 week). |

Step 2—Convert the sales budget to a plant production and shipping schedule. The scheduling group allocates production targets to the company's 14 plants to gain greatest production and distribution efficiencies. This group has one week to convert the sales budgets derived in Step 1 into unit production targets for each plant. Scheduling makes this conversion by analyzing the history of each product category and including such factors as product destination, delivery distance, and plant capabilities. It also takes into account current product inventories and adjusts or planned increases or decreases. After unit production targets are assigned, production managers begin budgeting their quarterly costs.

Step 3—Prepare cost/expense budgets. All the HON Company's functional areas are organized as either cost or expense centers. Separate budgets are prepared for research and development, SG&A, customer service, production, and distribution. In this step, area managers submit expense budgets that determine spending and efficiency targets for the upcoming quarter and year. Each area is expected to provide for improvements designated in the strategic plan. Managers have five working days to complete their expense budgets.

Preparation of a production plant's budget within one week requires widespread participation of department managers and employees and the full commitment of the plant accountant. The budget process pushes responsibility down to the lowest departmental levels within each plant. Department managers are expected to base their budgets on action plans that detail how improvements will be made. The plant accountant must prepare the direct and indirect salary budgets, consolidate department budgets into an overall plant budget, and prepare productivity performance measures. The plant manager helps to guide improvement efforts between departments and makes sure that overall outcomes agree with goals set forth in the strategic plan.

Company-wide productivity improvements begin with the production and distribution processes. Every department in these two areas is expected to initiate changes that allow more units to be processed without incurring added cost. For example, as unit sales increase, it is presumed that production plants will keep inventory levels constant by striving for a one-piece production flow through which products are processed, without

interruption, from the time they are started to the point of being loaded on delivery trucks. Similarly distribution is expected to reduce average costs by increasing use of freight container capacity.

The strategic plan specifies an allowable sales percentage for R&D, for SG&A expenses broken down by functional area (general administration, marketing, selling), and for customer service. At the beginning of the budget process, area managers are given general expense guidelines based on past history. Here, as in production, budget responsibilities are pushed down to department levels where guideline targets are refined to take into account the effects of improvements and new programs.

As improvement projects are implemented, SG&A areas are expected to trade spending authority among themselves. For example, if marketing were to find that a new product was to be delayed for one quarter, it could push back its planned expense for printing new literature and for new product training. SG&A managers then would prioritize needs to find where these funds might best be used while still meeting the allowable spending targets for all of SG&A. They may agree, for instance, that MIS can best use the free resources to bring in temporary workers to help speed up completion of a current high-priority project, such as putting customers on electronic data interchange.

Step 4—Consolidate budgets and compare with strategic plan. After individual budgets are completed by functional areas, they are forwarded to the HON Company headquarters. At this point, the company accounting group has one week to review the budget for obvious errors and assemble the final budget package. The budget is analyzed to ensure that strategic plans are being accomplished and that the plants and the SG&A departments are focused on the correct efforts. For example, the budget for the first two quarters of the year—when seasonal activity is low—should include adequate provision for periodic maintenance. If budgeted maintenance expenditures are low, a production plant may have under-budgeted preventive maintenance or neglected special overhaul projects which would require further budget revision.

Step 5—Prepare a budget package for parent company. The company's controller department has one week to prepare a complete set of financial statements plus a host of comparative data: budgeted return on assets employed, productivity measures, budgeted sales attributable to new product introductions, major tooling expenditures, and an analysis of list prices to net sales. These data first are analyzed to ensure that the HON Company's performance trends satisfy the targets set forth in the strategic plan. Normally, any shortfalls already would have been identified and corrected prior to this point in the process. If additional deficiencies are identified, however, the company controller first must correct problem areas before proceeding further.

Then the completed budget is sent to the parent company, HON Industries, for approval. If the parent does not approve the budget, the HON Company controller must investigate needed changes, such as additional cost cuts. In these cases, the HON Company president normally has one additional week to assure the parent company that the budget is the best that is attainable, or, if such arguments fail, the budget is trimmed further. This type of approach has proven effective because the HON Company's philosophy is that a change in the budget is not simply a change in numbers, but rather it means that the company's action plans also must be changed.

BUDGETING FOR COMMITMENT AND ACTION

The HON Company's continuous budgeting system enables senior managers to inspire and motivate the achievement of corporate strategies. Employees at all levels and in all departments are kept informed of new product and process developments, and they in turn update their own performance targets accordingly. By planning in three-month time frames, managers and front-line employees can make a fair assessment of their work improvements and thus can set realistic targets. This interactive approach pushes decisions down to the production floor, and, as a result, helps to gain employee commitment and faster adoption of productivity improvements. It also ensures that standard costs and variance reports are meaningful, an important consideration for helping employees gain the satisfaction of short-term victories in their work.

Does quarterly budget preparation consume a disproportionate amount of company time? Experience has shown that managers improve their budgeting skills over time and need no more time to do quarterly budgets than would be needed for one annual budget. Information technology advances also have shortened budget preparation time. A highly integrated computer budgeting system supplies each department manager with four-quarter histories and four-quarter projections of budget line items. Driver codes for revenue and cost targets are set by default, and, thus, managers need only change budgets for line items on an exception basis. The budget system speeds up information flows to higher levels, too, because proposed targets are rolled up to the next level immediately where they can be reviewed and revised quickly by senior management.

Most important, the HON Company's process of continuous quarterly budgeting unites senior-level strategy with a committed corporate culture. Corporate management best understands where energies need to be focused to enhance the firm's competitive edge, but attaining strategic goals depends on a workforce that can translate corporate strategies into a well-coordinated action plan. Continuous budgeting is the vehicle for ensuring both understanding and ownership by front-line workers by communicating a corporate vision, empowering employees to act on the vision, and targeting and tracking short-term wins.

The result is an attitude among employees that ongoing improvement is a way of life.[1]

ENDNOTE

1. For more on this perspective, see John P. Kotter, "Why Transformation Efforts Fail," *Harvard Business Review*, March–April 1995, pp. 59–67.

Ralph Drtina, CPA, is professor of accounting and management, Crummer Graduate School of Business, Rollins College, Winter Park, Fla. He is a member of Mid-Florida Chapter, through which this article was submitted.

Steve Hoeger, CMA, CPA, is manager of financial analysis, Speed Queen, a Raytheon Company, Ripon, Wis. He is a member of Illowa (Wis.) Chapter.

John Schaub, CMA, is assistant controller, the HON Company, Muscatine, Iowa. He is a member of Illowa Chapter.

QUESTIONS

10.1a Is HON's budgeting philosophy an aggressive one? Is there a downside to this philosophy? Explain.

10.1b How are HON managers able to develop their budgets without the process taking all of their time? Explain.

10.2 Budgeting Gamesmanship

*by Christopher K. Bart**

While most managers dislike having to deal with them, budgets are nevertheless essential to the management and control of an organization. Indeed, budgets are one of the most important tools management has for leading an organization toward its goals. As viewed in the literature, budgets are required to "institutionalize" a firm's goals, monitor the performance and progress of both the business and individual products, and measure the performance of managers.[1] While not all firms have five- or ten-year financial forecasts, practically all firms (beyond a certain maturity and size) have budgets.[2]

Given their unique role and importance in the overall planning process, it may seem superfluous to state that— budgets need to be rooted in reality. In fact, one of budgeting's main principles is that the budget numbers be challenging (yet realistic), honest, and accurate—given the best information available.[3] Otherwise, both the purpose of strategic planning in general and manager motivation in particular is destroyed.

The translation of strategic plans into measurable financial standards and goals for an organization, however, is not a precise science.[4] In the first place, there is always uncertainty in the business environment. Consequently, making precise predictions as to a firm's performance and position vis-à-vis the competition can be problematic. Second, it is generally assumed that lower-level managers are wont to "play games" in preparing their budget forecasts—resulting in distorted and even falsified information for those to whom it is reported.[5] Consequently, this "budgeting gamesmanship" is generally considered a form of dysfunctional behavior in that it frustrates both the planning process and the accuracy of business and manager evaluations. It is, therefore, typically recommended that senior managers actively strive to discourage and eliminate budgeting gamesmanship.[6]

PRIOR RESEARCH AND THEORY

The games that managers play with their budgets is a topic that has received only limited attention from business writers and academics. In addition, budgeting gamesmanship activities have been reported largely by way of anecdotal reference in qualitative and very limited studies.[7] What research there has been has tended to confirm the general notion that when budgets are used to evaluate managerial performance, they influence the attitude of managers toward accounting information. Some of the budget-related variables that researchers have investigated to determine their impact on managerial behavior include the degree of budget participation, the level of budget difficulty, and the frequency of budget feedback.[8]

Despite these efforts, the topic of budgeting games has generally remained an area of speculation among budgeting researchers and academics.[9] The nature and extent of budget games are still relatively unknown; most managers, therefore, do not know how widespread budgeting gamesmanship is within their organization. Unfortunately, some previous studies have also tended to confuse faulty accounting systems with the way that managers use the information provided by those systems.[10] Thus, while budgeting gamesmanship is of interest, it remains understudied and misunderstood.[11]

Relatively little is known about how budgeting activities operate at the product level within large, multiproduct firms. The business policy literature on the strategy formulation process and its associated budgeting activities has generally confined itself to the corporate level.[12] Fortunately, research at the product level is becoming more common.[13] However, given the diversification trend among firms generally and the widespread use of product managers by firms to manage their multiproduct circumstances,[14] it is important that "strategic processes and their related practices at the product level" be further explored.[15]

This article presents findings from some recently conducted clinical research that investigated budgeting gamesmanship at the product level in several large, diversified companies.

RESEARCH FINDINGS

Budgeting gamesmanship was found to be a widespread practice in six of the eight firms we examined— specifically, at the companies we will call Alpha, Beta, Delta, Kappa, Omega, and Phi. The types of games that product managers play in these firms; the size of the games; and the factors motivating, facilitating, and constraining the playing of games are examined in the following sections. Thereafter, the two firms where budgeting games were not found to exist (which we will call Gamma and Sigma) are discussed.

THE FIRMS WITH GAMES: THE CASES OF ALPHA, BETA, DELTA, KAPPA, OMEGA, AND PHI

The Games that Product Managers Play. Although they never referred to them as "games" per se, the product managers interviewed were not wanting for a rather extensive lexicon to describe their budgeting manipulations. "Cushion," "slush fund," "hedge," "flexibility," "cookie jar," "hip/back pocket," "pad," "kitty," "secret reserve," "war chest," and "contingency" were just some of the colorful terms used to label the games that managers played with their financial forecasts and budgets. For the most part, however, all of these terms could be used interchangeably.

We asked the product managers to expand on the specific types of games that were played with their budgets. A list of these games and their frequency of mention is provided in Exhibit 1. The responses show that the potential for budget games exists wherever a product manager is asked to make an estimate of his or her plans—in other words, practically anywhere. Their responses also suggest that some games are played more often than others (see rankings in Exhibit 1).

The Size of the Games. Product managers were asked to state the exact amount of "cushions and hedges" that they had built into their plans. The relevant statistics are displayed in Exhibit 2. As the exhibit shows, the size of the games can be quite substantial in absolute dollar terms and in relative terms as a percentage of sales. In some cases, the games could be said to have a material impact on overall company profitability. The overall average also appeared to be fairly large.

Facilitating Factors in Budgeting Gamesmanship. Product managers were quick to identify how certain situations facilitated—even encouraged—budgeting games in their strategic plans. The consensus was that the bigger the promotional budget, the greater the opportunity.

Product history was another factor identified as facilitating cushions. New products, in particular, seemed to provide greater latitude in negotiating volume estimates as the firm had no prior experience with the product.

Other managers claimed, however, that even among products with fairly long histories, the opportunity for budget games was there—though greater for some products than for others. Opportunity seemed to vary with the *strategic posture* of the product. For example, in the case of "growth" postured products, managers stated that the amount of competitive activity was higher than normal and that prices tended to be unstable. Senior management was seen as being committed in terms of spending money. It was, therefore, deemed easier to convince top management of the need for "spending even more."

Products with a "harvest" strategic posture, on the other hand, were said to be characterized by less environmental uncertainty and usually smaller promotional budgets. The "cushionability" of these products was consequently seen to be reduced considerably.

Another condition identified as facilitating budgeting games was the time constraints imposed on senior managers during the product plan review period. As one manager put it:

> "Senior management just doesn't have the time for checking every number you put into your plans …. So one strategy is to 'pad' everything. If you're lucky, you'll still have 50% of your cushions after the plan reviews."

Finally, product managers claimed that the less knowledgeable a group manager was about a product and the less experience he or she had, the less able he or she was at finding where the cushions were. One product manager was particularly candid in describing how his group manager's lack of experience was capitalized on:

> "We've got this new group manager this year who came to us from a consumer promotion house. This just means that I'll have to be especially careful in estimating the costs for my brands' consumer promotions. But I know that I'll be able to 'get him' when it comes to my advertising and trade promotion forecasts."

EXHIBIT 1. PRODUCT MANAGERS' BUDGET GAMES

Type of Game	Frequency of Mention	Rank
Understating volume estimates	48.5%	1
Undeclared/understated price increases	39.4%	3
Undeclared/understated cost reduction programs	36.4%	4
Overstated expenses		
—Advertising	48.5%	1
—Consumer promotions	45.5%	2
—Trade-related	33.3%	5
—Market research	27.3%	6
Undeclared line extensions	33.3%	5

EXHIBIT 2. THE SIZE OF THE BUDGET GAMES ($ IN 000)[a]

Company	Mean ($)	Range ($)	Mean (% of sales)	Range (% of sales)
Alpha	$83.2	$11–210	0.3%	0.2–1.5%
Beta	175.0	50–500	1.5	0.5–3.0
Gamma	0.0	0–0	0.0	0.0–0.0
Delta	93.3	80–100	1.2	1.0–1.7
Kappa	640.0	100–1,400	1.9	0.4–3.2
Omega	298.8	44–750	0.8	0.6–1.5
Phi	940.0	100–2,460	2.1	0.5–5.0
Sigma	0.0	0–0	0.0	0.0–0.0
Average[b]	$364.3	n.a.	1.4%	n.a.

[a] Calculations are per product manager or per product assignment.

[b] Overall average calculations exclude Gamma and Sigma because product managers in these firms did not have any cushions in their budgets.

Factors That Constrain Budget Games. Several factors appeared to aid senior managers in the detection of budget games. One was the historical promotional spending pattern of the products. If current promotional expenses—calculated as a percentage of sales—were significantly out of line with earlier figures, they would be closely examined by senior management. Surprisingly, not all firms required these calculations and, where they did, a few product managers actually admitted to manipulating them to avoid calling attention to their current budget numbers. Some also stated that they would take advantage of "rounding out effects" in their calculations to accomplish the same purpose.

Interestingly, while all the product managers recognized that glaring, obvious, or ridiculous cushions invited their detection, many claimed that their selective use sometimes served a purpose. As one manager pointed out:

"It doesn't hurt to have a few things that 'stick out.' Management thinks that you're hiding something, so it's good if you give them some things to find. Sometimes they're happy with it. Other times, they come back and ask you for still more [profit]."

Another factor contributing to the discovery—and often the elimination—of product managers' budgeting games was the practice among senior managers of telling product managers what their total assignment profit target had to be. In such circumstances, if a product manager were unlucky, his or her cushions would be wiped out instantly. A variation of this practice was for the group product manager simply to demand that he or she be informed of where the hedges were. Few of the product managers who had experienced this latter situation, however, admitted to "telling all."

Most product managers expressed the view that the greater the profit pressures on the company, the more the marketing vice-president and group product managers would be driven to "ferret out the cushions." And, as previously mentioned, many managers said that for products with a harvest strategic posture, it was much more difficult to play budgeting games. Several remarked, however, that because the environment for harvest-postured products was relatively stable, there was less need for cushions to begin with.

Why Product Managers Play Games with Their Budgets. There were a number of factors motivating product managers to play games with their budgets. The first involved the objective setting process itself. One product manager described the problem as follows:

"When a product manager puts together his plans, he usually has a fairly good idea of what he thinks his business can do next year in both volume and profit terms. However, most managers here know that when their forecasts and budgets are submitted, invariably they will be changed by senior management—often with the simple 'stroke of a pen.' Consequently, if a manager were to give a realistic 'call' on his numbers, he could wind up with an even higher volume target and also [fewer] promotional dollars to achieve it. In the end, the product manager would have a profit target that everyone tells him 'he set' but that he would be hard pressed to deliver. So, you have to learn how to play the game."

Along similar lines, many managers commented that arbitrary budget cuts by senior management during the year also prompted the necessity of hedges. And several product managers blamed the budgeting gamesmanship within their firms on senior management's request for forecasts so early in the planning process.

A second major factor motivating managers to put hedges into their plans was market uncertainty. If "unanticipated competitive activities" threatened a product's volume forecast—and if additional funds were not available to counter the attack—a product manager would use his or her hedge (for example, cancel some "approved" but "not intended to be used" marketing program) in order to meet his original profit commitments.

The main reason motivating product managers to play games with their plans, however, was the drive to achieve their product's profit targets. This drive was, in turn, nurtured by one of two factors:

1. *formal company systems* that specified the performance evaluation criteria for product manager salary adjustments and/or bonus payments; and 2. *informal company* practices that led product managers to perceive what the real performance evaluation criteria were within the organization.

At Beta, for example, product managers were rewarded with a bonus payment that was determined, in part, on their products' profit performance compared with the "original plan." Cushions were, therefore, considered a form of insurance for product managers in meeting their profit targets—and thus earning their bonus. As one product manager put it:

"Some of the more successful managers here last year were the ones that really got their profit targets as low as possible and then 'exceeded plans' in terms of results. Unfortunately, last year I called my numbers realistically and am now being penalized in terms of my bonus. You might say, though, that last year I was young and innocent. This year I'm older and wiser!"

In two of the other firms, Alpha and Delta, either the product manager's formal job description or his or her formally contracted salary performance evaluation criteria was used to reinforce the notion of profit responsibility. Consequently, product managers in both these firms placed a very high premium on achieving their products' profit objectives.

There were other firms, however, where such formal mechanisms were not used (Kappa, Omega, and Phi) and still product managers were strongly motivated to achieve their profit targets. In other words, product managers somehow perceived that it was incumbent on them to deliver their products' budgeted profit targets. As one of them expressed it:

"Sure, I don't have anyone telling me that I have to meet my targets but I know that it's the first thing that the boss looks at before he considers my performance appraisal. After all, that's what I'm really being paid to do. He may not even bring up the fact that I missed my targets in some areas but I just know he takes that fact into account when he tells me my salary increase—or worse!"

Interestingly, the method by which reward criteria were conveyed (formal/explicit or informal/implicit) did not appear to have any influence on the degree of product manager gamesmanship as shown in Exhibit 3. Consequently, it does not seem to follow that the more explicitly rewards (such as pay, promotion, and incentives) are tied to goal achievement, the more product managers will try to pad their budgets.

Senior Management Attitudes. Senior managers in the firms where product managers played budget games acknowledged that they were aware of such practices among their subordinates. But there were important differences in term of their acceptance of it. Two dominant attitudes seemed to prevail.

The situation at Alpha, Delta, and Omega. For the most part, the senior executives in these firms did not seem to be overly concerned that game playing at lower levels existed. The attitude frequently expressed was: "I like to know that my product managers have some flexibility built into their plans." Their reasoning seemed to parallel that of their subordinates—that is, senior executives want to feel assured that if a product manager's market environment does not turn out as forecasted, he or she will be able to cancel certain programs and still be able to deliver the "bottom line." This tacit acceptance, in turn, enabled senior executives to feel more confident about meeting their more macro targets.

There was much more concern expressed, however, about knowing the actual size of the product managers cushions. In fact, this was a traditional area of debate and negotiation among the various levels as senior managers tried to pinpoint just how much flexibility existed one level down. Top management's rationale in wanting to know was quite simple: "We've got to know so we can judge whether those guys down below have gone too wild—and in the process screwed up our inventory and capacity planning—or whether there is not enough slack built in." Given their profit responsibilities, however, it did not seem unusual that product managers were reluctant to disclose the scope of their game playing activities. After all, disclosure of the cushions could mean their reduction or removal.

The situation at Beta, Kappa, and Phi. The senior managers in these firms, however, were not so relaxed about allowing their product managers to build cushions into their plans. The attitude in these firms was that senior management should be the custodian of the company's cushions, not lower-level managers; that it was top management's job to balance the portfolio of products, not individual product managers and that it was senior management's prerogative to decide which—if any—product managers were to be excused for not meeting their profit targets. The view was frequently expressed that giving lower-level managers "tight numbers" enabled senior managers to "see what stuff [the product managers] were made of"; and that holding all cushions at the corporate level put pressure on product managers which produced higher creativity

EXHIBIT 3. EXPLICITNESS OF REWARD CRITERIA AND BUDGETING GAMESMANSHIP ACTIVITIES

	Reward Criteria	Budget Games	Return	Return
Company	Explicitness	(mean % of sales)	on sales (%)	on assets (%)
Alpha	Job Description	0. 3%	3.4%	8.8%
Beta	Bonus criteria	1.5	3.5	5.7
Delta	Merit criteria	1.2	8.2	12.2
Kappa	Perceived/implicit	1.9	5.1	7.2
Omega	Perceived/implicit	0.8	3.9	9.5
Phi	Perceived/implicit	2.1	2.4	7.0

EXHIBIT 4. SENIOR MANAGEMENT ATTITUDES, BUDGETING GAMESMANSHIP ACTIVITIES, AND PERFORMANCE

Company	Senior Management Attitudes	Budget Games (mean % of sales)	Return on sales (%)	Return on assets (%)
Alpha	Tolerate games	0.3%	3.4%	8.8%
Delta	Tolerate games	1.2	8.2	12.2
Omega	Tolerate games	0.8	3.9	9.5
Beta	Discourage games	1.5	3.5	5.7
Kappa	Discourage games	1.9	5.1	7.2
Phi	Discourage games	2.1	2.4	7.0

and energy than would otherwise be achievable. The role of product managers at these firms, in turn, was to present their best profit forecasts and then "work like hell" to achieve them since they knew (as in the case of Beta) or strongly suspected (as in the case of Kappa and Phi) that they were going to be held responsible for their product assignment's profit target.

Attitudes, Cushion Size, and Performance. Unfortunately, results did not match expectations in the cases of those firms where senior managers opposed product manager game playing. In fact, their opposition seemed to have the opposite effect as product managers at these firms appeared to be more determined than managers elsewhere to have cushions. As Exhibit 4 shows, Beta, Kappa, and Phi have much higher cushioning levels, on average, than firms where product manager game playing is not so actively discouraged (Alpha, Delta, and Omega).

Senior management attitude also seemed to be related to company performance in a number of ways. For example, Exhibit 4 shows that firms where senior managers tolerate the reasonable use of cushions by lower-level managers (Alpha, Delta, and Omega), out-perform the companies where game playing is discouraged—both in terms of profits as a percentage of sales and profits as a percentage of assets. It is also our impression that in the firms where senior managers were at odds with their subordinates on the use of cushions, there were both more morale problems and higher turnaround than in the companies where senior management and product managers were more of one mind on the issue.

FIRMS WITHOUT GAMES: THE CASES OF GAMMA AND SIGMA

In two of the firms examined (Gamma and Sigma), product managers were found not to use cushions in their budgets. There were a number of factors to explain this occurrence.

First, senior managers at these companies did not encourage product managers to pursue budgeting activities. But unlike their counterparts at Beta, Kappa, and Phi (who were prodded into disobeying their superiors because of the reward criteria), product managers at Gamma and Sigma were not formally or informally held responsible for their products' profit performance, nor did they perceive such responsibility. Instead, product managers in these firms stated that their performance evaluations tended to focus on three-areas: (1) personal development, (2) training of assistants, and (3) overall management of their products. Thus, there appeared to be no formal or informal signals prompting product managers to play games with their budgets. This does not mean, however, that the product managers at Gamma and Sigma did not strive to achieve their products' profit targets, because they did. The difference—as the product managers themselves explained—as that of being "profit conscious" as opposed to being "profit responsible":

"You have to ask yourself: Why is the product manager here? He is the person responsible for formulating and executing the objectives and strategies of the brands in his assignment. It's expected, then, that he's going to work toward—strive—to achieve the

financial targets in his plans. You don't have to tell him what his job is—he already knows. The key point is that the product

But profit consciousness without game playing also depended on one critical assumption. This product manager put it most succinctly:

"You have to believe that your boss isn't going to hurt you at performance evaluation time when you did everything humanly possible to hit your targets but still you missed them."

Thus it appeared that in the firms without budgeting gamesmanship, there was a good deal of trust between senior management and product managers. Senior managers trusted their subordinates to report honestly and to work ambitiously. Product managers, on the other hand, relied on their superiors to treat and judge them with fairness and understanding.

But how does this climate of trust maintain its balance? Why should product managers trust their bosses? Why shouldn't product managers in these firms try to put cushions into their plans and succeed? And why should they rely on their bosses not to betray them at performance evaluation time?

Essentially, the relationship of trust seemed to be sustained largely as a result of senior management effort. Senior managers at both Gamma and Sigma stated that they worked hard to maintain the climate of trust, that trust smoothed the relationship between superiors and subordinates; and that betraying the trust of lower-level managers had serious implications for both the prosperity of the firm and their own career paths. As one group product manager put it:

"The moment I betray my product manager, I've had it in this company. My bosses will be angry with me for being unfair. And my subordinates will never take my word at face value again. They'll start to play games with me and I'll have to try and catch them … and that sure can waste a lot of time!"

ATTITUDES, REWARD CRITERIA, AND PERFORMANCE

Throughout our study, the attitude of senior managers in conjunction with the product managers' reward criteria seemed to be related to both the scope of the games product managers played and the performance of the firm as a whole. Referring to Exhibit 5, the firms with the highest amount of game playing and the lowest performance were those firms in which the senior managers actively opposed budgeting games at lower levels and where the product managers felt that they had "profit responsibility" (at Beta, Kappa, and Phi). Lower

levels of budgeting gamesmanship and higher company performance, on the other hand, were associated with two different situations. In one situation (Gamma and Sigma), senior managers opposed budgeting games at lower levels but also took the steps necessary to ensure that product managers did not feel they had to play them for rewards. In the other situation (Alpha, Delta, and Omega), senior managers did not discourage game playing—they even tacitly encouraged it—but product managers were either formally or informally held responsible for their products' profits. It appears, therefore, that where budgeting games are concerned, as long as that attitudes of senior managers are consistent with the product managers' reward system, superior performance may result. And because game playing was found to occur in both high- and low-performing firms, it cannot be automatically, regarded as dysfunctional behavior among product managers.

SUMMARY AND CONCLUSIONS

The findings presented in this article attempt to shed light into the games that product managers play in the course of preparing their products' budgets. Our study has shown that product managers do indeed play games in their budgets, that the games are many and varied, that some games are preferred to others, and that the actual size of the budgeting games appears to be quite large on average. The study has also identified the factors that contribute to and facilitate the playing of budgeting games and those that frustrate and constrain their occurrence.

Four of the findings, however, deserve highlighting. First, the data suggest that formal and explicit performance evaluation criteria are no more likely to result in higher levels of budgeting gamesmanship than less formal and more implicit reward criteria. Second, the firm's reward system seems to have a greater influence over the behavior of product managers (insofar as budgeting games are concerned) than the verbal dictates of senior managers. In other words, lower-level managers will ignore the orders of superiors not to play budgeting games if they perceive that their performance evaluation will be based on whether they achieve their budget target. Third, the attitudes of senior managers in conjunction with the product managers' reward systems seem to be related to both the scope of the games that product managers play and the performance of the firm as a whole. Finally, the findings suggest that budgetary game playing by product managers does not necessarily constitute dysfunctional behavior as it is conventionally viewed in the management literature. Instead, budgeting games may simply be a form of tactical maneuver that product managers deploy to survive in what they consider to be a hostile environment.

EXHIBIT 5. SENIOR MANAGEMENT ATTITUDES, PRODUCT MANAGER SALES/PROFIT RESPONSIBILITY, BUDGETING GAMESMANSHIP, AND PERFORMANCE

Company	Senior Management Attitudes	Sales/profit Responsibility	Budget Games (mean % of sales)	Return on sales/assets (%)
Beta	Discourage games	Yes	1.5%	3.5/5.7%
Kappa	Discourage games	Yes	1.9	5.1/7.2
Phi	Discourage games	Yes	2.1	2.4/7.0
Gamma	Discourage games	No	0.0	9.5/44.3
Sigma	Discourage games	No	0.0	9.3/9.4
Alpha	Tolerate games	Yes	0.3	3.4/8.8
Delta	Tolerate games	Yes	1.2	8.2/12.2
Omega	Tolerate games	Yes	0.8	3.9/9.5

PERFORMANCE AND OPERATING STATISTICS FOR THE EIGHT RESEARCH FIRMS[a] (IN MILLIONS OF DOLLARS)

	Alpha	Beta	Gamma	Delta	Kappa	Omega	Phi	Sigma	Avg.
Sales	$110	$267	$94	$87	$201	$300	$1,900	$2,100	$632
Profit									
Percentage of sales	3.4%	3.5%	9.5%	8.2%	5.1%	3.9%	2.4%	9.3%	5.8%
Percentage of assets	8.8%	5.7%	44.3%	12.2%	7.2%	9.5%	7.0%	9.4%	8.9%
Total number of products	23	24	16	33	25	40	12	24	24.6
Number of "growth" products	9	9	8	11	10	22	4	8	10.1
Number of "harvest" products	14	15	8	22	15	18	8	16	14.5
Number of product managers/product assignments	5	9	4	9	7	9	10	4	7.1
Average product assignment size									
Number of products	4.6	2.7	4.0	3.7	3.6	4.4	1.2	6.0	3.5
Sales volume	$21.6	$15.9	$5.4	$5.1	$25.7	$30.0	$106.0	$375.0	$58.4
Product concentration	Food	Food	Health & Beauty Aids	Home & Beauty Aids	Food	Food	Beverages	Commodity Metals	

[a] Adapted from company data. Absolute numbers have been disguised. Key ratios, however, have been preserved.

RESEARCH METHODOLOGY

Budgeting Gamesmanship. This term is defined as the deliberate and premeditated manipulation of current year sales, cost, and profit forecasts by product managers to project an overly conservative image into their product budgets. To measure this variable, product managers in the study were simply asked whether they "played games" in their budgets. While most managers initially expressed reluctance to discuss such a sensitive matter, all eventually spoke candidly—on the understanding that individual identities would be kept strictly confidential.

Sample Selection and Size. The study was based on indepth interviews with product managers in eight large diversified firms. Firms engaged in diverse activities were selected to ensure a wide variety of situations and circumstances. Six of the firms (Alpha, Beta, Gamma, Delta, Kappa, and Omega) were wholly owned subsidiary divisions of major U.S.-based firms. The remaining two firms (Phi and Sigma) were single-division, stand-alone companies. A summary of key financial and operating performance statistics for the units is presented in the accompanying exhibit.

The unit of analysis was the individual product manager. The budgeting system in each firm was also mature.

Research Instrument. The following list of questions constituted the research instrument for the study on which this article is based:

- Do product-level managers play games with their budgets? If yes, why?
- How widespread are budgeting games among product managers?
- What exactly are the types and scope of budget games that product managers play?
- Are there preferred games?

- Is there a relationship between budgeting gamesmanship and different product strategies?
- What factors contribute to the detection of product managers' budget games by senior managers and what factors allow them to go undetected?
- How does the product managers' performance evaluation system influence budgetary game playing?
- Do senior managers encourage or discourage budget gamesmanship by their product managers?
- Do product manager budgeting games represent a form of dysfunctional behavior?

Data Collection. The point of entry into each company was the president or a divisional general manager. Data on the management of products were gathered by on-site interviews with product, product group, and corporate-level managers and by physical inspection of company documents (such as individual product plans). In total, 113 managers (including 41 of the firms' 57 product managers) were interviewed over a period of 151 hours.

Limitations. The research method restricted the sample size. The sample selection method (judgmental) and the sample size also limited the generalizability of the findings. The high response rate by company managers, however, gives the results high validity in spite of the small number of firms sampled. It should also be noted that the exploratory nature of this study precluded the testing of all possible variables.

ENDNOTES

The author wishes to express his appreciation to the Social Sciences and Humanities Research Council of Canada for funding this research study. The author is also indebted to Professors Robert Cooper, Peter Banting, Julie Desjardins, Wayne Taylor, and Frank Tyaack of McMaster University for their comments and suggestions on earlier versions of this article.

1. J. Bower, *Maintaining the Resource Allocation Process: A Study of Corporate Investment Planning*, Boston: Graduate School of Business, Harvard University, 1970; W. J. Bruns and D. T. DeCoster, *Accounting and Its Behavioral Implications*, New York: McGraw-Hill. 1969; A. Hopwood, *Accounting and Human Behavior*, Englewood Cliffs, NJ: Prentice-Hall, 1977; H. Koontz and C. O'Donnell, *Principles of Management: An Analysis of Managerial Functions*, New York: McGraw-Hill, 1964; P. Lorange and R. F. Vancil, *Strategic Planning Systems*, Englewood Cliffs, NJ: Prentice-Hall, 1977; G. A. Steiner, *Strategic Planning: What Every Manager Must Know*, New York: The Free Press, 1979; and G. A. Welsch, *Budgeting: Profit Planning and Control*, Englewood Cliffs, NJ: Prentice-Hall, 1976.

2. See W. J. Bruns and D. T. DeCoster. Endnote 1.

3. See W. J. Bruns and D. T. DeCoster, H. Koontz and C. O'Donnell, Steiner, and Welsch, Endnote 1.

4. See A. Hopwood. Endnote 1.

5. C. Argyris, *Impact of Budgets on People*, New York: Controllership Foundation, 1952; J. Cherrington and D. J. Cherrington. "Budget Games for Fun and Frustration," *Management Accounting*, January 1976, 28–32; F. Collins, "The Interaction of Budget Characteristics and Personality Variables with Budgetary Response Attitudes," *Accounting Review*, April 1978, 324–335; and H. Simon, H. Guetzkow, G. Kozmetsky, and C. Lyndall, *Centralization vs. Decentralization of the Controller's Department*, New York: Controllership Foundation, 1954.

6. See G. H. Hofstede's *The Games of Budget Control*, London: Tavistock Publications, 1968: Hopwood, Steiner, and Welsch, Endnote 1.

7. See C. Argyris. D. J. Cherrington et al., F. Collins, and H. Simon et al., Endnote 5: and P. Munter, F. Collins, and D. Finn, *Gameplay in Budgeting*, Oxford, OH: Planning Executives Institute, 1983.

8. S. Becker and D. Green, "Budgeting and Employee Behavior," *Journal of Business*, Vol. 35, October 1962, 392–402; W. J. Bruns and D. J. DeCoster, and A. Hopwood, Endnote 1; F. Collins, Endnote 5; D. Searfoss and R. Monczka, "Perceived Participation in the Budget Process," *Academy of Management Journal*, December 1973: and R. Sapp and R. Seiler. "Accounting for Performance: Stressful But Satisfying," *Management Accounting*, August 1980, 29–35.

9. P. Munter et al., Endnote 7.

10. A. Hopwood. "An Empirical Study of the Role of Accounting Data in Performance Evaluation," *Empirical Research in Accounting: Selected Studies*, 1972, supplement to the *Journal of Accounting Research*. Vol. 10, 156–182; R. Dew and K. Gee, *Management Control and Information*, New York: Macmillan, 1973.

11. P. Munter et al., Endnote 7.

12. D. E. Schendel and C. W. Hofer, *Strategic Management: A New View of Business Policy and Planning*. Boston: Little, Brown, 1979.

13. C. K. Bart, "Product Strategy and Formal Structure," *Strategic Management Journal*, 7, 1986, 293–312. J. Bower, Endnote 1.

14. *Current Advertising Practices: Opinions as to Future Trends*, New York: Association of National Advertisers, 1974.

15. T. J. Peters and R. H. Waterman, *In Search of Excellence: Lessons from America's Best Run Companies*, New York: Harper & Row, 1982.

Dr. Christopher K. Bart is a recognized expert in the areas of corporate strategic planning for turnaround situations, planning for performance, strategy implementation, and new venture management. He has a unique expertise in helping firms organize their internal structure better to achieve their goals. Dr Bart has been involved in examining the issues and problems associated with managing multibusiness firms in the consumer products industry. Currently, he is investigating the organizational practices that large, diversified firms use to manage and control product innovation.

Dr. Bart is an associate professor of business policy at the Faculty of Business, McMaster University, in Hamilton, Ontario, Canada. He has also recently been a Research Fellow at the newly created National Centre for Management Research and Development in London, Ontario, Canada. Professor Bart holds degrees in

business administration from York University (MBA, 1975) and the University of Western Ontario (Ph.D., 1982). A highly regarded lecturer, he has been named both "Outstanding Undergraduate Business Professor" and "MBA Professor of the Year," He has also received many academic awards and honors.

Among his other qualifications, Dr. Bart is a chartered accountant. He is a past director of the Planning Executives Institute and a member of numerous boards of directors and professional organizations.

QUESTION

10.2 What are some of the factors that constrain the budget games discussed by Christopher Bart? Explain.

10.3 Budgeting Made Easy

*by Steve Hornyak**

It's budget time!

In most companies, these three words strike fear in employees' hearts. Financial officers and management accountants brace themselves for reconciling ream of spreadsheets that may reveal wildly disparate data depending on order and configuration. Nonfinance employees in various divisions scurry to understand their role in the process and struggle to pull together the facts and figures they hope will appear attractive to management. And fast-approaching budget deadlines invariably will result in weeks of all-night numbers crunching if the process proves to be as bumpy as usual.

Managers in the modem mid- to large-sized company want to work a different way, and a number of additional factors are prompting a change in their philosophy regarding budgeting and planning. Many of these organizations are expanding rapidly, prompting managers to demand precise resource allocation to support growth plans. Operational managers are heavily involved in preparing the company's budget. A tight management plan is contingent upon a comprehensive and accurate budget. A company's officers want the budget completed on time and correct on the first round. And people in various departments want to know how their piece of the budget affects overall corporate

operations so they can do some "what if" scenarios and modeling.

Fortunately, new technology solutions are taking the toil, guesswork, and disparity out of the budgeting process. Enterprisewide budgeting and planning over the Internet ("e-budgeting") is a corporate service application that supports an organization's operations and efficiency. The "e" in e-budgeting refers to both "electronic" and "enterprisewide" and it represents a revolutionary new way for companies to plan for the future. Companies can implement a budgeting system that scales to the entire enterprise, and they can harness the power of the Internet from any location in the world to budget effectively. Some significant benefits e-budgeting offers an organization include:

- Reducing administrative costs and tasks.
- Increasing service levels to employees.
- Freeing the finance department to focus on strategy, not spreadsheets.

As financial managers and management accountants, you can help steer your company toward these new, Internet-based applications that can deliver immediate benefits, especially the streamlining of a previously

---

* From: S. Hornyak, "Budgeting Made Easy," *Management Accounting* (October 1998): 18–23. Reprinted with permission conveyed through Copyright Clearance Center, Inc.

cumbersome process. By discovering ways new e-budgeting technology can deliver business solutions, you can transform the budgeting and planning process from a chore of drudgery to a strategic luxury for your organization.

PITFALLS OF TRADITIONAL BUDGETING

First, let's look at the traditional budgeting process. Whether manual or performed via spreadsheets, in the past, the budgeting process has depended on the notion that everyone involved in the planning phase comes equipped with a baseline knowledge of accounting. This is rarely the case. Although few will admit it, many nonfinance participants in the budgeting process often don't know where to begin. They understand their jobs thoroughly—and how those functions fit into overall operations—but they have not been trained in any kind of budgeting procedures. And they have been told that all the tools anyone needs to develop a specific slice of a company's budget are a spreadsheet and a deadline. But a lack of guidance and knowledge of appropriate budgeting tools for nonfinance participants can hinder them when they try to develop a meaningful contribution to their company's master plan.

Another stumbling block results when different departments use a variety of spreadsheet or software program to pull together their part of the budget information. The finance department has to compile all the spreadsheets—that usually are not interpretable—and management accountants must weed through the resultant paperwork that has been generated in these disparate systems. It's an intensive, unnecessary extra step that begins to slow down the process.

The budgeting process also is prolonged because the finance department must account for any time lag in this input from remote-user participants. Management accountants and financial managers watch deadlines disappear while they wait for copies of spreadsheets via e-mail and "snail mail." Gridlock results. Waiting on the "latest and greatest" version of a manager's budget component and then trying to reconcile disparate numbers with others in the system can be a financial manager's worst nightmare. Never mind that numbers may have to be rekeyed every time a change is made because the data in different systems don't affect each other.

The biggest drawback of traditional budgeting systems is the inability of participating individuals to access and use historical data during the budgeting and planning process. In fact, employees or managers attempting to allocate their sliver of the company funds often work in a vacuum. Without access to historical budgeting information, creating a budget from the ground up or making alterations to the existing budget may become tedious—and sometimes futile—tasks for nonfinance users.

HOW E-BUDGETING WORKS

Although a company can use e-budgeting programs as stand-alone applications, they are most effective when integrated with financial systems, particularly with a general ledger application, so budgeters can "close the loop." Participants in the budgeting process can link back to past data, validate assumptions implicit in their budget area, and, at some levels, see how their numbers will affect others.

An e-budgeting solution completely automates the development of an organization's budget and forecast. From anywhere in the world, at all times, participants in the process can log on through the Internet to access their budget and any pertinent related information so they can work on their plans. Web-based enterprise budgeting systems offer a centrally administered system that provides easy-to-use, flexible tools for the end users who are responsible for budgeting. The Web functionality of these applications allows constant monitoring, updates, and modeling.

Pushing the initial phase of the budget process from the back office to corporate managers and front-fine employees frees up the finance department to focus on more strategic issues such as "what if" modeling, sales, and fiscal objectives. In fact, corporate service applications such as e-budgeting bolster employee productivity by reducing administrative tasks and supporting the day-to-day operation of an organization.

Although Web-based enterprisewide budgeting and planning solutions facilitate participation by a wide range of users, they rely on the finance department to maintain ultimate control. It's the management accountants and financial managers who will monitor the process continually from inception to the final working budget.

E-budgeting provides the flexibility demanded by modem organizations. For example, the finance department can request across-the-board reallocations of expenditures and model the result immediately. No longer do financial managers and management accountants have to go back and forth with other managers, reinputing data and retallying results. E-budgeting can eliminate the cumbersome accounting tasks of pulling numbers from disparate files, cutting and pasting, entering and uploading, and constantly performing reconciliation. Financial managers don't want to scroll through hundreds of spreadsheets; they simply want to see if the company is making money, how much it's making, and if actual income and expenditures are on track with budget projections. Web-based solutions bring everyone to "the same page" and free up the finance department for strategic decision making rather than paper pushing.

Also, a Web-based budgeting application lets managers access data from the office, home, or even the airport—wherever they happen to be working. It broadens the system's availability to the user community.

With Web deployment and distributed capabilities, new systems are accessible to users regardless of the technology at their workstations.

For maximum control, e-budgeting incorporates an automated "check-out/cheek-in" process that provides flexibility for highly distributed users (those famous road warriors) while maintaining strict security to sensitive information. All activity is logged and recorded to provide a complete audit trail, which allows the finance department to maintain ultimate control.

Because many employees outside finance may have little finance and budgeting experience, e-budgeting applications take into consideration the needs of various users and the types of budgets for which they are responsible. For example, a customer service manager needs to be able to do workforce planning. He needs the application to help him conduct detailed planning by individual employee, not just at the salary account level. He needs to be able to decide when each person on his team will get a salary increase and what that increase percentage will be. In addition to tabulating bonuses and overtime, an e-budgeting system will automatically calculate all related benefits percentages for his department behind the scenes.

Similarly, an IT director who makes important capital planning decisions for the company needs an easy tool that allows her to plan for new networks, new servers, and new PCs. With an e-budgeting system, she can easily ascertain which periods of the year capital additions will be needed and can plan for capital acquisitions by major category or even down to specific models of PCs. Also, e-budgeting automatically calculates the related depreciation expense associated with each type of capital item. It's just one more piece of the overall plan that is required to derive a realistic budget from which to manage. In all cases, companies can use an e-budgeting system to help build these diverse types of budgets—capital, expense, human resources, and revenue—with ease and flexibility.

E-budgeting solutions also facilitate flexible planning with their "what-if" modeling capabilities. For example, a controller could propose, "What would happen if we increase revenue by 10% or cut R & D by 2%?" The application would model the result. E-budgeting technologies also are capable of supporting mass updates and changes through top-down and bottom-up revisions, so individuals can quickly forecast a wide array of budgetary possibilities before deriving an accurate final projection.

BUDGETING FOR "OUR CORNER OF THE WORLD"

The intuitive interface of Web-based budgeting solutions recognizes that most users are nonaccountants who may prepare a budget only once a year. These users may not know how to develop a plan, or they may be proficient with planning but may not want to know the intricacies of how a budget system works. Take, for instance, a CIO (chief information officer) who is responsible for a considerable amount of a company's budget. He or she has control over investments in technology and is therefore accountable for the technology budget. The CIO does not necessarily want to be accounting savvy, but because this executive's department will be spending money from the annual budget, he or she is in charge of developing a budget forecast.

Now the CIO can use an intuitive e-budgeting application to submit his/her segment of the total corporate budget and save the aggravation of performing manual input. Members of the MIS department also can submit subsets of their collective budget through a standardized system. Other individuals, who are experts in their areas of the company's operations but who may not have an accounting background, can participate strategically whether they are in charge of workstation upgrades, new software, or the online services budget.

As you can see, an intuitive e-budgeting solution, which is based on artificial intelligence and business rules programmed into the software, integrates all the individual "pieces" into a well-developed composite of the corporate budget. Quite simply, it gives budgeters the necessary tools to plan accurately and efficiently and the finance department the mechanism to integrate all components into a streamlined "big picture" of how the company is expected to spend its money.

BENEFITS OF E-BUDGETING

Chief among the benefits of Web-based enterprisewide budgeting and planning are a dramatic reduction of administrative resources devoted to tasks and transactions, an overall increase in employee participation, and a significantly more strategic focus for the finance department. New e-budgeting solutions reduce the number of administrative tasks and the associated time and cost necessary to carry out the budgeting and planning process. By slashing the need for hundreds of spreadsheets and by eliminating the monotonous task of reconciliation, the e-budgeting process uses a variety of creative techniques to cut down the paperwork trail and save time for the finance department and other budget participants. Administrative costs and tasks are curtailed because fewer handoffs are required. E-budgeting provides check-out/check-in management and top-down/bottom-up revisions, so budgeters can fill out, print out, and exchange fewer reports. Everything is online. E-budgeting also offers analysis and reporting capabilities with the ability to drill down to details. This process provides automated consolidations and a clean audit trail.

E-budgeting also extends the budgeting process to a wider range of users. Corporate managers and employees with budget responsibility gain easy access and an intuitive interface via the Internet. For example, an employee can "check out" the budget on a laptop (like you check out books with your library card) and work on it while traveling on a plane. When finished with the changes, he or she can log back into the application via the Web and upload the changes to the application database. The new figures the employee inputs into the budget will immediately affect and be affected by other budget components when the employee "checks in" (returns) the information via the Internet. Web access with distributed/disconnected capabilities is a key enabler for this flexibility.

Now more than ever, companies are following strict budgets, and managers are being held accountable for their budget plans. Many companies actually base compensation plans on budgeting. Organizations often award merit pay increases or base promotions on a manager's ability to develop, implement, and meet budgets. E-budgeting systems provide these managers with the right tools to budget accurately and effectively.

All budgeting participants benefit from a user-definable interface that is customized to an employee's skill sets. E-budgeting systems also provide the historical data necessary for current budgeters in any department to make crucial decisions and allocations based on past forecasts and trends.

New e-budgeting solutions provide the tools for a variety of employees to help build different types of budgets, whether they are expense, capital, or payroll/HR. A corporate human resources executive planning a budget can take a close look at "the people costs" for each individual in the company, not just from the perspective of salary, but also taking into account other line item information such as forecasted bonuses and raises.

Most important, e-budgeting allows an organization's finance department to focus on more strategic activities instead of managing spreadsheet consolidations. They can shift their attention to business analysis and more proactive efforts to monitor critical issues in a company's growth cycle. For example, they can research how expanding a particular service in a geographic region would affect the revenue forecast and the associated expenses that would offset that effect. Or they can easily do top-down adjustments and take a look at the bottom line if expenses are reduced for each department by 5% or 10%. This "what-if?" modeling will help budgeters ascertain the impact of changes to the budget and make informed decisions about the status of the budget.

A STRATEGIC SOLUTION FOR THE ENTERPRISE

Organizations put a huge amount of time and energy into budgeting, but the process often is so labor intensive that the finance department gets bogged down in data consolidation and verification rather than planning and analysis. The major value of new e-budgeting solutions is that they turn budgeting into a management tool instead of an accounting chore. These powerful applications dramatically change how an organization's employees develop strategic budgets and plans.

E-budgeting solutions streamline and transform the strategic budgeting process for nonfinancial users. The applications empower front-line employees and corporate managers to participate in areas in which they have expertise and allow the finance department to perform its vital role of fusing information into strategic goals and objectives. New e-budgeting solutions can eliminate literally hundreds of spreadsheets and staff-hours from the budget process.

Budgeting should never be a full-time job, but many companies are moving toward "continuous budgeting" and away from an annual or quarterly plan. That means someone will be accessing budget data almost every day in some shape or form, especially when the potential for new business or products arises. A Web-based solution for the entire enterprise will let executives produce a more accurate and strategically sound budget than ever before.

CANADIAN COMPANY ADOPTS WEB-BASED BUDGETING PROGRAM

Last year Toronto Dominion Bank decided to use the World Wide Web to advance its business objectives. Since then more than 200,000 bank customers have used TD Access Web and PC Banking in Canada. In addition, the company launched TD Access Web Business, a comprehensive, secure, and easy-to-use Internet banking service for its Main Street Banking small business customers, and it introduced TD Access WebFunds, an Internet-based mutual fund trading service.

When executives at Toronto-Dominion Bank were searching for a new solution capable of handling the bank's enterprisewide budgeting and planning function, they once again turned to the Internet. The company selected Clarus Corporation's Web-deployed, enterprisewide Clarus™ Budget solution.

"In the past, we have compiled our business plan using hundreds of spreadsheets, and our analysts have spent a disproportionate amount of their time compiling and verifying data from multiple sources," said David Bickley, associate vice president and controller of Toronto-Dominion Bank's Corporate & Investment Banking Group. "Implementing a Web-based, enterprisewide budgeting solution will help us develop business plans and allow our analysts to be proactive in monitoring quarterly results."

Clarus Budget combines operating, capital, and personnel budgeting in one distributed application. Through reducing paperwork and pencil pushing associated with administrative tasks, providing intuitive tools to participants in the budget process, and enabling its finance department to focus squarely on strategy, Claris Budget is expected to provide a significant business payback for Toronto-Dominion Bank.

Steve Hornyak is vice president, marketing, for Clarus Corp. (formerly SQL Financials International, Inc.). He joined the company in 1994. Prior to joining Clarus Corp., he worked for Oracle Corporation and for Price Waterhouse LLP (now PricewaterhouseCoopers) in its Management Consulting Services Group. He can be reached at 770-291-3900 or via e-mail at hornyak@ claruscorp.com.

QUESTIONS

10.3a What are four of the pitfalls of traditional budgeting according to Steve Hornyak?

10.3b What are the major benefits that Hornyak envisions for e-budgeting?

10.4 Corporate Budgeting is Broken—Let's Fix It

Traditional budgeting processes waste time, distort decisions, and turn honest managers into schemers. It doesn't have to be that way—if you're willing to sever the ties between budgets and compensation.

by Michael C. Jensen*

Corporate budgeting is a joke, and everyone knows it. It consumes a huge amount of executives' time, forcing them into endless rounds of dull meetings and tense negotiations. It encourages managers to lie and cheat, lowballing targets and inflating results, and it penalizes them for telling the truth. It turns business decisions into elaborate exercises in gaming. It sets colleague against colleague, creating distrust and ill will. And it distorts incentives, motivating people to act in ways that run counter to the best interests of their companies.

Consider just two examples. At one international heavy-equipment manufacturer, managers were so set on hitting their quarterly revenue target that they shipped unfinished products from their plant in England all the way to a warehouse in the Netherlands, near the customer, for final assembly. By shipping the incomplete products, they were able to realize the sales before the end of the quarter and thus fulfill their budget goal and make their bonuses. But the high cost of assembling the goods at a distant location—it required not only the rental of the warehouse but also additional labor—ended up reducing the company's overall profit.

Then there's the recent debacle involving a big beverage company. The vice president of sales for one of the company's largest regions dramatically, underpredicted demand for an upcoming major holiday. His motivation was simple—he wanted to ensure a low revenue target that he could be certain of exceeding. But the price for his little white lie was extremely high: The company based its demand planning on his sales forecast and consequently ran out of its core product in one of its largest markets at the height of the holiday selling season.

Such cases of distorted decision making are legion in business. No doubt, you could list similar instances that you've observed—or perhaps even instigated—at your own company The sad thing is, these shenanigans have become so common that they're almost invisible. The budgeting process is so deeply embedded in corporate life that the attendant lies and games are simply accepted as business as usual, no matter how destructive they are.

But it doesn't have to be that way. Even if you grant that budgeting, like death and taxes, will always be with us, deceitful behavior doesn't have to be. That's because the budget process itself isn't the root cause of the counterproductive actions; rather, it's the use of budget targets to determine compensation. When managers are told they'll get bonuses if they reach specific performance goals, two things inevitably happen. First, they attempt to set low targets that are easily achievable. Then, once the targets are in place, they do whatever it takes to see that they hit them, even if the company suffers as a result.

Only by severing the link between budgets and bonuses—by rewarding people purely for their

---

accomplishments, not for their ability to hit targets—will we take away the incentive to cheat. Only then will we eliminate the budgeting incentives that drive individuals to act in ways that destroy corporate value.

CHEATERS PROSPER

Let's look more carefully at how budgets drive compensation and, in turn, behavior. In a traditional pay-for-performance incentive system, a manager's total cash compensation (salary plus bonus) is constant until a minimum performance hurdle is reached—commonly 80% of a budgeted target. (The target might be expressed as profits, sales, output, or any number of things; for our purposes, it doesn't matter what's being measured.) When the manager exceeds that hurdle, she receives a bonus—often a substantial one. The bonus then increases as performance mounts above the hurdle until the bonus is capped at some maximum level—120% of the target is usual. This system is illustrated in Exhibit 1 "A Typical Executive Compensation Plan."

The kinks in the pay-for-performance line—caused by the minimum hurdle bonus and the maximum cap—create strong incentives to game the system. As long as the manager believes she can make the minimum hurdle, she will naturally try her best to increase performance—by legitimate means or, if push comes to shove, by illegitimate ones. If the measure is profits, for instance, she will have a strong incentive to increase the current year's earnings at the expense of next year's, either by pushing expenses into the future (delaying purchases or hires, for example) or by moving future revenues to the present (booking orders early or offering special discounts to customers, for example).

If, on the other hand, the manager concludes that she can't make the minimum hurdle, her incentives flip 180 degrees. Now her goal is to move earnings from the present to the future. After all, her compensation doesn't change whether she misses the target by a little or a lot; she still gets her full salary (assuming she doesn't get fired, of course). But by shifting profits forward—by prepaying expenses, taking write-offs, or delaying the realization of revenues—she increases her chances of getting a large bonus the following year. This is a variation on the "big bath" theory of corporate financial reporting: If you're going to take a loss, take as big a loss as possible.

Finally, if the manager is having a great year and her performance is nearing the budget cap, she again has an incentive to push profits into the future. Because she's not going to get any additional compensation if performance exceeds the level at which the cap is set, accelerating expenses or postponing sales will have no negative impact on her current earnings, but it will raise the odds that she'll reap a high bonus next year as well. This perverse incentive becomes even stronger if her current year's performance is used in setting the following year's targets, as is often the case.

When these kinds of subterfuge simply move profits from one year to another—by changing accruals, for example—the adverse impact on company value is probably small. But rarely is the activity so benign. Usually, the shuffling of dollars results from decisions that change the operating characteristics of a company, and it generates high, if sometimes hidden, costs that erode the total value of the company. We saw such erosion in the two examples presented earlier. We see it as well in the common practice of channel stuffing—when managers ship loads of products to distributors to

EXHIBIT 1. A TYPICAL EXECUTIVE COMPENSATION PLAN

In a traditional pay-for-performance compensation plan, a manager earns a hurdle bonus when performance reaches a certain level (A). The bonus increases with performance until it hits a maximum cap (B). The kinks in the pay-for-performance line create incentives to game the system. When performance approaches the hurdle target, a manager has a strong incentive to accelerate the realization of revenue and profit. When performance hits the cap, the manager has a strong incentive to push revenue and profit into the next year.

meet immediate sales goals, even though they know many of the goods will soon come back as returns. And we see it in distorted pricing decisions. The managers of one durable-goods manufacturer, struggling to meet their minimum bonus hurdles, announced late one year that they would be raising prices 10% across the board on January 2. The managers made the price hikes because they wanted to encourage customers to place orders by year-end so they could hit their annual sales goals. But the price increase was out of line with the competition and undoubtedly ended up costing the company sales and market share.

Even more insidious effects are common. One of the main reasons that big companies have budgets in the first place is to help coordinate the disparate parts of their businesses. By openly sharing accurate information and basing decisions on a common set of numbers, the thinking goes, you ensure harmonious interactions among units, leading to efficient processes, high-quality products, low inventories, and satisfied customers. But as soon as you start motivating unit and department heads to falsify forecasts and otherwise hide or manipulate critical information, you undermine the salutary effects of budgeting. Indeed, the whole effort backfires. You end up with uncoordinated, chaotic interactions as people make decisions on the basis of distorted information they receive from other units and from headquarters. Moreover, since managers are well aware that everyone is attempting to game the system for personal reasons, you create an organization rife with cynicism, suspicion, and mistrust.

When the manipulation of budget targets becomes routine, moreover, it can undermine the integrity of an entire organization. Once managers see that it's okay to lie and conceal information to enrich themselves or simply to hold on to their jobs, they soon begin to extend their dishonest behavior to all parts of the company's management system and even to its relationships with outside parties. Managers start to feed misleading information to customers, suppliers, and employees, and the CEO and CFO begin to "manage the numbers" to influence the perceptions of board members and Wall Street analysts. Even boards of directors are drawn into the fray, as they end up endorsing deceptive reports to shareholders. Sometimes, outright fraud ensues, as we've seen recently in high-profile cases involving companies such as Informix, Sabratek, and Lernout & Hauspie.

The damage can go well beyond the walls of individual companies. Think about what happens, for example, during a boom. As financial analysts and investors raise expectations for growth beyond the capability of companies, many managers begin to borrow from the future to satisfy the present demands. This results in an overstatement of earnings and cash flows for many companies and an exaggeration of the extent of the good times. Conversely, during the early stages of an economic slowdown, as demand falls below predicted levels and inventories build up, managers often find themselves falling short of their bonus targets. When they and their companies all react in the same, predictable way—taking big baths by maximizing the bad news—the cumulative effect is to exaggerate the economic weakness, perhaps deepening or extending the recession. Macroeconomic statistics and even public policy are likely distorted in the process.[1]

GETTING THE KINKS OUT

The only way to solve the problem is to remove all the kinks from the pay-for-performance line—to adopt a purely linear bonus schedule, as shown in Exhibit 2 "A Linear Compensation Plan." Managers are still rewarded for good performance, but the rewards are independent of budget targets: The bonus a manager received for a given level of performance remains the same whether the budget goal is set at Target 1 (below actual performance) or at Target 2 (above actual performance). The linear bonus schedule, in other words, rewards people for what they actually do, not for what they do relative to what they say they can do.

That removes the incentives to game the system. Because unit managers no longer get a pile of cash for exceeding a target, they have no motivation to feed falsified information into the budgeting process in order to lowball their goals. As a result, senior management receives unbiased estimates of what can be accomplished in the future, and the quality of planning and coordination improves considerably. At the other end of the process, managers are no longer rewarded for moving revenues and expenses around when the end of a budget period approaches. Because their bonuses are always determined by their actual performance, an extra dollar of revenue or profit (or whatever measure is used) will generate the same bonus this year as it will next year. Not only will this remove the costs of gaming, it will also free managers from all the time they traditionally had to devote to it. They can dedicate that time to their real jobs: maximizing the performance and value of their businesses.

Two additional points should be made here. First, nonmonetary rewards also have to be independent of budget targets. Handing out promotions or public accolades based on the ability to hit budget numbers, for example, will provide a continued incentive for gaming. That practice has to stop. All rewards must be based purely on actual performance.[2] Second, since pay will still go up as performance improves, dishonest managers may continue to lie about their numbers in order to increase their bonuses. That, of course, is a risk that companies have always had to watch out for. A linear bonus schedule does not reduce the need for good control systems and attentive executives.

Removing the kinks from the compensation system allows the budgeting process to do what it's intended to

EXHIBIT 2. A LINEAR COMPENSATION PLAN

The solution to the budget gaming problem: Adopt a purely linear pay-for-performance system that rewards actual performance, independent of budget targets. A manager receives the same bonus for a given level of performance whether the budget goal happens to be set beneath that level (Budget Target 1) or above it (Budget Target 2). Removing the kinks eliminates the incentives for managers to game the process.

do: provide the basis for good business decisions and enable the effective coordination of disparate units. But many managers will reflexively object to this proposal. Yes, they'll say, a linear bonus schedule will remove the incentive to game the system, but won't it also remove the motivational effects of performance targets? It's a legitimate question, and it's one that is difficult to answer with hard numbers. Empirical evidence shows that tying goals to rewards does enhance performance. A recent survey of more than 500 studies, for example, indicates that performance increases by an average of approximately 16% in companies that establish targets.[3] But even if we assume such findings are accurate, we don't know whether the performance increase is itself a result of gaming, as managers rush to overstate their results to meet the new targets.

Nor do we know definitively the long-term costs of gaming. No comprehensive study has been done, and such a study would be hard to carry out, given how pervasive and well-hidden these costs are. However, Donald Roy conducted a landmark study, published in the *American Journal of Sociology* in 1952, of an analogous situation: the use of piecework targets to determine the bonuses of factory workers. Based on his findings, Roy estimated that productivity in the factory he studied would increase by 33% to 150% if the targets were discontinued. Based on that research, as well as my own observations of the widespread, destructive effects of gaming, I conclude that the costs of budget-based bonuses far outweigh the benefits in most, if not all, situations.

Finally, it's important to note that setting extremely aggressive stretch goals, as is so common in business today, can itself have damaging repercussions. By establishing the expectation that managers will constantly push to exceed reasonable growth and profitability targets, senior executives can end up creating a dysfunctional organizational culture in which all the problems I've described are amplified. That's what happened recently at one prominent multinational corporation. A new CEO came in, and he suspected that unit heads were routinely lowballing their budget targets and then delivering mediocre results. He quickly reorganized the company to establish clearer accountability down the line, and then he launched an intensive campaign to get everyone to set stretch goals for the coming year, with their bonuses hanging in the balance. The effort blew up in the CEO's face.

The budget-setting process became a year-long exercise in internecine warfare. Knowing that their bonuses hinged on their ability to hit the new targets, line managers battled over the way the overall corporate stretch goals for revenues and profits should be allocated among the business units. Each, of course, tried to reduce his or her unit's target. Every time revised goals were circulated, new arguments broke out. And when the targets were eventually finalized, things got even worse. Within months, most unit heads realized they wouldn't be able to reach their stretch goals, and they let the year fall into the tank in a way that is consistent with pushing revenues and profits out to the future. They were clearly hoping that by taking a bath this year they would be given lower targets next year. Needless to say, the CEO's tenure was short.

MAKING THE SWITCH

It's not going to be easy for companies to adopt a linear compensation system. Target-based bonuses are deeply ingrained in the minds of managers and in the managerial codes of most organizations. Getting managers to give them up will be tough, and getting them to give up promotions or reputational rewards for "beating budget" will be even tougher. Most difficult of all, though, will be getting them to break free of the cynicism that surrounds the entire budgeting and bonus-paying system. But the benefits are so great—in terms of a company's long-run economic and organizational health—that the journey will be well worth the time and effort. And there are some guidelines that can help the transition proceed more smoothly.

Get the details right. The design of compensation programs lies outside the scope of this article. But it is important to emphasize that the success of a linear bonus program, like that of any pay system, hinges on its details. There are three key considerations: the performance measures used, the positioning and slope of the bonus line, and the establishment of minimum and maximum compensation levels.

In establishing performance measures, executives run the risk of distorting managerial decisions, even under a linear bonus system. One example is the use of multiple measures of performance. This practice can motivate managers to think more broadly and carefully about the operating and economic drivers of business success. But it also adds complexity to the system in a way that can impede decision making. Suppose, for example, a manager is told to increase both profits and market share in the coming year. If, after some point, market share can be increased only by cutting prices, and thus profits, the manager no longer has a basis for making reasoned decisions. The conflicting goals eliminate his ability to act purposefully. When using multiple performance measures for individual managers, companies should be careful to establish a single, clearly defined measure of overall business success, such as economic value added. That will give managers a basis for making trade-offs among performance measures when they come into conflict.[4]

A second example is the use of ratios as performance measures. Here I can be blunt: Don't do it. Using ratios, such as sales margin or return on assets, inevitably produces gaming. That's because managers can increase the measure in two ways: by increasing the numerator or decreasing the denominator. If, for example, a company tracks performance according to margin as a percentage of sales, managers can increase their pay by simply cutting back sales (selling only the highest margin products) instead of working to increase the margins on all products. The result: Total dollars of profit fall, and company value erodes.

The positioning and slope of the bonus line work in tandem to determine the amount of money a manager received for a given level of performance. Moving the line to the right on the performance scale, for instance, makes it harder to get an additional dollar of bonus, while providing a steeper slope makes it easier to get that dollar. In setting the line, executives have a tendency to focus on the short term. In particular, they often position the line based on the prior year's performance. That reduces the risk that managers will be overcompensated for overly conservative projections of performance (a high bonus in one year makes it harder to get a high bonus the next year), but it also reduces incentives for increasing performance. Because managers know that an increase in performance this year will result in higher targets for succeeding years, the motivation to make the extra effort is dampened—unless the current year's bonus is extraordinarily large. A better way is to look further into the future, setting bonus lines for a number of years out based on longer-term projections for growth and profitability. This is harder to do, but it reduces the potential for manipulation.

In general, it is extremely important that companies model the economic impacts of different positionings and slopes for their bonus lines. As in any compensation system, the right balance must be struck between the rewards delivered to employees for incentive purposes and the capital retained for reinvestment or for distribution to investors or other owners.

Finally, there's the issue of limits on compensation. Ideally, you wouldn't have any—all pay would be directly related to actual performance. But there are strong pressures to limit both the upside and the downside for employees and managers. Most companies have to pay salaries in order to attract and retain employees (thus defining the lower bound of compensation), and most feel compelled to set some upper limit to bonuses. What's important is to try to set the upper and lower limits outside the range of likely outcomes to minimize their potential for setting off gaming. In many cases, this will require companies to raise bonus caps well above traditional levels, which is sure to create organizational discomfort. For example, a manager will inevitably end up paying certain high-performing subordinates more than he himself makes. Also, some managers may complain that certain people are being paid inordinately large amounts just because they happened to get lucky. (Of course, luck is extremely hard to distinguish from talent, and much of the griping will simply be a sign of jealousy.) Managing such conflicts—by clearly articulating the philosophy underlying the pay plan, for example—is one of the difficult but necessary challenges in moving to a more rational compensation scheme.

Don't backtrack. Even after managers become intellectually convinced that a linear bonus schedule is desirable, they may still argue for a compromise plan that again allows budget targets to influence compensation. In a number of companies I have worked with, executives have, for instance, proposed replacing the new linear schedule with a curvilinear one. By making the pay-for-performance line curve upward more steeply after the budget goal is reached (and less steeply before it is reached), bonuses begin to increase more rapidly for every incremental improvement in performance beyond the target. That may appear to fulfill the psychological need of many managers to "get something more" after surpassing a goal, without putting any obvious kinks back into the system. But, in fact, curvilinear schedules reintroduce a strong incentive for gaming.

To see why, look at Exhibit 3 "The Impact of a Curvilinear Compensation Plan." In the example portrayed here, a manager whose profit performance in two succeeding years exactly matched the budget goal would receive a bonus of $12,000 in each year, for a total of $24,000. But if she could manipulate that same amount of profit so that she hit 80% of the goal in one year and 120% in the next, she would receive $10,000 in one year and $20,000 in the other, for a total of $30,000. The curvilinear plan, in other words, has given her a strong monetary incentive to start fudging the numbers again, and, in this case, she would be rewarded for increasing the variability of performance. What's more, she would be willing to do this even if it lowered overall performance within some range. In contrast, under a truly linear scheme, the manager would receive the same total ($30,000) in both scenarios.

Last January, Chrysler Motors introduced a new dealer-incentive plan that was based on a curvilinear pay-for-performance scale. The plan paid dealers a monthly bonus ranging from zero (for those who achieved less than 75% of their sales targets) to $500 per car sold (for those who achieved more than 110% of the target). When car sales began to slow in April, many Chrysler dealers realized that they were unlikely to exceed the targets for the month and therefore they reduced inventories, shifting sales of cars from April to May, when they could be much more certain to earn the $500 per car bonus. In the end, Chrysler's CEO had to announce that company sales fell 18% in April as a result of its dealer bonus program, while overall industry sales were down only 10%.

Lead from the top. Given the complexity of designing a new pay system, as well as the controversy it inevitably sets off, CEOs will feel a natural desire to hand off responsibility for the effort to the human resources department. That would be a mistake, probably a fatal one. HR has neither the standing nor the influence to make a fundamental business change that will have a profound impact on the decisions of line managers. And that's exactly the kind of change that I'm talking about: All members in the organization will have to shift their thinking about the role and use of both budgets and incentives. Performance measures will have to be changed, and bonus levels will have to be recalculated. Since these issues are as sensitive as any within a company, strong leadership is essential. Only the CEO has the credibility to make the business case for the changes and to rally the troops behind them.

The CEO should recognize that the new plan will meet with intense resistance, even at the highest reaches of the organization. Some of the strongest objections, I have found, tend to come from CFOs and their teams. Finance executives naturally fear that reducing the importance of budget targets in motivating line managers will make it more difficult to control results and avoid surprises. It will be the CEO's responsibility to make sure the CFO, not to mention Wall Street analysts, understands that the new approach will improve the quality of both the information provided and the

EXHIBIT 3. THE IMPACT OF A CURVILINEAR COMPENSATION PLAN

Curvilinear pay-for-performance plans are no cure for gaming. They encourage managers to increase the variability of year-to-year performance measures. In this example, a manager makes more by achieving 80% of a budget target one year and 120% the next than by hitting the target both years. Under the linear plan, by contrast, the manager would earn the same in both scenarios.

incentives paid to managers. And better information and better incentives will lead to better results. Yes, there may be greater uncertainty in quarter-to-quarter results—as there will no longer be any motivation to set artificially low targets and then do everything possible to meet them—but the long-run profits will be superior.

Finally, every line manager will have to understand the new system and the theory behind it and be prepared to explain it and defend it against opposition and opportunism from the ranks. There are no shortcuts through the education process. Organizations don't change overnight, particularly when the very frame through which we see the business is involved. Remember, it has taken many years to weave lying and deceit into the fabric of our business; cleansing the fabric will take time as well.

ENDNOTES

1. See M. C. Jensen, "Paying People to Lie: The Truth About the Budgeting Process," working paper (Harvard Business School, April 2001). Available on-line at http://ssrn.com/paper=267651.
2. To read more on how goals can distort behavior, even in the absence of ties to tangible rewards, see M. Schweitzer, L. Ordonez, and B. Douma, "The Dark Side of Goal Setting: The Role of Goals in Motivating Unethical Behavior," working paper (Wharton School, University of Pennsylvania, 2001).
3. See Edwin A. Locke, "Motivation by Goal Setting," in Handbook of Organizational Behavior, ed. Robert T. Golembiewski (Marcel Dekker, 2001). Also see Edwin A. Locke and Gary P. Latham, A Theory of Goal Setting and Task Performance (Prentice Hall, 1990).
4. See Michael C. Jensen, "Value Maximization, Stake-holder Theory, and the Corporate Objective Function," Business Ethics Quarterly, January 2001. Available on-line at http://ssrn.com/paper=220671.

The author thanks Joseph Fuller, Michael Gibbs, Jennifer Lacks-Kaplan, and Edwin Locke for their contributions to this article.

To further explore the topic of this article, go to www.hbr.org/explore.

Michael C. Jensen, the Jesse Isidor Straus Professor of Business Administration, Emeritus, at Harvard Business School in Boston, is the managing director of the organizational strategy practice of the Monitor Group, a collection of global professional services firms with headquarters in Cambridge, MA.

QUESTION

10.4 Discuss the typical executive compensation plan, the linear compensation plan, and the curvilinear compensation plan. According to the author, which of these plans *solves* the budget gaming problem?

10.5 Beyond Budgeting

The traditional performance management model is too rigid to reflect today's fast-moving economy. Two new approaches—devolution and strategic performance management—have risen in popularity, but they are equally frustrated by unyielding budgeting systems.

by Jeremy Hope and Robin Fraser*

In an age of discontinuous change, unpredictable competition, and fickle customers, few companies can plan ahead with any confidence—yet most organizations remain locked into a "plan-make-and-sell" business model that involves a protracted annual budgeting process based on negotiated targets and resources and that assumes that customers will buy what the company decides to make. But such assumptions are no longer valid in age when customers can switch loyalties at the click of a mouse.

Organizations need to find a new model that effectively empowers front-line managers to make fast decisions based on current information. The "Beyond Budgeting" model represents a set of information-age

* From: J. Hope and R. Fraser, "Beyond Budgeting" *Strategic Finance* (October 2000): 30–35. Reprinted with permission conveyed through Copyright Clearance Center, Inc.

best practices—from organization design and devolution of authority to planning and performance management—that leading-edge companies are now using to respond much faster to customer demands. Understanding what these practices are and what you need to do to adopt them is increasingly likely to determine whether or not your company is able to compete effectively in the new economy.

Such companies as Svenska Handelsbanken (see Exhibit 1), Volvo Cars, IKEA, Borealis, Fokus Bank, and Boots have all abandoned the budgeting model in one form or another in recent years. And the momentum is gathering pace. Ericsson, Diageo, and British cider maker Bulmers are among the latest companies to see the light. Such is the current interest that in 1998 a Consortium for Advanced Manufacturing-International (CAM-I) research forum known as the Beyond Budgeting Round Table (BBRT) was established to understand and report on these developments.

After two years' research and numerous case visits, the BBRT has concluded that not only do firms need more effective strategic management, but they also need to redesign their organizations to devolve authority more effectively to the front line. Crucial to success, however, is the recognition that these two elements of the beyond budgeting model must be given equal attention.

ORGANIZATION DESIGN AND DEVOLUTION

Most attempts at redesigning organizations and devolving decisions making have focused on flattening hierarchies, reengineering processes, and introducing team working. Invariably, such approaches simply lead to the delegation of control within a strict regime of coordination and accountability, with budgets as the primary weapon for policing this control.

Delegation and coordination don't make comfortable bedfellows. A constant battle is being waged in most large organizations between the forces of decentralized initiative (usually the losers) and the forces of centralized coordination (invariably the winners). The difference is the centralizing power of the budgeting system that emphasizes coercion rather than coordination (you *will* cooperate, *won't you*?), focuses on cost reduction rather than value creation, stifles initiative, and keeps planning and execution apart, thus reinforcing the separation between thinkers and doers. Other symptoms of failure include cost allocations that are nonnegotiable and middle managers who remain "commanders and controllers."

In the information economy, it's not so much decentralization that's required but *autonomy within boundaries*. Autonomy is much more than decentralization and a few steps beyond empowerment. Autonomy is a Greek word meaning self-governance. It means the freedom to act *and* the capability to act. The key to autonomy isn't to try to empower cost centers (it doesn't work) but to give more responsibility and accountability to a greater number of business units for value creation. Effective devolution is tough, and it takes many years of painstaking effort to hold back the forces of centralization, but such efforts usually prove worthwhile as they lead to a self-renewing organization with strong values, dispersed responsibilities, and a

EXHIBIT 1. SVENSKA HANDELSBANKEN—A MODEL FOR THE NEW ECONOMY

Since 1972, annual contributions to the Handelsbanken groupwide profit-sharing fund have been based on the margin by which it beats the average return on capital of all its Nordic rivals, and, apart from 1973, it has always made significant contributions. **Yet inside the firm there is no annual budget or target-setting process.** The bank and its constituent parts are all continuously striving to improve their place in a series of performance league tables geared to key measures such as return on capital, cost-to-income ratio, and profit per employee. It is these league tables and their constituent measures, underpinned by intense peer pressure, that drive continuous improvement at local and regional levels. Beating the competition rather than some negotiated budget goes to the heart of the Handelsbanken model.

Branch managers run their own business with high levels of freedom and responsibility. This means deciding which products to offer individual customers (there are no centrally imposed targets), which central services to use (services and prices are negotiated), and how many staff are needed. This freedom to act is supported by the capability to act. For example, there is a fast and open information system geared to measuring customer acquisitions and defections, work productivity, and customer and branch profitability. Information is online and is seen by local, regional, and group managers at the same time, but it is *how they use it* that's important. **Managers are empowered to make decisions and to fix mistakes** (higher-level managers only interfere when absolutely necessary). The result is a very flat organization with a multitude of semi-autonomous work units (600 for the whole bank) with peer pressure (using performance league tables) driving performance improvement.

The benefits are evident everywhere you look. Employee turnover is extremely low, reflecting high levels of satisfaction (redundancies are unknown). Talented graduates want to join Handelsbanken more than any other financial services company in Sweden, not because it offers the highest salaries and benefits but because young managers are given exceptional levels of responsibility within a radically decentralized structure. It is perhaps because **branches "own" their customers** (no matter where transactions take place), make fast decisions, and provide flexible products and services that Handelsbanken has the lowest number of complaints in its sector and consistently tops the customer satisfaction charts in Sweden. Costs are also the lowest in the industry (half the level of the European average taken as a percentage of assets). One reason is that costs are constantly challenged (rather than protected by the budgeting system); another is that bad debts are exceptionally low, largely due to the company's policy of devolving credit responsibility to front-line people who know the customer.

performance culture that no longer depends on one or two inspirational leaders at the top. Its features include:

- *Governing through shared values and clear boundaries*, enabling local managers to make fast decisions knowing that they are within agreed parameters.
- *Creating as many autonomous profit centers as possible*, providing enterprising people with the opportunity to "run their own business."
- *Coordinating the organization through market forces*, thus, for example, creating an "internal market" in which central services units see operating units as internal customers that must be serviced and satisfied.
- *Providing front-line managers with fast and open information networks* that convey up-to-the-minute knowledge about critical issues. Because everyone receives important information at the same time, controls are distributed (making them stronger) and bad news is shared immediately.
- *Giving managers the freedom to act and the responsibility to deliver results*, placing the onus of responsibility on front-line people to perform.
- *Giving managers the training and tools to think and act decisively*, providing managers with the capability to make fast decisions at the point of contact with the customer.

PERFORMANCE MANAGEMENT

In the latter decades of the twentieth century the role of budgets mutated from a set of coordinated financial plans to a wide-ranging management system for controlling the business, driving management behavior, and rewarding performance. As Figure 1 illustrates, the underlying thread was one of *control*. The vision of the chief executive was translated into the strategic plan by the planners and handed down the hierarchy to operational managers who prepared their budgets. Once these were agreed, all that was demanded was adherence to the plan. The head office didn't like surprises. Control reports were constantly fed back up the line, and if they showed that performance was veering off track, new directives would be issued from the head office. It isn't hard to see why the budgeting system became essential to success. It was the core management process and provided much needed stability and continuity in an increasingly competitive business world.

But despite attempts to fine-tune this model by introducing zero-base or faster (for example, quarterly) budgeting (neither of which takes the firm toward more effective devolution or strategic performance), such a model is now out of kilter with a fast-changing business world. A number of new approaches have been promoted over the past 10 years to overhaul the traditional model

and build performance management processes that enable managers to steer their firms toward clear strategic goals.

But despite the undoubted success of tools such as the Balanced Scorecard, there is often such a gulf between theory and practice that relatively few companies sustain their interest at the highest level. Most collide rather than connect with the budgeting process. The group finance people are often to blame. They see themselves as the guardians of the budget, and if a business unit or division is veering off its agreed performance track, then corrective action must be taken, and they are the ones that must enforce such action. This may well involve directives aimed at (unplanned) cost reductions. Of course, the first costs to be cut tend to be so-called discretionary investments in, for example, employee skills and management training, customer satisfaction programs, and "special" projects such as those that improve quality and increase the speed of operations. The trouble is that these are also the very investments that underpin the success of the medium-term strategy as laid down in the Balanced Scorecard. Other pitfalls await the inexperienced scorecard user.

For example, if the planning process remains locked into an annual cycle with a highly deterministic approach to strategy, then much of the promise from so-called strategic management will be unfulfilled. A "take that hill" strategy (to use a military metaphor) is of little value if the hill itself has moved in the meantime. Incentive schemes too heavily weighted toward achieving the fixed plan reinforce this inflexibility. Moreover, there's a fine line between "alignment" and "control," and there's a real danger of using the scorecard (wittingly or unwittingly) for top-down control (in the same way as a budget with some nonfinancial measures).

In the beyond budgeting model, an effective performance management system should be aimed at supporting self-governing business units (see Figure 1). Its principal features should include:

- *Targets* that are relative to the competition (internal or external) and thus are always self-adjusting and stretching the performance of the business unit.
- *Effective anticipatory management systems (including rolling forecasts)* that enable managers to continuously adjust strategy and manage investments and shareholder expectations.
- *A rolling strategy process* (with appropriate cycles) that is devolved to business unit teams and that operates within clear boundaries and values.
- *An investment management process* that forces managers to build flexibility and "exit routes" into their forecasts and in which execution is made at the latest possible time.

FIGURE 1.

THE BUDGETING MODEL	THE BEYOND BUDGETING MODEL

Culture: "Contract, compliance, and control"

Culture: "Responsibility, enterprise, and learning"

- *Distributed controls aimed at supporting front-line managers* and keeping senior managers informed (by exception).
- *Rewards based on relative performance* at a business unit or company level that encourage team performance and cross-company sharing at various levels.

THE BEYOND BUDGETING MODEL—MORE THAN THE SUM OF THE PARTS

To create new wealth, firms need both the benefits of effective devolution (such as fast decision making) and the benefits of effective performance management (such as fast, open, and relevant information). The power of this dual approach was recognized more than 25 years ago by Dr. Jan Wallander, the architect of the Svenska Handelsbanken business model.

Management books and journals are replete with success stories that support one management model or another, but how many can point to companies that have consistently beaten their rivals for almost 30 years without having a dominant market position (Handelsbanken only has 15% of the highly deregulated Swedish market)?

What's the reason for this sustained success? It's the combination of effective devolution and effective performance management that makes the Handelsbanken case so special and has pointed many more companies in the right direction. It paves the way for companies to simplify their performance management processes, reduce the cost and complexity of the organization, and create a firm that is strategically focused and much more innovative and responsive.

Yet the gravitational force of the budgeting system makes it extremely difficult for most firms to escape the world of compliance and control. This is *not* a comfortable message for a measurement industry that believes it alone has the power to drag the traditional model kicking and screaming into the information age. Only by over-coming the constraints of the traditional budgeting approach can managers build a business model that operates at high speed; is self-questioning, self-renewing, and self-controlling; and rewards innovation and learning.

The authors are program directors on the CAM-I Beyond Budgeting Round Table. Jeremy Hope is coauthor of Transforming the Bottom Line *and* Competing in the Third Wave, *both published by Harvard Business School Press. You can reach him at* lh23@dial.pipex.com. *Robin Fraser was until recently a management consulting partner in PricewaterhouseCoopers and led the development of their Priority base Budgeting and ABM practices in the UK. You can reach Robin at:* RobinFraser@Compuserve.com.

CAM-I Inc. is a not-for-profit international research consortium. To download a white paper or find out about joining the BBRT visit www.beyondbudgeting.org *or contact Peter Bunce by phone: +44 (0)1202-670717, fax: +44 (0)1202-680698, or e-mail:* Peter@cam-i.demon.co.uk.

QUESTION

10.5 What are the principle features of the "Beyond Budgeting Model"?

10.6 Games Managers Play at Budget Time

by Richard Steele and Craig Albright*

One of the most thoroughly studied questions in business is how, at budgeting time, large corporations should choose among investment opportunities. In-house economists, management advisors and even Nobel laureates have worked on this problem and come up with an impressive array of quantitative and process-oriented resource allocation systems. Why, then, are so many senior executives frustrated with the process and convinced that their companies' capital is not being invested as well as it could be?

One reason is that even the best-designed systems can be trumped by the power of personality. A forceful appeal sometimes carries more weight than even the most objectively accurate financial analysis built on highly reliable facts. It is now commonplace, in fact, for talented and charismatic managers to spin, manipulate and otherwise cajole senior management into funding their business ideas — often in the face of numbers that would, on their own, dictate a negative decision. Put another way, when people are economical with the truth during capital budgeting, the underlying economics get lost.

Having guided dozens of major corporations through the budgeting process and watched hundreds of presentations by line managers asking for capital, we have profiled five archetypes of bad behavior commonly used by managers to subvert decision-making standards and win resources. It is not uncommon for a manager to adopt more than one type, depending on how his or her plan is faring relative to others in the planning and budgeting process. Fortunately, there are ways for senior management teams to counteract such behavior directly during budgeting discussions and, over time, to instill values that lead to better use of investment capital.

THE SANDBAGGER

"There is no way that we, or anyone else, can grow by 10%."
Managers are sandbagging when they routinely come to the table with a business plan that is less ambitious than one they know they could probably fulfill. Sandbaggers argue that the market is so tough, the best the company could hope for is slight incremental improvement even with additional resources or the most heroic leadership. Of course, when such managers exceed their targets, as they usually do, they appear to be heroes themselves.

The president of a successful $700 million North American brokerage business, for example, was reluctant to commit to an earnings-growth target that the company's CEO had proposed. While the president thought the business had the potential to achieve the CEO's target, he did not want to risk missing the target and lose his group's bonuses. Instead of turning to his team for ideas on how to reach the goals, however, he dug in his heels and insisted that the business really could not meet them; he eventually negotiated a lower target. At the end of the year, the brokerage division announced earnings growth that was just above the reduced target.

Later, during the president's performance review, the CEO pointed to the repeated sandbagging and the time spent debating performance targets in the planning process as a serious problem. It was preventing the CEO and his team from spending time where they needed to most — with their employees and customers.

Sandbagging costs more than time, however: It also creates energy-sapping internal debate and, worse still, leads to people being overpaid for their performance as bonuses kick in even when low budget targets are met.

THE MAGICIAN

"There really are no weak spots in our business right now."
Sometimes division managers know things about their business that do not show up in the budget figures. They may have heard that a large customer was intending to defect, that a key manager was on her way out, or that market share numbers were starting to slip. But at budget time, magicians cover up faults in the business by conveniently leaving out uncomfortable facts and diverting attention to more positive aspects of the operation.

For instance, the manager of a European beverage company was taken aback when her colleagues noted several weaknesses in her plan for the core business. In response, she diverted their attention to a speculative new idea to launch store-branded products for discount retailers. A true magician, she alternately pointed to growth rates and customer surveys in that channel to support her claims that the new plan would significantly boost the company's top line. After several months of debate, the top management team remained hopelessly

---

*   From: R. Steele and C. Albright, "Games Managers Play at Budget Time," *MIT Sloan Management Review* (Spring 2004): 81–84. Reprinted with permission of publisher. Copyright © 2004 by Massachusetts Institute of Technology. All rights reserved.

deadlocked and frustrated at their inability to come to an agreement on the proposed new line of business. Meanwhile, the core business's performance was declining.

There should be no magic to the budget process, but some managers try to cast a spell rather than answer legitimate challenges to their proposals. If they are not brought back to reality, the inconvenient details they've forgotten to mention will reappear and expose what may turn out to have been disastrous decisions.

THE LONE AGENT

"Yes, but that principle does not apply to our business."
Some managers contend that their business cannot conform to corporate-budgeting conventions because of its supposedly unique character. In comparison with competitors, they say, it may be much bigger or much smaller, more international or more domestic, more high-tech or more low-tech. Driven by their fear of being managed to the norm, lone agents stonewall during meetings ("Yes, but …") and expect special treatment. They demand different standards for goals and performance that undermine trust and teamwork and make performance management across a company's businesses difficult.

The group executive of a Latin American wholesale bank, a unit of a financial services company, lost his temper when he was asked by the executive committee to cut operating costs by 5% as part of a groupwide exercise to identify funds that could be reinvested in new businesses. Believing the target to be at odds with the right strategy for the bank — its location in a developing market made it different from other units, he contended — the executive would not agree to the request. Rather than open his thinking to alternatives, he lashed out at those who had proposed the cost targets and any other executive who appeared to support them. Other top executives, in turn, saw the executive's behavior as divisive and an attempt to gain unfair privilege.

By claiming to merit special consideration, lone agents sow mistrust among their peers and superiors and, in the process, damage the top team's ability to debate the key strategic issues it faces in a mature and disciplined way.

THE VISIONARY

"I can't say exactly when, but this is going to be big — really big."
Managers who don't have the numbers on their side often appeal to emotions. Visionaries harp repeatedly on the "breakthrough" technology or service that will "revolutionize" the industry and remain on the "cutting edge" for years to come. The core of the argument often goes like this: "Given the enormous upside, which at this point cannot be quantified because it is 5 to 10 years out,

it will be worth putting up with poor short-term performance."

For example, an ambitious director of business development for an insurance company proposed a plan that would allow consumers to buy term life insurance directly from the company, rather than through agents. His boss told the director that while the vision was compelling, he was troubled by the deep investment required throughout the planning horizon in order to set up the technology, change processes, educate consumers and so on. The fact was, the director had very little to say about near- or medium-term performance and tried to meet objections by going back to the long-term opportunity his vision represented. The end result in this case was a stalemate among the top executives, although visionaries often do win the resources they need — at least for a year or two, until top management and stock-holders, frustrated by the lack of results, raise questions that lead to the plan's termination.

Companies need visionaries, to be sure. But visionaries should be standing on solid factual ground when they look to the future, not floating in the clouds. The challenge, then, is to find a way to marry the vision with a genuine commitment to delivering short-term performance.

THE HOSTAGE TAKER

"If we don't invest big right now, we'll be left on the sidelines."
Sometimes managers claim that they can deliver significant and immediate performance improvements if they are given a huge proportion of the available corporate capital. Hostage takers act as if the decision-making obstacle is not the management team but the chief executive, who in their view should be prepared to bet the company on their brilliant plan.

The managing director for a U.K. Internet company wanted to turn his business into a full-service Web-hosting service provider — a radical proposal that would require a huge investment in a risky market and direct resources away from other profitable lines of business. Although the chief executive respected the managing director's strategic and financial acumen, she was not convinced that the plan reflected the best use of the company's capital. Rather than force a broader discussion of options and alternatives, however, she allowed her attention to be captured by the hostage taker's ultimatum.

Consequently, the company invested hundreds of millions of pounds behind his growth plan and continued to do so for each of the next three years, even as the markets proved much more difficult than initially forecast. Other growth options were starved of investment during this time, leaving the company overexposed to a single high-risk opportunity.

Like lone agents, hostage takers want special treatment and, like visionaries, they appeal to emotions. But because of the percentage of corporate investment that they seek, they have the potential to do the most damage to the company's future if their plans do not turn out as projected.

WHY DO MANAGERS PLAY GAMES?

It is one thing to be able to identify the games managers play and quite another to be able to do something about them. Each of the six archetypes reflects organizational or individual shortcomings — be it a lack of critical thinking, a misalignment in ambition and purpose, a breakdown in corporate culture or poor incentives.

First, managerial game playing sometimes reflects a lack of skills and know-how rather than Machiavellian intentions. For example, managers may be weak strategic thinkers, have poor planning skills, or be inexperienced in valuing investment opportunities correctly. In such situations, the remedy would include training, coaching and other forms of management education.

Second, bad behavior can be a matter of deeper flaws. Some managers know full well what they are doing and are simply not team players; others lack a proper focus on short-term performance. These deficiencies require a firmer hand.

Third, managerial stratagems at budget time can also reflect a lack of clarity about performance goals and expectations. It is not always easy to get the executive team and business-unit management to agree on specific performance targets. More often than not, misunderstandings arise over the pace at which goals are to be met: Executive teams usually have a much shorter time frame in mind when it comes to most performance targets. The end result is that business-unit managers feel they have to tap dance their way through uncomfortable meetings. While this gap may never be fully closed, its existence should be acknowledged by top management in order to minimize inefficient behavior.

Finally, managerial antics may be a response to the environment — the corporate culture, incentives and values that shape the workplace. For example, if the company tends to promote hard-charging, sales-oriented types into senior management positions, the company may produce a surplus of lone agents and hostage takers. If the company's general managers came up through the finance function, there may be a tendency to produce sandbaggers and magicians — people who know how to manipulate financial data to their own advantage. In either case, senior management will have to use all the tools at its disposal — mission statements, compensation, promotions and training — to develop a more cooperative, forward-looking and results-oriented system within the company.

CHANGING THE RULES

Even in the most perfectly designed organization, managers are going to play the system, and executives need to be ready to deal with disruptive behavior when it arises. While this is clearly a long-term, complex issue, there are actions that senior management can take in the short term to reduce the tax that bad behaviors can levy on a company's capital. It's important to take action quickly, however, because managers who are successful game players will continue their behavior until it is checked — a sandbagger who gets his bonus one year will come up with new reasons for being unable to meet corporate targets the next time around.

1. **Get It on the Table.** Openly acknowledge at the beginning of each budgeting meeting — in a lighthearted way — the human tendency to twist the facts to one's favor. That will help diffuse tension and make it clear that the criteria for investment approval will be not only the hard numbers that make up the proposal but also the overall integrity with which the numbers are presented. Even if a business plan comes in with the highest internal rate of return of all the proposals, for example, it may not receive funding if the investment committee sees games being played that undermine the credibility of the analysis.

2. **Paint a Picture of the Ideal.** Create a profile of the behaviors and values that managers ought to reflect when presenting budgets for approval. Examples might include the ability to meet short- and long-term expectations, the ability to be candid about the condition of the business, the ability to make and reach stretch targets and so on. The development of such skills can be made a part of corporate training programs. At Cadbury Schweppes Plc, 150 top managers learned about the behaviors and capabilities necessary for success at the company by participating in simulated dialogues focused on resource allocation. To put some bite into the program, even the CEO took part, role playing both good and bad behaviors and making it clear that failure to meet the required standards could cost a manager his or her seat at the top table.

3. **Deal Positively With Disruptive Behavior.** Be willing and ready to respond to disruptive game playing during budget meetings. For each type of manipulation, there is both an inflammatory and a productive way to respond. (See "Neutralizing Disruptive Behaviors.") For example, when lone agents are demanding that a different set of rules be applied to their budgets, reemphasize the company's well-publicized decision-making standards. And

NEUTRALIZING DISRUPTIVE BEHAVIORS

For a variety of organizational and personal reasons, many managers will come to budgeting discussions with less than optimal proposals. But their discussions of these proposals can be disruptive, with repercussions for both employee and company performance. Top management needs to rein in such behavior, but angry criticisms are not the way to go about that task. Instead, top executives should neutralize the behavior with unemotional responses.

Disruptive Behavior	Inflammatory Response	Neutralizing Action
Sandbagger	Criticize the manager's lack of ambition	Refer to and enforce top-down corporate goals
Magician	Berate the manager for failing to reconcile conflicting datas	Refocus the manager's attention on trends in the core business
Lone Agent	Accuse the manager of failing to be a team player	Reinforce group standards as the price of a seat at the table
Visionary	Belabor the missing details in the manager's plan	Require the manager to demonstrate how and when the vision will be economically attractive
Hostage Taker	Claim that capital constraints rule out the proposal	Require the manager to develop several credible alternatives and to make trade-offs transparent

when managers are sandbagging, point to the existence of top-down goals, known to the sandbaggers well ahead of time.

4. **Put Peer Pressure to Work.** Require that all business-unit and general managers be present for key business reviews — and that they participate in the question-and-answer phase. General managers from other businesses may have firsthand knowledge
that will lead them to raise questions that executives may not have thought of. For example, a general manager who has seen business-unit magicians perform before may be able to redirect the meeting's attention away from the dazzle of a new market and ask whether the company really has the organization in place to compete within it.

Executives with their hands on the till need to keep one eye on the numbers and the other on the psychology of their managers — and be ready to respond in real time to disruptive behavior. Taking the veil off of bad behaviors, however, does more than just make budgeting discussions more productive. It also lays the foundation for addressing two larger and longer-term challenges. By taking the time to define which competencies and behaviors are required to make the capital-budgeting process more effective and efficient, senior executives create organizational discipline and a concrete way of establishing the highly sought-after performance-oriented culture. And by linking behaviors and values to strategy and capital-allocation decisions, senior executives tap into a proven way of delivering better performance. In the end, everyone wins when the means and the ends of delivering performance are aligned.

Richard Steele is a London-based partner with Marakon Associates, an international strategy-consulting firm. He can be reached at rsteele@marakon.com. Craig Albright was formerly with Marakon in New York City. He can be reached at craig489@optonline.net.

QUESTION

10.6 What are the five archetypes of bad budgeting behavior?

Chapter 11

Financial Control

In Reading 11.1, *Transfer Pricing with ABC*, Robert Kaplan, Dan Weiss, and Eyal Desheh trace Teva Pharmaceutical Industries' history in arriving at a transfer price that would satisfy senior management, division managers, and the financial staff. After considering numerous traditional approaches, they decided to follow an ABC approach. ABC allowed them to uncover numerous inefficiencies and misallocation of costs to products. Not only was the ABC-based transfer pricing system successful from a technical point of view, but there was also a dramatic reduction in conflicts among marketing and manufacturing managers.

In Reading 11.2, *What is EVA, and How Can It Help Your Company*, Paul Dierks and Ajay Patel present a primer on EVA and MVA. One of the benefits of this article is that the authors walk readers through the mechanics of calculating both EVA and MVA. Readers should work through the example given in Table 2 to obtain insight into how MVA and EVA are calculated from financial statement. The authors also discuss criticisms of both concepts, contrast them with other performance metrics, and present the benefits of EVA-based incentive plans.

M. Epstein and S. D. Young's, *"Greening" with EVA* (Reading 11.3), complements Reading 11.2 by presenting a checklist of what must considered before EVA is implemented. The checklist includes behavioral factors, such as the buy-in of the board and senior management, as well as technical factors such as how EVA will be tied to critical functions in the organization such as compensation, strategic planning and budgeting. The authors also discuss how Georgia-Pacific tied EVA to environmental responsibility. One senior executive is quoted as saying that the tie between the two concepts means, "integrating society's desire for a clean environment and shareholder expectations with financial concerns." Instructors might refer back to the material in chapter 7 on environmental issues and Chapter 11 on capital budgeting.

Reading 11.4 is *Evaluating Internal Operations and Supply Chain Performance Using EVA and ABC* by Terrance Pohlen and B. Jay Coleman. The authors provide a very clear dyadic linkage between the methods of ABC and EVA as applied to supply chain management. EVA is used to evaluate how process changes drive value in each firm and develops measures that align operations performance with supply chain objectives. ABC is used to determine what drives costs and performance and translates nonfinancial performance into activity costs and financial measures. A number of examples are used to illustrate how the two methods work together to provide a more integrated way to understand the entire supply chain of the organization.

In *The Demise of Cost and Profit Centers*, Reading 11.5, Robert Kaplan discusses how the Balanced Scorecard approach can be used to look at the way a company organizes itself. Specifically, Kaplan argues that the distinction between cost and profit centers is no longer significant because every unit, by contributing to effective strategy execution, has the opportunity to support and create profit.

Readings
Chapter 11

11.1 Transfer Pricing With ABC

Here's the story of how a multinational pharmaceutical company solved its transfer pricing problems by using activity-based costing.

by Robert S. Kaplan, Dan Weiss, and Eyal Desheh*

In the mid-1980s, Teva Pharmaceutical Industries Ltd. decided to enter the generic drug market. Already a successful worldwide manufacturer of proprietary drugs, the Israel-based company wanted to vie globally in this competitive new market, particularly in the United States. The move has proved lucrative so far, as sales have been increasing at an annual rate of nearly 20%. In 1996, Teva's worldwide sales were $954 million and its after-tax net income, $73 million.

As part of its new strategy, Teva reorganized its pharmaceutical operations into decentralized cost and profit centers consisting of one operations division and three marketing divisions. The operations division is made up of four manufacturing plants in Israel, which are organized as cost centers because plant managers have no control over product mix or pricing. The plants produce to the orders placed by the marketing divisions, and plant managers are responsible for operational efficiency, quality, cost performance, and capacity management.

The marketing divisions are organized into the U.S. market (through Teva's Lemmon subsidiary), the local market (Israel), and the rest of the world. All three have substantially different sales characteristics. The Lemmon USA division handles about 30 products, each sold in large quantities. The Israel division handles 1,200 products in different packages and dosage forms, with many being sold in quite small quantities. The division handling sales to the rest of the world works on the basis of specific orders and tenders [a request from a customer for a price/bid to deliver a specified product or service], some of which are for relatively small quantities. All three divisions order and acquire most of their products from the operations division, although occasionally they turn to local suppliers. The marketing divisions are responsible for decisions about sales, product mix, pricing, and customer relationships.

Until the late 1980s, the marketing divisions were treated as revenue centers and were evaluated by sales, not profit, performance. Manufacturing plants in the operations division were measured by how well they met expense budgets and delivered the right orders on time. The company's cost system emphasized variable costs, principally materials expenses—ingredients and packaging—and direct labor. All other manufacturing costs were considered fixed.

Teva's managers decided to introduce a transfer pricing system, which they hoped would enhance profit consciousness and improve coordination between operations and marketing. They were concerned with excessive proliferation of the product line, acceptance of many low-volume orders, and associated large consumption of production capacity for changeovers. They proposed a transfer pricing system based on marginal costs, defined to be just materials cost. Direct labor would not be included in the transfer price because the company was not expecting to hire or fire employees based on short-term marketing decisions. High costs were associated with laying off workers in Israel, and, more important, pharmaceutical workers were highly skilled. With Teva's rapid growth, managers were reluctant to lay off workers during short-term volume declines because if new employees had to be hired later, they would need up to two years of training before they acquired the skills of the laid-off workers.

But the proposed transfer pricing system generated a storm of controversy. First, some executives observed that the marketing divisions would report extremely high profits because they were being charged for the materials costs only. Second, the operations division would get "credit" only for the expenses of purchased materials. There would be little pressure and motivation to control labor expenses and other so-called fixed expenses or for improving operational efficiency. Third, if Teva's plants were less efficient than outside manufacturers of the pharmaceutical products, the marginal cost transfer price would give the marketing divisions no incentive to shift

* From R. S. Kaplan, D. Weiss, and E. Desheh, "Transfer Pricing with ABC," Management Accounting (May 1997): 21–28. Reprinted with permission conveyed through Copyright Clearance Center, Inc.

their source of supply. Finally, the executives concluded that using only a short-run contribution margin approach would not solve the problems caused by treating the marketing divisions as revenue centers. Measuring profits as price less materials cost would continue to allow marketing and sales-decisions to be made without regard to their implications for production capacity and long-run costs. An alternative approach had to be found.

WHAT EVERYONE WANTED

Teva senior management wanted a new transfer pricing system that would satisfy several important characteristics:

1. The system should encourage the marketing divisions to make decisions consistent with long-run profit maximization. The transfer price should not encourage actions that improved the profit or cost performance of a division at the expense of Teva's overall profitability.
2. The system should be transparent enough so that managers could distinguish costs relevant for short-run decisions—such as incremental occasional bids for orders—from long-term decisions—such as acquiring a new product line, deleting product lines, and adding to existing product lines.
3. The transfer prices could be used to support decisions in both marketing and operating divisions, including:

Marketing	Operations
■ Product mix	■ Inventory levels
■ New product introduction	■ Batch sizes
■ Product deletion	■ Process improvements
■ Pricing	■ Capacity management
	■ Outsourcing: make vs. buy

Division managers wanted a transfer pricing system with the following characteristics:

1. The transfer prices would report the financial performance of their divisions fairly.
2. Managers could influence the reported performance of their divisions by making business decisions within their scope of authority. That is, the reported performance should reflect changes in product mix, improved efficiency, investments in new equipment, and organizational changes.
3. The decisions made by managers of marketing divisions would reflect both sales revenue and associated expenses incurred in the operations division.
4. The system must anticipate that division managers would examine, in depth, the method for calculating transfer prices and would take actions that maximized the reported performance of their divisions.

Finally, the financial staff wanted a transfer pricing system such that:

1. The transfer prices and financial reports derived from them would be credible and could be relied upon for decision making at all levels of the organization without excessive arguments and controversy.
2. The transfer pricing system would be clear, easy to explain, and easy to use. Updating transfer prices should be easy, and the components of the transfer price calculation should promote good understanding of the underlying factors driving costs.
3. The system would be used for internal charging of costs from the operations division to the marketing divisions.

TRADITIONAL TRANSFER PRICE APPROACHES WOULDN'T WORK

Teva's managers considered but rejected several traditional methods for establishing a new transfer pricing system: market price, full cost, marginal cost, and negotiated price. Market price for the transferred product was not feasible because no market existed for Teva's manufactured and packaged pharmaceutical products that had not been distributed or marketed to customers. A full cost calculation including materials, labor, and manufacturing overhead was rejected because the traditional methods for allocating overhead (labor or machine hours) did not capture the actual cost structure in Teva's plants. Also, the accumulation of all factory costs into average overhead rates could encourage local optimization by each division that would lower Teva's overall profit. For example, manufacturing plants would be encouraged to overproduce in order to absorb more factory overhead into inventory, while marketing divisions might be discouraged from bidding aggressively for high-volume orders and encouraged to accept more low volume custom orders. Also, this system would not reveal the incremental costs associated with short-run decisions or the relative use of capacity by different products and different order sizes.

Using short-run marginal cost, covering only ingredients and packaging materials, was the system proposed initially, which the managers already knew was inadequate for their purposes. And, finally, senior executives believed strongly that negotiated transfer prices would lead to endless arguments among managers in the different divisions, which would consume excessive time on nonproductive discussions.

ACTIVITY-BASED COSTING IS THE ANSWER

In December 1989, Teva's senior management attended a presentation on the fundamentals of activity-based costing and decided to implement ABC in its largest production plant. They wanted to investigate the use of ABC for calculating transfer prices between that plant and the marketing divisions. Teva put together a multidisciplinary project team consisting of managers from the production, finance, and marketing divisions. The team worked for about six months to develop an activity dictionary, drive factory costs to activities, identify cost drivers for each activity, collect data, and calculate ABC based product costs. It took the team several more weeks to analyze the results. Table 1 shows a sample calculation (updated to reflect 1996 data) of the costs to produce 10 tablets of a pain reliever. With this information, managers believed they now had a defensible, quantifiable answer to a question about how much it cost to manufacture a special small batch for a customer.

After seeing how ABC worked at the first plant, in subsequent years the project team rolled out the ABC analysis to the remaining production plants. The ABC models were retrospective, calculating the activity costs, activity cost driver rates, and product costs for the prior year. By the end of 1993, senior managers wanted to use ABC prospectively, to calculate transfer prices for the coming year. In November, Teva built its ABC production cost model for 1994 using data from the first three quarters of 1993. But managers objected to calculating costs for 1994 based on 1993 historical data. The numbers would not incorporate the impact of new products, new machines, and expected changes in production processes. Also, the historical data contained volume and spending variances that occurred in 1993 but that were not expected to be representative of production operations in 1994.

The project team took this issue to the company's Financial Control Forum where representatives from the operations and marketing divisions and company headquarters met to discuss costing and financial reporting methodologies. After several meetings, the group decided to use the next year's (1994) forecasted costs—based on budgeted expense data, forecasted volume and mix of sales, and projected process utilization and efficiencies—to calculate the transfer prices.

THE ABC TRANSFER PRICE MODEL STRUCTURE

The structure of the early retrospective ABC models and the current prospective model recognizes the ABC hierarchy of unit, batch, product sustaining, and plant-level costs.[1] Unit liable costs represent all the direct expenses associated with producing individual product units such as tablets, capsules, and ampoules. These expenses principally include the cost of raw materials, packaging materials, and direct wages paid to production workers.

Batch-level costs include the expenses of resources used for each production or packaging batch, mainly the costs of preparation, setup, cleaning, quality control,

TABLE 1. PAIN RELIEVER 10 TABLETS, 250 MG

Annual Sales 1996—$2.1 million	
ABC Cost per package	
Material use	$1.50
Production costs	2.10
(The traditional production costs per package were only $1.50, 40% difference)	
Total:	$3.60

Production Cost Analysis:	
Resources	
Salaries	$0.86
Energy	0.27
Utilities	0.34
Depreciation	0.41
Administrative	0.22
Total	$2.10
Main Activities	
Storage	$0.25
Manufacturing	0.61
Packaging	0.71
Q.A.	0.42
Logistics	0.11
Total	$2.10
Cost Drivers	
Number of materials	$0.55
Batches	0.24
Labor hours	0.71
Machine hours	0.47
Samples	0.13
Total	$2.10

laboratory testing, and computer and production management. The lot sizes for pharmaceutical production usually are predetermined based on the capacity of containers in the production line,[2] but a second batch process, determined by customer orders, occurs for packaging the tablets or syrup. The costs of a production or a packaging batch can vary among different products and, of course, among different plants. For example, a small customer order can trigger the production of a large batch of tablets or syrup of which only a small portion may be packaged for the particular customer order.[3] Thus, the batch costs assigned to a particular order include two components: a pro-rata share of the batch cost of the production setup and the full batch cost of the packaging setup. The calculation of batch-level costs for several different types of customer orders is shown in Table 2.

Product-specific costs include the expenses incurred in registering the products,[4] making changes to a product's production processes, and designing the package. Plant-level costs represent the cost of maintaining the capacity of production lines including depreciation, cost of safety inspections, and insurance, as well as the general expenses of the plant such as security and landscaping. In many ABC applications, machine depreciation would be included in the unit and batch costs associated with producing products and changing

TABLE 2. BATCH-LEVEL TRANSFER PRICE

The batch-level transfer price has two components, the production setup and the packing setup. Consider the production and packaging process for a cough syrup. In the production process, the active ingredients, a syrup simplex, and flavors, are mixed together in a 600-liter container to produce the syrup solution. The cost of setup—labor, cleaning, maintenance, and quality control resources is $300. The setup cost is assigned proportionally to the entire output.

Subsequently, bottles are filled with the syrup solution and packed into cardboard boxes. The entire packaging process is performed on an automated filling and packing line. The setup of the line costs $500, which includes the cost of a skilled technician, cleaning, maintenance and quality control. Packing the same syrup into two different presentations such as different sized bottles (50 ml and 100 ml) or different packaging materials, requires two different setups.

The batch-level transfer price consists of the pro-rata share of the production setup and the full cost of the packaging setup. We illustrate the approach with three numerical examples:

Produce a full batch of 6,000 bottles of 100 ml syrup for a large order from a customer in the local market

$$[\$300/6,000] + [\$500/6,000] = \$.05 + \$.083 = \$.133/bottle$$
mixing   packing

Produce a small order of 1,000 bottles of 100 ml syrup, packed in special boxes, for a special tender in South America

$$[\$300/\$6,000] + [\$500/1,000] = \$.05 + \$.50 = \$.55/bottle$$
mixing   packing

Produce a full batch of 12,000 bottles of 50 ml syrup for a large order from a customer in the local market

$$[\$300/12,000] + [\$500/12,000] = \$.025 + \$.042 = \$.067/bottle$$
mixing   packing

---

from one product to another. Teva decided to treat equipment depreciation as a plant-level cost so the calculated unit and batch costs could be used to estimate more closely the marginal costs associated with producing one more unit or batch of a product.

USING ABC COSTS FOR TRANSFER PRICING

Teva bases its transfer price system on a prospective ABC calculation. Prices are set for the coming year based on budgeted data. The company calculates standard activity cost driver rates for each activity. During the year, these costs get charged to products based on the actual quantity of activities demanded during the year. The use of standard activity cost driver rates enables product costs to be calculated in a predictable manner throughout the year. It also eliminates monthly or quarterly fluctuations in product costs caused by variations in actual spending, resource usage, and activity levels.

Transfer prices are calculated in two different procedures. The first one assigns unit and batch-level costs, and the second assigns product specific and plant-level costs. The marketing divisions are charged for unit-level costs (principally materials and labor) based on the actual quantities of each individual product they acquire. In addition, they are charged batch-level costs based on the actual number of production and packaging batches of each product they order (see examples in Table 2). Now that Teva has the ability to analyze the costs of different presentations, the trend of having a large number of presentations for each product has slowed, For example, the marketing divisions realized that producing special sample packages of six tablets was very expensive and that it was cheaper to give physicians the regular packages of 20 tablets. In general, the procedure has given marketing managers the flexibility to decide when to accept a small order from a customer or how much of a discount to grant for large orders. Table 3 shows a sample calculation of the monthly unit and batch-level charges from a plant to a marketing division.

The product-specific and plant-level expenses are charged to marketing divisions annually based on budgeted information (see Table 4). The product-specific costs are easy to assign because each marketing division has specific products for its own markets. No individual product is sold to more than one marketing division. The plant-level (capacity-sustaining) expenses are charged to each marketing division based on the budgeted use of the capacity of the four manufacturing facilities.

Activity cost driver rates are calculated based on the practical capacity of each of the four plants. In this way, the rates reflect the underlying efficiency and productivity of the plants without being influenced by fluctuations in forecasted or actual usage. Analysts estimated the practical capacity by noting the maximum production quantities during past peak periods.

What about unused capacity? Unused capacity arises from two sources: (1) declines in demand for products manufactured on an existing line, and (2) partial usage when a new production line is added because existing production lines cannot produce the additional quantities requested by one of the marketing divisions. To foster a sense of responsibility among marketing managers for the cost of supplying capacity resources, Teva charges the marketing division that experienced the decline in demand a lump-sum assignment (see Table 4) for the cost of maintaining the unused production capacity in an existing line. When a marketing division initiates an increment in production capacity or manufacturing technology, it bears the costs of all the additional resources supplied unless or until the increment begins to be used by one of the other marketing divisions. At that point, each marketing division would be charged based on its percentage of practical capacity used.

TABLE 3. MONTHLY DEBIT MAY 1995

Product	Quantity Produced	Material (per package)	From Plant A to Local Market Division Unit Based Costs (Per Package)	Batch Based Costs (Per Package)	Total Costs† (Per Package)	Total Debit‡
Pain reliever 20 tablets, 500 mg.	1,000,000	$2.10	$0.22	$0.41	$2.73	$2,730,000
Pain reliever 30 capsules	1,200,000	1.60	0.20	0.32	2.12	2,544,000
Syrup 200 c.c.	200,000	0.81	0.43	0.11	1.35	270,000
•						•
•						•
•						•
Total						$15,100,200

† Total costs = material + unit based cost + batch based costs

‡ Total debit = total costs per package × quantity produced

TABLE 4. ANNUAL DEBIT—1995

Product	Annual Budgeted Quantity	From Plant A to Lemmon Marketing Division (USA) Product Based Costs (Per Package)	Plant Based Costs (Per Package)	Total Costs† (Per Package)	Total Debit‡
Pain reliever 20 tablets, 500 mg.	12,000,000	$0.10	$0.21	$0.31	$3,720,000
Pain reliever 30 capsules	20,000,000	0.12	0.20	0.32	6,400,000
Syrup 200 c.c.	3,500,000	0.14	0.12	0.26	860,000
•					•
•					•
•					•
Cost of used capacity					141,900,000
Cost of unused capacity					1,300,000
Total					$143,200,000

† Total cost = production based costs + plant based costs

‡ Total debit = total cost per package × annual budgeted quantity

The assignment of the plant-level costs (still referred to as "fixed costs" at Teva because of its long history with the marginal costing approach) receives much attention, particularly from the managers of the marketing divisions. They want to verify that these costs do indeed stay "fixed" and don't creep upward each period. By separating the unit and batch level costs from the product-sustaining and plant-level costs, the marketing managers can monitor closely the costs incurred in the manufacturing plants. In particular, the marketing managers make sure that increases in plant-level costs occur only when one or more of them requests a change in production capacity. The responsibility for the fixed cost increment is then clearly assignable to the requesting division.

The integrated budget process lets marketing managers plan their product mix with knowledge of the cost impact of their decisions. When they propose increases in variety and complexity, they know the added costs they will be charged because of their increased demands on manufacturing facilities. Active discussions occur between marketing and operations personnel about the impact of product mix and batch sizes.

Marketing managers now distinguish between products that cover all manufacturing costs versus those that cover only the unit and batch-level expenses but not their annual product-sustaining and plant-level expenses. Because of the assignment of unused capacity expenses to the responsible marketing division, the marketing managers incorporate information about available capacity when they make decisions about pricing, product mix, and product introduction.

One example illustrates the value of assigning product-sustaining and plant-level expenses to individual products in the new transfer pricing system. The initial and subsequent ABC analyses revealed that quite a few of Teva's products were unprofitable; that is, the revenues they earned were below the cost of the unit, batch, and product and plant-sustaining expenses associated with these products. But managers were reluctant to drop these products because many of the expenses assigned to them, including direct labor, would remain for some time even if production of the unprofitable products were to cease.

In the early 1990's, however, Teva's growing sales volume led to shortages in capacity. Teva eventually decided to sell 30 low volume products to another company. These products were not central to Teva's strategy, yet they consumed a great number of resources and managers' attention. By shifting the product mix away from the unprofitable products, Teva was able to use the freed-up capacity of people, machines, and facilities to handle the production of newly introduced products and the expanded sales of existing profitable products. While the debate about selling off the 30 products lasted three years, the ABC system contributed to the final decision by revealing that the cheapest source of new capacity was the capacity released by reducing the production and sales of currently unprofitable products.

ONGOING BENEFITS FROM ABC TRANSFER PRICING SYSTEM

With Teva's continued growth, requests for investments in new production capacity arise continually. ABC's high-lighting of unused capacity often reveals where production can be expanded without spending additional money. A second source is the capacity released by ceasing production of unprofitable products—when feasible without disrupting customer relations. Beyond these two sources, investments in a new production line can be assessed by simulating production costs if the line were to be installed. For example, a new line can reduce batch level costs because of less need for changeovers on both the existing and the proposed production lines. These cost reductions could provide the justification for the investment decision. In addition, the investment decision for a new production line explicitly incorporates the cost and assignment of responsibility for the unused capacity in the early periods while market demand has not yet built to long-term expected levels. Teva executives say that the discipline of recognizing and assigning unused capacity costs of new production lines provides valuable realism to the demand forecasts provided by the marketing divisions.

The transfer pricing system also motivates cost reduction and production efficiencies in the manufacturing plants. Managers in the different divisions now work together to identify ways to reduce unit and batch-level expenses. Manufacturing, purchasing, and marketing employees conduct common searches for lower-cost, more reliable, and higher-quality suppliers to reduce variable materials costs. Marketing managers compare Teva's production costs with those of alternative suppliers around the world. They share this information with manufacturing managers who learn where process improvements are required and may concur with a decision to outsource products where the external suppliers' costs are lower than Teva could achieve in the foreseeable future. These actions contribute to increasing Teva's long-term profitability.

The activity-based cost information also helps managers determine which manufacturing facility is appropriate for different types of products. For example (see Figure 1), Plant A has a relatively inflexible (high capital-intensive) cost structure with a high percentage of plant-level costs and a low percentage of unit costs. This plant is most appropriate for high-volume production of standard products. Plant B, with a significantly lower percentage of plant-level costs and a relatively high percentage of unit costs, is much more flexible and is appropriate for producing small batch sizes and test runs of newly introduced products. Thus, ABC information also is being used to determine operating strategy.

THE BEST NEWS: HARMONY IS GROWING

An unexpected benefit of the activity-based transfer price system is the ability to measure profit performance under changing organizational structures. Teva, like many other pharmaceutical companies, undergoes periodic organizational changes. By understanding cost behavior at the activity and product level, financial managers can forecast the potential performance of newly created profit centers and reconstruct what the past profit performance history would have been, assuming that the proposed profit center reorganization had existed for the past several years. The ABC system also enables senior executives to measure profit performance across organizational—cost and profit center—boundaries. For example, Table 5 shows the profitability of a significant product family whose individual products are manufactured in different plants and are sold by more than one marketing division.

TABLE 5. 10 PRODUCTS (SEGMENT A): 1995

	$ Million
Sales Revenue	50
Marketing expense	
USA Lemmon division	10
Local market division	9
Other export division	=
Total	19
Manufacturing expenses	
Plant A	11
Plant B	
Plant C	9
Plant D	
Total	20
Total expenses	39
Profit	11

FIGURE 1. STRUCTURE OF COSTS IN PLANT "A" AND PLANT "B"

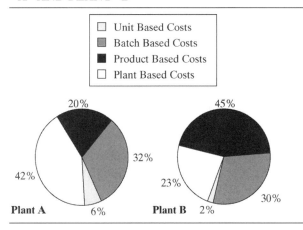

Jacob Winter, Teva's vice president of pharmaceutical operations, commented on the benefits derived from the ABC transfer price system:

In our changing environment, it is important for us to be able to understand and forecast our cost behavior. Some products remain in certain stages of production for a long time. These stages require resources of professional production and quality assurance staff, even when no direct labor is involved. On the other hand, since the supply of these resources is relatively fixed in the short run, we understand that we can use their capabilities for several small batch runs.

He also recognized that activity-based costs are not the primary information used for short-term operational decision making:

The ABC data provide an indication that must be supported by other information and facts. One cannot rely only on costing information when making operational decisions. Our short-term operational decisions focus on current bottlenecks and lead-time considerations. ABC provides guidance and insights about where we should be looking, but it is not the primary data for operational decisions.

Perhaps most important, the introduction of ABC-based transfer prices has led to a dramatic reduction in the conflicts among marketing and manufacturing managers. The managers now have confidence in the production cost economics reported by the transfer price system. Manufacturing managers who "sell" the product and marketing managers who "buy,' the product concur with the reasonableness of the calculated transfer prices. Teva's senior executives interpret the sharp reduction in intraorganizational conflicts as one of the most important signs that the use of activity-based transfer prices is succeeding.

ENDNOTES

1. R. Cooper, "Cost Classification in Unit-Based and Activity-Based Manufacturing Cost Systems." *Journal of Cost Management*, Fall 1990, pp. 4–14.
2. Production lot sizes can be expanded, if demand increases to a higher, sustainable level, by making technical changes to the production process and performing a quality control procedure to verify and validate that the product characteristics and quality have not been altered by the larger production batch.
3. At present, the Teva transfer price system does not charge the customer order for the full cost of setting up the production batch nor for the inventory carrying cost of the unused tablets or syrup. This is a refinement that could be added to the system in future years.
4. Registration costs include the costs of gaining and maintaining approval from governmental agencies for the right to manufacture each product.

Robert S. Kaplan is the Marvin Bower Professor of Leadership Development at the Harvard Business School. Dan Weiss is an instructor in the Industrial Engineering and Management Department of the Technion (Israel Institute of Technology) and partner, OIC Technologies Consulting Group. Eyal Desheh, formerly deputy chief financial officer at Teva Pharmaceuticals, is currently vice president and CFO of Scitex Corporation. Comments can be addressed to rkaplan@hba.edu.

QUESTIONS

11.1a Why wouldn't the traditional transfer-pricing approaches work at TEVA?

11.1b How did the new ABC transfer-pricing system affect the Marketing Division? Explain.

11.2 What Is EVA, and How Can It Help Your Company?

Economic value added (EVA) and market value added (MVA) arenot just performance metrics used to rank companies for investors—they can be used to manage your company better.

by Paul A. Dierks, CPA; and Ajay Patel*

Economic Value Added, or EVA, is a measure of financial performance that combines the familiar concept of residual income with principles of modem corporate finance—specifically, that all capital has a cost and that earning more than the cost of capital creates value for shareholders. EVA is after-tax net operating profit—NOPAT—minus a capital charge. If a company's return on capital exceeds its cost of capital, it is creating true value for the shareholder. Companies consistently generating high EVAs are top performers that are valued highly by shareholders.

Both EVA and MVA (Market Value Added) have been highly publicized in leading business magazines, but the focus usually is on what EVA and MVA are and how they are used externally to rank companies. Little detail is given on how the numbers in an EVA calculation actually are determined—which we propose to do here. Further, we demonstrate that these techniques have utility within a company in managing a company's operations, in guiding its strategy, and in providing incentives to its employees.

Key components of EVA are NOPAT and the capital charge—the amount of capital times the cost of capital. NOPAT is profits derived from a company's operations after taxes but before financing costs and noncash-book-keeping entries. It is the total pool of profits available to provide a cash return to those who provided capital to the firm. Capital is the amount of cash invested in the business, net of depreciation. It can be calculated as the sum of interest-bearing debt and equity or as the sum of net assets less noninterest-bearing current liabilities.[1]

The capital charge is the cash flow required to compensate investors for the riskiness of the business given the amount of capital invested. Reducing the amount of working capital or fixed assets required to run the business while holding profits steady increases EVA.

The cost of capital is the minimum rate of return on capital required to compensate debt and equity investors for bearing risk, e.g., cut-off rate to create value.

In formula form,

$$EVA = (r - c^*) \times capital;$$

where r = rate of return;and

c^* = cost of capital, or the weighted average cost of capital

Then, $EVA = (r \times capital) - (c^* \times capital)$;

$$EVA = NOPAT - c^* \times capital \; ; \; and$$

$$EVA = operating \; profits - a \; capital \; charge$$

Another perspective on EVA can be gained by looking at a firm's RONA—Return on Net Assets. For a firm, RONA is a ratio that is calculated by dividing its NOPAT by the amount of capital it employs (RONA = NOPAT/Capital) after making the necessary adjustments of the data reported by a conventional financial accounting system.

A convenient formulation of EVA is obtained by multiplying the total amount of net assets tied up by the spread between RONA and a threshold or minimum rate of return such as the cost of capital. Thus:

$$EVA = net \; investments \times$$
$$(RONA - required \; minimum \; return)$$

If RONA is above the threshold rate, EVA is positive.

Gains in shareholder wealth are driven by gains in EVA. The market price of a stock incorporates the current level of EVA and the expectation of future EVA. To increase the stock price, management must increase the current level of EVA and change the market's expectations of growth in future EVA.

In summary, EVA is really just another definition of earnings—sales less operating expenses—with one more item subtracted, a charge for the use of the capital involved. It is true economic profit consisting of all costs including the cost of capital.

WHAT IS MARKET VALUE ADDED (MVA)?

Market Value Added, or MVA, is a measure of the wealth a company has created for its investors. In effect, MVA shows the difference between what investors put in and what they can take out. EVA is the fuel that fires up a company's MVA. A company that has a positive EVA year after year will see its MVA rise, while negative EVA year in and year out will drag down MVA as the market loses faith that the company will ever provide a decent return on invested capital.

MVA is a cumulative measure of corporate performance that looks at how much a company's stock

* From P. A. Dierks and A. Patel, "What Is EVA, and How Can It Help Your Company? *Management Accounting* (November 1997): 52–58. Reprinted with permission conveyed through Copyright Clearance Center, Inc.

has added to (or taken out of) investors' pocketbooks over its life and compares it with the capital those same investors put into the firm. If MVA is a positive number, the company has made its shareholders richer. A negative MVA indicates how much shareholder wealth has been destroyed. Maximizing MVA should be the primary objective for any company that is concerned about its shareholders' welfare.

How is MVA calculated? First, all the capital a company took in over its span of existence is identified including equity and debt offerings, bank loans, and retained earnings, and the amounts are added up. Then, some "adjustments" are made that capitalize certain past expenditures, like R&D spending, as an investment in future earnings. This adjusted capital amount is compared to a firm's total market value, which is the current value of a company's stock and debt to get MVA or the difference between what the investors can take out (total market value) and the amount investors put in (invested capital). In formula form, MVA is calculated as follows:

MVA = [(shares outstanding × stock price) + market value of preferred stock + market value of debt] – total capital

MVA tends to move in tandem with the firm's stock market value. Stern Stewart, the consulting firm that developed and promoted EVA in the business community, contends that EVA is the sole measurement method that can be correlated with a firm's stock price. Many interesting movements of firms, some counter to one's expectations, can be seen in the Stern Stewart rankings of the top 1,000 firms in Lieber's, Fisher's, and Tully's *Fortune* articles.[2]

CALCULATING EVA AND MVA

As indicated earlier, EVA and MVA can be calculated using some very simplistic formulas, but the simplicity of these calculations can be misleading because the after-tax operating profit, NOPAT, and the amount used for capital are not readily available—that is, they don't come directly off the financial statements. The amount of equity equivalent reserves for certain accounts must be determined first, and the footnotes to the financial statements are the primary source for this information.

In The Quest for Value, G. Bennett Stewart calculates a firm's EVA in two ways: an Operating Approach and a Financing Approach.[3] These two approaches then are reconciled in a summary report. To understand how these approaches work, we first must understand the concepts of equity equivalent reserves or EEs.

Equity equivalents are adjustments that turn a firm's accounting book value into "economic book value, which is a truer measure of the cash that investors have put at risk in the firm and upon which they expect to accrue some returns."[4] In this way, capital-related items are turned into a more accurate measure of capital that better reflects the financial base on which investors expect to accrue their returns. Also, revenue- and expense-related equity equivalent adjustments are included in NOPAT—Net Operating Profit After Taxes—which is a more realistic measure of the actual cash yield generated for investors from recurring business activities.

Stern Stewart has identified a total of 164 equity equivalent reserve adjustments; however, only about 20 to 25 have to be addressed in detail, and only a portion of these actually may be made in practice. "In our published rankings and illustrations, we have chosen to make only a handful of such adjustments in the calculation of EVA and MVA—typically those which can be made with information contained in the Compustat database and easily explained to the general business reader."[5] It recommends making an adjustment only in cases that pass four tests:

- Is it likely to have a material impact on EVA?
- Can the managers influence the outcome?
- Can the operating people readily grasp it?
- Is the required information relatively easy to track and derive?[6]

An example of an equity equivalent adjustment occurs with R&D expenditures. Under accounting conventions, outlays for R&D are charged off in the period when they are incurred. These immediate charge-offs as operating expenses say there is no future value to be derived from R&D. As a result, the company's profits are reduced, and its capital is undervalued. For EVA purposes, all outlays over the life of successful R&D projects should be removed from the income statement, be capitalized into the balance sheet, and amortized against earnings over the period benefiting from the successful R&D efforts. Thus, in calculating EVA, R&D is seen as an investment, and amounts spent for it must be included in a firm's capital base to reflect accurately the true amount of capital employed. Only the portion of the R&D that no longer has future value should be charged to the income statement in order to properly reflect the costs (and profit) of a period.

Other examples of EEs are the LIFO and Deferred Income Tax Reserves. In periods of rising prices, companies save taxes by using a LIFO basis of inventory costing. Under LIFO, recently acquired goods are expensed, and the costs of prior periods are accumulated in inventory resulting in an understatement of inventory and equity. A LIFO reserve account captures the difference between the LIFO and FIFO value of the inventory and indicates the extent that the LIFO inventories are understated in value. Adding the LIFO reserve to capital as an equity equivalent converts inventories from a LIFO to a FIFO basis of valuation, which is a better approximation of current replacement cost. Also, adjusting NOPAT for the change in the LIFO reserve brings into earnings the current period effect of unrealized gain attributable to holding inventories that appreciated in value. Action(s) to be taken for an equity equivalent adjustment for a LIFO reserve are:

> Add to capital: amount of the LIFO reserve
> Add to (deduct from) NOPAT: the amount of increase (decrease) in the LIFO reserve

Changes in the LIFO reserve also can be viewed as a difference between LIFO and FIFO cost of goods sold. Including this change in reported profits converts a LIFO cost of goods sold expense to FIFO but LIFO's tax benefit is retained. Thus, the overall effect of treating a LIFO reserve as an equity equivalent is to produce a FIFO balance sheet and income statement but preserve the LIFO tax benefit.

Deferred taxes arise from a difference in the timing when revenues and expenses are recognized for financial reporting versus when they are reported for tax purposes. The difference between the accounting provision for taxes and the tax amount paid is accumulated in the reserve for deferred income taxes account. If long-term assets that give rise to tax deferrals are replenished, a company's deferred tax reserve increases, which is the equivalent of permanent equity. Adjusting NOPAT for the change in the deferred tax reserve results in NOPAT being charged only with the taxes actually paid instead of the accounting tax provision. This calculation provides a clearer picture of the true cash-on-cash yield actually being earned in the business. Action(s) to be taken for an equity equivalent adjustment for a deferred tax reserve are:

> Add to capital: amount of the deferred tax reserve
> Add to (deduct from) NOPAT amount of increase (decrease) in the deferred tax reserve

See Table 1 for additional examples of equity equivalents and their effect on capital and NOPAT.

As noted, Stewart recommends two methods of calculating a firm's EVA: an Operating Approach and a Financing Approach. The Financing Approach builds up to the rate of return on capital from the standard return on equity in three steps: eliminating financial leverage, eliminating financing distortions, and eliminating accounting distortions. As a result of the first two steps, NOPAT is a sum of the returns attributable to all providers of funds to the company, and the NOPAT return is completely unaffected by the financial composition of capital. What matters is simply the productivity of capital employed in the business, no matter the financial form in which the capital has been obtained.

The Operating Approach starts by deducting operating expenses—including depreciation—from sales, but other noncash-bookkeeping entries are ignored. Next, EE reserve adjustments are made. Interest expense, because it is a financing charge, is ignored, but other (operating) income is added to get pretax economic profits or Net Operating Profit Before Taxes (NOPBT). In the final step, an estimate of the taxes payable in cash on these operating profits is subtracted leaving NOPAT at the same amount as in the financing approach. (See Table 2—Calculating EVA and MVA.)

CRITICISMS OF EVA AND MVA

A problem with EVA is that it does not account for real options (growth opportunities) inherent in investment decisions. The market value of a firm's securities reflects the market's perception of the value of those growth opportunities. But EVA does not reflect this information. Therefore, when using EVA to analyze the financial performance of a company, analysts should keep in mind that focusing on year-to-year changes in EVA will be better for firms with substantial assets in place in mature industries with few growth opportunities (public utilities for instance). For firms with fewer assets in place and substantial growth opportunities, however, year-to-year changes in EVA are less likely to explain changes in firm value. Firms in the technology and biotech sectors, for instance, would fall into the latter category. This problem can be avoided by refocusing the firm on the present value of expected future EVA instead of on year-to-year changes in EVA. But doing so would eliminate the essential factors (simplicity and ease of use) that caused EVA to be preferred to NPV.

TABLE 1. EQUITY EQUIVALENT ADJUSTMENTS FOR CALCULATING EVA

Add Equity Equivalents to Capital for:	Add Increases in Equity Equivalents to NOPAT for:
Cumulative goodwill amortization	Goodwill amortization
Unrecorded goodwill	Increase in (not) capitalized intangibles
(Net) capitalized intangibles	Increase in full-cost reserve
Full-cost reserve	Unusual loss (gain) after taxes
Cumulative unusual loss (gain) after taxes	Increase in other reserves
Other reserves for such things as bad debts, inventory obsolescence, and warranties	

This list is taken from Stewart, *The Quest for Value*, p. 112.

TABLE 2. CALCULATE EVA AND MVA

1997 Balance Sheet—*Dollars in Thousands*		1997 Capital—*Dollars in Thousands*		1997 Capital—*Dollars in Thousands*	
Assets		**Operating Approach**		**Financing Approach**	
Cash	$35	Cash	$ 35	Short-term debt (10%)	$100
Receivables (net)	190	Receivable (net)	190	Long-term debt (8%)	150
Inventory	190	Inventory	190	Present value of noncapital leases	50
Other current assets	95	LIFO reserve	10	Other long-term liabilities	120
Total current assets	510	Other current assets	95	Total debt and leases	420
		Current assets	520	Common equity	425
Property, plant and equipment (net)	530	Accounts payable	150	Plus: equity equivalents	
Goodwill	75	Income taxes payable	20	Accumulated goodwill	
Other long-term assets	120	Other current liabilities	200	amortization	50
Total assets	$1,235	NIBCLs	370	LIFO reserve	10
		Net working capital	150	Deferred income taxes	70
Liabilities and Net Worth		Property, plant and equipment (net)	530	Sum of equity equivalents	130
Short-term debt (10%)	$ 100	Present value of noncapital losses	50	Adjusted common equity capital	555
Accounts payable	150	Adjusted property, plant and equipment	580		
Income taxes payable	20	Goodwill	75		
Other current liabilities	200	Accumulated goodwill amortization	50		
Total current liabilities	470	Adjusted goodwill	125		
Long-term debt (8%)	150	Other long-term assets	120		
Other long-term liabilities	120	Capital (operating approach)	$975	Capital (financing approach)	$975
Total liabilities	270				
Deferred income taxes	70				
Common equity	425				
Total liabilities and net worth	$1,235				

1997 Income Statement - *Dollars in Thousands*		EVA NOPAT via Operating Approach		EVA NOPAT via Financing Approach	
Net sales	$2,000	Net sales	$2,000	Income available to common	$30
Cost of goods sold	1,670	Cost of goods sold	1,670	Plus, equity equivalent adjustments	
Gross profit	330	Gross profit	330	Increase deferred Wet;	5
		Less: selling general & administration	185	Goodwill amortization	14
Less: selling, general & administration	185	Other operating expenses	50	Increase LIFO reserve	2
Depreciation	20	Increase LIFO reserve	2	Sum of equity equivalents	21
Goodwill amortization	15	Interest expense noncapital leases	4	Adjusted income to common	51
Other operating expenses	50	Net operating profit	101	Interest expense	22
Total operating expenses	270	Interest expense	22	Interest expense noncapital leases	4
Net operating profit	60	Other income	12		26
Interest expense	22	NOPBT	91	Tax savings on interest expense	10
Other income	12	Income tax provision	20	Interest expense after taxes	16
Income before taxes	50	Less increase in deferred taxes	5		
Less: axes (40%)	20	Plus tax savings on interest expense	10		
Net profit after taxes	$30	Cash operating taxes	25		
		EVA NOPAT via operating approach	$66	EVA NOPAT via financing approach	$66

1. Calculate Market Value Added (MVA)

	Share Price	#Shares		
Market:	$25.00	50,000	$1,250,000	Equity market value
Book value:	$11.10	50,000	$ 555,000	Economic book value*
Market Value Added (MVA) =			$ 695,000	

* Sum of Common Equity and Equity Equivalents

2. Calculate Economic Value Added (EVA)

   a. After-tax operating profit $ 66
   b. Less: cost of capital (CDC)

Weighted Average COC

	Amount	Weight	Percent
LT Debt	$270	17.8%	4.8%
Equity:	$1,250	82.2%	12.0%
		COC =	10.7%

Times: amount of capital =	$975	$105
c. Equals: Economic Value Added (EVA)		($ 39)

To capture the growth opportunities inherent in companies, managers also should focus on MVA. Because MVA is constructed off the market value of a firm's securities, it reflects the market's expectations of future opportunities for the firm. Using both EVA and MVA to evaluate performance allows companies to account for both the year-to-year and long-term changes in value.

The empirical research of academics to date has been limited, and the results have been inconclusive. In a study of 241 firms over the period of 1987 to 1993, Kenneth Lehn and Anil Makhija found "that EVA and MVA are significantly positively correlated with stock price performance attesting to their effectiveness as performance measures."[7] But a sidebar to a CFO article reports on a study by three University of Washington professors who found that "while EVA may add incremental information in some settings, as a performance measure it can't even outperform basic income before extraordinary items."[8] The James Dodd and Shimin Chen study of 566 companies for the years 1983–1992 showed that stock returns were correlated with EVA, but "the alignment is not nearly as perfect as suggested by recent articles." These authors also observed that residual income (RI) explained about the same variation as EVA and, thus, similar stock returns will result from performance measurement systems using EVA and RI performance measurements. They then concluded, "Therefore, the off-line adjustments to operating income necessary to calculate EVA may not pass a prudent cost-benefit analysis."[9]

OTHER PERFORMANCE METRICS

Although we focus here on EVA, other performance metrics exist—such as NPV, CFROI, and RI. CFROI (cash flow return on investment) is a rate of return measure calculated by dividing inflation-adjusted cash flow from the investment by the inflation-adjusted amount of the cash investment. While CFROI does adjust for inflation, it fails to account for risk and the appropriate required return on the project. In a sense, CFROI is similar to the internal rate of return (IRR), hence it measures the investment's return as opposed to the wealth created or destroyed by the investment.

EVA comes closest in theory and construct to net present value (NPV). The information requirements for both techniques are the same. For both techniques you need an appropriate risk-adjusted cost of capital. To determine the NPV of an investment decision, you need estimates of expected future cash flow. Similarly, to determine the economic value of the decision, you need the present value of expected future EVAs that are based on expected future cash flows of the firm. In other words, the NPV of an asset is simply the present value of the expected future EVA from the asset. Therefore the notion

of increasing or maximizing EVA each year is consistent with the goal of shareholder wealth maximization.

USING EVA AND MVA WITHIN A COMPANY

All managers are basically in the same business—putting scarce capital to its most promising uses. To increase their company's stock price, managers must perform better than those with whom they compete for capital. Then, once they get the capital, they must earn rates of return on it that exceed the return offered by other equally risky-seekers of capital funds. If they accomplish this goal, value will have been added to the capital that their firm's investors placed at their disposal. If they don't accomplish that goal, there will be a misallocation of capital, and the company's stock will sell at a price that discounts the sum total of the resources employed.

EVA is a financial management system that is well adapted to this kind of a situation because it focuses on creating shareholder value. In using the system, managers and employees focus on how capital is used and on the cash flow generated from it. It runs counter to the notion that long-term stock appreciation comes from earnings.

Focusing on EVA growth provides two benefits: Management's attention is focused more toward its primary responsibility increasing investor wealth—and, two, distortions caused by using historical cost accounting data are reduced or eliminated. As a result, managers spend their time finding ways to increase EVA rather than debating the intricacies of the fluctuations in their accounting for reported earnings.

EVA measures the amount of value a firm creates during a defined period through operating decisions it makes to increase margins, improve working capital management, efficiently use its production facilities, and redeploy underutilized assets. Thus, EVA can be used to hold management accountable for all economic outlays whether they appear in the income statement, on the balance sheet, or in the financial statement's footnotes. EVA creates one financial statement that includes all the costs of being in business, including the carrying cost of capital. The EVA financial statement gives managers a complete picture of the connections among capital, margin, and EVA. It makes managers conscious of every dollar they spend whether that dollar is spent on or off the income statement or on operating costs or the carrying cost of working capital and fixed assets.

Another very subtle benefit to a company that adopts EVA is that it creates a common language for making decisions, especially long-term decisions; resolving budgeting issues; evaluating the performance of its organizational units and its managers; and measuring the value-creating potential of its strategic options. An outgrowth of such an environment is that the quality of management also improves as managers begin to think like owners and adopt a longer horizon view.

EVA should not be viewed as "the" answer to all things. By itself, EVA doesn't solve business problems; managers must solve them. But having access to such a meaningful measure that is linked strongly to share price performance clarifies a manager's options and, in conjunction with MVA, provides a meaningful target to pursue for both internally and externally oriented decisions.

USING EVA TO FACILITATE THE MANAGEMENT OF THE COMPANY

Managers of EVA-adopting firms know their stock's price is tied to investors' expectations of the company's long-term cash flows; therefore, they will explicitly use value-added measures in guiding their firm's activities. In this way, greater emphasis will be placed on the operating profit needed to justify capital expenditures—or any expenditure, for that matter. It is this increased awareness of the efficient use of capital that eventually will produce additional shareholder value.

Value-added measures can be particularly effective for gauging the performance of subsidiaries, divisions, and other business units when a stock price measure is unavailable. By using value-added measures at the business unit level, companies can determine where capital will be invested most productively and the contribution each unit makes to the market value of the company. Unit managers then can be compensated on the basis of those contributions.

Under the aegis of "what gets measured gets managed": EVA concepts can lead to improvements in the overall management of a firm's everyday operations. Incorporating EVAs metrics into formal performance measurement systems facilitates both the use of measurements in areas that have been difficult to monitor and adds a degree of precision to measurements that previously have been taken and reported.

With a focus on EVA, managers can do a better job of asset management, which can free up cash for use in other areas of the business. For example, a good way to boost EVA is to increase inventory turns, which reduces the amount of cash tied up in raw materials. Also, the effects of increasing inventory turns can be readily evaluated against the costs of running out of materials, shipping products late, or otherwise failing to satisfy the customer. On a more microlevel, manufacturing employees will readily comprehend that by reducing waste they help create economic value.

Companies that have adopted EVA find they use it as a basis for decision making at all levels—whether it is at the strategic level of acquisitions, a new market entry, or even in thinking about day-to-day trade-offs in their business. In these situations, EVA provides a rather simplistic means of assessing the alternatives under review because there are only three basic means of raising a company's EVA:

1. Raise profit levels without raising the amount of capital spent—most obvious method is cost cutting, but imaginative man will always look for other methods.
2. Use less capital. That means looking for improvements in the way a business is run such as streamlining operations.
3. Invest capital in high-return projects. Any project should meet the minimum criterion of earning more than the cost of capital invested.[10]

EVA also has been found to be a worthy adjunct to other management change programs such as total quality management, quick response, and total customer development. Rather than being at odds with the aims of those efforts, EVA's quantification of results in financial terms helps to energize them by demanding and getting continuous financial improvement.

With a company-wide adoption and use of EVA concepts, all employees begin to think like, act like, and be paid like owners and feel responsible for and take part in the economic value of the firm. Teamwork will be fostered, and everyone will "care" about what is going on and how business is progressing on a daily basis.

BENEFITS OF EVA INCENTIVE PLANS

To this point, the emphasis has been on how focusing on EVA may help managers increase shareholder wealth. For the metric to help in creating shareholder wealth, however, managers must behave in a manner consistent with wealth creation. One powerful way to align managers' interests with those of the shareholders is to tie their compensation to output from the EVA metric. In fact, it is not just for managers but may be used for *all* employees. When implemented correctly, the basic notion of increasing shareholder value will permeate the entire organization, and employees at all levels, will begin to act in concert with upper levels of management.

Implementing an EVA-based incentive plan is fundamentally a process of empowerment—getting employees to be entrepreneurial, to think and act as owners; getting them to run the business as if they owned it; and giving them a stake in the results they achieve.

The overall, company-wide objective is to generate a persistent increase in EVA. To achieve that, employees must understand the role they play in increasing a firm's EVA. A key factor in sustaining a continuing interest in EVA, and in making it work, is to revise the compensation system to focus on creating value. It has been shown that one of the critical components in successfully using EVA to improve a company's MVA is tying it to bonuses and pay schemes. Designing an incentive compensation system that pays people for sustainable improvements in EVA, in concert with an understanding of what drives EVA and what drives economic returns, is what transforms behavior within a company.

A good way to get started quickly is to increase insider ownership of the firm's stock. One way to do this is to turn old profit-sharing plans into employee stock ownership plans.

If an incentive system is to work, it must have certain distinctive properties:

1. An objective measure of performance—one that cannot be manipulated by one of the parties who may benefit. For example, in many existing plans, the budget is a commonly used target for performance, but the manager usually is heavily involved in negotiating that budget. If the manager negotiates well, the budget target can be easily "beatable."
2. It must be simple so even employees far down in the organization will understand how EVA is tied to economic value so they can follow it well.
3. Bonus amounts have to be significant enough in amount for employees to alter their behaviors.
4. It must be definitive—which means the target stays fixed and the goalpost won't be moved after the plan gets under way.

Other conditions that are suggested strongly by members of the Stern Stewart organization are:

5. There should be no limits (caps) placed on the plan. The sky is the limit. Having caps will develop into operating a seasonal business—when the target is reached, slow down.
6. Seek sustainable performance by not paying the full bonus amount in one year. This procedure would entail setting up an incentive plan bank account where the entire bonus is deposited, but some (smaller) portion is paid now, and a larger portion is paid later—and the amount to be paid out later can be subject to a loss. The objective is to keep EVA positive and not have the focus on achieving that goal only one time. Anyone can do it once.
7. Include a cancellation clause. If a person resigns, the banked bonus is lost. But if he or she retires, the balance is converted into a deferred bonus account.

For middle and senior people, take a certain amount of each year's cash payment, pay most of it in cash (say, 80%) and the rest in stock options (to get an equity interest). In establishing the ground rules for the plan, the pay-for-performance ratio should be steeply sloped—meaning that a manager's reward is higher on the upside of performance.

Incorporating a long-term perspective into an incentive plan is another important feature to consider. To get managers to focus on creating real value for the shareholders, a portion of the stock options available to managers can be priced at a premium over the market price on the date of the grant, Thus, managers first must earn the hurdle rate for the shareholders before they can exercise their own options for a gain. Therefore, the managers' financial incentives are aligned with the shareholders', resulting in the impetus needed to get managers to think aggressively and long term.

Finally, the structure of the incentive system should be team based to focus more on individual or small work group results and should still capture a larger, longer-term perspective based on the company's performance. The proper weighting of these elements can provide different motivation to different people depending on their ability to influence the item being measured.

IMPLEMENTING EVA

Transitioning to value-added measures is an extensive (and expensive) process. It can require a year or more of planning by internal and external financial and compensation experts. Advocates of value-added measures justify the substantial costs by pointing to the benefits of optimizing the company's strategy for value creation.

A transition to value-added performance measurement must start with a serious commitment of the board of directors and senior executives to use these measures to manage the business. The interests of lower-level managers and the employees they supervise must be cultivated carefully so they "buy in."

Success with value-added performance measures also requires a massive education and communication effort directed at executives, line managers, and hourly employees. Although it probably will require a great deal of training time and money to educate everyone on the basic theory underlying the notion of creating economic value, doing it in a structured, unhurried manner probably will be the most productive way in the long run.[11]

ENDNOTES

1. The latter item, given the acronym NIBCLS, appears in an EVA financial statement prepared under an Operating Approach. See G. Bennett Stewart III, *The Quest for Value*, HarperCollins Publishers, Inc., 1991, pp. 92, 100.
2. Ronald B. Lieber, "Who Are the Real Wealth Creators?" *Fortune*, December 9, 1996; Shawn Tully, "The Real Key to Creating Wealth," *Fortune*, September 20, 1993; Anne Fisher, "Creating Stockholder Wealth," *Fortune*, February 5, 1996.
3. These approaches are very detailed, and the reader is referred to G. Bennett Stewart's book for a more thorough coverage of them. See G. B. Stewart, pp. 87–110.
4. G. B. Stewart, p. 91.

5. G. Bennett Stewart III, "EVA: Fact and Fantasy," *Journal of Applied Corporate Finance*, pp. 73–74.

6. *Ibid.*, p. 74.

7. Kenneth Lehn and Anil K. Makhija, "EVA & MVA as Performance Measures and Signals for Strategic Change," *Strategy & Leadership Magazine*, May/June 1996, pp. 34–38.

8. Randy Myers, "Metric Wars," *CFO*, October 1996, p. 44.

9. James L. Dodd and Shimin Chen, "EVA: A New Panacea?" *B&E* Review, July/September 1996, pp. 26–28.

10. Shawn Tully, "The Real Key to Creating Wealth," *Fortune*, September 20, 1993, p. 50.

11. An excellent "how to" article on implementing EVA, including several specific steps and rules to follow, titled "How to Implement EVA and Make Share Prices Rise: Economic Value Added" by Mark Gressle, was published in *Cashflow Magazine*, March 1996, p. 28.

Paul A. Dierks, CPA, is an associate professor of management in the Babcock Graduate School of Management at Wake Forest University. He is a member of the Piedmont Winston-Salem Chapter, through which this article was submitted. He can be reached by phone at (910) 759-4579 or e-mail at paul_dierks@ mail.mba.wfa.edu. Ajay Patel is an assistant professor of management at the Babcock Graduate School of Management at Wake Forest University.

QUESTIONS

11.2a What exactly is EVA? Can it be labeled "true economic profit?"

11.2b Define MVA. What is the relation between MVA and EVA?

11.3 "Greening" With EVA

Now you can use Economic Value Added and other shareholder value measures to improve your corporate capital investment decisions.

by Marc J. Epstein and S. David Young*

Many companies are spending hundreds of millions of dollars a year on environmentally related operating costs and capital investments. But their accounting, costing, and capital investment systems don't identify and measure environmental costs properly. Instead, they hide these costs in various administrative and overhead accounts. Further, well-developed capital investment tools that companies use throughout their organizations are rarely employed for environmental capital investments. If used properly, shareholder value measures such as economic value added (EVA®), an increasingly popular performance metric, can significantly improve corporate decision making in the realm of environmental management and can improve both environmental and general capital investment decisions.[1]

Companies often make their investment decisions about environmentally-related projects based on incomplete data and incomplete analysis. If companies undertake the projects because they have to comply with an environmental regulation, they usually don't scrutinize them as much as they do capital projects. The main reason is the lack of financial expertise in environmental health and safety (EH&S) departments and the attitude, shared by managers throughout the corporate world, that they have no choice because they must comply with the regulations. We think this attitude produces substantially inferior decisions and compromises efforts to design, implement, and manage a corporate environmental strategy. It continues to foster reactive approaches to environmental management and inhibits the development of proactive approaches that can lead to substantially reduced environmental impacts and dramatic improvements in long-term corporate profitability.

WHAT ARE THE USUAL PROCEDURES?

While discounted cash flow (DCF) analysis is common in most corporate capital investment projects, companies approve many environmental projects with only a simple payback analysis. Lack of financial expertise encourages the use of payback, and some finance departments believe DCF analysis isn't necessary in regulatory projects because the projects must be completed without regard to whether they are financially sound.

The result is that companies do not identify or analyze the impacts of such projects. Not only is this approach common for projects driven by regulatory

---

mandate, but it often is applied to voluntary projects. Further, companies typically require payback periods that are substantially shorter than for other capital investments and don't subject the projects to the rigorous analysis the capital investment process usually entails. One study of environmental capital investments found that "payback periods were short; in nearly two-thirds of the activities, companies recouped their investments in six months or less."[2] By requiring extremely short payback periods; by avoiding the typical corporate technical, environmental, and financial screens; and by ignoring a full understanding of future costs and benefits, companies often make improper capital investment decisions.[3]

But when they complete a DCF analysis that considers all the impacts of a project on the company through the entire life cycle, they are encouraged to think through the impacts and possibly examine process and product redesign. They can accomplish this task through cross-functional groups that examine all of the impacts and consider likely changes in regulations, technology, cost of technology, consumer demand, and the impacts of those changes on the proposed capital investment.[4] Financial professionals should use the same techniques they use to forecast cash inflows and outflows for traditional investment projects to estimate the likely future cash flows related to the environmental impacts of general corporate capital investments, plant sitings, and both voluntary and regulatory environmental capital investments.

Obviously, the decision process for regulatory projects and voluntary projects should be different, but the analysis of alternatives and impacts should not. Too often, companies focus only on minimizing costs instead of maximizing net benefits. Too often, they calculate only the payback period without considering the time value of money, the broad array of constituencies affected, or the significant future benefits and costs likely to arise from environmentally related capital projects. Choosing projects based only on the shortest payback period will not yield the best choices.

EVA, which can show the contribution of environmental investments to shareholder value and can be tied to compensation and long-term divisional improvement, is one way to go.

WHAT IS EVA AND HOW IS IT CALCULATED?

EVA is similar to conventional measures of profit but with two important differences: EVA considers the cost of all capital, and it is not constrained by the generally accepted accounting principles (GAAP) that govern corporate financial reporting. The net income figures reported in company income statements consider only the most visible type of capital cost—interest—while ignoring the cost of equity finance. Financial accountants do not measure the cost of finance provided by the

company's shareholders because these costs, like all opportunity costs, can't be observed directly. But they are real, nonetheless. Although estimating the cost of equity is a highly subjective exercise, measures of performance that ignore such costs can't reveal how successful a company has been in creating value for its owners. One way to describe EVA is that it represents a company's profits net of the cost of both debt and equity capital. It is economic profit or residual income. But EVA doesn't stop there. It also corrects for potential distortions caused by GAAP. Very simply, the user of EVA can abandon any accounting principles that are viewed as distorting the measurement of wealth creation.

To understand EVA, you need to understand Market. Value Added (MVA).[5] MVA is the difference between the market value of the firm and its invested capital (including equity and debt) contributed to the firm:

MVA = Market value – Invested capital

Managers want to maximize MVA, not the value of the firm, which is accomplished easily enough by investing ever-increasing amounts of capital. For example, if a company raises $20 million in capital and invests it in projects that are expected to earn the cost of capital, both total value and total capital have increased by $20 million, and MVA is unchanged. MVA increases only when invested capital earns a rate of return greater than the cost of capital. When a company invests newly raised capital in value-creating projects—those with a positive net present value—MVA increases. When that capital is invested in value-destroying projects (those with a negative net present value), MVA decreases. So how does EVA relate to MVA? MVA is the present value of the firm's expected future EVAs. EVA generates more attention than MVA because, as we will explain later, it is more amenable to periodic performance measurement. EVA is calculated as follows:

	Net sales
–	Operating expenses
=	Operating profit
–	Taxes
=	Not operating profit
–	Capital charges
=	EVA

Capital charges equal a company's "invested capital" (or "capital employed") times the weighted-average cost of capital. Invested capital is the sum of all the company's financing apart from noninterest-bearing short-term liabilities, such as accounts payable, accrued wages, and accrued taxes.

If GAAP distorts the measurement of capital or operating income, it can be adjusted as necessary. Most of the adjustments are in the form of "equity equivalents." The logic behind these adjustments is that when companies apply GAAP, certain items are charged to income, such as provisions, deferred taxes, and goodwill, which artificially—and misleadingly—reduce stated capital. Unless these charges are restored to equity, capital charges will be understated, and operating income will be misstated.

The potential number of adjustments is practically limitless. EVA consultants have already identified more than 150 changes that can be made to operating profit and invested capital. But most companies that use EVA or similar measures make fewer than five adjustments (and many make none at all) for fear that the evaluation and reward system based on EVA would become impossibly complicated.

IMPLEMENTING EVA

Although the idea of using EVA is often proposed by the CFO or the corporate controller, the implementation process begins with the board and the CEO. The CFO's office may spearhead implementation, but the profound attitude shifts that are possible from value-based management practices require commitment at the highest levels. Why expect employees to accept EVA and all that goes with it if the CEO doesn't appear totally committed to the concept?

As shown in Table 1, after the board, the CEO, and other top managers have accepted value-based management and the use of EVA, a steering committee must be established to make the important strategic decisions regarding program design. The members of this committee should include the CFO, at least one senior level operating manager other than the CEO, and the corporate head of human resources. Other candidates might include a senior strategic business unit or product line manager, the corporate controller, and the head of investor relations. This committee will be tasked with determining, subject to board approval:

- Which corporate activities will be driven expressly by value-based management and which activities will be tied to EVA. A fully committed company incorporates value-based management into its strategic planning, capital allocation, operating budget, and compensation processes and systems. Investor relations also will be affected.
- How far down in the organizational hierarchy EVA will be calculated. The general rule of thumb is to continue until the arbitrariness of transfer pricing and/or overhead allocation policies offset the advantages of improving line of sight through the direct measurement of EVA for lower-level managers.
- EVA (or value) drivers will be used for levels in the hierarchy below those for which EVA is calculated

and how they will be identified. The balanced scorecard is a popular approach for this purpose.
- How EVA will be calculated.
- If a single cost of capital figure will be used to calculate capital charges or if the cost of capital will be calculated separately for each division.
- Which managers and employees will have bonuses linked to EVA and how the bonus plan will work.

TABLE 1. A CHECKLIST FOR IMPLEMENTING EVA

Step 1:	Establish buy-in at the board and top management levels.
Step 2:	Set up a steering committee that will make the major strategic decisions on the EVA program (subject to board approval).
Step 3:	The steering committee formulates a strategy. What functions will be tied to EVA? Compensation Strategic planning Operating budgets Capital budgets Investor relations How far down the hierarchy will EVA be calculated? How will EVA be calculated? Management compensation Who will be covered? How will the bonus plan work? Relation to nonfinancial measures
Step 4:	The steering committee appoints a working committee to implement the strategy.
Step 5:	Set up a training program.

A working committee also should be appointed. This committee will implement the strategy set forth by the steering committee and approved by the board. The members of this committee should include, at a minimum, a senior representative from the CFO's office (probably an accountant), a human resources professional (with extensive experience in management training), and a senior-level line manager (but below the executive board level). For medium-sized and smaller companies, a single committee may be tasked with both the key strategic issues in EVA program design and with implementation of the program. Large, global companies are more likely to separate these tasks into two committees.

Whether performed by the steering committee or a working committee, one of the most delicate tasks in EVA implementation is designing a training program that draws genuine commitment to value creation from the company's employees.

EVA AND FINANCIAL MANAGEMENT

EVA is innovative in three important ways. First, because it is not bound by GAAP, its users are willing to make whatever adjustments are needed to produce more economically valid numbers. Second, proponents have been pushing companies to bring EVA into lower levels of the organization on the assumption that all employees, not just senior managers, must undertake their tasks with the overriding goal of creating shareholder value. Third, EVA offers a means of measuring and communicating performance that can be used in the capital markets, for capital investment appraisal, and in the evaluation and compensation of managerial performance. Instead of using, say, earnings per-share to communicate with security analysts, internal rates of return for capital investment appraisal, and return on net assets for the evaluation of managerial performance, companies can use EVA for all three.

Consider a typical capital investment. We undertake the investment when the net present value is positive and reject it when the NPV is negative. NPV is calculated by subtracting the capital to be invested from the present value of the net cash flows, or

$$\text{NPV}_{project} = \text{Present Value}_{project} - \text{Capital}_{project}$$

Now, consider the formula for MVA:

$$\text{MVA} = \text{Total Value} - \text{Total Capital}$$

In effect, MVA is equivalent to the present value of the cash flows to all capital providers (the value of the firm) net of the capital invested in the firm. Or it is the net present value for the entire firm. Remember that MVA, whether for the entire firm or just a single capital investment project, equals the present value of future EVAs.

When you view it in this way, you can see that firms can use EVA/MVA to evaluate capital investment proposals because these measurement tools will yield the same answer as NPV. That means the same terminology that companies use to communicate with shareholders can also be used internally for decision making. For capital budgeting proposals, nothing is lost by using EVA instead of discounted cash flow approaches because EVA produces equivalent results.

If the discounted present value of future EVAs yields the same answer as NPV, what does EVA offer that NPV doesn't? From a valuation standpoint, nothing. But EVA does have an important advantage. The problem with NPV (and MVA, for that matter) is that it is what economists call a "stock" or "wealth" measure; it is not a "flow." It measures the total amount of wealth that is expected to be created from undertaking an investment or activity, not performance. Managerial performance is evaluated over periods of time, say, three months, six months, or a year, not at a point in time. Because NPV and MVA are equivalent, and MVA is the present value of future EVAs, EVA becomes the means by which we can convert the stock measure of NPV (or

MVA) into a flow. By linking management bonuses to EVA, companies reward managers for undertaking positive net present value projects, which is exactly what they want them to do.

EVA, CAPITAL INVESTMENT DECISIONS, AND ENVIRONMENTAL IMPACTS

To improve the quality of capital investment decisions, companies must be careful to consider the impacts of their products, services, and activities on their constituents over the life of the investment. Many companies make capital investment decisions on both environmental issues and general capital investments without considering the broad lifecycle impacts that will affect long-term corporate profitability. If companies want to improve capital investment decisions, they need to estimate future costs and benefits that probably will be internalized.[6] One such example is the cost of product take back. Already common in Europe and globally in some industries, these are costs that corporations incur when they take back and dispose of products they produced after consumers use them. Such costs should be included in both product costing and capital investment decisions.[7]

Once a company completes its analysis of future financial impacts, it should include those results in an NPV or EVA analysis. Corporate environmental health and safety managers often complain that the analysis of EH&S investments, both mandated and voluntary, are incomplete because they don't include a broad integration of impacts. But they also find that senior corporate managers don't see the value of these investments and, for this reason, often reject them.

This dilemma can be resolved through EVA because it can communicate the potential contribution of a project in language that is consistent with what many consider to be the most important of all corporate concerns: maximizing shareholder value.

BARRIERS AND CHALLENGES TO EVA IMPLEMENTATION

Companies adopt EVA because it can encourage managers to think and act more like owners. When managers are paid based on metrics other than EVA or similar value-based measures, there is a substantial risk that they will undertake activities, such as growth for its own sake, which might increase their own compensation at the expense of shareholder wealth creation. When companies link pay to EVA, and especially to improvements in EVA, managers soon learn that the surest way to high pay and advancement is creating as much wealth as possible for shareholders over the long term. But while the idea is simple enough, implementation is often complicated and frustrating.

Successful implementation of EVA requires:

- A full commitment from top management, especially the CEO. Not only must the value creation philosophy be integrated with all of the company's key systems—including strategic planning, capital budgeting, and management compensation—it must constantly be reinforced in management meetings, training seminars, company newsletters, performance reviews, and in communications with external parties such as security analysts and the financial press.

- A decision on which, if any, adjustments are to be made to the GAAP-based accounting numbers. Companies have a delicate balancing act to perform, managing the increased precision that comes from making more and more adjustments against the need to keep the measurement system easy and understandable.

- A careful consideration of transfer pricing and overhead allocation policies and their impact on EVA calculations. These issues are crucial because they can interfere with one of EVA's most potent advantages: its ability to get all managers, not just the most senior ones, to think more like owners. The power of EVA to accomplish this mission depends largely on the calculation of divisional EVA. But as any management accountant knows, different transfer pricing and overhead allocation policies can lead to wildly different divisional performance numbers. These issues are especially troublesome when large portions of managerial pay are linked to these numbers. Companies can sidestep the problem by calculating EVA only at the group level or for large stand-alone units. Unfortunately, when bonuses are linked to EVA at the corporate level, the compensation system becomes little better than conventional profit-sharing plans. Its ability to act as a motivator for employees at all levels becomes seriously blunted because, for all but the most senior managers, corporate EVA is too remote from their day-to-day activities.

- Intensive training for any manager or employee whose bonuses will be linked to EVA. In addition to explaining the imperative of value creation, and why it must go to the top of the corporate agenda, employees must understand how their unit EVAs will be calculated and how, in detail, the EVA numbers will be linked to compensation.

Management accountants and financial managers can make a major contribution to corporate profits by using their skills in measurement and analysis to improve capital investment decisions. On the environmental front, that includes identification and measurement of impacts related to a broader set of constituencies and a broader set of impacts than most companies now consider. It also means communicating this information effectively throughout the organization and demonstrating the relationship of the various impacts on shareholder value. EVA can be an important tool in this effort.

ENDNOTES

1. EVA is a registered trademark of Stern Stewart & Company.
2. Mark H. Dorfman, Warren R. Muir, and Catherine G. Miller, *Environmental Dividends: Cutting More Chemical Wastes*, Inform, 1992.
3. An extensive discussion of this topic can be found in Marc J. Epstein and Marie-Josee Roy, "Integrating Environmental Impacts into Capital Investment Decisions," *Greener Management International: The Journal of Corporate Environmental Strategy and Practice*, Spring 1997, pp. 69–87.
4. See, for example, Srikant Datar, Marc J. Epstein, and Karen White, "Bristol-Myers Squibb: The Matrix Essentials Product Life Cycle Review," *Stanford Business School Case*, 1997.
5. This section is largely adapted from Economic Value Added, INSEAD technical note 01/98-4667, and "Economic Value Added: A Primer for European Managers," *European Management Journal*, August 1997, both by S. David Young.
6. Additional details on incorporating life-cycle costing and total stakeholder analysis in product and project analysis (PPA) can be found in Marc J. Epstein, *Measuring Corporate Environmental Performance: Best Practices for Costing and Managing an Effective Environmental Strategy*, 1996.
7. Marc J. Epstein, "Accounting for Product Take Back," *Management Accounting*, August 1996.

Marc J. Epstein is visiting professor in the Jones Graduate School of Management at Rice University in Houston. Formerly a professor at Harvard and Stanford Business Schools, he has written extensively for Management Accounting *and is the author of the award-winning IMA book*, Measuring Corporate Environmental Performance: Best Practices for Costing and Managing an Effective Environmental Strategy. *His latest book,* Counting What Counts: Turning Accountability to Competitive Advantage, *will be released in April. He can be reached at epatein@rice.edu.*

S. David Young is professor of accounting at INSEAD. His research focuses on performance measurement and value based management. He is now writing a book on measuring and implementing Economic Value Added and can be reached by e-mail at david.young@insead.fr.

QUESTION

11.3 What factors must be considered before implementing EVA?

11.4 Evaluating Internal Operations and Supply Chain Performance Using EVA and ABC

Terrance L. Pohlen and B. Jay Coleman *

INTRODUCTION

Firms cannot exist in isolation and must rely on other firms to perform a complex chain of interdependent activities from source-of-supply to the end-user. One company rarely controls an entire supply chain, and success depends on how well the combined capabilities of these firms can be integrated to achieve a competitive market-place advantage (Cook, DeBree, and Feroleto, 2001). Managers must extend their "line of sight" to understand system-wide performance and the contribution of each firm (Lummus and Vokurka, 1999). They subsequently need to develop measures for on meeting end-user requirements and aligning firm behavior with supply chain objectives. The ability to develop such measures is a major challenge to supply chain management (Pohlen, 2003).

Performance measures are critical to the success of the supply chain (Deloitte, 1999). Companies can no longer focus on optimizing their own operations to the exclusion of their suppliers' and customers' operations (Lummus, Vokurka, and Alber, 1999). By tying manufacturing and supply chain activities to performance outcomes, operations managers and senior executives can make more informed decisions regarding the allocation of scarce resources and the initiatives and partners that are best for the overall supply chain. Managers across an entire supply chain must collaborate to improve performance and obtain the greatest mutual benefit. Performance measures are needed to keep the trading partners aligned with the enterprise-wide goals so supply chain performance can be optimized.

Effective supply chain management requires measures capable of capturing inter-firm performance (van Hoek, 1998) and integrating the results to depict overall supply chain performance (McAdam and McCormack, 2001). Performance must be measured simultaneously across multiple firms, and the measures must demonstrate how each firm's behavior affects the others and the value delivered to the end-user. Supply chain performance measures must translate nonfinancial performance into financial terms and shareholder value

(Ellram and Liu, 2002). Supply chain management will affect more than costs, and managers must be able to sell the value created to senior executives, trading partners, and shareholders. Although most managers acknowledge the importance of designing metrics and rewards, they lack an adequate framework for developing suitable performance measures (Kallio, 2000, Simatupang and Sridharan, 2002).

Few firms have measures capable of capturing performance across multiple companies (Keebler, 1999, Lambert and Pohlen, 2001, Lee and Billington, 1992, McAdam and McCormack, 2001, and Simatupang and Sridharan, 2002), and most are not satisfied with the measures they currently use for supply chain performance (Deloitte, 1999). In many instances, the measures identified as supply chain metrics are actually measures of internal operations or logistics performance (Lambert and Pohlen, 2001). Other approaches, such as the total cost of ownership (TCO) or the supply chain operations reference (SCOR) model, measure the effect of suppliers or other trading partners on performance within the firm. They do not measure performance across multiple firms or the overall supply chain.

In an effort to address this shortcoming, we apply a general framework introduced by Lambert and Pohlen (2001) to show how operations performance can be evaluated with a multi-firm, supply chain perspective. The framework can help operations managers achieve supply chain objectives such as "increased shareholder value" and "improved customer service" by providing a concrete roadmap. The focus is on increasing shareholder value for each firm in the supply chain by establishing within-company and cross-company links between actions (i.e., prospective value drivers) and profits. Senior executives can use the framework to determine whether operational-level actions did, indeed, create value, to demonstrate what requires measurement, to focus attention, and to align behavior within each firm with supply chain objectives. The framework differs from other approaches by simultaneously measuring and analyzing interfirm performance and linking operational

---

* From: R. L. Pohlen and B. J. Coleman, "Evaluating Internal Operations and Supply Chain Performance Using EVA and ABC," *SAM Advanced Management Journal* (Spring 2005): 45–58. Reprinted with permission of SAM Advanced Management Journal (www.samnational.org).

performance measures directly to the drivers of shareholder value.

APPLYING THE FRAMEWORK

The framework employs a dyadic economic value added (EVA) analysis and activity-based costing (ABC). The dyadic EVA analysis 1) evaluates how process changes simultaneously drive value in each firm, and 2) develops measures that align operations performance with supply chain objectives. ABC determines what drives costs and performance (Krumwiede and Roth, 1997, Buckingham and Loomba, 2001) and also translates nonfinancial performance into activity costs and financial measures. EVA and ABC enable managers to optimize and better coordinate the performance of activities across the entire supply chain (Dekker and Van Goor). The framework was adapted for an operational environment by developing five steps, each of which is performed by operations management personnel:

- Establish strategic objectives for the supply chain.
- Map the firms composing the supply chain.
- Examine operational decisions (i.e., potential value creators) using a dyadic EVA analysis.
- Translate process objectives into costs and operational performance measures using ABC.
- Measure and extend analysis to other trading partners.

1. *Establish strategic objectives for the supply chain*

The corporate strategy of the firm demonstrating the greatest leadership and power provides the most likely starting point for establishing supply chain objectives. Operations managers should look first at strategy when setting objectives and determining what to measure (Neely et al, 2000; Keegan et al, 1989; and Wisner and Fawcett, 1991). The corporate strategy reflects management's choices and trade-offs in its drive to achieve a unique competitive position and maximize shareholder value (Rappaport, 1987). Supply chain strategy flows directly from corporate strategy and the selected target markets by determining the configuration of the processes and companies that best meet end-user requirements and provide the greatest competitive advantage (Lummus, Vokurka, and Alber, 1999). Beginning with the consumer, management works backwards through the supply chain to consider what combination of trading partners best serves the target markets.

During this stage, operations managers perform a competitive analysis of the attractiveness of their industry and their position relative to their competitors. They seek to understand how alternative manufacturing strategies affect the firm's competitive position and the value created. The analysis leads to the selection of strategies that should best achieve corporate objectives

and increase shareholder value. The resulting strategic plan and the company's mission statement provide direction and control for subsequent tactical planning and management of daily operations (Stock and Lambert, 2001).

2. *Map the firms composing the supply chain*

Mapping identifies the companies composing the supply chain from end-users to the raw material suppliers, after step 1 is completed and the most appropriate processes and strategic partners are identified (Stock and Lambert, 2001). Supply chain maps typically appear as a complex web like the branches and roots of an uprooted tree (Lambert and Pohlen, 2001). They rarely resemble the linear pipeline diagrams in most illustrations. This complexity makes it extremely difficult to understand what is actually happening and to communicate objectives across a supply chain (Keebler, 1999, McAdam and McCormack, 2001). Mapping enables managers to better understand their supply chains; however, few firms actually map them (Gardner and Cooper, 2003). Managers use the maps to achieve a competitive advantage — determining which branches or roots generate the most profit, pose the greatest risk, incur unnecessary cost and time, and require focused attention. The maps frequently reveal, previously undetected opportunities. For example, several tier-one suppliers may purchase critical components from the same tier-two supplier. Operations managers can leverage this information and negotiate a single ordering agreement with the tier-two supplier on behalf of their tier-one suppliers. They may also discover opportunities to reduce set-up times, eliminate waste, remove unnecessary intermediaries, and cut cycle times. Analyzing each link in the chain identifies many opportunities for improvement (Lummus, Vokurka, and Alber, 1998), but the value created by these opportunities must be demonstrated and sold to executives in the other firms to secure their buy-in and to align behavior with supply chain objectives.

3. *Examine operational decisions (potential value creators) using a dyadic EVA analysis* \

Several processes span each link in the supply chain (Croxton, 2001), and a dyadic EVA analysis shows simultaneously how process changes drive value in multiple firms (Lambert and Pohlen, 2001). EVA has the advantage of providing "…a measure of wealth creation that aligns the goals of divisional or plant managers with the goals of the entire company" (Brewer, 1999). A dyadic EVA takes this a step further by measuring value creation across multiple companies and aligning management decisions with the objectives of the supply chain (Pohlen and Goldsby, 2003). A value-based approach expands the analysis beyond a simple "cost-cost" analysis by examining the effect on revenues, cost-of-goods sold, expenses, and assets. In many instances, a process change will affect activities in multiple companies. A dyadic analysis provides the capability to simultaneously determine the effect of any changes from the supplier's and customer's perspectives (Figure 1).

To illustrate how the value of an operational decision can be assessed within and across firms in the supply chain, consider a manufacturer who is attempting to implement a new manufacturing strategy or production initiative, such as lean production. As part of lean production, the manufacturer must reduce waste or, according to lean production doctrine, nonvalue-added items such as inventory, over-production (producing more units than needed to fill current orders), correction or rework (due to quality defects), the waiting of product during the production process, and overly long processing times. The lean focus also requires the manufacturer to increase its production flexibility.

In partial response to these needs, suppose the manufacturer decides to implement procedures to reduce production setup time. This will reduce setup costs, which are largely a function of production downtime caused by the setup, and thereby reduce production run sizes (i.e., less overproduction). With lower production quantities, average inventory levels will naturally go down as well, since order quantities directly influence the size of cycle stock, thus reducing that element of waste. These smaller production runs will also generate shorter order cycles (or time between orders) for the manufacturer. The shorter cycles, in turn, increase manufacturing flexibility, with a direct benefit for downstream customers. If a particular item is out-of-stock when ordered by a customer, the manufacturer will be able to launch a job to produce the needed item much sooner than if the manufacturer were tied to long production runs. The manufacturer can also afford to implement *heijunka* (Coleman and Vaghefi, 1994) – that is, the ability to make a little bit of everything every day, as opposed to making only one thing for a while before changing over to make something else. As a result, production plans can be set to make workloads much smoother across departments or work centers, and across time periods.

Wastes associated with waiting, processing, and correction also are improved. With shorter setup times and cycles, the likely waiting time for customer orders entering the production process is also reduced, as is the waiting time of work-in-process as it enters production queues. Also, reduced setup times will mean more time available for production, meaning the firm may be able to produce more during a given period, and possibly meet demand it is currently missing. With better designed setups, the scrap generated during and immediately after setups (due to testing) will be reduced. In sum, the potential benefits of a program to reduce setup times are substantial and permeate nearly all of the objectives of a lean production program.

However, note that the preceding concentrates on nonfinancial measures of performance. Ultimately, the performance changes should affect traditional financial measures within the firm. To illustrate, Figure 2 takes the supplier's perspective (the left half of Figure 1), and details the value drivers box. Also added is a box listing many aforementioned effects on various operational measures associated with reduced setup time and how they align with the firm's value drivers and financial metrics. As shown, setup time reduction should lead to a commensurate reduction in many of the expenses associated with inventory, including insurance; utilities; personnel directly associated with handling, maintaining, and auditing the inventory; interest (on any borrowing done to finance inventory); write-offs associated with inventory shrinkage due to damage, theft, or obsolescence; and scrap loss formerly experienced during and immediately following inefficient setups, etc. (Courtis, 1995). As a result, cost of goods sold and total expenses should decrease for the manufacturer, leading to a higher gross margin and net profit, respectively, and therefore a higher net operating profit after taxes (NOPAT). These effects are illustrated in the top half of Figure 2.

These benefits typically do not come without a price. In the short term, an investment in personnel time may be required to study setup practices and recommend changes. If a team approach is chosen for major setups, there may be an associated increase in personnel expenses and more employee training may be involved. Improved setups also may require modification of the product design itself to facilitate changeovers, which entails its own set of expenses. These and other costs will to some extent offset the previously noted improvements and will thereby affect the gross margin, net profit, and NOPAT, as shown in Figure 2.

But restricting the analysis to costs wouldn't be appropriate. As Courtis (1995) also notes, the reduction in time and expense, along with the increase in flexibility, should also benefit the revenue side. If cost savings are translated into lower prices for customers, sales volume and total revenue may increase. As noted, an increase in total output by converting setup time to productive time may allow the firm to meet demand it might not otherwise meet, and customer backorders may be reduced or eliminated. The gains in manufacturing flexibility and response time may generate increased business. In addition, the manufacturer may be able to reduce previously imposed minimum order quantities, thereby gaining a wider range of customers. As a result, the firm will see beneficial effects on sales revenue, gross margin, net profit, and NOPAT, over and above those associated with cost improvement (see Figure 2).

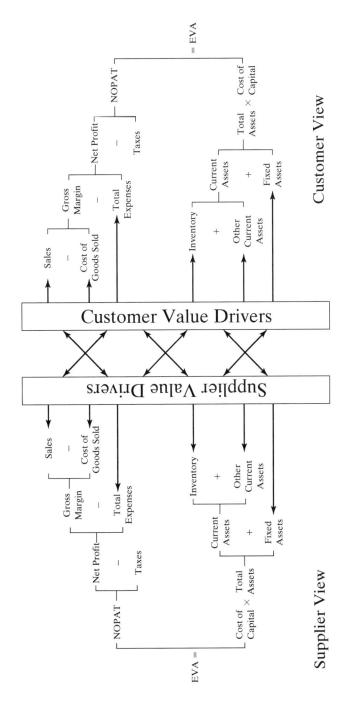

Supplier View

Customer View

Adapted from Stern, Joel M. and John S. Shiely with Irwin Ross, *The EVA Challenge*, New York: John Wiley & Sons, Inc., 2001, Figure 7.2, p. 120 and Pohlen, T. L. and Goldsby, t. J. (2003), "VMI and SMI Programs: How Economic Value Added Can Help Sell the Change," *International Journal of Physical Distribution and Logistics Management*, 33(7), 565-581.

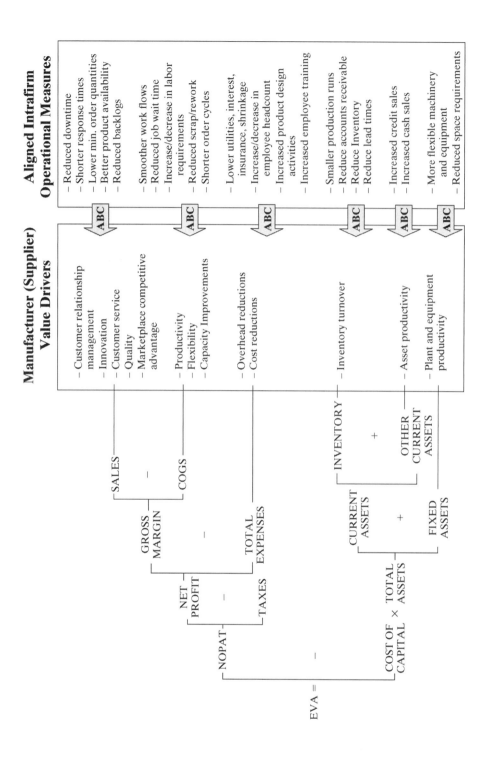

Figure 1: Using Dyadic EVA Analysis to Demonstrate the Effect of Collaborative Action on Value Drivers in the Supplier and Customer Firms

Figure 2: Evaluating the Manufacturer's Value Propositions of Reduced Setup Time

Again, however, the analysis shouldn't stop there. Restricting the analysis to revenues versus expenses ignores the impact on a firm's fixed and current assets. Although major investment is not necessarily required to improve setups (Shingo, 1985), this initiative may well require additional investment in fixed assets, such as newer and more flexible equipment (Courtis, 1995) and machinery that can be changed over more easily. Current assets will also be affected; the primary benefit will be the reduction in inventory already documented. However, this will likely be offset somewhat — and, according to Courtis (1995), perhaps completely — by higher cash balances and accounts receivable.

So, how does the firm factor in the classical profit and loss financial information with the changes in total assets? That is the advantage of opting for an EVA approach to see whether the setup reduction initiative generates value for the firm. As illustrated in Figures 1 and 2, the change in total assets is multiplied by the firm's weighted average cost of capital to determine the necessary benchmark return for the assets invested in the venture. If the changes in NOPAT exceed this benchmark, then the initiative creates economic value for the manufacturer.

However, stopping at the firm level would fail to account for the true influence on the manufacturer's supply chain partners and would likely not appropriately capture the total value of the initiative. Consider the corresponding view of one of the manufacturer's key retail customers, and the "mirror image" of Figure 2 that determines the retailer's own value propositions (in Figure 3). Recall that one of the benefits of setup savings is the possible reduction in prices that the retail customer must pay the manufacturer. When translated into the retailer's EVA analysis, the lower prices result in decreased costs of good sold, and a corresponding increase in gross margin, net profit, and NOPAT. Moreover, the manufacturer's faster production capabilities generated through more production uptime and increased flexibility translates into greater on-shelf availability for the retailer and a possible corresponding increase in retail sales and market share. The resulting increase in sales positively affects all profit measures as well.

There are also effects on the retailer's asset base. Suppose that as a result of the setup time savings the manufacturer can ship finished products more frequently and, in smaller quantities. (Perhaps the manufacturer had been requiring large minimum orders, which can now be greatly reduced). With smaller order quantities, the retailer's own cycle stock is reduced. Furthermore, the retailer's safety stock levels potentially could be reduced, since these are partially a function of lead time from the manufacturer.

With better manufacturing response times and reduced backlogs, safety stocks for the retailer can be lowered. The reduction in storage space requirements for the retailer also lowers the percentage of distribution center space allocated to the manufacturer's product. If significant enough, the retailer might even be able to eliminate distribution centers. All of this would have a positive impact on the retailer's total assets. When simultaneously evaluated against the retailer's changes in its own NOPAT, the change in EVA for the retailer can be estimated.

There are tangible benefits for the manufacturer associated with extending the analysis to its trading partner in the manner described. Suppose the manufacturer believes that an increase in selling price is needed to partially justify the investment in setup reduction. This obviously would run counter to the potential price reduction advantages to the retailer mentioned earlier in the section. However, a complete analysis of advantages to the retailer associated with the manufacturers' changes (e.g., in on-shelf availability and improved sales prospects), along with an illustration of the total asset reductions and corresponding increase in EVA for the retailer, could go a long way in selling the price increases to the retailer. It would also avoid the strict cost-versus-cost discussions that classically take place between supply chain partners.

Similar scenarios could also arise in which a member of the supply chain needs inter-firm visibility to make appropriate decisions or to sell trading partners on new initiatives. Suppose the manufacturer, as part of the lean initiative, wants to increase standardization (another lean production concept) by reducing the number or variety of products in its product line. Such a move would make it easier for the manufacturer to deal with the setup issues but would reduce the variety of product offered to the retailer. The retailer will typically view such a move negatively, as it would tend to imply reduced sales volume at the retail level. However, suppose the manufacturer promises a corresponding price decrease, as well as a minimum order reduction. Using the dyadic EVA analysis described, both parties can identify whether the reduction in the product line will pay off.

The dyadic EVA analysis demonstrates how working together to achieve supply chain objectives drives value in both firms. A holistic view of the supply chain facilitates communication and enables problems to be identified more easily (Cook, 2001). By incorporating all of the drivers of shareholder value, managers can move beyond cost-cost discussions, where one firm "loses" and another "wins," to identifying interfirm opportunities that create value for both firms and the entire supply chain.

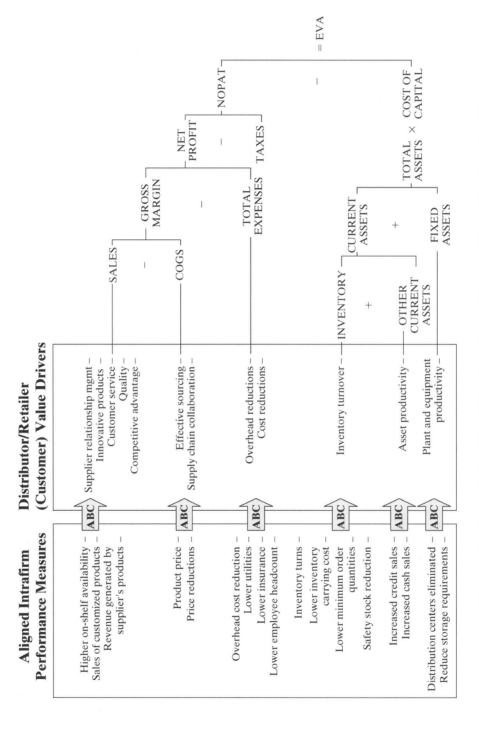

Aligned Intrafirm Performance Measures

Distributor/Retailer (Customer) Value Drivers

Higher on-shelf availability –
Sales of customized products –
Revenue generated by supplier's products –

ABC → Supplier relationship mgmt –
Innovative products –
Customer service –
Quality –
Competitive advantage –

SALES

Product price –
Price reductions –

ABC → Effective sourcing –
Supply chain collaboration –

COGS

GROSS MARGIN

Overhead cost reduction –
Lower utilities –
Lower insurance –
Lower employee headcount –

ABC → Overhead reductions –
Cost reductions –

TOTAL EXPENSES

NET PROFIT

Inventory turns –
Lower inventory carrying cost –
Lower minimum order quantities –
Safety stock reduction –

ABC → Inventory turnover –

INVENTORY

Increased credit sales –
Increased cash sales –

ABC → Asset productivity –

OTHER CURRENT ASSETS

CURRENT ASSETS

Distribution centers eliminated –
Reduce storage requirements –

ABC → Plant and equipment productivity –

FIXED ASSETS

TOTAL ASSETS × COST OF CAPITAL

NOPAT

– = EVA

TAXES

Figure 3: Evaluating the Retailer's Value Propositions of Reduced Setup Time by its Supplier

286

However, successful inter-firm collaboration will directly depend on the ability to accurately measure and assign any resulting cost changes by product, customer, supplier, or supply chain (Zank and Vokurka, 2003) and on the development of measures that align internal performance with supply chain objectives. This is the role and contribution to the framework performed by activity-based costing.

4. *Translate process objectives into costs and operational performance measures using ABC*

The financial and performance views of ABC support accurate costing and the development of supporting operational performance measures (Turney, 1991). The cost assignment, or vertical view, of ABC (Figure 4) assigns costs to the activities performed within an organization. An activity-based approach uses multiple drivers to reflect how resources and activities are actually consumed. The use of multiple drivers provides a more accurate assignment of costs than traditional cost systems that typically rely on a limited number of volume-based measures, such as direct labor hours or sales volume (Krumwiede and Roth, 1997). Operations managers can use this view to determine the costs of activities composing their firm's supply chain processes. ABC assigns the costs to the customers, suppliers, products, and supply chains involved in these activities. This cost information can be inserted directly into the dyadic EVA analysis when assessing performance and value resulting from conducting business with a specific customer.

Activity-based management (ABM), or the process view of ABC (Figure 5), decomposes supply chain processes into the specific activities performed within each firm. Operations managers can use this view to develop and align intrafirm performance measures that support the supply chain objectives. The horizontal perspective increases management understanding of activity performance by breaking down activities into measurable tasks, developing nonfinancial performance measures, and identifying the factors driving activity performance and cost. Management can act on this information to improve activity cost and performance.

An activity-based approach is essential for determining the inputs into the dyadic EVA framework. Reconfiguration of internal operational processes (such as setup time reduction) will drive changes in activities within the firm. ABC captures the effect of these changes in nonfinancial performance, translates the changes into costs, and updates the changes into financial performance and statements. The firm's impact on supply chain partners is also captured through ABC. Changes in performance are translated into assignable cost information that can be applied to the particular partner being studied. Additionally, the determination of assignable nonfinancial performance information helps the firm identify the effect of an activity on factors that cross the supply chain, such as quality, cost, flexibility, dependability, and innovation (Wisner and Fawcett, 1991).

ABC provides the necessary mechanism to link operational measures (shown in the performance measure column) in Figures 2 and 3 with the associated value drivers and financial measures shown in those figures. The measures and cost information obtained through ABC are traced to each of the value drivers, as illustrated by the large arrows. The linkage demonstrates how improved performance at the activity level leads to value creation and increased profitability at the corporate level. The cascading of objectives to value drivers to operational measures ensures the alignment of intrafirm performance with interfirm strategy. It also promotes more effective communication by identifying exactly what each individual must accomplish to meet corporate and supply chain objectives. The framework enables operations managers to work backwards from the objective to reconfigure processes, redistribute activities, align performance, measure progress, and demonstrate improvement in profitability.

5. *Measure and expand analysis to other trading partners*

Expanding the dyadic EVA analysis from the supplier-customer relationship to include trading partners across the entire supply chain enables management to see how each firm contributes to achieving supply chain objectives and whether corporate behavior is properly aligned to improve performance and generate additional value. A dyadic upstream and downstream view is necessary to allow the manufacturer's leadership team to fully evaluate initiatives or proposals. For example, suppose the manufacturer is asking a tier 1 supplier for reductions in delivery quantities and quicker response to synchronize with the manufacturer's objective of smaller production quantities. The tier 1 supplier maintains that comply a significant investment is required to move distribution centers closer to the manufacturer. This will entail an associated price increase. If viewed myopically, the manufacturer simply could not capture the true value of a new arrangement, nor could they determine what a reasonable price increase would be. Using a dyadic EVA analysis, the manufacturer could assess the impact of the investment for the supplier, could examine the value drivers (e.g., lower raw material inventory) generated for itself by the results of that investment, assess the resulting EVA changes, and in the process assess the EVA impact that would be passed along to its own customers. Only then could an appropriate decision be made.

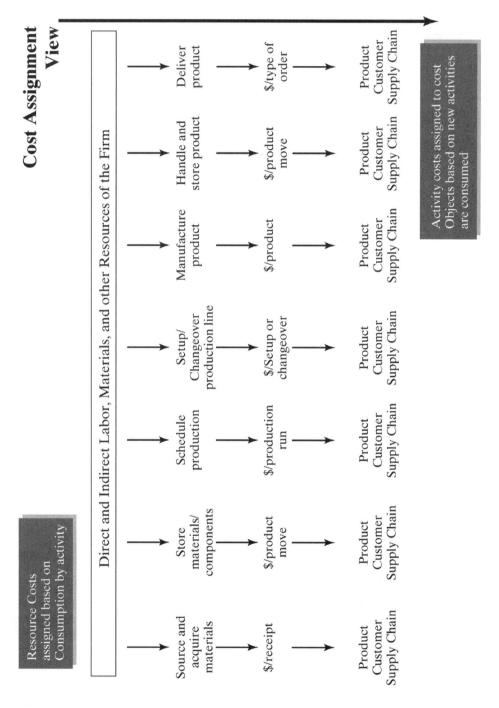

Cost Assignment View

Resource Costs assigned based on Consumption by activity

Direct and Indirect Labor, Materials, and other Resources of the Firm

Source and acquire materials	Store materials/ components	Schedule production	Setup/ Changeover production line	Manufacture product	Handle and store product	Deliver product
$/receipt	$/product move	$/production run	$/Setup or changeover	$/product	$/product move	$/type of order
Product Customer Supply Chain	Product Customer Supply Chain	Product Customer Supply Chain	Product Customer Supply Chain	Product Customer Supply Chain	Product Customer Supply Chain	Product Customer Supply Chain

Activity costs assigned to cost Objects based on new activities are consumed

Adapted from Turney, P. B. B. (1991), *Common Cents*, Hillsboro, OR: Cost Technology and Kaplan, R. S. (2001), "Integrating Shareholder Value with Activity-Based Costing with the Balanced Scorecard," *Balanced Scorecard Report, 3*(1), 3-6

Figure 4: Vertical, or Cost Assignment, View of Activity-Based Costing

Process View

Cost Drivers	Activities	Performance Measures
Vendor performance Component quality Inventory visibility	Source and acquire materials	Quality Cost Leadtime
Order frequency Minimum lot size Forecast accuracy	Store materials/ components	Inventory turns Inventory carrying cost Storage requirements
Equipment availability Changeover cost Lot size	Schedule production	Production run size Response time Backlogs
Equipment flexibility Product design Employee training	Setup/ changeover production line	Changeover time Reduced job wait time Employees trained/qualified
Component quality Product design Equipment maintenance	Manufacture product	Throughout rate/time Reduced scrap/rework Lower minimum quantity Employee headcount
Forecast accuracy Demand visibility Leadtimes Product run size	Handle and store product	Finished inventory turns Storage space requirement Inventory carrying cost
Product design Demand visibility Customer service Transp equipment availability	Deliver product	Shorter order cycles Reduce accounts receivable Better product availability

Adapted from Turney, P. B. B. (1991), *Common Cents*, Hillsboro, OR: Cost Technology

Figure 5: Activity-Based Management—the Horizontal, or Process View, of Activity-Based Costing.

Extending the dyadic EVA analysis beyond the supplier-customer dyad to include multiple trading partners provides several benefits. Managers can measure how effectively each firm has implemented the strategy and the supply chain's effect on shareholder value. Operations managers across multiple companies can identify opportunities where collaborative action could increase sales, eliminate duplicating or non-value-added activities, and reduce inventories. Executives obtain a better understanding of how their decisions affect upstream or downstream performance and costs. The focus shifts from negotiating lower prices and driving cost reductions to how to increase value for the end-user and the entire supply chain. An extended analysis also provides a more appropriate vehicle for assessing whether an equitable allocation of costs and benefits has occurred across the supply chain.

Although the previous discussion illustrates the effects of implementing one type of operations initiative within a supply chain, a similar process could be followed to analyze any operational changes made by any trading partner, including just-in-time (JIT), quick response (QR), flexible manufacturing systems (FMS), distribution requirements planning (DRP), material requirements planning (MRP), Six-Sigma, statistical process control (SPC), zero quality control (Shingo, 1986), collaborative planning, forecasting, and replenishment (CPFR), vendor managed inventory (VMI), sole/single sourcing, or concurrent engineering (CE, involving the supplier in product development). This is particularly recommended for initiatives that span the boundaries of multiple firms, as do JIT, QR, VMI, CPFR, and CE.

Working collaboratively with suppliers and customers on any of these will result at a minimum in ripple effects on EVA across a supplier-customer dyad and likely beyond to further branches of the supply chain. Quality improvement initiatives like CE, SPC, Six-Sigma, or zero quality control improve the ability to deploy new, innovative, higher-quality products faster than the competition. The customer's sales rise with increased market share and penetration into new markets resulting from the sale of new or better products, thereby producing additional sales revenue for the supplier. The exchange of information associated with CPFR will reduce cost-of-goods sold for a supplier through better production planning, ordering of materials, and workforce utilization. The customer's cost-of-goods sold can also decline as the supplier passes along cost savings. The supplier's current assets decrease as it holds less inventory due to improved forecasting and production scheduling. Accounts receivable may also decrease as the customer agrees to faster, electronic payments in return for off-setting cost reductions. Fixed assets decline due to

improved scheduling and better utilization of plant, equipment, and warehouse assets. In VMI, expenses decrease as the supplier eliminates non-value-added activities between the two firms: sales people no longer call on purchasing, orders are received electronically, shipments are scheduled to maximize truckload rates and leverage cross-docking opportunities, and warehousing and handling of finished goods inventories are reduced (Pohlen and Goldsby, 2003). The customer's current assets drop as the supplier assumes inventory ownership, and the customer's fixed assets drop through eliminating distribution centers and material handling equipment. Some customer expenses may increase if the supplier must be paid more quickly, or if it must purchase technology necessary for communicating with the supplier.

IMPLEMENTATION ISSUES

Several issues will confront managers attempting to implement the dyadic EVA and ABC framework. For example, other trading partners may be unwilling or unable to exchange the information needed to support the implementation of supply chain initiatives. However, this can be overcome by identifying common goals and providing objective information to a reluctant trading partner. In a value chain analysis examining interfirm relationships, Dekker (2003) found that improved discussion of outcomes and possible courses of action increased the interaction between trading partners. The objective nature of cost information eased communications and negotiations. As the consequences of changes in supply chain operations became more transparent, the trading partners perceived less risk that they would end up with inequitable outcomes or having their shares of the benefits appropriated. This approach applies even when the firms do not exchange financial information (Dekker and Van Goor, 2001). The ability to demonstrate the direction and magnitude of value creation provides a compelling argument for change. The dyadic EVA analysis does this by identifying mutually desirable objectives for the supply chain and providing objective information regarding the effects of changes in cost and performance on the affected trading partners.

The need to generate immediate results may preclude managers from investing in supply chain initiatives when there is a lag between investment and the subsequent benefits, even for changes with high payback. EVA overemphasizes the need to generate immediate results (Brewer, 1999), and increasing investments in assets has a negative effect on EVA-based metrics. The costs and expenses associated with any initiative are recognized when incurred; however, the associated benefits may not be realized for several years. The inability of some firms to accurately assign the benefits and costs to a specific supply chain initiative further exacerbates the situation. Managers can partially overcome this issue by using the framework to demonstrate how, over the longrun, supply chain investments will create value for the firm. However, without a balanced set of metrics that emphasize and reward investment in innovation and process improvement, EVA-based measures could act as a disincentive to managers weighing projects that do not provide immediate returns (Brewer, 1999).

The dyadic EVA and ABC approach may also produce a bias toward the development of financial and cost-based performance measures. The integration of EVA and ABC with the balanced scorecard (BSC) can overcome this situation. The BSC overcomes the limitations of managing only with financial measures (Davig, Elbert, and Brown, 2004). The BSC framework ensures a balanced set of measures by viewing performance from four perspectives: financial, customer, internal processes, and innovation and learning (Kaplan and Norton, 1992).

Robert Kaplan (2001), one of the principal architects of the BSC, argues that the BSC, EVA, and ABC are highly compatible and that organizations can greatly benefit from their integration. EVA takes into account the quantity of capital used to generate financial returns and can be used to organize the financial perspective of the BSC. However, EVA must be combined with other approaches, such as ABC, that can analyze activities and translate non-financial into financial performance. The first stage of ABC assigns the resources consumed in performing the activities and processes within an organization. Kaplan suggests the activity costs can be directly linked to the internal processes perspective in the BSC. The activity-based information demonstrates how reducing setup time and employing flexible manufacturing affects costs and process performance. The subsequent assignment of activity costs to determine cost-to-serve, supply chain profitability, or customer profitability, provides a linkage to the customer and financial perspectives of the BSC. ABM provides the link to the fourth perspective, innovation and learning, by identifying the factors that drive activity costs such as product design, employee training, and new product development, and the measures for assessing activity performance: percent of employees qualified/trained, change-over time, quality, and number of new product introductions. The BSC can integrate ABC, EVA, and ABM into a single framework that provides a balanced perspective between financial and nonfinancial results as well as long-term versus short-term performance. However, the BSC has been used only to integrate intrafirm performance measures, and its application across multiple firms requires further research.

CONCLUSION

Successful supply chain management ultimately comes down to the ability to create more value than the competition. The configuration of firms, processes, and activities composing the supply chain drives value creation. Operations managers and senior executives confront the problem of determining the configuration yielding the greatest value for the end-user and each trading
partner. They need to evaluate how the operational capabilities of each firm contribute to attaining supply chain objectives and the level of value created. The value of collaborative action must be measured and sold across each link to obtain trading partner buy-in and to align intrafirm performance with supply chain objectives. Despite the need to measure and align performance across multiple firms, most managers view performance from an internal perspective, or at best, how it is affected by their immediate upstream or downstream trading partners. Complexity and the interdependent nature of the supply chain make interfirm performance measurement extremely difficult; however, firms that act first to apply interfirm measures and align their performance with supply chain value objectives will achieve a sustainable advantage their competitors may be unable to emulate.

Dr. Pohlen, who retired from the U.S. Air Force with over 20 years of logistics experience, has published in leading logistics journals. His articles focus on the costing and financial management of logistics and supply chain performance measurement. Dr. Coleman is actively involved in research on the mathematical modeling of managerial decisions and has published over 40 articles.

REFERENCES

Brewer, P. C., Chandra, G., and Hock, C. A. (1999). Economic value added (EVA): Its uses and limitations. *SAM Advanced Management Journal, 64*(2), 4–11.

Buckingham, M., and Loomba A. (2001). Advantageous cost structure: A Strategic costing case study. *Production and Inventory Management Journal, 42*(1), 12–18.

Coleman, B. J., and Vaghefi, R. M. (1994). Heijunka (?): A key to the Toyota production system. *Production and Inventory Management Journal, 35*(4), 31–35.

Cook, J. S., DeBree, K., and Feroleto, A. (2001). From raw materials to customers: Supply chain management in the service industry. *SAM Advanced Management Journal, 66*(4), 14–21.

Courtis, J. K. (1995). JIT's impact on a firm's financial statements. *International Journal of Purchasing and Materials Management, 3*(1), 46–50.

Croxton, K. L., García-Dastugue, S. J., Lambert, D. M., and Rogers, D. S. (2001). The supply chain management processes. *International Journal of Logistics Management, 12*(2), 13–36.

Davig, W., Elbert, N., and Brown, S. (2004). Implementing a strategic planning model for small manufacturing firms: An adaptation of the balanced scorecard. *SAM Advanced Management Journal, 69*(1), 18–24.

Dekker, H. C. (2003). Value chain analysis in interfirm relationships: A field study. *Management Accounting Research, 14*(1), 1–23.

Dekker, H. C., and Van Goor, A. R. (2003). Supply chain management and management accounting: A case study of activity-based costing. *International Journal of Logistics: Research and Applications, 3*(1), 41–52.

Deloitte Consulting. (1999). Energizing the supply chain: Trends and issues in supply chain management. Retrieved June 21, 2004 from http://www.deloitte.com/ dtt/research/0,2310,sid%253D2222%2526cid%253 D35758,00.html

Ellram, L. M., and Liu, B. (2002). The financial impact of supply management. *Supply Chain Management Review, 6*(6), 30–37.

Gardner, J. T., and Cooper, M. C. (2003). Strategic supply chain mapping approaches. *Journal of Business Logistics, 24*(2), 37–64.

Holmberg, S. (2000). A systems perspective on supply chain measurements. *International Journal of Physical Distribution and Logistics Management, 30*(10), 847–868.

Kaplan, R. S. (2001). Integrating shareholder value and activity-based costing with the balanced scorecard. *Balanced Scorecard Report, 3*(1), 3–6.

Kaplan, R. S., and Norton, D. P. (1992). The balanced scorecard—measures that drive performance. *Harvard Business Review, 70*(1), 71–79.

Keebler, J. S., Manrodt, K. B., Durtsche, D. A., and Ledyard, D. M. (1999). *Keeping score*. Oakbrook, IL: Council of Logistics Management.

Kallio, J., Saarinen, T., Tinnila, M. and Vepsalainen, A. P. J. (2000). Measuring delivery process performance. *International Journal of Logistics Management, 11*(1), 75–87.

Kaplan, R. S., and Norton, D. P. (1996). *The balanced scorecard*. Boston, MA: Harvard Business School Press.

Keegan, D. P., Eiler, R.G., and Jones, C.R. (1989, June). Are your performance measures obsolete? *Management Accounting*, 45–50.

Krumwiede, K. R., and Roth, H. P. (1997). Implementing Information technology innovations: The activity-based costing example. *SAM Advanced Management Journal, 62*(4), 4–12.

La Londe, B. J., and Pohlen, T. L. (1996). Issues in supply chain costing. *International Journal of Logistics Management, 7*(1), 1–12.

Lambert, D. M., and Pohlen, T. L. (2001). Supply chain metrics. *International Journal of Logistics Management, 12*(1), 1–19.

Lee, H. L., and Billington, C. (1992, Spring). Managing supply chain inventory: Pitfalls and opportunities. *Sloan Management Review, 33*(3), 65–73.

Lummus, R. R., and Vokurka, R. J. (1999). Managing the demand chain through managing the information flow: Capturing moments of information. *Production and Inventory Management Journal, 40*(1), 16–20.

Lummus, R. R., Vokurka, R. J., and Alber, K. L. (1998). Strategic supply chain planning. *Production and Inventory Management Journal, 39*(3), 49–58.

Neely, A., Mills, J., Platts, K., Richards, H., Gregory, M., Bourne, M., and Kennerly, M. (2000). Performance measurement system design: Developing and testing a process-based approach. *International Journal of Operations and Production Management, 20*(10), 1119–1145.

McAdam, R., and McCormack, D. J. (2001). Integrating business processes for global alignment and supply chain management. *Business Process Management Journal, 7*(2), 113–130.

Pohlen, T. L. (2003). A framework for evaluating supply chain performance. *Journal of Transportation Management, 14*(2), 1–21.

Pohlen, T. L., and Goldsby, T. J. (2003). VMI and SMI programs: How economic value added can help sell the change. *International Journal of Physical Distribution and Logistics Management, 33*(7), 565–581.

Rappaport, A. (1987). Linking competitive strategy and shareholder value analysis. *The Journal of Business Strategy, 7*(4), 58–67.

Shingo, S. (1986). *Zero quality control: Source inspection and the poka-yoke system.* Stamford, Conn.: Productivity Press.

Shingo, S. (1985). *A revolution in manufacturing: The SMED system.* Stamford, Conn.: Productivity Press.

Simatupang, T. M., and Sridharan, R. (2002). The collaborative supply chain. *International Journal of Logistics Management, 13*(2), 15–30.

Stock, J. R., and Lambert, D. M. (2001). *Strategic logistics management*, 4th Ed, New York: McGraw-Hill Irwin, 684.

Turney, P. B. B. (1991). *Common cents*. Hillsboro, OR: Cost Technology.

van Hoek, R. I. (1998). Measuring the unmeasureable—measuring and improving performance in the supply chain. *Supply Chain Management, 3*(4), 187–192.

Wisner, J. D., and Fawcett, S. E. (1991). Linking firm strategy to operating decisions through performance measurement. *Production and Inventory Management Journal, 32*(3), 5–11.

Zank, G. M., and Vokurka, R. J. (2003). The Internet: Motivations, deterrents, and impact on supply chain relationships. *SAM Advanced Management Journal, 68*(2), 33–40.

QUESTION

11.4 What are the five steps involved in applying the EVA/ABC framework?

11.5 The Demise of Cost and Profit Centers

*by Robert S. Kaplan**

The Balanced Scorecard offers a previously unrecognized benefit: a whole new way of looking at organizational units. Specifically, observes Robert Kaplan, the distinctions between cost and profit centers are no longer significant. Every unit, by contributing to effective strategy execution, has the opportunity to support and create profit. This capability has important implications for specifying objectives and evaluating the performance of all organizational units.

In the early 1970s, as a young assistant professor of operations research at Carnegie Mellon University's business school, I was asked to learn how to teach the required accounting course. This worked out better than the dean or I might have expected. Soon I graduated to teaching MBA electives in management accounting— and faced the need to expand my knowledge of management accounting theory and practices. I came across a text and case book entitled Management Control Systems, written in 1965 by three Harvard Business School faculty members: Robert Anthony, John Dearden, and Richard Vancil.[1]

Management Control Systems (herein, "MCS") contained an exciting new approach to describing different decentralized organizational units. It examined the relationship between the design of decentralized organizations and the motivations of and incentives for those who manage them, based on the metrics used to measure the units' performance. MCS identified five different types of decentralized organizational units.

1. The profit center. Many operating unit managers have responsibility and authority for both production and sales. They make decisions about what products and services to produce; how to produce them; and their quality level, price, and sales and distribution systems.

But these managers may not have the authority to determine the level of capital investment in their facilities. In these cases, operating profit may be the single best (short-term) performance measure for how well the managers are creating value from the resources the company has put at their disposal. Such a unit, in which the manager has almost complete operational decision-making responsibility and is evaluated by a straightforward profit measure, is called a profit center.

2. The investment center. When a local manager has all the responsibilities described above as well as the responsibility and authority for his or her center's working capital and physical assets, the manager is running an investment center. The performance of such a unit is best measured with a metric that relates profits earned to the level of physical and financial assets employed in the center. Investment center managers are evaluated with such metrics as return on investment (ROI) and economic value added.

3. The standard cost center. A standard cost center is a production or operating unit in which someone other than the local manager determines the outputs that will be produced as well as the expected inputs required to produce each unit of output. Industrial engineers and cost accountants specify the quantity and price

---

standards for the materials, labor, energy, and machine time required to produce each widget (the generic term for a manufactured good). The cost center manager's job is to produce the demanded quantity and mix of widgets in an efficient manner, as determined by the standard cost system. Standard cost centers are also found in service industries, such as the fast food business, banking, and health care, where cost accountants establish standard costs for producing hamburgers and milk shakes, processing checks and deposits, or performing laboratory and radiological tests. The performance of a cost center manager is evaluated by a complex system of cost variances that compare actual to budgeted cost performance.

4. The revenue center. A revenue center, typically a marketing or sales unit, has the responsibility for selling the finished goods produced by a manufacturing division (a standard cost center) or the products offered by a service organization. Because a revenue center generally has discretion in setting the selling price (or in negotiating discounts off the list price), it is held accountable for generating targeted levels of gross revenues. It often compensates its salespeople with commissions based on the gross revenues they generate.

5. The discretionary expense center. Staff units, including general and administrative (G&A) departments such as finance, human resources, and legal; research and development (R&D) departments; and marketing units such as those responsible for advertising and promotion, are usually treated as discretionary expense centers. The output from these units is not easily measured in financial terms, and the relationship between the resources they expend (inputs) and the outcomes they produce is weak. Companies control these discretionary expense centers by negotiating and eventually authorizing an annual budget and then monitoring whether their actual spending remains within the budgeted amounts.

The MCS taxonomy reveals that decentralization can take many forms—a compelling discovery. And the management control systems course I taught based on this framework was a wonderful teaching—and learning—experience. Students analyzed cases of actual organizational units and debated which organizational form was most appropriate for the unit. The discussion, of course, took place within the traditional financial control paradigm dominant through the 1970s (and prevalent well into the present), which used only financial metrics—cost, revenue, gross margin, profits, or ROI—to motivate, align, and reward decentralized operating and support units.

THE BALANCED SCORECARD REVOLUTION

When Dave Norton and I introduced the Balanced Scorecard in the early 1990s, we described the limitations of financial metrics such as profits and ROI in motivating and evaluating the performance of profit and investment centers. We claimed that financial metrics were no longer sufficient for measuring the annual performance of the managers of these units and for motivating them to create long-term value. We contended that the performance of such managers must be measured by a variety of nonfinancial metrics designed to capture how well the unit's intangible assets built and expanded relationships with targeted customers; improved the quality and responsiveness of operating processes; created and introduced new products and services; enhanced the motivation and capabilities of employees; leveraged investments in databases and information technology; and aligned the culture and climate linked to the unit's vision, mission, and strategy.

The BSC soon proved to be a more general and powerful performance management framework for units previously treated as profit and investment centers. Less well appreciated, however, is how the BSC has actually eliminated the need to treat the remaining decentralized units as standard cost centers, revenue centers, or discretionary expense centers. By linking their activities to strategy execution, all units become, in effect, strategic business units. Let's see how as we examine each in turn.

TRANSFORMING THE COST CENTER

Empire Glass[2] was one of the most provocative cases I taught from MCS. The Empire Glass company treated a manufacturing plant that had no authority for pricing, marketing, or sales activities—a classic cost center—as a profit center. The class discussion always started with students actively criticizing this choice. Treating this manufacturing unit as a profit center violated all the rules they had just learned about what constituted a profit center. During the course of class discussion, however, students came to realize that the manufacturing plant actually had a substantial influence on sales and margins. Producing the right volume of product at high-quality levels and delivering the order on time contributed to satisfied, loyal customers. The profit measure helped the manufacturing manager appreciate how his plant contributed to current and future sales. If he were to be evaluated only by how much he beat the standard cost budget for the actual volume and mix of products demanded, the plant manager might instead have emphasized long production runs, ignored sales requests for expedited production and delivery, and failed to recognize the consequences of late deliveries, an incorrect product mix, or producing products that did not conform to specified quality standards.

While the thinking behind such a decision seemed reasonable at the time, we now understand that forcing a plant such as the Empire Glass plant to be a profit, rather than a cost, center was a suboptimal solution, caused by having to select only a single financial measure to evaluate the plant's performance. Today, with more than a decade of BSC experience, we would instead ask students to construct a strategy map and Balanced Scorecard for the Empire Glass plant. The primary financial metrics would include a comparison of actual to standard costs for the volume and mix of products produced. But the financial perspective would also include metrics for sales revenue and margins. These alert the manager to how the plant's quality, lead time, and on-time delivery performance influence revenues and profits. And beyond this richer set of metrics in the financial perspective, students can draw upon three other nonfinancial perspectives—customer, process, and learning and growth—to select leading indicators of the plant's performance.

In the customer perspective, we would include the metrics that capture the performance desired by Empire's most important customers; for example, short lead times, on-time delivery, and zero defect rates. For the process perspective, we would not only include metrics for manufacturing cost improvements, but also metrics for process cycle times, defect rates, and yields. We could also introduce metrics of flexibility and ease of introducing new product varieties into large-scale manufacturing. For the learning and growth perspective, we would measure the percentage of employees trained in Six Sigma and employees' awareness of how the plant's production and delivery performance influences customer satisfaction. What a revolution in thinking and in practice! The plant is neither a cost nor a profit center; it is a strategic operating unit whose alignment with company strategy can be comprehensively but succinctly visualized, measured, motivated, and evaluated.

REVISITING THE REVENUE CENTER

Let's next consider the revenue center, which has historically been measured by the dollar volume and mix of products sold. In building a Balanced Scorecard for a revenue center, we specify, in the customer perspective, objectives for market and account share, for customer satisfaction and loyalty, and for growth in targeted customer segments, accounts, and channels. These customer metrics provide more specificity and guidance for marketing and sales units. The process perspective focuses on customer management processes: acquisition, retention, and growth. And the learning and growth perspective identifies the skills and knowledge required for promoting, branding, and selling the company's products and services; emphasizes the development of customer databases and the capabilities for customer data-mining analytics; and signals the importance of a customer-focused culture.

Just as manufacturing and operations units like Empire Glass can now, through the BSC, internalize their impact on revenues, sales and marketing units should think about their impact on costs. These units, with their metrics on customer outcomes, customer processes, and customer learning and growth metrics, may become too customer-focused. They may attempt to generate customer orders and loyalty by offering excessive product and service customization, highly responsive delivery options, and expanded post-sales customer services. All these offerings are welcomed by customers and lead to more satisfaction and increased business. But the customization, responsive delivery, and expanded post-sales services also raise costs throughout the company. Engineering must design the new product variants and the processes to produce them; manufacturing and operations incur high costs to produce the customized products in short production runs; distribution incurs costs for frequent, expedited deliveries on short lead times; and the field-service and home-office support units must devote considerable resources to achieve promised levels of customer service. Marketing and sales decisions thus have profound consequences for costs incurred elsewhere in the company. As with Empire Glass, the choice of financial measures for evaluating the performance of the marketing and sales units is no longer an "either-or" choice between revenues and profits. These units can measure both. The Balanced Scorecards for the marketing and sales units could include metrics on profitability, cost-to-serve for key customers, frequency and magnitude of losses in unprofitable customer relationships, and changes in operating costs associated with providing special features or services. Activity-based costing (ABC) makes it feasible to calculate the costing of every customer order and the profit or loss of every customer relationship.[3] Companies can now use profits, not just sales, to measure the performance of their marketing and sales units.

THE NEW DISCRETIONARY EXPENSE CENTER

Perhaps the greatest breakthrough in measuring, evaluating, and motivating the performance of decentralized units occurs in discretionary expense centers— corporate overhead departments— which have historically been controlled only by comparing their actual spending to somewhat arbitrarily determined budgets. (See Figure 1.) Activity-based costing and the Balanced Scorecard enable discretionary expense units to be evaluated by the same tools as those used for profit, revenue, and cost centers. First, ABC helps them connect their expenses to the specific services they provide. For example, consider the accounts receivable (A/R) department within finance. By analyzing the time demands on the

FIGURE 1. GENERIC SUPPORT UNIT STATEGY MAP

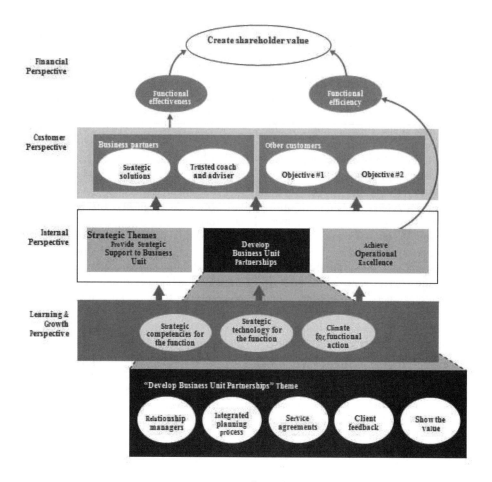

employees in A/R, we can assign A/R's costs simply and accurately to the operating units that create the work, using such cost drivers as number of invoices issued, number of cash collections processed, number of customer credit checks performed, and number of customer files maintained. Furthermore, time-driven ABC systems can measure the unit costs of the repetitive processes done within HR (training, employee benefit counseling, performance management appraisals) and IT (providing CPU capacity, storage capacity, and connect time). The ABC innovation enables these resource costs to be charged out to operating units just as the outputs from manufacturing units are charged out, via standard costs, to marketing and sales units. In effect, ABC enables discretionary expense centers to become cost centers with a financial goal of breaking even—to recover their expenses through cost-recovery pricing schemes based on the actual demands made by operating units on the support units' resources.

But organizations needn't stop there. An entire chapter of the recent Kaplan-Norton book, Alignment, explains how strategy maps and scorecards can be developed for such units as finance, IT, and human resources, among many others. Now, every corporate support unit can be treated not as a discretionary expense center—not even as a break-even cost center—but as a strategic business unit in its own right. How can an organization accomplish this dramatic transformation?

Starting with the financial perspective, the organization can continue to demand that support units stay within their budget. The units can also have an objective to lower the cost of supplying services to their customers—the operating and support units. The organization can also require them to break even by ensuring they recover their expenses by pricing their services on a cost basis. Beyond the cost focus, many support units add corporate- and business-unit revenue and profit objectives to their scorecards to reflect the role they play in contributing to operating units' financial objectives. While support units neither produce products nor service external customers, they can strive to help make the operating units they serve more productive and more profitable with these customers.

Support units must understand their internal customers' strategies and align their service offerings to contribute to their customers' success, just as operating units do with their external customers. These objectives typically appear in the support unit's BSC customer perspective. Many support unit scorecards therefore include an objective to become "their customers' trusted adviser" and measure this objective with metrics from service-level agreements and customer feedback. Just as they might employ revenue and profit metrics in their scorecard's financial perspective, some support units may even incorporate external customer metrics in their scorecards to recognize how they can directly create value for the operating units' customers. For example, an IT shared-services unit can create new platforms and new capabilities for servicing customers that help strategically differentiate the company's operating units.

Several support units may have additional customers to consider in their strategy maps and scorecards. HR units treat employees as their customers, providing them with competency and leadership development training, career development advice, performance management systems linked to their units' strategy, and competitive compensation and benefit packages. Finance units treat the company's investors, analysts, regulators, and tax authorities as their customers. Finance offers them reporting and disclosures about the company's financial progress, risk management and internal-control processes; it also offers tax reporting that demonstrates that the company minimizes tax payments while remaining within the laws and regulations of the countries in which it operates.

All support units can identify the critical processes they perform to deliver services to internal and external customers, processes highlighted in the Balanced Scorecard's process perspective. Though often routine and transactional, these processes—such as operating the general ledger and accounts receivable function (finance), the compensation and benefit system (HR), and the computing and networking infrastructure (IT)—are nonetheless vital. Support departments should constantly strive to lower the cost and raise the reliability and quality of their basic support services. But they should not stop there. Support departments should expand their scope to identify the processes that enable them to become trusted advisers to operating unit leaders and help those leaders achieve their differentiating strategies. If a support unit does not offer some differentiating services to its internal customers, it runs a high risk of the company eliminating it and outsourcing the function to a lower cost external provider.

Finally, the support units' customer-focused strategies require upgrading the skills and capabilities of their employees so they are equipped to be trusted advisers to business unit heads and relationship managers in the units they support. This generally requires significantly enhanced information technology capabilities, and almost always a shift in mindset and culture—from being a central and captive provider of functional expertise to being a customer-focused shared service unit.

MAKE EVERY UNIT A STRATEGIC BUSINESS UNIT

The development of strategy maps and Balanced Scorecards has transformed the foundation of management control systems. The leading paradigm of organizational structure and control of just a generation ago, based on cost, profit, investment, revenue, and discretionary expense centers, has been replaced by a robust, powerful framework in which every organizational unit—whether line or staff, whether centralized or decentralized—can be considered a strategic business unit. The management control system is no longer based on the budget— whether for profits, ROI, costs, revenues, or discretionary expenses. Companies now use the more general and powerful strategy management system, built upon the framework of strategy maps and Balanced Scorecards, to motivate, align, and evaluate the performance of diverse organizational units.

ENDNOTES

1. R. Anthony, J. Dearden, R. Vancil, Management Control Systems (Richard D. Irwin, 1965). At the time I could not have imagined that 13 years later, all three would be my colleagues. The book is now in its 12th edition.
2. Empire Glass Co. (A), Harvard Business School Case, by David F. Hawkins (April 10, 1964: 9-109-043). The case, written by my HBS colleague, is still being taught in many business schools.
3. R. S. Kaplan and S. R. Anderson, "Time-Driven Activity-Based Costing," Harvard Business Review (November 2004): 131–138. Kaplan and Anderson's new book on the subject is due out from Harvard Business School Press in the spring of 2007.

QUESTION

11.5 Why does Robert Kaplan say that the distinction between traditional cost and profit centers is no longer meaningful or significant?